T0300583

NON-STATE ACTORS AS STANDARD SETTERS

This analysis of 'globalised' standard-setting processes draws together insights from law, political sciences, sociology and social anthropology to assess the authority and accountability of non-state actors and the legitimacy and effectiveness of the processes. The essays offer new understandings of current governance problems, including environmental and financial standards, rules for military contractors and complex public–private partnerships, such as those intended to protect critical information infrastructure. The contributions also evaluate multi-stakeholder initiatives (such as the Extractive Industries Transparency Initiative), and discuss the constitution of public norms in stateless areas. A synopsis of the latest results of the Worldwide Governance Indicators research project (WGI), arguably one of the most important surveys in the area today, is included.

ANNE PETERS is Professor of Public International Law and Constitutional Law at the University of Basel and Vice President of the Board of the Basel Institute on Governance. She was also visiting professor at Sciences Po, Paris.

LUCY KOECHLIN is Head of Public Accountability at the Basel Institute on Governance, and Lecturer in Development Studies at the Institute of Sociology and the Centre for African Studies Basel (CASB), University of Basel, Switzerland.

TILL FÖRSTER is a member of the Board of the Basel Institute on Governance and holds the chair for social anthropology at the University of Basel. He is also director of the CASB.

GRETTA FENNER ZINKERNAGEL is a member of the Advisory Board of the Basel Institute on Governance after having been the Institute's Executive Director for three years. She currently advises international organizations and governments on anti-corruption and governance issues.

NON-STATE ACTORS AS STANDARD SETTERS

Edited by
ANNE PETERS,
LUCY KOECHLIN,
TILL FÖRSTER,
and
GRETTA FENNER ZINKERNAGEL

CAMBRIDGE
UNIVERSITY PRESS

CAMBRIDGE UNIVERSITY PRESS
Cambridge, New York, Melbourne, Madrid, Cape Town,
Singapore, São Paulo, Delhi, Tokyo, Mexico City

Cambridge University Press
The Edinburgh Building, Cambridge CB2 8RU, UK

Published in the United States of America by Cambridge University Press, New York

www.cambridge.org
Information on this title: www.cambridge.org/9780521114905

First published 2009

A catalogue record for this publication is available from the British Library

ISBN 978-0-521-11490-5 Hardback

CONTENTS

FIGURES

TABLES

CONTRIBUTORS

DAN ASSAF Doctoral Candidate, Faculty of Law, University of Toronto, Canada; LLB, BA (Economics) (Tel Aviv).

JULIA BLACK Professor of Law and Research Associate, Centre for Analysis of Risk and Regulation, London School of Economics and Political Science; DPhil., BA (Hons) Jurisp. (Oxon).

MONICA BLAGESCU Policy Services Coordinator, Humanitarian Accountability Partnership (HAP) International, Switzerland; MA (International Affairs, International University of Japan); BA (Political Science and Mass Communications, American University in Bulgaria).

RICHARD CALLAND Associate Professor of Public Law, University of Cape Town; Director, Economic Governance Programme, IDASA, South Africa; Member, International Advisory Group, Medicines Transparency Alliance.

LINDSEY CAMERON Doctoral Candidate and Research Assistant, Faculty of Law, University of Geneva; LLM (International Humanitarian Law, University of Geneva); LLB (McGill); MA (History, University of Toronto).

GRETTA FENNER ZINKERNAGEL Executive Director, Basel Institute on Governance, Switzerland; BA (Institut des Hautes Etudes de Sciences Politiques, Paris), BA, MA (Political Science, Free University Berlin).

TILL FÖRSTER Professor of Social Anthropology and Chair of the Department of Social Anthropology, University of Basel, Switzerland; DPhil. (Free University Berlin); Member of the Board, Basel Institute on Governance, Switzerland.

STÉPHANE GUÉNEAU Research Fellow, CIRAD (French Agricultural Research Centre for International Development), Montpellier; Visiting Professor, Sciences Po, Institute for Sustainable Development and International Relations (IDDRI), Paris; MSc (Economics, University of Montpellier); Doctoral Candidate (Management and Administration in

Environmental Sciences and Policies, Paris Institute of Technology for Life, Food and Environmental Sciences (AgroParisTech).

PETER HÄGEL Assistant Professor, Department of International and Comparative Politics, The American University of Paris, France; BA, MA (Political Science, Free University Berlin).

DANIEL KAUFMANN Senior Fellow, Global Economy and Development, Brookings Institution; BSc, Economics and Statistics, Hebrew University of Jerusalem; MA, PhD, Economics, Harvard.

EVA KOCHER Associate Professor (*Privatdozentin*), Faculty of Law, University of Hamburg, Germany; Director, Labour Studies Academy (Akademie der Arbeit), University of Frankfurt/Main, Germany; Dr. iur. (University of Hamburg).

LUCY KOECHLIN Head of Public Accountability, Basel Institute on Governance, Switzerland; Lecturer, Institute of Sociology, University of Basel; Lic. phil., MSc (LSE).

AART KRAAY Lead Economist, Development Research Group, The World Bank; BSc University of Toronto; MA, PhD Harvard.

ROBERT LLOYD Global Accountability Project Manager, One World Trust, United Kingdom; MA (Governance and Development, Institute of Development Studies, University of Sussex); BA (Geography, King's College London).

MASSIMO MASTRUZZI Economist, World Bank Institute, The World Bank; MA, MS, Georgetown University.

MICHAEL MIKLAUCIC BA University of California; MSc London School of Economics.

DIETER NEUBERT Professor of Sociology and Chair of Development Sociology, Department of Sociology, University of Bayreuth, Germany; DPhil. (University of Mainz).

ANNE PETERS Professor of Public International Law and Constitutional Law, Faculty of Law, University of Basel, Switzerland; Dr. iur. (University of Freiburg, Germany), LLM (Harvard); Vice-Chair of the Board, Basel Institute on Governance, Switzerland.

MARK PIETH Professor of Criminal Law and Criminology, Faculty of Law, University of Basel, Switzerland; Dr. iur. (University of Basel); Chairman,

OECD Working Group on Bribery in International Business Transactions; Chair of the Board, Basel Institute on Governance, Switzerland.

MARCUS SCHAPER Visiting Assistant Professor of Political Science, Reed College, United States; PhD, MA (Government and Politics, University of Maryland); Dipl Pol (Political Science, University of Potsdam).

EGLE SVILPAITE Dr. iur. (Mykolas Romeris University, Lithuania); LLM (European Law, University of Lund, Sweden).

ULRIKE WANITZEK Professor of Law, Institute of African Studies, Faculty of Law and Economics, University of Bayreuth, Germany; Dr. iur. (University of Bayreuth).

STEVEN WHEATLEY Reader in International Law and Director of the Centre for International Governance, University of Leeds; LLM (Nottingham, UK); LLB (University of Central England).

ACKNOWLEDGEMENTS

The idea of this publication arose from a conference on a similar topic that was organised by the Basel Institute on Governance in February 2007 in Switzerland. We thank the speakers and participants of this conference for the rich debate that has inspired this book, as well as the conference's sponsoring partners.

The dedicated work of Claudia Jeker from the Law Faculty of the University of Basel, and of Radha Ivory, Daniela Winkler and Nina Schild from the Basel Institute on Governance in the planning and organising of this publication, as well as in editing, proofreading and formatting is very gratefully acknowledged. Without their help this book may never have seen the light of day. Finally, our thanks go to Cambridge University Press, especially to Finola O'Sullivan for her perseverance, patience and guidance.

The Basel Institute on Governance, under the umbrella of which we publish this book, has funded much of the work that went into the publication. The Institute received financial support for this from the 'Stiftung zur Förderung der rechtlichen und wirtschaftlichen Forschung an der Universität Basel' (Foundation for the promotion of legal and economic research at the University of Basel). This contribution is gratefully acknowledged, as is the seed funding from the Danzas Foundation, without which the Basel Institute on Governance would not be able to operate.

The editors

ABBREVIATIONS

ABIOVE	Associação Brasileira das Indústrias de Óleos Vegetais (Brazilian Association of Vegetable Oil Industries)
ADM	Archer Daniels Midland Company
AI	Amnesty International
ALNAP	Active Learning Network for Accountability and Performance in Humanitarian Action
ANEC	Associação Nacional Dos Exportadores De Cereais (National Association of Grain Exporters)
BCBS	Basel Committee on Banking Supervision
BIAC	Business and Industry Advisory Committee to the OECD
BOND	British Overseas NGOs for Development
CBD	Convention on Biological Diversity
CEN	European Committee for Standardization
CENELEC	European Committee for Electrotechnical Standardization
CESR	Committee of European Securities Regulators
CI	Critical Infrastructures
CIA	Central Intelligence Agency
CII	Critical Information Infrastructures
CIIP	Critical Information Infrastructure Protection
CITES	Convention on International Trade in Endangered Species
CoE	Council of Europe
COST	Construction Sector Transparency Initiative
CPN(M)	Communist Party of Nepal (Maoist)
CSA	Canada Standard Association
CSO	Civil Society Organisation
CSR	Corporate Social Responsibility
DAC	Development Assistance Committee
DCAF	Geneva Centre for the Democratic Control of Armed Forces
DDoS	Distributed Denial of Service
DFID	Department for International Development
DHS	Department of Homeland Security
DRSC	Deutsches Rechnungslegungs Standards Committee (Accounting Standards Committee of Germany)

ECA	Export Credit Agency
ECG	Export Credit Group
ECHR	European Convention of Human Rights
ECOSOC	United Nations Economic and Social Council
EFTA	European Free Trade Association
EITI	Extractive Industries Transparency Initiative
EPFI	Equator Principles Financial Institution
ERO	Electric Reliability Organisation
ETI	Ethical Trading Initiative
ETSI	European Telecommunications Standards Institute
EU	European Union
EUI	European University Institute
FAO	Food and Agriculture Organization
FARC	Fuerzas Armadas Revolucionarias de Colombia (Revolutionary Armed Forces of Colombia)
FATF	Financial Action Task Force
FCPA	Foreign Corrupt Practices Act
FERC	Federal Energy Regulatory Commission
FinCEN	Financial Crimes Enforcement Network
FIU	Financial Intelligence Unit
FLA	Fair Labour Association
FLEG	Forest Law Enforcement and Governance
FOI Act	Freedom of Information Act
FORCOMS	Forest Concession Monitoring System
FSC	Forest Stewardship Council
G7	Group of Seven
GAP	Global Accountability Project
GC	Global Compact
GDP	Gross Domestic Product
GEF	Global Environment Facility
GIGA	German Institute of Global and Area Studies
GRI	Global Reporting Initiative
HAP	Humanitarian Accountability Project
HAPI	Humanitarian Accountability Partnership International
HICs	High Income Countries
HIPCs	Heavily Indebted Poor Countries
HPCR	International Association for Humanitarian Policy and Conflict Research
IAF	International Accreditation Forum
IAG	International Advisory Board
IASB	International Accounting Standards Board
IBRD	International Bank for Reconstruction and Development

ICC	International Chamber of Commerce
ICME	International Council on Metals and the Environment
ICRC	International Committee of the Red Cross
ICTR	International Criminal Tribunal for Rwanda
IDA	International Development Association
IDASA	Institute for Democracy in South Africa
IDDRI	Institute for Sustainable Development and International Relations
IFA	International Framework Agreement
IFC	International Finance Corporation
IFIA	Interafrican Forest Industries Association
IFRC	International Federation of Red Cross and Red Crescent Societies
IFRS	International Financial Reporting Standards
IGOs	Intergovernmental Organisations
IHL	International Humanitarian Law
ILA	International Law Association
ILO	International Labour Organization
IMF	International Monetary Fund
IMO	International Maritime Organization
INGO	International Non-Governmental Organisation
IOE	International Organisation of Employers
IOSCO	International Organization of Securities Commission
IPOA	International Peace Operations Association
IPS	Illicit Power Structure
IR	International Relations
ISAC	Information Sharing and Analysis Centre
ISAF	International Security Assistance Force
ISO	International Organization for Standardization
ITTA	International Tropical Timber Agreement
ITTO	International Tropical Timber Organization
LDC	Least Developed Country
LFMI	Lithuanian Free Market Institute
LMIC	Lower Middle Income Country
LRA	Lord's Resistance Army
MAC	Marine Aquarium Council
MAI	Multilateral Agreement on Investment
MDB	Multilateral Development Bank
MEJA	United States Military Extraterritorial Jurisdiction Act
MeTA	Medicines Transparency Alliance
MIGA	Multilateral Investment Guarantee Agency
MNE	Multinational Enterprise
MSC	Marine Stewardship Council
MSI	Multi-Stakeholder Initiative

NATO	North Atlantic Treaty Organization
NCTT	Non-Cooperative Countries and Territories
NEPA	National Environmental Policy Act
NERC	North American Electricity Reliability Corporation
NGO	Non-Governmental Organisation
NRDC	National Resources Defense Council
NWF	National Wildlife Foundation
OAS	Organization of American States
ODA	Official Development Assistance
OECD	Organisation for Economic Co-operation and Development
OFAC	Office of Foreign Assets Control
OLICs	Other Low Income Countries
ONF	Office National des Forêts (State Forestry Office)
OPEC	Organization of the Petroleum Exporting Countries
PACI	Partnership against Corruption Initiative
PCIJ	Permanent Court of International Justice
PEFC	Pan-European Forest Certification Scheme
PEFC	Programme for the Endorsement of Forest Certification Schemes
PGA	Peoples' Global Action
PIANC	International Navigation Association
PMC	Private Military Company
PPAH	Pollution Prevention and Abatement Handbook
PPM	Production Process and Method
PPP	Public–Private Partnership
PR	Public Relations
Quango	Quasi Non-Governmental Organisation
RENAMO	Resistência Nacional Moçambicana (Mozambique National Resistance)
RSPO	Roundtable on Sustainable Palm Oil
RTRS	Roundtable on Responsible Soy
SAR	Suspicious Activity Report
SCS	Scientific Certification Systems
SDR	Special Drawing Rights
SFI	Sustainable Forestry Initiative
SIPRI	Stockholm International Peace Research Institute
SKAL	Certification Organic Production (the Netherlands)
SLIMF	Small and Low-Intensity Managed Forest
SME	Small and Medium Enterprises
SPA	Seven Party Alliance
STSC	Sustainable Tourism Stewardship Council
SWIFT	Society for Worldwide Interbank Financial Telecommunications
TBT	Technical Barriers to Trade
TFTP	Terrorist Finance Tracking Programme

TNCs	Transnational Corporations
TRC	Truth and Reconciliation Commission
UK	United Kingdom
UMICs	Upper Middle Income Countries
UN	United Nations
UNCCD	United Nations Convention to Combat Desertification
UNCITRAL	United Nations Commission on International Trade Law
UNDP	United Nations Development Programme
UNEG	United Nations Evaluation Group
UNEP	United Nations Environment Programme
UNFCCC	United Nations Framework Convention on Climate Change
UNFF	United Nations Forum on Forests
UNGA	United Nations General Assembly
UNHCR	United Nations High Commissioner for Refugees
UNICEF	United Nations Children's Fund
UNIDROIT	International Institute for the Unification of Private Law
USC	United States Code
US(A)	United States of America
USAF	United States Air Force
USAID	United States Agency for International Development
WCD	World Commission on Dams
WCSDG	World Commission on the Social Dimension of Globalisation
WHO	World Health Organization
WIPO	World Intellectual Property Organization
WTO	World Trade Organization
WWF	World Wide Fund for Nature
WWII	Second World War
YCL	Young Communist League

PREFACE

The increasing pace of economic globalisation and liberalisation has made it obvious that the traditional nation state is no longer alone in the driving seat of regulation, especially in international trade relations. So-called 'non-state actors', a broad term encompassing intergovernmental organisations, non-governmental organisations, transnational corporations, as well as new forms of mixed standard setters such as 'public–private partnerships' (PPPs) or 'multi-stakeholder groups', are becoming increasingly involved in the business of regulation.

With the new actors come new forms of standard setting: the classic divide between state regulation, on the one hand, and self-regulation, on the other hand, is giving way to hybrid forms of co-regulation. The methodology of regulation is also changing rapidly. Especially at the international level, task forces are applying soft law and peer review mechanisms. Likewise, in the private sector, codes of conduct secured by para-judicial means are being introduced in many areas.

Furthermore, social scientists are rightly pointing out that for too long the legal discourses have focused on formal regulation only. They refer to the essential role of para-legal standard setting. The emergence of new actors, processes and regulatory types can be observed in many economically sensitive areas (competition, environmental, labour rules, etc.), as well as in human rights standards. Non-state actors, however, also play a key role in replacing formal governance in so-called 'failing states'.

This book gives a broad insight into the multifaceted world of standard setting by non-state actors. It goes well beyond description. In a unique international and interdisciplinary effort, it attempts to extract the common features of this evolution and to formulate crucial research questions, bringing together the three too-frequently disconnected discourses of the legal, social and political science.

In my roles as member of the Financial Action Task Force on Money Laundering and Chairman of the OECD Working Group on Bribery, I have had direct experience of the implications of the increasing involvement of non-state actors in standard setting both from a theoretical and a practical perspective. It is key how the legitimacy of soft law instruments or of 'PPPs' can be secured: what replaces the rule of law and democracy of the nation state in international regulation or amongst private actors? The book goes a step further to discuss how discourses of accountability and of legitimacy may compete and place the actors in dilemmas that could, in the extreme case, jeopardise their survival.

By highlighting such challenges, and by discussing methods to evaluate the accountability of institutions, this book takes us into the heart of current debate about standard setting.

MARK PIETH*

* Professor of Criminal Law and Criminology, Faculty of Law, University of Basel, Switzerland; Chair, OECD Working Group on Bribery in International Business Transactions; Chair of the Board, Basel Institute on Governance, Switzerland; Dr. iur. (University of Basel).

Non-state actors as standard setters: framing the issue in an interdisciplinary fashion

ANNE PETERS,* LUCY KOECHLIN,** AND
GRETTA FENNER ZINKERNAGEL***

1. Background and context

On all levels of governance, standard setting (norm formation or regulation), is no longer the exclusive domain of states or governmental authorities. The role and the capacity of increasingly diverse and polymorphous non-state actors involved in standard setting are expanding.[1] Also, the processes by which norms are shaped are becoming more varied. Finally, the rapidly growing number of national, sub-national, and international standards has increased these standards' diversity, but also regulatory overlap and norm conflicts.

The context in which the proliferation of non-state actors' standard setting occurs is well known. Globalisation, liberalisation and privatisation waves which swept the globe in the 1980s and 1990s have contributed to shifting the focus away from the state as the sole source of regulation. The result is the often referenced blurring of the public and the private sectors.[2] The integration of national economies into a world economy has diminished or at least modified the authority of the state[3] and has pushed its regulatory capacity to its limits both in substance and

* Prof Dr. iur., LLM (Harvard), University of Basel; Basel Institute on Governance.
** Lic. phil., MSc (LSE), Basel Institute on Governance and Institute of Sociology, University of Basel.
*** BA (Institut des Hautes Etudes de Sciences Politiques, Paris), BA, MA (Political Science, Free University Berlin), Basel Institute on Governance.

[1] United Nations 2004, *We the Peoples: Civil Society, the United Nations and Global Governance, Report of the Panel of Eminent Persons on United Nations–Civil Society Relations* ('Cardoso Report'), A/58/817 (11 June 2004), paras 11–14.
[2] See, e.g., Nye and Donahue (eds.), *Governance*; Peters, 'Privatisierung, Globalisierung'.
[3] Strange, *The Retreat of the State*; but see for a reassertion of the states' role Weiss, *States in the Global Economy*; Paul, Ikenberry and Hall (eds.), *The Nation State in Question*.

in terms of territorial scope. Policy issues that have formerly been treated at the level of nation states, for instance environmental pollution, migration, or organised crime, are increasingly understood as phenomena with global scope and global roots which cannot be tackled in a satisfactory manner through national standard setting.

One reaction to this has been standard setting in inter-state fora. Here states remain the principal standard-setting actors, but the international processes of standard setting differ from traditional unilateral regulation at the national level. Second, often triggered by regulatory attempts at governmental or inter-governmental level, standard setting is at least in part taken over by the private sector, in particular in areas where inter-governmental efforts fail, or where stakeholders, such as civil society or private business, feel that regulation by international treaty does not adequately take into account their concerns. Numerous initiatives have been established as Public Private Partnerships (PPPs[4]) between the public and private (business or civil society) sectors. An innovative example of a PPP in which governments play an active part in the standard-setting process is the Extractive Industries Transparency Initiative.[5] Conventionally, PPPs have described service-delivery and infrastructure projects. Hence EITI is an exceptional (and maybe indicative) example of a 'new' form of PPP – or multi-stakeholder initiative, as these forms of collaborations are increasingly being called (see Lucy Koechlin and Richard Calland, Chapter 4). This initiative brings together governments, companies, civil society groups, investors and international organisations with the aim of improving governance in resource-rich countries through the verification and full publication of company payments and government revenues from oil, gas and mining.

Some multi-stakeholder regulatory initiatives, such as the Partnership against Corruption Initiative (PACI) or the Wolfsberg Anti-Money Laundering Principles, are constituted without any direct participation of the State.[6] They move a step beyond the typical PPP towards private self-regulation. However, as these initiatives often principally serve to

---

[4] PPPs are defined by the UN General Assembly as follows: 'Voluntary and collaborative relationships between various parties, both State and non-state, in which all participants agree together to achieve a common purpose or undertake a specific task and to share risk and responsibilities, resources and benefits' (UN General Assembly 2005, *Enhanced Cooperation Between the United Nations and All Relevant Partners, in Particular the Private Sector. Report of the Secretary General* (A/60/214), para. 8). See in scholarship Börzel and Risse, 'Public–Private Partnerships'.
[5] www.eiti.org.   [6] See Pieth, 'Multi-Stakeholder Initiatives'.

assist its member institutions in implementing or pre-empting (missing but anticipated) governmental norms, public entities are still indirectly involved in the standard-setting process, and certainly so when it comes to the hard enforcement of the norm by governmental action (as opposed to soft enforcement mechanisms as implemented by the initiatives themselves).

The standard-setting activity of both state and non-state actors, comprising voluntary agreements within the purely private sphere and multisectoral initiatives, seems to be driven by two main objectives: to solve problems more effectively and to gain public confidence (social legitimacy[7]), as illustrated by the financial institutions' environmental standards (analysed by Marcus Schaper in Chapter 11).[8]

These forms of regulation, novel in terms of actors and processes, testify that the effectiveness of national regulation has reached its limits and needs to be supplemented, though not necessarily replaced, by standards or norms originating from other processes and other actor constellations, in particular in policy areas which are linked to the globalisation of economic activity. The new standard setting appears to respond to the increasing complexity of societal steering functions and to reflect the (relatively or absolutely) diminishing power and resources of the state. Inversely, the new types of standard setting themselves affect the distribution of political decision-making power within and across societies, the relationship between public and private actors, and our established understandings of public functions.

All these developments are generally acknowledged and recounted in all academic disciplines which this volume represents, in particular law, sociology, and political science. However, it appears that we have not yet fully understood this phenomenon, and that there continues to be disagreement, within and among disciplines, about the actual importance of the development, and about the sustainability or, conversely, reversibility of the trend. In order to appreciate the nature as well as the extent and the impact of the novel standard-setting processes, we need to define more accurately the actual role of non-state actors therein. Further, we need a

---

[7] See for the notion of legitimacy below, 3.4.

[8] See for another manifestation of these intentions, e.g. IOE, ICC & BIAC (2006), *Business and Human Rights: The Role of Business in Weak Governance Zones – Business Proposals for Effective Ways of Addressing Dilemma Situations in Weak Governance Zones. Submission to the Special Representative of the UN Secretary-General for 'Business and Human Rights'* (December 2006); see also the *Voluntary Principles on Security and Human Rights* 2000, available at www.voluntaryprinciples.org/.

better understanding of current standard-setting processes, and to find out how they differ from the more traditional public regulatory approach. We also need to assess how this influences the quality, accountability, and legitimacy of standards and their authors. This inter-disciplinary endeavour requires a very brief overview of the state of the debates on standard setting by non-state actors in our three fields.

2.   State of debates and emerging questions

2.1   Law

Standard setting by non-state actors has so far not been explicitly treated in international legal scholarship. There is, however, a solid body of legal literature on the creation of international law on the one hand, and on non-state actors, on the other hand. While traditional scholarship focused on the production of international rules in form of the traditional sources (treaty-making and the emergence of customary law), recent scholarship has paid some attention to the role of non-state actors in those processes.[9]

The currently burgeoning legal literature on non-state actors at least in passing deals with those actors' norm-making activity. Novel and comprehensive works on the first type of non-state-actors, international organisations, have recently been published, but only one monograph explicitly focuses on 'international organisations as law-makers'.[10]

Second, some international lawyers have studied the legal role of business actors as authors or co-producers of norms. A traditional field of interest for contract lawyers has been the so-called *lex mercatoria*,[11] whose *problématique* was in the 1990s linked to the globalisation debate.[12] A different strand of legal scholarship, notably in the 1970s and 1980s, examined state contracts between firms and states.[13] Later, lawyers have taken an interest in corporate self-regulation in the form of codes of conduct, often in the context of corporate social responsibility

---

[9] See Hofmann (ed.), *Non-State Actors as New Subjects of International Law*; Schuppert (ed.), *Global Governance*; Boyle and Chinkin, *The Making of International Law*, 46–52 on 'non-state actors and law-making'.

[10] Alvarez, *International Organizations*.

[11] See, e.g., López Rodríguez, *Lex Mercatoria*; Röthel, 'Lex Mercatoria'.

[12] The seminal work is Teubner (ed.), *Global Law without a State*. Within the discipline of international relations, see Cutler, *Private Power*.

[13] The seminal work is Böckstiegel, *Der Staat als Vertragspartner*. For a comprehensive discussion, see Kischel, *State Contracts*.

and corporate citizenship.[14] Legal scholars have barely analysed the elaboration of technical or product standards by industrial sectors, professional associations, technical experts and government officials.[15] The role of transnational corporations (TNCs) as formants of ordinary international hard law has been studied only recently.[16]

Most academic attention has been devoted to the third group of non-state actors, NGOs.[17] There is abundant scholarship on the increasingly important role of NGOs in the international legal process, analysing their direct lobbying at intergovernmental conferences, the organisation of parallel non-state fora, and NGO involvement in compliance control (for example in the form of *amicus curiae* briefs in international judicial proceedings, or by furnishing shadow reports in human rights monitoring).[18] It is generally admitted that NGO-activism has been a decisive factor in the adoption of important recent multilateral treaties. Notably, the Anti-Torture Convention of 1984, the Landmines Convention of 1997, and the ICC-Statute of 1998 would have probably not come into being without the intense work of transnational NGO coalitions. Inversely, NGO resistance was a crucial contribution to the failure of the projected Multilateral Agreement on Investment (MAI) in 1998. Most scholarly contributions concentrate on the NGO activity in special fields of international law, notably in environmental law,[19] human rights law,[20] and – due to the unique legal role of the International Committee of the Red Cross – in international humanitarian law, and to a lesser extent in international labour law, international criminal law, trade law and peace and security law. The growing impact of NGOs on the formation of international law has also triggered investigation into their legitimacy in a legal and ethical perspective.[21]

---

[14] Mullerat (ed.), *Corporate Social Responsibility*; Zerk, *Multinationals and Corporate Social Responsibility*; Dilling, Herberg and Winter (eds.), *Responsible Business?*
[15] Schepel, *The Constitution of Private Governance*. For legal analysis of technical standards in the EU context, mostly in the 1990s, see below note 62.
[16] Nowrot, *Normative Ordnungsstruktur*; Tully, *Corporations and International Law-Making*.
[17] See Charnovitz, 'Nongovernmental Organizations'.
[18] See, on the impact of NGOs on international law-making, Breton-Le Goff, *L'Influence des Organisations*; Lindblom, *Non-Governmental Organisations*; Dupuy and Vierucci (eds.), *NGOs in International Law*. See also Boyle and Chinkin, *The Making of International Law*, 46–52.
[19] See, e.g., Oberthür *et al.*, *Participation of Non-Governmental Organisations*.
[20] See, e.g., Schwitter Marsiaj, *The Role of International NGOs*; Cohen-Jonathan, and Flauss (eds.), *Les organisations non gouvernementales*.
[21] See, e.g., Vedder (ed.), *The Involvement of NGOs*. See also the University of Chicago Law School 2002, 'Symposium on NGOs and Democratic Accountability', *Chicago Journal of International Law*, vol. 2, 155–205 with contributions by P. Wapner, P. Spiro, D. Spar, J. Dail, and B. Kingsbury.

International organisations have in the 1990s begun to concern themselves with the role of non-governmental international actors in the international political and legal process. Key documents in that regard have been issued by UN bodies, by the OECD, and on a regional level by the Council of Europe and the EU. These documents deal with NGOs (for example their registration or participatory status),[22] with transnational corporations (for example their environmental and human rights obligations,[23] notably in the context of corporate social responsibility),[24] and with PPPs.[25] Most of these texts are not legally binding. In political terms, however, they demonstrate how seriously non-state actors' involvement in global and European governance is being taken. Notably, the most powerful inter- and supranational organisations have made the integration of non-state actors into their law-making activity an integral feature of their broad strategies of institutional reform. During the recent UN reform debate, the UN Secretary General solicited an expert report on United Nations–civil society relations (the 2004 Cardoso Report).[26] Within the EU, self-regulation by business actors and co-regulation with the European institutions is a core element of the current attempts to improve European regulation.[27]

---

[22] UN ECOSOC, *Consultative Relationship Between the United Nations and Non-Governmental Organizations* (UN Doc A/RES/1996/31) (resolution passed at the 49th plenary meeting of 25 July 1996). For the Council of Europe, see the *Convention on the Recognition of the Legal Personality of International Non-Governmental Organisations of 24 April 1986* (ETS 124); CoE, *Fundamental Principles on the Status of Non-Governmental Organisations in Europe and Explanatory Memorandum* (November 2002); CoE, *Participatory Status for International Non-Governmental Organisations with the Council of Europe* (Res(2003)8 of 19 November 2003) (adopted by the Committee of Ministers at the 861st meeting of the Ministers' Deputies); CoE, *Status of Partnership Between the Council of Europe and National Non-Governmental Organisations* (Res(2003)9 of 19 November 2003) (adopted by the Committee of Ministers at the 861st meeting of the Ministers' Deputies).

[23] OECD Guidelines for Multinational Enterprises (DAFFE/IME/WPG(2000)15/FINAL); ILO, *Tripartite Declaration of Principles Concerning Multinational Enterprises and Social Policy*, 17 November 2000, ILM, vol. 41, 186; UN ECOSOC Sub-Commission on the Promotion and Protection of Human Rights, *Norms of the Responsibilities of Transnational Corporations and Other Business Enterprises*, 13 August 2003 (UN Doc E/CN.4/Sub.2/2003//12/Rev. 2).

[24] Commission of the European Communities, *Green Paper – Promoting a European Framework for Corporate Social Responsibility* (COM(2001) 366 final); Commission of the European Communities, *Communication Implementing the Partnership for Growth and Jobs: Making Europe a Pole of Excellence on Corporate Social Responsibility (European Alliance)* (COM(2006) 136 final).

[25] UN General Assembly 2005, above note 4.   [26] Cardoso Report, above note 1.

[27] Mandelkern Group on Better Regulation 2001, *Final Report*, available at: http://ec.europa.eu/governance/impact/docs/key_docs/mandelkern_report_en.pdf; European Parliament, Council & Commission, Interinstitutional Agreement on Better Law-making (2003/C

International legal scholarship naturally focuses on the production of international law, as opposed to non-legal norms. But since the emergence of the concept of international soft law in the 1970s, legal scholars have paid some attention to the creation of 'informal' or 'para-legal' norms, which are situated outside the realm of international law or in a grey zone between law and politics.[28] Crucially, most of the norms or standards made by or with the contribution of non-state actors fall into this group. They do not necessarily pertain to the traditional and 'official' sources of international law, escape typical legal categorisation and therefore pose an extraordinary challenge to legal analysis. Legal research on various types of extra- or para-legal norms[29] is therefore especially important for our theme.

2.2   Sociology

Sociological literature has long recognised the importance of extra- or para-legal norms. Classic sociology emanated from a prime interest in multiple and overlapping norm systems shaping and mediating societal tensions by analysing the emergence and functionality of specific integrative processes and the conditions for the generation of social order. The capacity of certain actors to exercise power over others and processes of (particularly state, but also non-state) domination are of central concern to understanding the resources, norms and patterns that shape social stratification and societal power.[30] An influential stream of current sociology seeks to understand the conditions and outcomes of specific institutional configurations, and to this end explores the embeddedness and relative autonomy of the state with regard to social networks and forces.[31] Drawing on comparative empirical research, the core issue is the robustness of state institutions in terms of generating social order in a

---

321/01), OJ C 321/1; Commission of the European Communities 2003, *Action Plan Simplifying and Improving the Regulatory Environment: Report from the Commission on European Governance*, Office for Official Publications of the European Communities, Luxembourg.

[28] The seminal work is Baxter, 'The Infinite Variety'; see, critically, Weil, 'Relative Normativity?'.

[29] See, notably, Brown-Weiss (ed.), *International Compliance*; Shelton (ed.), *Commitment and Compliance*; Kirton and Trebilcock (eds.), *Hard Choices*. See, on 'standards', below, 3.1.

[30] For an influential re-framing of classic sociological theory, see Giddens' theory of structuration in Giddens, *Central Problems*. For an exemplary contribution on the interplay between state and non-state political and economic groups see Rueschemeyer *et al.*, *Capitalist Development*.

[31] Importantly, see Granovetter, 'Economic Action'.

globalising world. It is argued that '[a]utonomy complements embeddedness, protecting the state from piecemeal capture, which would destroy
the cohesiveness of the state itself and eventually undermine the coherence of its social interlocutors. The state's corporate coherence enhances
the cohesiveness of external networks and helps groups that share its
vision overcome their own collective action problems. Just as predatory
states deliberately disorganise society, developmental states help organise it.'[32] The underlying understanding is that the developmental outcomes of specific state-society dynamics are shaped by the capacity of
the state to maintain its relative autonomy and organisational power in
the context of transformed resource bases, the shifting influence of non-
state actors, and the permeability of local, national and international
norms.

The sites and patterns of these struggles are the object of sociological
research, contributing to a contextualised understanding of power
relations between the public and private sphere, and as such both
shaping the conceptual public/private-divide as well as transcending
it.[33] For instance, Joel Migdal's image of 'state in society' poignantly
illustrates the dynamics and reciprocal constitution of state and society,
not by putting the sovereignty, authority, or legitimacy of the state on
centre-stage, but, by highlighting the 'actual practices of its multiple
parts'.[34] Till Förster illuminates this point in his case study
(Chapter 12).

The ultimate objective of these approaches is to gain a nuanced understanding of the actors, structures and processes shaping state–society relationships. They also seek to understand the conditions which produce stable
and productive structures and agency relationships, or conversely lead to
the fragmentation and implosion of state capacity and authority.[35] Drawing
on insights from comparative social and political sciences, such antagonist

---

[32] See Evans, *Embedded Autonomy*, 235. Seminal on state authority and embeddedness is
Evans, Rueschemeyer and Skocpol, *Bringing the State Back In*.

[33] For a recent contribution on the current transformations of statehood and governance
processes on local levels, see Corbridge *et al.*, *Seeing the State*; and (for states in advanced
capitalism) Brenner, *New State Spaces*. For a case study on the actors and processes
shaping the permeation of local and global standards, see Randeria, 'Domesticating Neo-
Liberal Discipline'.

[34] Migdal, *State in Society*, 6.

[35] This issue is in more politicised terms discussed under the heading of failed states. See
Zartmann (ed.), *Collapsed States*; Beissinger and Young (eds.), *Beyond State Crisis?*;
Rotberg, *When States Fail*; Mason, 'Constructing Authority Relationships'; for further
case studies, see Kaarsholm (ed.), *Violence, Political Culture*.

forces of fragmentation and integration in contemporary governance dynamics have aptly been called 'fragmengration'.[36]

Notably the analysis of seemingly extreme cases of disintegration of authority and social order and of a proliferation of 'new' licit and illicit actors (see Michael Miklaucic, Chapter 7) might illuminate core issues and reveal patterns which may be less visible, but nonetheless present in all contemporary state–society relationships in a globalised world. As Goran Hyden states, 'the question of how rules are handled and regimes established and sustained is an empirical question of universal validity'.[37] The central sociological issues of this book are the practices through which the rules of the political arena are formulated, enforced and managed, the arena in which the state and non-state actors operate and interact to make authoritative decisions. Essentially, the sociological concern is the 'who' and 'how' of rule-setting in the exercise of power and in the settlement of conflicts over such rules.

2.3   Political science

Among the three disciplines combined in this volume, political science has probably most extensively acknowledged and analysed the appearance of new (non-state) actors and their growing role at all levels of society.[38] Susan Strange and others have compared this development to the medieval to modern transition from feudal agriculture to capitalist industry.[39] Initially, the literature concentrated mainly on the potentially diminishing sovereignty of the state and on the shift away from the state as sole proprietor of power and authority. The role of non-state actors in regulation has more recently been addressed by a growing number of authors.[40] At first, the relevant political science literature focused on the transition from domestic governmental regulation to inter-governmental regimes.[41] Soon the growing importance of corporations and (financial) markets in replacing or complementing the state as source of power was

---

[36] Rosenau, *Distant Proximities*, 11.
[37] See Hyden, 'Governance and the Reconstitution', 186.
[38] E.g.: Keohane and Nye (eds.), *Transnational Relations*; Krasner, 'Structural Causes'; Rosenau and Czempiel (eds.), *Governance without Government*; Kooiman, *Modern Government*; Rosenau, *The Study of World Politics*.
[39] Strange, *The Retreat of the State*.
[40] See notably Cutler, Haufler and Porter (eds.), *Private Authority*; Haufler, *A Public Role*.
[41] E.g. Keohane and Nye (eds.), *Transnational Relations*; Krasner, 'Structural Causes'.

noted.[42] But only in the late 1990s and early twenty-first century has a substantial body of political science literature begun to recognise the eminence of non-state actors other than international organisations and corporations, that is, global civil society and transnational NGOs, in global governance.[43] This analytical interest reflects the proliferation of NGOs and the increased economic power and concomitant level of professionalisation of civil society organisations. They have become pivotal agenda-setters for new policy issues such as human rights, bribery or climate change, and have accordingly acquired a key (if not always clearly defined) role in standard setting.[44]

However, political scientists still disagree on the degree of influence and importance of non-state actors in standard setting. It is controversial whether in some fields they come close to replacing the state as a source of regulation or whether they are simply complementing state regulation. Jan Kooiman, for instance, defines governance in modern societies as emerging from a plurality of governing actors rather than as a form of governmental control of society.[45] Robert Keohane and Joseph Nye formulated a theory of 'complex interdependence' for explaining this phenomenon both on the national and global level.[46] Growing interdependence between nation states and new, non-state actors is also how Charles Kegley and Eugene Wittkopf describe the development.[47] Thomas Biersteker has found the role of the state to be transformed by the appearance of non-state actors in the regulatory sphere, but rejects the suggestion that the state is eroding, as this would fail to adequately reflect the realities.[48]

Explicitly discussing the role of non-state actors in regulation, Bridget Hutter points out that our concept of regulation has been broadened. She explains this with the decreasing impact which public law can have on increasingly complex and internationalised policy issues, and with the ongoing decentralisation and outsourcing of public functions.[49] Finally,

---

[42] Strange, *Sterling and British Policy*; Strange, *The Retreat of the State*.

[43] Prakash and Hart (eds.), *Globalization and Governance*; Arts, Noortmann, and Reinalda (eds.), *Non-State Actors*; Hall and Biersteker (eds.), *The Emergence of Private Authority*.

[44] Hall, 'Private Authority'.   [45] Kooiman, *Modern Government*.

[46] Keohane and Nye, *Power and Interdependence*.

[47] Kegley and Wittkopf (eds.), *The Global Agenda*.

[48] Biersteker, T. 2004, *The Emergence of Private Authority in Global Governance*, speech held at the Confederation of Indian Industry, New Delhi, on 31 March 2004 and published in part in the Financial Express of 6 April 2004: www.financialexpress.com/old/fe_full_story.php?content_id=56416.

[49] Hutter, 'The Role of Non-State Actors'.

one of the most influential authors, James Rosenau, observing that the late twentieth century and the turn to the twenty-first century have been characterised by shifting boundaries, relocated authorities, weakened states and proliferation of non-state actors at all levels of society,[50] confirms that the state has not been entirely replaced but is rather joined by other players. The state remains a significant actor in a world that is marked by an increasing diffusion of authority and, consequently, by a diminution of hierarchy.

These findings run counter to the claims of traditional regime theorists who insist that, despite the fact that non-state actors such as corporations and civil society organisations play an increasing role at international, national and regional levels, regimes are ultimately made up of governments only.[51] And, despite the wealth of literature on the matter, it seems, first, that the current principal theoretical concepts of political sciences have only begun to capture the growing complexity of the role of non-state actors in standard setting, in part as a response to civil society actors and new forms of multi-stakeholder partnerships. Second, the potential lack of accountability resulting from the new forms of standard setting has emerged as a key challenge for political scientific analysis.

2.4   Three research questions

Drawing from these disciplinary debates there is no doubt about the pertinence of the topic. However, it is equally evident that there remains a great need for further in-depth disciplinary as well as cross-cutting interdisciplinary inquiry that responds to open and unresolved questions. In particular the following three core issues surrounding non-state actors as standard setters have emerged:

- Which new actors and processes can be identified in contemporary standard setting? (Part I).
- In the context of the demonopolisation of governmental standard setting, what is the legitimacy and accountability of (both state and non-state) actors and standards? (Part II).
- Finally, what can be said about the authority and effectiveness of standards, their authors and their enforcement? (Part III).

---

[50] Rosenau, *The Study of World Politics*.
[51] Waltz, *Theory of International Politics*; Krasner, 'Sovereignty'; James and Jackson (eds.), *States in a Changing World*; Skolnikoff, *The Elusive Transformation*.

In an effort to contribute to a comprehensive understanding of current standard-setting processes, this volume seeks to explore these three broad questions. The contributions are grouped accordingly. The three parts of the book provide the analytical structure for a comparative and coherent assessment.

3.   Key concepts

Before tackling those questions, we need to clarify the key concepts which are central to them. This is all the more important as the concepts may have different meanings in the three core disciplines, and are used in different senses in the various contributions.

3.1   Standard setting

This book is about standard setting as opposed to law making, because the concept of 'standard' is broader than the concept of 'law', and transcends important analytical categories. As Harm Schepel has put it: 'Standards hover between the state and the market; standards largely collapse the distinction between legal and social norms; standards are very rarely either wholly public or wholly private; and can be both intensely local and irreducibly global.'[52] It is widely agreed that standards are often created outside or beyond the state, and by or at least with the help of non-state actors.

Standards oscillate between facts and norms. Standards, notably technical ones, may even be purely descriptive. This book primarily deals with standards in the sense of 'a rule, principle, or means of judgment or estimation; a criterion, measure'.[53]

The term 'standard' is often used in legal documents and scholarly writing, but with quite different meanings.[54] Standards play a part in technical harmonisation ('technical standards'),[55] in administrative law, and in torts, anti-trust, product safety, and copyright law. Notably in the common law tradition, there is a specific understanding of standards (or principles) as opposed to rules.[56]

---

[52] Schepel, *The Constitution of Private Governance*, 3.
[53] *The Oxford English Dictionary*, 504, 505.
[54] See, for a good overview, Riedel, 'Standards and Sources'.
[55] Schepel, *The Constitution of Private Governance*, 24.
[56] Schlag, 'Rules and Standards'; Kaplow, 'Rules versus Standards'.

In the international sphere, the concept of standards has gained currency in international economic law,[57] in environmental law,[58] and in human rights law.[59] Technical, sanitary and phytosanitary standards, as endorsed and referred to by the TBT and the SPS Agreements, play a role in world trade law. The International Labour Organisation has adopted 'core labour standards'.[60] Standard setting is especially important in the financial domain (see in this book Marcus Schaper (Chapter 11), and Peter Hägel (Chapter 13)).[61] Within the EU, the harmonisation of technical standards is employed to remove trade barriers and to further economic, and ultimately legal, cultural, and social integration.[62]

What matters for lawyers is that standards, as already pointed out, are not necessarily legal norms. They are in a grey zone of law, morals, economics and politics. Not surprisingly, most of the standards treated in this book belong to the non-legal or para-legal realm (see for an exception Ulrike Wanitzek's Chapter 17, which examines the interaction between state law and other forms of law in Tanzania). Standards may be considered more or less law-like, depending on one's concept of law. The legal and sociological discourse on standards therefore inevitably raises the question of the meaning and nature of law. It has thereby promoted a wider, less state-centred, understanding of law, and here meets with legal pluralism.

In practical terms, standards often accompany and spell out 'hard' legal obligations. They may be stricter than those obligations. For instance, standards established by firms which assume corporate social responsibility (CSR), as dealt with by Eva Kocher (Chapter 15), and Egle Svilpaite (Chapter 16), are generally conceived as voluntary engagements by

---

[57] See Schwarzenberger, 'The Principles and Standards', on the minimum standard, the standard of preferential treatment, the most-favoured-nation standard, the national standard, the standard of identical treatment, the standard of the open door, and the standard of equitable treatment.

[58] Contini and Sand, 'Methods to Expedite Environment Protection'.

[59] Riedel, *Theorie der Menschenrechtsstandards*.

[60] ILO 2003, *Guide to International Labour Standards*, ILO Office, Geneva; ILO 2003, *Fundamental Rights at Work and International Labour Standards*, ILO Office, Geneva; Nussberger, *Sozialstandards im Völkerrecht*.

[61] See further Kerwer, 'Banking on Private Actors'; Bradley, 'Private International Law-Making'; Levit, 'A Bottom-Up Approach'; Barr and Miller, 'Global Administrative Law'; Grote and Marauhn (eds.), *The Regulation of International Financial Markets*.

[62] Cf. European Commission 2000, *Guide to the Implementation of Directives Based on the New Approach and the Global Approach*, Luxembourg: European Commission. See, in the academic literature, Rönck, *Technische Normen*; Falke, 'Standardization'; Joerges, Schepel and Vos, *The Law's Problems*; Egan, *Constructing a European Market*.

business beyond what is required by law.[63] Ultimately, these engagements may well pave the way for new, more demanding law.

3.2   Non-state actors

'Non-state actor' is a term of political science and sociology, but no legal term of art.[64] It seems no coincidence that the term 'non-state actor' does not contain a positive attribute, but is – so to speak – an empty term. It comprises actors which apparently only have in common that they are not the state, and not governmental. This terminology manifests academic helplessness vis-à-vis the great differences among those actors, and also reveals that scholars are still focused on the state as the most important point of reference of governance.[65] Most of these actors are not fundamentally new, but only new in the regulatory arena and/or new in their constellation, that is, in the way they co-operate and build ad hoc or more permanent consortiums in the context of norm formation, norm monitoring or norm enforcement.

The actors can be categorised in different ways, for instance in relation to their place on the regulatory continuum between purely public and purely private forms of regulation or actor constellations, as proposed by Dan Assaf (Chapter 3). Other authors distinguish the actors according to their place in the three-sector model of state, private sector and civil society. The most important non-state actors we examine in this book are intergovernmental or international organisations,[66] non-governmental organisations (NGOs), and finally multinational or transnational enterprises or corporations (in the following TNC[67]). Chapters 9 and 10 cover all three types of actors: Julia Black examines all types of legal governmental, non-governmental and commercial organisations involved in regulatory relationships; Monica Blagescu and Robert Lloyd deal with NGOs, TNCs, and international organisations.

---

[63] See the definition of CSR in the European Commission's Green Paper 2001, above note 24, at para. 20. See in scholarship Henningfeld, Pohl and Tolhurst (eds.), *The ICCA Handbook.*

[64] On the legal implications, see below, text with notes 74–75.

[65] It seems worth noting that politicians and activists hardly speak of non-state actors, but rather specifically denominate them.

[66] International organisations, mostly composed of states, are non-state actors in the sense that they are distinct from their member states (see below, text after note 74).

[67] We employ the term 'transnational corporation' (TNC) in conformity with the terminology used in United Nations documents and publications. In contrast, ILO and OECD texts use the expression 'multinational enterprise' (MNE).

An international organisation is, in a definition given by the International Law Commission, 'an organisation established by treaty or other instrument governed by international law and possessing its own international legal personality'.[68] International organisations are treated in Steven Wheatley's Chapter 8, and in Peter Hägel's Chapter 13 on international financial organisations.

With the term 'Transnational Corporation' (TNC),[69] we refer to a variety of cross-border arrangements and alliances. This understanding is in conformity with the OECD Guidelines on Multinational Enterprises of 2000, which apply to 'companies or other entities established in more than one country and so linked that they may co-ordinate their operations in various ways. While one or more of these entities may be able to exercise a significant influence over the activities of others, their degree of autonomy within the enterprise may vary widely from one multinational enterprise to another. Ownership may be private, state or mixed.'[70] TNCs are the main focus of Lindsey Cameron's Chapter 5 on military contractors, of Egle Svilpaite's Chapter 16 on firms in a transition state, of Eva Kocher's Chapter 15 on business producing in the Global South, and finally of Marcus Schaper's Chapter 11 on multilateral development banks, export credit agencies, and private banks financing projects in Southern countries.

By NGOs,[71] we mean bodies that are non-governmental in the sense that they are not established by governments. They are – at least

---

[68]   Art. 2 of the *Draft Articles on the Responsibility of International Organizations, Report of the International Law Commission*, Fifty-fifth session, 2003 (UN Doc A/58/10, 38).

[69]   See, on the concept of multinational or transnational enterprise, Muchlinski, *Multinational Enterprises*, 5–8; Zerk, *Multinationals and Corporate Social Responsibility*, 49–54.

[70]   OECD Guidelines for Multinational Enterprises of 8 November 2000 (DAFFE/IME (2000)20), concepts and principles, para. 3.

[71]   'Non-Governmental Organisations' lack a generally accepted definition in international law. The Council of Europe's Fundamental Principles on NGOs of 2002 characterise their object as follows: '1. NGOs are essentially voluntary self-governing bodies and are not therefore subject to direction by public authorities. ... 2. NGOs encompass bodies established by individual persons (natural and legal) and groups of such persons. They may be national or international in their composition and sphere of operation; 3. NGOs are usually organisations which have a membership but this is not necessarily the case; 4. NGOs do not have the primary aim of making a profit. ... 5. NGOs can be either informal bodies or organisations which have legal personality. They may enjoy different statuses under national law ...': Council of Europe 2002, *Fundamental Principles on the Status of Non-Governmental Organisations in Europe and Explanatory Memorandum* of 13 November 2002. See, for other definitions in international documents, Art. 1 of the *Convention on the Recognition of the Legal Personality of International Non-Governmental Organisations of 24 April 1986*, ETS 124; UN ECOSOC 1996, Res. 1996/31 – *Consultative Relationship Between the United*

formally – free from government interference, and do not wield governmental powers. Their relevance, operational modes and interactions with other actors are discussed by Dieter Neubert in Chapter 2, Lucy Koechlin and Richard Calland in Chapter 4, and Monica Blagescu and Robert Lloyd in Chapter 10, amongst others. We do not consider entities that have profit as their primary objective, political parties, and entities which promote or use violence or have clear connections with criminality as NGOs.[72] However, as Dieter Neubert maps out in his analysis of so-called 'marginal' actors, these entities are also relevant non-state actors with significant standard-setting authority. They are treated in Michael Miklaucic's Chapter 7 on illicit power structures on a sub-national level.

In functional terms, these three groups of non-state actors cannot always be readily distinguished. For instance, some TNCs create foundations in the public interest. NGOs and governments may form quasi-non-governmental organisations (quangos). Some intergovernmental organisations resemble private business, for example the International Finance Corporation. Moreover, the various actors increasingly co-operate, as already mentioned above, in the form of PPPs[73] (see Dan Assaf on PPPs in the protection of critical information infrastructure, Chapter 3; and Stéphane Guéneau on states, NGOs, companies and other private actors in the Forest Stewardship Council, Chapter 14; and Daniel Kaufmann, Aart Kraay, and Massimo Mastruzzi on the private–public governance nexus, Chapter 6).

Despite these functional overlaps and mergers, from a legal perspective it still matters whether an actor is a legal person or not.[74] Most standard-setting actors which are covered in this book do not enjoy international legal personality. This is different only for international (intergovernmental) organisations. There is a legal presumption that they possess international legal personality. This personality entails, depending on the functions entrusted to the concrete international organisation in its founding document, a limited treaty-making power. International organisations are therefore capable of creating standards in the form of binding international agreements.

Nations and Non-Governmental Organisations (UN Doc A/RES/1996/31), 49th plenary meeting of 25 July 1996, paras 1–17.

[72] See, in the literature, Lindblom, *Non-Governmental Organisations*, 36–52, esp. 47.

[73] See above, note 4.

[74] In international legal scholarship, the New Haven school has since the 1950s blurred the distinction between international legal persons and (other) actors by focusing on the 'participants' in the international legal process. This approach has not been espoused by other legal scholars.

In contrast, NGOs and TNCs are not generally deemed to enjoy international legal personality.[75] Doctrinally, this means that NGOs and TNCs cannot create international binding law themselves, but may only function as lobbyists, consultants, or otherwise catalyse the formation of 'hard' international law. By themselves, they can only produce other types of norms, such as guidelines or codes of conduct. These are, in a legal perspective, at best para-law, soft law, or – as we call it – 'standards'. However, these non-state norms or standards intensely interact with state- or inter-state law, by inspiring or interpreting it. Inversely, their standards may also forestall (inter-state)-law. This is shown in Chapter 14 by Stéphane Guéneau on the standard-setting activity of the Forest Stewardship Council, which has allowed states to shy away from the burdensome negotiation of binding international agreements about sustainable forest management.

Most importantly, NGOs and business have been increasingly collaborating in 'civil regulation'.[76] This joint regulatory activity started in the field of environmental protection, and meanwhile also covers labour and human rights standards. TNCs and NGOs here act in public–private co-operations in order to fill the regulatory gap between traditional legal regulation by the territorial state and the increasingly transnational character of business activities.

3.3   Governance

Standards and actors are, respectively, modes and authors of governance. Governance, as opposed to government, is a new term which stresses that state–society relationships and the rules, procedures and processes which order these relationships have been fundamentally transformed. Governance, as defined by the Report of the Commission on Global Governance,[77] and as used in this volume, for example by Steven Wheatley (Chapter 8), refers to the totality of ways in which individuals, public and private institutions regulate or order their common affairs. Governance is performed not only by institutionalised mechanisms, but it also consists of non-institutionalised processes. Hence, regulatory tools

---

[75] This is a different matter from their legal status under domestic law, which may be formalised (an NGO may, e.g., be incorporated, or registered as an association), or not.

[76] Murphy and Bendell, 'Towards "Civil" Regulation'.

[77] Commission on Global Governance 1995, *The Report of the Commission on Global Governance, Our Global Neighbourhood*, Oxford University Press, 2.

are not only formal laws, but also informal rules and standards involving all societal actors and expanding to all levels of governance, from local, sectoral, public to global governance. Most of these facets are illustrated in this volume.

Global governance,[78] as opposed to national governance, is characterised by the absence of some overarching governmental authority.[79] It consists not only of the system of interstate relations, but also in the combination of attempts at regulation by international organisations, NGOs, and TNCs with differing territorial scope. The structure of global governance is polycentric, not hierarchical, but network-like. Typical modes of global governance are not command and compulsion, but setting up incentives, persuasion, the stimulation of self-regulation, in short 'soft' instruments.

Chapter 6 by Daniel Kaufmann, Aart Kraay, and Massimo Mastruzzi shows how the Worldwide Governance Indicators draw from reports and views of many tens of thousands of stakeholders (the vast majority non-state, including citizens and entrepreneurs). The indicators have in some sense become a standard setter for measuring and monitoring (and benchmarking) country governance over time, and across space. And in measuring and monitoring, non-state actors such as local NGOs and the media utilise these indicators for making governments more accountable and for advocating governance reforms.

3.4   Legitimacy

Part II of this book deals with the issue of legitimacy. The question is whether, how, and to what extent, both the actors and the standards produced by them can be considered legitimate. 'Legitimacy' is multi-dimensional. It is on the one hand a social concept, and on the other hand a normative one.[80] By social legitimacy, we mean the acceptance of a political order, or – in our context – of actors and standards by the persons concerned.[81] Social legitimacy thus is an empirical fact. In contrast, any statement about normative legitimacy is based on judgments which can be ethical or moral, but also legal. Thus, ethical or moral

---

[78] See, e.g., Behrens, 'Global Governance'; Marks and Hooghe, 'Contrasting Visions'; Koenig-Archibugi and Zürn (eds.), *New Modes of Governance*.

[79] Rosenau, 'Governance, Order', 7.

[80] See in more detail Peters, Förster and Koechlin, Chapter 18, 4.1.

[81] Compare Weber, *Economy and Society*, 212 et seq.

legitimacy is a standard of moral rightness which is applied to make moral claims about law, political institutions, and about the exercise of power.[82] Alternatively or cumulatively, the normative judgment may be a legal-positivist one. A norm, including a standard, is legitimate in that sense when it originates from a formally correct source, and/or when it has been adopted in conformity with the correct procedures. Legitimacy here flows from legality.

In the context of the demonopolisation of governmental standard setting, all dimensions of legitimacy play a role.[83] A standard-setting actor, for example an NGO, may be socially legitimate because it enjoys wide popular support, as manifested in donations and membership. It may be considered morally legitimate, because its agenda is to protect a universally agreed good, for example the climate. It may possess legalist legitimacy, because it has been accredited for a global conference or has an official consultative status with the UN Economic and Social Council. Ideally, the three dimensions of legitimacy play together and to some extent converge. Also, they might arguably complement each other, so that the weakness of legal-positivist and procedural legitimacy in standard setting might be compensated for by other types of legitimacy.

On the other hand, the different legitimacies may also be in conflict, as Julia Black (Chapter 9) demonstrates with regard to the legitimacy and accountability discourses surrounding complex regulatory regimes. She concludes that there are different legitimacy communities, comprising actors within and outside the regulatory regime who have different perceptions as to the relevance and validity of different legitimacy claims with respect to different regulatory actors. Their different legitimacy claims, and associated discourses, are not always compatible but may compete. The differences between communities may be such that organisations can face a legitimacy dilemma: that actions that they need to take to render them legitimate for one legitimacy community are in direct opposition from those they need to adopt to satisfy another. Different legitimacy mechanisms (or rather relationships) are not necessarily substitutable, as not all will satisfy every legitimacy community. It is not therefore always possible to maintain legitimacy by replacing one

---

[82] Habermas, *Communication and the Evolution of Society*, 178: 'Legitimacy means that there are good arguments for a political order's claim to be recognized as right and just; a legitimate order deserves recognition. Legitimacy means a political order's worthiness to be recognized.'

[83] See, e.g., Dingwerth, 'The Democratic Legitimacy'; Bernstein and Erin, 'Non-State Global Standard Setting and the WTO'.

with another when the first one fails, unless the replacement is recognised by that legitimacy community. Finally, how organisations respond to competing legitimacy demands is structured by the particular institutional context.

Dieter Neubert (Chapter 2) points out that the new standard-setting actors may draw their legitimacy from a wide variety of sources. The source of legitimacy may be tradition or religion, the capacity to deliver certain public goods as, for instance, security. Last but not least, legitimacy may derive from elections. Neubert also asks how the actors legitimise their practices in the negotiation of standards, and how these legitimising strategies change over time.

Steven Wheatley (Chapter 8) relies on Jürgen Habermas' deliberative model of democracy and argues that the key to a more legitimate exercise of political authority by international organisations and other non-state actors is a transparent decision-making process that provides opportunities for debate and political dialogue, with participation by those representing a broad range of views. Such participation may substitute for the missing democratic legitimacy and accountability which elections provide.

Applying this model to a concrete field, Marcus Schaper (Chapter 11) demonstrates that international environmental standards defined by international financial agencies, private banks and/or export credit agencies suffer from a legitimacy deficit, because they are not devised with any input from or participation by members of the polities in which they are implemented. He argues that this gap can only be bridged by the endorsement of those standards by relevant international bodies, and, ideally, through deliberation within and participation of the recipient countries.

Stéphane Guéneau (Chapter 14) argues that most of the actors draw their legitimacy from their own social basis, claiming that they represent the interests of the general population in an intact natural environment and its sustainable use that maintains the biodiversity and productivity of forests and forest land. A side effect of the establishment of FSC standards is that the legitimacy of the private actors is strengthened while the legitimacy of public actors is questioned because of their failure to establish such standards and to influence the process significantly.

Ulrike Wanitzek (Chapter 17) describes adoption processes whose legitimacy is based on the one hand on the legitimacy of so called 'customary' law that is still embedded in the fabrics of the daily life-world of the ordinary people in Tanzania. They draw another, at times stronger legitimacy from the religious sphere, in particular Islamic law whose prescriptions are often considered universal and unquestionable. On the other hand, the processes are linked to the international interactions at state level and the bi- and multilateral agreements that the states have signed. However, many actors question precisely this legitimacy when it contradicts the basic social and cultural norms of their own societal milieu.

Finally, two contributions analyse the legitimacy of standards set by business actors. Eva Kocher shows that private social standards in transnational production draw a certain amount of legalist legitimacy from their reference to universal legal principles and national law (Chapter 15). Egle Svilpaite, in contrast, highlights that social standards established by firms in a transition state lack legitimacy due to their wide, vague, blurry content, because of their contradictory, watered-down and double-sided implementation, and because of non-disclosure practices or dormant publicity (Chapter 16).

3.5   Accountability

The new ways of generating and maintaining legitimacy described in this volume are intimately connected with issues of accountability. It is therefore not surprising that accountability discourses relating to all aspects of state- and non-state standard setting are currently proliferating. Mark Bovens has defined accountability as 'a relationship between an actor and a forum, in which the actor has an obligation to explain and to justify his or her conduct, the forum can pose questions and pass judgment, and the actor may face consequences'.[84] In other words, accountability does not only imply ex post scrutiny, but has ex ante preventive effects.

In this book, Julia Black (Chapter 9) describes the relationship between accountability and legitimacy as follows: '[The] perceptions of the right to govern ('legitimacy') may depend (in whole or in part) on whether the actor is accepted as having an appropriate accountability relationship with others, often including, but not necessarily confined to, the person whose perception is in question.' On this premise, Monica Blagescu and Robert Lloyd (Chapter 10) search means to judge and evaluate the quality of accountability of influential international actors.

---

[84]   See Bovens, 'Analysing and Assessing Accountability', 450; see also Grant and Keohane, who define accountability as the implication that some actors have the right to hold other actors to a set of standards, to judge whether they have fulfilled their responsibilities in light of these standards, and to impose sanctions if they determine that these responsibilities have not been met: Grant and Keohane, 'Accountability and Abuses', 29.

In the 'amorphous global public sphere', state and non-state actors (namely international organisations, TNCs, and NGOs) are each mandated to govern in certain spheres. In their Global Accountability Project (GAP), Blagescu and Lloyd argue that accountability principles have become generalisable and apply to all three sectors (public, business, civic). They also show that the actual application of key accountability principles can be measured. Thereby, the accountability of all three types of actors in all three sectors can be compared and subjected to civic debate and regulation.

3.6   Authority and power

As the standard-setting authority was traditionally incumbent on states,[85] the emergence of new sites and actors begs the question of their authority.[86] Therefore, Part III of this book deals with the authority, and also with the closely related problems of power and effectiveness of non-state actors as standard setters. The concept of authority is ambiguous. It is frequently, both in political science and in sociological discourses, also in some contributions to this book, co-equalled or associated with power. For instance, Eva Kocher (Chapter 15) uses legal authority and 'regulatory capacity' as synonyms. A different conceptualisation is to distinguish authority from power, and rather to link it to legitimacy. In that perspective, authority is not the capacity to enforce obedience, but the right (or title) to legitimately influence action, opinion, or belief.[87] This understanding is informed by the insight that authority is co-constituted by some kind of recognition (acknowledgement), while power can exist and be exercised without such recognition. Standard-setting activity requires both theoretical – or what Steven Wheatley (Chapter 8) calls epistemic authority[88] – in the sense of expertise (in matters of ideas and beliefs), and practical authority in the sense of the right to rule (and thus to influence behaviour).

---

[85] Green, *The Authority of the State*; Pauly and Grande, 'Reconstituting Political Authority'.

[86] Higgott *et al.* (eds.), *Nonstate Actors and Authority*; Hall and Biersteker (eds.), *The Emergence of Private Authority*; Cashore, 'Legitimacy'.

[87] Raz (ed.), *Authority*, 2–3. In this sense also Hall and Biersteker (eds.), *The Emergence of Private Authority*, 4: 'What differentiates authority from power is the legitimacy of claims to authority.'

[88] According to Wheatley (Chapter 8), relying on G.-U. Charles, epistemic authority is concerned with who should be believed, under what circumstances, and with respect to what issues.

Today, the authority to set standards is dispersed amongst and between actors. These actors operate on a continuum between state and non-state spheres. The fact that we have such a continuum also indicates that the structures from which the actors or combinations of actors derive their authority are shifting. The fragmentation and multiplication of authorities does not in a linear way erode state authority. It is not true that the more actors emerge, the less authority the state enjoys, as many if not all of the chapters of this book demonstrate. For instance, Peter Hägel's key questions are whether the delegation of authority to private actors may be reversed, and when declining control (of the state) leads to a loss of overall authority (Chapter 13). He considers crucial the ensuing conflicting authority and control claims between private actors and state actors.

The more fluid and amorphous understanding of the constitution and empirical reality of authorities is keenly illustrated in Dieter Neubert's contribution (Chapter 2). Neubert coins the term 'islands of order' to highlight the de-linkage of such authorities from spatial and functional ranges defined by the state. These 'islands of order' respond to what has been termed by James Rosenau 'demands for governance',[89] and are – at least in part – shaped by actors and processes of setting standards. Overall, the materialisation of such islands of order in factually open contexts is contingent on both global and local conditions.[90]

Steven Wheatley (Chapter 8) argues that the political authority of non-state actors depends on a combination of three factors, whose relative weight varies with the circumstances of the particular case: the first factor is the source of political authority (that is, the constitutive instrument or mechanism); the second factor is the extent to which it is accepted that the non-state actors are pursuing good governance aims and methods. The third factor is, in circumstances of imperfect knowledge and reasonable disagreement, the epistemic authority of the non-state actor. Wheatley points out that non-state actors do not enjoy inherent epistemic authority, and therefore must make a claim to know better than anyone else what should be done, that is, which normative standards should be applied to which actors in which circumstances. Finally, Wheatley argues that epistemic authority must be understood democratically.

---

[89] Rosenau, 'Strong Demand', 31–48.
[90] Order can of course also be generated through other modes of governance than through standard setting, for instance through technical and financial resources which are furnished, e.g. by international financial institutions, foreign aid donors, or TNCs.

Democratic epistemic authority is provided by democratic decision-making procedures: inclusive, consensus-seeking processes of reasoned deliberation, with reasons for decisions made public and subject to scrutiny by external actors.

Eva Kocher and Egle Svilpaite (Chapters 15 and 16) examine the authority of business standard setters. Egle Svilpaite describes the basically schizophrenic attitude of business vis-à-vis government: on the one hand the public sector is viewed with deep mistrust, but on the other hand it is expected to regulate social standards and ensure a level playing field. Eva Kocher demonstrates that, although private social standards refer to universal norms (for example to labour standards by the ILO), universalism is not sustained when the standards are actually applied. Ultimately, the content of a social standard in its concrete application is established by reference to local customs, practices and legal standards. Thus, in the implementation of that standard, its universalist legitimacy is not effectively translated into a corresponding authority. Legal authority, understood by Kocher as regulatory capacity, does not mean compliance at shop-floor level. Legal authority does not presuppose enforcement, but merely legal enforceability; and this in turn implies enforceability by way of (para)legal proceedings. According to Kocher, juridification creates a specific legal connection between legitimacy in standard setting and authority in enforcement: legal arguments explicitly refer back to imputedly legitimate standards, on the one hand, and implicitly point to enforcement mechanisms, on the other hand. By invoking the legitimacy of international and local national law, corporate standards compete with national legal systems – without guaranteeing the appropriate authority. This produces a risk of erosion. Independent monitoring and effective national and international complaint mechanisms are necessary to prevent such erosion. Local actors, especially employees and their representatives, must be empowered to participate in implementation and monitoring. Therefore, freedom of association emerges as the most important vehicle for the provision of greater authority.

3.7   Effectiveness

Standard setting is effective when the standards are attended with results, are complied with, and in fact generate the desired order. Depending on a given actor's authority to set standards, the mechanisms to generate compliance will differ. Compliance is a key indicator of effective (if not necessarily legitimate) governance.[91] Julia Black (Chapter 9) argues that the organisational effectiveness of regulatory bodies in polycentric regulation relationships varies with their role and responses within the multiple and often competing discourses on accountability and legitimacy, and she sketches out a typology of possible organisational responses dealing with such trilemmas.

Marcus Schaper (Chapter 11) argues first that the effectiveness of international financial standards is contingent on the market power of the financial institutions formulating the policies. This is an important example of the 'market authority' of such standards. Second, the authority of the standards depends on the capacity and composition of the NGOs policing them. This linkage places a huge and largely informal responsibility for the actual implementation and enforcement of such standards on potentially under-resourced actors.

Standard-setting bodies need not enjoy authority in the sense of legitimacy to be effective. Indeed, illicit or extra-legal entities may well exercise power highly effectively, through coercive and/or remunerative means of control, rather than through deliberative or normative mechanisms. This is demonstrated in the contributions of Dieter Neubert (Chapter 2) and Michael Miklaucic (Chapter 7).

Lacking effectiveness is evident in the governance of privatised military and security activity, as Lindsey Cameron (Chapter 5) shows. Despite the introduction of an enforcement mechanism which allows any individual to make a written complaint, 'it would be at best unreasonable and at worst hopelessly naïve to expect self-regulation to suffice when it comes to PMCs [Private Military Companies]', she writes. Put more sharply, the security companies' pledges to adhere to the International Peace Operations Association's (IPOA's) code of conduct have proved 'woefully inadequate'.

In Chapters 15 and 16, Eva Kocher and Egle Svilpaite examine the effectiveness of standards established by business actors. Egle Svilpaite shows that the effectiveness of self-regulatory mechanisms is doubtful, as the case of Lithuania demonstrates: the CSR standards are too weak, nonbinding, and define no real responsibility for a concrete group of people or problems. Svilpaite concludes that business standards are not effective unless embedded in appropriate state regulation and scrutinised by a responsible, critical civil society.

---

[91] See Barker, *Political Legitimacy*.

In the same vein, Kocher expands on social standards in transnational production in the form of codes of conduct or framework agreements that are applied and enforced mostly by transnational companies themselves. Judicial or para-judicial enforcement mechanisms are often lacking. In some cases, standards are even breached on a systematic basis. Consequently, it has not yet been demonstrated that self-regulated social standards have actually led to an improvement in working conditions. However, there are conditions under which such norms can be given stronger teeth. International framework agreements involving trade unions effectively promote the freedom of association and organisation of trade unions at a local level. By strengthening the creation and activity of important local actors, the agreements create a reflexive mechanism that contributes to the involvement of local actors in norm implementation and is thus able to further effectiveness of norm enforcement. Collective representation partly steps in and may, in some cases, even be an adequate functional equivalent to implementation and enforcement via third-party delegation. Nevertheless, mechanisms for the enforcement of transnational social standards remain essentially political in nature. Societal pressure continues to be one of the key reasons for compliance. Kocher's conclusion raises the fundamental question of the motives driving business to set standards, and the issue of the mandate and capacity of NGOs in this context.

In the following three parts of this book, methods, approaches, and knowledge of three academic disciplines are used in order to answer our three main questions. Pulling these insights together will enable us to grasp the phenomenon of standard setting by and with the help of non-state actors better and in a more comprehensive way.

References

Alvarez, J. 2005, *International Organizations as Law-Makers*, Oxford University Press.

Arts, B., Noortmann, M. and Reinalda, B. (eds.) 2001, *Non-State Actors in International Relations*, Aldershot, Ashgate.

Barker, R. 1990, *Political Legitimacy and the State*, Oxford University Press.

Barr, M. and Miller, G. 2006, 'Global Administrative Law: The View from Basel', *European Journal of International Law*, vol. 17, 15–46.

Baxter, R. 1980, 'The Infinite Variety of International Law', *International and Comparative Law Quarterly*, vol. 48, 546–66.

Behrens, M. 2004, 'Global Governance' in A. Benz (ed.), *Governance – Regieren in komplexen Regelsystemen*, Wiesbaden, VS Verlag für Sozialwissenschaften, 103–24.

Beissinger, M. and Young, C. (eds.) 2002, *Beyond State Crisis? Post-Colonial Africa and Post-Soviet Eurasia in Comparative Perspective*, Washington DC, Woodrow Wilson Centre Press.

Bernstein, S. and Erin, H. 2008, 'Non-State Global Standard Setting and the WTO: Legitimacy and the Need for Regulatory Space', *Journal of International Economics*, vol. **11**, 575–698.

Böckstiegel, K. 1971, *Der Staat als Vertragspartner ausländischer Privatunternehmer*, Frankfurt am Main, Athenäum.

Börzel, T. and Risse, T. 2005, 'Public–Private Partnerships: Effective and Legitimate Tools of International Governance?' in L. Grande and E. Pauly, *Complex Sovereignty: Reconstituting Political Authority in the 21st Century*, University of Toronto, 195–216.

Bovens, M. 2007, 'Analysing and Assessing Accountability: A Conceptual Framework', *European Law Journal*, vol. **13**, 447–68.

Boyle, A. and Chinkin, C. 2007, *The Making of International Law*, Oxford University Press.

Bradley, C. 2005, 'Private International Law-Making for the Financial Markets', *Fordham International Law Journal*, vol. **29**, 401–53.

Brenner, N. 2004, *New State Spaces, Urban Governance and the Rescaling of Statehood*, Oxford University Press.

Breton-Le Goff, G. 2001, *L'influence des organisations non gouvernementales (ONG) sur la négociation de quelques instruments internationaux*, Bruxelles, Bruylant.

Brown-Weiss, E. (ed.) 1997, *International Compliance with Nonbinding Accords*, Washington DC, The American Society of International Law.

Cashore, B. 2002, 'Legitimacy and the Privatization of Environmental Governance: How Non-State Market-Driven (NSMD) Governance Systems Gain Rule-making Authority', *Governance: An International Journal of Policy, Administration and Institutions*, vol. **15**, 503–29.

Charnovitz, S. 2006, 'Nongovernmental Organizations and International Law', *American Journal of International Law*, vol. **100**, 348–72.

Cohen-Jonathan, G. and Flauss, J.-F. (eds.) 2005, *Les organisations non gouvernementales et le droit international des droits de l'homme*, Bruxelles, Bruylant.

Contini, P. and Sand, P. 1972, 'Methods to Expedite Environment Protection: International Ecostandards', *American Journal of International Law*, vol. **66**, 37–59.

Corbridge, S. *et al.* 2005, *Seeing the State – Governance and Governmentability in India*, Cambridge University Press.

Cutler, C. 2003, *Private Power and Global Authority: Transnational Merchant Law in the Global Political Economy*, Cambridge University Press.

Cutler, C., Haufler, V. and Porter, T. 1999 (eds.), *Private Authority and International Affairs*, State University of New York Press.

Dilling, O., Herberg, M. and Winter, G. (eds.) 2007, *Responsible Business? Self-Governance and the Law in Transnational Economic Transactions*, Oxford, Hart Publishing.

Dingwerth, K. 2005, 'The Democratic Legitimacy of Public–Private Rule Making: What Can We Learn from the World Commission on Dams', *Global Governance*, vol. **11**, 65–83.

Dupuy, P. and Vierucci, L. (eds.) 2008, *NGOs in International Law*, Northampton, Elgar.

Egan, M. 2001, *Constructing a European Market. Standards, Regulation, and Governance*, Oxford University Press.

Evans, P. 1995, *Embedded Autonomy: States and Industrial Transformation*, Princeton University Press.

Evans, P., Rueschemeyer, D. and Skocpol, T. 1985, *Bringing the State Back in*, Cambridge University Press.

Falke, J. 1996, 'Standardization by Professional Organizations' in G. Winter (ed.), *Sources and Categories of European Union Law*, Baden-Baden, Nomos, 645–75.

Giddens, A. 1986, *Central Problems in Social Theory: Action, Structure, and Contradiction in Social Analysis*, Berkeley, University of California Press.

Granovetter, M. 1985, 'Economic Action and Social Structure: The Problem of Embeddedness', *American Journal of Sociology*, vol. **91**, 481–510.

Grant, R. and Keohane, R. 2005, 'Accountability and Abuses of Power in World Politics', *American Political Science Review*, vol. **99**, 29–43.

Green, L. 1989, *The Authority of the State*, Oxford University Press.

Grote, R. and Marauhn, T. (eds.) 2006, *The Regulation of International Financial Markets: Perspectives for Reform*, Cambridge University Press.

Habermas, J. (T. McCarthy, transl.) 1979, *Communication and the Evolution of Society*, Boston, Beacon.

Hall, R. 2005, 'Private Authority: Non-State Actors and Global Governance', *Harvard International Review*, 22 June 2005.

Hall, R. and Biersteker, T. (eds.) 2002, *The Emergence of Private Authority in Global Governance*, Cambridge University Press.

Haufler, V. 2001, *A Public Role for the Private Sector: Industry Self-Regulation in a Global Economy*, Washington DC, Carnegie Endowment for International Peace.

Henningfeld, J., Pohl, M. and Tolhurst, N. (eds.) 2006, *The ICCA Handbook on Corporate Social Responsibility*, Chichester, John Wiley & Sons.

Higgott, R. A. *et al.* (eds.) 2000, *Nonstate Actors and Authority in the Global System*, London, Routledge.

Hofmann, R. (ed.) 1999, *Non-State Actors as New Subjects of International Law: from the Traditional State Order towards the Law of the Global Community*, Berlin, Duncker & Humblot.

Hutter, B. 2006, 'The Role of Non-State Actors in Regulation' in F. Schuppert (ed.), *Global Governance and the Role of Non-State Actors*, Baden-Baden, Nomos, 63–79.

Hyden, G. 1999, 'Governance and the Reconstitution of Political Order' in R. Joseph (ed.), *State, Conflict and Democracy in Africa*, Boulder, Lynne Rienner, 179–95.

James, A. and Jackson, R. (eds.) 1993, *States in a Changing World: A Contemporary Analysis*, Oxford University Press.

Joerges, C., Schepel, H. and Vos, E. 1999, 'The Law's Problems with the Involvement of Non-Governmental Actors in Europe's Legislative Processes: The Case of Standardisation under the "New Approach"', *EUI Working Paper LAW* 99/9.

Kaarsholm, P. (ed.) 2006, *Violence, Political Culture and Development in Africa*, Oxford, James Currey.

Kaplow, L. 1992, 'Rules versus Standards: An Economic Analysis', *Duke Law Journal*, vol. **42**, 557–629.

Kegley, C. and Wittkopf, E. (eds.) 1995, *The Global Agenda: Issues and Perspectives*, New York, McGraw-Hill.

Keohane, R. and Nye, J. (eds.) 1972, *Transnational Relations and World Politics*, Cambridge, Harvard University Press.

Keohane, R. and Nye, J. 1989, *Power and Interdependence: World Politics in Transition*, 2nd edn, Boston, Little, Brown.

Kerwer, D. 2004, 'Banking on Private Actors. Financial Market Regulation and the Limits of Transnational Governance' in A. Héritier, M. Stolleis and F. Scharpf (eds.), *European and International Regulation after the Nation State*, Baden-Baden, Nomos, 205–23.

Kirton, J. and Trebilcock, M. (eds.) 2004, *Hard Choices, Soft Law: Voluntary Standards in Global Trade, Environment and Social Governance*, Aldershot, Ashgate.

Kischel, U. 1992, *State Contracts*, Stuttgart, Boorberg.

Koenig-Archibugi, M. and Zürn, M. (eds.) 2006, *New Modes of Governance in the Global System: Exploring Publicness, Delegation and Inclusiveness*, Houndmills, Palgrave Macmillan.

Kooiman, J. 1993, *Modern Government: New Government-Society Interactions*, London, Sage Publications.

Krasner, S. 1982, 'Structural Causes and Regime Consequences: Regimes as Intervening Variables', *International Organization*, vol. **36**, 185–205.

Krasner, S. 1988, 'Sovereignty: An Institutional Perspective', *Comparative Political Studies*, vol. **21**, 66–94.

Levit, J. 2005, 'A Bottom-Up Approach to International Law-Making: The Tale of Three Trade Finance Instruments', *Yale Journal of International Law*, vol. **30**, 125–209.

Lindblom, A.-K. 2005, *Non-Governmental Organisations in International Law*, Cambridge University Press.

López Rodríguez, A. 2003, *Lex Mercatoria and Harmonization of Contract Law in the EU*, Copenhagen, DJØF Publishing.

Marks, M. and Hooghe, L. 2005, 'Contrasting Visions of Multi-Level Governance' in I. Bache and M. Flinders (eds.), *Multi-Level Governance*, Oxford University Press, 15–30.

Mason, A. 2005, 'Constructing Authority Relationships on the Periphery: Vignettes from Colombia', *International Political Science Review*, vol. **26**, 37–54.

Migdal, J. 2001, *State in Society: Studying how States and Societies Constitute and Transform one Another*, Cambridge University Press.

Muchlinski, P. 2007, *Multinational Enterprises and the Law*, 2nd edn, Oxford University Press.

Mullerat, R. (ed.) 2005, *Corporate Social Responsibility: The Corporate Governance of the 21st Century*, The Hague, Kluwer Law International.

Murphy, D. F. and Bendell, J. 2002, 'Towards "Civil" Regulation: NGOs and the Politics of Corporate Environmentalism' in P. Utting, *The Greening of Business in Developing Countries*, London, Zed Books/UNRISD, 245–67.

Nowrot, K. 2006, *Normative Ordnungsstruktur und private Wirkungsmacht: Konsequenzen der Beteiligung transnationaler Unternehmen an den Rechtssetzungsprozessen im internationalen Wirtschaftssystem*, Berlin, Berliner Wissenschaftsverlag.

Nye, J. and Donahue, J. (eds.) 2000, *Governance in a Globalizing World*, Washington, Brookings Institution Press.

Oberthür, S. *et al.* 2002, *Participation of Non-Governmental Organisations in International Environmental Co-operation: Legal Basis and Practical Experience*, Berlin, Schmidt.

Oxford Dictionary 1989, vol. 16, Oxford, Clarendon.

Paul, T., Ikenberry, G. J. and Hall, J. (eds.) 2003, *The Nation State in Question*, Princeton University Press.

Pauly, L. and Grande, E. 2005, 'Reconstituting Political Authority: Sovereignty, Effectiveness, and Legitimacy in a Transnational Order' in L. Grande and E. Pauly, *Complex Sovereignty: Reconstituting Political Authority in the 21st Century*, University of Toronto, 3–21.

Peters, A. 2006, 'Privatisierung, Globalisierung und die Resistenz des Verfassungsstaates' in P. Mastronardi and D. Taubert (eds.), *Staats- und Verfassungstheorie im Spannungsfeld der Disziplinen*. Beiheft Archiv für Rechts- und Sozialphilosophie 105, Stuttgart, Franz Steiner, 100–59.

Pieth, M. 2007, 'Multi-Stakeholder Initiatives to Combat Money Laundering and Bribery' in C. Brütsch and D. Lehmkuhl (eds.), *Law and Legalisation in Transnational Relations*, London, Routledge, 81–100.

Prakash, A. and Hart, J. (eds.) 1999, *Globalization and Governance*, London, Routledge.

Randeria, S. 2003, 'Domesticating Neo-Liberal Discipline: Transnationalisation of Law, Fractured States and Legal Plurality in the South' in W. Lepenies (ed.), *Shared Histories and Negotiated Universals*, Frankfurt and New York, Campus & St. Martins Press, 146–82.

Raz, J. (ed.) 1990, *Authority*, New York University Press.

Riedel, E. 1986, *Theorie der Menschenrechtsstandards*, Berlin, Duncker & Humblot.

Riedel, E. 1991, 'Standards and Sources', *European Journal of International Law*, vol. **2**, 58–84.

Rönck, R. 1995, *Technische Normen als Gestaltungsmittel des Europäischen Gemeinschaftsrechts*, Berlin, Duncker & Humblot.

Rosenau, J. 1992, 'Governance, Order, and Change in World Politics' in Rosenau and Czempiel (eds.), 1–29.

Rosenau, J. 2003, *Distant Proximities – Dynamics Beyond Globalisation*, Princeton University Press.

Rosenau, J. 2005, 'Strong Demand – Huge Supply: Governance in an Emerging Epoch' in I. Bache and M. Flinders (eds.), *Multi-Level Governance*, Oxford University Press, 31–48.

Rosenau, J. 2006, *The Study of World Politics: Globalization and Governance*, London, Routledge.

Rosenau, J. and Czempiel, E.-O. (eds.) 1992, *Governance without Government: Order and Change in World Politics*, Cambridge University Press.

Rotberg, R. 2004, *When States Fail: Causes and Consequences*, Princeton University Press.

Röthel, A. 2007, 'Lex Mercatoria, Lex Sportiva, Lex Technica', *Juristen-Zeitung*, vol. **62**, 755–63.

Rueschemeyer, D. *et al.* 1992, *Capitalist Development and Democracy*, University of Chicago Press.

Schepel, H. 2005, *The Constitution of Private Governance, Product Standards in the Regulation of Integrating Markets*, Oxford, Hart Publishing.

Schlag, P. 1985, 'Rules and Standards', *UCLA Law Review*, vol. **33**, 379–430.

Schuppert, G. (ed.) 2006, *Global Governance and the Role of Non-State Actors*, Baden-Baden, Nomos.

Schwarzenberger, G. 1966, 'The Principles and Standards of International Economic Law', *Recueil des Cours de l'Académie de la Haye*, vol. **117**, 1–98.

Schwitter Marsiaj, C. 2004, *The Role of International NGOs in the Global Governance of Human Rights*, Zurich, Schulthess.

Shelton, D. (ed.) 2000, *Commitment and Compliance: The Role of Non-Binding Norms in the International Legal System*, Oxford University Press.

Skolnikoff, E. 1994, *The Elusive Transformation: Science, Technology, and the Evolution of International Politics*, Princeton University Press.

Strange, S. 1996, *The Retreat of the State: The Diffusion of Power in the World Economy*, Cambridge University Press.

Strange, S. 1971, *Sterling and British Policy*, Oxford University Press.

Teubner, G. (ed.) 1997, *Global Law without a State*, Dartmouth, Aldershot.

Tully, S. 2007, *Corporations and International Law-Making*, Boston and Leiden, Martinus Nijhoff.

Vedder, A. (ed.) 2007, *The Involvement of NGOs in International Governance and Policy: Sources of Legitimacy*, Leiden, Martinus Nijhoff.

Waltz, K. 1979, *Theory of International Politics*, Reading, Mass., Prentice Hall, Addison-Wesley.

Weber, M. 1968, *Economy and Society* (ed. by G. Roth and C. Wittich), New York, Bedminster Press.

Weil, P. 1983, 'Towards Relative Normativity in International Law?', *American Journal of International Law*, vol. 77, 413–42.

Weiss, L. (ed.) 2003, *States in the Global Economy: Bringing Democratic Institutions Back in*, Cambridge University Press.

Zartmann, I. (ed.) 1995, *Collapsed States: the Disintegration and Restoration of Legitimate Authority*, Boulder, Lynne Rienner.

Zerk, J. 2006, *Multinationals and Corporate Social Responsibility, Limitations and Opportunities in International Law*, New York, Cambridge University Press.

PART I

New actors and processes in contemporary standard setting

2

Local and regional non-state actors on the margins of public policy in Africa

DIETER NEUBERT[*]

1. Introduction

When we ask about new actors and processes in contemporary standard setting we, at least implicitly, assume that the state has a core position as law maker and the government acts as the institution which formulates and implements basic structures of the economy and society in the sense of a regulatory policy. The division of tasks and the different ways of acting between the state and the non-state actors are often captured with the classical three-sector model of society with state as first sector, market/economy as the second so-called 'private sector' and a third 'non-profit' sector.[1] This common model dominated the scholarly and political discussion in the 1980s and 1990s and is still important both for the description of modern liberal democracies as well as for the political programme for developing and transforming countries promoted by the World Bank and other international development agencies. However, the three-sector model comes with hidden assumptions:

- The state's existence is taken for granted, as is its dominant role in standard setting.
- This three-sector model is a widely shared political objective for the constitution of a modern liberal and democratic society in which the existence of non-state actors is seen as positive. There are differences concerning the balance between the three sectors and the specific role for each one of them, but all three are seen as necessary.

---

[*] Professor of Sociology and Chair of Development Sociology, Department of Sociology, University of Bayreuth, Germany; Dr. phil. (University of Mainz).
[1] See Brock, *The Nonprofit Sector*; DiMaggio and Anheier, 'Sociological Conceptualization of Non-Profit'; Evers, 'Welfare Mix'; Powell, *The Non-Profit Sector*; Weisbrod, 'Voluntary Non-Profit Sector'.

- International political support for non-state actors, especially in transformation and developing countries carries the implication that these actors are new in some parts of the world and that their role has to be promoted to overcome traditional social structures or outdated socialist regimes.
- It is assumed that political processes are bound by the rule of law. Therefore, standard setting is seen as a procedure for making laws and by-laws or as the formulation of formal rules and regulations.

Beside the fact that non-state actors are still highly regarded, a controversial discussion on non-state actors has been taking place. In the centre of this debate is either the blurred distinction between enterprises and the state or between NGOs (non-governmental organisations) and the state. Critics talk of the erosion of the public–private divide especially in the sense that enterprises or NGOs influence public policy via effective agenda setting and domination of the public political discussion or via lobbying and using corporatist structures.[2] However, this discussion is somehow limited by the three-sector model. This prevents focus from being shifted to other types of non-state actors on the margins of conventional public policy, such as traditional leaders, cross-territorial traders or criminal organisations.

In strong states, like Western liberal democratic states, or well-organised dictatorships, these actors play only a limited role.[3] These non-state actors at the margins of public policy can become remarkably politically relevant in weak and failing states[4] because there the 'margins of public policy' are much wider than in well-organised strong states with a functioning bureaucracy in the Weberian sense. In considering the role of non-state actors in these weak and failing states, we are forced to rethink the hidden assumptions in a more fundamental way. In doing this I will draw from African examples because Africa offers an extremely wide range of non-state actors on the margins of conventional public policy.

The main objections against the hidden assumptions in the three-sector model are:

---

[2] For corporatism, see Lehmbruch and Schmitter (eds.), *Corporatist Policy Making*; Zimmer, 'Corporatism Revisited'.

[3] However, there are exceptions, e.g. at least in the twentieth century the Mafia in Italy had considerable influence on political processes.

[4] For failing states see Rotberg, *When States Fail*; Milliken and Krause, 'State Failure, State Collapse'.

- The discussion of weak and failed states shows that the state cannot be taken for granted. Especially, in weak states and in failed states the roles can change dramatically in favour of some of the non-state actors.
- From a worldwide perspective, the three-sector model does not capture the diversity of non-state actors. In particular, non-state actors, such as warlords, criminal organisations or vigilante organisations do not fit into the political programme of democratisation or good governance linked to that model.
- The blurred distinction between state and non-state is not at all new. At least in Africa, the diversity of non-state actors is as old as the modern territorial state itself.[5]
- The procedure of standard setting often differs from the ideal rule of law. In weak or failing states laws and formal regulations are hardly implemented and effective standards in everyday life may not be set in formal procedures according to the rule of law. They may instead result from powerful action either by state or non-state actors.

Against this background, it seems that non-state actors in Africa cannot be understood in a kind of analytic opposition between them and the state. Many of the African non-state actors gain room and a role due to the weakness of the state or even to its absence. In this situation, non-state actors are in some sense natural standard setters. In doing so, they are filling one of the gaps left open by a weak or failing state.

This chapter focuses on the role of non-state actors in this specific situation where the public sector is weak or even absent.[6] In the first section, I will try to show the diversity of non-state actors beyond the conventional three-sector model. In the second section, I will present a short history of how this diversity of non-state actors came into being. In the third section, I will examine the role of non-state actors in weak and failing states with a focus on standard setting. Finally, in my conclusion, I will briefly argue that the challenge facing us in understanding the nature of politics is not only the blurred distinction between the private and the public, but also the weakness or even absence of a conventional public policy in Africa.

---

[5] This may be true for Western liberal states, too. However, this is not of concern in this chapter.

[6] The purpose of this chapter is to give a first insight into the diversity of non-state actors. Therefore, the references will offer examples; a comprehensive and systematic review of literature, for instance of the growing literature on NGOs or neo-traditional leaders in Africa, is not intended.

2.   The diversity of non-state actors: a tentative typology[7]

If we are to take the concept of 'non'-state actors seriously, we should treat it as actually meaning 'non-state' and 'actor'.[8] Actors, in this sense, act on the political or societal level, but even with this limitation the range of non-state actors is extremely wide.

For an overview, we may start within the conventional three-sector model. However, we will see that there are actors who do not fit into this model, either because they transcend the analytical differences between the sectors or they do not fit at all into this frame.

The African non-profit sector differs dramatically from country to country, but the basic types of actors may be named.[9] At first we find the typical range of NGOs that we already know from Western liberal democracies (welfare organisations, youth and women's associations, religious organisations, for example Christian, Muslim or Hindu, and development organisations). The non-profit sector in developing countries (as well as in some post-socialist transformation countries) has very strong international links. Especially in African countries, a considerable part of the resources required for their functioning comes from international donors. In a number of countries, such as Rwanda, Mozambique or Malawi, the now-diversified non-profit sector is the result of a supply-driven policy.[10] The constituency of African NGOs is often weak and many of these organisations would not survive without foreign funding.

Because of their considerable importance, religious organisations, in particular, need to be appraised in detail. The Catholic Church and the mainstream protestant churches are like other non-profit sector NGOs closely linked to their international partners. African churches and their welfare and development activities often depend on international funds, too. But in contrast to other NGOs, churches have a social basis of their own.[11] Especially Pentecostal and revivalist churches and missions have managed to build up a strong constituency that functions as the main

---

[7] Like in any typology of social phenomena I will present ideal types in the Weberian sense.

[8] For a more detailed discussion of the concept see Josselin and Wallace, 'Non-State Actors in World Politics'.

[9] See Neubert, 'Development Utopia'; Neubert, *Entwicklungspolitische*; Neubert, 'Nichtregierungsorganisationen'; Igoe and Kelsall (eds.), *Between a Rock and a Hard Place*.

[10] See Glagow's studies on the mushrooming of NGOs in these countries, see Glagow *et al. Indigenous Non-Governmental Organizations*; Glagow, Ruffert and Chokani, *Nichtstaaliche Trägerstrukturen*. For Rwanda see Neubert, *Entwicklungspolitische*.

[11] For Madagascar see Randrianja, 'Madagascar, FFKM and Politics' for Kenya and Rwanda see Neubert, *Entwicklungspolitische*.

resource for the organisation. And some of these African churches invest the funds generated by their constituency in well-run enterprises, which add to their income.[12]

In Islamic countries or regions, Islamic groups have increasingly gained importance. They mobilise their followers often into social movements and may receive support from Saudi Arabia, Libya, or, in the case of the Ismaelites, from Pakistan from the Aga Khan Foundation.[13]

Community-based groups such as self-help groups, co-operatives, committees of local traders, artisans, rotating saving groups, or neighbourhood committees are a specific feature of the non-profit sector in African societies (just as is the case in developing countries as a whole). Usually, they are seen as part of the third sector. However, co-operatives overlap with the private sector and neighbourhood committees, or the so-called 'civics' in South Africa, have taken over local administrative functions.[14]

The non-profit sector is open in the sense that there are organisations that overlap with the state sector and the private sector. Additionally, there are social and political opposition groups and/or political movements that question the existing political structures fundamentally. They are mostly ignored by the three-sector model and are usually not even considered as part of civil society. Some of them fight these structures using violence. We find separatist movements more or less along the lines of the radical communist groups we used to find in the West. Of these, Islamic movements are the most prominent ones. They may act on a political stage or they may fight as guerrilla movements with armies or as terrorists.[15]

The new generation of terrorists now acts on a world scale. They may use supporters in the country of action, but they see themselves in an

---

[12] See Bornstein, 'Transcending Politics'; Gifford, *Ghana's New Christianity*; Hearn, 'The "Invisible" NGO'; Tukahebwa, 'Privatization as a Development Policy'.

[13] See Kaiser, *Culture, Transnationalism and Civil Society*; Renders, 'Ambiguous Adventure'; Weiss, 'Reorganizing Social Welfare'.

[14] See Adler, *Small Beginning*; Beck and Demmler, *From Resistance to Development*.

[15] For a better understanding of non-state actors using violence, one can specify these actors according to the descriptive criteria of (political) objectives, main types of fighting and violence, weaponry, resources for fighting, degree of professionalisation of fighters, authority and command structure, co-ordination of strategy, links between fighters and population, 'ethics of war' and occurrence of extreme war crimes (Neubert, 'The Peacemakers' Dilemma'). See also Miklaucic (Chapter 7), who develops a systematic typology of illicit power structures using the dimensions of behaviour, motivation, modality and morphology.

international, rather than in a merely national conflict. The most prominent example are Islamic terrorists and fighters, who unfortunately tend to be summed up under the rather imprecise heading of al Qaeda, though to be sure this is not only an Islamic phenomenon: the left wing terrorists of 1970s und 1980s in Europe already had the vision of an international movement.[16]

The African private sector is much more diversified than its counterpart in modern Western democracies. Besides the typical formal sector it includes the so-called 'informal sector' of micro-enterprises. In terms of economic strength, more important are illegal economic activities such as small- and large-scale smuggling and drug trafficking. In weak states like Zaire under Mobutu or Sierra Leone or Liberia, often medium- and some large-scale enterprises in farming and mining form a parallel economy besides the formal sector, a phenomenon that has already been described in detail by Janet MacGaffey.[17] This parallel economy works and acts according to similar strategies as those employed in the formal economy and still fits the concept of the private sector.

In failing states, in particular, we find entrepreneurs who hardly represent a typical private sector actor. They draw their economic power from the use and control of violence.[18] Therefore, I will call them 'violence entrepreneurs'. Often, they are referred to as 'warlords', but this conceals the role of 'markets of violence' described by Georg Elwert.[19] The use and non-use of violence is a commodity which can be bought. Violence entrepreneurs often do not pursue political objectives, but use violence to control resources, trading networks or make money from protection or ransom.

As far as these violence entrepreneurs are concerned, the weak state is an enabling environment. Their actions produce instability and violence, which in turn creates conditions within which they can pursue their actions.

Another peculiarity, which we do not find in modern Western liberal democracies and one which reaches beyond the three-sector model, is the existence of local 'neo-traditional' actors, such as local leaders and local authorities and associations, including specific local communal

---

[16] This also holds true for the communist movement in the nineteenth and early twentieth centuries, which was right from the beginning a global movement. However, the national movements acted locally or nationally. International solidarity supported them politically and militarily, but the conflicts remained more or less national.

[17] See MacGaffey, *Entrepreneurs and Parasites.*

[18] See Mair, *Die Globalisierung Privater.*   [19] See Elwert, 'Markets of Violence'.

structures. These are local chiefs or 'kings', councils of elders, secret societies, and local groups of young fighters who defend their community and/or carry out cattle raids in neighbouring communities.[20] The term 'neo-traditional' refers to their source of legitimacy, which is derived from tradition. This does not mean that they are always relics from former, pre-colonial or pre-modern times. Some may have been in existence for a long time, but not necessarily all. Often, they have changed and have been transformed extensively. Tradition as a source of legitimacy might be, and often is, combined with other sources. To be more precise, one should say that they are local actors who use a traditional garb. With that in mind, I will refer to those actors who use tradition as a dominant source of legitimacy simply as 'local "neo-traditional" actors'.[21]

These non-state actors outside the conventional three-sector model do not form a distinct fourth sector. Some share characteristics with organisations from other sectors. The violence entrepreneurs partly follow strategies we know from the private sector. Local neo-traditional actors combine elements of self-organisation, which we would link to the non-profit sector, with elements of a local level authority, which may be in lieu of some state functions on this level. They may even draw their legitimacy from official or semi-official functions delegated by the state. The particular relationship to the state and the division of functions is the result of ongoing processes of negotiations.[22]

Most of these actors are restricted to a local or sub-national level. Additionally, all of them are somehow located outside the formal institutions of a modern liberal democracy. I will address them with the rather weak label of 'informal non-state actors'. This underlines their distance from the conventional three-sector model and from the formal institutions of a modern state.

We should keep in mind that the types of non-state actors presented here are ideal types in a Weberian sense. In reality, these types overlap and a specific organisation may have features of several types at the same time. In particular, the different types of informal non-state actors presented here cannot completely cover all possible forms. These

---

[20] See Bellagamba and Klute, 'Emergent Powers'; Skalník, 'Chiefdom'.

[21] Neo-traditional actors are important because the reference to tradition may not only be used at the local level but is also successfully applied in relation to the state or to outside actors like development organisations or companies.

[22] See Lund, 'Public Authority and Local Politics'.

informal actors emerge mostly out of specific local settings that differ too much for us to be able to predict every possible type. Those presented here are already known and can be found in quite different settings.

3. What's new? A short look into the history of the diversity of non-state actors in Africa

Before we can examine the roles of non-state actors in standard setting today, it is helpful to reconsider briefly the history of non-state actors in Africa. This should remind us that non-state actors have been involved in standard setting since their existence.

The three-sector model started to make sense with the establishment of the modern territorial state in the nineteenth century. Since then we have had, of course, a private market sector as well as third-sector organisations. From their inception some NGOs have been involved in the process of standard setting, either as watchdogs or as lobby groups. The most prominent examples in industrial countries from the nine-teenth century are the anti-slavery societies in Britain and the USA and the Red Cross Society.[23]

NGOs were not only a European and North American phenomenon. In India, the first welfare associations were founded in the nineteenth century[24] and in some African colonies, like Kenya, the first NGOs emerged in the 1920s.[25]

We should also be aware that the mission societies and Christian churches were at the forefront of colonisation and established themselves in the colonies. Although they worked closely together with the colonial administration they acted independently of the colonial authorities and often presented themselves as representatives of the indigenous population. European churches were localised step by step (with local priests and later local bishops) and, especially in Africa, new African churches were founded.

The indigenous institutions in the colonies like chiefdoms, councils of elders, secret societies as well as indigenous forms of law changed their role with the establishment of colonisation. Depending on the colonial policy these institutions could be integrated into the state apparatus as part of indirect rule to become state actors by definition. In other cases

---

[23] See Curti, *American Philanthropy Abroad*; Lissner, *Politics of Altruism*.

[24] See Sen, 'Non-profit Organisations in India', 175–94; Sheth and Sethi, 'The NGO Sector in India'.

[25] See Neubert, *Entwicklungspolitische*, 104–10.

they were pushed aside as tradition and custom became of dwindling relevance or they were seen as politically dangerous and abandoned. For a long time the co-existence of state administration and jurisdiction and local customary institutions and law was accepted. Protest movements were obviously another type of non-state actor. They were often interpreted as revival movements referring to pre-colonial values. Pre-colonial institutions and those of protest movements were seen as a transitional phenomenon that would end after full modernisation (or 'transition' or 'civilisation').[26]

Against this historical background we can ask what is new concerning non-state actors in the Third World and particularly in Africa. There are two trends we should be aware of. First, concerning third-sector organisations, for nearly twenty years we have been observing a rising interest in their work and a re-evaluation of their role. Under the heading of support for civil society, this led to a policy of enabling the foundation and financing of these organisations. The result is a supply-driven increase in these organisations as already mentioned.

Second, pre-colonial or 'traditional' institutions still remain in place. Even after independence and after the establishment of democratic regimes they are there and often as strong as ever. They do not just disappear. Some African governments even reinstalled local chiefs in the administrative system.[27] Especially in countries where the state is weak or in so-called 'failed states' or on the peripheries where the political influence of the central government is weak, these neo-traditional non-state actors have been regaining power. They are filling the gap of public authority left open by a dwindling state.[28]

The existence of this type of non-state actor is not new, but it is only in recent years that we have discovered that their important role persists. This persistence attracts scholarly interest. Particularly in social anthropology these local forms of power are currently a highly valued object of research.[29] Whereas anthropologists tend to be fascinated by these

---

[26] For example the Mau Mau Movement has been interpreted this way in different terminologies (Mühlmann, 'Zwischen Erweckung und Terror'; Rosberg and Nottingham, *The Myth of Mau-Mau*; Buijtenhuijs, *Le Movement Mau Mau*.) Ranger gives a historical overview on the different interpretations of protest movements in general (Ranger, 'Religious Movements').

[27] For example, Mozambique: Buur and Kyed, 'Contested Sources of Authority'; Uganda: Nsibambi, 'Restoration of Traditional Rulers'.

[28] See Lund, 'Public Authority and Local Politics'.

[29] See Bellagamba and Klute, 'Emergent Powers'; Lund, 'Public Authority and Local Politics'; McIntosh, *Beyond Chiefdoms;* Skalník, 'Chiefdom'.

institutions and often argue in favour of them, political scientists are mostly more sceptical and take them as an indicator of problems of state building and complain about the decline of the state. Both positions risk being led by a certain sympathy for one or the other side (either the state or the autonomous local institutions), which may inhibit a more detailed risk analysis of the relationship between the state and the local institutions.

Additionally, even warlords are not an entirely new phenomenon. The concept was first applied to describe the situation in China at the beginning of the twentieth century.[30] Even if this term has been used in Africa only since the 1990s the phenomenon is by no means new and has existed since the pre-colonial slave trade where African middlemen acted sometimes like warlords.[31]

Irrespective of the evaluation of the role of these non-state actors, it should be acknowledged that they are a matter of fact in Africa and should be taken into account as political and social factors.

4.   Standard setting by non-state actors in a weak or failing state: islands of order

The role of non-state actors in Africa in a reasonably working state is fairly well known. In weak or failing states or on the margins of the sphere of influence of the state, the roles of non-state actors change. The political space left open by the state is contested between the state and different non-state actors who are driven by different motives and follow different strategies.

Standard setting is not the main issue, but an effect of this contest and the resulting new structuring of the political space with new divisions of spheres of influence and areas of overlapping authorities of state and non-state actors. A weak or failing state simply lacks the means to set binding standards. In a situation like this, laws, by-laws, rules or regulations formulated by the state lack implementation and the population may often be unaware of their existence.

We have to bear in mind that there are several ways of standard setting. First, there is law or rule making using the polity to set standards according to formal procedures linked to the rule of law. This is what we

---

[30] See Osterhammel, 'Musterfall der Kriegsfürsten'.
[31] However, the numbers of warlord-like violence entrepreneurs have risen with the increase of decentralised conflicts.

have in mind when we are talking about standard setting in Western liberal states. Second, there is rule making without reference to the rule of law, strict formal procedures and fixed codification. In these cases, rules may be set either arbitrarily by powerful actors or negotiated inside a community.[32]

Third, standards may be set indirectly and informally by action. One example is service provision by NGOs. In countries where NGOs offer reliable educational and health services, they influence the expectations of the people. People will compare the availability and the quality of government services with those of the NGOs. If government services are worse, the government will lose reputation and a process of creeping de-legitimisation may take place.[33] The NGOs' action produces standards for service provision.[34]

Another example may be violent actors like warlords or violence entrepreneurs, rebels, terrorists or violent political activists. Constant attacks and use of violence may change the perception of violence. In particular, failure to pursue or punish those responsible for attacks may cause a culture of impunity to develop.[35] This amounts to the establishment of new standards for the use of violence.

Here, the main concern is on this informal type of standard setting alongside the formal procedures under a rule of law, looking at rule making in a very basic sense. Every social order is based on standards and rules defining basic values, ways to live together and things that are permitted and things that are not. In a situation where the state is too weak to impose rules or is even absent, non-state actors can fill this gap. Therefore, weak and failed states offer us a kind of laboratory to find out the different forms of standard setting by non-state actors, which might otherwise be hidden behind the dominating role of the state.

However, not every social situation is an 'order' in this sense. In short, order needs a certain number of people and includes notions of authority and obedience and a certain stability over time. Order in this sense creates a space of predictability.[36] This space of predictability offers the opportunity for rational action, in that the reactions and results of agency

---

[32] For a simple typology of political systems see Macamo and Neubert, 'When the Post-Revolutionary'; Neubert, 'Globalisierung der Demokratie?'

[33] Neubert, 'Development Utopia'; Neubert, 'Entwicklun gspolitische'.

[34] *Ibid.* Also see Bornstein, 'Transcending Politics'; Jackson, *The State Didn't Even Exist.*

[35] Neubert, 'Die ambivalenten Rollen'.   [36] See Elwert, 'Schmuckendes Gerede', 284.

(in the sense of social action) can be predicted and taken into consideration which leads to an action plan.

The examination of standard setting in this open political space helps us to understand weak and failing states better. The impression of anarchy and anomie, which often goes together with failed states, is much too simple to describe the social situation. We will see that different forms of order, often very fragile, are established. Most of these orders are limited in space and often in time, they are more or less temporary islands of order below the level of the state, which partly drive out anarchy and anomie.

For the description of non-law making processes of standard setting, we can start with formal Western-type organisations, such as international companies and aid organisations. For the structure of the presentation of examples we can simply make a distinction between 'formal' organisations and more or less 'informal' organisations. However, we must remember that a strictly systematic categorisation along this line is not possible.

Even in failed states we can observe that some kind of formal organisation remains and pursues its objectives, even though no public services are available, no public security is guaranteed and the official courts are not working properly. Mining, oil or timber companies in Africa explore natural resources often when the political situation is unstable or the country is at war. They use private security companies to protect their business, including the places were they work and those where their employees live. Cabinda, the enclave where Angola's oil is extracted, produced all through the Angolan civil war protected by private security.[37] The companies that mined coltane and diamond and harvested timber in the Democratic Republic of Congo, Liberia and Sierra Leone, worked mostly during war. They tried to protect themselves through hired guards and, often, they collaborated with one of the warring factions. The companies bought security from these violence actors by paying protection money. As long as business was profitable, they kept on producing. Security was calculable in costs. Often, they gained from the absence of the state, which was unable to collect taxes. Additionally, the companies were mostly free from ecological regulations and limited licences for exploration.

---

[37] For the private security firms see Bendrath, 'Söldnerfirmen in Afrika'; Coker, 'Outsourcing War'.

In 'its' territory the company has ultimate authority. It provides the necessary services, it guarantees protection and all decisions on law and order in the camp are in its hands. However, the territory controlled by private companies is extremely limited and usually does not reach beyond the production plant or the mining site and the employees' quarters.

Humanitarian aid and refugee organisations often are active in areas of weak state presence or where the state is actually absent. Usually, they come in when the state is no longer able to take care of its citizens, displaced persons or refugees. Especially in the case of displaced persons and refugees, aid organisations set up special camps. Usually, they need permission from the government, but aid organisations run the camps by themselves. In most cases, the camps are used for months at least – sometimes, however, for years. Refugee camps and sometimes also camps for internally displaced persons are under the authority of the UNHCR (United Nations High Commissioner for Refugees). The UNHCR regulates life government-like in the camps. This includes all questions of security, jurisdiction, political functions including setting the rules for self-representation of the inhabitants, and service provision like the care for basic needs (food, water, housing, medical treatment, sanitation, schools etc.). Functions of service delivery may partly or completely be delegated to NGOs. With these functions UNCHR and its co-operating partners gain far-reaching authority, which makes them the main standard setters in these camps. In many cases, aid organisations put some participatory structures in place for representation of camp-dwellers. These spokespeople may or may not be elected. However, aid organisations have space for taking their own decisions and for making their rules.[38]

Under these circumstances aid organisations acquire a quasi-state function. This is not intended and it puts an extra burden on their work. But their ability to provide for basic needs, the need to organise the day-to-day life in the camp and the need to decide who gets support under what conditions, put them in this powerful position. Like the companies, aid organisations establish a new order, which includes a set of norms and regulations. The norms themselves draw from human rights regulations and from practical needs and experience.

As in the case of companies, the territory under the authority of aid organisations is limited and usually does not extend beyond the camp

---

[38] See Jackson, 'The State Didn't Even Exist'; Turner, 'Under the Gaze of the "Big Nations"'; Turner, 'Negotiating Authority'.

itself. In both cases, that is, company sites and aid camps, we find clearly marked 'islands of order' with their particular rules and regulations and a limited spatial authority. Companies and aid organisations gain legitimacy from the guarantee of basic security and the provision of a place where people can live. From the perspective of the refugees or internally displaced persons, this practical legitimacy counts much more than the formal legitimation of the UNHCR by the United Nations (UN) regulations.

For an aid organisation to establish aid camps and aid facilities and to secure its existence, it must make some arrangement with the host state. But at the fringes of the state's sphere of influence or, in cases where the state is simply absent (as is true for large parts of Somalia), aid organisations must negotiate with all actors who are, or may become, strong enough to intervene. Although aid organisations usually try to take a strictly neutral position in conflicts, this always entangles them in the politics of a conflict. They help people to survive in the war; they can never be sure that they will not take care of fighters seeking short-term refuge in the camps. The organisation has to pay protection money to the groups who may attack them and it has to accept that fighters may partake of aid, too. This has been extensively described for the Horn of Africa or for the Sudan and led to a crisis of legitimation of humanitarian aid in the case of Rwandan refugees after the 1994 genocide.[39, 40]

Another case is the role of the NGO CARE in Mozambique during the civil war in the 1980s. CARE was at that time responsible for food aid for Mozambique. This aid was essential for the survival of civilians. With this strategic resource, CARE could dictate terms and ways of delivery of the aid. According to Joseph Hanlon,[41] CARE used this position to undermine the socialist policy of Mozambique and interfered, therefore, in the political system of the country. Formulated according to the discussion in this volume CARE influenced basic processes of standard setting. From Hanlon's left-of-centre perspective, CARE acted more or less willingly as a kind of Trojan horse for US foreign policy.

Apart from these formal organisations we find a wide spectrum of more or less informal non-state actors, whose roles even differ from country to country or from situation to situation. Therefore, it is only possible to show some typical actors. This overview cannot be complete

[39] See DeWaal, *Who Fights?*
[40] See Brauman, *Hilfe als Spektakel*; Whitman and Pocock, *After Rwanda.*
[41] Hanlon, *Mozambique. Who Calls the Shots?*

and the specific patterns of standard setting presented here are realised in different localities and are highly variable depending on the local situation.

Warlords, rebels or an elaborate parallel economy are linked to the phenomenon of weak or failing states. Warlords or violence entrepreneurs and small rebel groups or so-called militias are particularly often associated with anarchy and the complete absence of order. A situation of this type arose in December 2006, when the union of Islamic courts was chased away from Mogadishu by the Ethiopian army; anarchy prevailed briefly until the Ethiopians and the transitional government took over.[42]

However, this picture of anarchy is too simple and cannot be seen as a general feature of warlordism. For a start, an order exists inside these groups. It is set often arbitrarily by the leader, but it has to be followed. Additionally, rebel groups, militias and even warlords have a local refuge as a base for action. This is the place where their entourage stays during fighting.[43] This creates an island of order somewhat similar to the refugee camps or protected company sites. The order established in these refuges does not have to be very stable, nor does it need to automatically protect civilians or guarantee some kind of justice or effective policing. Only violence entrepreneurs with some political ambitions will look for a more stable order.

Most of the people live outside these havens for fighters and camps of aid organisations or companies. They try to organise themselves in the absence of the state. Even during ongoing civil wars, local communities try to keep some kind of order according to local principles. Especially in rural Africa, local neo-traditional actors act in these cases as the main forces of order. These neo-traditional leaders, councils of elders, or community groups are usually already in place. In remote areas, the state is not present on the local level even in times of peace so that these local neo-traditional actors may be uncontested.

However, a situation of civil war, which we often find in failed states, makes a difference. In peace, there is crime and there may even be raids, but the action of groups using violence is limited either by the state or by the local communities who are able to protect themselves. During civil wars, rebel groups and militias grow stronger and cannot be controlled

---

[42] See Weber, 'Alte Karten Neu Gemischt'.   [43] See Klute, *Kleinkrieg und Raum*.

by local communities or the weakened state. In this type of war civilians are the main victims.[44]

The local neo-traditional actors also gain importance in post-war situations. They can be seen as a nucleus of a post-war order. One example of the re-establishment of order by local neo-traditional actors is the end of the Tuareg rebellion in Northern Mali.[45] In the early 1990s, the Tuareg rebelled against the Malian state. Later in the conflict, the Tuareg were divided by internal disagreements and different factions began to fight one another. When the constant warring led to a kind of civil war and became a threat to the Tuareg population themselves, the fighters lost the support of their local communities. The Tuareg elders saw themselves responsible for restoring peace and started negotiations among the Tuareg factions and between the Tuareg and the Malian state. The elders succeeded in regaining control over the young fighters and, in the end, a peace agreement was negotiated. The young fighters were demobilised and were supported by an aid programme.[46] The interesting point was that the Malian state agreed to give the Tuareg, at least informally, a kind of semi-autonomy.

Actually, the Tuareg accepted the Malian state. In turn, in the Tuareg region, authority was held by Tuareg elders and not by the Malian state. The result is a structure described by Klute and Trotha[47] as 'parastatal' authority. Tuareg elders installed themselves as the main political authority in their region. The presence of the Malian state in the region is more or less symbolic and the Tuareg are quasi-autonomous. Traditional Tuareg nobles rule according to their interpretation of Tuareg norms and values that are not covered by the Malian constitution and do not refer to Malian laws. From a juridical point of view, the norms are at best part of what we might call customary law. This local Tuareg order was rather successful in providing local peace and political stability by ignoring or even violating the legal norms of Mali with the consent of the Malian Government. This order and its norms are lent legitimacy by the reference to 'Tuareg tradition' which, in turn and simultaneously, is

---

[44] We have to admit that our knowledge about local order during civil wars is extremely limited. The situation of civil war simply makes organised field research impossible. Interestingly, we are also missing ex post studies on the organisation of everyday life during war. One example is given by Macamo (2006) who shows that even under conditions of civil war people develop ways of keeping some kind of normal ordinary everyday life.

[45] See Klute and Trotha, 'Wege zum Frieden'; Klute and Trotha, 'Roads to Peace'.

[46] See Papendieck and Rocksloh-Papendieck, 'Peace and Aid'.   [47] Ibid.

interpreted by the local leaders themselves.[48] From time to time, this order is challenged by new groups of fighters who carry out violent attacks against government police stations. It is an open question whether they really contest the order as such or whether they are merely trying to gain political importance to push for new peace talks and concessions by the government.

In urban areas we find other forms of community security. In these cases, newly formed groups of young men are used to fill the gap left by an absent or corrupt police as a kind of local security or police force. These vigilante groups provide some order according to locally declared rules. At times, they are related to the public authorities; more often than not they act as a substitute for the missing or failing state police and jurisdiction. In Uganda, this local security force is appointed and controlled by a local security committee formed by the people with a formally elected board. Ugandan law binds the security committees, but the committees interpret and define rules and norms according to local perceptions. However, violations of laws by these security groups do happen.[49] In post-conflict Sierra Leone, young ex-combatants formed a security force which acted in a widely autonomous and rather arbitrary manner. However, they fulfilled the function of maintaining some order.[50]

Another example is that of the Nigerian city of Aba at the end of the 1990s. The threat of crime grew so dire that traders established a troop of young men as a local force, namely the 'Bakassi boys'.[51] They are paid by the traders of the town and act as a *de facto* police. Neighbouring towns followed this example and engaged the Bakassi boys as a local security force, too. They pursued criminals and, as a demonstration of their power, organised public executions and acted as police and court at the same time. The regular police still existed. In the beginning they tried to block the actions of the Bakassi boys, but gradually they were forced to accept them as a powerful reality and did not interfere any more. People supported the Bakassi boys because, unlike the police, they were not corrupt. The Bakassi boys did not only fight criminals, but also witchcraft. The order established by the Bakassi boys did not follow Nigerian

---

[48] This hybrid situation where local neo-traditional leaders act more or less autonomously but with the consent of a state is a widespread feature; see Lund, 'Twilight Institutions'.
[49] See Baker, 'Beyond the State Police'.   [50] *Ibid.*
[51] See Harnischfeger, *Die Bakassi-Boys in Nigeria*; Harnischfeger, 'Fighting Crime in Nigeria'.

laws. Quite apart from the fact that the Bakassi boys elicited compliance through force, their standards of wrong and right were consistent with local concepts and were therefore accepted by the people.[52]

Religious groups and churches play an important role as standard setters, especially in weak and failing states. One attraction of these religious groups is the promise of morality and the guarantee that members of a religious group will lead their lives according to this morality. Inside the movement, this creates a space of mutual trust and offers security.[53] Outside the religious group, members often obey the same norms. These intrinsic norms are an important factor of order in place and provide spaces of security. Again, Nigeria offers numerous examples of this process either carried out by Christian churches or by Islamic groups. In a wider sense, the long history of Shari'ah jurisdiction in Nigeria is another example.[54]

The last cases presented here underline how hard it is to differentiate systematically between formal and informal actors. This distinction is blurred in reality. Actors often act as hybrids, as in the para-statal Tuareg arrangement. In some cases, we may find a combination of formally divided roles. One case is described by Luca Jourdan (Jourdan forthcoming) from field research in North Kivu (Democratic Republic of Congo). In the war ravaged Kivu region, Eugene Serufuli was Governor from 2000 up to the parliamentary elections in 2007. At the same time, he ran an NGO with the promising name 'Tout pour la Paix et le Développement' and a militia called the 'Local Defence Forces'. This chameleon-like institutional representation offered Serufuli the possibility of choosing the role most conducive to pursuing a specific objective. At the same time, he was able to act under any set of conditions. If violence and civil war broke out again, he could rely on his fighters. If peace stabilised, the NGO business profited from the typical development peace dividend. Then, his position as Governor gave him security in more stable times. Only the free elections undermined his strong position because he did not manage to stay in office.

---

[52] In the South African town of Port Elizabeth a local force of young men (Amdalozi) formed during the anti-Apartheid struggle tries in a similar way to act as police and court. However, in this case the police still try to stop their activity (Buur, 'Reordering Society'.)

[53] Even ethnic movements may play this role as a normative counter-force against a society seen as immoral (Elwert, 'Ausdehnung der Käuflichkeit'; Elwert, 'Nationalismus und Ethnizität').

[54] See Anderson, *Law Reform in the Muslim World*; Ostien, Nasir and Kogelmann (eds.), *Comparative Perspectives*.

From the perspective of standard setting this multiple-role player presents a highly ambiguous figure. Depending on the role he took, the norms which he upheld may be completely contradictory. As long as all the different roles were an option, one cannot expect that he consistently represented the law and order as Governor. However, using his official role he could pursue rival warlords in the name of law and security.[55]

The last examples, like the Bakassi boys, the religious groups and the hybrid figure of the violence-entrepreneur-governor-NGO-leader point out that not every order constitutes an isolated and clearly demarcated island (of order). First, between the islands there is an open political space. Second, especially in urban areas we may find overlapping and competing orders, for example the order represented by the Bakassi boys and the order represented by the regular police. Third, some orders cannot be linked to a territorial space but to a social space, like the morality created by a religious group. In these cases, we may use the wider term 'spheres of order'.[56]

In all these cases we find a situation similar to legal pluralism (see Wanitzek in this volume). The actors in spaces of overlapping orders have to negotiate which order they will follow. This negotiation is by no means an open process, but rather one which is influenced by the power of the actors involved.

5.   Conclusions

The cases presented here point to a general problem in weak and failing states or in post-conflict situations: as the state is no more or not yet able to guarantee a minimum of public security and order, all kinds of non-state actors – religious communities, local neo-traditional actors, community groups, aid organisations and even companies – are involved in retaining order.

In this situation, we often cannot speak of a public–private divide, but of a public vacuum. Non-state actors take over the state function of standard setting. They fill the space left open by the state. In doing this, the state risks losing even more ground and its legitimacy may be further eroded.

---

[55] This is not an exceptional case. Kabila senior started his career as a smuggler, became a warlord, and with the help of his allies at the time, i.e. Rwanda and Uganda, he was installed as President of the Congo. Bemba, who ran unsuccessfully for the Congolese presidency in 2006 against Kabila, gained his political power after having started off as a warlord, too.

[56] I thank Till Förster, who proposed this term.

However, the non-state actors cannot fill the gap of an absent state. If they are successful they can create islands of order. But these islands of order follow completely different patterns and hardly set standards following formal procedures. (One exception is the UNHCR, whose procedures follow formal rules for the treatment of refugees.) The result of the often competing standards in the different islands of order may be an incomplete patchwork of overlapping standards. This patchwork of orders depicts the situation of a weak or failed state.

It is obvious that the patchwork of orders carries the potential for conflict, complicates travel and business and creates general insecurity. The question is whether and how this patchwork could be overcome. We have to accept that any attempt to construct a new overall order does not start from zero, but has to take into account the patchwork of existing orders. One possibility is a strengthening of the state and a re-conquering of political space. This has been tried in Sierra Leone or Liberia with some success. Another possibility is that some of the non-state actors are strong enough to become political actors in their own right and to gain the ability to negotiate with the state or with other similar powerful actors to create a new order that replaces the old one and a new state. Somaliland after the civil war may be an example of that.[57]

In any case, if we want to have a fuller understanding of non-state actors' role in standard setting in weak or failing states we need to study these local arenas. We must accept that these processes are not restricted to a few exceptions, but are, at least currently, part and parcel of standard setting in large parts of Africa and some other parts of the world too.

In these processes the formality or informality of the non-state actors is of minor importance because in the process of establishing a new order and standard setting informal actors may gain a formal role. It is more important to know where the actors come from, or whether the non-state actor can claim indigenous links. Aid organisations and companies may be highly efficient in running their islands of order, but they neither want to nor are they in a position to reinstall an overall and sustainable order on their own.

For further studies it will be necessary to look deeper into the ways in which new standards and order are established:

• Where do the standard setters draw legitimacy for themselves and for the order they set? In the examples given here legitimacy is based on

---

[57] See Bradbury, Abokor, and Yusuf, 'Choosing Politics Over Violence'; Bryden, *Rebuilding Somaliland*; Kulessa and Heinrich, 'Dekonstruktion von Staaten'.

tradition, spiritual power, coercion, the ability to offer security or on action (provision of security and services), in one case even on election (security committees in Uganda).

- How are the standards formulated and put in place? Are the standards codified and produced according to formal procedures or set more or less arbitrarily or open to negotiations and manipulation by power?
- What values form the basis of the new order? In the examples given here order referred to tradition, religion, human rights.
- How is order implemented and how are standards upheld? In the examples given here this is done by violence, by belief or by creating commitment but not bounded by the rule of law.

Our overview of the role of local and regional non-state actors on the margins of public policy in Africa leads to four concluding points:

- First, in the situation of a public vacuum left open by weak and failed states, standard setting is linked to the fundamental societal process of stabilising or re-establishing order.
- Second, the non-state actors who are involved in this process range from humanitarian aid organisations through local chiefs and community groups to violence entrepreneurs with an extremely diverse set of motives and values. Many of the values on which the orders to be established rest contradict liberal democratic normative orientations.
- Third, the bottom-up production of order is neither automatically just, nor does it lead to stable order every time. In short, these processes are part and parcel of African reality, but there is no reason either to romanticise them or to condemn non-state actors who do not live up to liberal democratic expectations.
- Fourth, these extreme cases show that the state could hardly be substituted by non-state actors completely.[58]

References

Adler, E. 1974, *A Small Beginning. An Assessment of the First Five Years of the Programme to Combat Racism*, Geneva, World Council of Churches.
Anderson, J. N. D. 1976, *Law Reform in the Muslim World*, London, Athlon Press.
Baker, B. 2006, 'Beyond the State Police in Urban Uganda and Sierra Leone', *Afrika Spektrum*, vol. **41**, no. 1, 55–76.

---

[58] I thank Elìsio Macamo for his comments.

Beck, C. R. and Demmler, S. L. 2000, *From Resistance to Development. Kontinuität und Wandel Basisnaher Nichtregierungsorganisationen in Südafrika*, Hamburg, Lit.

Bellagamba, A. and Klute Bellagamba, G. 2008, 'Tracing Emergent Powers in Contemporary Africa – Introduction' in A. and G. Klute (eds.), *Beside the State. Emerging Forms of Power in Contemporary Africa*, Amsterdam, Brill, 1–34.

Bendrath, R. 1999, 'Söldnerfirmen in Afrika – Neue Politische Vergesellschaftungsformen Jenseits des Modernen Staates' in W. R. Vogt (ed.), *Friedenskultur statt Kulturkampf. Strategien Kultureller und Nachhaltiger Friedensstiftung*, Baden-Baden, Nomos, 251–88.

Bornstein, E. 2005, 'Transcending Politics Through the Kingdom of God and Free Markets: A Case Study of Religious NGOs in Zimbabwe' in J. Igoe and T. Kelsall (eds.), *Between a Rock and a Hard Place. African NGOs, Donors and the State*, Durham, Carolina Academic Press, 63–92.

Bradbury, M. *et al.* 2003, 'Somaliland: Choosing Politics Over Violence', *Review of African Political Economy*, vol. **30**, no. 97, 455–78.

Brauman, R. 1995, *Hilfe als Spektakel. Das Beispiel Ruanda*, Berlin, Rotbuch.

Brock, K. L. 2001, *The Nonprofit Sector and Government in a New Century*, Montreal, Queens University.

Bryden, M. (ed.) 2005, *Rebuilding Somaliland: Issues and Possibilities*, Lawrenceville, Red Sea Press.

Buijtenhuijs, R. 1971, *Le Mouvement Mau Mau une Révolte Paysanne et Anti-Coloniale en Afrique Noire*, Paris, Mouton.

Buur, L. 2006, 'Reordering Society: Vigilantism and Expressions of Sovereignty in Port Elizabeth's Townships', *Development and Change*, vol. **37**, no. 4, 735–57.

Buur, L. and Kyed, H. M. 2006, 'Contested Sources of Authority: Re-claiming State Sovereignty by Formalizing Traditional Authority in Mozambique', *Development and Change*, vol. **37**, no. 4, 847–69.

Coker, C. 2001, 'Outsourcing War', in D. Josselin and W. Wallace (eds.), *Non-State Actors in World Politics*, Basingstoke, Palgrave, 189–202.

Curti, M. 1963, *American Philanthropy Abroad: A History*, New Brunswick, Rutgers University Press.

DeWaal, A. 2000, *Who Fights? Who Cares? War and Humanitarian Action in Africa*, Trenton, World Press.

DiMaggio, P. J. and Anheier, H. K. 1990, 'Sociological Conceptualization of Nonprofit Organizations and Sectors', *Annual Review of Sociology*, 137–59.

Elwert, G. 1987, 'Ausdehnung der Käuflichkeit und Einbettung der Wirtschaft. Markt und Moralökonomie', *Kölner Zeitschrift für Soziologie und Sozialpsychologie* (Special issue: Soziologie Wirtschaftlichen Handelns), 300–21.

Elwert, G. 1989, 'Nationalismus und Ethnizität. Über die Bildung von Wir-Gruppen', *Kölner Zeitschrift für Soziologie und Sozialpsychologie*, vol. **41**, 440–64.

Elwert, G. 1997, 'Schmückendes Gerede und Reale Entwicklungsbedingungen – Über Soziokulturelle Bedingungen der Entwicklung' in M. Schulz (ed.), *Entwicklung: die Perspektive der Entwicklungssoziologie*, Opladen, Westdeutscher Verlag, 261–90.

Elwert, G. 1999, 'Markets of Violence' in G. Elwert *et al.* (eds.), *Dynamics of Violence. Processes of Escalation and De-Escalation of Violent Group Conflicts*, Berlin, Duncker & Humblot, 85–102.

Evers, A. 1995, 'Part of the Welfare Mix: The Third Sector as an Intermediate Area Between Market Economy, State and Community', *Voluntas*, vol. **6**, no. 2, 159–82.

Gifford, P. 2004, *Ghana's New Christianity: Pentecostalism in a Globalising African Economy*, London, C. Hurst.

Glagow, M. *et al.* 1992, *Indigenous Non-Governmental Organizations in Mosambik – Gesellschaftliche Selbstorganisation im Entwicklungsprozeß*, Materialien: Nr. 34 Forschungsprogramm Entwicklungspolitik, Universität Bielefeld.

Glagow, M. *et al.* 1993, *Nichtstaaliche Trägerstrukturen in Malawi. Gesellschaftliche Selbststeuerung im Prozeß der Demokratisierung und Entwicklung*, Universität Bielefeld.

Hanlon, J. 1991, *Mozambique. Who Calls the Shots?*, London, James Currey.

Harnischfeger, J. 2001, *Die Bakassi-Boys in Nigeria. Vom Aufstieg der Milizen und dem Niedergang des Staates*, Bonn, Konrad Adenauer Stiftung – Auslandsinformationen (KAS – AI).

Harnischfeger, J. 2003, 'The Bakassi Boys: Fighting Crime in Nigeria', *Journal of Modern African Studies*, vol. **41**, no. 1, 23–49.

Hearn, J. 2002, 'The "Invisible" NGO: US Evangelical Mission in Kenya', *Journal of Religion in Africa*, vol. **32**, no.1, 32–60.

Igoe, J. and Kelsall, T. (eds.) 2005, *Between a Rock and a Hard Place. African NGOs, Donors and the State*, Durham, Carolina Academic Press.

Jackson, S. 2005, '"The State Didn't Even Exist": Non-Governmentality in Kivu, Eastern DR Kongo' in J. Igoe and T. Kelsall (eds.), *Between a Rock and a Hard Place. African NGOs, Donors and the State*, Durham, Carolina Academic Press, 165–96.

Josselin, D. and Wallace, W. 2001, 'Non-State Actors in World Politics: A Framework' in D. Josselin and W. Wallace (eds.), *Non-State Actors in World Politics*, Basingstoke, Palgrave, 1–20.

Jourdan, L. (forthcoming), 'New Forms of Political Order in North Kivu. The Case of the Governor Eugene Serufuli' in A. Bellagamba and G. Klute (eds.), *Beside the State. Emerging Forms of Power in Contemporary Africa*, Amsterdam, Brill.

Kaiser, P. J. 1996, *Culture, Transnationalism and Civil Society – Aga Khan Social Service Initiatives in Tanzania*, Westport, Conn., Praeger.

Klute, G. 2006, *Kleinkrieg und Raum*, Bayreuth, Manuskript.

Klute, G. and Trotha, T. v. 2000, 'Wege zum Frieden. Vom Kleinkrieg zum Parastaatlichen Frieden im Norden von Mali', *Sociologus*, vol. **50**, no. 1, 1–36.

Klute, G. and Trotha, T. v. 2004, 'Roads to Peace: From Small War to Parasovereign Peace in the North of Mali' in M.-C. Foblets and T. v. Trotha (eds.), *Healing the Wounds. Essays on the Reconstruction of Societies after War*, Oxford, Hart, 109–44.

Kulessa, M. and Heinrich, W. 2004, 'Dekonstruktion von Staaten als Chance für Neue Staatlichkeit? Das Beispiel Somalia und Somaliland' in J. Hippler (ed.), *Nation-Building – ein Schlüsselkonzept für Friedliche Konfliktbearbeitung*, Bonn, Dietz (in English: *Nation Building – A Key Concept for Conflict Transformation*, London, Pluto 2005).

Lehmbruch, G. and Schmitter, P. C. (eds.) 1982, *Patterns of Corporatist Policy Making*, London, Sage.

Lissner, J. 1977, *The Politics of Altruism. A Study of the Political Behaviour of Voluntary Development Agencies*, Genf, Lutheran World Federation.

Lund, C. (ed.) 2006, 'Twilight Institutions', *Development and Change* (special issue), vol. **37**, no. 4.

Lund, C. 2006, 'Twilight Institutions: Public Authority and Local Politics in Africa (special issue)', *Development and Change*, vol. **37**, no. 4, 685–705.

Macamo, E. 2006, 'Accounting for Disaster: Memories of War in Mozambique', *Afrika Spektrum*, vol. **41**, no. 2, 199–219.

Macamo, E. and Neubert, D. 2004, 'When the Post-Revolutionary State Decentralises – The Case of Mozambique', *Cadernos de Estudos Africanos*, no. 5/6 (July 2003/June 2004), 53–74.

MacGaffey, J. 1987, *Entrepreneurs and Parasites. The Struggle for Indigenous Capitalism in Zaire*, Cambridge University Press.

Mair, S. 2002, *Die Globalisierung Privater Gewalt. Kriegsherren, Rebellen, Terroristen und Organisierte Kriminalität* (SWP Studie 10 2002), Berlin, Stiftung Wissenschaft und Politik.

McIntosh, S. K. (ed.) 1999, *Beyond Chiefdoms. Pathways to Complexity in Africa*, Cambridge University Press.

Milliken, J. and Krause, K. 2002, 'State Failure, State Collapse, and State Reconstruction: Concepts, Lessons and Strategies', *Development and Change*, vol. **33**, no. 5, 753–74.

Mühlmann, W. E. 1961, 'Zwischen Erweckung und Terror: Der Mau-Mau-Aufstand in Kenya' in Mühlmann, W. E. (ed.), *Chiliasmus und Nativismus. Studien zur Psychologie, Soziologie und Historische Kasuistik der Umsturzbewegungen*, Berlin, Reimer, 105–40.

Neubert, D. 1997, 'Development Utopia Re-Visited. Non-Governmental Organisations in Africa', *Sociologus*, vol. **47**, 51–77.

Neubert, D. 1997, *Entwicklungspolitische Hoffnungen und Gesellschaftliche Wirklichkeit. Eine Vergleichende Länderfallstudie von Nicht-Regierungsorganisationen in Kenia und Ruanda*, Frankfurt am Main, Campus.

Neubert, D. 2003, 'Nichtregierungsorganisationen in der Diskussion', *Gesellschaft – Wirtschaft – Politik (GWP)*, vol. **52**, no. 2, 259–86.

Neubert, D. 2004, 'The Peacemakers' Dilemma. The Role of NGOs in Processes of Peace-Building in Decentralised Conflicts' in M.-C. Foblets and T. v. Trotha (eds.), *Healing the Wounds. Essays on the Reconstruction of Societies After War*, Oxford, Hart, 47–82.

Neubert, D. 2004, 'Die Ambivalenten Rollen von Staat und Selbstorganisation' in K. Beck *et al.* (eds.), *Blick Nach Vorn. Festgabe für Gerd Spittler*, Köln, Rüdiger Köppe Verlag, 53–66.

Neubert, D. 2004, 'Globalisierung der Demokratie? Klientelismus in Mehrparteiensystemen in Afrika Südlich der Sahara' in V. Lühr *et al.* (eds.), *Sozialwissenschaftliche Perspektiven auf Afrika. Festschrift für Manfred Schulz*, Köln, Lit, 207–23.

Nsibambi, A. 1995, 'The Restoration of Traditional Rulers', in H. B. Hansen and M. Twaddle (eds.), *From Chaos to Order: The Politics of Constitution-Making in Uganda*, Kampala, Fountain Publishers, 41–59.

Osterhammel, J. 1995, 'Musterfall der Kriegsfürsten. Das China der Warlords zwischen Krieg, Zerfall und Modernisierung', *Der Überblick*, vol. **31**, no. 2, 38–40.

Ostien, P. *et al.* (eds.) 2005, *Comparative Perspectives on Shari'ah in Nigeria*, Ibadan, Spectrum Books.

Papendieck, H. and Rocksloh-Papendieck, B. 2004, 'Peace and Aid: The Programme Mali-Nord and the Search for Peace in Northern Mali' in M.-C. Foblets and T. v. Trotha (eds.), *Healing the Wounds. Essays on the Reconstruction of Societies After War*, Oxford, Hart, 109–44.

Powell, W. (ed.) 1987, *The Non-Profit Sector*, New Haven, Yale University Press.

Randrianja, S. 2007, 'Madagascar, FFKM and Politics', in *Non-State Actors as Standard Setters: The Erosion of the Public-Private Divide*, Conference Proceedings, Basel 8.-9.2.2007 (on CD-Rom).

Ranger, T. O. 1986, 'Religious Movements and Politics in Sub-Saharan Africa', *African Studies Review*, vol. **29**, no. 3, 1–69.

Renders, M. 2002, 'An Ambiguous Adventure: Muslim Organisations and the Discourse of "Development" in Senegal', *Journal of Religion in Africa*, vol. **32**, no. 1, 61–82.

Rosberg, C. G. and Nottingham, J. 1966, *The Myth of Mau-Mau*, New York.

Rotberg, R. I. (ed.) 2004, *When States Fail. Causes and Consequences*, Princeton University Press.

Sen, S. 1992, 'Non-Profit Organisations in India: Historical Development and Common Patterns', *Voluntas*, vol. **3**, no. 2, 175–94.

Sheth, D. L. and Sethi, H. 1991, 'The NGO Sector in India: Historical Context and Current Discourse', *Voluntas*, vol. **2**, 49–68.

Skalník, P. 2004, 'Chiefdom: A Universal Political Formation?', *Focaal – European Journal of Anthropology*, vol. **42**, 76–98.

Tukahebwa, G. B. 1998, 'Privatization as a Development Policy' in H. B. Hansen and M. Twaddle (eds.), *Developing Uganda*, Oxford, James Currey, 59–73.

Turner, S. 2004, 'Under the Gaze of the "Big Nations": Refugees, Rumours and the International Community in Tanzania', *African Affairs*, vol. **103**, 227–47.

Turner, S. 2006, 'Negotiating Authority Between UNHCR and "the People"', *Development and Change*, vol. **37**, no. 4, 759–78.

Weber, A. 2007, 'Alte Karten Neu Gemischt. Stabilität kann in Somalia nur durch eine Repräsentative Regierung erreicht werden', *SWP-Aktuell 2007/A 04*, Berlin, Stiftung Wissenschaft und Politik, Deutsches Institut für Internationale Sicherheit und Politik.

Weisbrod, B. A. 1975, 'Toward a Theory of the Voluntary Non-Profit Sector in a Three-Sector Economy' in E. S. Phelps (ed.), *Altruism, Morality, and Economic Theory*, New York, Russel Sage Foundation, 171–95.

Weiss, H. 2002, 'Reorganising Social Welfare Among Muslims: Islamic Voluntarism and Other Forms of Communal Support in Northern Ghana', *Journal of Religion in Africa*, vol. **32**, no. 1, 83–109.

Whitman, J. and Pocock, D. (eds.) 1996, *After Rwanda. The Coordination of United Nations Humanitarian Assistance*, New York, St. Martin's Press.

Zimmer, A. 2001, 'Corporatism Revisited: The Legacy of History and the German Nonprofit Sector' in H. K. Anheier and J. Kendall (eds.), *Third Sector Policy at the Crossroads: An International Nonprofit Analysis*, London, Routledge, 114–25.

3

Conceptualising the use of public–private partnerships as a regulatory arrangement in critical information infrastructure protection

DAN ASSAF*

1. Introduction

Critical information infrastructure protection (or 'CIIP') is a concept 'du jour' in many developed countries. Faced with the inherent vulnerability of critical information infrastructures to cyber-attacks,[1] governments around the world have become preoccupied with their state of security.

The term 'Critical Information Infrastructures' (or 'CII') incorporates two terms: 'Critical Infrastructures' (or 'CI') and 'Information Infrastructures'. According to the USA Patriot Act, 'critical infrastructures' are:

> those systems and assets, whether physical or virtual, so vital to the US that the incapacity or destruction of such systems and assets would have a debilitating impact on security, national economic security, national public health or safety, or any combination of those matters.[2]

Considered to be critical infrastructures, for example, are telecommunications networks, power grids, water supply systems, banking and finance institutions, transportation systems, and oil and gas storage facilities and pipelines.

The term 'Information Infrastructures' usually describes the combination of computer and communications systems that serve as the underlying infrastructure for organisations, industries and the economy, including components such as telecommunications, computer hardware and software, the Internet and other computer networks,

---

* Doctoral Candidate, Faculty of Law, University of Toronto, Canada; LLB, BA (Economics) (Tel Aviv).
[1] McAfee Virtual Criminology Report, *Cybercrime: The Next Wave* (discussing the increasing threat to critical national infrastructure and hence to national security), 2007.
[2] 42 U.S.C. § 5195c(e) (2001).

supervisory and control systems, telecommunication satellites, fibre optics and the like.[3]

Altogether, critical information infrastructures are those parts of the information infrastructure that are essential for the continuity of critical infrastructure services. In other words, they are the communications and information networks, systems, software and facilities (including supervisory and controlling devices) underlying critical infrastructures.

Threats to critical information infrastructures could come from nation states and terrorist organisations. Both could exploit the heavy reliance of developed countries on information and communications technology by attacking their critical information infrastructures. This modus operandi is a key part of a concept known as 'information warfare'. It is considered to be asymmetric warfare as it allows a weaker opponent to outweigh the military and strategic superiority of stronger powers at relatively low cost through cyber-attacks against vulnerable critical information infrastructures. The potential damage from a cyber-attack on a country's critical infrastructure is aggravated by the interdependency and interoperability between critical infrastructures, that is, the co-relation between the condition of one critical infrastructure and the condition of another critical infrastructure.

An example would be useful. Suppose Iran fears that the United States plans to attack its nuclear facilities and promote a military revolt against the fundamentalist regime currently in control. Acknowledging that it cannot withstand a full American military assault, Iran decides to initiate a series of asymmetric attacks against the United States that will serve to diminish America's strategic advantages in the conventional military sphere. These attacks combine physical attacks against American facilities (for example embassies and military bases) around the world with cyber-attacks on American critical infrastructures (for example power grids, telecommunications networks, oil and gas facilities and pipelines). The physical attacks cause 500 casualties. However, the cyber-attacks produce an electric power blackout in the north-east corner of the United States, which adversely affects telecommunications services, energy production facilities, air and land transportation, banking and finance services, emergency services and so on. In other words, it brings major industries to a complete stop and causes enormous losses in productivity. At the same time, the Iranian military, exploiting havoc and panic in

---

[3] Dunn and Wigert, *International CIIP Handbook*.

America, opens a surprise pre-emptive attack against United States forces in the Persian Gulf. By combining physical and cyber-attacks, it is able to succeed against the otherwise superior American military power in the Gulf.

This example illustrates how cyber-attacks on critical infrastructure can be used as part of a military campaign. However, information operations may be used independently of military action just to cause disruption, as demonstrated by the 2007 cyber-clash between Russia and Estonia. In this case, the websites of various Estonian institutions (parliament, ministries, banks, media outlets etc.) were disabled for days by a concentrated 'distributed denial of service' (DDoS) attack. While no one died as a result, the damage to the Estonian economy was tremendous.[4]

Concerned with the vulnerability of their critical information infrastructures to information warfare, numerous governments around the world have come to understand the importance of protecting their critical information infrastructures. Dunn and Wigert, for example, survey twenty designated national CIIP policies, as well as various supra-national efforts.[5]

The choice of regulatory arrangement in securing critical information infrastructures is complex and important, especially in developed countries where most critical infrastructures are owned and operated by the private sector. Should government intervene in the market and mandate security measures in critical infrastructures? Should the private sector (in essence, the market) be left alone to decide on such measures? Or should there be an intermediate solution such as self-regulation, enforced self-regulation or even negotiated rule-making by a public agency?

The complexity of these issues would seem to foreclose quick policy decisions. However, it seems that policy makers in a number of countries have already followed the United States down the path of minimal government intervention. The United States was the first state to address the need for critical information infrastructure protection and its endorsement of a market-based approach involving self-regulation and public–private partnerships (PPPs) has apparently spilled over to other developed countries, including Australia, Canada and some states in the European Union, without any meaningful debate.[6]

---

[4] See, for example, Krebs, 'Estonia Incident Demonstrated Power of Russia-Based Cyber Networks'; Traynor, 'Russia Accused of Unleashing Cyberwar to Disable Estonia'.
[5] Dunn and Wigert, *International CIIP Handbook.*   [6] *Ibid.*

This chapter critically analyses the policy of conferring regulatory powers on private entities and endorsing the creation of PPPs as a governing mechanism in the protection of critical information infrastructure. It points to the problems inherent in the architecture of such arrangements and its implications for accountability and transparency. Further, it argues that better design is required to enhance the accountability of private, for-profit organisations to the broader public interest.

The rest of this chapter is structured in five parts. First, it discusses the general concept of the PPP and describes various ways in which PPPs have been defined and understood. In this section, special emphasis is placed on the relationship between PPPs and regulation. Second, it discusses various definitions of the concept and shows that the objectives of public and private parties in entering a collaborative project do not necessarily coincide. It also analyses the special case of PPPs in regulatory structures. Third, it analyses the United States' use of this mechanism in the context of critical information infrastructure protection. In this framework, it is argued that the design of PPPs in critical information infrastructure protection is much closer on the regulatory continuum to market mechanisms than to government regulation. Fourth, it calls attention to the potential accountability and transparency problems that result from using PPPs as a governance mechanism in protecting critical information infrastructure. Finally, this contribution questions whether PPPs can bridge the gap between private and public interests in securing critical information infrastructure and calls for regulatory arrangements to be restructured so they enhance accountability to public values.

2.   The regulatory continuum and public–private partnerships

The problem of protecting critical information infrastructure is similar in essence to many other social problems. And like other social problems, it requires governments to address and remedy it, either by intervening directly (in various ways) or by ensuring that the problem is remedied by other actors, such as the private 'for-profit' sector or not-for-profit organisations.

Governments may employ a variety of institutional arrangements to protect critical information infrastructure, thereby solving or mitigating a public problem. These arrangements are characterised by varying degrees of government intervention, from protection solely by the state, to collaborative arrangements between the state and the private sector, through to protection of critical information infrastructure solely

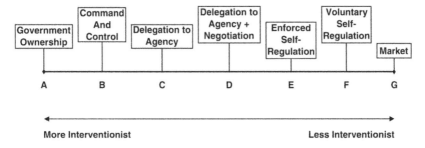

Figure 3.1 The Regulatory Continuum and Public–Private Partnerships

by the market (in which case, the state theoretically has no role at all). These positions can be placed on a continuum.

Figure 3.1 portrays the regulatory continuum and illustrates this point. At the left end of the continuum (point A), governments opt for 'in-house' protection of critical information infrastructures through government ownership. For example, states can decide that national electricity companies cannot be privatised because protecting their information systems is such an important interest. In effect, governments retain the responsibility of protecting critical infrastructure for themselves. This is, of course, the most interventionist (not to say centralist) way for governments to achieve adequate levels of protection for critical information infrastructure.

Moving right on the continuum to point B, we arrive at 'command and control' regulation, in which the state mandates clear and precise cyber-security standards through legislation (and sometimes statutory instruments) and monitors and enforces these standards through the criminal law. For example, the state could determine through legislation a set of comprehensive security requirements and require adherence by operators of critical infrastructure. Failure to comply with these standards would lead to criminal action against the operators that could conclude, for example, with the imposition of large fines. This is also a very interventionist mode of action, as the state dictates to the private sector how critical information infrastructures are to be protected.

A further move to the right (C) brings us to delegation of rule-making powers to central, specialised public agencies with discretionary powers to set standards, monitor and enforce compliance. The idea is that such a regulatory agency would have more expertise and independence from politics (at least in theory). Once again, the degree of intervention is high.

So far, points (A) to (C) have been characterised (amongst other things) by high levels of state intervention in the market. In each scenario, rule-making powers, as well as responsibilities for monitoring and enforcement, remain in the hands of the state and the role of the private sector is limited to compliance with the regulatory requirements. By contrast, the next set of points on the continuum is characterised by public and private collaboration, to varying degrees, in rule-making, monitoring and enforcement processes.

Point (D) represents a situation in which the state, through a public agency, consults and sometimes even negotiates with regulated entities. Direct regulations are tailored to individual firms or trade associations that agree to work with the government to achieve common goals. While the state retains its discretionary power, it seeks greater acceptance (and hence compliance) from the market.

Point (E), 'Enforced Self-Regulation', is a point of conceptual change: although some coercion is involved, the state adopts a less prescriptive and more facilitative role. Risk-, process-, management-, and performance-informed approaches attempt to confer the role of rule-making on the private sector, with some oversight or ratification by government entities.[7] The legislature, for example, could empower a regulatory agency to compel a company, or a trade association, to draft cyber-security rules specifically designed to address the contingencies facing this entity. The agency would then ratify and approve those rules.[8] Enforcement of those rules is usually done internally, with minimal intervention by the agency. In some cases, the agency may privatise only one of its roles (either rule-making or enforcement) and so leave more discretion with the government. This is perhaps what Elsig and Almaric term 'co-regulation': a partnership of equals, in which the public and private sectors act collaboratively to achieve a common goal and in which risks and opportunities are shared.[9]

The next point of interest on the continuum is 'Voluntary Self-Regulation' (F). Standards are developed and enforced privately without (or almost without) government involvement. Compliance with those standards is expected as a matter of good practice. It should be emphasised that, in many cases, self-regulatory entities are based on existing trade associations that have the power to compel their members to comply with standards.[10]

---

[7] Braithwaite, 'Enforced Self-Regulation'.   [8] *Ibid.*
[9] Elsig and Almaric, 'Business and Public–Private Partnerships'.
[10] Aviram and Tor, 'Overcoming Impediments'.

The last point on the continuum is regulation by the market (G). Here, the idea is that the market will self-adjust to reach socially optimal objectives on its own. The role of the government, if any, is limited to encouraging and inducing market transactions. For example, in the case of critical information infrastructure protection, consumers might be willing to pay more for more reliable electricity, which is resilient to cyber-attacks. On this argument, the profit incentive of the private companies would induce them to invest more in cyber-security measures. Competition would then drive all electricity providers to invest in such measures. The government's role, if any, would be to provide a stable legal framework for market transactions.

3. Public–private partnerships and regulatory arrangements

This brings us to the definition of public–private partnerships, which is also fairly muddled. Scholars use various definitions and it is rather hard to find agreement on the precise meaning and categorisation of PPPs. Some define it (rather obviously) as 'a voluntary co-operation between public and private actors on a common project'.[11] This definition emphasises the voluntariness of these partnerships. Others, like Elsig & Almaric, emphasise another attribute of partnerships – that of equality.[12]

Emanuel Savas, one of the main proponents of PPPs, introduced a definition which seems to be much more precise though much broader. Savas asserts that PPPs include various public–private interactions that differ by the degree of privatisation and reliance on the market. In other words, PPPs encompass '... any arrangement between a government and the private sector in which partially or traditionally public activities are being performed by the private sector'.[13] In other words, almost all forms of privatisation can be grouped under the rubric of PPPs.

Savas' definition is preferable to the previous two definitions for one main reason. Both Malm & Andersson's and Elsig & Almaric's definitions assume that the collaboration is designed to achieve a common goal or objective.[14] But this is not necessarily the case for every PPP. In fact, in most cases the objectives differ, especially when a for-profit private entity is involved. As I elaborate in section 5, the private, for-profit sector is motivated by profit-maximisation, whereas the public sector is usually

---

[11] Andersson and Malm , 'Public–Private Partnerships', 166–67.
[12] Elsig and Almaric, 'Business and Public–Private Partnerships'.
[13] Savas, 'Privatization', 4.   [14] Andersson and Malm, 'Public–Private Partnerships'.

motivated by other reasons. For example, a PPP in the area of private housing is a collaborative project between the government, whose object-ive is to provide a certain social service to economically and socially disadvantaged families or individuals and a private company, whose objective is to maximise the return for investors. The PPP arrangement is clearly voluntary and it seems reasonable to presume that the parties are equal, although this is not as straightforward. The objectives of the two parties differ. And yet, this does not undermine the collaborative effort. As long as the government presents the private entity with a good business case (that is, the potential to generate shareholder value), there will be collaboration. This example shows that the profit motive of private entities, although based on self-interest, can produce socially desired objectives.

What, then, of the relationship between PPPs and regulation? Regulation is an instrument for collaboration between public and private sectors. Applying Savas' definition to the regulatory continuum in Figure 3.1, points (D)–(F)[15] can be included within the concept of a PPP. These points represent privatisation or outsourcing of the state's regulatory function (rule-making, monitoring and/or enforcement) to varying extents. Evidently, the role of the state declines as we move on the continuum to the right, and the role (and discretion) of the private sector rises accordingly.

Collaboration in regulatory arrangements does not have to be volun-tary nor equal. Full voluntariness is achieved only in voluntary self-regulation. State coercion is present in enforced self-regulation and, of course, as we move further to the left along the regulatory continuum. Even in the case of voluntary self-regulation, the state may threaten regulatory intervention if the private sector takes no action, thus coercing industry self-regulation (for industry, still preferable to hierarchical regulation). The mere 'shadow of hierarchy' induces self-regulation.[16] Moreover, collaboration is entailed in the extreme case in which the state induces industry to self-regulate by providing economic incentives (such as subsidies or tax deductions).

Hence, in designing a regulatory arrangement that entails public–private collaboration to address the issue of critical information

---

[15] Some might say that even point (G), in which there is in theory no regulation at all, is a privatisation if it reflects a move along the continuum.

[16] Börzel and Héritier, 'Fostering Regulation?'.

infrastructure protection, policy makers have an array of strategies to choose from. As we shall see in the next part, American policy makers have adopted a rather narrow interpretation of the concept of a PPP and this is influencing the decisions by other policy makers in other parts of the world.

4. The American policy on critical information infrastructure protection – a privately dominated partnership

The American policy on critical information infrastructure protection has its origins in the mid 1990s. The 1993 bombing of the World Trade Center, together with the Oklahoma City bombing two years later, generated greater awareness of the threat to critical infrastructures from terrorist attacks.[17] Since then, a large and steady stream of high-level task forces, policy documents and laws has reflected the government's commitment to this issue.

From its inception, the *leitmotif* of the American policy on critical information infrastructure protection has been that the government should refrain from intervening in the market and instead seek voluntary co-operation from the private owners and operators of critical infrastructure. The government opted for a 'hands-off' approach in relying on market mechanisms to motivate those actors to take protective actions, improve the resilience of particular items of infrastructure and share information about vulnerabilities, threats and risks.[18, 19]

The main objective of these policies has been to '[p]romote a partnership between government and infrastructure owners and operators beginning with increased sharing of information relating to infrastructure threats, vulnerabilities, and interdependencies'.[20] Thus, the American policy heavily relies on the private sector to adequately protect critical information infrastructure. It attempts to promote voluntary self-regulation by industry sectors comprising American critical

---

[17] Lopez, 'Critical Infrastructure Protection'.   [18] *Ibid.*

[19] See also later on in two important strategies released by the White House. US President George W. Bush 2002, *National Strategy on Homeland Security.* Available at www.dhs. gov/interweb/assetlibrary/nat_strat_hls.pdf, and US President George W. Bush 2003, *The National Strategy for the Physical Protection of Critical Infrastructures and Key Assets.* Available at www.dhs.gov/interweb/assetlibraryhysical_Strategy.pdf.

[20] President's Commission on Critical Infrastructure Protection, *Critical Foundations: Protecting America's Infrastructures.* Available at http://fas.org/sgp/library/pccip.pdf.

infrastructure and, at the same time, establish PPPs for the purpose of information sharing between government and the private sector.[21]

Hence, the private sector was left with responsibility for determining or developing standards on critical information infrastructure protection, such as requirements for a documented management cyber-security policy, electronic perimeter security, access control, raising security awareness and training personnel and the issuance of recovery plans in case of cyber-attacks.

In order to achieve this goal, government endorsed the creation of Information Sharing and Analysis Centres (ISACs). ISACs are membership organisations usually housed in existing self-regulatory industry trade associations. They are intended to collect, analyse and share information related to critical information infrastructure protection. The main ISACs include the Financial Services ISAC (which comprises the large banks, investment companies and insurance companies), the telecommunications industry ISAC (which operates through the existing National Coordinating Center) and the electricity sector's ISAC (which operates through the North American Electricity Reliability Corporation or 'NERC'). The rationale for endorsing this kind of group, in terms of regulatory policy, was to foster voluntary industry self-regulation in the area of critical information infrastructure protection. In choosing this option, the government sought to play a very limited role in the creation of cyber-security standards for critical infrastructures, a role that would require it, at the utmost, to facilitate private rule-making by private institutions.

In addition to the ISACs, various public–private partnerships were established to encourage the sharing of information related to critical information infrastructure protection between industry and government. InfraGard, the Partnership for Critical Infrastructure Security, the National Cyber Security Partnership and the National Cyber Security Alliance are examples of such mechanisms.

Information sharing between and among industry and government is an important element of the American approach to critical information infrastructure protection. Information regarding vulnerabilities and flaws in information systems, about new and emerging threats and about security tools must be shared between owners and operators of the critical information infrastructure and between those owners and

---

[21] See, generally, Dunn and Wigert, *International CIIP Handbook*.

government entities. In other words, for the American model to succeed, information must freely flow horizontally and vertically.

To stimulate action by the PPPs and the flow of information from the private sector, Congress enacted the Critical Infrastructure Information Act of 2002 (CII Act). The CII Act promotes information sharing by exempting from disclosure under the Freedom of Information Act (FOI Act) information related to critical infrastructure security which has been shared voluntarily. This mechanism and its implications for transparency are further elaborated below. For now, the reader may recall the regulatory continuum described above. It is rather obvious that American policy makers interpreted the PPP very narrowly. In fact, it would not even be regarded as a PPP on Elsig & Almaric's interpretation.

4.1   A (minor) deviation from non-intervention

That said, there are two relatively recent exceptions to the American policy of complete non-intervention in critical infrastructure protection, one in the chemical sector and another in the energy sector.

In the first case, Congress recently mandated federal security standards (including cyber-security regulations) designed to secure high-risk chemical facilities through Section 550 of the Homeland Security Appropriations Act of 2007.[22] The Act authorised the Department of Homeland Security (DHS) to promulgate 'interim final regulations' to assure the security of high-risk chemical facilities. Following this, in April 2007, DHS issued an interim final rule, which came into effect on 8 June 2007, establishing risk-based performance standards and requiring thousands of chemical facilities that use or store significant quantities of toxic chemicals to perform vulnerability assessments and take steps to secure the facilities, both physically and virtually.

In the second case, the Federal Energy Regulatory Commission (FERC) is currently approving a number of cyber-security standards developed by the NERC.[23] Here Congress authorised regulatory activity through the Energy Policy Act of 2005 (EP Act).[24] According to the EP Act, FERC certified NERC as an Electric Reliability Organisation (ERO). Its mission is to develop and enforce, subject to FERC approval, mandatory reliability standards in bulk power systems, including cyber-security rules.

---

[22] Pub. L. 109–295.
[23] See NERC's official website. Available at http://www.nerc.com/cip.html.
[24] Electricity Modernization Act of 2005, Pub. L. No. 109–258.

It is not surprising that the first two sectors in which we observe deviation from the 'hands off' policy are the chemical and the energy sectors. The chemical sector is a hazardous industry per se; hence, the risk associated with an attack on a chemical facility can be perceived easily. The risks associated with an attack on bulk power systems are also quite apparent (the 2003 blackout in north-east America is a recent reminder of this). Thus, direct command-and-control regulation (in the first case) and enforced self-regulation, which is officially sanctioned by the government (in the second case) have been introduced as more intervening regulatory tools.

And yet, these two exceptions are limited in scope, mainly targeted at simplifying voluntary self-regulation and information sharing with the private sector. If we recall Savas' definition of PPP as various public–private interactions that differ by the degree of privatisation and reliance on the market and the regulatory analysis in section 2, we see that American policy on critical information infrastructure protection relies heavily on the private sector and that the 'private' in 'PPP' dominates.

5. The accountability challenge to the American approach to critical information infrastructure protection

The literature on privatisation and PPPs stresses the normative challenges associated with achieving a public goal through private or combined public–private action. These challenges are said to arise with respect to accountability and, to a certain extent, transparency. Not surprisingly, these challenges are also present in the use of PPPs as a means of ensuring critical information infrastructure protection. As shown below, the accountability challenges result from the different objectives (and values) which guide the public and the for-profit, private sectors.

Accountability is a popular concept especially in the debate between those who support current privatisation processes and those who oppose them (or at least, are less supportive). All parties to the debate agree that accountability considerations should not be the sole or primary justification for decisions to intervene in the private market or to privatise governmental duties. They also agree that accountability must be a factor in the calculus of such a decision, and moreover, that mechanisms should be put in place to ensure principal–agent accountability in decentred regimes. Their dispute relates to the form these mechanisms should take.[25]

---

[25] Minow, 'Public and Private Partnerships'; Trebilcock and Iacobucci, 'Privatization and Accountability'.

What exactly is accountability? Accountability, in its plainest sense, is the state of being answerable to someone. It means, roughly, that one actor must provide explanations or justifications to another actor regarding his/her actions and that the second actor could reward or punish the first based on his/her performance. This definition, in turn, raises another set of questions: accountability to whom and for what?

At least initially, 'accountability to whom' seems (somewhat misleadingly) to be a technical matter. It is a question of selecting a designated actor who could best monitor the actions of the accountable person or organisation. Accountability for what, on the other hand, seems to be more substantial and value-driven. In Prof Black's words, it asks, in essence, what conception of the good should be pursued.[26] The answer to the first question directly affects the answer to the second question, specifically in the context of protecting critical information infrastructure. The choice of actor to whom an entity is accountable has consequences for the outcome to which that entity is accountable, and hence is quite substantial. This point is further elaborated below.

There are various accountability mechanisms that could be used to assure that socially optimal outcomes are generated in a concrete setting. This part discusses the debate between opponents and proponents of current privatisation processes and transparency and voting as accountability mechanisms in relation to critical information infrastructure protection.

5.1   The debate about accountability and privatisation

Objections to current privatisation processes are often made on grounds of accountability. In general, opponents of privatisation processes argue that the lack of proper public accountability in decentred regimes undermines public commitments. In other words, the scope and content of public values is adversely affected by inappropriate accountability mechanisms. Proponents of current privatisation processes respond to this challenge by arguing that, in most instances, the market can provide substitute accountability mechanisms to ensure that the desired goals are met.[27] It should be noted that the manner in which these parties address

---

[26] See in this volume Black, Chapter 9.
[27] The symposium entitled 'Public Values in an Era of Privatization' at Harvard Law School in 2002 provided a useful example for such debate. See the proceedings in *Harvard Law Review*, vol. 116, no. 5, 1211–1498 (2003).

the issue of accountability assumes principal–agent accountability. In this model, the agent is required to demonstrate that his/her actions conform to the demands, intentions and interests of the principal.[28]

For the opponents of privatisation, Prof Minow noted that '[p]rivatisation creates possibilities of weakening or avoiding public norms that attach, in the legal sense, to "state action" or conduct by government'.[29] While she acknowledged that there are reasons to endorse the current processes and hence did not insist on direct public provision of goods and services, Prof Minow explained that privatisation and PPPs require 'explicit oversight and accountability to public values'. In other words, accountability is a central issue requiring 'more public involvement and identity' in privatisation settings.[30] Therefore, these processes should be designed with mechanisms that would ensure that private actors respond to public interest as well as their private preferences, or *rather than* their private preference in case of substantial divergence between the two.[31]

Profs. Trebilcock and Iacobucci critique Prof Minow's thesis. Their basic argument is that, in most cases, private firms are just as able to motivate their agents through profit incentives. This is mainly because private corporations may not survive in the face of poor performance. The risk of loss of jobs or liquidation induces private agents to reach the necessary objectives. The accountability structures that private firms face are usually characterised as 'downwards' in nature in that private firms are accountable to their shareholders and other stakeholders and are often susceptible to takeover by other actors.[32] All such actors have increased interest in scrutinising the private firms' performance.

Hence, Trebilcock & Iacobucci assert that there should be a limited role for direct government intervention in the market as private for-profit entities are in general superior to state institutions in their ability to motivate their agents to create profits and thereby generate socially optimal incentives. One interesting conclusion from this analysis is that the more the interests of the public and private sectors are aligned, the easier it would be for governments to design a PPP with minimal intervention that still provides accountability not only to private values (profit maximisation) but also to broader public interests. On the other hand, the less the interests are aligned, the harder it would be to design such an arrangement with minimal intervention.

---

[28] Dowdle, 'Public Accountability'.   [29] Minow, 'Public and Private Partnerships', 1246.
[30] *Ibid.*, 1237.   [31] Minow, *Partners, Not Rivals.*
[32] Scott, 'Accountability in the Regulatory State'.

The next sub-section questions whether private accountability mechanisms are adequate for the critical information infrastructure protection market. It will illuminate the problems associated with private provision of critical information infrastructure protection and question the burgeoning enthusiasm for self-regulation and PPPs in providing adequate levels of protection for critical information infrastructures.

5.2   The market for critical information infrastructure protection and the profit motive in cyber-security

If we are to conclude that market mechanisms and competition can drive the private sector to provide forms of accountability, we first must assume that market mechanisms operate well and that competition, one of the prerequisites for a perfect (or nearly perfect) market, exists.

There are two problems associated with the current market-oriented policy promoted by the United States. As we have seen, it is based on the conception that private, for-profit firms are superior to public entities in their ability to motivate agents to generate profit. I have shown elsewhere that the market for CIIP is susceptible to a number of failures, namely public goods, externalities and information deficits.[33] Further, and equally important, it is questionable whether the profit incentive in this market (and in the cyber-security market, more generally) actually exists.

These two points require further elaboration. Welfare economics suggests that government intervention is required only when market failures are present. The characteristics of the market for critical information infrastructure protection indicate a number of market failures (public goods, negative externalities and information deficits), all of which lead to under-provision of security and security-related information. Basic microeconomics suggests that the presence of one or more of these failures will cause the market to operate sub-optimally, despite (perhaps because of) private firms' attempts to maximise profits. Where the profit motive generates social costs (and hence maximisation of profits does not maximise social welfare), it should be constrained.

The second problem with relying on the profit incentive is the dubious nature of the business case for more secure critical information infrastructure and cyber-security, more generally. The business case is questionable for various reasons. First, businesses tend to behave reactively, rather than proactively, in mitigating vulnerabilities. Since cyber-attacks

---

[33] Assaf, 'Government Intervention'.

have not caused significant visible damage to critical information infrastructure thus far, business may find the costs associated with cyber-
security investment hard to justify. Second, an increase in cyber-security
investment implies fewer resources for income-generating investments,
which usually increase the company's value to its shareholders. Third,
and related to the first two reasons, cyber-security investments reduce
costs rather than create value (return on investment). All in all, the
business case for cyber-security investment is not clear.

These two problems are unique to the market for critical information
infrastructure protection and taken together they lead to a conclusion
that, in many cases, there will be a discrepancy between the amount of
money owners and operators of critical infrastructure are willing to
spend on cyber-security for business continuity and the amount of
investment that would be socially optimal. Hence, the chances for convergence between the interests of the private sector and the interests of
the public (profit maximisation and enhanced cyber-security) are rather
low. Naturally, under these circumstances, the accountability mechanisms of the private sector would not have the same effect as public
accountability mechanisms in ensuring that socially desired outcomes
are reached. It might even be the case that the profit-induced accountability mechanisms would lead cyber-security initiatives in the opposite
direction.

This understanding necessitates a conclusion that downward accountability mechanisms are insufficient for ensuring the public interest
(security) as well as, or rather than, the private interest (profit) in the
protection of critical information infrastructure. Therefore, these
mechanisms must be supplemented, perhaps even replaced, by explicit
public accountability and oversight mechanisms.

To sum up the issue of accountability incentives, it would be naïve to
expect private actors to take into account the interests of other entities
(other critical infrastructures operators, the security apparatuses, or the
citizenry as a whole) or in Stephen Linder's words 'embrace public
interest considerations and expect greater public accountability'.[34] By
relying on private owners and operators of critical infrastructures to
provide an adequate level of protection against cyber-attacks, including
explicitly anticipating that they set cyber-security standards, American
policy-makers vest substantial power and discretionary authority in
these private actors that are not ultimately responsible for national

---

[34] See Linder, 'Coming to Terms'.

security. Presumably, such authority and power should be accompanied by public accountability mechanisms designed to assure proper perform-ance. With this in mind, it is rather striking that the decision to favour a 'hands off' approach to critical information infrastructure protection was not accompanied by the creation of public accountability mechanisms that would enable proper oversight.

5.3   Additional public accountability mechanisms in relation to critical information infrastructure protection

An important aspect in the public–private accountability debate is that public actors are usually held accountable through a number of addi-tional mechanisms that do not apply to private actors. The requirement of transparency in public policy and decision making and the mechanism of elections are examples of such mechanisms. The next paragraphs discuss these mechanisms in relation to critical information infrastruc-ture protection.

5.3.1   The problem of transparency

Issues of transparency frequently arise in privatisations, as private actors are generally not required to adhere to the visibility requirements expected of public actors. Transparency and accountability are related. In fact, many consider transparency to be one mechanism by which public accountability is achieved. Recent concerns with transparency go back to the 1960s and 1970s, when the American public in particular became sceptical about the degree to which the professionalisation and rationalisation of the bureaucracy or judicial review could induce public officials to act in the public interest.[35] The idea behind freedom of information statutes was to make political decision making far more visible so to allow a much wider range of civil society actors to hold public officials to account even without directly participating in the political process.[36] Examples of this development are the Freedom of Information Act of 1966, which generally requires federal agencies to release their records to the public upon request, and the Government in the Sunshine Act of 1976, which requires federal agencies to hold their meetings regularly in public sessions. As Dowdle explains, the FOI Act was subordinated to the requirements of the bureaucratic government

---

[35] See Dowdle, 'Public Accountability'.   [36] Ibid.

itself through the enactment of broad exemptions. But even in its constrained shape, it still plays an important part in subjecting actors vested with authority and power to supervision by 'the people'.

A lack of transparency is one consequence of the American government's decision to keep its 'hands off' in the area of critical information infrastructure protection and to allow the private sector to formulate critical information infrastructure protection standards and rules. Only the private sector possesses important information about the vulnerability of its information systems to cyber-warfare. And, without such information, the public sector cannot assess whether tighter standards are required or whether further investment should be mandated.

But even if the public eye does not have a chance to 'glance' at this important information, one would expect the government to be able to do so, at least, to carry out its responsibility to secure the homeland. This, as we shall see, is a futile expectation.

The market for critical information infrastructure protection suffers from the problem of information deficits.[37] One of the most important elements of cyber-security and specifically critical information infrastructure protection is the information flow between all stakeholders – owners and operators of critical infrastructures, the government and other entities dealing with security – regarding security flaws, threats, vulnerabilities and so on. The problem is that of too little openness ('under-openness') in information sharing regarding security-related issues among private owners of critical infrastructures themselves and between them and the public sector, particularly security apparatuses. 'Under-openness' implies that both the public and private sectors are reluctant to share with each other important information related to critical information infrastructure protection, such as threats, warnings, security incidents, etc.

The private sector's reluctance to share information with the government is explained by its fear that information disclosed to the government will find its way to the public (or, even worse, to competitors) through freedom of information rules. The private sector may also fear that, by providing information to government, it will alert regulators to the real levels of protection for critical information infrastructure and that regulation will follow.

Because the standard-setting process takes place amongst private actors, government relies on the private sector to voluntarily supply it

[37] Assaf, 'Government Intervention'.

with relevant information. In light of this, the American government sought to promote the efficient sharing of information relating to critical information infrastructure protection between the public and private sectors using institutions such as ISACs. These institutions were designed to play the role of 'agora', a place for various stakeholders to share and exchange information. However, their effectiveness is yet to be proved.[38]

Pushed by the private sector, Congress enacted the Critical Infrastructure Information Act of 2002, which attempts to promote information sharing by exempting from disclosure under the FOI Act information which has been voluntarily submitted. Obviously, this exemption was supposed to induce the private sector to submit information related to critical infrastructure to the government. Alas, in the time since its enactment, the Act failed to fulfil its purpose.[39] Critical infrastructure owners and operators seemed to take the idea of 'voluntariness' too seriously and very little information found its way from the private sector to the government. Moreover, the little information provided was now exempt from the FOI Act, meaning that the public's ability to critically follow this issue decreased substantially. Hence, the government's decisions to subordinate freedom of information laws in order to encourage more transparency from private CII providers did not produce the desired outcome and, in fact, only resulted in less transparency in both the public and private sectors.

In sum, the consequence of the transparency problem is less public accountability. Diminished transparency impedes the ability of the public (as well as the legislature) to fully evaluate whether the private sector, responsible for enhanced protection of critical information infrastructure, acts efficiently and effectively and provides an adequate level of protection.

5.3.2   Voting

In trying to avoid government intervention on the grounds of accountability, market enthusiasts may argue that we cannot expect accountability from the public sector regarding the protection of critical information infrastructure because politicians are rarely elected on the basis of their CIIP activities. In other words, public agents are insulated

---

[38] Auerswald *et al.*, 'Leadership: Who Will Act', 397–98.
[39] Bagley, 'Critical Infrastructure Security'.

from the risk of failures in critical information infrastructure. As voting is a primary mechanism of accountability, the public sector may fail too.

There are two possible answers to this kind of argument: first, while voting is indeed an important accountability mechanism (the first accountability mechanism, to be sure),[40] there are others, including a rationalised and professionalised bureaucracy, judicial review, and transparency. The monitoring of issues of critical information infrastructure protection by the American Government Accountability Office is an evident example for such a mechanism. Second, even if they have previously escaped evaluation based on their ability to enhance critical information infrastructure protection, Hurricane Katrina and the events that followed may have changed the way politicians view possible catastrophes, such as an attack on the nation's critical information infrastructure. The public anger that resulted from Hurricane Katrina required the Bush administration to take concrete and strong measures to address the risk inherent in natural disasters. So it would be reasonable to assume that the concept of homeland security has gained sufficient 'popularity' within the electorate that politicians will be attentive to it and take the associated risks seriously. The broad discussion of homeland security issues (including critical information infrastructure protection) during the election for Congress held in 2007 is the first sign of this growing attention.

6.   Conclusion

This chapter attempted to shed light on an interesting phenomenon: the choice of American policy makers to rely on privately dominated regulatory structures in securing an important component of American national security: the security of critical infrastructure. It tried to illuminate the problems associated with the reliance on the private sector to achieve a socially desired objective. These problems are the result of the American government's failure to understand the gap that exists between the broader public interest (national security) and the narrower interest of the private sector (business continuity, as long as it generates shareholders' value).

This chapter did not argue that the goal of national security is more important than the goal of profit maximisation (or economic efficiency),[41] but rather that the broader value of national security should

---

[40] Dowdle, 'Public Accountability'.

[41] Although I suspect that in the face of a clear and immediate threat most people would prefer security to profit.

be considered in the design of regulatory arrangements in critical information infrastructure protection – and not only business continuity. In Prof Donahue's words, 'architecture or design [of the governing arrangement] ... motivates private actors to be more accountable to public values'.[42]

By designing regulatory structures that have overlapping accountability mechanisms policy makers can reduce the centrality of private accountability mechanisms and better ensure proper accountability for the values of both security and profit maximisation.

Reinforcing the 'public' in public–private partnership and creating a better balance between public and private values is a good place to start. The move from self-regulation to enforced self-regulation in the energy and chemical sectors, described in Section 4, served to alter the incentive structures of the private owners and operators of these critical infrastructures, albeit to a limited extent (profit maximisation remains their main objective). The private sector is still developing and setting cyber-security standards but the requirement to obtain the government's approval for those standards, together with the threat of government enforcement, changes the way in which management considers cyber-security issues and so enhances accountability to public values or interests.

And yet, the shift in regulatory policy is relevant only to a small part of what comprises the American critical infrastructure. Without a real commitment towards this path, whatever its challenges are, from both the public and private sectors, America (as well as other countries that adopted the same or similar regulatory model) will remain vulnerable to attacks on its critical infrastructures.

References

Andersson, J. J. and Malm, A. 2006, 'Public–Private Partnerships and the Challenge of Critical Infrastructure Protection' in M. Dunn and I. Wigert (eds.), 139–68.

Assaf, D. 2007, 'Government Intervention in Information Infrastructure Protection' in E. Goetz and S. Shenoi (eds.), Critical Infrastructure Protection, New York, Springer, 39–49.

Auerswald, P. E. et al. 2006, 'Leadership: Who Will Act – Integrating Public and Private Interests to Make a Safer World' in P. E. Auerswald et al. (eds.), Seeds of Disaster, Roots of Response: How Private Action Can Reduce Public Vulnerability, New York, Cambridge University Press, 483–505.

---

[42] See Donahue, 'Market-Based Governance', 8.

Avant, D. D. 2005, *The Market for Force: the Consequences of Privatizing Security*, New York, Cambridge University Press.

Aviram, A. and Tor, A. 2004, 'Overcoming Impediments to Information Sharing', *Alabama Law Review*, vol. **55**, 231.

Bagley, N. 2006, 'Benchmarking, Critical Infrastructure Security, and the Regulatory War on Terror', *Harvard Journal on Legislation*, vol. **43**, no. 1, 47–100.

Börzel, T. A. and Héritier, A. 2007, 'Fostering Regulation? Corporate Social Responsibility in Countries with Weak Regulatory Capacity', *Non-state Actors as Standard Setters: the Erosion of the Public–Private Divide* (conference), Basel Institute on Governance.

Braithwaite, J. 1982, 'Enforced Self-Regulation: A New Theory for Corporate Crime Control', *Michigan Law Review*, vol. **80**, no. 7, 1466–1507.

Branscomb, L. M. and Michel-Kerjan, E. O. 2006, 'Public–Private Collaboration on a National and International Scale' in P. E. Auerswald *et al.* (eds.), *Seeds of Disaster, Roots of Response: How Private Action Can Reduce Public Vulnerability*, New York, Cambridge University Press, 395–403.

Donahue, J. D. 2002, 'Market-Based Governance and the Architecture of Accountability' in J. D. Donahue and J. S. Nye Jr. (eds.), *Market-Based Governance: Supply Side, Demand Side, Upside and Downside*, Washington DC, Brookings Institution Press, 1–25.

Dowdle, M. W. 2006, 'Public Accountability: Conceptual, Historical, and Epistemic Mappings' in M. W. Dowdle (ed.), *Public Accountability: Designs, Dilemmas and Experiences*, Cambridge University Press, 1–29.

Dunn, M. and Wigert, I. 2006, *The International CIIP Handbook: An Inventory and Analysis of Protection Policies in Fourteen Countries*, Zurich, Center for Security Studies, ETH.

Elsig, M. and Almaric, F. 2008, 'Business and Public–Private Partnerships for Sustainability: Beyond Corporate Social Responsibility?' *Global Society*, vol. **22**, no. 3, 387–404.

Krebs, B. 2007, 'Estonia Incident Demonstrated Power of Russia-Based Cyber Networks', *Washington Post.com*, 13 October 2007. Available at http://www. washingtonpost.com/wpdyn/content/article/2007/10/12/AR2007101201700. html.

Linder, S. H. 2000, 'Coming to Terms with Public–Private Partnership: A Grammar of Multiple Meanings' in P. Vaillancourt-Rosenau (ed.), *Public–Private Policy Partnership*, Cambridge, MA, The MIT Press.

Lopez, B. 2006, 'Critical Infrastructure Protection in the United States Since 1993' in P. E. Auerswald *et al.* (eds.), *Seeds of Disaster, Roots of Response: How Private Action Can Reduce Public Vulnerability*, New York, Cambridge University Press, 39–50.

Minow, M. 2002, *Partners, Not Rivals: Privatization and the Public Good*, Boston, Beacon Press.

Minow, M. 2003, 'Public and Private Partnerships: Accounting for the New Religion', *Harvard Law Review*, vol. **116**, no. 5, 1229–70.

Morgan, B. and Yeung, K. 2007, *An Introduction to Law and Regulation: Text and Materials*, Cambridge University Press.

Ogus, A. 2002, 'Regulatory Institutions and Structures', *Annals of Public and Cooperative Economics*, vol. **73**, no. 4, 627–48.

President's Commission on Critical Infrastructure Protection, *Critical Foundations: Protecting America's Infrastructures*. Available at http://fas. org/sgp/library/pccip.pdf.

Salamon, L. E. (ed.) 2002, *The Tools of Government: A Guide to the New Governance*, New York, Oxford University Press.

Savas, E. S. 2000, *Privatization and Public–Private Partnerships*, New York, Chatham House Publishers.

Scott, C. 2000, 'Accountability in the Regulatory State', *Journal of Law and Society*, vol. **27**, no. 1, 38–60.

Traynor, I. 2007, 'Russia Accused of Unleashing Cyberwar to Disable Estonia', *The Economist*, 17 May 2007. Available at www.guardian.co.uk/russia/article/ 0,,2081438,00.html.

Trebilcock, M. J. and Iacobucci, E. M. 2003, 'Privatization and Accountability', *Harvard Law Review*, vol. **116**, no. 5, 1422–54.

US President George W. Bush 2002, *National Strategy on Homeland Security*. Available at www.dhs.gov/interweb/assetlibrary/nat_strat_hls.pdf.

US President George W. Bush 2003, *The National Strategy for the Physical Protection of Critical Infrastructures and Key Assets*. Available at www. dhs.gov/interweb/assetlibraryhysical_Strategy.pdf.

4

Standard setting at the cutting edge: an evidence-based typology for multi-stakeholder initiatives

LUCY KOECHLIN* AND RICHARD CALLAND**

1. The line of inquiry

The notion of 'multi-stakeholdism' is a fashionable one. 'Partnership' is a new mantra in the vocabulary of global politics. In the past ten years, a fast-growing array of multi-stakeholder initiatives (MSIs) was created as a 'means of filling "governance gaps" where existing national legislation and/or enforcement were not enough to prevent corruption or human rights abuses'.[1] At their high water mark, MSIs represent an alternative governance model and a possible platform for building democratic accountability in places where traditional democratic institutions and processes are weak. The trend reflects both frustration with progress at intergovernmental level and, perhaps, a more pragmatic approach on the part of some of the key actors, especially in the private and non-governmental sectors. It seems that 'multi-stakeholdism' has a 'feel-good' aspect to it. But do MSIs do any good? And, in order to evaluate the question of whether MSIs deliver on their promise, how does one go about measuring their performance? Given the apparently enduring support for the idea of MSIs, it would be valuable for policy makers, activists and academics alike to establish a model for evaluating their efficacy and impact.

* Head of Public Accountability, Basel Institute on Governance, Switzerland; Lecturer, Institute of Sociology, University of Basel; Lic. phil., MSc (LSE). The author would like to thank Gretta Fenner Zinkernagel for her substantial contribution towards the development of the typology.
** Associate Professor of Public Law, University of Cape Town; Director, Economic Governance Programme, IDASA, South Africa; Member, International Advisory Group, Medicines Transparency Alliance.
[1] Morrison and Wilde, *The Effectiveness of Multi-stakeholder Initiatives*, 2.

The spectrum of so-called multi-stakeholder processes is extremely broad, given the wide range of functions and forms operating in very different contexts. Some of the best-known ones have become increasingly present and visible in areas of weak and complex governance, addressing regulatory problems that are beyond the capacity of the individual governments to develop or enforce, such as ecological regimes or resource management. Examples such as the EITI (Extractive Industries Transparency Initiative) or the Voluntary Principles on Security and Human Rights spring to mind. In spite of much public attention, the actual (positive or negative) impact of such initiatives has not, however, so far been the subject of much in-depth analysis and a systematic and comprehensive assessment.

The overarching purpose of this chapter is to begin a discussion about how best to develop a rigorous methodology for measuring the impact of multi-stakeholder strategies in setting standards.[2] In order to fill this gap, this chapter addresses the emergence of MSIs within their context and delineates the fuzzy term 'MSI'. Second, an attempt is made to capture the key determinants of MSIs by developing a preliminary outline of an MSI-typology. Third, the concrete experience of one MSI, the EITI, is examined as a case study, with specific regard to its standard-setting potential, and as an opportunity to test the viability of the typology as a framework for analysis and evaluation. This includes such research questions as: What are the consequences and effects of multi-stakeholder processes on national and international governance? Under what conditions can and will civil society organisations as well as corporate actors get engaged? And, not least, when are multi-stakeholder processes suitable and effective?

2.   Towards a conceptual understanding of multi-stakeholder initiatives

The concept of MSI is notoriously vague, and perhaps derives part of its current appeal from this very vagueness. Broadly speaking, MSIs can be circumscribed as 'collective initiatives between governments, inter-governmental bodies, the private sector and NGOs'.[3] The term was initially coined in the follow-up process to the Rio conference in 1995 with regard to addressing environmental problems. However, in the past decade, such collective initiatives across sectors have been increasingly

---

[2] For an attempt at a cross-sectoral definition and measurement of accountability principles see the Global Accountability Project (see in this volume Blagescu and Lloyd, Chapter 10).

[3] Martens, *Multistakeholder Partnerships*, 4.

used in other areas, such as human rights regimes (for example UK–US Voluntary Standards on Security and Human Rights) or accountability and transparency initiatives (for example the EITI). By incorporating all relevant actors in a joint process, MSIs seek to achieve a comprehensive approach to individual and common problems facing each actor and to find appropriate collective solutions. Some of the virtues ascribed to such collective initiatives are that they present an effective and efficient alternative to government regulation for solving complex problems, in recognition of a) the global and interconnected nature of new problems (for instance arising from negative environmental or social effects of globalisation); b) the slow and winding pace and often inappropriate instruments of global negotiation processes; and c) the interdependencies between the various stakeholders and their actions.

Furthermore, 'rapid economic expansion and an increasing lack of government actions, due to financial limits, political "regulatory chill" effects or other impediments call for greater involvement of societal forces. Market or governmental failure or both stand out as prerequisites for the setting up of these hybrid institutions.'[4] Hence the ever-more important role of businesses and civic organisations (as the chiefly concerned actors and actor groups in markets and states) in formerly government-dominated areas of policy making, in particular rule setting, rule implementation and, in some instances, service provision.[5] The roles of the participating actors and sectors are not fixed, but depend on the origins, process and aim of the initiative.[6]

As Jens Martens discusses, a 'new form of multilateral co-operation beyond intergovernmental diplomacy has gained increasing importance. In this new paradigm of international co-operation, "global partnerships", "multi-stakeholder initiatives" and "global public policy networks" are perceived as the future of international co-operation, moving beyond traditional nation–state multi-lateralism'.[7] However, such multi-sectoral partnerships and public–private co-regulations come in many different

---

[4] Elsig and Amalric, 'Business and Public–Private Regulation Arrangements', 392.

[5] Service provision is an activity mainly attributed to conventional PPPs (see below for further elaboration); however, it is conceivable that it could be part of an MSI.

[6] This is an explicit differentiation from the understanding of multi-stakeholder partnerships that the UN coined, which refer to partnerships between advocacy organisations and the business community, with governments and IGOs taking a merely facilitating role (see for instance Haufler (ed.), *UN Global Compact*. It also differs from the concept of multi-stakeholder roundtables or platforms, which represent a more institutionalised type of body (cf. Warner, 'Multi-stakeholder Platforms'; or Turcotte and Pasquero, 'The Paradox') – whereas, as argued further down, MSIs feature a more process-oriented character.

[7] Martens, *Multistakeholder Partnerships*, 4.

shapes and sizes, so the term MSI needs to be distinguished from other similar terms. Public–Private Partnerships (PPPs) have become an increasingly common type of cross-sectoral co-operation, especially with regard to the regulation and the provision of certain public goods.[8] Here, the tasks and responsibilities of each party are subject to a clear and usually formalised agreement. A key feature of PPPs is the delegation of a public function to a private actor, such as infrastructure maintenance, energy provision or similar. Service provision is an activity mainly attributed to a PPP. On the other end of the spectrum so-called multi-sectoral networks can be found, which also address governance challenges, but in a far more fluid and dynamic form. Characterised by interdependence, flexibility and complementarity, these networks have facilitating roles, co-ordinative functions or pursue standard-setting objectives.[9]

MSIs comprise a form of multi-sectoral networks, characterised by a process-oriented, joint approach to benchmarking, rule making and implementation.[10] Frequently, though, no sharp distinction between PPPs and MSIs can be drawn. Especially in environmental and social regulation, bi-partite public–private forms of co-regulation at some point involve other actors, such as NGOs or international organisations. An interesting example is the 'International Cyanide Management Code for the Manufacture, Transport and Use of Cyanide in the Production of Gold', which began as a private self-regulatory initiative of the gold mining industry, but only coalesced into a voluntary code under the guidance of the United Nations Environmental Programme (UNEP) and the International Council on Metals and the Environment (ICME). In the meantime, the code enjoys official government support by the Chief Inspector of Mines in South Africa.[11]

---

[8] For instance, PPPs are defined by the UN General Assembly as follows: 'Voluntary and collaborative relationships between various parties, both State and non-state, in which all participants agree together to achieve a common purpose or undertake a specific task and to share risk and responsibilities, resources and benefits' (UN General Assembly (2005)). *Enhanced Cooperation Between the United Nations and all Relevant Partners, in Particular the Private Sector*. Report of the General Secretary A/60/214. For an early and important discussion on PPPs see Linder and Vaillancourt Rosenau, 'Mapping the Terrain'. For a current case study on PPPs in critical information technology infrastructure protection see in this volume Assaf, Chapter 3.

[9] See Benner *et al.*, 'Multi-sectoral Networks', 196.

[10] For a detailed illustration in the field of development co-operation see for instance Zammit, *Development at Risk*.

[11] Their own words reflect the pioneering spirit and ground-breaking achievement: 'The Code was developed under the auspices of the United Nations Environment Programme (UNEP) and the International Council on Metals and the Environment (ICME). In May

Table 4.1 *Types of Governance*[1]

Actors Involved/ Steering Modes	Public Actors only	Public and Private Actors	Private Actors only
Hierarchical: Top-down; (threat of) sanctions	–traditional nation–state –supranational institutions (EU)		
Non-hierarchical 1: Positive incentives, bargaining	Intergovernmental bargaining	*–delegation of public functions to private actors (PPPs)* *–public–private networks and partnerships with a specific formal or informal policy objective*	*–private interest government / private regimes* *–self-regulation*
Non-hierarchical 2: Non-manipulative persuasion (learning, communicating, arguing etc.)	Institutional problem-solving	*–(multi-sectoral networks, PPPs, MSIs* *–benchmarking (MSIs)*	*–private/private collaborations (e.g. NGOs and business companies)*

[1] This table is adapted from Börzel and Risse, 'Public–Private Partnerships', Figure 9.1, 197.

In Table 4.1, different steering modes and actors are distinguished, carving out the underlying logics as well as the types of governance regimes emanating from these logics. MSIs, as defined here, are only to be found in the second column, where public and private actors convene

2000, at a joint UNEP/ICME-sponsored international workshop in Paris, cyanide producers, financial institutions, regulatory personnel, gold mining companies and environmental advocacy organizations from around the world met and recommended that a multi-stakeholder Steering Committee be formed by participants from the gold mining industry, governments, non-governmental organizations, labor, cyanide producers and financial institutions to deliberate on appropriate factors to include and to develop a Code. This project represents the first time that such a multi-stakeholder group has worked co-operatively to generate an international, globally based voluntary program for improvement of an industry activity.' See their website at www.cyanidecode.org/about_faq.php#15 (last accessed 26 September 2008).

in non-hierarchical ways. Although the level of institutionalisation may differ, MSIs are characterised by the co-operative and voluntary relationship between governmental and intergovernmental bodies, profit-making firms and non-profit organisations. In other words MSIs comprise tri-sector partnerships, in which governmental institutions, civic organisations and private companies are included as equal partners.[12] Such an extension of collaborative models is crucial to framing appropriate problem-solving solutions that transcend limited sectoral interests and rationales.

Another useful categorisation derives from the level of state involvement, or the regulatory stage that such multi-sector collaborations engage in.[13] Within the matrix developed in Table 4.1, MSIs fall into the category of the co-regulation of public and private actors. Although the true joint decision-making power of all the participating actors may not be given, the distinctive feature of such collaborations still is that the role of non-state actors has become legitimate at the negotiation table in the making and implementing of governance regimes. In other words, non-governmental (civic or private) stakeholders are not merely consulted, but all parties take an active and engaged role in shaping the process and outcomes through bargaining and argumentative (that is, non-manipulative) persuasion. This is an important distinction, as the type of partnership influences both the behaviour as well as the roles of the involved actors.[14]

Against the backdrop of global and national regulatory complexities, 'the importance of allegiances which straddle state boundaries'[15] has become tangible, especially in areas in which governments – and particularly governments characterised by weak governance in terms of rule of law, accountability and regulatory capacity – are struggling or unwilling to address key issues such as security, environmental risks or human rights. With corporate as well as civic actors generally taking on new responsibilities and roles in policy and standard setting,[16] MSIs constitute a particular

---

[12] Conventional PPPs, on the other hand, traditionally relate to partnerships that involve stakeholders from only two sectors, i.e. the state or an intergovernmental organisation working together with either the private sector or the non-profit sector (see Linder and Vaillancourt Rosenau, 'Mapping the Terrain', 9).

[13] See Elsig and Amalric, 'Business and Public–Private Regulation Arrangements', 390.

[14] See Börzel and Risse 2005, 'Public–Private Partnerships', 199–206, in particular Figure 9.2., 200.

[15] Migdal and Schlichte, 'Rethinking the State', 36.

[16] Of course, this statement also holds true for OECD countries, where privatisation and deregulation processes of the last thirty years have also contributed to radical re-configurations between state and society, such as for instance in the United Kingdom. For a detailed discussion of the public–private boundary see in this volume Förster, Chapter 12.

form of co-operative problem solving. As a consequence of their inclusive and comprehensive nature they are well placed to fill regulatory voids, overcome apparently zero-sum-game policy dilemmas and trade-offs, and not least address the much-lamented democratic deficit of global governance regimes in terms of accountability and participation.[17]

An indicative and unique strength of MSIs is their process-oriented character. They act as a medium of dialogue, confidence-building, exchange and what Tanja Börzel and Thomas Risse term 'non-manipulative persuasion' (see Table 4.1 above) through learning, communication and argumentation across sectors, actors and interests. This has the inherent benefit of providing mediating platforms for the negotiation of controversial issues. Additionally, they create the conditions for the generation and co-ordination of resources to sustain the process and implement solutions.

3. Typologising multi-stakeholder initiatives

Based on the above thoughts, arguably MSIs should be evaluated in terms of both their legitimacy and their effectiveness; more precisely, their ability to increase a) the democratic accountability and b) the capacity of specific regulatory regimes shaped by MSIs. There seems to be a consensus that such initiatives can play a valuable role in addressing and contributing to both key dimensions. However, existing theoretical frameworks, useful as they may be to understanding governance forms and types of public–private collaborations, are not geared towards a systematic analysis and comparison of MSIs. Their impact on increasing transparency, accountability and regulatory order through non-hierarchical policy networks, consensual benchmarking and co-operative models is still underexplored, with very little empirical evidence to draw from.[18] In an effort to fill this gap, we shall first endeavour to strengthen the analytical framework. Having clarified the rationales underlying MSIs, the next step will be the identification of the main determinants that characterise MSIs, as well as the main factors that affect their effectiveness (problem-solving capacity) and legitimacy (democratic accountability). The objective is to refine the typology of MSIs, so that individual MSIs can be

---

[17] For a seminal collection of articles relevant to the debate on the democratic deficit see Keohane, *Power and Governance*.

[18] For an interesting discussion of case studies in environmental regulation see Mazurkiewicz, 'Corporate Self-regulation'.

analysed and rendered comparable with regard to their effectiveness and legitimacy. One of the challenges of this typology is to capture the process-oriented, dynamic nature of such initiatives.

Tentatively, four analytical categories are proposed, namely a) function of MSI; b) momentum of MSI (drivers and motives); c) status and composition of partners within MSI; and d) area of intervention.

3.1   Function of MSI

As indicated above, MSIs can cover a broad range of implicit or explicit purposes and functions. Characteristically, they co-exist with other forms of governance, but fill governance gaps in areas where other governance forms – unilateralism, intergovernmental multi-lateralism, private regulation or similar – prove inadequate. So what functions within governance regimes do MSI implicitly or explicitly fulfil? In an ideal-typical differentiation, the following functions seem most significant:

- dialogue/forum
- institution building
- rule setting
- rule implementation
- rule monitoring.[19]

The sequencing of the above dimensions has a certain chronological rationale. Although the mediating role of MSIs constitutes one of their key features by creating a forum for trust relations and policy dialogue, the purpose of MSIs may shift as they develop over time. For instance, the World Commission on Dams (WCD), one of the early and renowned MSIs, embodies this processual nature in its organisational design as well as in the way the final report was worded: 'In writing the [final] report, the Commission recognized that it would not be the final word, but the start of a new process of re-evaluation, constructive multi-stakeholder discussions and of implementation and adaptation of the guidance provided to suit local contexts'.[20] As the WCD exemplifies, a typical cycle might be that after an initial phase of dialogue and confidence building, certain voluntary principles may be agreed upon, which may

---

[19] The term 'rules' is understood here in a broad sense, encompassing both formal and informal norms and standards.

[20] See the WCD website at www.dams.org/commission/project.htm (last accessed 22 September 2008).

become more formalised and subject to stricter monitoring agreements. In other words, the dynamics of such initiatives are crucial to their function of building bridges and (often progressively) filling complex governance gaps.[21]

3.2   Momentum of MSI: drivers and incentives

This category endeavours to capture the dynamics of MSIs. One dimension relates to the initiator or driver behind a particular initiative. It is intuitively plausible that many MSIs need a primary driver to kick the process off and perhaps even to keep the momentum up. For instance, in the case of EITI this was the British government, or in the case of the Voluntary Initiative on Human Rights and Security it was the UK Foreign Office and the US Department of State who convened the first meeting between stakeholders. Both examples raise the question whether the 'shadow of hierarchy' or, rather, governmental leadership constitutes an important condition for success. Does it matter who is in the driving seat? Does it affect the degree to which different stakeholders take responsibility? It is empirically open whether and how the legitimacy and effectiveness of an initiative is affected by its origins. This is salient, for many initiatives are criticised for the mere fact that they are business-driven, or government-driven, the implication being that the drivers behind the initiative bias the degree of democratic participation and oversight. On the other hand, the issue of drivers also begs the question of leadership.

A second dimension incorporates the motives of the stakeholders. As voluntary initiatives, MSIs are 'coalitions of the willing' – but what motives drive stakeholders to engage in MSIs and remain willing coalition partners? 'Some see these initiatives as best practices for in-country performance. Some see them as establishing new tools of governance – a "third way" between regulation and laissez-faire. Others see them as useful levers for mobilising greater action from host Governments. While others hope to see them lead to new law',[22] as a review report on MSIs in the Oil and Gas sector concludes. In spite of the fact that this aspect seems crucial for their impetus and impact, it is seriously underexplored. An explicit analytical focus on the motives would allow the exploration of questions such as whether the type of motive plays a

---

[21] Underlining this point see Pieth, *Multi-stakeholder Initiatives*.
[22] Morrison and Wilde, *The Effectiveness of Multi-stakeholder Initiatives*, 4.

significant role in shaping the outcome of the MSIs. Does the initial incentive structure underlie dynamics of change and adaptation that affect the internalisation of new values and commitment to the process? Do expectations of stakeholders need to be managed with regard to key objectives and outcomes? Is it possible to identify conditions under which the key stakeholders of each sector will take ownership and stay engaged?

3.3   Status and composition of partners within MSIs

MSIs seem to be characterised by a certain paradox, in that stakeholders are seen to be equal partners in principle, but in practice there are a multitude of different formal and informal roles that the partners take. Hence, although MSIs are defined by the participation of representatives of all three sectors, these do not necessarily have an equal status within the initiative. Frequently, governments are still accorded a prioritised status over civil society, as will be discussed in the case of EITI. Even if the formal status is equal, the asymmetric resources and operating modes of the stakeholders can lead to confrontations and the reversion into former patterns of adverse and unco-operative behaviour: NGOs will use a strategy of carrot and stick by co-operating to a degree, but with the underlying threat or the actual exertion of public pressure on the companies and governments, whom they accuse of cherry-picking and window-dressing;[23] whereas companies and governments will not treat NGOs as serious and responsible partners, demanding that NGOs should make clear 'whether they are willing or able to assist in the implementation of specific multi-stakeholder initiatives. [...] Fundamentally, NGOs should be clear about their commitment to these initiatives – whether they are fully in or fully out'.[24] On the other hand, MSIs excel precisely as a result of this cocktail of diverse interests and profiles, with 'group

---

[23]   A good illustration of these problems from an NGO-perspective is provided by a review of Voluntary Standards by the director of Human Rights Watch: 'As voluntary initiatives, they are wholly dependent on the willingness of companies or governments to adopt their standards. Many companies and governments do not subscribe to these efforts ... Even when parties sign on to these efforts, it can be difficult for the initiatives to maintain rules that ensure compliance ... If voluntary initiatives falter in 2007, relationships between government, industry and NGOs could fray. NGOs might abandon some multi-stakeholder initiatives and exclusively pursue regulatory and other measures' (Ganesan, 'Is 2007 the End for Voluntary Standards?').

[24]   Morrison and Wilde, *The Effectiveness of Multi-stakeholder Initiatives*, 6. The report was sponsored by BP plc.

diversity [being] one of its greatest strengths, both in process and prod-uct',[25] as experiences from the Global Reporting Initiative (and others) show. In other words, it is an open question as to whether and at which critical junctures the formal status matters, or how far dialogue and communication alone shape the outcomes.

3.4   Area of intervention

One could compile a laundry list of areas in which MSI have evolved, from global fair trade (such as the Ethical Trading Initiative (ETI)[26]) to local peace building (such as the National Peace Committees in South Africa[27]). Still, certain areas seem to be more amenable to successful initiatives than others. These are in particular areas characterised by a high degree of contestation, such as the implementation of human rights in weak governance zones, and areas with high regulatory complexity, such as global environmental regimes. In an exemplary fashion, Table 4.2 combines areas of intervention with the function of MSIs. This distinc-tion and combination should allow a comparative analysis of MSIs, and a better understanding of specific governance problems – coupled with governance functions – that may be particularly suitable to address through MSIs.

In the following section, the typology will be applied to one of the most well-known MSIs, namely the Extractive Industry Transparency Initiative (EITI). It is highly topical, as it addresses one of the most serious governance problems fuelling corruption, social inequalities, and in many cases, con-flicts. Moreover it affects resource-rich (but often income-poor) countries, international companies, their home governments, as well as national and global civil society organisations alike; and lastly its solution requires a high degree of co-operation across sectors to identify the most perti-nent problems, and develop and implement appropriate regulatory measures.

---

[25] Richards and Dickson, 'Guidelines by Stakeholders'.

[26] Strictly speaking, the ETI is not an MSI according to our tri-sectoral condition; its members consist of NGOs, companies, and Trade Unions. However, the Department for International Development (DFID) was instrumental in setting up ETI; also, inter-national organisations such as the International Labour Organization play a key role in the ETI, both indicating a substantial involvement by national and international govern-ment organisations.

[27] For a detailed discussion see Gastrow, *Bargaining for Peace*.

Table 4.2 *Types of MSIs*

Purpose/Area of Intervention	Dialogue/Forum	Institution-building	Rule-setting	Rule-implementation	Rule-monitoring
Natural resource management	EITI, World Commission on Dams (WCD)	EITI, Global Reporting Initiative (GRI)	World Commission on Dams (WCD), EITI, GRI	EITI, GRI	EITI, GRI
Conflict financing	EITI		EITI, Kimberley Process	EITI	Kimberley Process
Human rights	Voluntary Principles on Security and Human Rights		Voluntary Principles on Security and Human Rights		

4.   The Extractive Industries Transparency Initiative (EITI)

4.1   The background and cornerstones of the initiative

The EITI, launched in 2002 at the World Summit on Sustainable Development in Johannesburg, breaks new ground, one in which government, civil society, corporations and investors are all directly involved in the development and governance of the initiative with the technical and financial support of international financial institutions (IFIs). The grand purpose of the EITI is that by requiring transparency over both payments by extractive companies and revenues received by governments the EITI makes it more likely that resources will be well managed. As DFID Secretary of State, Hilary Benn, put it: 'a vision of increasing transparency, based on a very simple principle: publish what you pay and publish what you receive'.[28]

The EITI represents a suitably searching case study for this inquiry. The rationale for multi-stakeholder approaches to problem solving is as simple as the problems that are sought to be addressed are complex: namely, problems such as the corruption and secrecy surrounding the extractive industries – the so-called 'resource curse'[29] – may appear to be so intractable that without the participation of all the most powerful actors, committed to a common objective and an agreed process, little or no progress will be possible. The Extractive Industries certainly represent a very tough problem to solve. Three and a half billion people live in countries rich in oil, gas or minerals. These natural resources provide great opportunities to improve the lives of poor people. But bad management and lack of transparency of these resources can lead to poverty, conflict and corruption. There are powerful, ruthless vested interests at stake; there is a history of exploitation, conflict and corruption; the actors tend to be multinational/cross-territorial; where they often operate within very weak/failed states and, therefore, within a very weak regulatory/enforcement environment.

Clearly, it represents an acute, multi-dimensional problem. Despite this, ordinarily, one might legislate to confront the problem. But in this context, the law – both domestic and international – represents a very blunt instrument. There are a number of reasons for this. First, the corporate actors involved in the global extractive industries 'possess an

---

[28] International Advisory Board Group of the EITI (2006). *Final Report*. September 2006, 8.
[29] For seminal contributions on this topic see Collier *et al.*, *Breaking the Conflict Trap* or Watts, 'Resource Curse?'.

enormous amount of raw economic and social power';[30] invariably, companies such as ExxonMobil, Shell and Total are economically and technologically much more powerful than the host governments where they operate. As Williams notes, in 1999, ExxonMobil's revenues were $185 bn, compared to gross domestic products of $1.6 bn and $43.3 bn, respectively, in Chad and Nigeria, two countries in which the company operated. Second, legal regimes in such host countries may well be too feeble to enforce statutory responsibilities. Third, as many scholars have noted, global governance is in a transient state, seeking to keep up with the rapid pace of the new wave of economic globalisation of the past ten to twenty years.[31]

Hence, attention has turned towards finding innovative, voluntary approaches to new standard setting and, therefore, the imperative for getting the appropriate stakeholders committed to a process of dialogue and joint problem-solving has grown. This chapter seeks to add to the body of studies that argue that it is in the realm of voluntary standard and norm setting, in contrast to mandatory regimes, that the most significant and positive advances have been made in recent years. Where successful, domestic law making can take advantage of the consensus that has been negotiated through the complex array of global initiatives. Like Cynthia Williams,[32] we would concur with Anne-Marie Slaughter when she advances the idea of 'regulation by information', whereby the 'basic paradigm for global regulatory processes is the promulgation of performance standards, codes of practice, and other aspirational models based on compiled comparative information'.[33]

Along with initiatives such as the Global Reporting Initiative, the EITI is a prime example of such a regime. In the seven years since its launch, 23 out of 53 such governments of resource-rich countries in Africa, Asia, Latin America and Central Asia have endorsed the EITI. Each of the 23 countries cited by the EITI secretariat as 'candidate' countries face governance challenges, many of them severe; none of the 23 countries appears in the top third (60 countries) in the 2008 Corruption Perception Index (CPI) of Transparency International,[34] while 15 of them are to be found in the bottom third (see Table 4.3 below).

---

[30] Williams, 'Civil Society Initiatives', 458.
[31] See, for example, Slaughter, 'Global Government Networks', 1041.
[32] Williams, 'Civil Society Initiatives', 463.
[33] Slaughter, 'Global Government Networks', 1046–47.
[34] www.transparency.org/news_room/latest_news/press_releases/2008/2008_09_23_cpi_2008_en.

Table 4.3 *EITI Candidate Countries and CPI Rating*

EITI Candidate Country	Transparency International 2008 Corruption Perception Index Listing (out of 180 countries)
Azerbaijan	158
Cameroon	141
Cote d'Ivoire	151
DRC	171
Equatorial Guinea	171
Gabon	96
Ghana	67
Guinea	173
Kazakhstan	145
Kyrgyzstan	166
Liberia	138
Madagascar	85
Mali	96
Mauritania	115
Mongolia	102
Niger	115
Nigeria	121
Peru	72
Republic of Congo	158
São Tomé e Príncipe	121
Sierra Leone	158
Timor-Leste	145
Yemen	141

The basic system of the EITI is to invite host countries to apply to be 'compliant'. In order to meet this standard, a validation process must be completed, whereby individual 'candidate' countries undertake a validation process. If all the validation indicators are met satisfactorily within two years, then the country is said to be 'compliant'. As we write, only one of the 23 countries – Azerbaijan – has reached the 'compliant' stage; but the EITI secretariat has announced that all 23 countries have validation deadlines in 2010 and have embarked upon their journey towards compliance.[35]

---

[35] www.eitransparency.org/files/news/EITI%20Newsletter%20-%20August%202008.pdf.

The March 2005, second EITI conference in London established six criteria, which it still refers to as the 'EITI criteria', namely: (a) regular publication of all payments by companies to governments ('payments') and by governments to companies ('revenues'); (b) credible, independent auditry of these payments and revenue; (c) audit reconciliation; (d) all companies, including state-owned companies, to be encompassed; (e) civil society actively engaged as a participant in the design, monitoring and evaluation of this process; (f) a public, financially sustainable workplan for all the above to be developed by the host government. These six principles should be seen as the overarching framework for the EITI. They should be seen as the 'minimum entry requirements for joining the game'.[36]

As the EITI has moved forwards so the compliance criteria have been extended and refined. Now, the emphasis is on a more ornate set of validation criteria, contained within the 'Validation Guide',[37] which the candidate countries must follow and implement as they aim to be 'compliant'. According to the EITI secretariat, validation is EITI's 'quality assurance mechanism and an essential feature of the EITI process. It serves two critical functions. First, it promotes dialogue and learning at the country level. Second, it safeguards the EITI brand by holding all EITI implementing countries to the same global standard'.[38] The validation is not an audit, however; the EITI secretariat emphasises that 'it does not repeat the disclosure and reconciliation work that is carried out to produce EITI reports. Validation has broader objectives: it evaluates EITI implementation in consultation with stakeholders, it verifies achievements with reference to the EITI global standard, and it identifies opportunities to strengthen the EITI process going forward'.[39] The validation process is one that is undertaken with the multi-stakeholder group, which appoints the validator, who then works with the group to assess the quality and accuracy of the information disclosed by the government and company participants, and thereby to evaluate the extent to which the country workplan – a document that is produced by the multi-stakeholder

---

[36] Note: in the most recent iteration of the validation process, these 'sign-up principles' have been simplified to four questions that must be answered in the affirmative by the candidate countries, see: http://issuu.com/eiti/docs/validationguide (last accessed 19 April 2009).

[37] http://issuu.com/eiti/docs/validationguide (last accessed 19 April 2009).

[38] EITI website: www.eitransparency.org/eiti/implementation/validation (last accessed 28 September 2008).

[39] EITI website: www.eitransparency.org/eiti/implementation/validation (last accessed 28 September 2008).

group – has been followed. The workplan bridges the 'sign-up' phase and the 'preparation' phase that immediately preceeds the implementation phase (disclosure and dissemination). It should also provide for both the role and the composition, especially the civil society representation, of the multi-stakeholder group. The preparation phase is largely concerned with process, especially the multi-stakeholder group, its representivity, and the country workplan. Thereafter, the countries move into the disclosure phase, which is focused on the disclosure of revenue payments made by oil and gas companies on the one hand, and received by host governments on the other. As noted, none of the candidate EITI countries have yet got through this stage, but are currently at various stages of implementation. The disclosure phase is thus eagerly awaited, as is the final phase – dissemination of the information disclosed.

4.2   Lessons and critique of the EITI

The EITI has, therefore, established itself as a plausible, and to a large extent, credible, voluntary governance model, though it is still too early to say whether it has yet had a positive impact.[40] A key element of the original governance model established by the UK Department of International Development (DFID) as a founding father of the EITI, and now replicated in its sequel MSIs (the Medicines Transparency Alliance [MeTA], and the Construction Sector Transparency Initiative [COST], both of which were launched by DFID in 2008), was an oversight and advisory structure called the International Advisory Group (IAG). Chaired by Peter Eigen, the founder of Transparency International, the EITI IAG was formed in July 2005 and initially comprised members from six governments, four major corporations, one investor group, and four NGOs.[41] The IAG was subsequently re-constituted as the EITI Board in 2006 and now comprises around 20 members drawn from three main stakeholder groups: governments (implementing and supporting); oil and

---

[40] Susan Aaronson from Georgetown University has made an initial attempt to answer the question 'Can Transparency in Extractive Industries break the resource curse?' Aaronson asserts that in some of the candidate countries corruption is reduced; she concludes tentatively that 'the data does not show that the EITI is causing these changes; but EITI is associated with these changes. The EITI seems to facilitate creation of a feedback loop between business, citizens and their government, which could gradually spill over into the polity as a whole'. A version of the paper appears on the EITI website: http://eitransparency.org/node/444.

[41] International Advisory Board Group of the EITI 2006, above note 29, 11.

gas corporations and associations, including institutional investors; and civil society. Given the relative international prominence of the EITI, its governance model and its progress should attract both attention and scrutiny, so that the lessons for other MSIs can be absorbed. The report of the IAG, and the changes that have arisen from the report, suggest that an advisory board can exert significant influence, both in terms of the legitimacy and credibility it may provide and the clout that the expertise of its membership may carry with international organisations, potential donors, and the key corporate and government partners themselves.

While the (new) EITI Board has clearly been given a different mandate from the IAG, in that it is responsible for leading the initiative and making decisions about the strategic direction and advocacy of the EITI, the EITI IAG charged itself with responsibility for leading a process of developing guidelines, criteria, and governance structures essential to the initiative, and answering three questions that are pertinent for the inquiry of this chapter, namely: How can we judge that countries are doing what they say they are in implementing EITI? How can EITI better understand and communicate the incentives for different stakeholders in EITI? What management and governance arrangements will best ensure the achievement of EITI's object-ives (that is, international best practice)? It attempted to do so in four areas: validation of EITI, incentives for implementing EITI, future challenges for EITI, and future arrangements for EITI. Their approach to validation appears sound, with a focus on validation of implementation of EITI, nothing more: it identifies and sets out in detail a validation process, the first step within which is the appointment of a validator by a multi-stakeholder group. The report emphasises the importance of this group and what it can and should comprise in terms of diversity of membership.

Section 2 deals with incentives and is far less convincing; the specific recommendation is that 'EITI should develop clearer evidence of the benefits of implementing EITI as part of broader governance reform; and other benefits, such as improved energy security and a better business climate'. The report concedes that 'Transparency initiatives such as EITI are relatively young and few academic studies have been carried out on which to analyse the actual impact of transparency'. This is a challenge for all ATI/transparency advocates and policy makers, and has recently been recognised at the Carter Center international conference,[42] whose

---

[42] The Declaration and Plan of Action of the Carter Center conference is available at www.cartercenter.org/documents/Atlanta%20Declaration%20and%20Plan%20of%20Action.pdf.

declaration called for a much more systematic approach to the measurement and evaluation of the impact of greater transparency.

Two of the main early critiques of the EITI stand out: the first, from the International Advisory Group;[43] the second, from civil society, namely the Publish What You Pay Campaign and Revenue Watch.[44] Published around the same time in autumn 2006, the two reports illustrate the potential benefits of a multi-stakeholder commitment to a complex process such as the EITI. International civil society has played a leading role in coordinating the participation of civil society in the EITI, drawing in 300 members from over 30 countries. This is significant for shifting the perpetually adversarial relationship between INGOs and multinational corporations (MNCs). Even so, the *Eye on EITI* notes that: 'In about half of the 21 endorsing countries, governments have been slow to match rhetorical commitments with any concrete actions to implement EITI. The failure to close the gap between rhetoric and reality fuels the perception that governments are paying lip-service to the principle of transparency embodied in the EITI in order to achieve other economic and political objectives'.[45] It is, however, a calm, considered review of progress, backed by a number of professional contributions. The most important of these consist of a series of reports named *Beyond the Rhetoric*,[46] which offer an innovative framework and index to assess actual compliance. One finding was, for example, that only two companies out of thirty scored more than 50 per cent.[47]

The most striking thing is the level of intersection between the two sets of recommendations (see Table 4.4 below). Not only is there a moderation of language, but also a relatively high level of consensus-finding – which is rare in MNC–Government–INGO relations. There is overlap/

---

[43] See International Advisory Board Group of the EITI 2006, above note 29.

[44] See Publish What You Pay/Revenue Watch (PWYP/Revenue Watch) 2006, *Eye on EITI – Civil Society Perspectives and Recommendations on the Extractive Industries Transparency Initiative*, London and New York.

[45] See Publish What You Pay/Revenue Watch (PWYP/Revenue Watch) 2006, above note 45, 7.

[46] See the reports by Revenue Watch: *Beyond the Rhetoric: Measuring Transparency in the Extractive Industries*, which are products of The Measuring Transparency project. This project has developed a standard to assess the performance of companies and governments in support of revenue transparency. It also provides a framework to track their progress over time. For the reports on goverments and companies see their website under http://archive.revenuewatch.org/reports/pwyp032805c.shtml (last accessed 28 September 2008).

[47] Save the Children 2005. *Beyond the Rhetoric: Measuring Revenue Transparency in the Oil and Gas Sectors*, London, available at www.savethechildren.org.uk/en/54_5101.htm.

Table 4.4 *Table Comparing Recommendations of the International Advisory Group of EITI (September 2006) with those of the Publish-What-You-Pay/Revenue Watch Institute, Eye on EITI Report (October 2006)*

Civil Society (Eye on EITI)	IAG (Final Report)
Validation	
Protect credibility of EITI by ensuring that rhetorical commitments are matched by concrete actions (1)*	The governments of implementing countries should ensure that implementation is in accordance with the EITI principles and criteria (1)
In each country, appoint a leader with the time, bureaucratic skill, and political influence to drive EITI implementation (2)	
	After committing to implement EITI, countries should be required to validate their progress on a regular basis (2)
Disaggregate data by company and by payment/revenue type in reconciled reports of company payments and government receipts (9)	Oil, gas and mining companies operating in countries implementing EITI should be validated as part of country validation. Companies that commit at the international level should complete a self-assessment form (3)
Participation/Future Arrangements	
Recognise that genuine civil society participation is a requirement of EITI and support its active engagement in each critical step of the EITI process (3)	EITI should establish a multi-stakeholder board, supported by a secretariat, to manage EITI at the international level (10)
Ensure that no civil society campaigner is harassed or intimidated for their work to promote transparency (4)	
	Support for implementing EITI should be country-driven and sustainable, while focusing on results and working in partnership (9)

Table 4.4 (*cont.*)

Ensure that civil society representatives are genuinely from that sector and not from those representing the interests of others such as political parties or companies (5)	
Increase financial and technical support to build civil society's capacity to participate in EITI (6)	
Incentives	
	EITI should develop clearer evidence of the benefits of implementing EITI as part of broader governance reform; and other benefits, such as improved energy security and a better business climate (4)
Future Challenges	
	EITI should pay more attention to the specific context of the mining sector (5)
Support the mainstreaming of EITI aims and approaches into other mechanisms that will increase and sustain government and company financial transparency (11)	EITI and EITI-implementing countries should identify appropriate opportunities to work with other transparency, anti-corruption, development and energy security programmes (6)
Create sub-national reporting schemes over the coming year (13)	EITI should undertake further work on the possibility of sub-national implementation (7)
Allocate sufficient funds to cover EITI costs in annual budgets and ensure that these are disbursed in time to support planned activities (7)	
	EITI should work with emerging economy governments to encourage their greater engagement with EITI (8)
Provide adequate technical and, in certain cases, financial support to governments implementing EITI (8)	

Table 4.4 (*cont.*)

Institutionalise EITI in statutory law to
   help ensure continuity and long-term
   sustainability (10)
Encourage and support EITI
   implementing governments in
   establishing mechanisms that
   promote transparent and accountable
   expenditure management (14)
Support contract transparency as an
   essential step toward achieving
   revenue transparency and
   accountability (12)

---

*The numbers in brackets correspond with the recommendation number in each
of the two respective reports.

consensus on four important issues: real implementation ˙by governments, validation by companies (including disaggregation), the need
to deepen the multi-stakeholder approach and to deepen the sub-
national system of EITI. The main differences are on incentives – only
the general recommendation from IAG (as mentioned above) with
nothing specific from civil society, except that clearly it has this in
mind with recommendation 14: 'Encourage and support EITI implementing governments in establishing mechanisms that promote transparent and accountable expenditure management'. This is a potentially
profound point that needs to be asked of all revenue transparency
initiatives: Having opened up the payments, where does the money go
and what is it used for?

The IAG report rather tentatively put forward a theoretical framework
for asserting direct and indirect benefits for implementing governments,
in particular in the areas of economic growth, governance, development
and 'reputation management'. They quote Alain Grisay, Chief Executive,
F & C Asset Management plc: 'Corruption and poor governance make
it risky and expensive to do business in the world's emerging resource-
rich nations. By embracing EITI, these governments will send a clear
signal to the capital markets that they are serious about creating a
stable prosperous society based on accountability and the rule of law.
EITI means lower risk for investors, cheaper capital for developing

nations, more transparent corporate practices and a better life for local citizens'.[48]

This is neatly put, but how do you measure these things? And, what are the best yardsticks for measuring change and progress? There are two ways of looking at this. The first is to focus solely on the EITI as a process-orientated, standard-setting voluntary governance model. The alternative is to go beyond the 'regulation by information' idea, and to test the ends against the means. This is not to ask whether greater transparency delivers greater socio-economic justice – the 'end' that many civil society activists attach to the initiative – but rather to ask whether, in fact, the EITI process delivers on its simple goal: transparency in revenue payments (open disclosure of what you pay and what you receive, for each of the two main actors – the corporation and the government). This dilemma has important ramifications for not just how the EITI itself should be evaluated, but how future MSIs should measure their progress in achieving their objectives. The new Medicines Transparency Alliance (MeTA), for example, goes further than the EITI in that its primary aim is stated to be increased access to affordable medicines for the poor. The implication is that the objective is not limited to greater transparency in the medicines supply chain – though that may be the target of its work – but the socio-economic outcome of greater access to affordable medicines. It is noteworthy, therefore, that the EITI IAG recommendations on validation were directed at validation of the implementation of the EITI – essentially process-orientated steps towards revenue payment transparency – the 'means', one might say, rather than the 'ends'. This may not represent a prudent if less ambitious approach, but also one that is loyal to the underlying, core fundamental of an MSI – that it is, and should be evaluated as, a process-orientated governance model.

4.3   Applying the MSI-typology to the standard-setting model of the EITI

If process is the main preoccupation, then the question of both legitimacy in a general sense, and the specific legitimacy that derives from the participation of all the main stakeholders from the three sectors, is a crucial one. The main concerns of the civil society paper relate to concerns around civil society participation, both 'cheating' with bogus representation by corporations and especially host governments, and

---

[48] International Advisory Board Group of the EITI 2006, above note 29, 23.

being marginalised, thus showing the need for a consistent approach to process rules. The second concern is the self-selection of CSO participants plus evidence of harassment in some cases.[49] As the process moves into its final, crucial validation phase, however, the main preoccuptions of all of the main stakeholders are likely to be the participation and security of civil society in the implementing countries.

There was also the argument that the EITI should be institutionalised by statute.[50] This is a broader issue and suggests that civil society stakeholders are unable to disguise their scepticism about the voluntary approach and are wanting to back up the principles with a legal platform. And, lastly, there were concerns about the funding of the EITI, where clear differences emerge: at this earlier point, the IAG appeared to prefer the idea of a shared funding model, while civil society indicated a preference for state funding because of its innate concerns about co-option.[51]

These concerns, amongst others, reflect some core problems in the implementation of the EITI – though it should be noted that an MSI such as the EITI is a very dynamic process, where the predominant issues change often; earlier proccupations can rapidly be overtaken by new, more pressing concerns. However, if the main points of dissent or disagreement were not to be addressed over the middle-to-longer term it is likely that the EITI would lose considerable credibility, with the real danger of NGOs withdrawing their support, and, conceivably, corporations then disengaging from the process. One of the main problems seems to be the passivity of Southern (host) governments, whose rhetorical compliance is not matched with an equal degree of regulatory compliance. All stakeholders, and especially the EITI board, are tasked with finding ways and means to increase governmental engagement – the real proof of the pudding will be in the validation process. However, in spite of these weaknesses it must be underlined that the EITI is still a considerable success in terms of the standards necessary to regulate a governance blind-spot.

Applying the typology developed in this chapter, the progress made by the EITI can be assessed more clearly. Zooming in on the first dimension elaborated above (see 3.1.), it has fulfilled several key functions: it has established a dialogue and forum which included all relevant stakeholders, internationally and from all sectors. It has established institutions on an

---

[49] See PYWP/Revenue Watch 2006, above note 45, Recommendations 11, 13, 14.
[50] See PYWP/Revenue Watch 2006, above note 45, 22.
[51] See PYWP/Revenue Watch 2006, above note 45, 18.

international level, mainly the EITI board, and a Secretariat with a dedicated and capable leadership, to guide the development and implementation of the initiative. Furthermore, although they may not have lived up to the high expectations of all the Board members and other EITI-watchers, the institutional arrangements have allowed the EITI to take some substantial steps to strengthen and substantiate its goals. In particular, this applies to the validation process, where clear and operational criteria have been formulated and are ripe to be applied. Lastly, it has set relevant standards in a consensual and co-operative fashion, and is in the process of 'hardening' these standards and negotiating monitoring mechanisms.

One key point that comes out of the examination of the EITI is, however, that there may be diverging views on what precisely the main purpose of an initiative constitutes. As was observed above, the core objective of the EITI is transparency in revenue payments, not the far broader objective of socio-economic justice, although it is hoped that the EITI will contribute to this overarching meta-goal. The diverse stakeholders attach differing importance to this goal, which also impacts on what functions they see as crucial for the effectiveness and legitimacy of the EITI. This remains an area of contestation.

The second dimension (see 3.2. above) incorporates the drivers of EITI, and a closer look shows the success of an initially government-driven initiative spreading its wings and gaining the support of, and engagement with, all key stakeholders. It should not be neglected, however, that the precondition for this take-off was the purposeful intervention by the UK government and the funds invested by them and other public actors. At the stage it is now, the EITI has lost some of its initial dynamics, bogged down by the difficult negotiation and enforcement of concrete, detailed actions. The stakeholders all still seem to be on board, however, if with varying degrees of engagement. Nonetheless, even southern governments seem to be driven by the necessity of shoring up their regulatory capacity and, not least, their international credibility. Currently, the driving force of the initiative seems to have passed to the EITI board, with strong push and pull factors coming from national and international civil society organisations.

The third dimension, status and composition (see 3.3. above), is perhaps most salient with regard to the effectiveness of EITI standard setting. With the initial phase of trust and confidence building over, the key issue now is implementation of standards and their validation. The IAG report recommended under the heading 'Future Arrangements' that EITI should establish a multi-stakeholder board, supported by a Secretariat, to manage EITI at the international level, which presents an interesting challenge for some stakeholders. As noted, the Board has now been established and has already met on five occasions. As the Board institutionalises, and becomes the fulcrum of the EITI, the vital importance of independent scrutiny should be not lost; there is always the danger of 'group-think'. Moreover, the specific modes of representation and participation of civil society are still heavily contested, and in some cases pose a risk of government manipulation. Evidently, both the quality and the legitimacy of the standards and their implementation are seriously affected by the elimination or obstruction of civil society participation. A further area of concern regards the integration and 'mainstreaming' of the propagated transparency mechanisms on a sub-national, national and international level. Although this is not made explicit in the discussed reports, the EITI will have to think about ways of expanding the participation in the initiative to be responsive to these needs without losing its sense of purpose and operational power.

On the fourth and last dimension, the area of intervention (see 3.4. above), the discussion of the EITI underlines that resource management, and especially resource revenue management on an international level, does indeed pose a highly interdependent, fraught and core governance problem. The issues attached to it by the various stakeholders – from global transparency standards over public accountability to economic prosperity – emphasise how strongly it is intermeshed with key economic, political and social problems, both nationally and globally. Tentatively, the conclusion is that the EITI has at least managed to map the messy and tangled area of the governance of natural resource revenues, and identify priority issues and methods of intervention, even if it has not yet achieved a coherent and strong regulatory regime.

5. Conclusions

Multi-stakeholder initiatives such as the EITI are probably not only a 'good thing' but are an essential governance innovation – necessary, but not necessarily sufficient for addressing an acute multi-dimensional problem such as the 'resource curse'. The EITI represents a pivotal case study from which many lessons can be learnt. Yet, multi-stakeholder approaches should be seen as complementary to, and not in substitution of, civil society advocacy and activism on the one hand and legislation on the other hand. The EITI shows the central importance of good process and full agreement about the rules of the game; but it also indicates how difficult this process of negotiation of 'good rules' remains, rubbing up against the different, and often competing interests of stakeholders. There are lessons about the bureaucracy of a multi-stakeholder process and the dangers of co-option. And yet the EITI case study – a 'hard case' (as a lawyer might put it) – shows that with adequate levels of political will and the backing of sufficiently powerful drivers, it is possible to establish a plausible multi-stakeholder governance institution, even in the face of the most demanding of policy challenges, as the control of natural resources and revenue opacity. The EITI is established, with clear rules of the game, clear objectives, and a plan of action in terms of implementation; the stakeholders are still on board, if not all with the same unwavering degree of commitment. The validation element is crucial and undoubtedly where the EITI's future impact will further strengthen or weaken; there is a full appreciation of this from a range of key stakeholders close to the process, as well as ongoing concern about this crucial aspect of the process from various civil society actors. The question of how you go about ensuring real implementation as opposed to fig-leaf implementation will become pivotal to assessing both its effectiveness and its legitimacy. In terms of the typology posited above, there is enough evidence to suggest that the EITI has succeeded in establishing itself as a viable and legitimate locus for dialogue and for standard setting. The extent to which the EITI can in the longer term address and overcome the validation question will determine whether it can also be regarded as an effective standard-implementation and standard-monitoring body.

Hence, it is possible to conclude that there is already sufficient evidence that a MSI approach to a governance deficit can succeed in establishing consensus amongst the most important actors on new standards. The primary finding is the moderation of language and the potential for building of consensus around action and strategy, and law and policy, from a range of usually bitterly opposed actors. With effective leadership and a diligent approach to process and the legitimacy and representation of the participants, a MSI represents a plausible model for achieving new standards. Without further research it is impossible to go further and draw any encompassing conclusions from the emergence and engagement of MSIs in environments of weak governance. However, the typology outlined here should provide a useful tool to structure further research on the composition, the process, the impact, and the conditions of success of MSIs. It is a first attempt at understanding the analytical and policy-related issues of MSIs in greater depth, and forms the basis of an evidence-based comparative analysis of MSIs in environments of weak governance. The underlying concern of these inquiries is whether the development of new standards, especially voluntary ones, are mere window-dressing, or whether and how a genuine transformation of social and legal norms is taking place. This is especially salient with regard to rendering both global economic activities as well as public institutions in weak states more transparent and accountable.

Lastly, the need to develop the capacity for producing credible evidence, based on a rigorous research methodology, remains – and on this there is an ongoing role for the academy. There are currently hardly any tools measuring the impact of greater transparency and consequently little solid evidence on the impact of transparency standards and standard-setting processes. The development of these tools requires greater attention and systematic empirical research.

References

Benner, Th. *et al.* 2004, 'Multi-sectoral Networks in Global Governance: Towards a Pluralistic System of Governance', *Government and Opposition*, 191–210.

Börzel, T. and Risse, T. 2005, 'Public–Private Partnerships: Effective and Legitimate Tools of International Governance?' in L. Grande and E. Pauly, *Complex Sovereignty: Reconstituting Political Authority in the 21st Century*, University of Toronto, 195–216.

Collier, P. *et al.* 2003, *Breaking the Conflict Trap: Civil War and Development Policy*, Oxford University Press.

Elsig, M. and Amalric, F. 2008, 'Business and Public–Private Regulation Arrangements: Beyond Corporate Social Responsibility?' *Global Society*, vol. **22**, 387–404.

Ganesan, A. 2006, 'Is 2007 the End for Voluntary Standards?', *Business for Social Responsibility Weekly* on 13 December 2006 (members only); available under http://hrw.org/english/docs/2006/12/12/global14872.htm (last accessed 23 September 2008).

Gastrow, P. 1995, *Bargaining for Peace: South Africa and the National Peace Accord*, Washington, United States Institute of Peace Press.

Haufler, V. (ed.) 2002, *UN Global Compact – Case Studies of Multistakeholder Partnership. Policy Dialogue on Business in Zones of Conflict*, New York, UN Global Compact.

Keohane, R. 2002, *Power and Governance in a Partially Globalised World*, London, Routledge.

Linder, S. and Vaillancourt Rosenau, P. 2000, 'Mapping the Terrain of the Public–Private Policy Partnership' in P. Vaillancourt Rosenau (ed.), *Public Private Policy Partnerships*, Boston, MIT Press, 1–18.

Martens, J. 2007, 'Multistakeholder Partnerships – Future Models of Multilateralism? Dialogue on Globalization', Occasional Papers 29, Bonn, Friedrich Ebert Stiftung.

Mazurkiewicz, P. 2005, 'Corporate Self-regulation and Multi-stakeholder Dialogue' in E. Croci (ed.), *The Handbook of Environmental Voluntary Agreements – Design, Implementation and Evaluation Issues, Environment and Policy* vol. 43, Dordrecht, Springer, 31–47.

Migdal, J. S. and Schlichte, K. 2005, 'Rethinking the State' in K. Schlichte (ed.), *The Dynamics of States – the Formation and Crises of State Domination*, Aldershot, Ashgate, 1–40.

Morrison, J. and Wilde, L. 2007, *The Effectiveness of Multi-stakeholder Initiatives in the Oil and Gas Sector – Summary Report*, twentyfifty, at 2, available at   www.corporateaccountability.org/eng/documents/2007/effect_of_multi_stakeholder_inis_in_oil_and_gas.pdf.

Pieth, M. 2007, 'Multi-stakeholder Initiatives to Combat Money Laundering and Bribery' in C. Brütsch and D. Lehmkuhl (eds.), *Law and Legalisation in Transnational Relations*, London, Routledge. 81–100.

Richards, T. and Dickson, D. 2007, 'Guidelines by Stakeholders, for Stakeholders – Is it Worth the Effort?', *Journal of Corporate Citizenship*, vol. **25**, 19–21.

Slaughter, A.-M. 2003, 'Global Government Networks, Global Information Agencies, and Disaggregated Democracy', *Michigan Journal of International Law*, vol. **24**, 1041–74.

Turcotte, M.-F. and Pasquero, J. 2001, 'The Paradox of Multistakeholder Collaborative Roundtables', *The Journal of Applied Behavioral Science*, vol. **37**, no. 4, 447–64.

Warner, J. 2005, 'Multi-stakeholder Platforms: Integrating Society in Water Resource Management?' *Ambiente & Sociadade*, vol. **VIII**(2), 1–19.

Watts M. 2005, 'Resource Curse? Governmentability, Oil and Power in the Niger Delta, Nigeria' in P. Le Billon (ed.), *The Geopolitics of Resource Wars: Resource Dependence, Governance and Violence*, London, Routledge, 50–80.

Williams, C. 2004, 'Civil Society Initiatives and "Soft Law" in the Oil and Gas Industry', *International Law and Politics*, vol. **56**, 457–502.

Zammit, A. 2003, *Development at Risk – Rethinking UN-Business Partnerships*, Joint Publication by South Centre and UNRISD, Geneva, UNRISD.

5

New standards for and by private military companies?

LINDSEY CAMERON[*]

1. Introduction

Private military companies (PMCs) are becoming a well-known phenomenon. The fact that the employees of private military companies, taken together, make up the second largest contingent in Iraq – now estimated to number at least 48,000, second only to the US armed forces[1] – has sparked enormous debate among policy makers, military leaders, non-government organisations and academics on the role of these actors in situations of armed conflict. Observers and critics have especially expressed concerns regarding the responsibility of private actors for human rights violations and the wisdom of being able to rely only on a commercial contract to compel a person to remain in a war zone and carry out life-threatening tasks. For some, the privatisation of large-scale violence may signal the beginning of a massive change in the concept of the essential, necessary components of statehood.[2] As for the

---

[*] Doctoral Candidate and Research Assistant, Faculty of Law, University of Geneva; LLM (International Humanitarian Law, University of Geneva); LLB (McGill); MA (History, University of Toronto). The author wishes to extend warm thanks to Marco Sassòli and Théo Boutruche at the University of Geneva for many fruitful discussions and helpful suggestions during the preparation of this chapter.

[1] US GAO study, *Rebuilding Iraq: Actions Still Needed to Improve the Use of Private Security Providers*, testimony of William Solis, Director, Defense Capabilities and Management before the Subcommittee on National Security, Emerging Threats and International Relations, Committee on Government Reform, US Government Accountability Office, 13 June 2006. Available at www.gao.gov/new.items/d06865t.pdf. A recent report from a UK non-government organisation alleges that the UK government wants to '"privatise the war" as part of its exit strategy': see Sengupta, 'UK: Blair'.

[2] For a thorough discussion of this issue, see Leander, *Eroding State Authority?*, esp. 138; Peter Singer, one of the first political scientists to study PMCs in depth, does not see these forces as changing the state but as a significant actor in a 'transformed' 'international environment'. See Singer, *Corporate Warriors*, 242.

companies, instead of hiding as shadowy mercenaries, they now hold international conferences attended by former dignitaries.[3] For lawyers, governments and political scientists, the accountability and regulation of private military companies are the key issues that urgently need to be addressed, implying a tacit acceptance that these companies are here to stay and do not need to be outlawed.[4]

Private military companies exploded onto the international scene in 2004 largely due to two incidents in Iraq, aside from their sheer numbers: first, the brutal execution of four employees of the PMC 'Blackwater' in Fallujah, which led to the US response in that city using overwhelming force and, second, the torture of detainees at Abu Ghraib prison carried out with the involvement of PMC employees.[5] These two incidents exemplify in horrific terms both the vulnerability and potential power of PMC employees. Both have led to legal proceedings in US courts[6] and the latter incident in particular to a flurry of academic writing on the

---

[3] The US trade association of PMCs held a conference in Jordan 2006 and the UK equivalent held a conference in October 2006 attended by Sir Malcolm Rifkind.

[4] United Kingdom, Green Paper 2002, *Private Military Companies: Options for Regulation*, The Stationery Office, London; Swiss Federal Council, Rapport du Conseil fédéral sur les entreprises de sécurité et les entreprises militaires privées, 2006 and contra UN Special Rapporteur on Mercenaries, Enrique Ballasteros, Question of the use of mercenaries as a means of violating human rights and impeding the exercise of the right of peoples to self-determination, UN Doc. E/CN.4/2004/15 esp. at para. 57 (2003).

[5] These two examples have been officially recognised by the former Special Rapporteur on the Right of Peoples to Self-Determination and its application to peoples under colonial or alien domination or foreign occupation: Use of mercenaries as a means of violating human rights and impeding the exercise of the right of peoples to self-determination, Mrs Shaista Shameem, in her annual report. See UN Doc. E/CN.4/2005/14 at para. 50 (2004). Both the Fay Report and Taguba Report recommended referral to the US Department of Justice for potential criminal prosecution for these events. See Major General George R. Fay, AR 15–6 Investigation of the Abu Ghraib Detention Facility and 205th Military Intelligence Brigade 130–34, 23 August 2004, online: www4.army.mil/ocpa/reports/ar15-6/index.html (last visited 26 March 2008). The report enumerates incidents in which private contractors were allegedly involved, including (but not limited to) rape (Incident 22), use of 'unauthorised stress positions' (Incident 24) use of dogs to aggress detainees (Incidents 25 and 30), humiliation (Incident 33). See also 131–34 for M-G Fay's findings regarding the civilians (private military company employees) he investigated. See also www.dod.mil/pubs/foi/detainees/taguba/ (last visited 26 March 2008) for the report of Major General Antonio M. Taguba, Article 15–6 Investigation of the 800th Military Police Brigade (hereafter Taguba Report).

[6] On Abu Ghraib, see the cases *Ibrahim* v. *Titan*, Civil Action No. 04–1248 (JR), *Saleh* v. *Titan* Case No. 04CV1143 R (NLS). On the families suing Blackwater for failing to ensure the security of the employees, see *Richard Norden et al.* v. *Blackwater Security LLC et al.*, No. 5:05-CV-48-FL(1) 382 F. Supp. 2d 801. The vulnerability should not be understated: as of August 2007, an estimated 770 civilian contractors have been killed in Iraq.

responsibility of private actors for such acts.[7] Further reports have demonstrated that employees of these companies do more than meet the catering needs of the armed forces – they participate in combat operations with uncertain regularity.[8]

Contrary to what some assert, however, PMCs do not operate in a legal vacuum.[9] In fact, it is erroneous and potentially harmful to state that 'these [private military companies] act in a void, virtually free from legal restraints'.[10] Nevertheless, for lawyers, the advent of these actors in theatres of armed conflict – especially those who engage in combat or have combat roles[11] – represents a challenge in terms of fitting PMCs into the legal framework that applies in armed conflicts with an eye to encouraging increased regulation of these companies by states. Admittedly, mechanisms for *implementing* existing legal obligations have been a particularly thorny problem.[12] This chapter will therefore outline the framework of international humanitarian law that is central to PMC issues and illustrate the aspects that can make regulation a somewhat tricky exercise. In particular, it will consider whether the employees of PMCs are combatants, mercenaries or civilians under international humanitarian law and sketch the consequences of their status when it comes to regulating what PMCs may do in situations of armed conflict. It will then provide an overview of current attempts at regulation of PMCs – states, international organisations and the companies themselves are all actively engaged in exploring ways to regulate the industry. The crux of the matter is that PMCs cannot set international standards themselves when it comes to activities that are already regulated by international humanitarian law; rather, they may merely regulate in order to achieve better compliance with existing standards. It is conceivable, however, that they may set standards for matters that are not already governed by applicable

---

[7] See, for example, Bina, 'Private Military Contractor Liability', 1237; Carney, 'Prosecuting the Lawless', 317; Dickinson, 'Government for Hire', 135; for a pre-Abu Ghraib article, see Forcese, 'Deterring "Militarized Commerce"', 171.

[8] In addition, technological developments make remote participation in combat by civilians a reality. See Heaton, 'Civilians at War', 155.

[9] See, e.g., Singer, 'War, Profits and the Vacuum of Law', 521.

[10] Carney, 'Prosecuting the Lawless', 323.

[11] This is not limited to offensive combat. See below, section 3.1.

[12] Department of Defense Instruction No. 5525.11 of 3 March 2005 on 'Criminal Jurisdiction Over Civilians Employed by or Accompanying the Armed Forces Outside the United States, Certain Service Members, and other Service Members' attempts to address the gap in criminal jurisdiction. However, the fact remains that, despite recommendations by Taguba Report and others, no civilian contractor has yet been prosecuted for the events in Abu Ghraib. Moreover, this applies only to those contracted by the US Department of Defense, which is far from a majority of these actors.

international law. It should be noted that a legal analysis of PMCs is based on their functions and activities rather than on whether they are called private security companies or private military companies. Finally, this chapter does not seek to condemn or to condone PMCs – it merely seeks to clearly explain international humanitarian law with a view to PMCs so that regulation can proceed in a manner that is commensurate with the long-standing principles and rules of that law. Rather than simply asserting that new law is needed, this chapter strives to assess PMC issues under existing IHL and show its relevance for effective regulation.

2. International humanitarian law – combatants, civilians, mercenaries

2.1   What is international humanitarian law?

International humanitarian law (IHL) is the body of public international law that applies to and in situations of armed conflict. IHL provides comprehensive rules for the protection of individuals in situations of armed conflict and also regulates the conduct of hostilities. It applies independently of the legality of the resort to the use of force by either party and it is somewhat unusual in international law in that its rules and obligations apply directly to all individuals who find themselves in a territory on which there is an armed conflict, whether they are state or non-state actors.[13] The employees of private military companies operating in situations of armed conflict are therefore clearly bound by IHL. The key components of IHL applicable to private military companies and their employees (operating in armed conflicts) are the Geneva Conventions of 1949, their Additional Protocols of 1977 and customary international law.[14] Despite increasing convergence in

---

[13] This is confirmed by the fact that non-state actors have and can be found individually criminally responsible for violations of international humanitarian law. See ICTR *The Prosecutor* v. *Jean-Paul Akayesu*, Case No. ICTR-96-4-I, Judgment (Appeals Chamber), 1 June 2001, para. 444. This applies for non-international and international armed conflicts. Admittedly, the extent to which individuals bear obligations under IHL other than those carrying a criminal sanction is not as yet clearly established in law.

[14] See especially Geneva Convention relative to the Treatment of Prisoners of War (adopted 12 August 1949) 75 UNTS 135 [Geneva Convention III]; Geneva Convention relative to the Protection of Civilian Persons in Time of War (adopted 12 August 1949) 75 UNTS 287 [Geneva Convention IV]; Protocol [No. I] Additional to the Geneva Conventions of 12 August 1949 relating to the Protection of Victims of International Armed Conflicts (adopted 8 June 1977) 1125 UNTS 3 [hereafter, Protocol I]. In addition, other IHL treaties that would apply include arms control treaties, treaties banning specific weapons, etc.

the law, distinctions relevant to PMCs persist between the IHL applicable to international armed conflicts and non-international armed conflicts; paramount among these is the fact that, in the IHL of international armed conflicts, it is imperative to analyse the status of persons as either civilians or combatants. IHL also defines mercenary status and provides rules for the treatment of mercenaries. In non-international armed conflicts, on the other hand, no combatant status exists, so a distinction must be drawn between those who actively and directly participate in hostilities and those who do not.

2.2   Combatant status

One of the fundamental principles of the IHL of international armed conflicts is that one must distinguish between civilians and combatants, since it is only lawful to target combatants.[15] The principle of distinction is crucial to IHL's ability to protect civilians from the violence of armed conflict. Furthermore, only combatants may lawfully directly participate in hostilities: this is the 'combatants' privilege'.[16] The fact that combatants may lawfully directly participate in hostilities means that they are immune to prosecution for lawful acts of war – for example, killing enemy soldiers – but not immune from prosecution for commission of violations of IHL. If captured, combatants have the right to be prisoners of war unless they have failed to distinguish themselves from the civilian population while fighting.[17] The flipside to this 'privilege' is that combatants may be directly targeted and killed with impunity by opposing enemy combatants.

Examples abound of PMC employees directly participating in hostilities and lobbying by the companies indicates that some seek a more robust role in combat operations generally;[18] consequently, it is imperative to determine whether they are combatants under international humanitarian law such that they may benefit from 'combatants' privilege'.

Members of the armed forces of a (state) party to a conflict are combatants.[19] As one author notes, this 'confirms that lawful combatants

---

[15]   Article 48 Protocol I.   [16]   See Article 43(2) Protocol I.

[17]   In fact, Article 4A of Geneva Convention III defines who has a right to be a prisoner of war, not who has a right to be a combatant, although it is understood that they are one and the same.

[18]   War on Want, Corporate Mercenaries: The threat of private military and security companies, October 2006.

[19]   See Article 4A(1) of Geneva Convention III on Prisoners of War and Article 43(1) of Protocol I.

act in a public capacity'.[20] International humanitarian law does not set out the steps that states must take in order to incorporate individuals into their armed forces; that is a matter of internal law.[21] However, it does set out certain minimum requirements for those forces: they must be organised under a command responsible to a party to the conflict and subject to an internal disciplinary system.[22] Incorporation of a PMC employee into the armed forces of a party to a conflict therefore depends on the will and internal legal regime of the state in question. It would be entirely possible for states to incorporate PMCs into their armed forces if they choose to do so; if they did, PMC employees would have combatant status. However, the will of an individual to be a member of a state's armed forces, without more, is not sufficient for that individual to be a part of the armed forces.[23] The fact that some official form of incorporation is necessary is evidenced by the fact that a specific provision in the article of Protocol I defining combatants stipulates that states that incorporate their own police forces *or other paramilitary forces* into their armed forces must inform the opposing side.[24] This also suggests that international humanitarian law anticipates that even though it is a matter of domestic law as to how members of armed forces are recruited and registered within a state, it should be understandable to opposing forces precisely who constitutes those forces.

The example from Iraq has shown that states hiring PMCs rather tend to emphasise that those individuals are civilians. The US Department of Defense Instruction on 'Contractor Personnel Authorized to Accompany the US Armed Forces' of 2005 defines the status of contractors as 'civilians accompanying the force', confirming an earlier Joint Chiefs of

---

[20] Watkin, 'Warriors Without Rights?', 25.

[21] The ICRC Commentary to Article 50 Protocol I states that 'armed forces … constitutes a category of persons which is now clearly defined in international law and determined in an indisputable manner by the laws and regulations of States'. See Sandoz, Swinarski and Zimmermann, *Commentary on the Additional Protocols of 8 June 1977*, 611, para. 1914 (hereafter: ICRC Commentary). See also Ipsen, 'Combatants and Non-Combatants', 67.

[22] Article 43(1) Protocol I; it is difficult to say to what extent Article 43 alters the existing regime of Article 4A of Geneva Convention III. Nevertheless, combatants must also distinguish themselves from civilians in order to have the right to status as a prisoner of war, although IHL does not specifically prescribe uniforms. See Pfanner, 'Military Uniforms', 93.

[23] Sassòli, 'Combatants'.

[24] Article 43(3) Protocol I. Louise Doswald-Beck does not believe this to be a constitutive requirement: see ICRC, *Report on the Second Expert Meeting on Direct Participation in Hostilities under International Humanitarian Law*, The Hague, 25–26 October 2004, 13.

Staff publication on the issue.[25] In addition to this official position, the regulations passed by the Coalition Provisional Authority in Iraq only obliged PMCs to comply with human rights law, which would be sorely inadequate if the US, as an occupying power, knew or believed that they were part of its armed forces.[26] There are also reports of PMC employees killed in action who received a military burial and were later stripped of those honours on the grounds that they were not members of the US armed forces. Furthermore, writing by US military officers on the subject treats PMC employees as civilians, not combatants.[27] Finally, it is consistent with doctrine that a mere commercial contract is not sufficient to incorporate a person and therefore a PMC into the armed forces of a party.[28] Thus, the PMCs contracted by the US armed forces in Iraq are not members of its armed forces. A similar exercise would necessarily have to be conducted for each state's contractors but it is generally

---

[25] US Department of Defense Instruction 3020.41, 3 October 2005, para. 6.1.1, 'International Law and Contractor Legal Status', and Joint Chiefs of Staff, Joint Publication 4.0, Doctrine for Logistic Support of Joint Operations, Chapter V, 12a (6 April 2000). It should be noted, however, that the latter document goes on to say that civilians accompanying the force 'are neither combatants or [sic] noncombatants', a conclusion which is untenable under IHL and which does not reappear in the later document. The POW status of such civilians is consonant with Article 4A(4) of Geneva Convention III.

[26] Order 17 passed by the Coalition Provisional Authority in Iraq, CPA/ORD/27 June 2004/17 (Revised), available online: www.cpa-iraq.org. Otherwise, the Order should also have clearly referred to IHL obligations binding on the companies. It is worthy of note that Article 51 of Geneva Convention IV prohibits an occupying power from forcibly recruiting protected persons into its armed forces and even prohibits 'pressure or propaganda which aims at securing voluntary enlistment'. One could query whether the US or UK would be in breach of that provision considering the thousands of Iraqis that have been hired by private military companies in a climate of disastrous unemployment to perform tasks such as guarding oil pipelines if one were to consider that private military companies were incorporated into the armed forces of the then occupying powers.

Note: One must be careful not to confuse the rules on attribution for the purpose of holding a state responsible for the acts of private contractors it hires with the rules on government agents that legally have combatant status. Even though it may be possible to attribute the acts of an employee of a private military company to a state, that relationship to a state, although perhaps sufficient for purposes of state responsibility, is not sufficient to make an individual part of a state's armed forces. See the International Law Commission's Draft Articles on the Responsibility of States for Internationally Wrongful Acts, UN GAOR 55th Sess. Supp. No. 10, A/56/10 (2001), especially Draft Articles 5 and 8.

[27] See Major Guillory, 'Civilianizing the Force', 111; Lieutenant Colonel Maxwell, 'The Law of War and Civilians on the Battlefield'; Major Turner, USAF, Civilians at the Tip of the Spear. See also Heaton, 'Civilians at War'.

[28] Ipsen, 'Combatants and Non-Combatants', 69.

reasonable to presume that PMCs are not incorporated into a state's armed forces.

A person may also have combatant status if he or she belongs to a militia or volunteer force that (1) belongs to a party to a conflict and (2) fulfils specific criteria.[29] In addition to the requirement of 'belonging to a Party to the conflict', the four conditions that must be collectively fulfilled by the group (in order for its individual members to benefit from combatant and POW status) are 'a) that of being commanded by a person responsible for his subordinates; b) that of having a fixed distinctive sign recognisable at a distance; c) that of carrying arms openly; d) that of conducting their operations in accordance with the laws and customs of war'.

The determination as to whether each PMC (firm, not individual) meets these five requirements would have to be made on a case-by-case basis – not an inconsequential issue considering that there are scores of PMCs operating in Iraq presently.[30] While anecdotes abound regarding the paramilitary nature of PMCs and photographs occasionally depict individuals in distinctly military-like uniforms, experts conclude that 'civilian contractors' of the sort currently in Iraq would only rarely fulfil all of the latter four requirements. In particular, many lack uniforms and are not subject to a responsible command.[31]

With regard to the criteria of 'belonging to a Party to a conflict', one may be tempted to imagine that all those hired by the United States or the United Kingdom (or Iraq, for that matter) meet this requirement by virtue of the contract between the government and the company but the

---

[29] Article 4A(2) of Geneva Convention III.

[30] Reports from the UK indicate that as many as 181 British PMCs are currently in Iraq. A number of Senators in the United States have requested the Comptroller General of the United States to investigate the use of Private Military Firms in Iraq by the DoD and the CPA: Letter to Comptroller Walker from Senators C. Dodd, R. Feingold, J. Reed, P. Leahy and J. Corzine of 29 April 2004. In addition, Ike Skelton, a Ranking Democrat in the Committee on Armed Services of the US House of Representatives, has written to Donald Rumsfeld, Secretary of Defense, to request 'a breakdown of information regarding private military and security personnel in Iraq. Specifically … which firms are operating in Iraq, how many personnel each firm has there, which specific functions they are performing, how much they are being paid … what the chain of command is for these personnel, what rules of engagement govern them and how disciplinary or criminal accusations are handled if any such claims are levied against them'. See also Letter from the Honorable Ike Skelton to Secretary of Defense Donald Rumsfeld, 2 April 2004. As yet, there seems to be no clear figure.

[31] Schmitt, 'War, International Law and Sovereignty', 527 et seq. See also Watkin, 'Warriors Without Rights?', 67.

fact that the official position of those states is that they are civilians makes this an untenable argument. Moreover, when one considers the complex chains of subcontracts with reconstruction companies and aid agencies hiring their own PMCs to protect their worksites and aid convoys, the relationship becomes much less clear.[32]

A consideration of the purpose of recognising this class of combatants in law further indicates that it is inappropriate to rely on that provision to define PMC employees as combatants. The historical purpose of the provision was to allow for the partisans in the Second World War to have prisoner of war status.[33] The partisans of WWII are much more easily assimilated to the remnants of defeated armed forces or groups seeking to liberate an occupied territory than to PMCs. Indeed, the 'resistance' role of these militias was a factor in granting them prisoner of war status.[34] Granting combatant status to security guards hired by an occupying power appears to subvert the aims of the drafters of the Convention when recognising this category of combatants, which was to make room for resistance movements and provide them with an incentive to comply with international humanitarian law. The very definition of mercenaries thirty years later that seeks to remove combatant status from precisely such private forces (see below) provides further support that the original purpose of this provision remained paramount through the 1970s. Of course, there is no obligation to restrict the interpretation of this provision to its historical purpose but advertence to that historical purpose provides some indication of the inadequacy and inappropriateness of using that provision in the context of modern private military companies.

Status determination is not always straightforward, even for some regular armed forces; however, the proliferation of a significant number of PMCs with an ambiguous status exacerbates the problem. In particular, the plethora of companies means that it will be extremely difficult for an enemy to comply with IHL in terms of knowing who may be directly targeted, considering that probably only very few PMCs will have combatant status but they may closely resemble the many other PMCs

---

[32] See also Schmitt on belonging to a party to the conflict, *ibid.*, 525.

[33] Pictet, *The Geneva Conventions of 1949*, 52 et seq.

[34] *Ibid.*, 53–59. When one considers the loosening of requirements in Article 44 to enable certain guerrilla fighters to have combatant status, it is evident that the incentive to do so remains essentially the same: to enable those engaging in anti-colonial wars, that is, fight against a more powerful oppressor, to be protected as combatants under humanitarian law if they respected the threshold requirements.

operating in the conflict zone. It would be a crime for an enemy to target civilian PMC employees directly but the inability to distinguish the civilian PMCs from combatant PMCs may discourage any attempt to comply with IHL and contribute to an erosion of the principle of distinction.

In summary, it is very unlikely that many PMC employees would have combatant status under IHL. Some authors, envisioning a bevy of beneficial uses of PMCs (such as in peace operations where states hesitate to send their own troops) seem to presume that it would not be a big step for states to incorporate PMCs into their armed forces and thereby ensure their combatant status.[35] However, reality belies this presumption – one of the reasons states have recourse to PMCs in certain contexts is precisely to get around national laws that would prevent them from sending their own armed forces: a frequently cited example is the use of PMCs by the US in Colombia to battle the FARC due to a law prohibiting official US intervention.[36] It is thus essential to take privatisation as a serious signal that states would be at the very least quite reluctant to incorporate PMCs into their armed forces. Consequently, it is imperative to determine the status of PMC employees under IHL if they are not combatants. A straightforward application of IHL leads to the conclusion that if they are not combatants, they are civilians.

2.3   Civilian status

Under IHL, one must be either a combatant or a civilian. This is confirmed by Article 50 of Additional Protocol I, which defines a civilian as 'any person who does not belong to one of the categories of persons' defining combatants. Furthermore, the Commentary to the Geneva Conventions of 1949 states:

> Every person in enemy hands must have some status under international law: he is either a prisoner of war and, as such, covered by the Third Convention, a civilian covered by the Fourth Convention, or again, a member of the medical personnel of the armed forces who is covered by the First Convention. There is no intermediate status; nobody in enemy hands can be outside the law.[37]

---

[35] Wither, 'European Security and Private Military Companies', esp. 122.
[36] Singer, *Corporate Warriors*, 206–07.   [37] Pictet, *The Geneva Conventions of 1949*, 51.

Therefore, if PMC employees are not combatants, they must be civilians.[38] Within the broad category of civilians, there is a narrower category of 'protected persons' (based largely on nationality) who benefit from more detailed rules regarding their treatment in the hands of the enemy. Nevertheless, all civilians, including those who are not 'protected persons', are protected against attack as long as they do not actively or directly participate in hostilities.[39]

It is important to note here that in some circumstances, some members of PMCs providing services to the armed forces of a party to a conflict would have prisoner of war status if they fell into enemy hands, even though they are civilians. This treatment is prescribed for 'persons who accompany the armed forces without actually being members thereof, such as ... supply contractors, members of labour units or of services responsible for the welfare of the armed forces'.[40] In order for such persons to have POW status, however, they must have authorisation from the armed forces which they accompany (and usually an identity card indicating that authorisation) and they must refrain from directly participating in hostilities.

There may be some situations in which this either-or qualification seems unsatisfactory, as perhaps is the case with heavily armed and uniformed PMC groups. Indeed, in law, hard cases often push at the boundaries of existing legal definitions and lead to strange results. Nevertheless, under the current state of the law, anomalies do not call into question the overall framework for classifying persons under IHL.

2.4 Mercenaries

Private military companies are often referred to as 'mercenaries', so a brief explanation of mercenaries under IHL and other international treaties is in order. In common parlance, a mercenary is a person who 'serves merely for wages' and/or a soldier who is hired into a foreign

---

[38] As will be explained in more detail below, civilians who directly participate in hostilities do not, through that action, become 'combatants' for the purposes of IHL, as that would imply that they have the right to participate in hostilities and to POW status. Rather, they remain civilians and remain entitled to the protections accorded to civilians, with the exception of the protection against attack, which is suspended for such time as they directly participate in hostilities.

[39] See Article 13 of Geneva Convention IV, Article 50 Protocol I.

[40] Article 4A(4) of Geneva Convention III.

service.[41] The concept of 'soldiers of fortune' may be unpalatable politically, such that the term 'mercenary' used in reference to PMCs may
influence the debate on whether to regulate or prohibit these actors.
However, the term 'mercenary' also has a legal meaning: 'mercenaries'
are defined in Protocol I and also in two different international treaties
that criminalise mercenarism.

The definition of a mercenary under IHL is:

> (2) Any person who:
> a) Is specially recruited locally or abroad in order to fight in an
>   armed conflict;
> b) Does, in fact, take a direct part in the hostilities;
> c) Is motivated to take part in the hostilities essentially by the desire
>   for private gain and, in fact, is promised, by or on behalf of a Party
>   to the conflict, material compensation substantially in excess of
>   that promised or paid to combatants of similar ranks and func-
>   tions in the armed forces of that Party;
> d) Is neither a national of a Party to the conflict nor a resident of
>   territory controlled by a Party to the conflict;
> e) Is not a member of the armed forces of a Party to the conflict; and
> f) Has not been sent by a State which is not a Party to the conflict on
>   official duty as a member of its armed forces.[42]

These six criteria must be fulfilled *cumulatively* in order for a person to meet the
legal definition of being a mercenary. For this reason, commentators argue
that this definition is 'unworkable'[43] and that anyone who manages to get
caught by it 'should be shot and their lawyer beside them'.[44] The consequence of being held to be a mercenary is established in the first paragraph of
Article 47: 'A mercenary shall not have the right to be a combatant or a
prisoner of war.' However, Protocol I specifies that even if someone has been
unlawfully participating in hostilities and does not have the right to prisoner
of war status, that person nonetheless benefits from the protection of Article
75 of the Protocol (fundamental guarantees).[45]

---

[41] The Shorter Oxford English Dictionary defines a mercenary as 'A professional soldier
serving a foreign power'. The American connotations of the word include an absence of
ethics.
[42] Article 47 of Protocol I.
[43] See in particular Hampson, 'Mercenaries', 14–16. See also Aldrich, 'Guerrilla Combatants', 881 for a concise but accurate overview of the technicalities of Article 47.
[44] Private correspondence from a person within the PMC industry to Peter Singer, cited in
Corporate Warriors, 238.
[45] The extension of this protection to those who do not enjoy combatant status is specified
in Article 45 Protocol I. Under international humanitarian law, it is the detaining power
that would make the determination whether a person is a mercenary by establishing a

The two treaties seeking to criminalise mercenaries essentially reiterate the definition quoted above.[46] Those conventions (which have not been ratified by many states)[47] then establish the elements of related crimes: individuals who meet the definition of being a mercenary and who directly participate in hostilities commit an offence,[48] and even those who attempt direct participation also commit an offence under the UN Convention. In addition, Article 2 of the UN Convention stipulates that '[a]ny person who recruits, uses, finances or trains mercenaries ... commits an offence for the purposes of the Convention', thus adding a number of ways to participate in the crime without actually being present and fighting in a theatre of hostilities.[49]

Using examples from private military companies operating in Iraq in 2003 and early 2004 (that is, while the conflict could still unquestionably be classified as international), one can conclude that some individuals working for these companies may get caught by Article 47 of Protocol I and by the mercenary conventions. For example, a South African employee of a PMC guarding L. Paul Bremer, earning $1,500 per day and firing at resistance fighters who attack Bremer, could conceivably meet all the criteria of the definition. It is up to the party that detains him to make this determination.[50] However, the tens of thousands of Iraqi,

---

'competent tribunal' when prisoner of war status is called into question. Article 5(2) Geneva Convention III obliges a detaining power to constitute 'a competent tribunal' to determine the status of an individual who claims POW status in case of any doubt. Article 45 of Protocol I imposes the same requirement.

[46] International Convention against the Recruitment, Use, Financing and Training of Mercenaries (adopted 4 December 1989, entered into force 20 October 2001) UNGA Res A/RES/44/34 (hereafter, UN Convention); Convention for the Elimination of Mercenarism in Africa, Organisation of African Unity, Libreville (adopted 3 July 1977, entered into force 22 April 1985) CM/817 (XXXIX), Annex II, Rev. 3 (hereafter, AU Convention). The AU Convention definition repeats Article 47 of Protocol I verbatim; the UN Convention leaves out Article 47(2)(b) but then adds it as an element of the offence.

[47] The UN Convention has been ratified by only 28 states and entered into force in 2001. Ratifications as of 7 September 2006. The African Union Convention entered into force in 1985. None of the states that have significant numbers of PMCs operating from or on their territory are state parties. The lists of states that have ratified the UN Convention and the AU Convention are available at www.icrc.org.

[48] Article 3 of the UN Convention and Article 1(3) of the AU Convention.

[49] Each Convention has an additional definition of 'mercenary' specifically aimed at situations where the goal is to overthrow a government and, in the case of the African Union Convention, there are special provisions relating to the involvement of state representatives in such cases. Article 5 of the AU Convention.

[50] Article 5 Geneva Convention III provides that if a person's status is in doubt, that person must be treated as a prisoner of war until his 'status has been determined by a competent

US and UK nationals who work for PMCs in Iraq would escape the definition of being a mercenary due to paragraph d) of the definition cited above (being a national of a party to the conflict).

Under IHL, it is not a crime or a violation of the Geneva Conventions per se to be a mercenary. There is no distinct IHL crime of 'mercenarism'.[51] Under the mercenary conventions or a state's domestic law, mercenarism may be a separate crime attracting prosecution but it is not a crime under IHL itself. However, if detained, mercenaries have no right to prisoner of war status, which puts them in essentially the same position as civilians who directly participate in hostilities.

The narrowness of the definition clearly makes the concept of mercenarism an inadequate tool for the regulation of PMCs. That being said, it is imperative to bear in mind that whether or not PMCs meet the legal definition of mercenaries by no means disposes of the issue of whether their participation in combat situations in armed conflicts is lawful. Many commentators make the mistake of apparently believing that as long as it can be demonstrated that PMCs do not meet the definition of mercenaries under the mercenary conventions or IHL, states may simply proceed with regulatory schemes,[52] but the fact that PMC employees do not have combatant status (because they are not members of the armed forces or members of armed groups belonging to a party to a conflict) means that they may not participate directly in hostilities, even if they are not mercenaries. As will be shown, the consequences for directly participating in hostilities are virtually identical if one is a mercenary or a civilian. Since the vast majority of PMC employees are civilians (and not mercenaries or combatants), it is essential to explore the repercussions of PMCs having civilian status under IHL.

3.   Consequences of civilian status of PMCs under IHL: a challenge for regulation

There is no problem under IHL with PMC employees having civilian status as long as they do not directly participate in hostilities. But if PMC employees, as civilians, directly participate in hostilities, they lose the

tribunal'. For a fuller discussion of PMCs with regard to mercenarism under international law, see Cameron, 'Private Military Companies'.

[51] Rome Statute of the International Criminal Court (adopted 17 July 1998, entered into force 1 July 2002) 2187 UNTS 90.

[52] See, for example, Carney, 'Prosecuting the Lawless'; Zarate, 'The Emergence of a New Dog of War', 75; Coleman, 'Constraining Modern Mercenarism', 1493.

protection from attacks normally accorded to civilians during the time that they participate. Enemy combatants may legally target and kill them during their participation in the same way that they may target and kill other combatants. Moreover, they may also be prosecuted and punished for the mere fact of having participated in hostilities.[53] If they kill enemy combatants, the black letter law of IHL even allows them to be sentenced to death following a trial.[54] One could argue that such a vulnerable position is the price PMC employees must pay for their apparently high salaries and choice to participate in conflict situations in this way. But that is admittedly not a very humanitarian view and it does not address the problems associated with increased participation in hostilities by civilians.

Therefore, one may seek to regulate these companies in order to limit their potential to negatively affect the principle of distinction and to reduce the risks to the employees themselves. However, several aspects of IHL make this endeavour particularly difficult. This section will illustrate the three main quirks of IHL affecting regulation of PMCs aimed at reducing their participation in hostilities. First, IHL does not distinguish between 'defensive' and 'offensive' attacks for the purpose of determining whether a person is directly participating in hostilities, such that regulations that constrain PMCs to 'defensive' roles or operations will not get around this problem. Second, the nature of what constitutes a military objective is not static under IHL, making it impossible to resolve this problem merely by prohibiting PMC employees from being employed as guards of 'military objectives'. Finally, there is not yet a clear, established definition of precisely which acts constitute 'direct participation in hostilities', thus making it difficult to propose a simple list of things that PMCs cannot do in order to prevent their participation.[55] Each will now be explained in more detail, with suggestions on how these issues may be addressed by regulations.

3.1 Direct participation in hostilities

First, the fact that IHL does not distinguish between attacks made in offence and defence is clearly stated in Protocol I. Article 49(1) provides:

---

[53] Article 51(3) Protocol I indicates this loss of protection. Marco Sassòli argues that it is implicit in IHL that it is prohibited but not a war crime.

[54] Article 68 of Geneva Convention IV allows the death penalty to be pronounced under specific circumstances against protected persons if those persons are guilty of 'serious acts of sabotage against the military installations of the Occupying Power'.

[55] For a brief but excellent overview of the legal concept of direct participation in hostilities, see Quéguiner, *Direct Participation*.

'"Attacks" means acts of violence against the adversary, whether in offence or in defence.' This means that former US Secretary of Defense Donald Rumsfeld's protestation that PMCs are used only in defensive roles, while perhaps important to make PMCs more palatable politically, is totally irrelevant for IHL in terms of the legality of actions of PMC employees.[56] The problems posed by the lack of distinction between offensive and defensive attacks are best illustrated by the use of private military companies as security guards. Private security guards are commonly seen outside of armed conflicts patrolling shopping malls, public buildings and banks. However, the use of such private security guards cannot be easily transposed to a situation of armed conflict without creating the possibility that they will be led to participate directly in hostilities. A private security guard who fires back in defence, if the attacking party is a party to the conflict, is directly participating in hostilities, even if he otherwise had no intention of carrying out an offensive military action against that party.

This is not to say, however, that a party to a conflict could not hire a PMC to guard against *criminal* activity: if the attack on the security guard is carried out by common criminals for general criminal reasons, then the private military company employee need not fear that engaging with those criminals raises the spectre of direct participation in hostilities.[57] This is because criminals are generally not parties to a conflict and because their actions lack a *nexus* with the armed conflict. It should be noted, however, that this distinction may be extremely difficult to grasp since occupying powers and states may enact laws outlawing and criminalising resistance fighters. If a PMC employee engages with individuals from an outlawed resistance group, the fact that they are also criminals under the occupying power's laws does not mean that the PMC employee fighting against them is participating in a police operation rather than directly participating in hostilities. Consider also the example of the 17,000 Iraqi individuals hired by a PMC in Iraq to guard oil pipelines: how do they know whether attacks on the pipelines they are guarding are the work of criminals simply trying to loot petrol or enemy forces attempting to diminish the other side's access to oil (and therefore a

---

[56] See the Reply of Secretary of Defense Rumsfeld to the Honorable Ike Skelton of 4 May 2004, available at www.house.gov/skelton/5-4-04_Rumsfeld_letter_on_contractors.pdf (last accessed 1 October 2006).

[57] The fact that security operations by these actors often goes beyond mere police operations is illustrated by numerous news reports as well as the fact that many are known to arm themselves with grenades and other non-police-type arms.

military operation)? When the PMC employees fire back in defence, does that make it lawful for the other group to target them individually? It is both the nature of the operation combined with the status of the individual (or capacity in which he fights) that is determinative. PMC employees must therefore be highly trained to distinguish between police operations and military operations, especially if they want to avoid directly participating in hostilities. Moreover, PMCs should not be used to guard objects or places that are military objectives or that are likely to become military objectives, a recommendation which leads to a discussion of the second 'quirk' of IHL.

Things can become military objectives according to their *nature, location, purpose* or *use*.[58] There is no set list of military objectives.[59] Almost anything can become a military objective. If an object being guarded by a PMC employee suddenly becomes a military objective by its use (for example, a building normally used for civilian purposes is, unbeknown to him, temporarily filled with combatants) and he continues to guard it, he may be a civilian who is unlawfully participating in hostilities. This would mean that the enemy could lawfully target the PMC employee directly, in addition to the building itself. But what happens when the object ceases to be used as a military object and he continues to guard it? Does he cease to participate in hostilities? How can such a change in status reasonably be expected to be understood and taken into account by opposing forces? Specifying in any regulatory scheme that PMCs may not be used to guard any objective that is military in nature would help to diminish this problem but it cannot eliminate it altogether. PMCs should also not be used as security guards in highly unstable zones where hostilities may occur, which may defeat the purpose of hiring them altogether in many instances. Similar problems may arise with respect to driving convoys to supply armed forces if PMC employees take action to defend convoys that come under attack (beyond individual self-defence).

Finally, the whole concept of what constitutes direct participation in hostilities, aside from actually fighting against opposing forces and guarding military objectives, remains undefined, thus making it hard to list in an exhaustive way the activities that must be banned for PMCs. The ICRC Commentary characterises direct participation in hostilities as 'acts of war which by their nature or purpose are likely to cause actual

---

[58] Article 52 Protocol I.
[59] See Sassòli and Cameron, 'The Protection of Civilian Objects', esp. 39–41.

harm to the personnel and equipment of the enemy armed forces'.[60] However, the Commentary continues, '[t]here should be a clear distinction between direct participation in hostilities and participation in the war effort'.[61] Participation in the war effort is perhaps best exemplified by munitions factory workers: while these individuals certainly help the war, their activities are not legally considered to constitute direct participation *in hostilities*.

Many activities carried out by PMCs, such as support and logistics activities, that is, catering and construction and maintenance of bases, are *not* direct participation in hostilities. As noted above, Article 4A(4) of Convention III foresees that civilians will perform tasks such as supplying the armed forces with food and shelter but that those persons retain their civilian status. This indicates that PMC employees may not be perceived as directly participating in hostilities merely for performing such support services. However, it is imperative that their roles be restricted to those duties, which may be problematic. At times, logistics personnel (when they are members of the armed forces) are called in to support troops if those troops need extra help in a tight battle.[62] If the kitchen staff is left to guard the military base due to short staffing and the kitchen staff are employees of a private military company, they are put in the awkward position of guarding and fighting for a legitimate military objective, which probably means that they are directly participating in hostilities. In the discourse on PMCs, the problem of a lack of back-up armed forces (logistics staff) is perceived as merely a strategic issue. However, increased reliance on civilian contractors in these roles has important implications under IHL if they are indeed called upon to act in a way that could be construed as direct participation in hostilities.

Moreover, many of the new activities handled by PMCs may constitute direct participation in hostilities. These activities may be less obvious and more difficult to identify because a PMC employee does not need to be on a battlefield firing a gun to be directly participating in hostilities; rather, a person may be sitting at a computer far away programming a weapon to

---

[60] ICRC Commentary, to Article 51(3) Protocol I at para. 1944.

[61] *Ibid.* Note that, while the present author does not agree with all of its conclusions in the matter, the High Court of Justice of Israel canvassed some of the literature and state practice on what constitutes 'direct participation in hostilities' in the judgment cited below at note 64, paras. 34–37.

[62] Peter Singer notes that this occurred during WWII at the Battle of the Bulge but it also occurred as recently as the mission in Somalia in the early 1990s. See Singer, *Corporate Warriors*.

strike certain targets. It would be lawful for enemy forces to target that individual directly even an ocean away, just as it would be lawful for them to target a person in front of them pulling a trigger. Changes in technology have led to an increased potential for participation in hostilities by civilians. Complex weapons may be furnished with a civilian to maintain and operate them and other forms of attack may demand sophisticated technical knowledge and input supplied by the private sector.[63] PMCs may also provide these services and their employees would therefore be directly participating in hostilities.

It is essential to note that it is not only what one might label 'humanitarian do-gooders' who seek to lessen direct participation in hostilities by civilians. In fact, the legal battle raging in the United States at the present time over the status and treatment of the 'unlawful combatants' held in Guantánamo Bay arises precisely out of US consternation regarding persons without combatant status fighting against US forces. In the context of the 'war on terror', US authorities insist that those who engage in hostilities against US armed forces who do not have combatant status are 'unlawful combatants'; some furthermore argue that such individuals should benefit from a severely limited scope of rights as compared with prisoners of war or protected civilians when they fall into US hands.[64] Since the debate on private military companies raises the central issue of who is a combatant (and therefore who is a civilian) under international humanitarian law, as well as the consequences for direct participation in hostilities, this debate should be viewed as an integral part of the debate on 'unlawful combatants'. The principle of equality of belligerents and the need for incentive to comply with IHL demands consistency when interpreting the law vis-à-vis insurgents in Iraq, al Qaeda fighters in Afghanistan and PMC employees.

---

[63] See Heaton, 'Civilians at War' for a full discussion of changes in technology leading to increased direct participation by civilians in combat activities.

[64] See Dörmann, 'The Legal Situation', for a comprehensive overview of this issue. It should be noted that in a recent high-profile judgment, the High Court of Justice of Israel explicitly refused to accept the existence of such a third category of persons in international armed conflicts. Having established that civilians taking direct part in hostilities lose protection from attack during such participation, regarding any further difference in treatment as compared with normal civilians, the Court opined, 'The question before us is not one of desirable law, rather one of existing law. In our opinion, as far as existing law goes, the data before us are not sufficient to recognize this third category.' See HCJ 769/02, The Public Committee against Torture in *Israel et al.* v. *The Government of Israel,* 11 December 2005, especially at paras. 26, 28 and 31.

There are clearly myriad ways in which civilian employees of PMCs can find themselves directly participating in hostilities, even without their intention or desire to do so. There are at least three crucial reasons why we should be concerned about this distinct possibility for increased direct participation in hostilities by civilians. First, it may lead to an erosion of the principle of distinction, thus lessening the protective power of that principle for peaceful civilians.[65] The impact of this cannot be stated strongly enough: the principle of distinction 'is the foundation on which the codification of the laws and customs of war rests'.[66] Second, PMCs may lack a disciplinary structure normally inherent to combatant groups, which allows for and in fact demands the sanctioning of violations of IHL by commanding officers, thereby putting peaceful civilians at greater risk from the effects of hostilities. Commanding officers normally have immense power to punish their soldiers immediately to stop violations of IHL from occurring but it is unthinkable (and highly undesirable) that a PMC would allow one of its employees to shoot and kill another employee for disobeying orders. Nevertheless, the lack of an effective disciplinary mechanism puts civilians at risk. Finally, direct participation in hostilities places the PMC employees themselves in an extremely vulnerable position: aside from the fact that they may be directly targeted, they may be tried and executed if they kill an enemy combatant, a result which may be shocking to them. Thus, at the very least, they should be informed of their precarious position. On a final note, some US military officers argue in the context of PMCs that 'a state using civilians in violation of the law of war will be in breach of its responsibilities under that law'.[67] Although there is no explicit prohibition in IHL treaties for civilians to participate directly in hostilities, one may argue that such participation violates the spirit of the law and thus entails state responsibility.

4.   Regulation

From the foregoing, it should be clear that there is very little room in this context for this particular category of non-state actors to be 'standard

---

[65] US military officers are also concerned about an erosion of the principle of distinction vis-à-vis their own civilian contractors accompanying the forces, aside from peaceful civilians. See Maxwell, 'The Law of War and Civilians on the Battlefield'; Heaton, 'Civilians at War'; Guillory, 'Civilianizing the Force'.

[66] ICRC Commentary, 558.

[67] Heaton, 'Civilians at War' at beginning; see also Maxwell, 'The Law of War and Civilians on the Battlefield'.

setters', at least as far as carrying out tasks and fulfilling roles that are already defined and regulated by IHL is concerned. PMCs may not set a standard for conduct that is below what is required by existing international law. Beyond regulating the conduct of hostilities, IHL provides hard and fast legal rules on the treatment of persons, including those subject to detention and interrogation, activities in which PMCs have been actively (and very controversially) involved.[68] In addition, any vague provisions of IHL are filled out by applicable international human rights law. The content of possible regulations in terms of what PMCs may do and how they may do it is therefore fairly well established under existing international law, although further efforts may be necessary to determine the precise contours of the obligations for PMCs. However, there are many possible ways of promoting the respect of IHL and human rights law and PMCs may participate in the process of developing regulations for their industry to that end.

It can be expected that armed forces hiring PMCs will have carefully defined rules on when they may directly participate in hostilities or be engaged in activities likely to lead to such participation.[69] However, a PMC employee hired by a reconstruction company to guard a construction site or hired by an NGO to guard a food convoy may also end up unlawfully participating in hostilities and needs to be subject to regulation. Given the constraints illustrated above, what kind of regulation is feasible?

4.1   International level

Some authors advocate for the adoption of an international convention for PMCs, including one author who takes the approach that the transfer of military services can be regulated much in the same way as the transfer of military goods.[70] However, drafting, negotiating and adopting a new international convention on PMCs is not a very practical means of proceeding. It tends to take a long time to get states to agree to the terms of, and become parties to, international conventions – too long, in this case, to be an effective means of dealing with the immediate proliferation of the

---

[68] See, for example, Article 3 common to the four Geneva Conventions, Articles 27–34 and 118–135 of Convention IV.

[69] Indeed, the US has elaborate instructions. See DoD Instructions, above notes 25 and 12.

[70] See Milliard, 'Overcoming Post-Colonial Myopia', 1, Appendix A: Proposed Draft Convention: International Convention to Prevent the Unlawful Transfer of Military Services to Foreign Armed Forces.

companies. Others have sought to regulate PMCs on the international level by proposing changes to the definition of what is a mercenary in international treaties.[71] However, it is highly unlikely that the Additional Protocols will be amended to make such a change given resistance on the part of all parties to open it up for revision and the relatively taboo nature of mercenaries. The international treaty approach is therefore unlikely to be fruitful when it comes to regulating PMCs.

Another approach that is international in scope and hopefully in effect, yet which does not go as far as concluding a treaty, is the innovative Swiss initiative on PMCs. Through that initiative, states are provided a forum to achieve inter-state co-ordination in the regulation of PMCs. Informal discussions between states, PMC representatives and academic experts, along with the International Committee of the Red Cross, enable states to reaffirm the existing applicable legal framework (IHL and human rights law), to clarify their own international legal obligations when engaging or licensing PMCs and to collectively examine best practices in promoting respect for IHL and human rights law by PMCs. Crucially, however, it remains entirely up to states participating in the process to develop and implement their own national laws as best they see fit. No binding international legal instrument is envisioned as a result of this process of dialogue.[72]

Voluntary co-ordination is fundamental to the potential success of this approach. States should indeed be encouraged to regulate companies registered and/or headquartered in their jurisdiction, hired by them or hired by other corporations registered in their jurisdiction, as the Swiss

---

[71] See, for example, Frye, 'Private Military Firms'. She proposes to redefine mercenaries so that PMC operatives fall within the definition of a mercenary and are criminalised under the UN Mercenary Convention. Her definition would catch only those PMC employees who are not citizens or subjects of the territory/country in which they are acting. However, we know that many security companies in Iraq have hired local Iraqis to act as security guards. This poses very different problems for the schema of IHL civilians/combatants but nonetheless remains outside the framework.

[72] Since this chapter was submitted for publication, the Montreux Document has been endorsed by 29 states. See www.eda.admin.ch/eda/en/home/topics/intla/humlaw/pse/psechi.html (accessed 19 June 2009). Note that the Working Group on the use of mercenaries as a means of violating human rights and impeding the exercise of the right of peoples to self-determination also advocates a multi-state party series of 'Round Tables' exploring state monopoly on the use of force and has also recommended that states licensing and hiring PMCs adopt legislation to allow sanctioning of companies for human rights violations. See the Working Group report, 'Implementation of General Assembly Resolution 60/251 of 15 March 2005 entitled "Human Rights Council"', UN Doc A/HRC/4/42 at p. 21 and following.

initiative recommends. Moreover, it is imperative that as many states as possible adopt such regulations to avoid migration of the companies to countries without regulations and ideally there will be a high degree of harmony between states in terms of the content of their regulations to avoid facilitating PMCs' gravitation to the state with the loosest regulations. The fact that, to date, states with the highest PMC user-rates are participating in this process,[73] in addition to some PMCs themselves, suggests that this kind of approach may be a worthwhile mechanism for dealing with the challenges presented by such non-state actors in future. Nonetheless, as any international endeavour, it remains dependent on the will of states to be effective, which is both its greatest strength and weakness.

4.2   States

The unique context in which this industry operates makes states and lawmakers extremely wary of allowing PMCs to drive the standard setting alone. Even prior to the Swiss initiative, concerned states have been adopting national laws and regulations in efforts to control the industry and regulate their activities. Non-state advocates of this approach maintain that the national laws regulating the companies should, as a minimum, include licensing and oversight mechanisms.[74] South Africa has one of the strictest laws on PMCs (amounting to a virtual ban, largely for historical-political reasons),[75] while the United Kingdom has been considering legislation for several years[76] and the United States has adopted and is considering a variety of legislative acts and amendments to deal with PMCs,[77] to name a few. Still in nascent

---

[73] See the Expert Meeting of Governmental and other Experts on Private Military and Security Companies, 13–14 November 2006, Montreux, Switzerland, *Chair's Summary*, 22 July 2007, available online, *ibid.*

[74] See e.g. Holmqvist, *Private Security Companies*; Schreier and Caparini, *Privatising Security*. See also Cottier, 'Elements for Contracting', for an overview of the approaches of key states.

[75] Regulation of Foreign Military Assistance Act 15 of 1998 (20 May 1998), Republic of South Africa Government Gazette, vol. 395, no. 18912. In addition, in August 2006, the lower house of the South African parliament passed the Prohibition of Mercenary Activity and Regulation of Certain Activities in Areas of Armed Conflict Bill.

[76] UK Green Paper, above note 4.

[77] This includes the Department of Defense Instruction, above notes 25 and 12, in addition to the extension of the Military Extraterritorial Jurisdiction Act over private contractors, above note 78, and a number of other proposals.

stages, one proposed law would extend the US *Military Extraterritorial Jurisdiction Act* (MEJA) to cover contractors under Federal contracts, which would essentially allow the United States to exercise criminal jurisdiction over contractors operating outside of US territory.[78] While not exactly a regulatory measure and while not without faults, this is one measure that could conceivably enhance PMC compliance with IHL, especially when it comes to indiscriminate shooting of civilians. However, the only prosecution of a private contractor in Iraq under the MEJA to date involved possession of child pornography, not offences related to violations of IHL.[79] Two other bills (one from the Senate and one from the House) of a more regulatory nature were introduced in Congress early this year; though distinct, by and large they take the same approach, specifying reporting requirements regarding descriptions of hiring processes for PMC personnel and the activities to be carried out, as well as requiring the Joint Chiefs of Staff to 'issue rules of engagement regarding the circumstances under which force may be used by contract personnel performing private security functions ...'.[80] However, despite the seemingly pressing nature of the problem of getting a handle on the PMC industry in light of Iraq, neither of the latter two bills seems to be making much headway in its respective legislative process.[81]

In the case of the United States, some of the proposed laws have been drawn up in consultation with PMCs themselves.[82] This demonstrates a co-operative approach between governments and these non-state actors

---

[78] MEJA Expansion and Enforcement Act of 2007 (Bill) (House of Representatives) H.R. 2740 110th Congress 1st Session 15 June 2007. This bill has been scheduled for debate in the House of Representatives.

[79] Elsea and Serafino, 'Private Security Contractors', 19. There are, however, concerns regarding the constitutionality of using Courts Martial to prosecute civilians (under the Uniform Code of Military Justice), such that the extension of the latter Code to civilians may not be an appropriate solution.

[80] See Transparency and Accountability in Military and Security Contracting Act of 2007 (Bill) (Senate) S.674 110th Congress 1st Session 16 February 2007, especially sections 5 and 6, and Transparency and Accountability in Security Contracting Act of 2007 (Bill) (House of Representatives) 10 January 2007, H.R.369 110th Congress 1st Session.

[81] Both bills are currently 'in committee' and have been for the better part of a year. However, the Congressional Research Service has prepared a Report for Congress and there are a number of other bills in the works. See CRS Report, above note 79. Note that just as this work was going to press, one of the bills was passed by the House of Representatives in a flurry of activity following the shootings in Baghdad in September 2007.

[82] David Price, who introduced one of the bills in the House of Representatives, states this. See August Cole, 'Fresh bid to lift veil on security work', Market Watch (16 May 2005).

that recognises that PMCs are powerful actors and that regulation by states requires their participation and buy-in in order to be effective. At the same time, states are acutely aware of their own obligations under international law and of the fact that they may continue to be on the line for any transgressions committed by the companies they license or hire. Balancing these competing yet symbiotic interests in a way that preserves the existing IHL framework will not be easy to achieve, as the following example illustrates. Above, it was implied that regulatory schemes should seek to limit direct participation in hostilities by PMCs. In fact, the South African *Foreign Military Assistance Act* explicitly prohibits direct partici-pation in hostilities;[83] the passage of that act led to the prompt dissolu-tion of a major South African PMC. Nonetheless, many South Africans continue to work for PMCs operating in Iraq. Thus, companies and their employees will clearly take advantage of the fluid global reality and the inherently international environment in which they operate. While they may continue to perceive their own legitimacy as central to their market value and sustainability, such that they will not seek to escape what they see as reasonable regulatory constraints, regulations that prevent them from taking advantage of lucrative opportunities may indeed lead to company migration. This truth both reinforces the desirability of a co-ordinated inter-state approach to regulation and sheds light on some of the likely sticking points for all-party negotiations.

4.3   Others

An alternative way to regulate PMC activity is by making the terms of the contract as detailed and comprehensive as possible. Considering that not only states but also NGOs and intergovernmental organisations operat-ing in conflict zones may hire PMCs, the possibility to control a PMC and clearly define applicable standards, obligations, training and what will occur in case of breach through contracts can be an effective means of regulating them on a case-by-case basis.[84]

   Regulation by contract should not be confused with 'market regula-tion', which is sometimes touted as the best mechanism to ensure that PMCs act responsibly and in compliance with international law. 'Market regulation' is rather synonymous with doing nothing and hoping that PMCs will conduct themselves in conformity with the law as a means of

[83] Foreign Military Assistance Act, above note 75, section 1.
[84] Cottier, 'Elements for Contracting', 640–46.

ensuring their competitiveness through a good reputation. However, as one author astutely points out, there will always be a market for PMCs that do not respect the law or at the very least are extremely aggressive, illustrating the naivety of this approach.[85]

4.4   Self-regulation

A number of companies within the industry itself have proposed their own code of conduct, seeking to demonstrate a will to self-regulate.[86] This gesture is laudable but people handling weapons in situations of armed conflict clearly need to be bound by more than a voluntary code of conduct. Moreover, as has been explained above, regardless of whether PMCs have, for example, adhered to the voluntary code of conduct of the PMC trade association International Peace Operations Associations (a code that incorporates the Geneva Conventions and their Additional Protocols), they are bound by that body of law when they are active in armed conflict situations. Indeed, any civilian who directly participates in hostilities must nonetheless comply with the rules on the conduct of hostilities and PMCs are no exception.

The International Peace Operations Association has even adopted an 'Enforcement Mechanism', which apparently allows 'any individual' to make a written complaint against any PMC member of the trade association. The complaint may then be reviewed at a number of levels, and sanctions, such as expulsion from the trade association, may be adopted against an offending member. While such initiatives are commendable, they must not be mistaken for true regulation, oversight or justice: the IPOA Enforcement Mechanism specifically only grants a right of appeal against any decision *to the PMC member*; an individual whose complaint has been rejected is explicitly not allowed to appeal that decision.[87] Equally, complainants may not make any appeal regarding the nature of the sanctions decided against any PMC (but again, the PMC may do so).[88] This small example clearly shows that it would be unreasonable

---

[85] Perrin, 'Promoting Compliance', 622–23. See also Walker and Whyte, 'Contracting out War?', 685–86.

[86] See the website of the umbrella organisation, International Peace Operations Association: www.ipoaonline.org and in particular, their Code of Conduct of 31 March 2005. For a discussion of this Code of Conduct, see Perrin, 'Promoting Compliance', 634–35.

[87] IPOA Enforcement Mechanism, section 4.7. See also section 4.8, which forbids a complainant to re-submit a complaint (adopted 15 December 2006).

[88] *Ibid.*, sections 6.17 and 6.16.

at best and hopelessly naïve at worst to expect self-regulation to suffice when it comes to PMCs.

4.5 Content of regulations

With regard to the content of national regulations, serious and careful work needs to be done to unpack the obligations in IHL and elucidate their application to and by PMCs. Nonetheless, in broad terms, the following recommendations can be made: companies should have to go through very strict licensing procedures.[89] States must ensure that these companies and their employees are trained in international humanitarian law, even if the state has to offer to provide such training.[90] If a PMC is deployed in a region where a state's armed forces are already active, the licensing regime could provide for an extension of that state's normal military jurisdiction so that violations of humanitarian law and human rights law can be dealt with effectively *sur place*. However, in the case of a PMC being deployed where none of the home state's armed forces are present, there is no easy solution for maintaining discipline and enforcing humanitarian law.[91] A licensing scheme could require that a state contracting and importing services from a PMC be prohibited from granting immunity for criminal violations of law. It should also create a mechanism to facilitate the hearing of claims and provision of remedies for violations of human rights and humanitarian law by populations residing in places where licensed PMCs are active. However, one can surmise that a state having recourse to large numbers of PMCs will not likely be in a position to enforce the law on a large scale.

The proposed convention of one author admits for the possibility that some contractors may take a direct part in hostilities but, despite the fact that the proposing author is a military lawyer, his only solution is that, 'Engaging in direct combatant activities shall subject the licensed military service provider to the highest scrutiny by the Authorising State and the United Nations High Commissioner for Human Rights, including, but not limited to, enhanced reporting requirements and deployment of

---

[89] Most political scientists approve of the idea of a licensing regime. See above note 74.

[90] This obligation of the state can be drawn from Article 1 common to all four Geneva Conventions, in which 'The High Contracting Parties undertake to respect *and to ensure respect for* the present Convention in all circumstances' (emphasis added).

[91] This may be the case, for example, in Afghanistan should the US withdraw all its forces yet leave the PMCs it has hired and that are already operating there to remain in support of NATO and/or ISAF.

monitoring teams from the Authorising State, United Nations or International Committee of the Red Cross.[92] It is unclear why the author of this proposal would advocate the High Commissioner for Human Rights as ideal for scrutinising direct combat, except perhaps for want of a better candidate. Nonetheless, designation of a monitoring body or other monitoring mechanisms is an important element. Not all violations of IHL are crimes or war crimes but a consistent practice of abiding by all its rules is integral to preventing more serious violations by impeding the development of a culture of impunity. In addition, the companies themselves should be obliged to disclose to employees their potentially vulnerable position if, in the course of their work, they do participate directly in hostilities. Ideally, in order to avoid creating a privileged category of 'unlawful combatants', any state wishing to employ a PMC whose employees are likely to engage in combat would integrate those individuals into its armed forces through its normal recruitment procedures. To avoid weakening democratic control over armed forces, regulations should require oversight by elected representatives and the requirement that legislators receive notification of and approve contracts with PMCs should not be subject to the contract price.[93] Finally, special rules for incorporating such companies may also help to avoid additional (non-IHL) problems that are associated with the industry, such as trafficking in individuals in order to increase the labour pool.[94]

Clearly, the issues are complex and control of non-state actors in conditions of armed conflict is not easy. Nevertheless, such regulatory measures would go a long way to improving the compatibility of PMCs with IHL and would provide important mechanisms to implement the law and enhance its capacity to protect peaceful civilians who have the misfortune of finding themselves in dire situations. Some of the innovative ways that states and the private sector are working together to regulate this industry could provide a useful model for regulatory processes.

---

[92] See Milliard, 'Overcoming Post-Colonial Myopia', Proposed Draft Article 1(5).

[93] For example, although the US has legislation on exporting military services, Congress does not have to be notified of contracts for less than $50 million, which provides a means to escape transparency by simply cutting a contract with a company into several smaller deals.

[94] US Department of State Trafficking in Persons Report 2006, 19 June 2006. Available at www.state.gov/g/tip/rls/tiprpt/2006 (last viewed 20 September 2006).

5. Conclusion

Five years after the second US invasion of Iraq, new incidents continue to propel PMCs back into the international spotlight. Towards the end of 2007, employees of the PMC Blackwater who were guarding a diplomatic convoy opened fire in a busy intersection in Baghdad, killing as many as 17 civilians and injuring 24 more. In addition to triggering a major diplomatic incident between the US and Iraq, the killings sparked pointed questions regarding the regulation and accountability of PMCs.[95]

In the US, the House Committee on Oversight and Reform held a hearing and invited testimony from the company president. A memorandum on the company provided to Committee members prior to the hearing revealed, in tragic detail, the previous record of a lack of accountability of either the company or its employees for killing patently innocent, non-combatant Iraqis. For example, one employee who shot and killed an Iraqi official's bodyguard in December 2006 was flown out of Iraq within 36 hours (with the knowledge of the State Department) and his contract was terminated on the grounds that he had been in possession of a firearm while intoxicated.[96] Nearly a year later, he has still not been charged with a criminal offence. The State Department and the company agreed that Blackwater should provide $15,000 in compensation to the family, which, to date, is the extent of the accountability of the company or employee in the matter.[97] The memorandum furthermore showed that, according to the company's own records, 122 employees (out of some 800) had had their contracts terminated; the most common cause was for 'weapons related incidents', including for 'inappropriately firing at Iraqis, ... threatening Iraqis with a firearm, ... negligent or accidental weapons discharges and one termination for proposing to sell weapons to the Iraqi government'.[98] Needless to say, under the normal rules of IHL, 'inappropriately firing at' civilians should draw more severe consequences than mere contract termination. In addition, the memorandum cites a number of occasions in which company

---

[95] Despite the extension of criminal jurisdiction over Department of Defense contractors discussed above, the contractors in question may remain beyond the reach of the law since they were hired by the Department of State.

[96] US House of Representatives, Committee on Oversight and Government Reform, 'Memorandum on Additional Information about Blackwater USA', 1 October 2007, 2.

[97] *Ibid.*, 12.   [98] *Ibid.*, 13.

employees fled shooting scenes, leaving injured persons without medical attention, a further potential violation of IHL rules.

It should be borne in mind that, although it has a reputation for aggressiveness, the company in question is generally viewed as highly professional and it has pledged its adherence to the IPOA Code of Conduct discussed above but these factors have proved woefully inadequate. In his testimony before the Committee, the company president insisted on the fact that none of the diplomats under his protection had been killed over the course of the contract, suggesting that the standard of service his company was providing was beyond reproach.[99] However, in the context of armed conflicts, where chaos often reigns and the safety of civilians is extremely precarious, this chapter has shown that other standards obviously must also be respected. When we consider whether such non-state actors are the appropriate actors to set standards in this context, we must first think carefully about whether they and states have the same 'standards' in mind.

The Iraqi government's reaction to the September shootings, which was to suspend Blackwater's operating licence for several days, effectively brought US Embassy activity in Iraq to a standstill since its employees could not leave the protected 'Green Zone' without a Blackwater escort. Calls for control over the PMC industry from US legislators have intensified. For its part, the Iraqi government is now looking into passing legislation to be able to try the contractors under Iraqi criminal law. Such public outcry for accountability in both countries, as long as it is sustained, may thus push forward regulations both in the state hiring PMCs and in the state in which they are operating. This is along the lines of the model for regulation advocated by the Swiss initiative, suggesting that that model accurately reflects accountability and regulatory needs. In an ideal world, effective regulation will prevent the occurrence of such events in future; at the very least, it should make individuals and companies aware of their obligations and accountable for any transgressions.

References

Aldrich, G. 1982, 'Guerrilla Combatants and Prisoner-of-War Status', *American University Law Review*, vol. **31**, 871–82.

---

[99] Broder, 'Chief of Blackwater'.

Bina, M. 2005, 'Private Military Contractor Liability and Accountability after Abu Ghraib', *John Marshall Law Review*, vol. **38**, 1237–63.

Broder, J. 2007, 'Chief of Blackwater Defends His Employees', *New York Times*, 3 October 2007.

Cameron, L. 2006, 'Private Military Companies: Their Status under International Humanitarian Law and its Impact on their Regulation', *International Review Red Cross*, vol. **88**, 573–98.

Carney, H. 2006, 'Prosecuting the Lawless: Human Rights Abuses and Private Military Firms', *George Washington Law Review*, vol. **74**, 317–44.

Coleman, J. 2004, 'Constraining Modern Mercenarism', *Hastings Law Journal*, vol. **55**, 1493–1538.

Cottier, M. 2006, 'Elements for Contracting and Regulating Private Security and Military Companies', *International Review Red Cross*, vol. **88**, 637–63.

Dickinson, L. 2005, 'Government for Hire: Privatizing Foreign Affairs and the Problem of Accountability under International Law', *William and Mary Law Review*, vol. **45**, 135–237.

Dörmann, K. 2003, 'The Legal Situation of "Unlawful/Unprivileged Combatants"', *International Review Red Cross*, vol. **85**, 45–74.

Elsea, J. and Serafino, N. 2007, 'Private Security Contractors in Iraq: Background, Legal Status, and Other Issues', *Congressional Research Service Report for Congress*, **19**.

Forcese, C. 1999/2000, 'Deterring "Militarized Commerce": The Prospect of Liability for "Privatized" Human Rights Abuses', *Ottawa Law Review*, vol. **31**, 171–211.

Frye, E. 2005, 'Private Military Firms in the New World Order: How Redefining "Mercenary" can Tame the "Dogs of War"', *Fordham Law Review*, vol. **73**, 2607–64.

Guillory (Major), M. 2001, 'Civilianizing the Force: Is the United States Crossing the Rubicon?', *Air Force Law Review*, vol. **51**, 111–42.

Hampson, F. 1991, 'Mercenaries: Diagnosis before Proscription', *Netherlands Yearbook of International Law*, vol. **22**, 3–38.

Heaton, M. R. 2005, 'Civilians at War: Reexamining the Status of Civilians Accompanying the Armed Forces', *Air Force Law Review*, vol. **57**, 155–208.

Holmqvist, C. 2005, 'Private Security Companies: The Case for Regulation', *SIPRI Policy Paper*, no. 9.

Ipsen, K. 1995, 'Combatants and Non-Combatants' in D. Fleck (ed.), *Handbook of Humanitarian Law in Armed Conflicts*, Oxford University Press, 65–101.

Leander, A. 2006, *Eroding State Authority? Private Military Companies and the Legitimate Use of Force*, Rome, Rubbetino.

Maxwell (Lieutenant Colonel), M. D., US Army 2004, 'The Law of War and Civilians on the Battlefield: Are We Undermining Civilian Protections?', *Military Review*, 17–25.

Milliard, T. 2003, 'Overcoming Post-Colonial Myopia: A Call to Recognize and Regulate Private Military Companies', *Military Law Review*, vol. **176**, 1–95.

The Shorter Oxford English Dictionary 2002, 5th edn, Oxford University Press.

Perrin, B. 2006, 'Promoting Compliance of Private Security and Military Companies with International Humanitarian Law', *International Review Red Cross*, vol. **88**, 613–36.

Pfanner, T. 2004, 'Military Uniforms and the Law of War', *International Review of the Red Cross*, vol. **86**, 93–124.

Pictet, J. 1952, *The Geneva Conventions of 1949: Commentary, III Geneva Convention*, Geneva, ICRC, 52 et seq.

Quéguiner, J.-F. 2003, 'Direct Participation in Hostilities under International Humanitarian Law', *HPCR Working Paper*, available at www.ihlresearch. org/portal/ihli/alabama.php.

Sandoz, Y., Swinarski, Ch. and Zimmermann, B. 1987, *Commentary on the Additional Protocols of 8 June 1977 to the Geneva Conventions of 12 August 1949*, Geneva and Dordrecht, ICRC and Martinus Nijhoff.

Sassòli, M. (forthcoming), 'Combatants' in R. Bernhardt, *Encyclopedia of Public International Law*, Heidelberg, Max Planck Institute for Comparative Public Law and International Law.

Sassòli M. and Cameron, L. 2006, 'The Protection of Civilian Objects – Current State of the Law and Issues de lege ferenda' in N. Ronzitti and G. Venturini (eds.), *The Law of Air Warfare – Contemporary Issues*, Utrecht, Eleven International Publishing, 35–74.

Schmitt, M. 2005, 'War, International Law and Sovereignty: Re-Evaluating the Rules of the Game in a New Century: Humanitarian Law and Direct Participation in Hostilities by Private Contractors or Civilian Employees', *Chicago Journal International Law*, vol. **5**, 511–46.

Schreier, F. and Caparini, M. 2005, *Privatising Security: Law, Practice and Governance of Private Military and Security Companies*, Geneva, DCAF, available at www.dcaf.ch.

Sengupta, K. 2006, 'UK: Blair Accused of Trying to "Privatise" War in Iraq', *The Independent*, 30 October 2006.

Singer, P. 2003, *Corporate Warriors: The Rise of the Privatized Military Industry*, Cornell University Press.

Singer, P. 2004, 'War, Profits and the Vacuum of Law: Privatized Military Firms and International Law', *Columbia J Transnational Law*, vol. **42**, 521–49.

Turner (Major), L. 2001, *USAF, Civilians at the Tip of the Spear: Civilian Issues Commanders Encounter During Deployments*, Alabama, Maxwell Airforce Base.

Walker, C. and Whyte, D. 2005, 'Contracting out War? Private Military Companies, Law and Regulation in the United Kingdom', *International & Comparative Law Quarterly*, vol. **54**, 651–89.

Watkin, K. 2005, 'Warriors Without Rights? Combatants, Unprivileged Belligerents, and the Struggle over Legitimacy', *HPCR, Occasional Paper Series*, **25**.

Wither, J. 2005, 'European Security and Private Military Companies: The Prospects for Privatized "Battlegroups"', *The Quarterly Journal*, 107–26.

Zarate, J. C. 1998, 'The Emergence of a New Dog of War: Private International Security Companies, International Law and the New World Disorder', *Stanford Journal of International Law*, vol. **34**, 75–162.

6

Governance matters VII: aggregate and individual governance indicators 1996–2007

DANIEL KAUFMANN*, AART KRAAY** AND MASSIMO MASTRUZZI***

1. Introduction

This paper presents the latest update of the Worldwide Governance Indicators (WGI) research project.[1] The indicators measure six dimensions of governance: Voice and Accountability, Political Stability and Absence of Violence/Terrorism, Government Effectiveness, Regulatory Quality, Rule of Law, and Control of Corruption. They cover 212 countries and territories for 1996, 1998, 2000, and annually for 2002–2007.[2]

* Director, Governance and Anti-Corruption, World Bank Institute, The World Bank Group; Senior Fellow, Brookings Institution; BSc, Economics and Statistics, Hebrew University of Jerusalem; MA, PhD, Economics, Harvard.
** Lead Economist, Development Research Group, The World Bank; BSc University of Toronto; MA, PhD Harvard.
*** Economist, World Bank Institute, The World Bank; MA, MS, Georgetown University.
    The views expressed here are the authors' and do not necessarily reflect those of the World Bank, its Executive Directors, or the countries they represent. The Worldwide Governance Indicators are not used by the World Bank for resource allocation. We would like to thank B. Parks, S. Rose, M. Camerer, M. Carballo, C. Cilley, N. Meisel, J. Ould-Auodia, R. Fullenbaum, Z. Nyiri, L. Fessou, M. Seligson, F. Marzo, C. Walker, P. Wongwan, G. Grein, P. Priestley, S. Sarkis, J. Langston, L. Abruzzese, S. Hatipoglu, D. Cingranelli, D. Richards, J. Zveglich, M. Lagos, R. Coutinho, S. Mannan, F. Paua, J. Blancke, Z. Tabernacki, J. Auger, L. Mootz, and D. Cieslikowsky for providing data and comments, and answering our numerous questions. Financial support from the Knowledge for Change Program (KCP) of the World Bank is gratefully acknowledged.
[1] This paper is the seventh in a series of estimates of governance across countries. Documentation of previous rounds can be found in Kaufmann, Kraay and Zoido-Lobatón 1999a, b, 2002, and Kaufmann, Kraay and Mastruzzi 2004, 2005, 2006a, 2006b and 2007b.
[2] A few of the entities covered by our indicators are not fully independent states (e.g. Puerto Rico, Hong Kong, West Bank/Gaza, Martinique, French Guyana and others). A handful of very small independent principalities (e.g. Monaco, San Marino, Liechtenstein and Andorra) are also included. For stylistic convenience all 212 entities are often referred to in this paper as 'countries'.

The indicators are based on several hundred individual variables measuring perceptions of governance, drawn from 35 separate data sources
constructed by 32 different organisations from around the world. We
assign these individual measures to categories capturing these six dimensions of governance, and use an unobserved components model to construct
six aggregate governance indicators in each period.

As in the past, we complement our estimates of governance for each
country with margins of error that indicate the unavoidable uncertainty
associated with measuring governance across countries. These margins
of error have declined over time with the addition of new data sources to
our aggregate indicators, and are substantially smaller than for any of the
individual sources. We continue to encourage users of the governance
indicators to take these margins of error into account when making
comparisons of governance across countries, and within countries over
time. In particular, a useful rule of thumb is that when confidence intervals
for governance based on our reported margins of error overlap in comparisons of two countries, or a single country over time, this suggests that the
data do not reveal statistically (or for that matter practically) significant
differences in governance.

The margins of error we report are not unique to the WGI, nor are
they unique to perceptions-based measures of governance on which we
rely. Measurement error is pervasive among all indicators of governance
and institutional quality, including individual indicators as well as
'objective' or fact-based ones – if these are available at all. Unfortunately,
typically little if any effort is devoted to estimating, let alone reporting, the
substantial margins of error in any other governance and/or investment
climate indicators – objective or subjective, aggregate or individual.
A key advantage of the WGI is that we are explicit about the accompanying margins of error, whereas in most other cases they are often left
implicit or ignored altogether.[3]

Despite these margins of error, the WGI are sufficiently informative
that many cross-country comparisons result in statistically (and probably also practically) significant differences in estimated governance. In
comparing governance levels across countries, for example, we document that over 65 per cent of all cross-country pair-wise comparisons
using the WGI for 2007 result in statistically significant differences at the

---

[3] The only other governance-related indicators that we are aware of that now report
margins of error are the Transparency International Corruption Perceptions Index and
the Global Integrity Index.

90 per cent significance level, and nearly 74 per cent of comparisons are significant at the less stringent 75 per cent significance level. In assessing trends over time, we find that 31 per cent of countries experience significant changes over the decade 1998–2007 in at least one of the six indicators (roughly evenly divided between significant improvements and deteriorations). This highlights the fact that governance can and does change even over relatively short periods such as a decade. This should both provide encouragement to reformers seeking to improve governance, as well as warn against complacency in other cases as sharp deteriorations in governance are possible.

The aggregate indicators that we report constitute a useful way of organising and summarising the very large and disparate amount of information on governance embodied in all our underlying data sources. The specific aggregation procedure we use also allows us to calculate explicit margins of error to capture the inherent uncertainties in measuring governance. At the same time, we recognise that for some purposes the information in the many individual underlying data sources can be of interest to users. For example, several of these provide highly specific and disaggregated information about particular dimensions of governance that could be of interest for monitoring particular reforms. For this reason, we report country scores on the individual indicators underlying our aggregate governance indicators, on the WGI website at www.govindicators.org. These disaggregated underlying indicators are presented for the entire time period covered by the aggregate indicators, from 1996 to 2007. As a new feature this year, these data are available both interactively on a country-by-country basis as it has been in the past, as well as in downloadable spreadsheets reporting the data from all countries for each data source.

As in past years, the WGI are based on subjective or perceptions-based data on governance reflecting the views of a diverse range of informed stakeholders including tens of thousands of household and firm survey respondents, as well as thousands of experts working for the private sector, NGOs, and public sector agencies. As such, the WGI predominantly relies on the reports from non-state actors. We rely on the reports of these stakeholders, which reflect their judgments and perceptions, for three main reasons.

First and most basic, perceptions matter because agents base their actions on their perceptions, impression, and views. Consider two types of non-state actors, namely citizens and enterprises. If citizens believe that the courts are inefficient or the police are corrupt, they are unlikely to avail themselves of their services. Similarly, enterprises base their investment decisions – and citizens their voting decisions – on their perceived view of the investment climate and the government's performance. Second, in many areas of governance, there are few alternatives to relying on perceptions data. This is most particularly so for the case of corruption, which almost by definition leaves no 'paper trail' that can be captured by purely objective measures. Third, we note that even when objective or fact-based data are available, often such data may capture a de jure notion of laws 'on the books' that differs substantially from the de facto reality that exists 'on the ground'.[4]

And finally, virtually all measures of governance and the investment climate rely on judgment in some measure, so that the distinction between 'subjective' and 'objective' data is somewhat of a false dichotomy.[5] Rather, a more useful distinction is between efforts to measure formal rules as distinct from their implementation in practice, recognising that changes in formal rules (often associated with so-called 'actionable' indicators) need not lead to desired changes in outcomes.

The WGI project has evolved in several directions over the past decade. A key feature of the WGI is its effort to develop more precise or informative measures of broad concepts of governance by drawing on a diverse set of underlying indicators. One important dimension of this evolution is a basic one – a steady expansion in the number of underlying data sources on which the WGI are based. In our very first effort,[6] the WGI were based on just 13 data sources covering only 173 countries. Since then we have added sources each year as they have become available, and made backwards revisions to the earlier data as well to incorporate these sources, until the current round of the WGI which now covers 212 countries and is based on 35 separate data sources.

As the number of data sources has expanded, the aggregate WGI have become more informative about the broad notions of governance they seek to capture. In particular, the average standard error associated with the governance estimates has declined by more than a third since the first round of the indicators in 1996. Another important innovation three years ago was that we began to make the individual indicators underlying

---

[4] In fact, in Kaufmann, Kraay and Mastruzzi 2005 we document sharp divergences between de jure and de facto measures of business entry regulation and find that corruption explains a good deal of the extent to which the former are subverted in practice.

[5] See in more detail Kaufmann and Kraay 2008.

[6] Kaufmann, Kraay and Zoido-Lobatón 1999a, b.

the aggregate WGI publicly available through the WGI website, including data from a large number of commercial sources. This makes the
WGI project one of the largest cross-country datasets on governance
available.

The WGI have also evolved in terms of the accompanying analytic
work on relevant data issues. In our first effort[7] we extensively discussed
alternative approaches to constructing aggregate indicators, and over the
years we have addressed further aggregation issues. For example, we
analysed extensively the possibility that expert assessments might make
correlated perceptions errors in their assessments of governance and that
this would distort the weighting of sources in the aggregate WGI.[8] We
showed that there was in fact very little evidence for such correlated
perceptions errors, and moreover that the WGI were very robust to
simple alternative weighting schemes, including just straight unweighted
averaging of the underlying data sources.

We have also investigated the empirical relevance of other potential
problems with expert assessments, for example, the hypotheses that
expert assessments are tainted by ideological biases, or are biased
towards the views of the business elite, or are biased by the recent
economic performance of the countries in question (that is, so-called
'halo effects'). In each case we proposed specific empirical tests and
showed that such biases were for the most part not present, or at most
were quantitatively unimportant.[9]

Another area where we have refined the WGI over time is in the
interpretation of changes over time in the aggregate indicators. We first
developed a dynamic version of the unobserved components model on
which the WGI are based and used it to develop formal statistical tests of
the significance of changes in governance based on changes in the
aggregate indicators.[10] It turned out that a very simple rule of thumb
using data from the static version of the WGI was a good approximation
to this more complex and formal method of assessing significant
changes: if 90 per cent confidence intervals in the two periods being
compared do not overlap, the observed change in the aggregate WGI is
unlikely to signal a statistically – or practically – significant change in

---

[7] Kaufmann, Kraay and Zoido-Lobatón 1999a, b.
[8] Kaufmann, Kraay and Mastruzzi 2006a, 2007a.
[9] See Kaufmann, Kraay and Mastruzzi 2004 for a discussion of ideological biases,
Kaufmann, Kraay and Mastruzzi 2005 for a discussion of halo effects, and Kaufmann,
Kraay and Mastruzzi 2007b for a discussion of business elite biases.
[10] Kaufmann, Kraay and Mastruzzi 2005.

governance. We have also continuously monitored changes in world averages of governance on our individual data sources, finding no evidence of significant trends in one direction or the other, as a way of validating our choice of units for the aggregate indicators in which world averages are set to be the same over time.[11]

We contrast this careful attention to the significance of changes in governance indicators with the practice followed by the vast majority of governance and investment climate related datasets, which report no margins of error whatsoever and hence can provide no guidance to users as to circumstances under which observed changes in the data are likely to signal meaningful changes in unobserved governance. More generally, recognising the importance of margins of error and the imprecision of country rankings, we do not follow the popular practice of producing precisely ranked 'top ten' or 'bottom ten' lists of countries according to their performance on the WGI, recognising that such seemingly precise 'horse races' are of dubious relevance and reliability.

As a consequence of their increased visibility and use by policymakers and scholars worldwide, the WGI have also attracted considerably scrutiny by others. This natural and healthy process of scholarly debate over data and methodology has resulted in several written critiques of the WGI, to which we have provided detailed responses and rebuttals.[12]

Finally, we reiterate, as we have with each previous round of the WGI, that the composite indicators we construct are useful as a first tool for broad cross-country comparisons and for evaluating broad trends over time. In contrast, the aggregate WGI are often too blunt a tool to be useful in formulating specific governance reforms in particular country contexts. Such reforms, and evaluation of their progress, need to be informed by much more detailed and country-specific diagnostic data that can identify the relevant constraints on governance in particular country circumstances. We therefore view the WGI as complementary to a large number of other efforts to construct more detailed measures of governance, often just for a single country.

We begin by describing the data used to construct this round of the governance indicators in section 2. In this current update, we have added

---

[11] We also adjust for (small) compositional effects driven by (small) increases in the number of countries covered by the governance indicators since 1996.

[12] Interested readers can refer to Kaufmann, Kraay and Mastruzzi 2007a for a detailed response to several critiques of the WGI that have been raised by other authors, as well as the exchange over the WGI in the April 2007 issue of the Journal of Politics.

two data sources to the WGI. The first is the Institutional Profiles Database, an expert assessment of governance and institutional quality in 85 countries produced by the Treasury and Economic Policy Directorate General of the French Ministry of the Economy, Industry and Employment and the French bilateral aid agency Agence Française de Développement. The second consists of the AmericasBarometer household surveys conducted by the Latin America Public Opinion Project at Vanderbilt University. Details on both new sources are provided below. We have also made numerous minor revisions to the past data from several of our underlying sources in order to make them more fully comparable over time. These revisions have resulted in minor changes to our previous estimates for 1996–2006, and so the entire new dataset described here supersedes previous releases. In Section 3 we briefly describe cross-country differences and changes over time in governance as measured by our aggregate indicators. Section 4 concludes.

2.   Methodology and data sources for 2007

In this section we briefly describe the latest update of the WGI. Our methodology for constructing aggregate governance indicators has not changed from past years, and a detailed description can be found in Kaufmann, Kraay and Mastruzzi (2004).

We define governance broadly as the traditions and institutions by which authority in a country is exercised. This includes the process by which governments are selected, monitored and replaced; the capacity of the government to effectively formulate and implement sound policies; and the respect of citizens and the state for the institutions that govern economic and social interactions among them. The six dimensions of governance corresponding to this definition that we measure are:

1. Voice and Accountability (VA) – measuring perceptions of the extent to which a country's citizens are able to participate in selecting their government, as well as freedom of expression, freedom of association, and a free media.
2. Political Stability and Absence of Violence (PV) – measuring perceptions of the likelihood that the government will be destabilised or overthrown by unconstitutional or violent means, including politically motivated violence and terrorism.
3. Government Effectiveness (GE) – measuring perceptions of the quality of public services, the quality of the civil service and the degree of

its independence from political pressures, the quality of policy formulation and implementation, and the credibility of the government's
commitment to such policies.

4. Regulatory Quality (RQ) – measuring perceptions of the ability of the
   government to formulate and implement sound policies and regulations that permit and promote private sector development.

5. Rule of Law (RL) – measuring perceptions of the extent to which
   agents have confidence in and abide by the rules of society, and in
   particular the quality of contract enforcement, property rights, the
   police, and the courts, as well as the likelihood of crime and violence.

6. Control of Corruption (CC) – measuring perceptions of the extent to
   which public power is exercised for private gain, including both petty
   and grand forms of corruption, as well as 'capture' of the state by elites
   and private interests.

In brief, our methodology consists of identifying many individual
sources of data on governance perceptions that we can assign to these
six broad categories. We then use a statistical methodology known as an
unobserved components model to construct aggregate indicators from
these individual measures. These aggregate indicators are weighted
averages of the underlying data, with weights reflecting the precision of
the individual data sources. Crucially our methodology also generates
margins of error for the estimates of governance for each country, which
need to be taken into account when making comparisons of governance
across countries and over time.

2.1 Underlying data sources

We rely on a large number of individual data sources that provide us with
information on perceptions of governance of a wide range of stakeholders. These data sources consist of surveys of firms and individuals,
as well as the assessments of commercial risk rating agencies, non-
governmental organisations, and a number of multilateral aid agencies
and other public sector organisations. A full list of these sources is
presented in Table 6.1. For the 2007 round of the WGI, we rely on a
total of 340 individual variables measuring different dimensions of
governance. These are taken from 35 different sources, produced by
32 different organisations. A detailed description of each data source,
and a description of how we have assigned individual questions from
these data sources to our six aggregate indicators, can be found at

Table 6.1 *Sources of Governance Data Used in 2007 Update of WGI*

Code	Source	Type*	Public	Country Coverage	Representative	1996	1998	2000	2002	2003	2004	2005	2006	2007
ADB	African Development Bank Country Policy and Institutional Assessments	Expert (GOV)	Partial	52			×	×	×	×	×	×	×	×
AEO	OECD Development Center African Economic Outlook	Expert (GOV)	Yes	33		×	×	×	×	×	×	×	×	×
AFR	Afrobarometer	Survey	Yes	18				×	×	×	×	×	×	×
ASD	Asian Development Bank Country Policy and Institutional Assessments	Expert (GOV)	Partial	25				×	×	×	×	×	×	×
BPS	Business Enterprise Enviornment Survey	Survey	Yes	27				×	×	×	×	×	×	×
BRI	Business Environment Risk Intelligence Business Risk Service	Expert (CBIP)	Yes	50		×	×	×	×	×	×	×	×	×
BTI	Bertelsmann Transformation Index	Expert (NGO)	Yes	120					×	×	×	×	×	×
CCR	Freedom House Countries at the Crossroads	Expert (NGO)	Yes	63							×	×	×	×
DRI	Global Insight Global Risk Service	Expert (CBIP)	Yes	142	×	×	×	×	×	×	×	×	×	×

Abbrev.	Source	Type	Available	No.									
EBR	European Bank for Reconstruction and Development Transition Report	Expert (GOV)	Yes	29		×	×	×	×	×	×	×	×
EGV	Global E-Governance Index	Expert (NGO)	Yes	196	×		×	×	×	×	×	×	×
EIU	Economist Intelligence Unit	Expert (CBIP)	Yes	154	×	×	×	×	×	×	×	×	×
FRH	Freedom House	Expert (NGO)	Yes	197	×	×	×	×	×	×	×	×	×
GCB	Transparency International Global Corruption Barometer Survey	Survey	Yes	62		×	×	×	×	×	×	×	×
GCS	World Economic Forum Global Competitiveness Report	Survey	Yes	125	×	×	×	×	×	×	×	×	×
GII	Global Integrity Index	Expert (NGO)	Yes	41			×	×	×	×	×	×	×
GWP	Gallup World Poll	Survey	Yes	130	×	×	×	×	×	×	×	×	×
HER	Heritage Foundation Index of Economic Freedom	Expert (NGO)	Yes	157	×	×	×	×	×	×	×	×	×
HUM	Cingranelli Richards Human Rights Database and Political Terror Scale	Expert (GOV)	Yes	192	×	×	×	×	×	×	×	×	×
IFD	IFAD Rural Sector Performance Assessments	Expert (GOV)	Yes	100			×	×	×	×	×	×	×

Table 6.1 (*cont.*)

Code	Source	Type*	Public	Country Coverage	Representative	1996	1998	2000	2002	2003	2004	2005	2006	2007
IJT	IJET Country Security Risk Ratings	Expert (CBIP)	Yes	187	×						×	×	×	×
IPD	Institutional Profiles Database	Expert (GOV)	Yes	85	×								×	×
LOB	Latinobarometro	Survey	Yes	18		×	×	×	×	×	×	×	×	×
MIG	Merchant International Group Gray Area Dynamics	Expert (CBIP)	Yes	156	×				×	×	×	×	×	×
MSI	International Research and Exchanges Board Media Sustainability Index	Expert (NGO)	Yes	38					×	×	×	×	×	×
OBI	International Budget Project Open Budget Index	Expert (NGO)	Yes	59							×	×	×	×
PIA	World Bank Country Policy and Institutional Assessments	Expert (GOV)	Partial	136		×	×	×	×	×	×	×	×	×
PRC	Political Economic Risk Consultancy Corruption in Asis Survey	Survey	Yes	12			×	×	×	×	×	×	×	×

Code	Name	Type		Yes	N									
PRS	Political Risk Services International Country Risk Guide	Expert	(CBIP)	Yes	140	×				×	×	×	×	×	×
QLM	Business Enviornment Risk Intelligence Financial Ethics Index	Expert	(CBIP)	Yes	115	×			×	×	×	×	×	×	×
RSF	Reporters Without Borders Press Freedom Index	Expert	(NGO)	Yes	166	×					×	×	×	×	×
TPR	US State Department Trafficking in People report	Expert	(GOV)	Yes	153	×			×	×	×	×	×	×	×
VAB	Vanderbilt University Americas Barometer	Survey		Yes	22							×	×	×	×
WCY	Institute for Management and Development World Competitiveness Yearbook	Survey		Yes	53	×	×	×	×	×	×	×	×	×	×
WMO	Global Insight Business Conditions and Risk Indicators	Expert	(CBIP)	Yes	202	×	×	×	×	×	×	×	×	×	×

*CBIP – Commercial Business Information Provider, GOV – Public Sector Data Provider, NGO – Non-Governmental Organisation Data Provider

www.govindicators.org. Almost all our data sources are available annually, and we use the data only from the most recent year available from each source in our aggregate indicators. In a few cases, we use data lagged one or two years if current data are not available. In some cases we use several individual variables from a single data source in our aggregate indicators. When we do so, we first compute a simple average of these variables from a single source, and then treat the average of these individual questions as a single observation from that data source.

The WGI data sources reflect the perceptions of a very diverse group of respondents. Several are surveys of individuals or domestic firms with first-hand knowledge of the governance situation in the country. These include the World Economic Forum's Global Competitiveness Report, the Institute for Management Development's World Competitiveness Yearbook, the World Bank/EBRD's business environment surveys, the Gallup World Poll, Latinobarometro, Afrobarometro, and the AmericasBarometer. We refer to these as 'Surveys' in Table 6.1. We also capture the perceptions of country analysts at the major multilateral development agencies (the European Bank for Reconstruction and Development, the African Development Bank, the Asian Development Bank, and the World Bank), reflecting these individuals' in-depth experience working on the countries they assess. Together with some expert assessments provided by the United States Department of State and the French Ministry of Finance, Industry and Employment, we classify these as 'Public Sector Data Providers' in Table 6.1. We also have a number of data sources provided by various non-governmental organisations such as Reporters Without Borders, Freedom House, and the Bertelsmann Foundation. Finally, an important category of data sources for us are commercial business information providers, such as the Economist Intelligence Unit, Global Insight, and Political Risk Services. These last two types of data providers typically base their assessments on a global network of correspondents with extensive experience in the countries they are rating.

The data sources in Table 6.1 are evenly divided among these four categories. Of the 35 data sources, eight are from commercial business information providers and the remaining categories have nine data sources each. However, an important distinction is that the commercial business information providers typically report data for much larger country samples than our other types of sources. An extreme example is the Global Insight Business Conditions and Risk Indicators, which provides information on 203 countries in each of our six aggregate indicators. Primarily for reasons of cost, household and firm surveys typically have much smaller country coverage. Our largest surveys, the Global Competitiveness Report survey and the Gallup World Poll each cover around 130 countries in 2007, and several regional surveys cover necessarily smaller sets of countries. Some of the expert assessments provided by NGOs and public sector organisations have quite substantial country coverage, but others, particularly regionally focused ones, again have much smaller country coverage. Table 6.2 summarises the distribution of country-level data points for each of the six indicators in 2007. The 2007 WGI are based on a total of 11,852 country level data points (after averaging multiple questions from individual sources), of which 43 per cent come from commercial business information providers. The remaining data points are fairly evenly distributed between the remaining three types of data providers.

This year, we continue the practice we started in 2006 of reporting the underlying data from virtually all of the individual data sources that go into our aggregate indicators. The sources we have made available on our website are noted in Table 6.1. A number of our data sources, such as Freedom House and Reporters Without Borders, have always been publicly available through the publications and/or websites of their respective organisations. Several of our other sources provided by commercial risk rating agencies and commercial survey organisations have only been available for a fee. In the interests of greater transparency, these organisations have kindly agreed to allow us to report their proprietary data in the form in which it enters our governance indicators. All the individual variables have been rescaled to run from zero to one, with higher values indicating better outcomes.

These individual indicators can be used to make comparisons of countries over time, as all our underlying sources use reasonably comparable methodologies from one year to the next. They also can be used to compare different countries' scores on each of the individual indicators, recognising, however, that these types of comparisons too are subject to margins of error. We caution users, however, not to compare directly the scores from different sources for a single country, as they are not comparable. To take a specific example, it does not make sense to compare a question rated on a 1–10 scale from a data source covering only developing countries with a similar question rated on a similar scale, but covering developed countries, as the distribution of true governance is likely to be different in the two groups. For example, the same score of 7 out of 10 on the two sources might correspond to quite different levels of governance quality. As discussed in detail in Kaufmann, Kraay and

Table 6.2 Distribution of Data Points by Type of Data in 2007 WGI

	Commercial Business Information Providers	Surveys of Firms or Households	Non-governmental Organisations	Public Sector Organisations	Total
Number of Data Points					
Voice and Accountability	492	374	751	399	2,016
Political Stability/Absence of Violence	1,024	186	0	315	1,525
Government Effectiveness	840	388	321	393	1,942
Regulatory Quality	790	213	282	422	1,707
Rule of Law	955	409	439	737	2,540
Control of Corruption	954	493	282	393	2,122
Total	5,055	2,063	2,075	2,659	11,852
Shares of Total for Each Indicator					
Voice and Accountability	0.24	0.19	0.37	0.20	1.00
Political Stability/Absence of Violence	0.67	0.12	0.00	0.21	1.00
Government Effectiveness	0.43	0.20	0.17	0.20	1.00
Regulatory Quality	0.46	0.12	0.17	0.25	1.00
Rule of Law	0.38	0.16	0.17	0.29	1.00
Control of Corruption	0.45	0.23	0.13	0.19	1.00
Total	0.43	0.17	0.18	0.22	1.00
Weighted Shares of Total for Each Indicator					
Voice and Accountability	0.24	0.02	0.62	0.12	1.00
Political Stability/Absence of Violence	0.84	0.03	0.00	0.13	1.00
Government Effectiveness	0.65	0.11	0.06	0.18	1.00
Regulatory Quality	0.63	0.07	0.14	0.16	1.00
Rule of Law	0.67	0.10	0.12	0.10	1.00
Control of Corruption	0.65	0.13	0.11	0.11	1.00
Total	0.59	0.08	0.20	0.13	1.00

Mastruzzi (2004), our aggregation procedure provides a way of placing such different sources in common units that allows for meaningful aggregation across sources.

The only data sources we have not been able to obtain permission to publicise fully are the World Bank's Country Policy and Institutional Assessment, and the corresponding internal assessments produced by the African Development Bank and the Asian Development Bank. We do note, however, that starting in 2002 the World Bank began publishing limited information on its CPIA assessments on its external website. For the years 2002–2004 the overall CPIA ratings are reported by quintile for countries eligible to borrow from the International Development Association (IDA), the concessional lending window of the World Bank. Starting in 2005, the individual country scores for the IDA allocation factor, a rating that reflects the CPIA as well as other considerations, is now publicly available. The African Development Bank's CPIA ratings are also publicly available by quintile only since 2004, and are fully public since 2005, and the Asian Development Bank's scores have been fully public for its concessional borrowers since 2005.

Finally, as a new feature this year, we are also providing downloadable spreadsheets reporting further details of the available underlying source data for each indicator. These can be found on the Resources page of www.govindicators.org.

2.2   Revisions to underlying data sources

In this round of the governance indicators we have added two new data sources. The Institutional Profiles database is a relatively recent effort by the Treasury and Economic Policy Directorate General of the French Ministry of the Economy, Industry, and Employment and the French bilateral aid agency Agence Française de Développement. This data source covers 85 countries in 2006, with an earlier round covering 51 countries in 2001, and the latest version is documented in Meisel and Ould-Aoudia (2007). We have not used this source previously because of the long lag between the first and second rounds – in the WGI we use only data sources that are updated every three years or more frequently. However, the Institutional Profiles database is scheduled to be updated again in 2009, and so this year we use data from the 2006 database for 2006 and 2007. This dataset is an expert assessment, and the respondents are staff in the country offices of these two agencies in 85 developed and developing countries. Their views on various dimensions of governance and institutional quality are collected through an extensive questionnaire with 365 separate questions. These are combined into a number of sub-indices and indices by the authors of the dataset.

The second data source is the AmericasBarometer survey project of the Latin America Public Opinion Project at Vanderbilt University.[13] This source conducted household surveys in a set of 20 countries in Latin America in 2006.

As in past years, we have also made some minor revisions to the underlying data from our existing sources in previous years. In most cases this consisted of ensuring that when we average multiple questions from a single source, we choose questions that are available for as many years as possible so that the composition of these averages changes as little as possible over time. Also, one of our data sources, the Bertelsmann Transformation Index, has this year begun to release detailed subcomponents of its broader indices that we have used in the past. For example, they now separately report assessments of corruption, which we now use as a separate source in the Control of Corruption Indicator, while previously this variable was merged with other dimensions of the rule of law.[14]

These minor revisions to the historical data result in only trivial changes in the six aggregate WGI over the period 1996–2006 when compared with last year's data. In all but one case over the past 10 years, the correlation between the original and the revised indicators is 0.999 or higher. The only minor exception is Regulatory Quality in 1998, where the correlation is still extremely high at 0.97.

2.3   Aggregation methodology

We combine the many individual data sources into six aggregate governance indicators, corresponding to the six dimensions of governance described above. The premise underlying this statistical approach should not be too controversial – each of the individual data sources we have provides an imperfect signal of some deep underlying notion of governance that is difficult to observe directly. This means that as users of the individual sources, we face a signal-extraction problem – how do we isolate an informative signal about governance from each individual data source, and how do we optimally combine the many data sources to get

[13] See also Seligson 2008 for further details on Americas Barometer.
[14] Readers interested in the details of these changes can consult the papers documenting previous updates of the governance indicators available at www.govindicators.org.

the best possible signal of governance in a country based on all the available data? The statistical procedure we use to perform this aggregation, known as the unobserved components model, is described in detail in our past work.[15] The main advantage of this approach is that the aggregate indicators are more informative about unobserved governance than any individual data source. Moreover, the methodology allows us to be explicit about the precision – or imprecision – of our estimates of governance in each country. This imprecision is not merely a consequence of our reliance on subjective or perceptions data on governance – rather imprecision is an issue that should be squarely addressed in all efforts to measure the quality of governance, recognising the inherent complexity and imprecision associated with such a task.

The aggregation procedure we use in effect first rescales the individual indicators from each underlying source in order to make them comparable across data sources. It then constructs a weighted average of each of these rescaled data sources to arrive at an aggregate indicator of governance. The weights assigned to each data source are in turn based on the estimates of the precision of each source that are produced by the unobserved components model. In brief, the identifying assumption in the unobserved components model is that any observed correlation between two measures of corruption, for example, is due to their common, but unobserved, signal of corruption. From this assumption it follows that data sources that are more correlated with each other provide more reliable information about corruption, and so receive greater weight.[16] We have also documented that, since the underlying data sources on average are quite correlated with each other, the choice of weights used to construct the aggregate indicator does not substantially affect the estimates of governance that we report.[17]

[15] See for example Kaufmann, Kraay and Mastruzzi 2004.

[16] In past work, we have discussed in detail the merits of this approach – see particularly Kaufmann, Kraay and Mastruzzi 2006a, Section 3.

[17] Kaufmann, Kraay and Mastruzzi 2006a, 2007a. It is also worth noting that a far more consequential weighting decision is whether to include a data source or not. In the WGI we have for the most part opted to include as many data sources as possible, then allowing the data and aggregation procedure to select the weights. For example, household-survey-based data sources receive zero weight in the Transparency International Corruption Perceptions Index (TI-CPI) because the constructors of that measure have chosen to exclude all such data sources. Incidentally, while the WGI does include the disaggregate sources used by TI-CPI (and a number of other sources as well, which TI-CPI excludes) for the control of corruption aggregate component, the WGI does not include the TI-CPI itself, because it is also an aggregate poll of polls (in a similar vein to the recently launched Ibrahim Index of African Governance, which compiles individual sources).

Here we briefly report some summary information on the weights for the 2007 indicators. Table 6.3 reports the weights assigned to each data source in each of the six governance indicators in 2007.[18] This table reports the weights that would be used in the case of a hypothetical country appearing in all the available underlying data sources for each indicator. Because of gaps in the country coverage of all our data sources, no single country appears in all data sources. Nevertheless, the information reported in Table 6.3 is informative about the relative weights of the underlying indicators. The weights used to construct the aggregate governance indicators for any particular country are approximately equal to the relative weights reported in Table 6.3 for the subset of indicators in which that country appears.[19]

One noteworthy feature in Table 6.3 is that there are some systematic differences in the weights assigned to different types of sources. These are summarised in the bottom panel of the table. For each of the four types of data sources, we first report the share of each type in the total number of sources for each indicator. For example, for Control of Corruption, we rely on a total of 25 data sources, of which 7, or 28 per cent, are from commercial business information providers. We also report the share of the total weights accounted for by each type of indicator. Taking the same example of Control of Corruption, these seven data sources together receive a slightly higher share of the total weight in the indicator, at 35 per cent. The last column reports a simple average of these two figures across all six indicators. These show that data from commercial business information providers and data from non-governmental organisations receive weights that are somewhat higher than their proportion in the total number of data sources. NGO-based sources, for example, get 21 per cent of the total weight in the aggregate indicators but account for 16 per cent of the data sources. In contrast, survey-based indicators account for 13 per cent of the weight on average, but account for 27 per cent of sources; and indicators provided by public-sector organisations get almost exactly the same weight on average as their prevalence among the number of sources would suggest (25 versus 26 per cent).

---

[18] A full version of this table reporting the weights for all years in Excel format is available for downloading on the Resources tab of www.govindicators.org.

[19] The precise expression for the weights used for each country can be found in Kaufmann, Kraay and Mastruzzi 2004, Equation (2). Information on the estimated variance of the error term of each source required to construct these weights can also be downloaded together with the weights reported in Table 3 for all periods at www.govindicators.org.

Table 6.3 *Weights Used to Aggregate Individual Data Sources in 2007 WGI*

	VA	PV	GE	RQ	RL	CC	Average
Commercial Business Information Providers							
bri	..	0.058	0.092	..	0.067	0.006	0.056
dri	..	0.116	0.030	0.024	0.025	0.019	0.043
eiu	0.071	0.126	0.084	0.063	0.104	0.050	0.083
ijt	..	0.094	..	..	..	..	0.094
mig	..	0.074	0.040	0.038	0.052	0.126	0.066
prs	0.047	0.057	0.061	0.062	0.021	0.021	0.045
qlm	..	..	..	..	0.074	0.076	0.075
wmo	0.033	0.162	0.112	0.123	0.092	0.047	0.095
Surveys of Firms or Households							
afr	0.022	..	0.055	..	0.013	0.013	0.026
bps	..	..	0.001	0.000	0.001	0.021	0.006
gcb	..	..	..	..	..	0.006	0.006
gcs	0.007	0.029	0.065	0.042	0.060	0.045	0.041
gwp	0.002	..	0.006	..	0.003	0.006	0.004
lbo	0.001	..	0.001	..	0.004	0.000	0.001
prc	..	..	..	..	..	0.0064	0.064
vab	0.018	..	..	..	0.025	0.008	0.017
wcy	0.005	0.033	0.048	0.056	0.062	0.072	0.046
Non-Governmental Organisation Data Providers							
bti	0.120	..	0.047	0.084	0.013	0.042	0.061
ccr	0.177	..	..	..	0.006	0.002	0.061
egv	..	..	0.008	..	..	..	0.008
frh	0.178	..	..	..	0.110	0.176	0.155
gii	0.074	..	..	..	0.015	0.002	0.030
her	..	..	..	0.045	0.054	..	0.050
msi	0.048	..	..	..	..	..	0.048
obi	0.029	..	..	..	..	..	0.029
rsf	0.032	..	..	..	..	..	0.032
Public Sector Data Providers							
adb	..	..	0.079	0.170	0.045	0.045	0.085
aeo	0.001	0.032	..	..	..	..	0.017
asd	..	..	0.131	0.038	0.004	0.007	0.045
ebr	..	..	..	0.086	..	..	0.086
hum	0.035	0.067	..	..	0.013	..	0.038
ifd	0.005	..	0.026	0.030	0.013	0.015	0.018
ipd	0.080	0.116	0.050	0.033	0.064	0.082	0.071

Table 6.3 (*cont.*)

	VA	PV	GE	RQ	RL	CC	Average
pia	..	..	0.049	0.086	0.045	0.041	0.055
tpr	..	..	..	..	0.004	..	0.004
Commercial Business Information Providers							
Share of Sources	0.15	0.58	0.32	0.31	0.27	0.28	0.32
Share of Weights	0.15	0.71	0.43	0.32	0.44	0.35	0.40
Surveys of Firms or Households							
Share of Sources	0.30	0.17	0.32	0.19	0.27	0.36	0.27
Share of Weights	0.06	0.06	0.18	0.10	0.17	0.24	0.13
Non-Governmental Organisation Data Providers							
Share of Sources	0.35	0.00	0.11	0.13	0.19	0.16	0.16
Share of Weights	0.67	0.00	0.06	0.13	0.20	0.22	0.21
Public Sector Data Providers							
Share of Sources	0.20	0.25	0.26	0.38	0.27	0.20	0.26
Share of Weights	0.12	0.22	0.34	0.45	0.19	0.19	0.25

We can combine this information with the information on country coverage of data sources reported in Table 6.2. In particular, in the bottom panel of Table 6.2 we report the distribution of country-level data points, weighting each point by the weight it receives in the corresponding aggregate indicator for each country. In light of the higher weights assigned to data from commercial business information providers, we find that the weighted average share of country-level data points for this type of source rises from 43 per cent (unweighted) to 59 per cent (weighted). Correspondingly, the weighted share of household surveys declines somewhat from 17 per cent to 8 per cent, and for public sector providers from 22 per cent to 13 per cent.

We conclude this discussion of weighting by noting that while the weighting scheme we use has the attraction in principle of reducing the variance of the overall governance estimates, in practice this effect is relatively small, with the standard errors of the governance estimates declining by about 10 per cent relative to an unweighted benchmark.[20]

---

[20] Related to this, the main reason why standard errors vary across countries is because some countries appear in more data sources than others, and not because countries vary in the average precision of the data sources in which they appear.

Moreover, if we compare our precision-weighted estimates of governance with an alternative set of aggregate indicators based on simple averages of the underlying indicators, we find that the two estimates of governance are very similar, with correlations of 0.99 on average across all our indicators and periods. This reflects the fact that all our underlying data sources do, in most cases, provide fairly similar cross-country ratings of governance. We have also experimented with alternative weighting schemes that equally weight each type of governance indicator (of the four types identified in Table 6.1). Again, we find that the correlations are very high with our benchmark indicators.[21]

3. Estimates of governance 1996–2007

Data on the aggregate governance indicators and their underlying components are available at www.govindicators.org. The units in which governance is measured follow a normal distribution with a mean of zero and a standard deviation of one in each period. This implies that virtually all scores lie between –2.5 and 2.5, with higher scores corresponding to better outcomes.[22] This also implies that our aggregate estimates convey no information about trends in global averages of governance, but they are of course informative about changes in individual countries' relative positions over time. Moreover, as we discuss below, we find little evidence from our individual data sources of any systematic trends in world averages of governance. As a result, relative and absolute changes in countries' governance scores are likely to coincide quite closely.

Table 6.4 summarises some of the key features of our governance indicators. In the top panel we show the number of countries included in each of the six indicators and seven periods of WGI measurement since 1996. Depending on the governance component, for 2007 the indicators cover between 207 and 212 countries. Over time, there has been a steady increase in the number of sources included in each of our indicators. This increase in the number of data sources is reflected in an increase in the median number of sources available per country,

---

[21] See Kaufmann, Kraay and Mastruzzi 2007a, Critique 8, for details.

[22] These boundaries correspond to the 0.005 and 0.995 percentiles of the standard normal distribution. For a handful of cases, individual country ratings can exceed these boundaries when scores from individual data sources are particularly high or low. Note also that small adjustments to this distribution of scores are made for earlier years to correct for compositional effects driven by expansion of the sample of countries covered.

Table 6.4 *Summary Statistics on Governance Indicators*

	Voice and Accountability	Poilitical Stability/ Absence of Violence	Government Effectiveness	Regulatory Quality	Rule of Law	Control of Corruption	Overall
Number of Countries							
1996	194	180	182	183	171	154	177
1998	199	189	194	194	194	194	194
2000	200	190	196	196	196	196	196
2002	201	190	202	197	197	197	197
2003	201	200	202	197	202	198	200
2004	208	207	208	204	209	205	207
2005	208	208	209	204	209	205	207
2006	209	209	212	206	211	207	209
2007	209	209	212	207	211	208	209
Median Number of Sources Per Country							
1996	4	4	3	4	6	4	4
1998	5	5	4	5	7	5	5
2000	5	5	5	6	8	6	6
2002	7	6	8	8	11	7	8
2003	8	6	8	8	11	8	8
2004	8	7	9	8	12	9	9
2005	9	7	9	8	12	9	9
2006	10	8	10	9	13	11	10
2007	11	8	11	9	13	11	11
Proportion of Countries with Only One Data Source							
1996	15	16	21	11	6	18	15
1998	11	7	10	10	9	10	10
2000	11	8	8	7	7	8	8
2002	10	7	5	7	7	8	7
2003	3	10	5	7	5	7	6
2004	6	6	8	7	9	8	7
2005	6	5	8	7	8	7	7
2006	6	3	9	8	8	8	7
2007	6	3	8	9	8	8	7
Averages Standard Error							
1996	0.25	0.37	0.34	0.41	0.30	0.32	0.33
1998	0.27	0.31	0.18	0.30	0.22	0.24	0.25

Table 6.4 (*cont.*)

	Voice and Accountability	Poilitical Stability/ Absence of Violence	Government Effectiveness	Regulatory Quality	Rule of Law	Control of Corruption	Overall
2000	0.26	0.32	0.22	0.28	0.19	0.22	0.25
2002	0.21	0.30	0.22	0.25	0.19	0.22	0.23
2003	0.20	0.30	0.22	0.21	0.20	0.20	0.22
2004	0.21	0.29	0.23	0.21	0.19	0.20	0.22
2005	0.20	0.28	0.21	0.21	0.19	0.19	0.21
2006	0.18	0.26	0.23	0.21	0.19	0.19	0.21
2007	0.18	0.26	0.23	0.22	0.19	0.19	0.21

which, depending on the governance component, ranges from three to six in 1996, and from eight to thirteen in 2007. Thanks to the increase in sources, the proportion of countries in our sample for which our governance estimates are based on only one source has also declined considerably, from an average of 15 per cent of countries in 1996 to an average of only 7 per cent in 2007.

An important consequence of this expanding data availability is that the standard errors of the governance indicators have declined substantially, as shown in the final panel of Table 6.4.[23] In 1996 the average (for all countries and indicators) of the standard error was 0.33. In 2007 the standard error ranges from 0.18 to 0.23 for five of our six indicators, while for Political Stability it is slightly higher at 0.26 (vs. 0.37 in 1996), reflecting the somewhat smaller number of data sources available for this indicator. These substantial declines in standard errors (on average lowering them by over one-third) illustrate the benefits in terms of precision of constructing composite indicators based on an expanding number of data sources incorporating as much information as possible. Of course, since our aggregate indicators

---

[23] As described in detail in Kaufmann, Kraay and Mastruzzi 2004, the output of our aggregation procedure is a distribution of possible values of governance for a country, conditional on the observed data for that country. The mean of this conditional distribution is our estimate of governance, and we refer to the standard deviation of this conditional distribution as the 'standard error' of the governance estimate.

combine information from all these sources, they have greater precision than any individual underlying data source. Looking across all nine time periods, the median standard error of the individual data sources for the governance indicators was substantially higher at 0.6, with an interquartile range from 0.46 to 0.90.[24] In other words, on average the current set of aggregate WGI indicators exhibit standard errors which are less than one-half those of an individual indicator. This highlights the benefit of averaging data from many different sources when seeking to measure broad concepts of governance as we do. Moreover, the likelihood of encountering an extreme outlier in a country's aggregate governance score is commensurately lower than in any individual source.

3.1   Cross-country comparisons of governance using the WGI

We use Figure 6.1 and Figure 6.2 to emphasise the importance of taking these margins of error into account when making comparisons of governance across countries and over time. In Figure 6.1, we order countries in ascending order according to their point estimates of governance in 2007 on the horizontal axis, and on the vertical axis we plot the estimate of governance and the associated 90 per cent confidence intervals. These intervals indicate the range in which it is 90 per cent likely that the true governance score falls.[25] We do this for two of the six governance indicators, Political Stability and Absence of Violence/Terrorism, and Control of Corruption. The size of these confidence intervals varies across countries, as different countries appear in different numbers of sources with different levels of precision. The resulting confidence intervals are substantial relative to the units in which governance is measured. From Figure 6.1 it should also be evident that many of the small differences in estimates of governance across countries are not likely to be statistically significant at reasonable confidence levels, since the associated 90 per cent

---

[24] In an earlier paper (Kaufmann, Kraay and Mastruzzi 2004) we showed how to obtain margins of errors for other 'objective' measures of governance and found that they were as large, or larger than those of the individual subjective measures on which we rely for the WGI (and thus obviously (thanks to the aggregation)) we also found that the WGI had much lower margins of error than any 'objective' measure. This underscores the fact that all efforts to measure governance involve margins of error, often non-trivial.

[25] An x% confidence interval for governance can be obtained as the point estimate of governance plus or minus the standard error times the (100–x)/2th percentile of the standard normal distribution. For example, the 90% confidence intervals we report throughout the paper are the point estimate plus or minus 1.64 times the standard error.

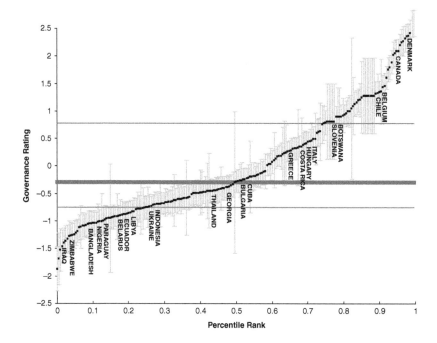

Figure 6.1

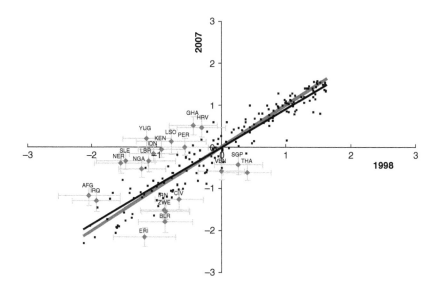

Figure 6.2

confidence intervals are likely to overlap. For many applications, instead of merely observing the point estimates, it is therefore more useful to focus on the range of possible governance values for each country (as summarised in the 90 per cent confidence intervals shown in Figure 6.1), recognising that these likely ranges often overlap for countries that are being compared with each other.[26]

This is not to say, however, that the aggregate indicators cannot be used to make cross-country comparisons. On the contrary, there are a great many pair-wise country comparisons that do point to statistically significant, and likely also practically meaningful, differences across countries. Our 2007 Control of Corruption indicator, for example, covers 208 countries, so that it is possible to make a total of 21,528 pair-wise comparisons of corruption across countries using this measure. For 65 per cent of these comparisons, 90 per cent confidence intervals do not overlap, signalling quite highly statistically significant differences across countries. And if we lower our confidence level to 75 per cent, which may be quite adequate for many applications, we find that 74 per cent of all pair-wise comparisons are statistically significant. In sum, the likelihood that a comparison between any given pair of countries does exhibit a reasonably significant difference in governance performance is close to three-quarters.

The benefit of improved precision of aggregate indicators with increased data availability over time can also be clearly seen from this calculation. Consider our 1996 Control of Corruption indicator, which was based on a median of only four data sources per country, as opposed to a median of 11 sources in 2007, implying substantially higher margins of error in 1996. Of the 11,781 possible pair-wise comparisons in 1996, only 46 per cent are significant at the 90 per cent confidence level, and only 59 per cent at the 75 per cent confidence interval (versus 65 per cent and 74 per cent respectively, in 2007).

We also emphasise that the WGI are unusual in that we generate and report these margins of error, which allow an explicit assessment of the significance of observed cross-country and over-time differences in

---

[26] Of course, asking whether 90% confidence intervals overlap or not corresponds to a hypothesis test at a significance level that is more stringent than 10%. The assumptions underlying our statistical model imply that the standard error of the difference between two country scores is the square root of the sum of the squared standard errors of the two sources, which is always smaller than the sum of the two standard errors themselves. It is more convenient – and more conservative – for users to simply inspect confidence intervals and see whether they overlap.

estimates of governance. Although rarely explicitly disclosed – or even acknowledged – all other measures of governance are subject to margins of error as well, which in our past work we have shown to be at least as large as those we calculate for our individual and aggregate indicators.[27] This underscores the need for caution in making cross-country comparisons with any type of governance indicator.

3.2   Changes over time in governance using the WGI

We now turn to the changes over time in our estimates of governance in individual countries. Figure 6.2 illustrates these changes over the decade 1998–2007. In both panels, we plot the 1998 score on the horizontal axis, and the 2007 score on the vertical axis. We also plot the 45-degree line, so that countries above this line correspond to improvements in governance, while countries below the line correspond to deteriorations in governance. The first feature of this graph is that most countries are clustered quite close to the 45-degree line, indicating that changes in our estimates of governance in most countries are relatively small over the ten-year period covered by the graph. A similar pattern emerges for the other four dimensions of governance (not shown in Figure 6.2), and, not surprisingly, the correlation between current and lagged estimates of governance is even higher when we consider shorter time periods than the decade shown here.

Nevertheless, a substantial number of countries do show significant changes in governance. Over this period, we find that for each of our six indicators, on average 9 per cent of countries experience changes that are significant at the 90 per cent confidence level. Looking across all six indicators, 31 per cent of countries experience a significant change in at least one of the six dimensions of governance over this period, roughly equally divided between improvements and deteriorations. We also note that the 90 per cent confidence level is quite high, and for some purposes a lower confidence level, say 75 per cent, would be appropriate for identifying changes in governance that are likely to be practically important. Not surprisingly this lower confidence level identifies substantially more cases of significant changes: 20 per cent of countries experience a significant change on each indicator on average, and 59 per cent of

---

[27] See Kaufmann, Kraay and Mastruzzi 2004.

countries experience a significant change on at least one dimension of governance.

In Figure 6.2 we have labelled those countries for which the change in estimated governance over the 1998–2007 period is sufficiently large that the 90 per cent confidence intervals for governance in the two periods do not overlap.[28] Examples of such substantial changes in governance estimates between 1998 and 2007 include significant improvements in Voice and Accountability in countries such as Ghana, Indonesia, Nigeria, and Peru, but also declines in that component in countries such as Belarus, Zimbabwe and Côte d'Ivoire. In Rule of Law we see improvements in countries such as Georgia, Liberia, Rwanda, and Estonia, contrasting with declines in countries such as Côte d'Ivoire, Eritrea, and Zimbabwe. Other examples of improvements in estimates of governance not shown in Figure 6.2 include Rwanda, Algeria and Angola in Political Stability and Absence of Violence/Terrorism, Afghanistan, Serbia and Ethiopia in Government Effectiveness, Georgia and the Democratic Republic of Congo in Regulatory Quality, and Liberia and Serbia in Control of Corruption.

In Table 6.5 we provide more detail on all the statistically significant (at the 90 per cent level) changes in our six governance indicators over the period 1998–2007. The first three columns report the level of governance in the two periods, and the change. The next three columns report on how the underlying data sources move for each case. In the column labelled 'Agree' we report the number of sources available in both periods which move in the same direction as the aggregate indicator. The columns labelled 'No Change' and 'Disagree' report the number of sources on which that country's score does not change or moves in the opposite direction to the aggregate indicator. For each country we also summarise the extent to which changes in the individual sources agree with the direction of change in the aggregate indicator by calculating the 'Agreement Ratio', or 'Agree'/('Agree' + 'Disagree'). The agreement ratio is quite high for countries with large changes in governance. Averaging across all countries and indicators, we find an average agreement ratio of 0.91 for the period 1998–2007, as reported in Table 6.5. This provides confidence

---

[28] While this is not a formal test of the statistical significance of changes over time in governance, it is a very simple and transparent rule of thumb for identifying changes in governance that are likely to be significant. In Kaufmann, Kraay and Mastruzzi 2005, 2006 we have shown in more detail how to assess the statistical significance of changes in governance, and that this simple rule of thumb turns out to be a fairly good approximation.

Table 6.5 *Significant Changes in WGI Estimates of Governance 1998–2007*

	Governance Score						Agree/	Sources	Balanced	Bal Chng/
	2007 (Level)	1998 (Level)	Change	Agree	No change	Disagree	(agree=Disagree)	Added	Change	Actual Chng
Voice and Accountability										
THAILAND	-0.61	0.40	-1.01	4	0	2	0.67	7	-0.75	0.75
ERITREA	-2.15	-1.18	-0.97	2	1	0	1.00	5	-0.75	0.77
BELARUS	-1.80	-0.86	-0.93	4	0	0	1.00	5	-0.94	1.01
SINGAPORE	-0.43	0.27	-0.69	3	0	3	0.50	5	-0.42	0.61
ZIMBABWE	-1.54	-0.86	-0.68	4	2	0	1.00	10	-0.88	1.28
IRAN	-1.52	-0.87	-0.65	2	2	1	0.67	6	-0.40	0.62
COTE D'IVORE	-1.26	-0.65	-0.61	5	1	0	1.00	4	-0.64	1.05
VENEZUELA	-0.58	0.00	-0.58	6	0	1	0.86	8	-0.82	1.41
PERU	0.00	-0.57	0.56	3	1	2	0.60	10	0.68	1.20
IRAQ	-1.29	-1.92	0.64	4	0	1	0.80	3	0.76	1.18
NIGERIA	-0.54	-1.22	0.68	5	1	0	1.00	11	0.55	0.80
CROATIA	0.47	-0.31	0.77	5	0	0	1.00	7	0.79	1.02
LIBERIA	-0.35	-1.12	0.77	4	0	0	1.00	5	0.77	0.99
KENYA	-0.06	-0.92	0.85	4	2	0	1.00	11	0.54	0.63
INDONESIA	-0.17	-1.04	0.87	5	0	1	0.83	9	1.03	1.18
AFGHANISTAN	-1.17	-2.04	0.87	3	0	0	1.00	5	1.01	1.16
LESOTHO	0.12	-0.77	0.90	1	1	0	1.00	6	0.73	0.81
GHANA	0.50	-0.43	0.94	6	0	0	1.00	9	0.95	1.01
SIERRA LEONE	-0.33	-1.47	1.14	3	0	0	1.00	8	1.18	1.03

Table 6.5 (*cont.*)

	Governance Score			Agree	No change	Disagree	Agree/ (agree=Disagree)	Sources Added	Balanced Change	Bal Chng/ Actual Chng
	2007 (Level)	1998 (Level)	Change							
NIGER	−0.38	−1.54	1.16	4	0	0	1.00	7	1.09	0.94
SERBIA	0.20	−1.14	1.34	5	0	0	1.00	6	1.37	1.02
Average				3.90	0.52	0.52	0.90	7.00		
Political Stability and Absence of Violence										
COTE D'IVOIRE	−2.12	−0.28	−1.84	5	0	1	0.83	3	−1.63	0.88
THAILAND	−1.07	0.37	−1.44	5	0	1	0.83	5	−1.37	0.95
GUINEA	−2.02	−0.58	−1.43	2	0	1	0.67	4	−1.43	1.00
NEPAL	−2.13	−0.73	−1.40	2	0	0	1.00	4	−1.07	0.76
NIGERIA	−2.07	−0.84	−1.23	4	2	0	1.00	4	−1.20	0.97
LEBANON	−2.09	−0.86	−1.23	3	0	2	0.60	3	−0.89	0.72
PHILIPPINES	−1.38	−0.15	−1.23	4	1	1	0.80	5	−0.92	0.75
KYRGYZSTAN	−1.11	0.01	−1.12	2	0	1	0.67	4	−0.80	0.72
PAKISTAN	−2.44	−1.33	−1.12	6	0	0	1.00	4	−1.10	0.99
BANGLADESH	−1.44	−0.49	−0.95	4	0	1	0.80	4	−0.96	1.01
UZBEKISTAN	−1.42	−0.48	−0.94	2	0	1	0.67	5	−0.84	0.89
ETHIOPIA	−1.72	−0.82	−0.90	5	0	0	1.00	4	−1.11	1.24
IRAN	−1.33	−0.45	−0.88	5	1	0	1.00	3	−0.84	0.96
VENEZUELA	−1.23	−0.38	−0.85	5	0	1	0.83	5	−0.80	0.95
ARMENIA	−0.01	−0.86	0.85	4	0	0	1.00	4	1.36	1.60

SOUTH AFRICA	0.18	−0.83	1.01	6	0	1	0.86	5	1.06	1.05
ALGERIA	−1.18	−2.33	1.15	5	0	1	0.83	4	1.31	1.14
SERBIA	−0.77	−1.96	1.18	4	0	0	1.00	4	1.41	1.19
CONGO	−0.83	−2.04	1.21	3	0	1	0.75	4	1.51	1.25
GUINEA-BISSAU	−0.41	−1.79	1.39	3	0	0	1.00	0	1.46	1.05
TAJIKISTAN	−0.87	−2.26	1.39	3	0	0	1.00	4	1.55	1.12
LIBYA	0.47	−1.23	1.70	5	0	0	1.00	4	1.74	1.02
ANGOLA	−0.46	−2.23	1.77	5	0	0	1.00	3	1.99	1.13
SIERRA LEONE	−0.30	−2.18	1.88	3	0	0	1.00	2	2.23	1.19
RWANDA	−0.19	−2.15	1.96	2	0	0	1.00	3	1.47	0.75
Average				*3.88*	*0.16*	*0.52*	*0.89*	*3.76*		
Government Effectiveness										
MALDIVES	−0.19	0.96	−1.15	2	0	0	1.00	3	−0.88	0.77
COTE D'IVOIRE	−1.37	−0.36	−1.01	6	0	0	1.00	4	−0.96	0.95
ZIMBABWE	−1.48	−0.48	−1.00	5	1	1	0.83	7	−0.79	0.79
CHAD	−1.45	−0.61	−0.84	3	0	0	1.00	8	−0.59	0.70
TOGO	−1.48	−0.68	−0.80	3	1	0	1.00	6	−0.76	0.95
BOLIVIA	−0.83	−0.04	−0.79	4	1	0	1.00	8	−0.62	0.79
BELARUS	−1.26	−0.51	−0.75	2	0	2	0.50	3	−0.84	1.33
SPAIN	1.22	1.70	−0.70	6	1	0	1.00	4	−0.63	0.89
QATAR	0.06	0.70	−0.63	2	0	2	0.50	3	−0.84	1.33
ITALY	0.33	0.92	−0.59	4	1	2	0.67	4	−0.59	0.99
ETHIOPIA	−0.45	−1.09	0.64	4	1	0	1.00	7	0.70	1.09
ALGERIA	−0.52	−1.16	0.64	5	1	0	1.00	6	0.83	1.29
RWANDA	−0.37	−1.15	0.78	3	0	0	1.00	5	0.66	0.84

Table 6.5 (*cont.*)

	Governance Score									
	2007 (Level)	1998 (Level)	Change	Agree	No change	Disagree	Agree/ (agree=Disagree)	Sources Added	Balanced Change	Bal Chng/ Actual Chng
SERBIA	-0.34	-1.18	0.84	3	0	0	1.00	8	0.93	1.10
HONG KONG	1.80	0.92	0.88	5	0	1	0.83	4	0.90	1.03
KOREA, SOUTH	1.26	0.36	0.90	7	1	0	1.00	5	0.82	0.91
AFGHANISTAN	-1.33	-2.27	0.95	1	0	0	1.00	6	0.94	1.00
Average				3.82	0.47	0.47	0.90	5.53		
Regulatory Quality										
ZIMBABWE	-2.24	-0.68	-1.56	8	0	0	1.00	4	-1.64	1.05
BOLIVIA	-1.18	0.30	-1.48	6	0	0	1.00	5	-1.58	1.07
VENEZUELA	-1.56	-0.15	-1.41	8	0	0	1.00	4	-1.63	1.16
ARGENTINA	-0.77	0.64	-1.40	8	0	0	1.00	3	-1.58	1.13
ERITREA	-1.95	-0.63	-1.32	3	0	0	1.00	3	-1.13	0.85
ECUADOR	-1.09	-0.05	-1.04	6	0	0	1.00	4	-1.18	1.13
COTE D'IVOIRE	-0.98	-0.07	-0.91	5	2	0	1.00	3.	-0.95	1.05
GEORGIA	0.21	-0.77	0.98	5	0	0	1.00	7	1.03	1.06
Congo, Dem. Rep.	-1.35	-2.43	1.08	5	0	0	1.00	4	1.14	1.06
LIBYA	-0.98	-2.20	1.21	5	0	0	1.00	3	1.32	1.09
IRAQ	-1.35	-2.76	1.41	3	1	0	1.00	3	1.49	1.06
Average				5.64	0.27	0.00	1.00	3.91		

Rule of Law

ZIMBABWE	-1.67	-0.50	-1.17	9	0	1	0.90	9	-1.17	1.01
ERITREA	-1.10	-0.22	-0.89	4	0	0	1.00	4	-0.61	0.69
VENEZUELA	-1.47	-0.69	-0.78	10	1	1	0.91	8	-0.79	1.01
BOLIVIA	-0.96	-0.30	-0.66	7	2	0	1.00	9	-0.61	0.93
COTE D'IVOIRE	-1.54	-0.90	-0.64	6	2	0	1.00	4	-0.59	0.93
TRINIDAD AND TOBAGO	-0.22	0.36	-0.59	6	0	1	0.86	4	-0.44	0.74
ARGENTINA	-0.52	0.04	-0.56	9	2	1	0.90	6	-0.58	1.03
ESTONIA	1.00	0.50	0.49	7	2	0	1.00	8	0.51	1.04
TAJIKISTAN	-1.13	-1.75	0.61	3	3	0	1.00	11	0.74	1.21
SERBIA	-0.57	-1.30	0.72	3	1	1	0.75	9	0.74	1.02
GEORGIA	-0.44	-1.18	0.74	4	2	1	0.80	11	0.75	1.01
RWANDA	-0.65	-1.47	0.82	4	1	0	1.00	6	0.74	0.91
LIBERIA	-1.06	-2.07	1.01	3	1	0	1.00	5	0.85	0.84
KIRIBATI	0.84	-0.69	1.53	1	0	0	1.00	3	0.77	0.50
Average				5.43	1.21	0.43	0.94	6.93		

Control of Corruption

ERITREA	-0.60	0.77	-1.37	2	1	0	1.00	4	-1.52	1.11
ZIMBABWE	-1.25	-0.38	-0.87	7	0	1	0.88	8	-0.898	1.01
COTE D'IVOIRE	-1.09	-0.38	-0.71	4	2	0	1.00	3	-0.64	0.94
KUWAIT	0.49	1.11	-0.61	2	2	1	0.67	4	-0.29	0.47
POLAND	0.14	0.60	-0.46	6	2	2	0.75	6	-0.45	097
UKRAINE	-0.73	-1.16	0.44	6	2	1	0.86	9	0.41	0.95
ESTONIA	0.94	0.42	0.52	5	1	1	0.83	7	0.26	0.50

Table 6.5 (*cont.*)

	Governance Score									
	2007 (Level)	1998 (Level)	Change	Agree	No change	Disagree	Agree/ (agree=Disagree)	Sources Added	Balanced Change	Bal Chng/ Actual Chng
TANZANIA	−0.45	−1.09	0.64	5	2	0	1.00	7	0.59	0.93
SERBIA	−0.41	−1.08	0.67	4	0	0	1.00	9	0.82	1.22
ICELAND	2.60	1.92	0.638	2	1	2	0.50	3	0.48	0.71
CAPE VERDE	0.76	−0.32	1.08	2	0	0	1.00	4	1.13	1.05
LIBERIA	−0.41	−1.72	1.30	3	0	0	1.00	4	1.32	1.01
Average				*4.00*	*1.08*	*0.67*	*0.87*	*5.67*		
Overall Average				4.35	0.55	0.47	0.91	5.47		0.98
								Cases>1.25	5	
								Cases >0.75	13	
								0.75 > Cases > 1.75	68	

Note: Shaded countries correspond to increases in WGI estimates of governance, and non-shaded areas correspond to declines.

that for countries with statistically significant changes in our aggregate governance estimates, these changes are reflected in a strong majority of the individual underlying data sources.

The last three columns of Table 6.5 further address directly the issue of adding sources over time. Averaging over all the significant changes, we find that for a typical change, between five and six new data sources were added between 1998 and 2007. One might reasonably wonder about the extent to which changes in the aggregate indicators are driven by the addition of sources whose ratings differed from those for 2007 provided by sources also available in 1998. It turns out, however, that this effect is small in most cases. To see this, in the second-last column, we have calculated the change that we would have seen in the aggregate indicators had we used only those same data sources available in both 1998 and 2007 for the indicated country. We refer to this as the 'balanced' (sources) change. The final column reports the ratio of this balanced change to the actual change reported in the third column of Table 6.5. If this ratio is less than one, the actual change exceeds (in absolute value) the balanced change, indicating that the addition of sources magnified the change relative to what would have been observed using only the balanced set of sources. And if this ratio is greater than one, the addition of new sources offsets the change observed among the balanced sources.

It turns out that these compositional effects are not large. For 68 of the 85 significant changes reported in Table 6.5, the ratio of the balanced change to the actual change is between 0.75 and 1.25, that is, the balanced change is within 25 per cent of the actual change. Another way to see the relative unimportance of compositional effects is to calculate the share of the variance of the actual significant changes that is accounted for by the variance in the balanced changes. When we do this, we find that 97 per cent of the variation in the observed changes is due to changes in underlying sources, and only 3 per cent is due to the addition of sources.[29]

Finally, it is worth noting that the agreement ratios for significant changes in governance are substantially higher than the agreement ratios for all changes in governance. This can be seen in Table 6.6, which computes the same agreement ratio, but for all countries over the period 1998–2007. The agreement ratio averages 69 per cent, compared with

---

[29] This is calculated as (VAR(Balanced Changes) + COV(Balanced Changes, Actual Changes))/ VAR(Actual Changes). This is also the slope of a regression of the balanced changes on the actual changes.

Table 6.6 *Agreement Ratio for Changes in WGI Estimates of Governance, 1998–2007*

| | ALL CHANGES | | | |
	Sample	Agree	No change	Disagree	Agree / (Agree + Disagree)
Voice and Accountability	199	2.4	0.9	1.1	0.68
Political Stability/ Absence Violence	189	2.6	0.6	1.0	0.72
Government Effectiveness	194	2.5	0.8	1.1	0.69
Regulatory Quality	194	3.0	0.8	1.3	0.70
Rule of Law	194	3.2	1.9	1.7	0.65
Control of Corruption	194	2.5	1.5	1.2	0.68
Average	194	2.7	1.1	1.2	0.69
	SIGNIFICANT CHANGES (90%)			
	Sample	Agree	No Change	Disagree	Agree / (Agree + Disagree)
Voice and Accountability	21	3.9	0.5	0.5	0.88
Political Stability/ Absence Violence	25	3.9	0.2	0.5	0.88
Government Effectiveness	17	3.8	0.5	0.5	0.89
Regulatory Quality	11	5.6	0.3	0.0	1.00
Rule of Law	14	5.4	1.2	0.4	0.93
Control of Corruption	12	4.0	1.1	0.7	0.86
Average	17	4.4	0.6	0.4	0.91

91 per cent for large changes, suggesting that for the more typical smaller changes in our governance estimates, there is relatively more disagreement across individual sources about the direction of the change than there is for large changes. Nevertheless, even for these smaller changes, typically the majority of underlying individual sources agree about the direction of the change. These examples underscore the importance of carefully examining the factors underlying changes in the aggregate governance indicators in particular countries.

3.3   Trends in global averages of governance

We conclude by reviewing the available evidence on trends in global averages of governance over the expanded time period that we now cover. As we have already noted, the WGI are not informative about trends in global averages because we assume that world averages of governance are zero in each period, as a convenient choice of units. While the aggregate indicators are of course informative about the relative performance of individual (or groups of) countries over time, in order to assess trends in global averages of governance we need to return to our underlying individual data sources.

In Table 6.7 we summarise trends in world averages in a number of our individual data sources. Most of the sources in this table are polls of experts, with data extending over the whole period 1996–2007 covered by the aggregate WGI. Other than expert polls, only one of them, GCS, is a survey with a sufficiently standard format to enable comparisons over a reasonable period of time, in this case from 2002 to 2007. The first column reports the number of countries covered by the source in each of the periods shown, and the next three columns present the average across all countries of each of the sources in each of the indicated years. The underlying data have been rescaled to run from zero to one, and for each source and governance component, we report the score on the same question or average of questions that we use in the aggregate indicator. The next two columns report the standard deviation across countries for each source. The final column reports the change in the global average of each indicator over the longest period for which it is available, together with a t-statistic associated with a test of the null hypothesis that the world average score has not changed.

The picture that emerges from Table 6.7 is sobering, as there appears not to be strong evidence of a significant trend of improvements in governance worldwide over the 12 years of data covered in the table. Over this period, the average change in the global averages of these indicators is very small at only 0.02, on a scale from zero to one. While two-thirds of changes are positive (27 out of 41), only one-third of the changes in either direction are significantly different from zero at the 90 per cent confidence level. Of these, five register declines and nine improvements. This quite mixed picture suggests that there is substantial disagreement among sources about even the direction of changes in global averages of governance. As a result, we cautiously conclude that

Table 6.7 *Global Trends in Governance Indicators 1996–2007 for Selected Sources*

	Sample Average			Std Dev Across Ctrys			
	Sample	1996	2007	1996	2007	Change 96–07[*]	T-stat
Voice and Accountability							
EIU	120	0.41	0.47	0.25	0.26	0.06	1.79
FRH	194	0.56	0.58	0.29	0.28	0.02	0.66
GCS (Press Freedom / Parliament)	94	0.57	0.46	0.15	0.16	−0.11	−4.76
HUM	155	0.63	0.62	0.34	0.30	−0.01	−0.33
PRS	140	0.63	0.67	0.25	0.25	0.04	1.28
WMO	182	0.54	0.58	0.27	0.25	0.04	1.28
RSF	137	..	0.71	..	0.22	..	..
Political Stability and Absence of Violence							
DRI	106	0.82	0.85	0.18	0.15	0.04	1.53
EIU	120	0.56	0.60	0.25	0.22	0.04	1.27
GCS (cost of terrorism)	95	0.66	0.75	0.17	0.13	0.09	3.98
HUM	155	0.63	0.59	0.29	0.26	−0.04	−1.34
PRS[*]	140	0.70	0.73	0.13	0.11	0.03	1.86
WMO	182	0.67	0.68	0.25	0.22	0.01	0.54
Government Effectiveness							
CPIA	125	0.41	0.50	0.16	0.13	0.09	4.87
DRI	106	0.57	0.73	0.28	0.21	0.16	4.75
EIU	120	0.43	0.37	0.31	0.26	−0.06	−1.69
GCS (infrastructure quality)	95	0.54	0.51	0.24	0.23	−0.03	−0.86
PRS[*]	140	0.58	0.54	0.24	0.28	−0.04	−1.33
WMO	182	0.53	0.57	0.24	0.23	0.04	1.54
Regulatory Quality							
CPIA	125	0.50	0.55	0.14	0.14	0.05	2.83
DRI	106	0.82	0.86	0.16	0.13	0.04	2.21
EIU	120	0.54	0.56	0.22	0.22	0.02	0.73
GCS (burden of regulations)	95	0.30	0.38	0.13	0.13	0.08	4.44

Table 6.7 (*cont.*)

	Sample	Sample Average		Std Dev Across Ctrys			
		1996	2007	1996	2007	Change 96–07[*]	T-stat
HERITAGE	153	0.54	0.51	0.17	0.19	−0.03	−1.36
PRS	140	0.41	0.72	0.13	0.23	0.31	14.23
WMO	182	0.55	0.60	0.25	0.25	0.04	1.68
Rule of Law							
CPIA	125	0.40	0.42	0.17	0.15	0.02	1.23
DRI	106	0.71	0.81	0.20	0.17	0.10	3.86
EIU	120	0.49	0.53	0.27	0.24	0.04	1.30
GCS (organized crime / police / independent judiciary)	94	0.57	0.60	0.21	0.19	0.03	1.18
HERITAGE	153	0.57	0.46	0.23	0.24	−0.11	−4.05
HUM	155	0.60	0.40	0.35	0.42	−0.20	−4.54
PRS	140	0.72	0.63	0.23	0.22	−0.09	−3.53
QLM	115	0.45	0.44	0.29	0.30	−0.01	−0.29
WMO	182	0.57	0.59	0.24	0.22	0.02	0.82
Control of Corruption							
CPIA	125	0.38	0.42	0.16	0.16	0.04	1.95
DRI	106	0.58	0.67	0.26	0.27	0.09	2.55
EIU	120	0.35	0.38	0.33	0.31	0.02	0.51
GCS (bribe frequency)	95	0.64	0.59	0.19	0.19	−0.05	−1.85
PRS	140	0.59	0.43	0.21	0.20	−0.16	−6.61
QLM	115	0.39	0.37	0.29	0.29	−0.02	−0.57
WMO	182	0.50	0.53	0.27	0.25	0.03	0.98
				Average	0.02		
				# Significant Increases	9		
				# Significant Decreases	5		

[*] Note that changes for GCS are calculated over 2002–2007 and for WMO and CPIA over 1998–2007

[**] Note that there are small increases in the number of countries covered between 1996 and 2007 on HER and PRS.

we do not have as yet any convincing evidence of significant improvements in governance worldwide. We also note that this evidence is consistent with our choice of units for the aggregate governance indicators, which are scaled to have a mean of zero in each period, and as a result relative and absolute changes in country scores on the WGI are likely to be quite similar.

4. Conclusions

In this paper we have reported on the latest update of the Worldwide Governance Indicators for 2007. The WGI are available biannually since 1996, and annually for the six-year period 2002–2007. These aggregate indicators reflect the views of a diverse range of informed stakeholders, including tens of thousands of household and firm survey respondents, as well as thousands of experts working for the private sector, NGOs, and public sector agencies. As such, the WGI predominantly relies on the reports from non-state actors. Further, we report the individual indicators underlying the aggregate WGI. It is our hope that this timely annual reporting, as well as providing access to individual indicators, are making the aggregate indicators more useful to users in academic and policy-making circles.

We nevertheless emphasise to all users the limitations of these measures of governance, which are shared by virtually all efforts to measure governance across countries and over time. The aggregate indicators we construct are useful for broad cross-country and over-time comparisons of governance, but all such comparisons should take appropriate account of the margins of error associated with the governance estimates. These margins of error are not unique to our perceptions-based measures but are present – if not explicitly acknowledged – in any effort to measure governance. They naturally reflect the inherent difficulty in measuring something as complicated and multifaceted as governance. However, we have shown the feasibility of using the aggregate indicators to make comparisons of governance across countries and over time, subject to appropriate consideration of margins of error. In this paper we also gave a brief account of the evolution of the WGI over the past decade or so, including how the margins of error have declined over time, mostly due to the increasing availability of individual sources. Thus, while margins of error remain non-trivial, it is worth noting that for the current 2007 data we see that 65 per cent of all cross-country comparisons result in highly significant differences (at 90 per cent confidence levels), and that about one-third of countries have experienced substantial changes in at least one dimension of governance between 1998 and 2007.

We also caution users that the aggregate indicators can in some circumstances be a rather blunt tool for policy advice at the country level. We expect that the provision of the underlying data will help users in identifying – and acting upon – more specific aspects of governance that may be problematic in a given country. And we also encourage using these aggregate and individual indicators in conjunction with a wealth of possibly more detailed and nuanced sources of country-level data and diagnostics on governance in formulating policy advice.

References

Kaufmann, D., A. Kraay and P. Zoido-Lobatón (1999a). 'Aggregating Governance Indicators'. World Bank Policy Research Working Paper No. 2195, Washington, D.C.

Kaufmann, D., A. Kraay and P. Zoido-Lobatón (1999b). 'Governance Matters'. World Bank Policy Research Working Paper No. 2196, Washington, D.C.

Kaufmann, D., A. Kraay and P. Zoido-Lobatón (2002). 'Governance Matters II – Updated Indicators for 2000/01'. World Bank Policy Research Working Paper No. 2772, Washington, D.C.

Kaufmann, D., A. Kraay and M. Mastruzzi (2004). 'Governance Matters III: Governance Indicators for 1996, 1998, 2000, and 2002'. *World Bank Economic Review.* **18**: 253–87.

Kaufmann, D., A. Kraay and M. Mastruzzi (2005). 'Governance Matters IV: Governance Indicators for 1996–2004'. World Bank Policy Research Working Paper No. 3630. Washington, D.C.

Kaufmann, D., A. Kraay and M. Mastruzzi (2006a). 'Measuring Governance Using Perceptions Data', in Susan Rose-Ackerman, ed. *Handbook of Economic Corruption.* Edward Elgar.

Kaufmann, D., A. Kraay and M. Mastruzzi (2006b). 'Governance Matters V: Aggregate and Individual Governance Indicators for 1996–2005'. World Bank Policy Research Working Paper No. 4012. Washington, D.C.

Kaufmann, D., A. Kraay and M. Mastruzzi (2007a). 'The Worldwide Governance Indicators Project: Answering the Critics'. World Bank Policy Research Working Paper No. 4149. Washington, D.C.

Kaufmann, D., A. Kraay and M. Mastruzzi (2007b). 'Growth and Governance: A Reply/Rejoinder'. *Journal of Politics.* **69**(2): 555–62.

Kaufmann, D., A. Kraay and M. Mastruzzi (2007c). 'Governance Matters VI: Aggregate and Individual Governance Indicators for 1996–2005'. World Bank Policy Research Working Paper No. 4280. Washington, D.C.

Kaufmann, D. and A. Kraay (2008). 'Governance Indicators: Where Are We and Where Should We Be Going?' World Bank Research Observer. Spring 2008.

Meisel, N. and J. Ould Aoudia (2007). 'A New Institutional Database: Institutional Profiles 2006'. Documents de Travail de la DGTPE 2007/09.

Seligson, M. (2008). 'The AmericasBarometer Approach to Measuring the Quality of Governance'. Lecture presented at the 'Actionable Governance Indicators Conference', World Bank, Washington, D.C. 24 April 2008.

7

Contending with illicit power
structures: a typology

MICHAEL MIKLAUCIC*

1. Framing the problem

Of the nearly $2 trillion of Official Development Assistance (ODA) given by the major industrialised states since 1950, the vast majority of those funds and associated efforts to improve the lot of people in developing countries have been directed at the formal governmental institutions of the developing states.[1] Historically, the World Bank and regional development banks, as well as many bilateral development agencies, being governmental or inter-governmental organisations themselves, have focused on national budget support, debt relief or capacity-building within state institutions. Over the past two decades, some donors have recognised the central role of the private sector, democracy and good governance in successful development and increased their emphasis on market development, the rule of law, elections, legislatures, local governments and local civil society organisations. These approaches were predicated on the thesis that developmental and governance failures result from deficits in the formal state institutions, or the under-development of markets and traditional civil society.

This chapter seeks to further a complementary thesis: while institutional and civil society deficits certainly contribute to state failure and the lack of development, there is an additional dimension populated by a rogue's gallery of organisations (referred to in this chapter as 'illicit power structures'). These structures inhabit the dark space of the political economy and operate often under the analytic radar. They subvert

---

* Center for Complex Operations, National Defense University, Washington DC; BA, University of California; MSc, London School of Economics.
[1] Organisation for Economic Co-operation and Development 2007, Table: Net ODA from DAC Countries from 1950 to 1960. Available at www.oecd.org/searchResult/0,3400, en_2649_201185_1_1_1_1_1,00.html (last visited 25 March 2008).

and impede democratic consolidation and successful development and they obstruct viable peace in the wake of internal conflict. Private militias, warlords, rogue intelligence networks and criminal enterprises enrich and sustain themselves through hidden economic transactions and disrupt – even subvert – the legitimate processes of governance. This creates an environment in which peace settlements seldom prosper and democracy and development cannot flourish. Like dark matter in astrophysics, the attributes, dispositions, structures and propensities of illicit power structures are not easily or directly detectable. This chapter seeks to shed some light on illicit power structures by looking closely at their ideologies, motivations, methods and morphologies. By examining these closely, it may be possible to get a better sense of their dispositions, propensities and vulnerabilities, and hence to identify more effective strategies and tactics to counter their subversive impacts.

These subversive impacts derive from the utter disregard shown by many illicit power structures towards the wider common interest or 'public good', as distinct from the narrow interests of their own identity group. These structures are predatory and often operate at the expense of the national or common interest as they pursue parochial, non-state and non-public interests; that is, the specific interests of individual clans, ethnic groups, criminal organisations, etc. Many illicit power structures exploit the seams of weak governance to capture wealth belonging to the common patrimony for private gain as well as enriching themselves through inherently illegal activities such as trafficking in contraband. Wealth belonging to the common patrimony might be in the form of minerals, or other natural resources such as timber or oil. Trafficking in contraband includes, in various locations, narcotics, human beings and weapons. Additionally, illicit power structures can capture monopoly control over otherwise legal economic activity, such as the exportation of timber or diamonds, through various corrupt means.

2.   Working definition

The literature on illicit power structures – whether specifically on warlords, mafias, gangs or militias – unanimously laments the absence of analytic precision in the terminology of the subject matter. The imprecision of our current understanding may easily lead to false diagnoses and inappropriate prescriptions. For example, Vinci argues that faulty analysis of the Lord's Resistance Army (LRA) by the Ugandan government resulted in counter-insurgency tactics that only alienated the local population – and essentially misunderstanding the nature of the LRA, which is/was not a popular insurgency, had little impact on its operations. Conversely, improving clarity in the definition and the precision of our understanding of the characteristics of illicit power structures will help field personnel to react to them more effectively.[2]

As a short definition, the following is proposed: *illicit power structures are sub-national, extralegal entities that seek power through the use of either actual or threatened coercion, illegal inducement or charismatic, anti-system leadership. Often supported by criminal economic activity, the leadership of these structures may be situated within or parallel to the state or they may constitute an armed opposition to it. Identity groups that benefit from their patronage will typically regard them as legitimate.* This definition intentionally excludes rogue states and transnational terrorist organisations. These are currently under intense and extensive examination by a plethora of agencies and scholars. Effective responses to such structures are likely to require all the elements of national power including substantial and high-level diplomatic and military contributions, while this framework focuses on how foreign assistance may be useful in neutralising illicit power structures.

3.   Towards a provisional typology

According to Schulz, Farah and Lochard, 'If the United States is to develop an effective policy and strategy to counter the threats posed by armed groups today and in the decades ahead, it must have a clear understanding of their characteristics.'[3] To be effective, a typology of illicit power structures must identify the aspects of an illicit power structure that most fully capture its essence while describing those characteristics that distinguish one from another. Numerous authors have proposed typologies of non-state armed groups. The common weakness of these proposed typologies is that they tend to stress only a single aspect or characteristic of the illicit power structure and thus miss their multi-dimensionality. For example, Stedman's typology of spoilers, while path-breaking and still relevant, distinguishes between organisations only on the basis of their stand with regard to a peace process: either they are implacably opposed to any agreement ('absolute spoilers'), opportunistic negotiators ('greedy spoilers') or reconcilable

---

[2] Vinci, 'The Problems of Mobilization'.   [3] Shultz *et al.*, note 2, at 2.

provided their specific demands are met ('limited spoilers').[4] Shultz, Farah and Lochard propose a taxonomy consisting of insurgents, terrorists, militias and organised crime.[5] Vinci criticises the static brittleness of such taxonomies, adding in warlords and guerillas, explaining that these labels fail to adequately define the proliferation of armed groups, which has emerged since the end of the Cold War. He then proceeds to create a typology based on the mobilising functions of armed groups. Despite his claims to the contrary, this does in fact appear to be 'another taxonomic system',[6] albeit based on the mobilisation of resources.

The typology proposed in this chapter examines illicit power structures through four successive analytic 'prisms', attempting to reach a progressively more granular and multi-dimensional understanding. The four prisms are 1) their ideologies, 2) motivations, 3) actions and 4) structures.

3.1   Ideology

From a field practitioner's vantage point – be the practitioner a state or international official or a third country diplomat or aid official – a critical characteristic of an illicit power structure is its 'ideology'. By that I mean the view its leaders have of the world, including its ideal configuration and their organisation's rightful role or place. If there is a common normative standard for contemporary ideology which defines accepted norms it is, I believe, the acceptance of a rule-based system of democratic states as the fundamental organising principle for the global architecture. This reflects the current evolution of the Westphalian system, governed as it is by the norms of international and domestic behaviour embodied in the UN Charter, the Geneva Conventions and the various conventions and agreements pertaining to state behaviour, prerogatives and responsibilities. Ideologies which do not meet this standard may be characterised by a desire for the radical restructuring of the international order, or sizable parts of the world, in a manner that de-emphasises the state in favour of other organising structures, such as communities of faith, class or ethnic identity. Others may accept the state system but cling to an

---

[4] Stedman, 'Spoiler Problems'.   [5] Shulz, note 2, at 2.
[6] Vinci, 'The Problems of Mobilization'.

earlier norm of sovereignty which permits total latitude by each state with respect to internal governance. Some of these restructurings may be supra-national, while others may be sub-national. However, they all contest the fundamental legitimacy of the existing state system with its associated norms of both internal and external behaviour and thus pose a profound challenge to the core beliefs around which the modern international system is built.

Ultimately what an illicit power structure can be reconciled with depends on the nature of the outcome it seeks and its determination to achieve that outcome. If its desired outcome is fundamentally incompatible with the underlying architecture of a rule-based system of democratic states, it would appear unlikely that an accommodation satisfactory to both the US and the illicit power structure is on the cards. For example, it is hard to imagine how groups seeking to do away with the state system altogether, such as those promoting a global proletarian revolution or a global Islamic caliphate, can be accommodated in a system based on the fundamental values of the so-called modern Westphalian or western system of sovereign individual states.

Pioneering work in analysing the orientations of illicit power structures to their political environment was done by Stedman, in his seminal 1997 paper referred to above.[7] Although this chapter does not argue that illicit power structures and spoilers are coterminous (discussed below), Stedman's conceptualisation is insightful and suggests a similar conceptualisation around the prism of ideology.

As summarized above, Stedman describes absolute spoiler behaviour as immutably and irrevocably opposed to the peace process; absolute spoilers cannot be co-opted or persuaded to participate genuinely by any strategy or tactic. Opposition to both just peace or to democratic consolidation is absolute in the sense that the 'spoilers' are unwilling to engage in the kinds of compromise behaviours necessary to achieve these objectives. In some cases their actions may appear irrational in that no cost seems too high to achieve their own parochial objectives including the ultimate cost of life itself. Therefore cost-benefit calculations are of no use in tempting absolute spoilers to attenuate their demands and requirements and join the process constructively. This

---

[7] Although Stedman wrote only about spoilers to peace processes, the same analysis can be applied to so-called 'governance spoilers'.

analysis can be extended to what I refer to here as absolutist illicit power structures.

There is little chance that an organisation genuinely dedicated to the destruction of the contemporary state system as a whole can be brought into a process of constructive negotiation within the context of that very system.

Limited spoiler behaviour in Stedman's analysis entails holding out for the purpose of leveraging participation for the achievement of specific and limited objectives. The fact that objectives are limited does not necessarily imply that they are insubstantial or easy to accomplish. Regional autonomy, representational quotas, a new constitution, criminal prosecution of current officials and historical reparations are examples of limited objectives that might be extremely difficult to negotiate. Yet, if a compromise can be reached whereby a critical mass of the spoiler's limited objectives can be achieved, the spoiler can be brought effectively into the peace process and into the democratic consolidation. What is of paramount importance to the limited spoiler is the achievement of the limited objective, not subversion of the process or utter defeat of the adversary, let alone destruction of the system itself. Their interests are theoretically compatible with a political solution based on compromise and with some of the interests of other parties to the just peace. The signing by the Mozambican National Resistance (RENAMO) of a peace agreement with the Government of Mozambique in 1992 is an example of the successful engagement of a limited spoiler that was prepared to join the peace process and the process of democratic consolidation in exchange for an assurance of its security and the recognition of its legitimacy.

Those Stedman refers to as 'greedy spoilers' position themselves to gain as much as possible through the negotiating process without threatening their core identity, security and interests. Greedy, or opportunistic spoilers will hold out until they are convinced that further obstruction of the peace process and democratic consolidation will result in an irreversible net loss to their interests. However, unlike limited spoilers, opportunistic spoilers will not be sated in their hunger for additional gain merely by the accomplishment of specific or limited objectives, at least in theory. They will continually weigh the balance of forces, seeking exploitable opportunities to win additional gains – if necessary, at the expense of delaying or risking the peace process and the democratic consolidation.

Stedman's typology has some shortcomings. For example, an organisation may enter, withdraw and re-enter a peace or democracy process in a given day. Moreover, it is generally not crystal clear whether or not participation is genuine, or just a play for time. An organisation's interests and demands tend to remain consistent, but they can also change over time. Can its interests be accommodated within a negotiation process leading to just peace and democratic consolidation? Or do its interests inherently exclude those of other parties with no hope of accommodation? In addition, the 'greedy' or opportunistic spoiler category is inherently difficult to distinguish from a limited spoiler – all parties to negotiations are opportunistic in that they seek the best possible deal for themselves and will negotiate until the point that further demands or dilatory behaviour might compromise the critical mass of gains they require.

The use of the term 'spoiler' itself has been debated widely. Some argue that this term embeds a particular and uni-dimensional normative and subjective content into the discussion that is unsuitable for the cold and rational diplomacy and negotiation required to navigate complex peace and stabilisation processes.[8] For these reasons, this chapter does not accept 'spoilers' and illicit power structures as coterminous. Some spoilers, though not all, are illicit power structures. All illicit power structures can be spoilers, though not all are.

A similar logic to Stedman's makes sense in analysing the disposition of an illicit power structure toward its geo-political context. Some illicit power structures can be coaxed to participate in the rule-based system of democratic states, while others cannot. Instead of absolute, greedy and limited spoilers, this framework distinguishes between those power structures whose ideology and associated interests can be reconciled within the context of the rule-based system of democratic states and those whose interests challenge the basic premises of that system. They will be referred to as absolutist illicit power structures and non-absolutist illicit power structures (see Figure 7.1).

While their disposition can be altered and change over time, absolutist illicit power structures are dedicated and determined to undermine the state system. As such they are recalcitrant and opposed to any compromise with state or international authorities which sustain the

---

[8] In a series of workshops organised by the Office of the Coordinator for Reconstruction and Stabilisation of the US State Department (S/CRS), from January through May 2006, in Washington, DC, General William Nash (Ret.) argued tirelessly against using the term 'spoiler' on the basis that a group which might seem to be a spoiler today might turn into an ally tomorrow and that a spoiler from one perspective might be a saviour from another.

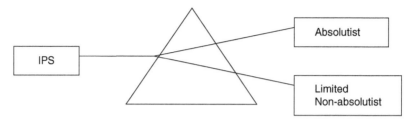

Figure 7.1   Prism 1 – Ideology

state-centric order. This presents a powerful and direct challenge to the prevailing international system.

3.2   Motivation

Motivation constitutes the second 'prism' for analysing the distinctions among illicit power structures. There is a burgeoning literature on economic motivations for civil war, with some arguing that greed is the central motivator, while others argue that grievance or need is the root source of conflict. There are also those who argue that conflict may be fuelled by creed (beliefs or ideology).

A common assumption among political scientists and international relations scholars has been that conflict is caused by deprivation either of a fair share of the public goods provided by state authorities or recognition of certain elements of the identity of sub-state groups. This assumption leads to the conclusion that material or 'identity needs' are the root of conflict and that if satisfied, the conflict might be resolved.

In studying the intra-state conflicts of the 1990s, scholars and some practitioners began to examine the causes of intractable conflicts and the motives of belligerents. In a paper published in 1998, British political scientist David Keen argued persuasively that we cannot assume resolution of the conflict, peace, the cessation of hostilities or, by extrapolation, democratic consolidation are objectives shared by all or any of the belligerents in a conflict.[9] Keen's insight was that some belligerents benefit substantially from conflict and therefore protect their material interests by fuelling and sustaining conflict. These are often referred to as 'conflict entrepreneurs'. The motivation of so-called conflict entrepreneurs is the same as any other entrepreneur: profit. This reflects the

---

[9] Keen, 'Economic Function'.

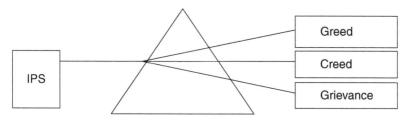

Figure 7.2   Prism 2 – Motivation

'greed' motivation, which has had some persuasive proponents. Paul Collier of the World Bank and Anke Hoeffler argue that conflict is fuelled and sustained by greed and economic considerations.[10] They conclude that opportunity (availability of finance, opportunity cost and risk) is the key explanatory factor in understanding conflict and thus dismiss as less important motivations based on need.

The work of Collier and Hoeffler engendered a significant counter-literature, which argued that identity politics remains a critical motivating factor in civil war, along with relative deprivation. Today the debate over the competing roles of 'need', 'greed', and 'creed' in fuelling internal conflict appears to have dissipated somewhat as further study and examination have produced a more nuanced understanding.[11] Another of Keen's insights is that motivations are subject to change over time: a conflict may originate in need or grievance and evolve into a conflict over access to, and profit, from resources. Zartman argues that trying to attribute motivation exclusively to greed, creed or need is fruitless, while stating that material considerations play a role in all political conflict is banal. His position is that it is the interplay between greed, creed and need that is of causal interest.[12]

It is assumed here that most conflict is probably motivated by a combination of key factors involving the interplay of greed, need and creed (see Figure 7.2). Nevertheless it still can be useful to attempt to identify the dominant factor at any given point in time in order to understand the dynamics behind an organisation's behaviour and especially to develop mitigating tactics.

---

[10] Collier and Hoeffler, 'Greed and grievance'.
[11] See for instance Ballantine, 'Conclusion'; or Collier, Hoeffler and Rohner, 'Beyond greed and grievance'.
[12] See Zartman, 'Need, Creed and Greed'.

3.3   Methods

Whatever the source of the power of an illicit power structure, it can exert that power through violence or coercion, through inducement or offering material reward, or through normative leadership, sometimes referred to as legitimacy. The sources of its power may determine the degree to which an illicit power structure can obstruct peace and democratic development as well as determining its modality. This is the proposed third analytic 'prism' for creating the typology. How does it maintain membership and internal discipline? How does it engage with other political elements in the political process? How does it attempt to intervene in the peace process or the democratisation process? Through violence or the threat of violence? Through bribery or offering economic rewards? Through evangelism for a higher conceptual basis for society or other-worldly cause?

The power of an illicit power structure – its ability to exert significant influence over the processes of peace and democratic consolidation – may derive from financial sources, weapons, propensity to engage in violent behaviour or the number and quality of fighters at its command. However, there are limited methods by which such assets may be applied to exercise power. As early as 1968, the sociologist Amitai Etzioni identified three modalities of the exercise of power by an organisation:

> Power, analytically, can be exhaustively classified according to the means of control applied. If they are symbolic, such as gestures and signals, we refer to the power as normative. If they are material objects, or cash used to obtain them, we refer to the power as remunerative. If they are physical means which entail contact with the body of those subjected to power, such as inflicting pain, deformity or death, we refer to coercive power.[13]

Although they will most frequently be used in combination, he argued that one modality will prevail for any given organisation based on its function.

Etzioni distinguished between assets and power. Nonetheless, it is obvious that the type of assets available to an organisation will be related to the way in which it exercises power. As illicit power structures mainly derive their power from financial or paramilitary resources, we should not be surprised that the most common modalities of exercising power are remunerative and coercive. However, for certain specific populations, a given illicit power structure may have legitimacy due to clan,

---

[13] Etzioni, 'Organizational Dimensions'.

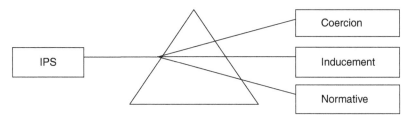

Figure 7.3   Prism 3 – Methods

ideological or patronage relationships and in such cases power may be of a normative nature (see Figure 7.3).

Though not proposed as a fundamental prism of analysis for this typology, it is nonetheless worth briefly discussing the range of sources of power. Financial revenues are discussed in more detail below. There are illicit power structures that do not have or need access to significant financial resources as their behaviour and activities are non-capital-intensive. For example, the LRA, which has terrorised the rural areas and villages of northern Uganda since the late 1980s, has done so with light weapons and low-cost terrorist tactics. Illicit power structures may depend on stolen weapons or inflict violence and terror with primitive weapons or they may exert influence through possession of especially lethal or feared weapons. They may influence processes of peace and democratic consolidation through the mere threat of violence by their minions.

It should be clear that to the extent that an illicit power structure utilises coercion to accomplish its political objectives, it challenges the state's monopoly on the *legitimate* use of force, according to which the state alone can legitimately discipline individuals and must protect individuals from coercion or violence applied by other agencies. By challenging the state's monopoly on the use of force, an illicit power structure also strikes at the state's unique capacity to provide the social good of security. Through the use of force, illicit power structures create a parallel system of social goods and social control upon which state legitimacy is based. Thus they undermine the state's legitimacy.

3.4   Morphology

Organisations can also be distinguished by the manner in which they are structured. This constitutes a fourth analytic 'prism' proposed for developing the typology of illicit power structures. Hierarchical organisations have a clear and generally linear chain of command, with well-defined superior/subordinate relationships and a series of levels of seniority with declining authority from the top down. Other organisations are radial based on a central command authority with linear relationships with a variety of satellite entities, which do not typically have relationships with each other. Some organisations evolve or devolve as leaderless networks the cells or elements of which operate with a very high degree of autonomy. Each of these has different propensities, operational methods and – perhaps most important – vulnerabilities. Does this small list exhaust the possible generic morphologies of illicit power structures? Undoubtedly not.

The study of organisational structure has recently been applied to the examination of terrorist organisations and this research sheds important light on the inner workings of illicit power structures. The importance of their organisational architecture will become evident as strategies for mitigating their influence are explored.

Dishman provides several basic topographies of terrorist organisations that can be usefully applied to illicit power structures, distinguishing between hierarchical, networked and leaderless organisations.[14]

Hierarchical organisations operate on the basis of top-down leadership and decision making with authority ultimately devolving from the top of the leadership pyramid (see Figure 7.4). The hierarchical organisation is structured to facilitate top-to-bottom guidance. The chain of command is generally clear and streamlined. Such organisations often have a fairly well developed division of labour and are subject to the bureaucratic phenomenon known as 'stove-piping'. Only the highest ranks are fully appraised of the extent of the activities, assets, interests, etc. of the organisation. At lower levels, personnel are often provided with information on a 'need to know' basis only. Yet, most elements within the organisation are aware of the structure and are familiar with both supervisory and subordinate elements, as well as lateral elements. Warlord militias are often structured in this fashion.

A networked, or decentralised, cell organisation is loosely structured and can have multiple leaders with shifting functions and responsibilities. Decision making is usually decentralised, encouraging autonomy, local initiative and flexibility. The durability of such a structure, however, is dependent on the degree to which the cells in the network share goals

[14] Dishman, 'The Leaderless Nexus'.

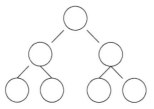

Figure 7.4   Hierarchical Organization

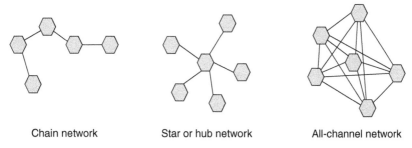

Chain network   Star or hub network   All-channel network

Figure 7.5   Networked Organizations (borrowed directly from The Advent of Netwar (Revisited))

and objectives and a similar level of commitment.[15] The Zapatista Movement that emerged in southern Mexico in the 1990s is an example of a networked power structure. Arquilla and Ronfeldt describe several variations of networked organisations, including chain, hub and all-channel networks.

The chain network, as seen in Figure 7.5, connects multiple nodes in a linear pattern, which permits communication or interaction only in a specified manner. Contact between nodes at either end must pass through intermediaries. In a star – or hub or radial – network, cells are each tied by a radial line to the leader, or 'hub', but have little or no connectivity amongst them or familiarity with, or awareness of, each other. Only the 'leader', or the hub element, is aware of the structure. The radial elements are more or less coequal in status, but each must go through the hub to communicate with any other. In the all-channel network all nodes are connected to all other nodes. The organisational

[15] Arquilla and Ronfeldt 2001, 'The Advent of Netwar'; Weiss and Bump, *Remittances in Conflict and Crises.*

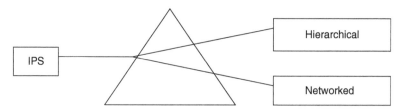

Figure 7.6   Prism 4 – Morphology

structure is generally flat and effectiveness depends on communication-intensive behaviour. The all-channel network can be mobilised very rapidly as direction and/or directives are disseminated nearly simultaneously to all cells (see Figure 7.5).

The so-called 'leaderless nexus' almost defies the common understanding of structure, as its internal relationships are very vague and often exceedingly fluid. In a leaderless organisation there are no leaders – only perpetrators – involved in an attack. Such an organisation lacks a clear chain of command or fixed hierarchy and its various cells are self-sufficient and autonomous. They typically operate ignorant of each others' identities but with resolute commitment to a common set of beliefs.[16] Current anecdotal observation suggests that such organisations are becoming more common as modern information and communication technology and capability spread widely throughout the world and the cost barriers to the use of this technology become easily surmountable.[17] For purposes of the proposed model these 'leaderless' organisations will be considered networked structures, though the emphasis might be understood as on the 'network' rather than on the 'structure'.

There are other elements to be considered in describing the morphology of an organisation (see Figure 7.6), for example its structural connectivity to external and other internal actors. How does it finance its illicit activity? Is it fuelled by remittances from a diaspora and/or from illegal natural resource exploitation, trafficking in contraband or black-market trading in ordinary commercial items? Is its personnel tribe- or clan-based, class-based, geographically localised or dispersed? How is it

---

[16] Asian Development Bank 2007, *Key Indicators*. Available at www.adb.org/Documents/Books/Key_Indicators/2007/pdf/Special-Chapter-2007.pdf, Tables 2.1 and 2.5 (last accessed 26 March 2008).

[17] Peoples' Global Action (or PGA) is an example. See www.nadir.org/nadir/initiativ/agp/index.html.

related to traditional forms of social organisation? What kinds of armaments does the illicit power structure have and from where and how are they obtained? These questions must be examined to fully articulate the morphology.

3.5   Conclusion on typologies

We are still in the early stages of understanding the phenomenon of illicit power structures. Previous efforts to develop typologies and taxonomies must be considered preliminary, as is the typology proposed here. In the social sciences we tend to fret over the difficulty of accurately describing our subject matter, but this problem is not limited to the social sciences. This was true for centuries in the so-called hard sciences and remains the case in many sub-disciplines of physics, astronomy and biology among others. The four successive analytic steps suggested in the preceding sections lead to a typology consisting of 36 variants or types of illicit power structures (see Figure 7.7). This typology acknowledges the unlikelihood or even impossibility of pure types. No illicit power structure will fit perfectly into any specific category. Each illicit power structure is likely to combine multiple characteristics at each stage of analysis and change characteristics over time as well.

Such a typology is most useful if it is used to create a narrative that leads to actionable conclusions and analytically supports specific strategic courses of action and tactics to neutralise the subversive impact of illicit power structures. The application of the proposed typology maps out an approach whereby the analysis of each successive prism brings us ever closer to an accurate description and understanding of the specific illicit power structure, even if we may never reach a perfectly accurate understanding. It is hoped that by examining illicit power structures through this set of prisms, field operators will have a better understanding of their propensities, vulnerabilities and capacities, leading to more effective strategies for dealing with them. More granular analysis can certainly elicit additional variants, therefore these categories cannot be considered to be comprehensive.

The effort is meant to compromise comprehensiveness in favour of manageability and yet cover a significant majority of the illicit power structures encountered in the process of establishing just peace and democratic consolidation.

The 36 variants of illicit power structures derived from this process are theoretical, that is, they are logical possibilities according to the model.

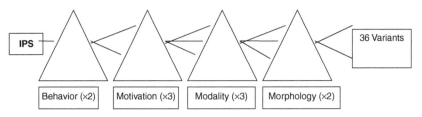

Figure 7.7   A typology of illicit power structures

However, they must be tested in the field to determine if they indeed describe satisfactorily existing illicit power structures. Some variants may not exist in real life. For example, it is difficult to imagine an absolutist illicit power structure whose behaviour is intransigent, motivated by greed, whose modus operandi is one of normative leadership structured as a leaderless network. Such an organisation does not appear to make sense at first glance: if motivated by greed, compromise with a dose of material reward (opportunism) rather than intransigence would seem more logical. The test will be in the field.

Field testing will also help identify effective strategies for countering the influence, or mitigating the negative impact, of illicit power structures the process of by providing insight into their strengths and vulnerabilities. This is of course the purpose of the typology – to assist in developing more effective responses to the challenges posed by illicit power structures to the establishment of peace and democracy.

4.   The case of the Communist Party of Nepal (Maoist)[18]

Nepal is a relatively small, extremely poor state, with a youthful population of approximately 25 million and a very modest natural economic endowment. The sources of conflict in Nepal are multiple and profound. They include an economic resource base that (in its current state) can only support the existing population at levels of destitute poverty, intrastate regional rivalries that pit North against South and both against the centre of the country, as well as a caste system that has historically disadvantaged large segments of the population. The Communist Party

---

[18] This brief review of the Communist Party of Nepal (Maoist), using the Illicit Power Structures analytic framework, is based on an in-country assessment in Spring 2007, by the author and Dr Thomas Marks, Chair, Department of Irregular Warfare of the National Defense University. The analysis presented here is that of the author.

of Nepal (Maoist) (CPN(M)) waged an insurgency beginning in 1996 that had resulted in over 13,000 deaths by the signing of the Comprehensive Peace Agreement in November 2006. Moreover the insurgency hobbled the country by making large swathes of it – as much as 75 per cent according to some accounts[19] – effectively ungovernable by national authorities.

Although the CPN(M) has always limited its activities to Nepal, it has participated since its origins in an international movement of revolutionary organisations. This ideology clearly fits within the parameters of the 'absolutist illicit power structures'. Over time, however, it appears that the ideology driving the CPN(M) has evolved from one fixed on a global Maoist revolution to a more 'nationalist' disposition,[20] a position that is more compatible with the existing international state system. CPN(M) engaged the so-called Seven Party Alliance (SPA) of traditional Nepali political parties in a negotiation process in April 2006, based on an agreement to marginalise the Nepali monarchy and conduct a Constituent Assembly or national constitutional congress. Arguably, this engagement signifies an acknowledgement of the legitimacy of a negotiated compromise outcome within the context of a rule-based, state-dominated system.

Some argue that the CPN(M)'s decision to enter negotiations and end hostilities resulted from a cold calculation that the military struggle had stalled and could not alone yield CPN(M)'s desired outcome. They argue forcefully that the shift from armed struggle to negotiation is merely tactical, disguising the ongoing objective of absolute and exclusive Maoist rule of Nepal. Whether or not this is true, the CPN(M) has accepted in practice the constraints of a negotiated process situated in a system of states. There is therefore a basis to believe the CPN(M) might be engaged in such a way that it either comes to accept the concept of a rule-based system of democratic states (in fact and principle), or finds itself tangled in an institutional web of commitments and relationships that result in behaviour consistent with such beliefs.

This has implications for field planners. Importantly the shift in CPN(M) behaviour, whether tactical or strategic, marks an improvement

---

[19] Asian Centre for Human Rights 2005, Nepal: The Maoists' conflict and impact on the rights of the child: An alternate report to the United Nations Committee on the Rights of the Child on Nepal's 2nd periodic report (CRC/CRC/C/65/Add.30) Geneva, Switzerland, New Delhi. Available at: www.achrweb.org/reports/Nepal/Nepal-CRC-0305.pdf.

[20] The CPN(M) was described as 'nationalist' in its outlook by Dr Jeffrey Key, at a briefing on 13 July 2007 in Washington, DC.

in the situation. As successful as the CPN(M) may have been in depriving the Government of Nepal of true sovereignty in much of the country, it was never itself able to hold any significant territory and the self-inflicted costs of the CPN(M) military approach ultimately became unsustainable. Here, the Government of Nepal's apparently effective strategy of applying the Nepal Army in a counter-insurgency mode for the past five years should be acknowledged. However, now that the CPN(M) has essentially abandoned the outright insurgency, the military counter-insurgency approach may well have accomplished all that it can accomplish. An evolution towards further inducement and co-optation should provide positive reinforcement to the CPN(M) leadership for embracing non-violent tactics and legitimate political competition.

What motivates the cadres of the CPN(M)? The question is simpler than the answer. The top leadership of the CPN(M), in particular Prachanda and Battarai, are educated Brahmins, who allegedly feel a strong commitment to the ideological principles of Maoism (however this is construed) and therefore may be understood to be driven by their beliefs or their creed. The CPN(M) foot soldiers, on the other hand, include a cross-section of the deprived within Nepal, drawing people from lower castes, ethnic and linguistic minorities and women. In a country as poor as Nepal, it requires no stretch of imagination to recognise the widespread experience of grievance and realise the driving power of need. The gap between the 'haves' and 'have-nots' in Nepal is the biggest in Asia and the fastest growing during the 1990s and 2000s of any other country in the region.[21] Thus, while there is a commitment to the Maoist ideological creed, the conclusion that the CPN(M) insurgency was need- or grievance-driven is credible. Even though the insurgency in the Nepali countryside has been brutal and economically devastating, there is little indication that CPN(M) leaders or rank-and-file members systematically used the insurgency for venal purposes, such as personal enrichment, casting doubt on any possible allegations of a widespread greed motivation.

If this thumbnail analysis is correct and the CPN(M) is driven primarily by need (or grievance), the obvious response is to examine and address the need (or grievance) to the greatest extent possible. Political development to create a more equitable dispensation of resources and more participatory and inclusive governance, accompanied by policies to create economic opportunity, will both ameliorate the suffering of those

---

[21] See above note 13.

with the most acute needs, while creating political space to air grievances and modify the social contract. If such policies can be effectively introduced in Nepal they should have potential to lessen the attractiveness of the CPN(M)'s revolutionary message, resulting in attrition among the CPN(M)'s ranks or adaptation of the CPN(M)'s message to reflect a less adversarial stance.

Throughout the decade of insurgency the CPN(M) effectively brutalised the Nepali countryside, eventually driving the state authorities out of a large part of the country. Their campaign embraced multiple lines of activity, following traditional Maoist doctrine, including the so-called 'mass line', 'united front', 'political warfare', 'international action' and military or armed violence. During the final several years there is no doubt that the predominant line of action was the armed struggle and the CPN(M) utilised both physical coercion and menace (the threat of coercion) as political tools to expand its influence. Since the ceasefire and Comprehensive Peace Agreement of November 2006, the level of armed violence has significantly decreased. However, as neither the CPN(M) nor its affiliates have abandoned armed violence and the threat of violence, this continues to be salient.

The CPN(M) has indicated its intent to compete for positions in the Constituent Assembly election (currently planned for November 2007). Critical questions are whether or not the CPN(M) will permit unimpeded campaigning by competitors in areas under its influence and whether or not it will rein in its affiliated Young Communist League (YCL)[22] and other front groups and stop menacing the local populations with intimidation and the threat of violence. The ongoing use of intimidation leads to the conclusion that coercion remains an important method of exerting its influence, even if no longer the predominant method. However, this development is not irreversible and efforts to discourage and raise the costs of violent and coercive behaviour should be sustained. Such efforts might work towards the conversion of the mindset of the CPN(M) cadres and leadership, or towards the creation of a web of institutional and personal commitments through public statements, legal agreements, etc., from which it would be difficult or embarrassing to withdraw.

The CPN(M) is a hierarchical organisation, like Maoist parties generally, and is led by its charismatic Chairman, Pushpa Kamal Dahal (also known as Comrade Prachanda). According to the South Asia Terrorism Portal,

---

[22] Although nominally independent there is little doubt that the YCL responds to the command of the CPN(M) leadership.

Structurally, the CPN-M consists of the standing committee at the top, followed by the politburo, central committee, regional bureaus, sub-regional bureaus, district committees, area committees, and cell committees. The Politburo issues directives with the assistance of an approximately 25-member central committee. The main armed component reportedly consists of six guerrilla battalions, which launch military action in response to instructions relayed through their individual chief commissars (one per battalion), who are central committee members. The politburo and standing committee reportedly formulate most of the political and strategic policies. The standing committee, with approximately ten members, is the most powerfully body in the CPN-M. There are five regional bureaus: Eastern, Central, Kathmandu Valley, Western and International department.[23]

There has allegedly been a loosening of the organisational hierarchy due to the engagement of the CPN(M)'s leadership in the peace process. Field cadres are said to be exercising a greater degree of autonomy. Although this may be the case, most interlocutors agree that CPN(M) remains a 'top-down' organisation in which major decisions, including those related to the peace process, organisational matters, overall direction and significant field activities, are reserved for senior leaders.

It is possible that those leaders currently have less direct control over the day-to-day behaviour of the cadres. For example, it is not clear that the CPN(M) leadership exerted operational control over Maoist cadres during the March 2007 Terai incidents, which resulted in substantial casualties.[24] Such decreased operational control could be a conscious attempt by leaders to create plausible denial where CPN(M) cadres use violence; however, we cannot know this with certainty. What we do know is that significant tension has appeared since the beginning of the peace process and that certain CPN(M) leaders and members have dissented from recent directions and developments.[25] There is also growing evidence of discord and even 'revolt' within the Maoist rank and file, with

---

[23] South Asia Terrorism Portal (07/27/07). Available at: satp.org/satporgtp/countries/nepal/terroristoutfits/index.html (last accessed 26 March 2008).

[24] International Crisis Group 2007, 'Nepal's Troubled Tarai Region', *Asia Report No. 136*, International Crisis Group, Kathmandu/Brussels, Available at: www.crisisgroup.org/library/documents/asia/south_asia/136_nepal_s_troubled_tarai_region.pdf (last accessed 26 March 2008).

[25] International Crisis Group 2005, 'Nepal's Maoists: Their Aims, Structure and Strategy', *Asia Report No. 132*, International Crisis Group, Kathmandu/Brussels. Available at www.crisisgroup.org/library/documents/asia/south_asia/132_nepal_s_maoists_purists_or_pragmatists.pdf.

local violent behaviour contradicting and embarrassing the national Maoist leadership.[26]

If it is real, the gradual loosening of the hierarchical rigidity of the CPN(M) has practical implications. It should no longer be assumed that any message sent out from the CPN(M) Politburo or even the Standing Committee will be rapidly transmitted to, or rigorously obeyed by, the field cadres. It can no longer be assumed that they are under tight control. A strategy aimed at exploiting the widening gaps between the CPN(M) leadership and the cadres might reinforce organisational attrition and dilute party discipline and reduce party membership.

What can we conclude from this abbreviated review of the current situation of the Communist Party of Nepal (Maoist)? Although originally possessed of a Maoist internationalist revolutionary world view, its recent behaviour indicates a possible evolution toward a state-based world view that is not fundamentally in conflict with the prevailing world view of the other political forces within Nepal, the region or the United States. It is motivated primarily by grievances about gross inequities in the distribution of national political and economic power, grievances that have been addressed successfully in other countries and regions. While not eschewing violent and coercive behaviour, the CPN(M) can be enticed into participating in a non-violent political process that may change the cost/benefit calculus for violence and convert those who are not 'die-hard' revolutionaries to more constructive participants in the political process. The apparent loosening of party discipline and top-down control presents opportunities for positive direct interactions with CPN(M) cadres that were foreclosed during the 'People's War'.

This abbreviated analysis of the CPN(M) lacks the granularity necessary for actual project planning. However, it does suggest how a comprehensive review of the CPN(M) would progress and how it could be used to design an effective strategy. There are indications that a strategy emphasising political engagement of the CPN(M) leadership and addressing the most pressing needs of the Maoist cadres through direct interaction could simultaneously bind the leadership to the democratic political process while detaching them from the cadre base and limiting their ability to cause systematic mischief.

---

[26] 'Out-of-control Nepal Maoists attack police post', *Nepal News.Net* (IANS), Friday 10 August 2007. Available at www.nepalnews.net/story/272278 (last accessed 26 March 2008).

Ideology	Motivation	Modality	Morphology
			Hierarchical
			Networked
		Coercive	
		Remunerative	Hierarchical
		Normative	Networked
			Hierarchical
			Networked
			Hierarchical
			Networked
	Creed	Coercive	Hierarchical
Absolutist	Greed	Remunerative	Networked
	Grievance	Normative	
			Hierarchical
			Networked
			Hierarchical
			Networked
		Coercive	Hierarchical
		Remunerative	Networked
		Normative	
			Hierarchical
			Networked
			Hierarchical
			Networked
		Coercive	Hierarchical
		Remunerative	Networked
		Normative	
			Hierarchical
			Networked
			Hierarchical
			Networked
	Creed	Coercive	
Limited	Greed	Remunerative	Hierarchical
	Grievance	Normative	Networked
			Hierarchical
			Networked
			Hierarchical
			Networked
		Coercive	Hierarchical
		Remunerative	Networked
		Normative	
			Hierarchical
			Networked

Figure 7.8   'Periodic' Table of Illicit Power Structures

Is this a significant departure from the current de facto strategy being pursued by the major international powers and donors? While considerable effort has been put into inducing the CPN(M) leadership into the competitive and non-violent political process, less has been done to address the broad socio-political grievances that sustained the insurgency or to accelerate the weakening of the Maoist party hierarchy. The Constituent Assembly process that is under way could change this dramatically by providing Nepal's various ethnic, regional and other interest groups with more direct and effective means of expressing their political preferences, thus diminishing the attractiveness of confrontational politics associated with the CPN(M).

References

Arquilla, J. and Ronfeldt, D. 2001, 'The Advent of Netwar (Revisited)' in J. Arquilla and D. Ronfeldt (eds.), *Networks and Netwars: The Future of Terror, Crime, and Militancy*, Santa Monica, RAND, 1–25.

Ballantine, K. 2005, 'Conclusion: Beyond Greed and Grievance – Reconsidering the Economic Dynamics of Armed Conflict' in K. Ballantine and J. Sherman (eds.), *The Political Economy of Armed Conflict – Beyond Greed and Grievance*. Boulder, CO, Lynne Rienner Publishers Inc, 259–283.

Collier, P. and Hoeffler, A. 2000, *Greed and Grievance in Civil War*, Policy Research Working Paper Series 2355, Washington, World Bank.

Collier, P, Hoeffler A. and Rohner, D. 2009, 'Beyond Greed and Grievance: Feasibility and Civil War'. *Oxford Economic Papers* vol. **61**(1), 1–27.

Dishman, C. 2005, 'The Leaderless Nexus: When Crime and Terror Converge', *Studies in Conflict and Terrorism*, vol. **28**, 237–52.

Etzioni, A. 1968, 'Organizational Dimensions and Their Interrelationships: A Theory of Compliance' in B. P. Indik and K. Berrien (eds.), *People, Groups, and Organizations*, New York, Teachers College, 94–109.

Keen, D. 1998, '*The Economic Function of Violence in Civil Wars*', Adelphi Paper 320, London, International Institute for Strategic Studies.

Schultz, R. H., Farah, and Lochard, I. V. 2004, *Armed Groups: A Tier-One Security Priority*, INSS Occasional Paper 57, Colorado, USAF Academy.

Stedman, S. J. 1997, 'Spoiler Problems in Peace Processes', *International Security*, vol. **22**, no. 1, 5–53.

Vinci, A. 2006, 'The Problems of Mobilization and the Analysis of Armed Groups,' *Parameters*, Spring, 49–62.

Weiss Fagan, P. and Bump, M. 2006, *Remittances in Conflict and Crises: How Remittances Sustain Livelihoods in War, Crises and Transitions to Peace*,

New York, International Peace Academy/Georgetown University, available at www.ipacademy.org/pdfs/Remittances_ERPT.pdf (last accessed 26 March 2008).

Zartmann, I. W. 2005, 'Need, Creed and Greed in Intrastate Conflict', in C. J. Arnson and I. W. Zartman (eds.), *Rethinking the Economics of War: the Intersection of Need, Creed and Greed*, Washington and Baltimore, The Johns Hopkins University Press, 256–283.

PART II

The legitimacy and accountability of actors and standards

8

Democratic governance beyond the state: the legitimacy of non-state actors as standard setters

STEVEN WHEATLEY[*]

1. Introduction

Non-state actors have emerged as standard setters in the globalised system without, in any formal sense, being legitimated by, or accountable to, those over whom they claim to exercise political authority. This has led to complaints of a 'democratic deficit', notably at the 1999 Ministerial Conference of the World Trade Organization when the 'international system's lack of transparency, accountability, and citizen inclusiveness became a major political issue'.[1] Global governance institutions are viewed as 'remote, bureaucratic, elite-driven and unresponsive to popular will'. To their critics, they appear to allow political and economic elites 'to bypass the onerous processes of persuasion and consensus-seeking that democracy requires'.[2] The focus of this chapter is the democratic deficit experienced by the citizens of democratic states as policy issues are decided outside of their direct control.[3] It outlines the domestic and international aspects of sovereign law-making, before examining the phenomenon of international governance by non-state actors, which sits outside of the Westphalian paradigm of state as 'self-legislator'.

The work argues that the political authority of non-state actors is provided by a recognition of their institutional competence and

---

[*] Reader in International Law and Director of the Centre for International Governance, University of Leeds; LLM (Nottingham, UK); LLB (University of Central England). My thanks to Anne Peters for her comments on a previous version; all errors and arguments remain the responsibility of the author.
[1] Strauss, 'Considering Global Democracy', i.
[2] Keohane, Macedo and Moravcsik, 'Democracy Enhancing Multilateralism', 3–4.
[3] Cf. Michelman, 'The 1996–97 Brennan Center Symposium Lecture', 412.

epistemic authority, which is concerned with 'who should be believed, under what circumstances, and with respect to what issues'.[4] At the level of domestic government, epistemic authority is provided by democratic law-making procedures.[5] Non-state actors do not enjoy inherent epistemic authority: they must make a claim to know better than anyone else what should be done, that is, which normative standards should be applied to which actors in what circumstances. The argument is that epistemic authority is provided by democratic decision-making procedures: inclusive, consensus-seeking processes of reasoned deliberation, with reasons for decisions made public and subject to scrutiny by external actors. The work concludes by highlighting the continuing importance of domestic democratic institutions in ensuring the protection and promotion of private and public autonomy in an age of global legal pluralism.

2.   Sovereign authority

Following the 1648 Treaty of Westphalia, global governance actors constituted a system of sovereign states that divided first Europe and later the entire world into territorial units with clear hierarchical structures of government. The settlement separated sovereignty authority, that is, legitimate(d) political authority, into its internal and external components: domestic and inter-nation law. Internal sovereignty is exercised within a constitutional framework, an idea that emerges following the American War of Independence and French Revolution, and, since the nineteenth century, in accordance with the 'democratic' will of the people, expressed in the idea of popular sovereignty or political self-determination. The territorial sovereign state defined the *demos*; democracy provided the justification for the exercise of coercive political authority in an act of collective *self*-determination in accordance with the principle of political equality of citizens: '*We the people*', and not others, make the laws.

Notwithstanding Robert Dahl's oft-repeated assertion that 'no-one has ever advocated, and no-one except its enemies has ever defined democracy to mean, that a majority would or should do anything it felt an impulse to do',[6] debates around the democratic legitimacy deficit of global governance institutions remain focused on the international

---

[4] Charles, 'Colored Speech', 610.   [5] Cf. Teubner, 'How the Law Thinks', 744.
[6] Dahl, *A Preface to Democratic Theory*, 36.

counter-majoritarian difficulty.[7] Majoritarian conceptions of democracy suggest that political legitimacy is provided by 'aggregating' the votes and/or preferences of citizens to identify where the majority lies on a particular issue. This is a misreading of democratic theory and practice, confusing 'people' and 'majority'.[8] The etymology of 'democracy' lies in the idea of 'popular government', or rule by the people.[9] Four factors combine to suggest a procedural approach to the democratic decision making:

1. reasonable disagreement and imperfect knowledge in political discussions;
2. the recognition of the importance of individual autonomy;
3. the liberal principle of legitimacy, which requires at least hypothetical consent for the exercise of political authority;
4. a commitment to collective decision making which takes into account the interests of others in the political community, but no requirement to take into account the interests of those outside of the political unit: democratic legitimacy requires that government to be responsive to the diverse people of the territory (and not *others*).

Democracy is an ongoing process of debate, deliberation and choice in a given community that provides the justification for the exercise of political authority. In the practice of democracy, it is not possible for all citizens to participate in the process of democratic will-formation: citizens will debate and deliberate in public, whilst law making is formally the responsibility of national parliaments.[10] Democratic legitimacy in the procedural sense focuses on the jurisgenerative process: the deliberative processes within and *between* institutions, the latter of which provides the rationale for the doctrine of the separation of powers and judicial review by courts: the foundational principle of democracy is the 'force of better argument'.[11]

---

[7] See, for example, Follesdal and Hix, 'Why there is a Democratic Deficit in the EU', 537: governance by the EU results in policies that are 'not supported by a majority of citizens in many or even most Member States'. Note the statist conception of majority rule: it is the perspective of majorities within EU Member States that is relevant (not a majority of 'European citizens').

[8] Bellamy and Castiglione, 'The Uses of Democracy', 76.   [9] Oxford English Dictionary.

[10] Habermas, 'Multiculturalism and the Liberal State', 851.

[11] Held, *Models of Democracy*, 18.

3.   Global governance

According to the positive orthodoxy, the hierarchical system of domestic government is complemented by a system of law 'operating between rather than above states'.[12] Public international law is constituted by a complex web of voluntary legal relationships between sovereign states, supplemented by 'pseudo-logical'[13] acts of interpretation of contract-like norms.[14] Law making is the preserve of states and judicial-like bodies that provide authoritative interpretations as to the meaning, scope and extent of international legal obligations. In the words of the Permanent Court of International Justice, the rules of international law binding on states 'emanate from their own free will'.[15] The democratic legitimacy of inter-nation law rests on the principle of sovereign equality, the nature of diplomatic communications, which requires inclusive deliberations through which states must seek a reasoned consensus and, at least in relation to democratic states, on the fact that consent to legal norms, and ongoing participation in legal regimes, constitutes an expression of democratic self-determination: sovereign (democratic) self-determination in the context of inter-nation law.

In the enlarged international community, law making 'is no longer the exclusive preserve of states'[16] (if it ever was). As Paul Berman observes, 'we inhabit a world of multiple normative communities, some of which impose their norms through officially sanctioned coercive force and formal legal processes, but many of which do not.'[17] The *Report of the Commission on Global Governance* refers to the 'many ways individuals and institutions, public and private, manage their common affairs', including 'formal institutions and regimes empowered to enforce compliance, as well as informal arrangements'.[18] Global governance includes both traditional forms of inter-state law making and new forms

---

[12] Gross, 'The Peace of Westphalia', 29.

[13] Morgenthau, 'Positivism, Functionalism', 263.

[14] The Westphalian system does not rest on sovereign consent alone. 'Constitutional' rules include those concerned with membership (i.e. the identification of 'sovereign' political units), the inherent rights of states (e.g. non-intervention) and rules for the establishment of legal relationships (*pacta sunt servanda*, etc.).

[15] Case of the SS 'Lotus', PCIJ, Ser. A, No. 10, 18.

[16] Boyle and Chinkin, *The Making of International Law*, vii.

[17] Berman, 'A Pluralist Approach', 302.

[18] Report of the Commission on Global Governance, *Our Global Neighbourhood* (1995), 2. See also Rosenau, 'Governance, Order', 4.

of international governance by non-state actors.[19] The latter include international organisations formally established by constitutive international law instruments but operating outside the effective control of state parties (the European Union and UN Security Council being the paradigmatic examples); informal 'networks' of national officials seeking to co-ordinate policy in a particular area (for example the Basel Committee on Banking Standards); public–private partnerships (the World Commission on Dams and the Global Fund to fight AIDS, Tuberculosis and Malaria); purely private institutions (the Internet Corporation for Assigned Names and Numbers) and 'communities'[20] of non-state actors, including multinational corporations (the 'Equator Principles') and international non-governmental organisations seeking to establish normative standards.

International governance norms do not fit within the traditional pedigree of international legal sources, as reflected in Article 38(1) of the Statute of the International Court of Justice: 'contract-like' agreements between states (treaties), the practices of states accepted as law (custom), generally accepted principles common to legal systems, and the writings of publicists and decisions of national and international tribunals on points of international law. The standard position is stated by Dinah Shelton: 'We take the view that international law is created through treaty and custom, and thus "soft law" is not legally binding per se.'[21] Soft law norms only become part of ('hard') international law when adopted in a treaty or when they emerge as part of customary international law.[22]

The problem with the standard position is that it fails to explain why 'soft' international law standards are framed in terms of 'law'. Both 'hard' and 'soft' forms of international law define legitimate state behaviour by reference to 'legal norms'; both influence domestic politics, as actors seek to rely on global governance norms in democratic debates; both rely on domestic governmental institutions for their effective implementation; and both rely on a complex 'interpretive community' of formal judicial bodies and other international law officials to 'judge' state conduct against the normative provisions, and in doing so to develop the law.

---

[19] Cf. Slaughter, Tulumello and Wood, 'International Law and International Relations Theory', 371.

[20] 'When several individuals share a common definition of what is legitimate, we say they constitute a community': Hurd, 'Legitimacy and Authority', 388.

[21] Shelton, 'Introduction', 6.   [22] Shelton, 'Editor's Concluding Note', 554.

The distinctive characteristic of soft law is not that it is 'soft', but that it is 'law'. Vaughan Lowe describes 'soft law' as 'norms that are not themselves legally binding but form part of the broader normative context within which expectations of what is reasonable or proper State behaviour are formed'.[23] Global governance norms, both 'hard' and 'soft', establish a 'shared expectation about appropriate behaviour held by a community of actors'.[24] Actions which are 'norm-breaking' generate 'disapproval or stigma'. Those in conformity with the norm receive praise, 'or, in the case of a highly internalised norm, because it is so taken for granted that it provokes no reaction whatsoever'.[25]

The defining characteristic of a non-state 'jurisgenerative' actor is its capacity to establish international governance norms that frame the context for action by states, corporate entities and individuals. To the extent that their jurisgenerative efforts have practical effect, non-state actors exercise political authority, an activity traditionally associated with the state. Law is a social practice concerned with the assertion of authority, where compliance is expected or assumed. Joseph Raz adopts the definition provided by John Lucas: 'A man, or body of men, *has authority* if it follows from his saying "Let X happen", that X ought to happen.'[26] Authority is the ability to change the 'normative situation' of other actors.[27] Law involves the issuing of instructions or 'directives', framed in terms of norms, rules, standards, principles, doctrines, etc. A person requires authority to command, but not to give advice, or request a certain course of action.[28] A person in a position of uncertainty may turn to an expert or expert body (an 'authority') for advice, and may decide to follow that advice, where the reasons advanced by the expert 'tip the balance' of reasons in favour of the outcome suggested. A command is not an additional factor trying to 'tip the balance'; it is expected that the addressee will follow the 'order' of the authority without regard to their own view of the merits of the case, indeed 'without even attempting to form a judgment on the merits'.[29]

In the modern age, the exercise of political authority through law requires justification. Law is a system of social control, but it is not the only system. The system of 'Fairtrade' labelling, which seeks to improve

---

[23] Lowe, *International Law*, 95–96.   [24] Finnemore, *National Interests*, 22.

[25] Finnemore and Sikkink, 'International Norm Dynamics', 892.

[26] Lucas, *The Principles of Politics*, 16, quoted in Raz, *The Authority of Law*, 11 (emphasis in original).

[27] Raz, 'The Authority of Law', 12.   [28] Ibid.,15.   [29] Ibid., 24.

the position of farmers and workers in the developing world through consumers making informed moral decisions, is not required to demonstrate its democratic legitimacy.[30] Effective political advocacy[31] and/or the 'mere' promulgation of standards does not constitute international governance: the exercise of political authority by non-state actors through law. In the identification of a system of 'law', H. L. A. Hart argued that in addition to primary rules of obligation, there must be secondary rules of change and adjudication, 'which specify the ways in which the primary rules may be conclusively ascertained, introduced, eliminated, varied, and the fact of their violation conclusively determined'.[32] The existence of secondary rules distinguishes legal systems from other systems of control, including morality. For Hart, the distinctive nature of law entails '*institutionalised* norm enforcement'.[33] Those systems of primary and secondary rules that are administered by legal officials are 'legal' systems.[34]

Brian Tamanaha accepts that Hart's idea of the union of primary and secondary rules is illuminating, but confines the idea to state law. According to Tamanaha: 'Law is whatever people identify and treat through their social practices as "law".' It does not require the participation of 'legal' officials: 'Any members of a given group can identify what law is, as long as it constitutes a conventional practice.'[35] Law is whatever we attach the label 'law' to, 'and we have attached it to a variety of multifaceted, multifunctional phenomena, including aspects of global governance'.[36] Tamanaha concludes that 'international law is clearly a kind of law'. He also makes reference to the emergent body of international human rights norms, and the role of non-state actors in pressuring governments and corporations through shaming and economic boycotts to eliminate human rights abuses. Although these are not formally part of international law, 'they may later be incorporated as such, and thereby

---

[30] Cf. Bernstein and Cashore, 'Can Non-State Global Governance be Legitimate?', 347.
[31] The action by Greenpeace (supported by a consumer boycott) to prevent the dumping of the oil storage rig Brent Spar was an act of political activism, not international governance, and was framed as such, with the environmental group claiming that the Shell oil company was engaged 'in an act of environment vandalism which future generations would find hard to forgive': quoted in Mankabad, 'Decommissioning of Offshore Installations', 613.
[32] Hart, *The Concept of Law*, 94. The conception is expressly statist, leading to doubts about the status of international law as 'law', 216.
[33] Tamanaha, *A General Jurisprudence*, 137.   [34] *Ibid.*, 142.
[35] *Ibid.*, 166.   [36] *Ibid.*, 193.

acquire the status of law'.[37] Tamanaha provides an illuminating contribution to an idea of law that is not confined to 'Westphalian' state and inter-nation law. His 'radical paring down of Hart's conception of law' is, however, as William Twining observes, ultimately flawed: it would recognise as a legal system any system of rules referred to as law, 'even if it has no functions, is ineffective, has no institutions or enforcement, involves no union of primary and secondary rules, and even if there is no normative element'.[38]

Law is a system of communications ('directives') framed in terms of law, that is, coded legal/illegal (or other binary equivalent),[39] issued by an authority to subjects of the legal regime,[40] with law-actors capable of interpreting the content and application of legal norms,[41] and consequently of developing the law. The interpretive community need not replicate Hart's institutionalised legal officials. In the context of international governance regimes, 'law-declaring fora' may include international institutions established under the international governance regime, domestic and international courts, as well as *ad hoc* tribunals, domestic and regional legislatures; executive entities, (formal) commissions of international publicists (and the 'invisible college of international lawyers'),[42] and international non-governmental organisations. As Harold Hongju Koh observes: 'Together, these law-declaring fora create an "interpretive community" capable of receiving a challenge to a nation's international conduct [and the conduct of other non-state actors], then defining, elaborating, and testing the definition of particular norms and opining about their violation.'[43] The defining features of an international governance regime are the capacity of non-state actors to consider and formulate responses to social, economic and political problems, to establish relatively precise standards (the doctrine of the rule of law), and the capacity, sometimes delegated to, or assumed by,

---

[37] *Ibid.*, 228.   [38] Twining, 'A Post-Westphalian Conception of Law', 221.

[39] See Luhmann, *Law as a Social System*, 93.

[40] The 'authority' may be assumed to exist by the subjects of the legal regime, even in the absence of any formal institutions. Consider for example rules of general international law (*pacta sunt servanda*, etc.). In the case of customary international law, the existence of international law norms is asserted by an 'interpretive' actor, who argues that a social practice in the international community of states and international organisation is binding in terms of law (the 'authority' of international law).

[41] Cf. Johnstone, 'Treaty Interpretation', 371.

[42] See Schachter, 'The Invisible College', 217.

[43] Koh, 'Bringing International Law Home', 650.

third parties, to interpret and apply those standards in relation to the activities of states, individuals and organisations.

The existence of a normative regime is not sufficient to designate the regime an 'international governance regime' for the purposes of global governance through law. A distinction must be made between the exercise of authority and the exercise of *legitimate* authority.[44] The ability to 'command' in terms of framing goals, directives and policies does not accord the right to command.[45] The exercise of global governance through law suggests the exercise of legitimate political authority, leaving the problem of identifying when a global governance institution is pursuing 'good governance' aims in accordance with 'good governance' methods.

Domestic institutions enjoy inherent 'sovereign' authority: the right to 'legislate' normative standards and an expectation that compliance will follow. As Brunnée and Toope observe, state law is inherently 'declaratory': 'the voice of authority speaking to the subject, whose role is to obey'.[46] Backed up by formal *governmental* institutions (and ultimately the possibility of coercive force), state institutions have the capacity to 'authoritatively enforce the law'. This is not the case in relation to non-state actors who must rely on 'non-hierarchical forms of steering'.[47] The authority of non-state actors, that is, the question as to whether or not what they say makes a 'practical difference', will depend in large part on an acceptance of their normative legitimacy on the part of those that they seek to regulate (states, organisations and individuals). Ian Hurd explains: legitimacy contributes to compliance 'by providing an internal reason for an actor to follow a rule. When an actor believes a rule is legitimate, compliance is no longer motivated by the simple fear of retribution, or by a calculation of self-interest, but instead by an internal sense of moral obligation'.[48] The rule 'takes on the quality of being authoritative over the actor. [It] is then in some sense hierarchically superior to the actor'.[49]

In order for non-state actors to exercise political authority (that is, to 'command') they must demonstrate their normative legitimacy, which is provided by evidence of their institutional competence and epistemic

---

[44] On the 'normative authority' of al Qaeda, see Michaels, 'The Re-State-Ment of Non-State Law', 1253.

[45] Cf. Rosenau, 'Governance and Democracy', 29.

[46] Brunnée and Toope, 'International Law and Constructivism', 42.

[47] Risse, 'Global Governance', 289.

[48] Hurd, 'Legitimacy and Authority', 387.   [49] *Ibid.*, 400.

authority. The introduction of international law norms can only be justified by reference to the need to respond to collective action problems, and even then the arguments for their introduction 'have to be of sufficient weight to override any disadvantages connected to the pre-emption of more decentralised rule-making' at the level of domestic government (or below).[50] The recognition of collective action problems (threats to the global environment and from international terrorism, etc.) provides the context and justification for global governance, but it does not tell us which issues should be dealt with by global governance institutions (and in a fragmented system of global governance, which institution) and which at the level of the state.[51] Anne-Marie Slaughter has referred to a foundational principle of 'legitimate difference' in transgovernmental co-operation, reflecting the premise that '"difference" per se reflects a desirable diversity of ideas about how to order an economy or society'.[52] The idea is reflected in the principle of subsidiarity: decisions should be taken as closely as possible to the citizen; consequently, 'the vast majority of governance tasks should still be taken by national government officials'.[53]

Arguments for accepting the legitimacy of international governance by non-state actors invariably concern either the fact that they have been constituted by (democratic) states at a 'constitutional moment' and therefore enjoy inherent political authority, and/or the fact that they promote certain global political and justice 'ends': a globalised economy, the development of 'good governance' practices, the protection of human rights, the eradication of hunger, poverty and preventable disease, the protection of the environment, etc. Additionally, it can be seen that the epistemic authority of non-state actors depends on their normative legitimacy: the voluntary acceptance of domination by actors 'on the grounds that they believe in its normative rightfulness'.[54] The definition combines both the idea of legitimacy as an empirical or social fact, reflected in the attitude of actors to the exercise of political authority, and the idea of 'normative legitimacy', which requires that legal norms are established in accordance with certain *democratic* rules and procedures.[55]

---

[50] Kumm, 'The Legitimacy of International Law', 921.
[51] Jackson, 'Quasi-States, Dual Regimes, and Neoclassical Theory', 519.
[52] Slaughter, 'Disaggregated Sovereignty', 178.
[53] *Ibid.*, 185.   [54] Steffek, 'The Power of Rational Discourse', 6.
[55] *Ibid.*, 5. See also Bernstein, 'Legitimacy in Global Environmental Governance', 142.

The constitutive mechanism and/or instrument establishing a non-state actor cannot by itself provide inherent political authority. First, not all non-state actors are established by a constitutive instrument. Second, even where a non-state actor is established by states through some formal mechanism (including the establishment of an international organisation or formation of a network of government officials) the democratic credentials of participating states is not always relevant and, from the perspective of democratic legitimacy, the participation of non-democracies is problematic. Third, where non-state actors are established by states they do not remain 'creatures' of the multilateral treaty regimes.[56] The 'delegation' of political authority does not absolve a non-state actor from providing a justification for the exercise of authority (and the manner in which authority is exercised) in the particular case. Finally, as Owen Fiss observes, the establishment of an international organisation by sovereign consent cannot provide the organisation with democratic legitimacy as 'consent lies properly within the domain of contracts, not democratic politics'.[57]

4.   International governance *for the people*

The justification for non-state actors exercising a governance function 'is primarily, if not exclusively, instrumental': they must demonstrate that they can provide 'benefits that cannot otherwise be obtained'.[58] Government *for the people*, as Fritz Scharpf observes, derives its legitimacy from its capacity to solve problems requiring collective solutions. It presupposes the existence of a 'constituency' connected by the perception of a range of common interests which justifies the institutional arrangements for collective action. Constituencies need not claim the exclusive, or even primary, loyalty of their members; they may be both territorial and sectoral.[59] As Hauke Brunkhorst observes, non-state actors may make a claim to output-legitimation, 'through the positive effect [they have] for the people or peoples of the world', but they lack input-legitimation due to the absence of direct democratic participation and control.[60] According to Thomas Nagel, the (input-) 'illegitimacy' of non-state actors is reflective of the development of government

---

[56] Charney, 'Universal International Law', 529.   [57] Fiss, 'The Autonomy of Law', 525.
[58] Buchanan and Keohane, 'The Legitimacy of Global Governance Institutions', 422.
[59] Scharpf, *Governing in Europe*, 11.
[60] Brunkhorst, 'Globalising Democracy without a State', 688.

institutions in domestic settings, where 'it appears that sovereignty usually precedes legitimacy.' For Nagel, 'the path from anarchy to justice must go through injustice', which in the context of global governance requires the development of 'effective but illegitimate institutions'.[61]

Andrew Moravcsik makes the point that it is important not to impose more stringent requirements for democratic legitimacy on non-state actors than state actors: the system of global governance should not be compared to some idealised democratic systems, but with 'real world' democracies.[62] Not all issues in domestic democratic settings are decided by directly elected and accountable institutions. Other decision-making institutions include markets, state bureaucracies, judicial bodies, quasi-public bodies, and private organisations.[63] Giandomenico Majone argues that issues are delegated to 'non-majoritarian' bodies because of the problem of credibility: elected governments, with one eye on forthcoming elections, are unlikely to adopt and maintain policies in the face of (short-term) antagonistic public opinion.[64] The fact of delegation suggests a distinction between 'political' issues, which should be decided by elected representatives, and 'administrative' ones, which rely on the ability of non-majoritarian institutions to deliver 'good results' in relation to clearly defined objectives established by democratic institutions (the central bank inflation target being the paradigm example). The legitimacy of non-majoritarian bodies does not depend on their direct political accountability to democratic publics, but on their 'expertise, professional discretion, policy consistency, fairness [and] independence of judgement'.[65]

Governance functions may be 'delegated' to, or 'assumed' by, non-state actors according to this argument where they are more likely to deliver 'good results' than directly elected and accountable majoritarian institutions. Moravcsik himself observes that European Union decision making,[66] including decision making by insulated national representatives, enjoys the greatest political authority in those areas (central banking, constitutional adjudication, economic diplomacy, etc.), in which many advanced industrial democracies 'insulate themselves from direct political contestation'.[67] In a democracy, all government functions are

---

[61] Nagel, 'The Problem of Global Justice', 147.

[62] Moravcsik, 'Is there a "Democratic Deficit" in World Politics?', 337.

[63] Shaffer, 'Parliamentary Oversight of WTO Rule-Making', 633.

[64] Majone, *Regulating Europe*, 41.   [65] *Ibid.*, 286.

[66] On the democratic legitimacy deficit in the European Union, see Goodhart, 'Europe's Democratic Deficits', 567.

[67] Moravcsik, 'In Defence of the "Democratic Deficit"', 613.

ultimately under the control of citizens and their representatives, but there is no requirement that they should be 'immanently under such control'.[68] As Moravcsik observes, modern democracies are 'not populist but constitutional' and constitutional democracy is enhanced by insulating certain issues from majoritarian decision making for the following reasons, alone or in combination:[69] the need for greater attention, efficiency and expertise in areas where most citizens remain 'rationally ignorant' or non-participatory,[70] to dispense justice for individuals and minority groups, notably in the protection of human rights by constitutional courts, and to provide majorities with unbiased representation and to protect against the capture of open political process by powerful (often economic) minority interest groups.[71]

Democratic will-formation, according to Moravcsik, requires that laws enjoy majority support, subject to the conditions that majority rule does not offend against settled constitutional norms, or violate the 'rights' of minorities. The difficulty with this analysis is the sense that the position of the majority can somehow be 'objectively' determined, and that constitutional norms and minority rights are 'objective' and settled, that is, that some issues are not 'political'. In an age of reasonable, and indeed unreasonable,[72] disagreement and imperfect knowledge there are no 'non-political' issues. In domestic settings, public pressure can be brought to bear on non-majoritarian bodies to ensure that they remain broadly responsive to public opinion.[73] Ultimately domestic expertocracies are subject to 'traditional forms of hierarchical supervision by elected representatives'.[74] This is not the case in relation to international governance institutions; as Peter Lindseth observes, there is no 'democratically legitimate hierarchical superior'.[75] Power-wielders in international governance institutions owe their loyalty to the regime, which seeks to overcome collective action problems, and not any people(s), or their representative institutions. There remains then a need to establish the normative legitimacy (and political authority) of a non-state actor, that is, to demonstrate why its claim to know better should be accepted in the particular case. Given that international organisations continue to

---

[68] Moravcsik, 'Conservative Idealism', 312.   [69] Moravcsik, 'What Can We Learn?', 238.
[70] See on this point Dahl, 'A Democratic Dilemma', 29.
[71] Moravcsik, 'In Defence of the "Democratic Deficit"', 614.
[72] See Wheatley, 'Minorities under the ECHR', 770.   [73] Bellamy, 'Still in Deficit', 728.
[74] Lindseth, 'Democratic Legitimacy', 634.   [75] Ibid., 634–35.

affirm that democracy is the only legitimate form of domestic government,[76] there must be an argument, according to Occam's razor,[77] that the epistemic authority of non-state actors is provided by some idea of democratic legitimacy rather than technocratic expertise.

5. International governance *by the people*

5.1 *Four possibilities*

In relation to arguments around the 'democratic legitimacy' of non-state actors, four possibilities emerge. First, democratic legitimacy can relate directly to an 'expression of majority will, making legitimacy a function of electoral success'.[78] With the exception of Members of the European Parliament (to an extent), power-wielders in global governance institutions do not enjoy 'direct' democratic legitimation through elections. This is problematic for Follesdal and Hix, who argue that democracy requires contestation for political leadership and over policy: competitive elections are essential to ensure that policies in fact represent the 'will of the people', which, moreover, is constructed through the process of political competition.[79]

Secondly, the 'overarching governance structure' can shape the legitimacy of policy choices in the form of 'Madisonian or systemic legitimacy', dispersing political authority as a way of protecting individual liberty, and ensuring 'triangulation on difficult policy choices (which is especially important under conditions of factual uncertainty or normative disagreement)'.[80] James Rosenau argues that the test for whether democracy is evolving in the 'globalised space' lies in the degree to which control mechanisms steer politics in the direction of more checks on the excesses of power, provide more opportunities for interests to be heard and impose 'more balanced constraints among the multiplicity of actors that seek to extend their command of issue areas'.[81]

Thirdly, the legitimate exercise of political authority can depend on decision-makers 'following the right process', which will help to 'clarify

---

[76] See, for example, UN General Assembly *2005 World Summit Outcome* A/RES/60/1 adopted without a vote 16 September 2005, para. 119.

[77] The principle that in explaining anything, no more assumptions should be made than are necessary.

[78] Esty, 'Good Governance at the Supranational Scale', 1515.

[79] Follesdal and Hix, 'Why there is a Democratic Deficit', 549–50.

[80] Esty, 'Good Governance at the Supranational Scale', 1519–20.

[81] Rosenau, 'Governance and Democracy', 49.

underlying issues, bring facts to bear, promote careful analysis of policy options, and engage interested parties in a political dialogue'.[82] It is significant that the application of public and administrative law principles to global governance institutions has focused on the 'democratic' legitimacy of the jurisgenerative process,[83] notably Krisch and Kingsbury's global administrative law principles of 'transparency, participation, reasoned decision [including principles of non-discrimination and non-arbitrariness] and review'.[84]

Fourthly, the idea of democratic legitimacy can be seen in terms of dialogue and deliberation. Daniel Esty makes the point that in the international policy arena, 'a transparent decision-making process that provides opportunities for debate and political dialogue, with participation by those representing a broad range of views, is a key to legitimacy, substituting for the missing democratic legitimacy and accountability that elections provide'.[85] The argument developed in this work is that the deliberative model of democracy associated with Jürgen Habermas provides the basis for beginning to think about the necessary conditions for the 'democratic' exercise of political authority by international organisations and other non-state actors.

5.2   Epistemic authority through democratic decision making

According to Habermas, a democratic order draws its legitimacy from the idea of collective self-determination: 'citizens must think of themselves as authors of the law to which they are subject as addressees'.[86] Law and the exercise of political authority is legitimate only to the extent that it has been agreed in a process of deliberative opinion- and will-formation. In ideal conditions, laws result from a process of reasoned deliberation amongst equal citizens, who reach a consensus.[87] The legitimacy of legal norms is provided by the 'rationality of the democratic procedure of political legislation[,] and above all by the fairness of the compromises involved'.[88] The idea of public reason is key: those seeking to demonstrate the 'political truth' of their position are required to rely on arguments supported by reasons in an attempt to convince others.

---

[82] Esty, 'Good Governance at the Supranational Scale', 1521.
[83] Sarooshi, *International Organizations*, 14.
[84] Krisch and Kingsbury, 'Introduction', 2. See also Lustig and Kingsbury, 'Displacement and Relocation', 413.
[85] Esty, 'Good Governance at the Supranational Scale', 1520.
[86] Habermas, *Between Facts and Norms*, 449.   [87] *Ibid.*, 158.   [88] *Ibid.*, 233.

Habermas attributes epistemic authority to the 'communicative community'.[89] Political truth equates to the consensus that would be arrived at through dialogue in an 'ideal speech situation',[90] in which positions are accepted as legitimate only where these are agreed through uncoerced discussions by those affected by the outcomes of the process. Michel Rosenfeld observes: the aim of the 'ideal speech situation' is 'to arrive at a rational consensus based on the force of the better argument'.[91] All those entitled to participate must be allowed to participate, each participant is entitled to propose and comment on proposals and no participant may be hindered in their participation by threats of force or deception.[92] Robert Keohane writes that input-legitimacy for non-state actors (specifically multilateral organisations) requires a 'diversity of representation and inclusiveness[.] If all voices are heard, more objections will be expressed, deliberation may be enhanced and decisions more widely accepted.'[93] Global governance institutions are required to establish 'institutionalised procedures for communication, insulated to a significant extent from the use and threats of force and sanctions, and sufficiently open to hinder manipulation'.[94] The ideal is that of 'rational persuasion'.[95]

The epistemic authority of non-state actors is provided by 'democratic' decision-making procedures that result in policy positions which can be justified to those subject to the international governance regime. Buchanan and Keohane refer to the need for international governance actors to 'offer public justifications of at least the more controversial and consequential institutional policies and must facilitate timely critical responses to them'.[96] The simplest and most effective method of improving the legitimacy and accountability of non-state actors is to require them to demonstrate that they have taken into account the impact of decisions on others, and that they have explained sufficiently their decisions.[97] Public justification allows global publics to engage with decision-making processes (not only the outcomes), make a judgment as to whether the decision-maker has sought to act in the

---

[89] Teubner, 'How the Law Thinks', 733.   [90] See Habermas, *Moral Consciousness*, 83–94.
[91] Rosenfeld, 'Affirmative Action, Justice, and Equalities', 845, footnote 120.
[92] Solum, 'Freedom of Communicative Action', 96.
[93] Keohane, 'The Contingent Legitimacy', 5.
[94] Keohane, 'Governance in a Partially Globalized World', 3.   [95] *Ibid.*, 2.
[96] Buchanan and Keohane, 'The Legitimacy of Global Governance Institutions', 428.
[97] Nicolaides, 'Improving Policy Implementation', 46, quoted in Cohen and Sabel, 'Global Democracy?', 778.

global public interest, and engage critically with the substantive rationale for decisions.

The theory and practice of democracy emerged in the context of the sovereign state which defined and delimited the people, or *demos*, on whose behalf representatives act, and to whom they are accountable. In relation to global governance institutions, 'there is no "taken-for-granted" connection between those establishing legal norms and those affected by the implementation of those norms'.[98] Following Habermas' principle of discourse, the 'democratic' legitimacy of an international governance regime requires that the non-state actors operate within a constitutional framework that recognises those subject to the normative regime as its authors, albeit indirectly. Law is legitimate 'only if all who are possibly affected could assent as participants in rational discourses'.[99] Deficits in democratic legitimacy 'result when the circle of all those involved in democratic decision making does not extend to cover the circle of all those affected by those decisions'.[100] There is no requirement that all affected persons do in fact participate (although there may be a recognition that those specially affected have a right to be consulted and to participate in discussions), but there is a 'warranted presumption ... that those whose interests are involved have an equal and effective opportunity to make their own interests (and their reasons for them) known'.[101]

Asserting a right for 'those affected' to take part in decision-making procedures is easier than identifying the relevant constituency – as Grant and Keohane observe, if being affected was a sufficient criterion for inclusion then 'anyone who buys gasoline would be entitled to participate in OPEC's deliberations'.[102] There is, however, an emergent acceptance on the part of non-state actors that they are accountable to those subject to their exercise of political authority: the acceptance by the Security Council of a requirement to provide reasoned justification for the listing of persons under the '1267 Sanctions Regime',[103] and establishment of the World Bank Inspection Panel[104] provide just two examples. In the absence of formal accountability mechanisms, most

---

[98] Goodhart, 'Europe's Democratic Deficits', 575.
[99] Habermas, *Between Facts and Norms*, 458.
[100] Habermas, 'Toward a Cosmopolitan Europe', 90.
[101] Nanz and Steffek, 'Global Governance', 321.
[102] Grant and Keohane 'Accountability and Abuses', 33.
[103] SC Res. 1735 (2006), para. 5.
[104] Bradlow and Grossman, 'Limited Mandates', 431–32.

international governance institutions have introduced informal mechanisms to engage (to some extent) with external actors, including international civil society organisations and those potentially affected by their policy decisions. Accessible websites are the clearest manifestation of this.

Where a non-state actor exercises political authority, there is a direct relationship between the relevant global governance institution and the actors to whom the normative provision is addressed (those subject to the international governance regime). As Cohen and Sabel observe, in 'an attenuated but significant way, the wills of all subject to the rule-making authority have been implicated, sufficiently much that rules of this type can only be imposed with a special justification'.[105] The international governance regime asserting political authority through law defines its own constituency and enters into an accountability relationship with that constituency. The standard definition of accountability is 'the process of being called "to account" to some authority for one's actions'.[106] The concept has expanded in recent years to include (amongst other things) the idea that governments should pursue the wishes or needs of their citizens – accountability as 'responsiveness'.[107] Increasingly, accountability is seen as a 'dialogical activity', requiring officials to 'answer, explain and justify, while those holding them to account engage in questioning, assessing and criticising'.[108] The hypothetical communicative community of an international governance regime – 'those subjected' – have the right to participate in decision-making processes, directly or through representatives. Engagement with international civil society actors, 'we the peoples' representatives', is understood to provide some form of legitimacy for the exercise of political authority, linking political institutions with the wider public in the process of collective will-formation to ensure that relevant interests and perspectives are included in decision-making processes, in particular those of hitherto marginalised or excluded groups. The establishment of an international governance regime constitutes a political community and defines its

---

[105] Cohen and Sabel, 'Extra Rempublicam Nulla Justitia?', 168. Thomas Nagel argues that there is only an obligation 'to accord equal status [i.e. citizenship and all that implies] to anyone with whom we are joined in a strong and coercively imposed political community': Nagel, 'The Problem of Global Justice', 133. Given that international organisations do not collectively enact or coercively impose laws in the name of those whose lives they affect, it makes no sense to talk about citizenship (and contingent, selective moral relations or justice) outside of the context of the nation-state (138).

[106] Mulgan, '"Accountability"', 555.   [107] Ibid., 556.   [108] Ibid., 569.

membership. In the *demos*/democracy debate, it is possible to develop a functioning democratic policy whose members (citizens) will subsequently recognise themselves as members of the same political community, providing democratic legitimacy for the exercise of political authority by the non-state actor.

6. Conclusion

This chapter has sought to outline an argument for the relevance of democratic legitimacy to standard setting by non-state actors. In common with domestic (governmental) authority, the political authority of non-state actors is dependent on a combination of three factors, which will be weighted according to the circumstances of the particular case:

1. the source of political authority (that is, the constitutive instrument or mechanism);
2. the extent to which it is accepted that the non-state actor is pursuing good governance aims and methods (for example 'least intrusive' and/or proportionate interferences in individual liberties); and
3. in circumstances of imperfect knowledge and reasonable disagreement, the epistemic authority of the non-state actor (that is, its claim to be the possessor of political truth).

A democratic understanding of epistemic authority (as proposed here) would focus on decision-making procedures, and the accountability of non-state actors to those subjected to the governance regime. This suggests areas for future research:

- the need to identify which non-state actors do in fact exercise a governance function (an issue addressed in this volume);
- the extent to which existing decision-making procedures can be regarded as 'democratic', at least in the sense employed here;
- the need to establish who is actually subjected (de jure or de facto) by the exercise of political authority, and thus entitled to have a say, and hold the relevant non-state actor to account;
- the practical need to develop effective mechanisms for the inclusion of otherwise marginalised individuals and groups in the decision-making procedures of non-state actors; and
- the importance of developing a theory of global legal pluralism consistent with the principle of democratic legitimacy.

The legitimacy, effectiveness and authority of international governance regimes require that non-state actors 'persuade' others to accept their governance functions. Moreover, non-state actors must rely on domestic governmental institutions for the enforcement of international governance norms: 'in a world of plural normative assertions, one crucial question will be whether a community's articulation of norms is sufficiently persuasive to convince those wielding coercive power to enforce such norms.'[109] The 'internalisation' of international governance norms by legislative embodiment, and/or executive acceptance,[110] implies a link to democratic publics and democratic debate: in order to be effective non-state actors must influence domestic deliberations and discourses. To the extent that global governance institutions promote more effective procedures at the domestic level for the exercise of political self-determination there is no democratic deficit. A difficulty occurs where non-state actors seek to establish substantive policy positions that are not (initially) accepted by democratic publics, and it is unlikely that democratic peoples will accept international governance norms that do not 'fit' with the values recognised in the system of global governance, including international human rights standards, or that are adopted in violation of the principle of democratic will-formation,[111] and the principle of public reason, whereby parties offer arguments and evidence in an attempt to persuade others.

Whilst international governance regimes sit outside the Westphalian paradigm of 'sovereign' law-making, they assert political authority in areas already subject to (or potentially subject to) state regulation. When there is more than one source of 'law' in a social field, more than one legal order, the social order can be said to exhibit legal pluralism.[112] Gunther Teubner argues that the globalisation of law requires that theories of legal pluralism shift their focus 'from groups and communities to discourses and communicative networks'.[113] In an age in which the state does not possess a monopoly on norm-creation, the definitive issue to consider is, 'where are concrete norms actually produced?'[114] In a subsequent article, Fischer-Lescano and Teubner refer to the idea of global legal pluralism,

---

[109] Berman, 'A Pluralist Approach', 319.   [110] See Koh, 'Why Do Nations Obey?', 2640.

[111] Risse and Ropp make the point that international norms are more likely to be implemented and complied with in the domestic context 'if they resonate or fit with existing collective understandings embedded in domestic institutions and political cultures': Risse and Ropp, 'International Human Rights Norms', 271.

[112] Griffiths, 'What is Legal Pluralism?', 38.   [113] Teubner, '"Global Bukowina"', 7.

[114] *Ibid.*, 11.

in which international organisations and regulatory regimes 'established themselves as autonomous legal orders',[115] generating 'highly specialised primary norms', and possessing 'their own procedural norms on law-making, law-recognition and legal sanctions [in cases of breach]'.[116]

The study of legal pluralism has focused on the 'jurisdictions, contra-dictions, and contestations' between different legal regimes.[117] Inconsistency cannot be resolved by an appeal to a higher 'authority' or rules of interpretation because the dispute turns on the question of supremacy. The recognition of pluralism implies an acceptance of 'inconsistent rules of recognition' between the laws of the sovereign state and those of international governance regimes. The argument here is that the 'jurispersuasive'[118] abilities of a non-state actor will depend on an evaluation of its epistemic authority: its claim to 'know better' than the people of the state, who in ideal circumstances reach domestic policy positions after 'deliberative' democratic decision-making procedures. The epistemic authority of non-state actors is grounded in a complex model of legitimacy reflecting the fact of its constitution in response to a collective action problem; the welfare-enhancing benefits, in terms of global justice ends, of international governance for the people; and, in circumstances of imperfect knowledge and reasonable disagreement the 'deliberative' democratic decision-making procedures, of the non-state actor.

In heterarchical conditions of legal pluralism, 'objective' political truth is not provided by the non-state actor or the people of the state: these are perspectives on political truth. This conflict and contestation between the political truths of the state and non-state actors allow social, economic, and political issues to be further problematised and further solutions proposed.[119] The fact of international governance by non-state actors creates sites in which political and legal contestation over the meaning of rights and other fundamental principles and the required responses to collective action problems can occur. In this way, international governance by non-state actors can contribute to the democratic legitimacy of globa-lised governance (including domestic government) consistent with a recognition of the importance of political participation in the establish-ment of legal norms and respect for individual human rights.

---

[115] Fischer-Lescano and Teubner, 'Regime Collisions', 1008.   [116] *Ibid*, 1015.
[117] Fiske and Ginn, 'Discourse and Defiance', 115.
[118] Compare Michaels, 'The Re-State-Ment of Non-State Law', 1242.
[119] See Merry, 'Anthropology and International Law', 108.

References

Bellamy, R. 2006, 'Still in Deficit: Rights, Regulation, and Democracy in the EU', *European Law Journal*, vol. **12**, 725.

Bellamy, R. and Castiglione, D. 2000, 'The Uses of Democracy: Reflections on the European Democratic Deficit' in E. Eriksen and J. Fossum (eds.), *Democracy in the European Union: Integration Through Deliberation?*, London, Routledge, 65.

Berman, P. 2007, 'A Pluralist Approach to International Law', *Yale Journal of International Law*, vol. **32**, 301.

Bernstein, S. 2005, 'Legitimacy in Global Environmental Governance', *Journal of International Law and International Relations*, vol. **1**, 139.

Bernstein, S. and Cashore, B. 2007, 'Can Non-State Global Governance be Legitimate? An Analytical Framework', *Regulation & Governance*, vol. **1**, 347.

Boyle, A. and Chinkin, C. 2007, *The Making of International Law*, Oxford University Press.

Bradlow, D. and Grossman, C. 1995, 'Limited Mandates and Intertwined Problems: A New Challenge for the World Bank and the IMF', *Human Rights Quarterly*, vol. **17**, 411.

Brunkhorst, H. 2002, 'Globalising Democracy without a State: Weak Public, Strong Public, Global Constitutionalism', Millennium, *Journal of International Studies*, vol. **31**, 675.

Brunnée, J. and Toope, S. 2000, 'International Law and Constructivism: Elements of an Interactional Theory of International Law', *Columbia Journal of Transnational Law*, vol. **39**, 19.

Buchanan, A. and Keohane, R. 2006, 'The Legitimacy of Global Governance Institutions', *Ethics and International Affairs*, vol. **20**, 405.

Charles, G.-U. 2005, 'Colored Speech: Cross Burnings, Epistemics, and the Triumph of the Crits?', *Georgetown Law Journal*, vol. **93**, 575.

Charney, J. 1993, 'Universal International Law', *American Journal of International Law*, vol. **87**, 529.

Cohen, J. and Sabel, C. 2006, 'Extra Rempublicam Nulla Justitia?', *Philosophy and Public Affairs*, vol. **34**, 147.

Dahl, R. 1956, *A Preface to Democratic Theory*, University of Chicago Press.

Dahl, R. 1994, 'A Democratic Dilemma: System Effectiveness versus Citizen Participation', *Political Science Quarterly*, vol. **109**, 23.

Esty, D. 2006, 'Good Governance at the Supranational Scale: Globalizing Administrative Law', *Yale Law Journal*, vol. **115**, 1490.

Finnemore, M. 1996, *National Interests in International Society*, Ithaca, Cornell University Press.

Finnemore, M. and Sikkink, K. 1998, 'International Norm Dynamics and Political Change', *International Organization*, vol. **52**, 887.

Fischer-Lescano, A. and Teubner, G. 2004, 'Regime Collisions: The Vain Search for Legal Unity in the Fragmentation of Global Law', *Michigan Journal of International Law*, vol. **25**, 999.

Fiske, J.-A. and Ginn, P. 2000, 'Discourse and Defiance: Law, Healing, and the Implications of Communities of Resistance', *Journal of Legal Pluralism and Unofficial Law*, vol. **45**, 115.

Fiss, O. 2001, 'The Autonomy of Law', *Yale Journal of International Law*, vol. **26**, 517.

Follesdal, A. and Hix, S. 2006, 'Why there is a Democratic Deficit in the EU: A Response to Majone and Moravcsik', *Journal of Common Market Studies*, vol. **44**, 533.

Goodhart, M. 2007, 'Europe's Democratic Deficits Through the Looking Glass: The European Union as a Challenge for Democracy', *Perspectives on Politics*, vol. **5**, 567.

Grant, R. and Keohane, R. 2005, 'Accountability and Abuses of Power in World Politics', *American Political Science Review*, vol. **99**, 29.

Griffiths, J. 1986, 'What is Legal Pluralism?', *Journal of Legal Pluralism and Unofficial Law*, vol. **24**, 1.

Gross, L. 1948, 'The Peace of Westphalia, 1648–1948', *American Journal of International Law*, vol. **42**, 20.

Habermas, J. 1986, *Between Facts and Norms* (transl. W. Rehg), Oxford, Polity.

Habermas, J. 1990, *Moral Consciousness and Communicative Action* (transl. C. Lenhardt and S. W. Nicholson), Cambridge (MA), MIT Press.

Habermas, J. 1995, 'Multiculturalism and the Liberal State', *Stanford Law Review*, vol. **47**, 849.

Habermas, J. 2003, 'Toward a Cosmopolitan Europe', *Journal of Democracy*, vol. **14**, no. 4, 86.

Hart, H. L. A. 1994, *The Concept of Law*, 2nd edn, Oxford, Clarendon Press.

Held, D. 1996, *Models of Democracy*, 2nd edn, Cambridge, Polity.

Hurd, I. 1999, 'Legitimacy and Authority in International Politics', *International Organization*, vol. **53**, 379.

Jackson, R. 1987, 'Quasi-States, Dual Regimes, and Neoclassical Theory: International Jurisprudence and the Third World', *International Organization*, vol. **41**, 519.

Johnstone, I. 1991, 'Treaty Interpretation: The Authority of Interpretive Communities', *Michigan Journal of International Law*, vol. **12**, 371.

Keohane, R. 2001, 'Governance in a Partially Globalized World', *American Political Science Review*, vol. **95**, 1.

Keohane, R. 2006, 'The Contingent Legitimacy of Multilateralism', *GARNET Working Paper* No. 09/06.

Keohane, R., Macedo, S. and Moravcsik, A. 2007, 'Democracy Enhancing Multilateralism', *Institute for International Law and Justice Working Paper*, no. **4**.

Koh, H. H. 1997, 'Why Do Nations Obey International Law?', *Yale Law Journal*, vol. **106**, 2599.

Koh, H. H. 1998, 'Bringing International Law Home', *Houston Law Review*, vol. **35**, 623.

Krisch, N. and Kingsbury, B. 2006, 'Introduction: Global Governance and Global Administrative Law in the International Legal Order', *European Journal of International Law*, vol. **17**, 1.

Kumm, M. 2004, 'The Legitimacy of International Law: A Constitutionalist Framework of Analysis', *European Journal of International Law*, vol. **15**, 907.

Lindseth, P. 1999, 'Democratic Legitimacy and the Administrative Character of Supranationalism: The Example of the European Community', *Columbia Law Review*, vol. **99**, 628.

Lowe, V. 2007, *International Law*, Oxford University Press.

Lucas, J. 1966, *The Principles of Politics*, Oxford University Press.

Luhmann, N. 2004, *Law as a Social System* (transl. K. Ziegert), Oxford University Press.

Lustig, D. and Kingsbury B., 2006, 'Displacement and Relocation from Protected Areas: International Law Perspectives on Rights, Risks and Resistance', *Conservation and Society*, vol. **4**, 404.

Majone, G. 1996, *Regulating Europe*, London, Routledge.

Mankabad, S. 1997, 'Decommissioning of Offshore Installations', *Journal of Maritime Law and Commerce*, vol. **28**, 603.

Merry, S. E. 2006, 'Anthropology and International Law', *Annual Review of Anthropology*, vol. **35**, 99.

Michaels, R. 2005, 'The Re-State-Ment of Non-State Law: The State, Choice of Law, and the Challenge from Global Legal Pluralism', *Wayne Law Review*, vol. **51**, 1209.

Michelman, F. 1998, 'The 1996–97 Brennan Center Symposium Lecture', *Californian Law Review*, vol. **86**, 399.

Moravcsik, A. 2004, 'Is there a "Democratic Deficit" in World Politics? A Framework for Analysis', *Government and Opposition*, vol. **39**, 336.

Moravcsik, A. 2006, 'What Can We Learn from the Collapse of the European Constitutional Project?', *Politische Vierteljahresschrift*, vol. **47**, 219.

Moravcsik, M. 2000, 'Conservative Idealism and International Institutions', *Chicago Journal of International Law*, vol. **1**, 291.

Moravcsik, M. 2002, 'In Defence of the "Democratic Deficit": Reassessing Legitimacy in the European Union', *Journal of Common Market Legal Studies*, vol. **40**, 603.

Morgenthau, H. 1940, 'Positivism, Functionalism, and International Law', *American Journal of International Law*, vol. **34**, 260.

Mulgan, R. 2000, '"Accountability": An Ever-Expanding Concept', *Public Administration*, vol. **78**, 555.

Nagel, T. 2005, 'The Problem of Global Justice', *Philosophy and Public Affairs*, vol. **33**, 113.

Nanz, P. and Steffek, J. 2004, 'Global Governance, Participation and the Public Sphere', *Government and Opposition*, vol. **39**, 314.

Nicolaides, P. *et al.* 2003, 'Improving Policy Implementation in an Enlarged European Union: The Case Of National Regulatory Authorities', 46, quoted in Cohen, J. and Sabel, C. 2006, 'Global Democracy?', *New York University Journal of International Law and Policy*, vol. **37**, 763.

Raz, J. 1979, *The authority of law*, Oxford, Clarendon Press.

Risse, T. 2004, 'Global Governance and Communicative Action', *Government and Opposition*, vol. **39**, 288.

Risse, T. and Ropp, S. 1999, 'International Human Rights Norms and Domestic Change: Conclusions', in T. Risse et al. (eds.), *The Power of Human Rights: International Norms and Domestic Change*, Cambridge University Press, 234.

Rosenau, J. 1992, 'Governance, Order, and Change in World Politics', in J. Rosenau and E.-O. Czempiel (eds.), *Governance Without Government: Order and Change in World Politics*, Cambridge University Press, 1.

Rosenau, J. 1998, 'Governance and Democracy in a Globalizing World' in D. Archibugi et al. (eds.), *Re-Imagining Political Community: Studies in Cosmopolitan Democracy*, Cambridge, Polity, 28.

Rosenfeld, M. 1985, 'Affirmative Action, Justice, and Equalities: A Philosophical and Constitutional Appraisal', *Ohio State Law Journal*, vol. **46**, 845.

Sarooshi, D. 2005, *International Organizations and Their Exercise of Sovereign Powers*, Oxford University Press.

Schachter, O. 1977, 'The Invisible College of International Lawyers', *Northwestern University Law Review*, vol. **72**, 217.

Scharpf, F. 1999, *Governing in Europe: Effective and Democratic?*, Oxford University Press.

Shaffer, G. 2004, 'Parliamentary Oversight of WTO Rule-Making: The Political, Normative, and Practical Contexts', *Journal of International Economic Law*, vol. 7, 629.

Shelton, D. 2000, 'Introduction', in D. Shelton (ed.), *Commitment and Compliance: The Role of Non-Binding Norms in the International Legal System*, Oxford University Press, 1.

Shelton, D. 2000, 'Editor's Concluding Note', in D. Shelton (ed.), *Commitment and Compliance: The Role of Non-Binding Norms in the International Legal System*, Oxford University Press, 554.

Slaughter, A.-M. 2004, 'Disaggregated Sovereignty: Towards the Public Accountability of Global Government Networks', *Government and Opposition*, vol. **39**, 159.

Slaughter, A.-M., Tulumello, A. and Wood, S. 1998, 'International Law and International Relations Theory: A New Generation of Interdisciplinary Scholarship', *American Journal of International Law*, vol. **92**, 367.

Solum, L. 1989, 'Freedom of Communicative Action: A Theory of the First Amendment Freedom of Speech', *Northwestern University Law Review*, vol. **83**, 54.

Steffek, J. 2000, 'The Power of Rational Discourse and the Legitimacy of International Governance', *EUI Working Papers*, RSC No. 2000, vol. **46**.

Strauss, A. 2007, 'Considering Global Democracy', *Widener Law Review*, vol. **13**, no. 2, i.

Tamanaha, B. 2001, *A General Jurisprudence of Law and Society*, Oxford University Press.

Teubner, G. 1989, 'How the Law Thinks: Toward a Constructivist Epistemology of Law', *Law and Society Review*, vol. **23**, 727.

Teubner, G. 1997, '"Global Bukowina": Legal Pluralism in the World Society' in G. Teubner (ed.), *Global Law Without a State*, Aldershot, Dartmouth, Aldershot, 3.

Twining, W. 2003, 'A Post-Westphalian Conception of Law', *Law and Society Review*, vol. **37**, 199.

Wheatley, S. 2007, 'Minorities under the ECHR and the Construction of a "Democratic Society"', *Public Law*, 770.

9

Legitimacy, accountability and polycentric regulation: dilemmas, trilemmas and organisational response

JULIA BLACK[*]

1. Introduction

It has been said that governments can 'puzzle as well as power'.[1] Shamelessly misappropriating this comment, it could be said that academic papers can do the same. Some puzzle their way through an issue, raising more questions than they answer; others 'power' on through, setting out the path that others must follow to find a solution to whatever problem is being addressed.

This chapter is of the former type. The issue that it considers is that of the accountability and legitimacy of decentred regulatory regimes. Decentred regulatory regimes are those in which the state is not the sole locus of authority or indeed in which it plays no role at all. They are marked by fragmentation, complexity and interdependence between actors, in which state and non-state actors are both regulators and regulated and their boundaries are marked by the issues or problems with which they are concerned, rather than necessarily by a common solution.[2] Such regimes pose a number of challenges which writers across a range of disciplines – law, political science, international relations, development studies – are all engaged in delineating and addressing. Indeed, the issues

[*] Professor of Law and Research Associate, Centre for Analysis of Risk and Regulation, London School of Economics and Political Science; DPhil, BA (Hons) Jurisp (Oxon). This contribution was presented at the ESRC Seminar on Administrative Justice, Liverpool, December 2006 and I thank the participants for their comments and Colin Scott for comments on the whole draft. Arguments have been elaborated in Black, J. 2008, 'Constructing and Contesting Legitimacy and Accountability in Polycentric Regulatory Regimes', *Regulation and Governance*, vol. 1.

[1] Heclo, *Modern Social Politics*.

[2] For a fuller discussion see Black, 'Decentring Regulation', 103–47. More generally on governance see Rosenau and Czempiel (eds.), *Governance without Government*.

to which the 'governance turn' is giving rise is drawing commentators like moths round a light.

These challenges include the functional, the systemic, the democratic and the normative. Functional challenges revolve around the problem of coordination: networks of organisations within a regulatory regime are characterised by complex interdependencies and can lack a central locus of authority.[3] There may not be a body whose role it is to act as the lead 'interpreter' of the regimes' rules or principles, for example, or to otherwise steer or co-ordinate the activities of the multiple participants in such a way that the regime moves towards the resolution of the problem which it both defines and is defined by and conflicts between regimes are resolved through jurisdictional appropriation. Systemic challenges revolve around issues of fragmentation of social systems.[4] For lawyers this is particularly the challenge posed to the identification and identity of law by the presence of numerous normative orders, an issue debated in terms of the nature of 'soft law' and the challenges of legal pluralism.[5] Democratic challenges arise from issues of representation: who should be involved in the decision-making structures of the various components of the network; to whom such bodies should be accountable and how.[6] Normative challenges stem from normative concerns as to the goals and operation of the regulatory regime: what conception of 'the good' is and should be pursued.[7] Of these, the functional, democratic and normative challenges in particular are often articulated in terms of the accountability and legitimacy of the regimes as a whole and the different actors within them.

For some engaged in that debate, the solution is to find functional equivalents to the structures of accountability which are to be found in constitutional settlements, at least of liberal democratic states. Checks and balances, dispute resolution processes, democratisation,

---

[3] For discussion see, e.g., Kickert, Klijn and Koppenjan (eds.), *Managing Complex*; Klijn and Koppenjan, 'Public Management and Policy Networks', 437; Klijn and Koppenjan, 'Public Management and Policy Networks. Foundations of a Network Approach to Governance', 135; Castells, *The Rise of the Network Society*.

[4] The leading work is Luhmann, *Social Systems*.

[5] See, e.g., Roberts, 'After Government?', 1; Teubner, '"Global Bukowina"; Chinkin, 'Normative Development'.

[6] See, e.g., Skelcher, 'Jurisdictional Integrity', 89.

[7] The re-description of international law in terms of 'governance' has been criticised as disguising or even seeking to neutralise the normative and political dimension of international legal regimes: Koskienniemi, 'The Fate of Public International Law', 1.

accountability networks – all are common features of the 'powering' solutions being advocated by commentators in a range of disciplines.[8]

This chapter takes a different perspective. The usual quartet of accountability questions – how, with respect to what, to whom and when – are not addressed, at least not directly. The chapter asks not what mechanisms are necessary to make actors in decentred regulatory regimes accountable or even legitimate, nor does it even ask in accordance with what values, or with respect to whom, they should be made accountable in the regulatory process. Rather it argues that to answer these questions we need to take the perspective of those on whom the demands are being made and ask how they respond. What happens when these different accountability and legitimacy demands are made and indeed what role do the objects of the accountability and legitimacy demands play in shaping those demands? This question is of interest in its own right; it is also logically prior to any 'powering' proposals.

The 'puzzling' proceeds in four main stages and has two key consequences, from which a number of further implications flow. First, it looks at the relationship between accountability and legitimacy and suggests that both are relational concepts that are socially and discursively constituted. Secondly, it suggests that actors within and outside the regulatory regime have different perceptions as to the relevance and validity of different legitimacy claims with respect to different regulatory actors – in other words, that there are different legitimacy communities. Thirdly, that different legitimacy claims, and associated discourses, are not always compatible but may compete. Fourthly, although organisations can often participate in a number of different legitimacy discourses simultaneously, and thus satisfy a range of different legitimacy communities, this can not only have a deleterious effect on the organisation (which may suffer 'multiple accountability disorder'), the differences between communities may be such that organisations can face a legitimacy dilemma: that actions that they need to take to render them legitimate for one legitimacy community are in direct opposition from those they need to adopt to satisfy another.

So far, so familiar, perhaps. However, the chapter then seeks to explore two main consequences of these propositions for regulatory accountability

---

[8] The literature is vast: for discussions at the national, EU and global level respectively, see, e.g., Scott, 'Accountability in the Regulatory State', 38; Papadoulous, 'Problems of Democratic Accountability', 469; Harlow and Rawlings, 'Promoting Accountability in Multi-Level Governance', 542; Keohane, 'Global Governance and Democratic Accountability'.

and legitimacy: first, that different accountability or legitimacy mechanisms are not necessarily substitutable, as some may suggest,[9] as not all will satisfy every legitimacy community. Secondly, and more importantly for this chapter, how organisations respond to these competing legitimacy demands is structured by the particular institutional context in which the regulatory regime and the individual organisation operate. Regulators are not ciphers – the insights of the 'ungovernability' of actors apply as much to them as those they seek to regulate. They can be active participants in the debate on their own accountability and legitimacy, not just a passive recipient. They may exhibit the same strategies of avoidance, defiance, manipulation, compromise or acquiescence in response to pressures for their accountability and legitimacy as any organisation does in response to any norms which others seek to impose on them.[10] This much is familiar from institutional theory, but its insights are often separated from the more normative or 'powering' prescriptions for accountability.

The chapter takes a further theoretical step and, pursuing the interplay of institutionalism with discourse theory, suggests one reason that a regulator (state or non-state based) may respond to some legitimacy communities but not to others. This analysis has implications for those who are seeking to get the organisation to respond to their accountability and legitimacy demands. Absent other key resources, the chapter suggests that those legitimacy communities whose demands have not been recognised will have to translate those demands into the discourses of those that have been recognised if they are to build the relationship of accountability with the organisation that they seek.

Finally, the chapter draws on the preceding analysis to offer a challenging empirical research agenda into the accountability and legitimacy of decentred regulatory regimes.

2.   The broad parameters of the accountability and legitimacy debates

Before embarking on the puzzle, it is worth reminding ourselves of the significance and wide-ranging nature of the contemporary debate over the accountability and legitimacy of organisations, including, but not limited to, non-state regulators. The accountability and legitimacy of

---

[9] See in particular Scott's redundancy model of accountability: Scott, 'Accountability in the Regulatory State'.
[10] See further below.

organisations, ranging from firms to national, international and supra-national governmental bodies, from charities to international non-governmental organisations (INGOs), from standard-setting bodies to investment arbitrators, is the subject of an intense debate.[11] The 'govern-ance turn' revealed a plethora of non-governmental actors who were performing what had been traditionally seen as core 'governmental' functions: welfare provision and regulation, or who in much broader terms are seen as exercising significant amounts of power over those both inside and outside them. The demands for corporate social accountabil-ity, the calls for improving the 'representativeness' or 'transparency' of international regulatory and standard-setting bodies or for enhancing the 'legitimacy' of INGOs all have the same central concern at their base: that power is being exercised in a way which is insufficiently accountable to others. As a result, organisations are, to use Power's evocative phrase, being turned 'inside out'.[12] The details of their internal decision-making structures and processes, including their incentive structures, audit and risk management processes, are seen as critically relevant to those out-side them.

These multiple demands for enhanced legitimacy and accountability can lead to a coalescence of norms with varying geographic and sectoral applicability. Firms, particularly multinationals, are the subject of a number of codes relating to corporate social responsibility and human rights, for example the UN Global Compact, the draft United Nations Norms on the Responsibilities of Transnational Corporations and other Business Enterprises, the OECD Guidelines for Multinational Enterprises and the ILO Tripartite Declaration of Principles concerning Multinational Enterprises and Social Policy. Firms are not alone. There have been increas-ing calls on INGOs to improve their legitimacy and accountability.[13] Partly in response, INGOs have developed their own codes of practice. Some of these are functional statements of best practice but they include provi-sions, albeit often in very general terms, which relate to accountability and transparency. For example, the One World Trust Global Accountability

---

[11] See, e.g., Schmidt, 'The New World Order Incorporated', 75; more generally on corpor-ate social responsibility, see, e.g., McBarnet, Voiculescu and Campbell (eds.), *The New Corporate Accountability*; on NGOs, see, e.g., Nyamugasira, 'NGOs and Advocacy', 297; Edwards and Hulme (eds.), *Non-Governmental Organisations*; on standard setters, see, e.g., Braithwaite and Drahos, *Global Business Regulation*.

[12] Power, *The Risk Management* (though Power's focus is on private for-profit corporations).

[13] Edwards and Hulme (eds.), *Non-Governmental Organisations*; Edwards, *NGO Rights and Responsibilities*.

Project identifies four dimensions of accountability – transparency, participation, evaluation and complaints and response – detailing operational
guidelines on how these can be translated into practice.[14] Other codes are
far narrower. Specific codes exist for INGOs giving disaster relief or
responding to HIV/Aids[15] or in specific countries or regions.[16] The above
are examples of self-imposed and self-managed codes. NGOs can also
be the subject of codes formulated by governments, for example the EC
Code of Conduct on Non-Profit Organisations, which focuses on the
potential use of non-profit organisations as vehicles for terrorist finance
or money laundering, although the range of its recommendations belies
this relatively narrow rationale: the registration, enhanced financial transparency, accountability and oversight of all non-profit organisations.[17]

Amongst this plethora of actors, non-state regulators occupy a curious
position. They may be campaigning NGOs, and as such occupy a dual
role as lobbyist and regulator, or they may focus primarily on a broad
'regulatory' function, at least in the sense that they set written norms for
others to follow. They may have a clear organisational structure, such as
Transparency International, the Forest Stewardship Council, the standard-
setting bodies such as the International Standards Organisation (ISO) or
the transnational financial regulatory organisations (IOSCO or BCBS, for
example).[18] Such structures may be federated, such as Responsible Care,
which has a central organisation but then allows regional bodies to develop
which shape the Code in ways that make it relevant for their own regions.[19]

---

[14] Blagescu, de la Casas and Lloyd, *Pathways to Accountability*.

[15] International Federation of Red Cross and Red Crescent Societies and the International
Committee of the Red Cross 1995, Code of Conduct for the International Red Cross, the Red
Crescent and NGOs in Disaster Relief: Annex VI to the resolutions of the 26th International
Conference of the Red Cross and Red Crescent, Geneva; Cabassi, *Renewing our Voice*.

[16] E.g. the BOND Statement of Principles available at www.bond.org.uk/aboutus/principles.
html. BOND stands for the 'British Overseas NGOs for Development'. It is a network of over
300 UK-based organisations working in international development. See further www.bond.
org.uk/index.html.

[17] Commission of the European Communities 1995, 'Recommendation for Member States
and a Framework for a Code of Conduct for Non-Profit Organisations to Enhance
Transparency and Accountability in the Non-Profit Sector to Prevent Terrorist
Financing and other types of Financial Abuse', *The Prevention and Fight Against
Terrorist Financing through enhanced national level coordination and greater transpar-
ency of the non-profit sector*, COM(2005) 620 final.

[18] IOSCO is the International Organisation of Securities Commissions; BCBS is the Basle
Committee on Banking Standards, part of the Bank of International Settlements.

[19] There is a minor industry in drawing up classificatory systems for such bodies: one of the
more influential is Slaughter, *A New World Order*.

In these cases, there is at least an organisation which 'owns' the norms or codes that are produced. However, it may be that there is no central organisational structure, rather there is a body of written norms which firms themselves have decided to apply, but there is no central locus of authority to which they can turn to discuss the proper interpretation or application of the principles. The Equator Principles provide a good example. These are a set of principles for sustainable development which many banks require the borrowers to comply with when issuing loans for infrastructure development, mainly in the energy sector (dams, pipelines etc.).[20] There is no one organisation which is responsible for issuing the Principles, interpreting or revising them, however. The 'regulators' are the banks, regulating both themselves and others to ensure compliance with the principles, at least in the initial loan documentation. Non-state regulatory regimes in this case have the organisational form of co-ordinated systems of corporate social responsibility, rather than taking the form of a single agency regulator which parallels a governmental body.

3.   Relationship between accountability and legitimacy

Although the 'crisis' of accountability of non-state regulators tends to tar all with the same broad brush, different types of non-state regulatory regimes can rather pose different challenges. In particular the absence of any single locus of authority within a regulatory regime enhances the challenges of functionality and of accountability and legitimacy discussed further below. Nonetheless, reliance on the traditional forms of accountability either of state-based regulators, or indeed of corporations, is simply inadequate for such systems of regulation. In these debates, as indeed so far in this chapter, the terms accountability and legitimacy tend to be conflated. It is worth spending a brief time exploring their relationship more fully, however, before moving on to examine the different forms that demands for each can take.

Definitions of accountability abound and there are almost as many definitions as there are articles on the subject. As Mulgan has commented, it is a word which 'now crops up everywhere, performing all sorts of analytical and rhetorical tasks and carrying most of the burden of

[20] The 'Equator Principles': financial industry benchmark for determining, assessing and managing social and environmental risk in project financing 2006. Available at www.equator-principles.com.

democratic governance'.[21] Or as Bovens puts it: 'As an icon, the concept has become less useful for analytical purposes, and today resembles a garbage can filled with good intentions, loosely defined concepts and vague images of good governance.'[22]

As Mulgan demonstrates, from its 'core' meaning of being called to account for one's actions through a social exchange by an external body or group which has authority over one, it has expanded to include 'internal' accountability to one's own conscience or to norms of professional ethics; 'responsiveness' by governments to demands made on them by citizens; 'control' over institutions through the checks and balances of political systems and 'dialogue' public discussion between citizens.[23] There is dispute over each dimension: whether accountability is internal or purely external;[24] whether it involves interpersonal, social exchange or whether accountability can be to the impersonalised operations of the market; whether it has to involve hierarchical relationships of authority, and whether accountability means control, as Scott argues for example,[25] or whether something less, such as responsiveness or the ability to impose consequences on the object of accountability suffices.[26]

It is suggested that contrary to being seen as a form of control, accountability should not be equated with control. Debates about whether a person is 'internally' accountable to their own moral sense, for example, are conflating 'accountability' with the constraints on action that are posed by institutional norms. Similarly notions of being 'accountable' to the market refer rather to the organisation's responsiveness to the actions of market actors; not that it explains itself to the market, or engages in any dialogic process at all.

Rather, a far narrower notion of accountability is suggested: to be accountable is to agree to subject oneself to relationships of external scrutiny which can have consequences.[27] Although his definition is arguably too prescriptive of the actual processes that should be adopted, Boven's definition expresses the kernel of accountability: 'a relationship between an actor and a forum, in which the actor has an obligation to

---

[21] Mulgan, 'Accountability', 555. For a useful exercise in classification, see Mashaw, 'Accountability and Institutional Design'.
[22] Bovens, 'Analysing and Assessing Public Accountability', 447.   [23] *Ibid.*
[24] Dubnick, 'Clarifying Accountability'; Sinclair, 'The Chameleon of Accountability', 219.
[25] Scott, 'Accountability in the Regulatory State'.
[26] E.g. Bovens, 'Analysing and Assessing Public Accountability'.
[27] See also Keohane, 'Global Governance and Democratic Accountability'.

explain and justify his or her conduct, the forum can pose questions and pass judgement, and the actor may face consequences.' The emphasis on the forum, and particularly in the form Bovens envisages, is too restrictive but it does highlight what it is suggested is one of the central aspects of accountability: a relational responsiveness to others.[28]

Accountability is usually in turn linked to another iconic word: legitimacy. Like accountability, legitimacy is a 'mother and apple pie' concept which no one can argue against. Also like accountability, there is a significant debate as to its meaning, but in this case one which occupies legal and political theorists more than it does those interested in public management. Again, a shortcut through the debate is proposed. It is suggested that by legitimacy is meant whether or not an institution or organisation is perceived as having a 'right to govern' both by those it seeks to govern and those on behalf of whom it purports to govern.[29] This need not be based in law, but more broadly in social acceptance. In this institutionalist conception of legitimacy, legitimacy may be an objective fact, but it is socially constructed.[30] It rests on the acceptability and credibility of the organisation to those it seeks to govern. Organisations may claim legitimacy, and may perform actions and enter into relationships in order to gain it. But legitimacy is rooted in the acceptance of that organisation by others.

Legitimacy is linked with authority. Here again a shortcut is taken through a thicket of political and legal theory. Relying on Raz, as developed by Coleman, by authority is meant whether or not what an actor says or requires makes a 'practical difference' to the way that others act or behave, and whether it does so simply by virtue of the actor saying it. In other words, does the mere fact that a particular actor stipulates that a particular course of conduct should be followed mean that others (though by no means all) will alter their conduct not as a result of a rationalistic pursuit of preferences but principally out of a sense of obligation, or because that actor is respected or esteemed within the community for whatever reason.[31] This does not imply that those subject to the legitimate authority of someone issuing directives have an obligation to

---

[28] E.g. Keohane, 'Global Governance and Democratic Accountability'. The notion has also entered the CSR debate, see, e.g., Painter-Morland, 'Redefining Accountability', 89.

[29] See discussions in Barker, *Political Legitimacy and the State*.

[30] Scott, *Institutions and Organisations*.

[31] The concept thus draws on the concept of authority developed in jurisprudence by Raz as elaborated by Coleman: Raz, *The Authority of Law*; Coleman, 'Incorporationism', 381.

obey; but that the authority is perceived as justified in issuing directives to them.[32]

Accountability is usually seen as a central element of legitimacy in the sense that to be legitimate, an actor has to be accountable. However, this is too general a characterisation of their relationship to be satisfactory. As discussed, legitimacy is a perceived right to govern: how and why that perception is forged is another, highly complex issue addressed in part below, but the reasons are grounded in social acceptance. Accountability, for its part, is a particular type of relationship between different actors, in which one gives account and accepts that the other has the authority to impose consequences as a result. In other words, that the response of the person to whom account is made will make a 'practical difference' to the conduct of the one who gives account, either retrospectively, prospectively or both. A more specific description of the relationship of the two concepts, at least as they are defined above, is therefore that perceptions of the right to govern (legitimacy) may depend (in whole or in part) on whether the actor is accepted as having an appropriate accountability relationship with others, often including, but not necessarily confined to, the person whose perception is in question.

4. Constructing accountability and legitimacy

The debate on the accountability and legitimacy of non-governmental regulators, especially at the transnational level, often depicts organisational actors which are somehow disconnected: autonomous bodies which are not grounded in any particular sector of society or even in any one state. However, as institutional theory emphasises, all actors are embedded in social institutions, from which in turn they derive their legitimacy. The conceptions of legitimacy and accountability outlined above have a strong affinity with institutional theory, or at least some branches of it.

A minimalist definition of institutions is that institutions comprise cognitive and moral structures, rules, norms, conventions or operating procedures which are regarded as socially or legally binding but which are not self-enforcing.[33] For political scientists institutions also comprise the key political structures: legislature, executive, voting system, legal

---

[32] See discussion in e.g. Sadursky, 'Law's Legitimacy', 377.

[33] Ikenberry, 'Conclusion'; DiMaggio and Powell, 'Introduction'; Jepperson, 'Institutions'; Scott, *Institutions and Organisations*.

system and bureaucracy. For economists, they also comprise markets, firms and other institutions which facilitate and constrain economic interactions. Institutions have four key dimensions, which receive differing degrees of emphasis in the various strands of institutionalism: a behavioural or regulative dimension (providing the norms of action which are externally enforced), a cognitive dimension (beliefs and understandings of cause and effect relations), a normative dimension (providing norms of appropriateness and legitimacy), and (some would add) a resource dimension (distributing resources and regulating access and agendas of decision making).[34]

The core notion is that 'institutions matter' to individual and social action and interaction because they provide the structure in which the action and interaction occurs. They provide shared conceptions of reality, meaning systems and collective understandings that guide decision making and which individuals take for granted. Actors articulate and define their policy problems and solutions by using institutionalised scripts, cues and routines that constitute their cognitive frameworks and empower them to act but on which they do not necessarily reflect.[35] Decisions are made to pursue goals, but often the reaffirmation of processes and rituals and the communication of symbols and legitimacy is equally, if not more, important.[36] Finally, institutions have both stabilising and facilitating effects: for example, they explain how collective action problems are overcome, the stability of political decision making and why, in a situation of multiple Pareto-optimal equilibria, one policy option is chosen over another.

In institutional theory, legitimacy is central to an organisation's survival and development. Legitimacy means social credibility and acceptability: 'a generalised perception or assumption that the actions of an entity are desirable, proper or appropriate within some socially constructed system of norms, values, beliefs and definitions'.[37]

The notion of accountability posited above as relational can also be developed from an institutionalist base. The argument presented here is that accountability is not an abstract, technical process. This conception of accountability runs counter to the 'invisible hand' of cybernetics and

[34] March and Olsen, 'The New Institutionalism', 734–49; Hall and Soskice, 'An Introduction to Varieties'; Scott, *Institutions and Organisations*.
[35] DiMaggio and Powell, 'Introduction'; Scott, *Institutions and Organisations*; Meyer, Boli and Thomas, 'Ontology and Rationalization'.
[36] Meyer and Rowan, 'Institutionalized Organizations', 340–63.
[37] Scott, *Institutions and Organisations*.

collibration or other mechanistic portrayals of accountability. Accountability is rather relational and dialogic.

Institutionalism captures and articulates the relational, situated character of legitimacy and accountability but not its dialogic component, as it lacks a strong communicative dimension. Here, discourse theory can be used to complement institutionalist analysis in a number of ways; institutionalism in turn provides analytical structures which explain how discourse can affect action more satisfactorily than discourse theory can itself.[38] A discourse theory of regulation argues that discourse constitutes regulation in that it builds understandings and definitions of problems (for example 'market failure', 'risk', 'accountability gap') and acceptable and appropriate solutions ('meta-regulation', 'precautionary principle', 'audit', 'participation'); it builds operational categories (for example 'compliance', 'transparency'), and produces the identities of and relations between those involved in the process. It is functional in that it is designed to achieve certain ends (for example the strategic use of rule design; the deployment of skills of argumentation and rhetoric by all involved at every stage). It is co-ordinating in that it produces shared meanings as to regulatory norms and social practices which then form the basis for action (for example the formation of regulatory interpretive communities, or of accountability relationships).

Discourse theory therefore suggests that different legitimacy claims and associated accountability relationships will be grounded and expressed in different discourses; that these discourses will build different understandings and definitions of the 'accountability' problem and appropriate solutions, such as audit, performance evaluation, participation, and operational categories, such as compliance, so as to produce different forms of accountability relationship. Most importantly for this discussion, discourse theory emphasises the role of power in regulation: discursive practices, events and texts arise out of and are shaped by power and ideology and struggles over them, suggesting that which legitimacy claims an organisation will respond to will be a reflection of the constellation of power relationships in which it is situated.

5. Competing claims of accountability and legitimacy

Thus far it has been argued that legitimacy is socially constructed through institutions, that accountability is a communicative relationship entailing responsiveness and that different legitimacy claims are expressed in

---

[38] See Black, 'Regulatory Conversations', 163–96.

different legitimacy discourses. This analysis is to an extent consistent with the 'principal–agent' conception of accountability relationships familiar from some political science,[39] in that relationships of authority are argued to underly accountability relationships, although it prefers the less dichotomous model of organisation and environment.

But where does this leave the familiar debates on the 'types', 'forms' or 'sources' of accountability and legitimacy? Categorisations of accountability are as numerous as its definitions. The familiar ones include: legal, financial, managerial, ethical, technical, democractic and procedural. Legitimacy criteria are just as well numerated and have been argued to include: legal mandate, due process, efficiency, effectiveness and expertise,[40] to which may be added representativeness and/or democratic mandate, and conceptions of justice.

Categorisation exercises can be helpful; they can facilitate analysis and thus aid understanding. However, what the analysis above suggests is that categorisation in itself does not answer the question 'is this body accountable or legitimate?', because those questions are inherently relational. They cannot be answered in the abstract. They have to be met with the response: 'accountable or legitimate to whom?' Discussions on categorisation which link types of accountability with different values go further in this respect, as do those which recognise that different forms of accountability conflict. But again the essentially constructed nature of accountability, and indeed legitimacy, is glossed over.

Nonetheless, these different typologies do draw attention to the differentiated, and indeed contested, nature of both accountability and legitimacy. Organisational environments are not homogenous, and what is considered to be 'desirable, proper or appropriate' varies considerably across them. The implication of this analysis is that what constitutes legitimacy for one part of an organisation's environment, or what I characterise here as different legitimacy communities, will differ from that which constitutes legitimacy for another. Moreover, different legitimacy communities may well be seeking different accountability relationships, directly or indirectly, with the relevant organisation.

It is suggested that there are four broad types of legitimacy claims[41] and associated accountability relationships: legality/regulative, justice,

---

[39] E.g. Keohane and Nye, *Power and Interdependence*.

[40] For discussion, see Baldwin and McCrudden, *Regulation and Public Law*, and Baldwin and Cave, *Understanding Regulation*.

[41] Legitimacy claims refer to claims made by the organisation for legitimacy and the bases of credibility or acceptability that an organisation has in different parts of its environment.

performance and representation.[42] Legitimacy based on legality refers here very broadly to conformance with written norms (thus embracing so-called 'soft law' or non-legal, generalised written norms), and actions in conformity with a procedural form of the 'rule of law', including legal values of procedural justice. Its application beyond law is signalled by the alternative term 'regulative'. Legitimacy claims rooted in justice refer to the normative values which the organisation is pursuing, including the conception of justice (republican, Rawlsian, utilitarian, for example, or the various religious conceptions of 'truth' or 'right'). Performance refers to the manner of functioning of the organisation: its conformity to ethical, managerial, financial, technical norms. Representation refers to the conformance of the organisation to different governance models: representative democracy, deliberative democracy and so on. Each of these broadly corresponds to the challenges outlined above: systemic, functional, normative and democratic.

All of these merit considerable elaboration in themselves; however, the point that I want to make here is that these legitimacy claims are both contested and contestable, not only between the different groups, but within them. Indeed, there may be more conflict within different conceptions of a particular legitimacy claim (justice, performance) than there is between them. Moreover, different legitimacy discourses will build, and be reinforced by, different types of accountability relationships.[43] Those of legality require, for example, conformance to written norms, an impartial forum where disputes over the application of those norms is determined, and rules to be clear, stable and prospective and to be applied impartially and in accordance with norms of fair procedure. There are in turn differences over conceptions of fair procedure, or what constitutes impartiality and so on. Accountability relationships which stem from discourses of functionality include, for example, those of audit, cost–benefit analysis, performance evaluation. Legitimacy claims related to representativeness require accountability relationships based on different conceptions of representative, participative or deliberate democracy, for example. Accountability relationships associated with legitimacy claims related to justice are built around competing conceptions of rights or 'the good'. Each of these broad groups of legitimacy

---

[42] See Dubnick 'Clarifying Accountability' for a similar breakdown.
[43] Accountability relationships should not be confused with accountability tools – audits, for example, are not just financial but can be social or ethical; they can be used in different forms of accountability relationship.

claims has internal fractures and divisions, resulting in ever more complex demands for different types of accountability relationships.[44]

6. Organisational responses to competing claims

It is not necessary for legitimacy claims to be interlinked or mutually supporting for them to be met by an organisation simultaneously. They simply have to be compatible. It may be that, just as for a firm the 'win-win' solution of sustainable development and profitability can in some circumstances be attained, a regulatory organisation can operate in accordance with accepted modes of procedural justice, for example, whilst also operating in a financially responsible manner. The development of management models such as balanced scorecards, for example, used by a number of UK government bodies, are just such attempts to structure, or at least provide a reporting framework, for the organisation's responsiveness to different aspects of its environment.[45]

However, the demands of legitimacy communities may well be directly opposed, such as to satisfy one will necessarily lead to dissatisfaction of the other. Representativeness is a good example. Non-state regulators face this problem to a significant degree. Frequently, in order to satisfy the legitimacy claims of those they are regulating, their main decision-making bodies need to be composed solely or mainly of representatives of those regulatees; however, to be legitimate to a wider section of civil society, those decision-making bodies need to be solely or mainly composed of representatives from other sections of civil society. The same debate occurs in the context of risk regulation: to be legitimate to scientists, regulators have to be composed of scientific experts or at least be governed by them in their decisions; however, to be legitimate to other sectors of society, regulators have to include a wider proportion of society in their decisions – the familiar debate on lay versus expert models of decision maker. There are other conflicts: between those demanding procedural

---

[44] In terms of how this maps on to the four types of control mechanism outlined by Hood *et al.*: hierarchy, mutuality, competition and random selection – accountability relationships stemming out of any of the legitimacy claims can take these forms. These four types of control mechanism can be seen as cutting across the different accountability relationships and legitimacy claims. See Hood, *Regulation Inside Government*.

[45] The idea originated with Kaplan and Norton, 'The Balanced Scorecard', 71–79; it is increasingly used by UK governmental regulators to report on performance, e.g. the Health and Safety Executive and the Environment Agency. They are also used by state and regional healthcare providers in the US, Canada and the UK.

justice and those demanding maximum speed and efficiency in decision making. Even within models of administrative justice there are conflicts, as Mashaw's familiar typology of bureaucratic, moralistic and professional models of administrative justice demonstrates.[46]

Organisations then face a legitimacy dilemma: what they need to do to be accepted by one part of their environment is contrary to how they need to respond to another part. Forming one set of accountability relationships can preclude forming others; it simply is not possible to have complete legitimacy from all aspects of its environment. It may be that this does not matter: the organisation does not need to meet the legitimacy claims of a particular legitimacy community in order to pursue its goals or to survive. But this is unlikely always to be the case. In particular in the regulatory context, non-state regulators must often compete with other regulators to have their norms accepted,[47] as well as trying to ensure behavioural changes in others who are under no legal obligation to take any notice of them at all. Satisfying multiple legitimacy communities is necessary if their authority is to be recognised and accepted, and thus for their continued survival as a regulatory body. These challenges are also faced by legally sanctioned state-based regulators, and it is well recognised that the degree to which those who are being regulated accept the legitimacy of the regulator has a significant impact on compliance,[48] but governmental regulators can borrow on the authority of the state to bolster their legitimacy claims in a way non-state regulators cannot. Non-state regulators need to build legitimacy from the start.

Even if the conflict between legitimacy communities does not lead to a dilemma, it can have a deleterious effect on the organisation as it seeks to respond to the multiple legitimacy and accountability demands being made on it: in Koppell's evocative phrase, the organisation may suffer 'multiple accountability disorder'.[49] In other words, its attempts to respond to the multiple demands may diminish its chances of survival. Edwards, for example, has noted that the increasing demands on NGOs to develop the accountability trappings of financial audit, transparency, and so on, can result in NGOs becoming bureaucratised and increasingly

---

[46] Mashaw, *Bureaucratic Justice*.

[47] Meidinger, *Competitive Supra-Governmental Regulation*.

[48] See in particular Tyler, *Why People Obey the Law*; Tyler, 'The Psychology of Legitimacy', 323–45; Braithwaite and Reinhart, 'Taxation Threat', 137; Braithwaite, 'Regulatory Styles', 363.

[49] Koppell, 'Pathologies of Accountability', 94.

distant from the communities they seek to engage with and represent.[50] Research into the effects of the introduction of new public management tools of accountability and evaluation in health care and education, for example, is replete with complaints from those within those sectors that the demands of audit, performance targets and other accountability and other managerial tools are distorting organisational priorities away from what others (doctors, teachers) think should be the central role for the organisation.[51] Conflicting pressures on the organisation lead to internal conflicts between different parts of the organisation and to the adoption of a range of responses, from transformation and acquiescence to defiance and manipulation.[52] Attempts to make an organisation accountable, and in turn legitimate, can end up in the accountability equivalent of the 'regulatory trilemma':[53] they are ignored, co-opted, or destroy that which it is they seek to make accountable.

7. Implications for the accountability and legitimacy of non-state regulators

What are the implications of this analysis for our understanding of the accountability and legitimacy of regulators, in particular non-state regulators? It is suggested that two main implications flow which have not yet received the research attention that they merit.

The first implication relates to the debate on the design of accountability mechanisms. These debates often assume that accountability is a technical issue; that what is necessary is to improve the design, enhance the mechanisms, structure the springs, in such a way that accountability will necessarily follow.[54] But to reiterate, legitimacy and accountability are constructed; gaining each is not a technical exercise; it is a relational one.[55] Those relationships are not necessarily substitutable one for the

---

[50] Edwards, *Future Positive*, esp. chapter 11; Slim, 'By What Authority?'

[51] See e.g. Lindkvist, 'Performance Based Compensation in Health Care', 89; Lapsley, 'Reflections on Performance Measurement'; Laughlin, Broadbent and Shearn, 'Recent Financial and Accountability Changes', 129–48.

[52] See Brignall and Modell, 'An Institutionalist Perspective', 281. On the distorting effects of targets see Hood, 'Gaming in Targetworld', 515; Bevan and Hood, 'What's Measured is What Matters', 517. On internal conflicts and the transformative effects of accounting in particular on newly privatised industries in the UK see Ogden, 'Transforming Frameworks of Accountability', 193; Dent, 'Accounting and Organizational Reality', 705; Conrad, 'A Structuration Analysis of Accounting Systems', 1.

[53] Teubner, 'Juridification'.   [54] Scott, 'Accountability in the Regulatory State'.

[55] See also Lister, 'NGO Legitimacy', 175.

other such that if one fails another can take its place.[56] Substitutability assumes homogeneity in legitimacy claims between different legitimacy communities within the organisation's environment. But as discussed above, those claims are heterogenous, and may indeed be mutually incompatible.

Far more could be said on that issue. However, it is the second set of implications on which I want mainly to focus. That is what the above analysis implies for the organisation which is the subject of the accountability and legitimacy claims. How does it respond to these competing claims? Here there is very little empirical research done on non-state regulators and others in polycentric regulatory regimes. There is a considerable body of research investigating questions such as why regulated firms respond in the way they do to the demands of regulators: why do firms develop environmental policies which extend beyond regulatory requirements,[57] for example, or why do they comply with non-legal codes of conduct relating to corporate governance, or on the reasons for and nature of their non-compliance.[58] There has also been research on the narrower question of the impact of new public management reforms on parts of the civil service and public service organisations, in particular in health, education and local government.[59] There is some work which focuses on INGOs, though for the most part this has been of the 'powering' type – offering blueprints for accountability and legitimacy, blueprints which themselves are usually rooted in particular legitimacy claims (managerial performance, participative democracy).[60] However, there has been very little sustained research on how either governmental or non-governmental regulators respond to competing accountability and legitimacy claims, and even less on how these responses may be affected by their relationship with other regulators in polycentric regulatory regimes.[61]

---

[56] Contrast Scott, 'Accountability in the Regulatory State'.

[57] On the latter, see Kagan, Gunningham and Thornton, 'Explaining Corporate Environmental Performance', 51.

[58] See e.g. Parker, *The Open Corporation*.   [59] Above note 52.

[60] For review see Slim, 'By What Authority?'

[61] It should be noted that there is also little research on how regulated organisations respond to competing regulatory norms, both legal and non-legal. Most research is done on a domain-specific basis: 'how did Organisation X respond to set of regulatory norms Y?', where 'Y' is environmental rules, or competition requirements or health and safety provisions, and so on. This is also true for studies of transnational regulation, both treaty-based and 'soft law' provisions, see e.g. Shelton (ed.), *Commitment and Compliance*. For a rare exception see Haines and Gurney, 'The Shadows of the Law', 353.

Table 9.1 *Organisational Responses to Institutional Processes*[1]

Strategies	Tactics	Example
	Habit	Following inevitable, taken-for-granted norms
Acquiescence	Imitate	Mimicking institutional models
	Comply	Obeying rules and accepting norms
	Balance	Balancing the expectations of multiple constituents
Compromise	Pacify	Placating and accommodating institutional elements
	Bargain	Negotiating with institutional stakeholders
	Conceal	Disguising nonconformity
Avoid	Buffer	Loosening institutional attachments
	Escape	Changing goals, activities or domains
	Dismiss	Ignoring explicit norms and values
Defy	Challenge	Contesting rules and requirements
	Attack	Assaulting the sources of institutional pressure
	Co-opt	Importing influential constituents
Manipulate	Influence	Shaping values and criteria
	Control	Dominating institutional constituents and processes

[1]Oliver, 'Strategic Responses to Institutional Processes', 152.

Building on the institutionalist and relational conceptions of legitimacy drawn above, it is suggested that institutionalist theories can be deployed to develop a hypothesis as to how regulators, particularly but not uniquely non-state regulators, will respond to multiple legitimacy claims and calls for multiple accountability relationships. Oliver's typology of organisational responses could be a useful starting point for such an empirical inquiry. In a synthesis of resource theory of organisations and institutional theory, and buttressed by empirical research,[62] Oliver identifies five types of strategic response by organisations to institutional processes (see Table 9.1).[63]

[62] And assuming a particular model of action: Giddens' 'structuration' (in which an organisation or individual has agency but that agency is structured by their institutional environment).

[63] Oliver, 'Strategic Responses to Institutional Processes', 145. For use and refinement of Oliver's model in the context of public sector management, see Brignall and Modell, 'An Institutionalist Perspective'; Modell, 'Performance Management and Institutional Processes', 437. Her categories are akin to those developed from empirical research and psychology by Valerie Braithwaite: capitulation; commitment/accommodation; disengagement, resistance and game playing: Braithwaite, 'Regulatory Styles'.

Acquiescence is accession to institutional pressures. Such acquiescence may be 'blind' in the sense that it is an unconscious adherence to taken-for-granted rules; or it may be more strategic – compliance with regulatory norms, for example, in order to gain credibility and thus reduce negative assessments of its conduct, product or services. Compromise is an attempt to balance, pacify or bargain with external constituents, where demands are competing, and/or where the organisation considers unqualified conformity unpalatable or unworkable. Avoidance is the attempt to preclude the need to conform, by concealing non-conformity, buffering itself from institutional rules or pressures by decoupling its technical activities from external contact, or escaping from the domain in which pressure is being exerted: 'exit' in Hirschmann's terms. Defiance is a more active form of resistance to institutional pressures, and can consist of dismissing or ignoring institutional rules or values; challenging them; or more directly attacking them. Finally, organisations may manipulate the environment by actively changing, seeking to change or exert power over the content of the expectations themselves or the sources that seek to express or enforce them.[64] This may be through co-opting the source of the pressure, attempts to manipulate the terms of debate,[65] or using controlling tactics: specific attempts to exert power or dominance over the external constituents that are applying pressure.

What determines which approach an organisation will adopt is the key research question. Response will be structured by the institutional environment and will be a function of both capacity and willingness to conform to different parts of its institutional environment. Oliver suggests that the scope of an organisation's willingness to respond is bounded by organisational scepticism, political self-interest and organisational control. The scope of an organisation's capacity to respond is bounded by organisational capacity, internal conflict and awareness. She suggests that organisational responses to institutional pressures to conformity will depend on five sets of categories, each with two dimensions. These are the nature of the pressures exerted/what the organisation gains from acquiescence (cause), which might be either social fitness or economic gain; who is exerting them (constituents), notably the multiplicity of claimants and the organisation's dependence on them; how consistent those demands are with the organisation's own goals (content), and

---

[64] *Ibid*, 152–59.
[65] Oliver does not note this, but discourse theory would suggest that this could be through deploying rhetorical tactics or otherwise seeking to change the discursive framing of an issue.

Table 9.2 *Oliver's Predictions of Organisational Responses*

Responses / Predictive Factor	Acquiesce	Compromise	Avoid	Defy	Manipulate
Cause					
Legitimacy	High	Low	Low	Low	Low
Efficiency	High	Low	Low	Low	Low
Constituents					
Multiplicity	Low	High	High	High	High
Dependence	High	High	Moderate	Low	Low
Content					
Consistency	High	Moderate	Moderate	Low	Low
Constraint	Low	Moderate	High	High	High
Control					
Coercion	High	Moderate	Moderate	Low	Low
Diffusion	High	High	Moderate	Low	Low
Context					
Uncertainty	High	High	High	Low	Low
Interconnectedness	High	High	Moderate	Low	Low

whether they are congruent with the organisation's goals and whether they constrain the organisation's discretion or not; the means by which they are imposed (control), by legal or non-legal means and whether the norms, values and practices are diffused or not throughout the environment; and the nature of the environmental context in which they occur (context), in particular whether it is characterised by uncertainty, and the degree of interconnectedness or degree of interorganisational relations within the organisational field.[66]

She then draws on sociological institutional theory, supplemented by organisational resource theory, to develop hypotheses on choice of strategy based on variation in the ten dimensions of these five categories (see Table 9.2).

The key set of hypotheses for our purposes is how will an organisation respond in a situation of uncertainty, in which uncertainty is increased by multiple, mutually incompatible or inconsistent demands,[67] for that is

---

[66] Oliver, 'Strategic Responses to Institutional Processes', 159.

[67] Incompatible here means the demands are by nature incompatible; inconsistent means that they are potentially compatible but are differently demanded over time.

the situation faced by many organisations, not least non-state regulators. Here the hypothesis suggests that responses will range from compromise to manipulation, depending on the degree of dependence, consistency, constraint, coercion, diffusion, uncertainty or interconnectedness in the organisation's environment. However, there is no set of hypotheses for the situation where legitimacy gains are perceived to be high in such a situation, presumably because it is assumed that overall legitimacy gains cannot be high in a situation of multiple and competing demands. However, it may still be the case that legitimacy gains may potentially be made to a number of different legitimacy communities (that is, is it always 'high'), but as it stands Oliver's hypotheses do not extend to situations where, although legitimacy gains might be high with respect to particular legitimacy communities, the organisation does not acquiesce. Arguably the hypothesis here would be that in a situation of multiple legitimacy claims, an organisation will not acquiesce even if legitimacy gains are high in situations where there is a low dependency of the organisation on that legitimacy community, the normative content of the claims are congruent only to a moderate or low degree, the constraints on discretion would be moderate or high, coercion is low, diffusion is low, uncertainty is high and interconnectedness is low.

Clearly, therefore, there is scope for elaboration and refinement of Oliver's model, but it is suggested that it could found the basis of fruitful empirical research into how regulators, especially non-state regulators, in fact respond to demands for legitimacy and accountability.

Still lacking from this analysis is any real conceptualisation of the role of power in accountability and legitimacy relationships – something which is often underplayed in sociological institutionalism.[68] However, it is suggested that the introduction of discourse theory into the analysis partly redresses this omission and in turn has implications for those who are seeking to make the organisation respond to their legitimacy claim. Discourse theory suggests that absent any other resource, the legitimacy community (or its constituent) will have to rely on discourse; in other words it will have to translate its demands into a discourse that the organisation already recognises in order to build relationships of accountability with the organisation that it seeks.[69]

---

[68] For emphasis elsewhere see Keohane and Nye, *Power and Interdependence*.

[69] For examples of this 'translation' in a regulatory context see Hajer, *The Politics of Environmental Discourse*; Morgan, *Social Citizenship*.

8. Conclusion

This chapter did not set out to provide an answer directly to the extraordinarily difficult questions: how to make actors in decentred or polycentric regulatory regimes, in particular, non-state regulators, accountable. It seeks to clear a path to answering it, however, by proposing that we understand better how such organisations themselves respond to the various legitimacy demands which are made upon them. Not only is such understanding of intrinsic interest, it should be the basis for forging answers to that initial, challenging question. It may also assist those who are seeking to increase regulators' responsiveness to their own legitimacy claims.

In order to begin to create that path, some conceptual groundwork had to be done. The chapter therefore examined the relationship between accountability and legitimacy, and suggested that both are relational concepts which are socially and discursively constituted. This in turn provides the basis for the second proposition, which is that there are different legitimacy communities, composed of actors within and outside the regulatory regime who have different perceptions as to the relevance and validity of different legitimacy claims with respect to different regulatory actors. This in turn led to a third proposition, which is that different legitimacy claims, and associated discourses, are not always compatible but may compete. Fourthly, we see that although organisations can often participate in a number of different legitimacy discourses simultaneously, and thus satisfy a range of different legitimacy communities, this can not only have a deleterious effect on the organisation (which may suffer 'multiple accountability disorder'), the differences between communities may be such that organisations can face a legitimacy dilemma: that actions that they need to take to render them legitimate for one legitimacy community are in direct opposition to those they need to adopt to satisfy another. In turn, attempts to make the organisation increasingly accountable may result in an accountability trilemma: they may be ignored, co-opted or destroy that which they seek to make accountable.

These propositions already find support in much of the current debates. The chapter then sought to explore two main consequences of these propositions for regulatory accountability and legitimacy. First, that different accountability or legitimacy mechanisms (or rather relationships) are not necessarily substitutable, as not all will satisfy every legitimacy community. It is not therefore always possible to maintain legitimacy by replacing one with another when the first one fails, unless the replacement is recognised by that legitimacy community. Second, that how organisations respond to competing legitimacy demands is structured by the particular institutional context in which the regulatory regime, and the individual organisation, operates. Regulators are not ciphers. They can be active participants in the debate on their own accountability and legitimacy, not just passive recipients. They may exhibit the same strategies of avoidance, defiance, manipulation, compromise or acquiescence in response to pressures for their accountability and legitimacy as any organisation does in response to any norms which others seek to impose on them. 'How to' proposals for accountability which ignore these different organisational response strategies are as weak as any proposal for a regulatory strategy which ignores how its prescriptions will be received.

Finally, the chapter proposes a further theoretical step and, pursuing the interplay of institutionalism with discourse theory, suggests that in acquiescing in, or at least reaching a compromise with, some legitimacy communities, the organisation indicates that it is prepared to recognise those, whilst refusing to recognise others. This has implications for those who are seeking to get the organisation to respond to their accountability and legitimacy demands. Absent other key resources, the chapter suggests that those legitimacy communities whose demands have not been recognised will have to translate them into the discourses of those that have been recognised if they are to build the relationships of accountability with the organisation that they seek. Together, it is suggested that these propositions could form the basis of detailed empirical research into how non-state regulators respond to competing demands for legitimacy and accountability, particularly in situations of uncertainty.

References

Baldwin, R. and McCrudden, J. C. 1987, *Regulation and Public Law*, London, Weidenfeld and Nicolson.

Baldwin, R. and Cave, M. 1999, *Understanding Regulation*, Oxford University Press.

Barker, R. 1990, *Political Legitimacy and the State*, Oxford University Press.

Bevan, G. and Hood, C. 2006, 'What's Measured is What Matters: Targets and Gaming in the English Public Healthcare System', *Public Administration*, vol. **84**, no. 3, 517.

Black, J. 2001, 'Decentring Regulation: Understanding the Role of Regulation and Self-Regulation in a "Post-Regulatory" World', *Current Legal Problems*, vol. **54**, 103–47.

Black, J. 2002, 'Regulatory Conversations', *Journal of Law and Society*, vol. **29**, no. 1, 163–96.

Blagescu, M., de la Casas, L. and Lloyd, R. 2005, *Pathways to Accountability: the GAP Framework*, London, Global Accountability Partnership, available at www.oneworldtrust.org.

Bovens, M. 2007, 'Analysing and Assessing Public Accountability: A Conceptual Framework', *European Law Review*, vol. **13**, no. 4, 447.

Braithwaite, J. and Drahos, P. 2000, *Global Business Regulation*, Oxford University Press.

Braithwaite, V. *et al.* 1994, 'Regulatory Styles, Motivational Postures and Nursing Home Compliance', *Law and Policy*, vol. **16**, no. 16, 363.

Braithwaite, V. and Reinhart, M. 2007, 'Taxation Threat, Motivational Postures and Responsive Regulation', *Law and Policy*, vol. **29**, nos. 1–22, 137.

Brignall, S. and Modell, S. 2000, 'An Institutionalist Perspective on Performance Measurement and Management in the New Public Service', *Management Accounting Research*, vol. **11**, 281.

Cabassi, J. 2004, *Renewing our Voice: Code of Good Practice for Responding to HIV/Aids*, Geneva, The HIV/AIDS Code of Practice Project, Geneva, available at www.hivcode.org/silo/files/code-of-good-practice.pdf.

Castells, M. 2000, *The Rise of the Network Society: Economy, Society and Culture*, Oxford, Blackwell.

Chinkin, C. 2000, *Normative Development in the International Legal System* in Sheldon (ed.), 21–42.

Coleman, J. 1998, 'Incorporationism, Conventionality and the Practical Difference Thesis', *Legal Theory*, vol. **4**, 381.

Conrad, L. 2005, 'A Structuration Analysis of Accounting Systems and Systems of Accountability in the Privatized Gas Industry', *Critical Perspectives on Accounting*, vol. **15**, 1.

Dent, J. 1991, 'Accounting and Organizational Reality: A Field Study of the Emergence of a New Organizational Reality', *Accounting Organizations and Society*, vol **16**, no. 8, 705.

DiMaggio, P. and Powell, W. 1991, 'Introduction' in W. Powell and P. DiMaggio (eds.), *The New Institutionalism in Organizational Analysis*, Chicago University Press, 1–40.

Dubnick, M. 1998, 'Clarifying Accountability: An Ethical Framework' in C. Sampford and N. Preston (eds.), *Public Sector Ethics*, Leichhardt/Annadale, Routledge, 68–81.

Edwards, M. 1999, *Future Positive: International Co-operation in the 21st Century*, London, Earthscan.

Edwards, M. 2000, *NGO Rights and Responsibilities: A New Deal for Global Governance*, London, Foreign Policy Centre.

Edwards, M. and Hulme, D. (eds.) 1995, *Non-Governmental Organisations: Performance and Accountability*, London, Earthscan.

Haines, F. and Gurney, D. 2003, 'The Shadows of the Law: Contemporary Approaches to Regulation and the Problem of Regulatory Conflict', *Law and Policy*, vol. **25**, no. 4, 353.

Hajer, M. 1995, *The Politics of Environmental Discourse*, Oxford Univeristy Press.

Hall, P. and Soskice, D. 2001, 'An Introduction to Varieties of Capitalism' in P. Hall and D. Soskice (eds.), *Varieties of Capitalism: The Institutional Foundations of Comparative Advantage*, Oxford University Press, 1–69.

Harlow, C. and Rawlings, R. 2007, 'Promoting Accountability in Multi-Level Governance: A Network Approach', *European Law Journal*, vol. **13**, no. 4, 542.

Heclo, H. 1974, *Modern Social Politics in Britain and Sweden*, New Haven, Yale University Press.

Hood, C. 2006, 'Gaming in Targetworld: The Targets Approach to Managing British Public Services', *Public Administration Review*, vol. **66**, no. 4, 515.

Hood, C. *et al.* 1999, *Regulation Inside Government: Waste-Watchers, Quality Police and Sleaze-Busters*, Oxford University Press.

Ikenberry, G. 1988, 'Conclusion: An Institutional Approach to Foreign Economic Policy' in G. Ikenberry, D. A. Lake and M. Mastanduno (eds.), *The State and American Foreign Economic Policy*, Ithaca, Cornell University Press, 219–43.

Jepperson, R. 1991, 'Institutions, Institutional Effects and Institutionalism' in W. Powell and P. DiMaggio (eds.), *The New Institutionalism in Organisational Analysis*, University of Chicago Press, 143–63.

Kagan, R., Gunningham, N. and Thornton, D. 2003, 'Explaining Corporate Environmental Performance: How Does Regulation Matter?', *Law and Society Review*, vol. 37, 51.

Kaplan, R. and Norton, D. 1992, 'The Balanced Scorecard – Measures that Drive Performance', *Harvard Business Review,* January–February, 71–79.

Keohane, R. 2003, 'Global Governance and Democratic Accountability' in D. Held and M. Koenig-Archibugi (eds.) *Taming Globalization: Frontiers of Governance*, London, Polity Press, 130–59.

Keohane, R. and Nye, J. 2001, *Power and Interdependence*, 3rd edn, New York, Addison-Wesley Longman.

Kickert, W., Klijn, E. and Koppenjan, J. (eds.) 1997, *Managing Complex Policy Networks*, London, Sage.

Klijn, E. and Koppenjan, J. 1995, 'Public Management and Policy Networks in the Public Sector: A Theoretical Study of Management Strategies in Policy Networks', *Public Administration*, vol. **73**, no. 3, 437.

Klijn, E. and Koppenjan, J. 2000, 'Public Management and Policy Networks. Foundations of a Network Approach to Governance', *Public Management*, vol. **2**, no. 2, 135.

Koppell, J. 2005, 'Pathologies of Accountability: ICANN and the Challenge of "Multiple Accountability Disorder"', *Public Administration Review*, vol. **65**, no. 1, 94.

Koskienniemi, M. 2007, 'The Fate of Public International Law: Between Technique and Politics', *Modern Law Review*, vol. **70**, 1.

Lapsley, I. 1996, 'Reflections on Performance Measurement in the Public Sector' in I. Lapsley and F. Mitchell (eds.), *Accounting and Performance Measurement: Issues in the Private and Public Sectors*, London, Paul Chapman Publishing, 109–28.

Laughlin, R., Broadbent, J. and Shearn, D. 1992, 'Recent Financial and Accountability Changes in General Practice: An Unhealthy Intrusion into Medical Autonomy?', *Financial Accountability and Management*, vol. **8**, 129–48.

Lindkvist, L. 1996, 'Performance Based Compensation in Health Care – A Swedish Experience', *Financial Accountability and Management*, vol. **12**, 89.

Lister, S. 2003, 'NGO Legitimacy: Technical Issue or Social Construct?', *Critique of Anthropology*, vol. **23**, no. 2, 175.

Luhmann, N. 1995, *Social Systems*, Stanford University Press.

March, J. and Olsen, J. 1984, 'The New Institutionalism: Organisational Factors in Political Life', *American Political Science Review*, vol. **78**, 734–49.

Mashaw, J. L. 1983, *Bureaucratic Justice: Managing Social Security Disability*, New Haven, Yale University Press.

Mashaw, J. L. 2007, 'Accountability and Institutional Design: Some Thoughts on the Grammar of Governance', *Yale Law School Research Paper*, no. 116, available at http://papers.ssrn.com/abstract=924879.

McBarnet, D., Voiculescu, A. and Campbell, T. (eds.) 2007, *The New Corporate Accountability: Corporate Social Responsibility and the Law*, Cambridge University Press.

Meidinger, E. 2007, 'Competitive Supra-Governmental Regulation: How Could it be Democratic?', *Buffalo Legal Studies Research Paper Series*, available at http://ssrn.com/abstract=1001770.

Meyer, J. and Rowan, B. 1977, 'Institutionalized Organizations: Formal Structure as Myth and Ceremony', *American Journal of Sociology*, vol. **83**, 340–63.

Meyer, J., Boli, J. and Thomas, G. 1994, 'Ontology and Rationalization in the Western Cultural Account' in W. Scott, J. Meyer *et al.* (eds.), *Institutional Environments and Organizations: Structural Complexity and Individualism*, Thousand Oaks (CA), Sage, 9–27.

Modell, S. 2001, 'Performance Management and Institutional Processes: A Study of Managerial Responses to Public Sector Reform', *Management Accounting Research*, vol. **12**, 437.

Morgan, B. 2003, *Social Citizenship in the Shadow of Competition*, Aldershot, Ashgate.

Mulgan, R. 2000, 'Accountability: An Ever Expanding Concept?' *Public Administration*, vol. **78**, no. 3, 555.

Nyamugasira, W. 1998, 'NGOs and Advocacy: How Well Are the Poor Represented?', *Development in Practice*, vol. **8**, no. 3, 297.

Ogden, S. 1995, 'Transforming Frameworks of Accountability: The Case of Water Privatization', *Accounting Organizations and Society*, vol. **20**, no. 2/3, 193.

Oliver, C. 1991, 'Strategic Responses to Institutional Processes', *Academy of Management Review*, vol. **16**, no. 1, 145.

Painter-Morland, M. 2006, 'Redefining Accountability as Relational Responsiveness', *Journal of Business Ethics*, vol. **66**, 89.

Papadopoulous, Y. 2007, 'Problems of Democratic Accountability in Multilevel Governance Systems', *European Law Journal*, vol. **13**, no. 4, 469.

Parker, C. 2001, *The Open Corporation*, Cambridge University Press.

Power, M. 2005, *The Risk Management of Everything*, London, Demos.

Raz, J. 1979, *The Authority of Law*, Oxford University Press.

Roberts, S. 2005, 'After Government? On Representing Law without the State', *Modern Law Review*, vol. **68**, 1.

Rosenau, J. and Czempiel, E. O. (eds.) 1992, *Governance without Government: Order and Change in World Politics*, Oxford University Press.

Sadursky, W. 2006, 'Law's Legitimacy and "Democracy Plus"', *Oxford Journal of Legal Studies*, vol. **26**, no. 2, 377.

Schmidt, V. 1995, 'The New World Order Incorporated: The Rise of Business and the Decline of the State', *Daedalus*, vol. **124**, no. 2, 75.

Scott, C. 2000, 'Accountability in the Regulatory State', *Journal of Law and Society*, vol. **23**, 38.

Scott, W. 2001, *Institutions and Organisations*, 2nd edn, Thousand Oaks (CA), Sage.

Shelton, D. (ed.) 2000, *Commitment and Compliance*, Oxford University Press.

Sinclair, A. 1995, 'The Chameleon of Accountability', *Accounting Organizations and Society*, vol. **20**, 219.

Skelcher, C. 2005, 'Jurisdictional Integrity, Polycentrism and the Design of Democratic Governance', *Governance*, vol. **18**, no. 1, 89.

Slaughter, A. M. 2005, *A New World Order*, Princeton University Press.

Slim, H. 2002, 'By What Authority? The Legitimacy and Accountability of Non-Governmental Organisations', *The International Council on Human Rights Policy International Meeting on Global Trends and Human Rights – Before and After 11 September*, Geneva, January 2002 (available at www.jha.ac/articles/a082.htm).

Teubner, G. 1987, 'Juridification – Concepts, Aspects, Limits, Solutions' in G. Teubner (ed.), *Juridification of the Social Spheres*, Berlin, de Gruyter, 3–48.

Teubner, G. 1997, '"Global Bukowina": Legal Pluralism in the World Society' in G. Teubner (ed.), *Global Law Without a State*, Aldershot, Dartmouth, 3–28.

Tyler, T. 1990, *Why People Obey the Law: Procedural Justice, Legitimacy and Compliance*, New Haven, Princeton University Press.

Tyler, T. 1997, 'The Psychology of Legitimacy: A Relational Perspective on Voluntary Deference to Authorities', *Personality & Social Psychology Review*, vol. 1, no. 4, 323–45.

10

Accountability of transnational actors: is there scope for cross-sector principles?

MONICA BLAGESCU* AND ROBERT LLOYD**

1. Why the accountability of transnational actors matters

Governance at levels beyond that of the nation state has become an unavoidable reality. A web of connections now binds us globally through trade, finance and communications. While this brings undoubted benefits to many, it also brings complex new problems such as financial instability, the spread of disease and international terrorism that transcend national boundaries and require collaborative global solutions. The growth in the number and scope of intergovernmental organisations (IGOs) reflects this growing need for greater state coordination. But the complexity and multiplicity of such problems has meant that IGOs alone are often unable and sometimes unwilling to respond to the myriad global problems we now face. Too often they lack the capacity, the knowledge or the political will to develop appropriate solutions and take collective action. As a result, non-state actors such as transnational corporations (TNCs) and global civil society organisations, particularly international NGOs (INGOs), have come to play an increasingly important role in the global public sphere, contributing their expertise in

* Monica Blagescu is currently the Policy Services Coordinator of Humanitarian Accountability Partnership (HAP) International, Switzerland. She was previously Accountability Programme Manager at the One World Trust and has an MA in International Affairs from the International University, Japan, and a BA in Political Science and Mass Communications from the American University, Bulgaria. She is based in Juba, South Sudan. This chapter draws on Blagescu, M. and R. Lloyd 2006, Global Accountability Report, One World Trust, London (UK). A follow-up report using the same methodology was published in 2007.
** Robert Lloyd is Global Accountability Project Manager at One World Trust. He has an MA in Governance and Development from the University of Sussex and a BA in Geography from King's College London.

addressing global issues, in advocating or influencing governmental bodies to take action.

Much of the influence of non-state actors within the global public sphere comes from their ability to affect new norms and standards on issues of societal concern. INGOs such as Transparency International, for example, have been instrumental in pushing the issue of corruption higher on the political agenda, and setting new standards. Likewise, Amnesty International has for over the past 20 years shaped and monitored compliance with international norms of human rights.

In some cases, non-state actors have adopted a more institutionalised role in standard setting at the global level. Actors such as the International Organisations for Standardisation develop and verify compliance with standards that some countries adopted as part of regulatory frameworks. Organisations worldwide are certified with compliance to ISO 9000 series (on quality management systems). Likewise, organisations such as Forest Stewardship Council or the Fairtrade Foundation have defined and certified compliance with new standards on the ethical sourcing of wood and ethical trade respectively.

Non-state actors are also setting standards for themselves through self-regulation. Corporations and increasingly INGOs are defining what is deemed ethical and accountable through self-regulatory arrangements such as aspirational codes of conduct, quality assurance and compliance verification schemes. Many functions are being assumed by non-state actors which were previously the preserve of the state.

2.   The rise of non-state actors and questions of their accountability and legitimacy

The dispersal of power to transnational non-state actors has also placed new problems on the global governance agenda; most notably it has led to concerns and questions over the legitimacy of decisions made and standards developed by these actors, given they lack a traditional mandate to govern. Related to this is also the question of who has the responsibility for making sure their actions are not harmful, but beneficial to the individuals and communities they affect.

Within the current global governance context, traditional forms of accountability are no longer appropriate. Fifty years ago, when societal regulation was undertaken primarily by states and international organisations were both small in number and limited in authority, state-based accountability was appropriate. In today's complex system of global governance, however, state-based accountability has become ill-equipped to provide those influenced and affected by transnational non-state actors with an adequate voice in how decisions at this level are made. What role can state regulation in one country play in ensuring Oxfam International, for example, is responsive to the people it provides humanitarian aid to in a different country and/or region? Likewise, what can states do to ensure the ISO takes on board the concerns of all key stakeholders (cross-border) in the development of their new CSR standard to be published in 2009? Can the state legislate for greater accountability of transnational non-state actors? Ultimately, global governance requires innovations that involve new principles of accountability, some which need to be applicable across a wide range of powerful transnational actors.

The legitimacy and effectiveness of global governance rests on our ability to address these accountability gaps and to tackle the challenge of ensuring meaningful inclusion of relevant stakeholders (especially the most marginalised) in the global public sphere. Mechanisms are required to hold transnational actors accountable and new approaches must be developed for translating principles of accountability into practice.

Non-state actors play an important role in the global public sphere; they are filling an important governance gap, setting and enforcing standards on a number of global public policy issues where none currently exist, and are pushing states to act on issues that too often are absent from the political agenda. They are playing a key role in the governance of societal affairs. Legitimacy can come from many sources.[1] Inter-governmental organisations, international NGOs and transnational corporations are increasingly taking on roles which have not always been delegated by those whom they affect; at times, such actors are not able to show that, and how, they are fit for purpose and that indeed they are effective in delivering their mission and vision. Stakeholder accountability – as explained below – can enable them to draw legitimacy from those whom they affect (by demonstrating how they are addressing needs of their stakeholders) and to strengthen effectiveness (by better protecting or responding to the needs of those whom they affect).

2.1   Intergovernmental organisations (IGOs)

The mobilisation of civil society, such as the demonstrations outside the World Trade Organisation (WTO) meetings in Seattle in 1999, reflects

---

[1] For an extensive discussion on types of legitimacy and their relation to accountability, please see Brown and Jagadananda, *Civil Society Legitimacy*.

the realisation that IGOs are performing an increasing range of tasks which go beyond their original mission and which affect an increasing number of people. However, it is not only 'mission creep'[2] that makes it difficult for stakeholders to hold IGOs to account, but also the fact that these institutions are so large that the chain of responsibility is difficult to understand.[3]

IGOs face accountability demands from different stakeholder groups, and are usually judged against three sets of potentially conflicting measures: whether they serve the interests of their member states; whether they serve the purposes for which they were established; and how their impact compares to evolving standards of benefits and harms.[4]

Formally, IGOs are accountable (supervisory and fiscal accountability) to their members – the nation states that fund them and make up their membership. However, the power imbalances that exist between members mean some nations have more influence and can demand more accountability than others. For instance, it is estimated that the developed countries make up 15 per cent of the world's population, yet account for over 60 per cent of voting strength in the World Bank and the IMF.[5] Given that power is often related to the amount of resources provided by members, industrialised countries are the main shareholders of IGOs, and their governments exercise decisive influence on important policy issues compared to other stakeholders.[6] The inequity of this situation is exacerbated further in cases where the less powerful states also lack the capacity to participate and effectively present their views within the decision-making processes.

Additionally, most citizens are unable to engage effectively with IGO decision-making structures, primarily because of the gap between constituencies, elected representatives and foreign policy decision making.[7] Elected representatives do not play an effective role at the national level in holding governments to account for their actions at IGOs, and the vast majority of IGOs (except NATO and the European Union) have no

---

[2] Einhorn, 'The World Bank's Mission Creep'.   [3] Woods, 'Unelected Government', 9–12.
[4] Grant and Keohane, 'Accountability and Abuses', 29–44.
[5] Helleiner, 'Markets, Politics and Globalisation', quoted in World Commission on the Social Dimension of Globalisation.
[6] WCSDG 2004, *A Fair Globalization: Creating Opportunities for All*, International Labour Organisation, Geneva.
[7] The One World Trust also promotes greater accountability of governments to national parliaments in relation to their actions at the global level. For information on the Parliamentary Oversight Project, which aims to enhance oversight of UK external policy by the British Parliament, please see www.oneworldtrust.org/?display=project)pid=11.

formal mechanism for democratically elected representatives to participate in decision making at the global level. There is therefore no adequate
route for citizens to participate in decisions taken by these organisations,
highlighting a lack of accountability to external stakeholders, particularly
to those who are most affected by the decisions of IGOs.

2.2   International NGOs

Perceived as having a moral legitimacy to speak on behalf of the less
powerful, INGOs have become adept at mobilising the media and generating public support for their causes. From trade justice to environmental protection, they have come to exert a growing influence at the
international level, shaping the policies and setting the agendas of a
number of multilateral institutions. At the same time, INGOs provide a
range of services in many developing countries from health care to water
provision. It is estimated, for example, that World Vision International
on its own supported over 100 million people in 96 countries in 2007.[8]
The growth in the scope of INGOs' activities and the increasing power
they wield in the international arena have given rise to concerns about
their accountability.

INGOs are accountable to government regulators and institutional
donors, those that provide them with a legal and financial base. Given the
leverage these actors have over INGOs, the responsibilities between
governments, donors and INGOs are generally clear and the mechanisms for ensuring accountability strong. INGOs' accountability *downwards* (to those that they affect, provide services to or speak on behalf of
in policy forums),[9] *inwards* (to their organisational mission, values,
members, supporters and staff) and *horizontally* (to their peers) often
lacks the same clarity and strength.[10] The fact that affected communities
often lack the power to make demands on INGOs means the accountability relationships with them are often seen to be weak. INGOs'
accountability to the general public is also weak with few organisations
openly communicating the real complexities of their work for fear of
jeopardising funding. The responsibility that INGOs owe to their peers

---

[8] JustGive.org 2008, *World Vision International.* Available at: www.guidestar.org/
pqShowGsReport.do?partner=justgive&npoId=2097.
[9] Najam, 'NGO Accountability'.
[10] Brown and Jagadananda, 'Civil Society Legitimacy'; Edwards and Hulme, 'NGO
Performance and Accountability'.

also lacks clarity. Although this should be high to uphold the reputation of the sector, norms or standards around what constitutes good practice have been underdeveloped until recently.[11] A growing number of NGOs are now engaging in self-regulation, most through negotiating common principles and a few through verifying compliance with agreed standards.[12]

2.3   Transnational corporations

Globalisation, deregulation and liberalisation have resulted in the increased power of TNCs in the global public sphere and their growing influence over activities which were traditionally the preserve of nation states. This has intensified as the number, scope and activities of TNCs have developed. The primary power of TNCs comes from their financial size and economic leverage. This enables them to engage in the political arena – lobbying with respect to regulation and licences, and supporting political parties – and gives them a degree of leverage over countries seeking their investment.[13] Both the decisions and actions of TNCs can have huge impact on a large number of people. TNCs, therefore, effectively operate in the global public sphere and their frequent denomination as 'private sector' businesses belies the reality of their true impact and reach.

TNCs face multiple calls for accountability – from shareholders, employees, suppliers, financiers, contractors, customers, government, the general public, groups affected by operations, peers, etc. – many of which compete or even conflict, and which must be balanced. The shareholders' position as owners of the company skews the accountability balance towards them, at the expense of accountability towards other groups that the TNC might affect.

The primary accountability mechanism for TNCs remains national regulatory requirements. The standards set by these regulations vary but, in general, protect only the interests of certain stakeholders; for instance, investors and creditors (financial reporting requirements), workers (labour standards), consumers (product safety standards) and the general public (for example environmental impact legislation). Although

---

[11] Brown, 'Building Strategic Accountability Systems', 31–43.
[12] See, for example, Sphere Project (aspirational standards); the HAP Standard in Humanitarian Accountability and Quality Management (linked to third-party compliance verification and certification). For an extensive list of initiatives see www.oneworldtrust.org/csoproject.
[13] Newell and Bellour, *Mapping Accountability*.

these remain critical accountability mechanisms for TNCs, the spread of globalisation has significantly weakened states' resolve (and sometimes ability) to intervene and enforce such regulations. This has exacerbated the accountability gaps between citizens and corporations.[14]

A number of international standards also apply which relate to, or have implications for, TNCs' accountability, although they are generally non-enforceable; for example the OECD Guidelines for Multinational Enterprises, the UN Global Compact and the Equator Principles. TNCs are also accountable to their peers, customers and investors. Increasingly, groups of businesses are developing self-regulation mechanisms or codes of conduct relating to certain issues, therefore encouraging peer accountability. Consumers have also played an important role in holding TNCs to account. Their influence has been particularly strong where a TNC has a high-profile brand and reputation to protect. Both institutional and individual investors are becoming more aware of their influence over TNCs and are taking into consideration social and environmental factors when making their investment decisions.

3.   Accountability – the conceptual framework

3.1   Understanding accountability

Accountability is for many a concept subject to multiple interpretations. An accountability relationship exists when a principal delegates authority to an agent to represent and act in their interests (the representative model and the principal–agent model). Within these models, holding an agent to account requires clearly defined roles and responsibilities, regular reporting and monitoring of behaviour against these roles, and the ability for principals to impose sanctions for breaches of responsibilities. According to this understanding, accountability is largely seen as an end-stage activity where judgement is passed on results and actions after they take place.

This understanding is too narrow; accountability needs to be more encompassing if it is to ensure organisations are truly answerable to those they affect. Accountability is no longer determined by delegation of authority alone. Although an individual may not have delegated authority to an organisation to act in their interest, the activities of the latter may impact substantially on them, enough to warrant the establishment

---

[14] Keohane, 'Global Governance and Democratic Accountability', 29–44.

of an accountability relationship. This view of accountability (the stakeholder model) emphasises that organisations have to respond to the needs of many stakeholders. For an organisation to be truly accountable for its decisions and actions, relevant stakeholders need to be involved at different stages of the decision-making process. Accountability is no longer an end-stage activity. Passing judgement after a decision is made limits the extent to which an organisation can be accountable. Organisations need to take into account the views of stakeholders, to give stakeholders an account of their actions and decisions, and to enable stakeholders to hold them to account.

Understanding accountability in this way extends the limits of the traditional concept beyond its role as a disciplinary mechanism and towards its use as a transformative process. An organisation that is accountable to multiple stakeholders not only ensures that decisions are effective in meeting the needs of those they affect, but also that decision-making processes are more equitable. This more open and participatory approach moves accountability away from 'policing' towards promoting learning and organisational change. Accountability pursued as a process opens us space for improvement: it enables organisations to learn and respond to the needs and views of different stakeholders when meeting its mission and vision.

When understood in this way, accountability is no longer simply a mechanism for disciplining power, but a process that enables organisational change and strengthens increased performance and effectiveness.

3.2   The Global Accountability Framework

After an in-depth analysis of accountabilities for transnational actors[15] and a pilot Index Report,[16] the Global Accountability Project (GAP) at the One World Trust defines accountability as:

> the processes through which an organisation makes a commitment to respond to and balance the needs of stakeholders in its decision-making processes and activities, and delivers against this commitment.

This definition emphasises the need for organisations to *balance* their response to accountability claims and *prioritise* between different stakeholder groups according to organisational missions and criteria such as *influence, responsibility* and *representation*. It is unrealistic to expect an

---

[15] For more details see Blagescu, *Pathways to Accountability*.
[16] For more details see Kovach, Neligan and Burall, *Power without Accountability?*.

organisation to use the same type of mechanisms at all times and to be equally accountable to all stakeholder groups; this would lead to paralysis.

The Framework identifies four core accountability dimensions that are critical to managing accountability claims from both internal and external stakeholders (see Figure 10.1):

Transparency: is the provision of accessible and timely information to stakeholders. To be transparent, an organisation must be open about activities and performance and provide information on what it is doing and how well it is doing it through financial statements, annual reports and performance evaluations. This is the basic information needed by stakeholders to monitor an organisation's activities and to hold it to account for its commitments, decisions and actions. It also relates to responding to information requests.

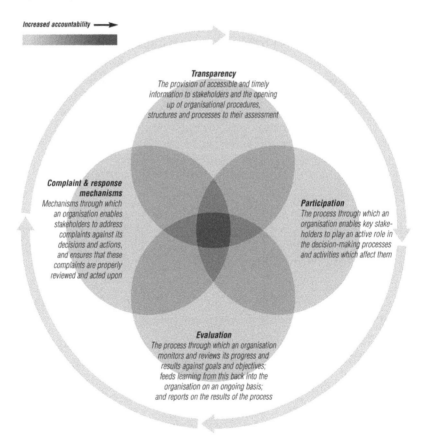

Figure 10.1   The Global Accountability Framework

Participation: is the active engagement of both internal and external stakeholders in the decisions and activities that affect them. Participation must allow for change; it has to be more than acquiring approval for, or acceptance of, a decision or activity.

Evaluation: in this context, evaluation refers to the processes through which an organisation, with involvement from key stakeholders, monitors and reviews its progress against goals and objectives; it incorporates learning into future planning; and it reports on the results of the process. Evaluation ensures that an organisation both learns from, and is accountable for, its performance.

Complaint and response mechanisms: provide the means through which an organisation enables stakeholders to file complaints on issues of non-compliance, or against its decisions and actions, and through which it ensures that these complaints are properly reviewed and acted upon. Complaint and response mechanisms should be seen as a last resort for ensuring accountability. *Transparency, participation* and *evaluation* processes should be used to minimise the need for complaint mechanisms.

4.   Measuring accountability

4.1   What is the Global Accountability Index?

The Global Accountability Index (the 'Index') is the first initiative to measure and compare the accountability of transnational actors from intergovernmental, non-governmental and corporate sectors. It assesses how accountable 30 of the world's most powerful organisations are to civil society, affected communities and the wider public, on the basis of four core dimensions of accountability: transparency, participation, evaluation, and complaint and response mechanisms.

It is the values, attitudes and behaviours of individuals that drive the culture and practice of accountability within organisations. Organisational capabilities[17] emerge from the presence of these values, attitudes and behaviours as well as the structures that support them – they foster the organisational culture and enable accountability claims to be managed. The Index documents the degree to which the headquarters or international secretariat of the assessed organisations have the capabilities in place to

---

[17] Policies, i.e. written organisation documents that guide performance, and the systems that support them. For more on this, see section 3.4.2.

enable accountability and responsiveness to both the communities they affect and the public at large. In doing so, the Index offers the first quantitative insight into how accountability values and principles are becoming embedded in the organisational capabilities of transnational actors. Complementing the ongoing need for more qualitative work in this area, the Index offers new angles for comparative analysis and practical improvement and provides a unique perspective on the emerging picture of accountability in the currently amorphous global public sphere.

The diverse missions, operating styles, organisational histories, cultures and resulting structures of transnational actors present unique challenges to any attempt to develop broadly applicable accountability indicators. Questions around to whom, for what and how an organisation ought to be accountable are complex and linked to the context in which they operate, their scale, the area of activity and sector of work. As a result, the accountability strategies organisations employ vary. In recognition of this, the Index does not measure organisations against a rigid one-size-fits-all set of accountability standards, nor does it dictate the specific structures through which these standards should be operationalised. It rather assesses the presence of *key accountability principles and values* in existing organisational capabilities (policies and systems), independent of the different shapes and forms in which they may manifest themselves. This approach is more suited to the cross-sector comparison, as it provides for greater flexibility in what is being measured and allows for a better capturing of organisation- and sector-specific capabilities that reflect emerging principles of accountability good practice.

4.2   How was the Index developed?

The development of the Global Accountability Framework took place over the course of five years and engaged representatives from non-governmental, corporate and intergovernmental sectors as well as a cross-reference group of their respective stakeholders. Workshops and online forums were convened that brought together representatives of these transnational actors to debate and discuss what accountability meant in practice. This was cross-referenced with minimum expectations of accountability on the part of these organisations' stakeholders. Through these discussions, a framework for accountability was developed. The four dimensions in the Global Accountability Framework – transparency, participation, evaluation, and complaint and response mechanisms – and the principles that underlie them represent those issues that stakeholders saw as integral to being accountable, irrespective of an organisation's sector of operation.

The indicators used in assessing the accountability of 30 of the world's most powerful organisations (the Global Accountability Index) have been developed based on this Framework. In doing so, the GAP attempts to put forward an emerging standard of accountability of transnational actors.

4.3   Important parameters for the interpretation of the Index

Whenever comparative assessments are undertaken, especially when they are of a quantitative nature and applied across different actors and sectors, questions of accurate and appropriate categorisation and scoring will arise. This Index is the first of its kind both to attempt cross-sector assessment and capture what to many is inherently qualitative information in a quantitative approach. The results of this work are therefore best interpreted within the following important parameters.

First, the purpose of this Index and its underlying framework of analysis is to provide a tool for meaningful analysis and practical pathways to strengthened accountability. We are aware that if applied with a heavy hand or in an inflexible manner, any quantitative model has the potential to hinder progress. However, if applied sensitively it will help to illuminate good practice, highlight accountability gaps, encourage cross-sector learning, and promote realistic reforms to bring powerful transnational actors closer to the people they affect.

Second, the Index captures the existence of and commitment to values and principles of accountability at the headquarters or international secretariat level of an organisation; and the internal capability to implement these principles across the wider organisation, network, federation or group *to ensure accountability to affected communities and the public at large.* The presence and quality of accountability policies and systems at this level is taken either as reflecting an already existing organisation-wide commitment to the issue, or as an indication that the headquarters or international secretariat recognises that these stated values and principles should be applied throughout the organisation as a matter of good practice.

Third, the Global Accountability Report does not attempt to measure the inevitable variations and differences between commitments that are made in organisational documents at the international office and what happens in practice at the field level. Depending on the type of organisations and governances structures that they have in place, such differences can be a reflection of decentralised organisations, loose links between international and field offices, or inadequate communication and management practices. The study therefore does not claim to present a full and definitive assessment of the overall accountability of indexed organisations. What happens in practice and at field level is obviously key for a more definitive assessment of any organisation's accountability and we are progressively developing indicators to capture these aspects.

Fourth, we recognise that accountability is a concept subject to multiple cultural or sector-specific interpretations and understandings. The Index does not claim to capture the breadth of manifestations that accountability principles may take across organisations. However, based on our work to date, there is recognition of the emergence of good practice principles of accountability that transcend all sectors.

Also it is important to establish a basis for comparison across organisations which operate in the same global public sphere. This is why the analytical framework is based on a defined set of underlying values and principles of accountability, and measures organisational commitments, policies and systems against these principles across sectors.

4.4   Why measure accountability?

In the same way that accountability of transnational actors matters, so does the need for sufficient and good-quality data on how accountability principles are operationalised in the currently amorphous global public sphere.

Debate and practice on the accountability of transnational actors is still an emerging area, with some organisations and policy makers only just beginning to grasp its relevance. With this in mind, there are a number of reasons why assessing global accountability is important.

First, measuring the accountability of transnational actors and documenting the systems and policies that are currently in place allow for the identification and dissemination of emerging good practice in accountability. In doing so, we can highlight and give credit to those organisations that have taken the necessary steps towards becoming more accountable and provide those that have yet to engage meaningfully with the issue with the incentive and the knowledge on how to move forward.

Second, measuring accountability will help shift debates around the accountability of transnational actors beyond purely theoretical and largely ideological (and rhetorical) understandings and help ground them in empirical analysis. It needs to be noted, however, that not all that can be measured matters, and not all that matters can be measured. There are important elements of accountability that cannot be easily captured in quantitative indicators.

Third, measuring accountability will help to identify accountability gaps within specific transnational actors, their sectors and, as our data set grows, the global public sphere more broadly. This knowledge will help organisations and their stakeholders identify where efforts and resources should be concentrated to strengthen accountability and, in doing so, increase the effectiveness of decisions and operations.

Fourth, finding and applying appropriate quantitative methods to measuring accountability generate new data and create meaningful opportunities for analysis. This does not just fill an important gap in our knowledge of the rapidly expanding transnational arena, but it also offers pragmatic options for addressing the existing accountability gaps.

4.5   The Index disaggregated

This section describes in more detail what the Index measures, how the nature and scope of different sectors and organisations have been taken into account in the assessment process, and lists the key indicators that have been used.

4.5.1   Flexibility in the assessment: accountability to whom and for what?

All the organisations assessed in the Index (see Table 10.1) have multiple internal and external stakeholders that they need to be responsive and accountable to (see Table 10.2). The Index does not attempt to capture an organisation's accountability to each of these in equal measure, but rather focuses on a select range based on the current imbalances that exist within the transnational actors' accountability systems. The nature and purpose of each of the three sectors have also been considered when answering the 'accountability to whom?' question, together with the specific scope of each individual organisation.

IGOs need to be accountable to civil society organisations as expression of citizen groups' interests, affected communities and also of societal

Table 10.1 *List of Assessed Organisations*

Intergovernmental organisations	International non-governmental actors	Transnational corporations
Bank for International Settlements (BIS)	ActionAid International (AAI)	Anglo American plc
Food and Agriculture Organization (FAO)	Amnesty International (AI)	Dow Chemical Company
Global Environment Facility (GEF)	Human Life International (HLI)	Exxon Mobil Corporation
International Labour Organization (ILO)	International Chamber of Commerce (ICC)	Microsoft Corporation
International Monetary Fund (IMF)	International Confederation of Free Trade Unions (ICFTU)	Nestlé
Organisation for Economic Cooperation and Development (OECD)	International Federation of Red Cross and Red Crescent Societies (IFRC)	News Corporation
World Health Organisation (WHO)	The Nature Conservancy	Pfizer Inc
World Intellectual Property Organisation (WIPO)	Oxfam International (OI)	RWE
World Bank/IBRD	World Vision International (WVI)	Toyota Motor Corporation
World Trade Organisation (WTO)	World Wildlife Fund International (WWF)	Wal-Mart Stores Inc

Table 10.2 *Internal and External Stakeholders that the Index Focuses on*

Sector	Internal stakeholder	External stakeholders
IGOs	Member states' staff	Relevant civil society organisations and the wider public
INGOs	National organisations' (sections, affiliates etc) staff	Affected communities and the wider public
TNCs	Shareholders' staff	Relevant civil society organisations, affected communities and the wider public

expectations more broadly. As public bodies, IGOs also need to be accountable to the general public. They are funded with citizens' tax contributions
and need to show accountability for their decisions and actions.

INGOs need to be accountable to affected communities, those that are
directly impacted by their activities, be it through the aid they deliver, the
projects they run or the position they assume in policy forums. These
groups are often integral to the values and mission of the organisation.
The Index also looks at INGOs' accountability to the wider public. The
legitimacy of INGOs is intricately linked to public trust; without the
public's financial support, and their willingness to volunteer and support
campaigns, INGOs would not be able to function.

TNCs need to maintain some level of accountability to relevant civil
society groups, as an expression of citizen groups' interests, communities
affected by their operations and of (changing) societal expectations more
broadly. They should also be accountable directly to communities that
they affect in multiple and profound ways. Having transformed how
people work and live, and with the increased impact on social and
environmental issues, they also need to be accountable to the public on
those issues of public interest.

In each of the sectors, organisations also need to be accountable to their
internal members, those that jointly 'own' the organisation, and also to staff
and other stakeholders that are formally part of the organisation.

We recognise that each sector and organisation will have more stakeholders than those focused on here under this broad categorisation;
however, these are the ones to whom accountability is often lacking the
most. While recognising that organisations in the three sectors are
accountable to some sets of stakeholders, it is to the groups below that
they also need to strengthen their accountability.

Based on this understanding, Table 10.3 identifies the overarching
questions asked across the dimensions in relation to the three sectors.

4.5.2   Assessing organisational capabilities that enable, support and foster accountability principles

In each of the four dimensions, indicators are grouped into two categories:

Policy: a written document/policy through which the organisation
   makes a commitment to the values and principles of transparency,
   participatory decision making, evaluation and learning, and handling
   and responding to complaints; and

Table 10.3 *What the Index Measures; by Dimension and Sector*

Sector	Transparency	Participation	Evaluation	Complaint and response
IGOs	Do they ensure public disclosure of information and respond to information requests on decision-making processes, policies and operations that have an impact on the *wider public*?	**Internal**: Do governing articles ensure equitable voice and control among *member states*? **External**: Do IGOs ensure that *civil society organisations are engaged in decision-making processes that affect them*?	Do they ensure evaluation of projects, programmes, policies and wider strategies, and integrate this learning in future planning?	Do they ensure a safe channel for *staff, partners, affected communities and the public at large* to file complaints for non-compliance with organisational policies and other commitments and do they offer them a response?
INGOs		**Internal**: Do governing articles ensure equitable voice and control among *national chapters, affiliates and other members*? **External**: Do INGOs ensure that *affected communities and relevant public are engaged in decision-making processes that affect them*?		
TNCs		**Internal**: Do governing articles ensure equitable voice and control among *shareholders*? **External**: Do TNCs ensure that *civil society organisations and affected communities are engaged in decision-making processes that affect them*?	Do they ensure evaluation of social and environmental impact and integrate learning in future planning?	

Systems: the management strategies and resources through which the organisation encourages, enables and supports the implementation of the commitment made in the policies above.

Together, these two groups of indicators reflect an organisation's capabilities to enable, support and foster accountability practice.

a. Policy   The presence of written organisational documents that guide performance in each of the four dimensions of accountability foster consistent implementation across the organisation, provides stakeholders with an understanding of how the organisation is addressing the issue and enables them to hold the organisation to account against stated commitments.

Here, we assessed both the existence of such policies and their quality – the good practice principles that underlie them. An organisation, for example, may make a general commitment to being transparent in its code of ethics, or in its organisational values; alternatively it may have a specific transparency policy or policy on public information disclosure, which provides details both to staff and external stakeholders on how, when and what information will be made available. While a general commitment to transparency is important, having written documentation that guides an organisation's approach to disclosure reflects a deeper understanding of the issues and will result in more consistent and coherent implementation. As a result, written policy documents are given more weight than general, more vague commitments. The quality indicators assess the breadth and depth of this commitment and vary across the four dimensions.

b. Systems   Indicators under this category capture three cross-cutting issues: leadership, training and accessibility.

Leadership refers to the commitment that exists at the highest level within an organisation to ensure effective implementation of key accountability principles. Without support from those in positions of power, there is little chance that accountability will take hold within an organisation; and even if it does, without high-level commitment, implementation will only ever be piecemeal, implemented in relation to individual projects, but never integrated throughout the organisation. It is therefore important that a senior manager or Board member has responsibility for overseeing implementation of relevant policies that enable accountability or (in the absence of a policy) for oversight of the accountability principles underlying the accountability dimension more broadly.

Training: the capacity of relevant staff to fulfil their responsibilities and to enable them to comply with organisational policies can be enhanced through training. Providing training on the implementation of accountability-related areas shows the organisation's commitment to invest resources and build the capacity of staff to become more accountable. Training and coaching are important steps towards ensuring that accountability values and principles become embedded into an organisation's culture, across the board.

Accessibility relates to the need for organisations to make accountability-related policies or positions available to external stakeholders through appropriate mediums and in relevant languages. Given that a core element of accountability is meeting stated commitments, it is essential that external stakeholders are aware of what these commitments are so they can hold organisations to account against them. In this regard, policies and other relevant documents need to be disseminated through different media and in different formats (online, print, workshops, etc.) and translated so as to be accessible to relevant stakeholder groups.

5.   Methodology

The indicators were scored based on publicly available data, questionnaires that were completed by the assessed organisations, internal documents and other information collected through semi-structured interviews with representatives of the assessed organisations and external experts or stakeholders of the organisations. The assessments are based on public data that was available as of June 2006, and internal information and feedback from external experts provided as of September 2006.

Ten organisations out of the 30 included in the assessment chose not to engage in the research; in these cases, the indicators have been scored solely based on public information and data collected from independent experts and stakeholders of the organisations. Consequently, in these instances, scores may not necessarily reflect their 'true' accountability but more accurately their lack of transparency. These organisations may have structures and policies in place to support accountability but they are not publicly disclosing this information. This is problematic in and of itself given the primacy of transparency to an accountable organisation and the need for affected communities and the wider public to know how accountability is fostered. Non-engaging organisations are identified in all the graphs and tables with an asterisk next to their name.

5.1   Data collection process

The research process consisted of five integrated stages: desk-based research, questionnaires, interviews, internal reviews, and feedback from organisations and their external stakeholders on the preliminary findings. In this last stage, valid and relevant information provided both by organisations and external stakeholders resulted in changes to the data and the scores.

Assessed organisations were contacted early in the process, invited to engage in the assessment and asked to commit to completing a questionnaire and to undertaking a follow-up interview. Twenty out of the thirty organisations agreed to participate although the level of engagement varied, with some dedicating more time and resources to the study than others.

A list of key primary documents used in the study is available at the end of this report. Full details of primary and secondary sources are available on the One World Trust's website.

5.2   Scoring

Indicators that measure the existence of policies or other written organisational documents that guide performance in relation to each of the dimensions have been scaled on the basis of the type of document(s) and the level of enforcement that they imply:

0 points: no organisational document is present that guides performance in relation to principles within the dimension

¼ point: a vague commitment to the dimension is present in organisational documents

1 point: a strong commitment to the dimension is provided in a specific policy or incorporated into multiple organisational documents

Indicators in relation to the principle that underlie these commitments and system indicators have been scored on the basis of whether a particular item or attribute (as described in Table 10.4) is present (1 point) or absent (0 points). Although this binary scoring system is potentially limiting, we maintained flexibility in how scores were assigned to accommodate the different nature of the three sectors and of individual organisations.

The majority of indicators were weighted equally, but those indicators which were judged to contribute more to organisational accountability were double-weighted. The scores for each organisation were totalled

Table 10.4 *Key Indicators by Dimension*

Dimension	Key indicators*
Transparency	Policy Does the organisation make a commitment to being transparent or have a document in place that guides public disclosure of information? Does the document(s) include: • A commitment to respond to requests for information and provide a justification for denial? • Clarity about the timeframe for responding to information requests? • A narrowly defined set of conditions for non-disclosure? • An appeal process in place if an information request is denied? Systems Does the leadership of the organisation assume responsibility for oversight of transparent practices within the organisation in compliance with the specific policy or other relevant documents? Do relevant members of staff receive training on information disclosure and responding to information requests? Is the specific policy or relevant document that guides information disclosure accessible to the public? Is there a specialised function on the organisation's website that allows the public to ask a question or request information?
Participation	Policy *External stakeholder engagement* Does the organisation make a commitment to engaging affected communities and other external stakeholder in decision-making processes or have a document in place that guides engagement? Does the document(s) include: • The conditions under which external stakeholders can expect to be engaged and at what level of decision making? • Details on how external stakeholders can initiate engagement on issues that are of concern to them? • A commitment that the organisation will clearly communicate in a timely manner the purpose of the engagement and that the results of engagement will be made public unless otherwise specified by external stakeholders?

Table 10.4 (*cont.*)

Dimension	Key indicators*
	• A commitment that the organisation will change policy or practice as a result of engagement else an explanation is provided to stakeholders?
	Internal member control Do the organisation's governing documents ensure equitable member control at the governing and executive body levels? Do the governing documents ensure a minority of members are not able to dominate decision making within the organisation?
	Systems Does the leadership of the organisation assume responsibility for overseeing compliance with the specific policy or other relevant documents on external stakeholder engagement? Do relevant members of staff receive training on external stakeholder engagement? Is the specific policy or relevant document that guides engagement accessible to external stakeholders? Has the organisation institutionalised the involvement of external stakeholders in high-level decision making?
Evaluation	Policy Does the organisation make a commitment to evaluate or have a document in place that guides evaluation? Does the document(s) include: • A commitment to engage external stakeholders in the evaluation of activities that have impacted them? • Commitment to use the results of evaluation to inform future decision making? • Commitment to be open and transparent about evaluation results? • Commitment to evaluate performance in relation to the strategic plan, key internal management and administrative policies, issue-specific policies, and operations?
	Systems Does the leadership of the organisation assume responsibility for oversight of evaluation within the organisation in compliance with the relevant documents?

Table 10.4 (*cont.*)

Dimension	Key indicators*
	Do relevant members of staff receive training on evaluation?
	Are the documents that guide evaluation accessible to external stakeholders?
	Is there a mechanism in place for disseminating lessons learnt within the organisation?
Complaint and response	Policy
	Does the organisation make a commitment to, or have a policy on, addressing complaints from external and internal stakeholders regarding issues of non-compliance?
	Do(es) the document(s):
	• Guarantee confidentiality, non-retaliation and independence of investigation from the complainant and the subject of the complaint?
	• Provide a clear description of how a complaint can be made and how it will be investigated?
	• Identify an independent appeal mechanism?
	• Include a commitment to reverse all negative consequences suffered by victims of proven whistleblower retaliation?
	• Require mandatory discipline for anyone found to have retaliated against a whistleblower?
	Systems
	Does the leadership of the organisation assume responsibility for compliance with the specific policy or other relevant documents on handling complaints?
	Do the relevant members of staff receive training on how to deal with and respond to complaints from internal and external stakeholders?
	Is the policy that guides complaint and response mechanisms accessible to internal and external stakeholders?
	Does the organisation have in place a functioning mechanism through which external stakeholders can file a complaint in relation to issues of non-compliance?

* A full list of indicators and sub-indicators can be accessed on the One World Trust's website at www.oneworldtrust.org/accountability.

and weighted out of 100 per cent for each dimension. There is an equal weighting between policies and systems, the two categories that cut across the dimensions. Both are integral to effective organisational capabilities.

Within the participation dimension, two different sets of organisational documents are being analysed under the policy category: those that guide external stakeholder engagement and the governing articles, which guide internal member control. Again, both are weighted equally. Also, within the complaint and response dimension, an equal weight is given to the policies and systems in place for dealing with complaints from internal and external stakeholders.

For the practice issues in relation to online disclosure of information and evaluation, the same weighting was used; scores were totalled and weighted out of 100 per cent.

5.3   Challenges of assessing cross-sector accountability

There are numerous challenges associated with trying to measure cross-sector accountability in relation both to the data collection process and indicator development. These are highlighted below.

First, although at the beginning of the study we attempted to capture practice across all four dimensions as a way of highlighting relevant correlations between accountability capabilities and the type of practice that they support, multiple challenges were encountered. For example, given the multitude of stakeholders and engagement processes that organisations undertake, a decision was made to use a case study approach to measuring the practice of external stakeholder engagement and seek plausible proof of the type and quality of the engagement. Organisations were asked to provide two examples of a high-level stakeholder engagement process they had undertaken in the past 12 months. Although a number of case studies were collected, the data was inconclusive in enabling comparisons between organisations and across sectors.

In relation to the complaint and response dimension, in order to provide a meaningful measure of the quality of practice, stakeholders that filed complaints would need to be contacted to offer their experiences of the process and identify if they were content with the redress they received. Given the confidentiality under which complaints are usually made, conclusive data on the quality and effectiveness of complaint and redress mechanisms could not be collected. A more in-depth analysis of procedures with focus on the type of response offered might be considered in the future.

Second, non-engagement by some organisations led to data gaps where the data necessary to score the indicators was not publicly available. While the lack of data is in and of itself an indication of unaccountable practices, given the score variation this creates across organisations from the same sector, positive accountability development and better performers are lost in aggregate scores. It is for this reason that non-engaging organisations are highlighted in the report and that average scores by sector need to be interpreted with caution.

Third, a decision was made not to offer an organisation-specific aggregate or average accountability score based on data across the four dimensions. As mentioned before, this is in recognition that aspects of accountability assessed in this study are not definitive and providing an accountability score might be misleading. For example, one dimension might be more relevant to an organisation than others in relation to a specific stakeholder group, depending on the nature of the relationship.

6.   Concluding cross-dimension analysis

This following section offers a short analysis of some of the high-level trends that have emerged from this study both across sectors and dimensions.

6.1   Seven organisations from the three sectors score above 50 per cent in at least three dimensions

Although each dimension is important in and of itself, there is a need for good performance across all dimensions for an organisation to be considered accountable. This is due to the inter-linkages that exist across the four dimensions. For example, an evaluation process underpinned by openness and transparency strengthens organisational accountability more than one that is conducted in secrecy. Similarly an organisation that has well-developed policies in place to foster participatory practices, but lacks similar capabilities in relation to complaint and response mechanisms, is not fully accountable; such an organisation does not offer stakeholders a channel through which they can file complaints and receive a response in relation to less adequate engagement processes.

Using the threshold of 50 per cent to differentiate between organisations that are developing their accountability capabilities and those that lag behind, it emerges that no organisation scores above 50 per cent in all

Table 10.5 *Organisations that Score more than 50 per cent Across Three of the Four Dimensions of Accountability*

	Transparency	Participation	Evaluation	Complaint and response
IGOs	GEF, OECD, World Bank/ IBRD	GEF, OECD	GEF, OECD World Bank/IBRD	World Bank/ IBRD
INGOs	ActionAid International	ActionAid International, World Vision International	ActionAid International, World Vision International	World Vision International
TNCs	Pfizer	Anglo American	Anglo American, Pfizer	Pfizer, Anglo American

four dimensions. Yet seven organisations manage this in three of the dimensions. While these organisations still have a way to go to meet existing good practice accountability principles, they have the most consistently developed capabilities across three of the four accountability dimensions.

The cross-sector balance of these seven organisations highlights that innovation and positive developments in accountability are not concentrated in one specific sector and that there are many areas where organisations from different sectors can learn from each other (see Table 10.5).

6.2   *Accountability systems are developed, but documents that guide them lack principles of good practice*

Across the four dimensions, the systems that organisations from all three sectors have in place to support accountability score on average better than the policies that guide their approach on these issues. Organisations are investing time and resources into developing the structures and capacity to strengthen their accountability, but the demonstrated quality of the principles that underpin their commitments remains low.

For each of the four dimensions, the policies that organisations currently have in place to guide their approach lack the good practice principles most crucial to strengthening accountability. For example, while all IGOs make a commitment to engaging with civil society actors in decision-making processes that affect them, none make a specific commitment that they will change policy or practice as a result of the engagement or else they will provide an explanation. This principle might be reflected in IGOs' practice of engaging with CSOs, but without embedding it into written organisational documents, it means that CSOs cannot hold them to account for the quality of that engagement. In addition, IGOs run the risk that a minimum level of good practice will not be implemented consistently across the organisation.

Across the three dimensions, the gap between policies and systems is greatest within transparency. This difference comes from the absence of coherent organisation-wide policies that guide disclosure of information among many of the organisations. While virtually all organisations make a commitment to being transparent and have senior managers that oversee public disclosure of information, few have in place a clear policy that provides guidance to both internal staff and external stakeholders on what information will be made available, when and how, and that identifies a narrowly defined set of conditions for non-disclosure. This highlights a shortcoming in many organisations' thinking on transparency. Most continue to see it as a one-way flow of standardised information such as financial accounts; but transparency also relates to responding to requests for information and engaging in dialogue with stakeholders regarding the information they need. Currently, the understanding among transnational actors seems to be that the obligation to justify why information should be made available ought to be on external stakeholders, rather than on the organisations themselves. This is at odds with emerging transparency norms that recognise access to information as a right.

The discrepancy between transparency policies and systems can also be explained by the well-developed external relations/PR and communications capacities of transnational actors. Many of the organisations assessed in the Index identified their external relations departments as having responsibility for overseeing organisation-wide transparency practice. Although these systems might perform well in terms of releasing information with the purpose of managing the image of the organisation, they are not always sufficient to govern and bring about the disclosure of information across the organisation that satisfies principles of good practice in this area.

The graph in Figure 10.2 provides the average dimension scores by sector and indicates that INGOs and TNCs each lead on one of the

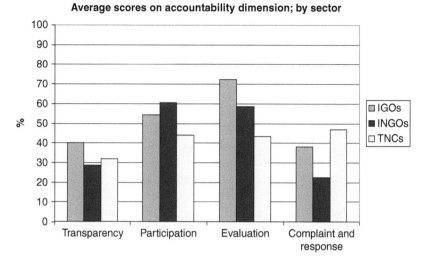

Figure 10.2 Cross-Dimension Performance in Accountability: Strengths and Weaknesses of Sectors

dimensions while IGOs are top for two. On average, both INGOs and TNCs scored last for at least one of the four dimensions, while IGOs are never last, although lagging in certain areas.

6.3   Of the four accountability dimensions, IGOs on average score highest on evaluation and lowest on complaint and response mechanisms

The good performance of IGOs in the evaluation dimension is a reflection of multiple factors; most noticeably the intense scrutiny IGO performance has come under from both civil society organisations and member states. Although the challenge of evaluating performance is considerable for IGOs, with many operating across multiple levels and geographical regions, the need to demonstrate impact and effectiveness has necessitated the strengthening of capabilities for assessing performance, ensuring learning and reporting results.

Within the World Bank and the IMF, for example, the pressures to demonstrate outcomes and results have led both institutions to establishing independent evaluation mechanisms that report directly to the Board and provide an independent objective assessment of project, programme and policy effectiveness within these institutions. The incentive to increase evaluation and learning capabilities within these was further strengthened by the International Financial Advisory Commission (Meltzer Commission), whose 2000 report argued that the World Bank was costly, inefficient, bureaucratic and unable to carry out their mission of poverty alleviation under current structures.[18] Both IGOs now have evaluation policies in place.

Within the UN system, agencies have faced similar pressures to provide evidence of their effectiveness; reflecting this, the focus among UN agencies has shifted from measuring inputs to measuring performance. As a consequence, there has been a greater focus on the need to strengthen accountability and evaluation capabilities. Of the four UN agencies assessed in the Index, three have policies in place that guide their evaluation practice (FAO, ILO, WHO) while the fourth is in the process of developing one (WIPO). Furthermore, two of the IGOs' policies meet existing principles of good practice (GEF and ILO).

The need to develop evaluation capabilities has been recognised by the General Assembly, which in December 2004 passed a resolution that stated that there is a 'need to optimize the linking of evaluation to performance in the achievement of developmental goals, and encourages the United Nations development system to strengthen its evaluation activities'.[19] In support of this, the UN Evaluation Group has also developed system-wide principles on evaluation that ensure evaluations within the UN follow agreed-upon basic principles. More recently, they have established a task force to examine issues concerning capacity development in evaluation (Task Force on Evaluation Capacity Development).[20]

The recent G8 commitment to increase development aid by $50 billion will undoubtedly place even greater pressure on IGOs involved in development to further strengthen their evaluation capabilities as a significant proportion of this money will be channelled through multilateral agencies. The publicity that surrounded this announcement will mean a wide range of stakeholders will be eager to see evidence of results.

---

[18] Metzler, *Report of the International Financial Institution Advisory Commission.*

[19] United Nations General Assembly 2004, *Triennial Comprehensive Policy Review of Operational Activities for Development of the United Nations System* (A/Res/59/250 of 17 December 2004). Available at www.daccessdds.un.org/doc/ UNDOC/GEN/N04/491/ 26/PDF/N0449126.pdf?OpenElement.

[20] The United Nations Evaluation Group (UNEG), *Evaluation Capacity Development: A Strategy*, Strategy Paper, United Nations Development Programme, New York. Available at http://cfapp1-docs-public.undp.org/eo/evaldocs1/uneg_2006/eo_doc_350011048.doc.

Of the four dimensions, IGOs' lowest average score was on complaint and response mechanisms. While all but one (WIPO) of the IGOs assessed have policies for receiving and responding to complaints from internal stakeholders, the good practice principles that underpin these policies vary. No IGO meets all of them. Except for the World Bank, no other IGO has formalised a process of handling and responding to complaints from external stakeholders, civil society groups in particular. While a number of organisations, such as GEF, the ILO and the OECD claim that there are multiple forums through which external stakeholders can raise concerns with them, this is not the same as having safe formal procedures in place that ensure external stakeholders can raise their concerns in confidentiality, without fear of retaliation and expect a response.

6.4   Of the four accountability dimensions, INGOs on average score highest on participation and lowest on complaint and response mechanisms

Participation is the area of accountability where INGOs in the study perform best, ahead of the other two sectors. Participation has a long history in the INGO sector: many development INGOs, for example, have been utilising participatory techniques to engage their stakeholders in the decisions that affect them for decades. Engaging individuals and communities and ensuring equality of voice in decision making are seen as crucial to challenging social injustices and inequalities; for progressive INGOs, these are core organisational values. Organisations such as Action Aid International, Oxfam International and World Vision International stand out in the sector for their developed capabilities to engage with external stakeholders.

These values are also reflected in the participation of internal members in INGOs' overall governance structures. Organisations such as ActionAid International, Amnesty International, the IFRC, Oxfam International and the WWF International all score 90 per cent on equitable internal member control of decision making. Yet not all INGOs share the same values. More conservative organisations such as Human Life International did not score well in this category. The ICC, too, does very poorly in the participation capabilities.

The low score on complaint and response mechanisms is a reflection of the underdeveloped practice of receiving and responding to complaints from external stakeholders through a formalised channel. Internal codes of conduct guide the process for dealing with complaints from internal stakeholders, staff in particular; in most contexts this is required by law. Processes are also generally in place to respond to negative feedback or complaints from institutional donors. But a formalised mechanism for responding to complaints from external stakeholders, affected communities in particular, is still a new concept.

Most INGOs are currently addressing grievances and concerns on an ad hoc basis through the everyday interaction between field staff and local communities or through the more general process of receiving feedback through monitoring and evaluations. Yet a formalised mechanism is more respectful and dignifying for users, particularly for INGOs that operate in highly volatile and changing environments, and some INGOs are starting to recognise this. As members of Humanitarian Accountability Partnership International (HAPI), World Vision International is the only INGO in the study that received a partial score for setting up capabilities to receive and respond to complaints from affected communities.

6.5   Of the four accountability dimensions, TNCs on average score highest on complaint and response mechanisms and lowest on transparency

The high score of TNCs for complaint and response mechanisms – the highest of all three sectors – is a reflection of the fact that this has become a regulated area of accountability for companies registered on the US stock exchange following the collapse of Enron and WorldCom. The Sarbanes–Oxley Act that followed these public scandals requires companies to have formal procedures for addressing complaints from both internal and external stakeholders relating to accounting and auditing matters and to afford protection to whistleblowers. All the companies that have these procedures in place handle complaints in relation to broader organisational issues, such as non-compliance with corporate codes of ethics/conduct. Nine out of the ten assessed companies have procedures in place that enable complaints from internal stakeholders to be made. A smaller number have in place capabilities to handle complaints related to non-compliance from external stakeholders; Anglo American, Microsoft, News Corp and Pfizer stand out in this regard.

The low score for TNCs in relation to transparency is a reflection of their underdeveloped policies on the issue. TNCs have well developed capabilities to ensure openness with shareholders and institutional investors – a reflection of the relative power of these stakeholders and the fact that disclosure of financial information is a regulated area. These same capabilities, however, are not as developed in relation to transparency on issues that affect the global public good.

7.   Conclusion

While each global organisation needs to address its accountability in a way that is appropriate to its own sphere of activity, the work of GAP has shown that there are common principles of accountability that are applicable to all global actors, irrespective of their form or function. As the number of global challenges continues to grow, global actors come to play an increasingly important role in our daily lives. As other forms of public assurance of the effectiveness and legitimacy of some such actors are slow to follow, the need to demonstrate stakeholder accountability at the global level will only increase. Unless we are able to ensure that individuals and communities are able to influence, input into and, when needs be, hold to account the global institutions that impact on them, global efforts to provide solutions to global issues will fail.

A better understanding of the current state of accountability at the global level is needed. The work of the One World Trust has been instrumental in this regard. By assessing the accountability capabilities of global organisations at headquarters, we are beginning to create the first picture of how far we have come in extending basic principles of accountability to the global level, but also how far we still need to go.

Across all organisations there is a need to further strengthen transparency capabilities. This research has found that, while organisations make a commitment to being open and transparent, few have transparency policies, and even fewer commit to good practice principles such as the presumption of disclosure. Without access to timely and relevant information on what an organisation is doing, it is very difficult for stakeholders to hold it to account. INGOs and intergovernmental organisations specifically need to focus their efforts on more effectively enabling affected communities to participate in decision-making processes and on developing robust complaints mechanisms for external stakeholders, such as beneficiaries and the general public. While in the past complaints have been dealt with on an informal basis, as INGOs in particular have evolved into transnational actors spanning multiple countries and with budgets of millions of pounds, the need to develop more formalised procedures for handling and responding to such complaints has strengthened. Corporations, on the other hand, need to strengthen their capabilities for engaging with external stakeholders such as NGOs. While it is becoming good practice among companies to engage with NGOs, this has largely been done on an ad hoc basis. Companies need to develop more structured and consistent ways of engaging with stakeholders, such as through stakeholder advisory panels.

All organisations need to ensure that those policies that support accountability are complemented by adequate management systems that translate such policies into practice. Accountability policies at the headquarters bring greater consistency and coherence to how accountability is viewed across the organisation, but without appropriate management systems – that span staff training to senior level oversight, resources to performance monitoring and evaluation, etc. – there is always the risk that policies and procedures amount to nothing more than window dressing.

References

Blagescu, M. et al. 2005, *Pathways to Accountability: The Global Accountability Framework*, London, One World Trust.

Brown, D. and Jagadananda 2007, Civil Society Legitimacy and Accountability: Issues and Challenges, Johannesburg, CIVICUS World Alliance for Citizen Participation and Center for Youth and Social Development.

Brown et al. 2004, 'Building Strategic Accountability Systems for International NGOs', *AccountAbility Forum* (special edition on NGO accountability), issue 2 (summer), 31–43.

Edwards, M. and Hulme, D. 2002, '*NGO Performance and Accountability: Introduction and Overview*' in M. Edwards and A. Fowler, NGO Management, London, Earthscan, 3–15.

Einhorn, J. 2001, 'The World Bank's Mission Creep', Foreign Affairs, September/ October, 22–35.

Grant, R. and Keohane, R. 2005, 'Accountability and Abuses of Power in World Politics', *American Political Science Review*, vol. **99**, 29–44.

Helleiner, G. 2001, 'Markets, Politics and Globalisation', Journal of Human Development, vol. 2, no. 1, quoted in World Commission on the Social Dimension of Globalisation 2004, A Fair Globalization: Creating Opportunities for All, Geneva, International Labour Organisation, Geneva.

Keohane, R. 2003, 'Global Governance and Democratic Accountability' in D. Held and M. Koenig-Archibugi (eds.), *Taming Globalization: Frontiers of Governance*, London, Polity Press.

Kovach, H., Neligan, C. and Burall, S. 2003, *Power without Accountability?*, London, One World Trust.

Lloyd, R. and de Las Casas, L. 2005, 'NGO Self-Regulation: Balancing and Enforcing Accountability', Alliance Extra, December, www.allavida.org/alliance/axdec05e.html.

Metzler, A. 2000, Report of the International Financial Institution Advisory Commission, available at www.house.gov/jec/imf/meltzer.pdf.

Najam, A. 1996, 'NGO Accountability: A Conceptual Framework', Development Policy Review, no. 14, 339–53.

Newell, P. and Bellour, S. 2002, Mapping Accountability: Origins, Contexts and Implications for Development, Working Paper 168, Brighton, Institute of Development Studies.

Woods, N. 2003, 'Unelected Government: Making the IMF and World Bank more Accountable', Brookings Review, vol. 21, no. 2, 9–12.

11

Non-state environmental standards as a substitute for state regulation?

MARCUS SCHAPER*

1. Background and context

Environmental impacts of large infrastructure, industry, and resource extraction projects have been a concern for a considerable time. The development of environmental legislation in the advanced industrialised countries of the North reflects this concern. Such legislation includes laws that have been created to address air and water pollution stemming from industrial production (for example, the US Clean Water Act and Clean Air Act), other statutes that regulate zoning and construction of new developments (for example, the EU Water Framework Directive), and a set of procedural rules that require the consideration of potential environmental impacts before new developments are undertaken (for example, the US National Environmental Policy Act). Such public environmental standards tend to be less detailed in transition and developing countries. Coalitions of actors concerned about the environmental performance of infrastructure, industry, and resource extraction projects in such countries have consequently sought other means of improving the environmental performance of projects. In the absence of state actors willing or capable of creating and enforcing strict environmental rules in their respective countries, these coalitions have targeted private sector and international actors that play crucial roles in the constructing and financing of projects in developing and transition countries.[1]

Financial institutions have been most prominent among the actors targeted by concerned activist coalitions. This chapter explores the effects of environmental rules for project finance and considers the possible impact

---

* Visiting Assistant Professor of Political Science, Reed College, United States; PhD, MA (Government and Politics, University of Maryland); Dipl. Pol. (Political Science, University of Potsdam).
[1] For a detailed discussion see Schaper, 'Leveraging Green Power'.

that rules among other parties involved with project development could have. It is argued that the effects of non-state rules depend not only on their nature and implementation, but also to a large extent on the presence of competing actors not bound by environmental requirements. Private governance regimes should thus be evaluated primarily by the coverage of their rules and only in a second step by their substantial content. Coverage appears to be affected by the vulnerability of a class of actors to public pressure, their servility to regulatory bodies, and the level of competition in their respective spheres of influence.[2] Before one can jump to discussions about the potential of private standards to supplement or replace public ones, a comparative analysis of these standards is warranted.

Environmental requirements imposed by financial institutions on infrastructure projects for which their support is sought provide a good opportunity to compare environmental policies of public and private international financial institutions, which are subject to different regulatory bodies with varying levels of authority and oversight. The World Bank, national export credit agencies (ECAs), and private banks have all adopted similar environmental review procedures to guide their project finance operations.[3] This proliferation of environmental rules in project evaluation is a remarkable trend but begs questions about the impact of these policies.

Ideally, a comparative evaluation of their rules would employ project-level data to assess the extent to which environmental rules have affected the environmental performance of supported projects. Even in the case of the World Bank projects, for which much project data is available, such a comprehensive analysis has not been possible due to the lack of project-specific data on environmental performance. Instead, scholars have employed anecdotal case-study data or have studied relative magnitudes of 'green' and 'dirty' portfolios.[4] Portfolio composition data on the project level has recently been made available in the PLAID database, but this data still does not allow an analysis of environmental performance.[5] Data for projects supported by ECAs and private banks is even

[2] Ibid.
[3] Görlach, Knigge and Schaper, 'Transparency, Information Disclosure', 241–58; Schaper, 'Export Promotion, Trade, and the Environment'.
[4] Nielson and Tierney, 'Delegation to International Organizations', 241–76; Gutner, 'Explaining the Gaps between Mandate and Performance', 10–37; Gutner, 'World Bank Environmental Reform', 773–83; Nielson and Tierney, 'Theory, Data, and Hypothesis Testing', 785–800.
[5] Hicks et al., Greening Aid?.

more difficult to come by, thus rendering a comparative project-level analysis next to impossible. This chapter takes an entirely different approach. Assuming that the implementation of the actors' environmental policies was perfect all the time, the effect of these policies would nevertheless be limited to those projects that receive financing. In other words, even in a world of perfect implementation and compliance, many projects would not be affected by these environmental standards because they are financed by other actors not subject to comparable environmental rules. The smaller the market-share of 'green' financial institutions is, the smaller the impact of their policies can be.[6] As long as 'dirty' financing is available, sponsors of environmentally problematic projects can seek support from financial institutions that do not require environmental impact assessments or costly environmental modifications. I contend that analysis of project-level environmental data would be desirable once we can be sure that the policies in question do affect a considerable share of the financial markets. Thus, this chapter compares the market shares of international financial institutions in African infrastructure projects as a first step in assessing the institutions' environmental performance on the ground.

2. The cases: environmental standards for international financial institutions

Support for development projects from Western financial institutions has become contingent on those projects fulfilling the respective institutions' environmental requirements. The World Bank has established such environmental rules in its *Safeguard Policies, Pollution Abatement Handbook*, and *Operations Manual*. Export Credit Agencies in OECD countries are subject to this organisation's *Recommendation on* Common Approaches *to the Environment and Officially Supported Export Credits*. Private banks have established the *Equator Principles* as a 'financial industry benchmark for determining, assessing and managing social and environmental risk in project financing.'[7] All these rules follow the same logic requiring environmental assessment of projects, classification of projects according to potential environmental impact, and support decisions based on projects' environmental performance. The similarity of their provisions is a consequence of their common history: all three sets of

---

[6] Wright and Rwabizambuga, 'Institutional Pressures, Corporate Reputation', 89–117.
[7] www.equator-principles.com/principles.shtml.

rules are the result of campaigns by a largely similar group of activists. Nonetheless, implementation of these rules varies, depending on the type of actor.[8]

All financial institutions adopted their rules because they proved vulnerable to public pressure. World Bank environmental policies were created after US activists managed to leverage Congressional power over World Bank funding. US contributions to replenishment of the World Bank Group's International Development Association (IDA) funds could only go ahead once the Bank committed itself to environmental reform. Environmental policies among ECAs are also a result of campaigns by similar groups of activists. At first, they targeted the US Export–Import Bank through litigation over environmental rules. Later, they broadened their advocacy campaign to lobby for environmental rules for ECAs in other OECD countries as well. Thus, the World Bank and ECA rules are the result of activist campaigns targeted at state actors, which in turn brought about environmental rules for these agencies. Private banks, however, were targeted directly. Activists exploited banks' vulnerability to boycotts of their consumer banking and credit card business. Mindful of the importance of their reputation in a business with little product differentiation, banks responded by creating the *Equator Principles* as a tool to manage reputational risks associated with environmentally problematic projects in their portfolios.[9]

Though their vulnerability to public pressure made these institutions easy targets for activists, it remains to be seen whether these actors are able to effect the desired environmental outcomes. By making financial support conditional on environmental performance criteria, all three sets of policies mandate environmental considerations in project development in an indirect manner. The development of environmentally harmful projects remains possible, but access to financing is hampered by poor environmental performance. The effectiveness of these policies depends on two factors: the quality of their implementation and the availability of alternative financing for environmentally problematic projects.

---

[8] Schaper, 'Leveraging Green Power'; Schaper (under review), *Delegated Delegation*.

[9] On the World Bank policies see: Rich, *Mortgaging the Earth*; Wade, 'Greening the Bank', 611–733; Fox and Brown (eds.), *The Struggle for Accountability*; Gutner, *Banking on the Environment*. For more details on ECAs consult: Görlach, Knigge and Schaper, 'Transparency, Information Disclosure'; Schaper, 'Leveraging Green Power'; Schaper, *Delegated Delegation*. On the *Equator Principles* see: Amalric, 'The Equator Principles'; Wright and Rwabizambuga, 'Institutional Pressures, Corporate Reputation'.

Implementation as well as monitoring and enforcement arrangements are addressed elsewhere.[10] This analysis addresses the availability of alternative sources of financing and, by assuming perfect implentation, attempts to gauge the maximum impact financial institutions' environmental policies could have.

2.1   Regulation by international organisations: environmental policies of the World Bank Group

Multilateral development bank (MDB) environmental policies apply to projects throughout the developing world, but not all MDB policies are created equal. The World Bank Group was the first international financial institution to be targeted by NGOs to incorporate environmental considerations into its coverage decisions. Environmental reforms at the Bank started in the 1970s and, by the 1990s, had led to the development of fairly comprehensive environmental policies.[11] Pressure by activists on the Bank may have eased somewhat over time, but the development and effectiveness of its environmental policies are still closely scrutinised.[12]

Being the first MDB to be pressured into adopting environmental policies, World Bank policies are considered stronger than many regional development bank rules.[13] For the analysis pursued in this chapter, one would have to consider the share of projects supported by MDBs with more lenient environmental rules than the World Bank. The higher the World Bank's 'market' share for multilateral financing in a given segment is, the higher the impact of its policies can be. Conversely, the more financing is provided by MDBs with lesser environmental rules, the smaller the impact of World Bank policies is expected to be. However, all MDBs operate under some derivative of World Bank policies. Any race to the bottom on environmental project performance is therefore limited to the most lenient MDB policy, while races over ECA and private bank support may have no bottom at all. Consequently, a comparison of MDB portfolios is omitted from this chapter.

---

[10] Görlach, Knigge and Schaper, 'Transparency, Information Disclosure'; Schaper, *Delegated Delegation*.
[11] Rich, *Mortgaging the Earth*; Wade, 'Greening the Bank'.
[12] Fox and Brown (eds.), *The Struggle for Accountability*; Clark, Fox and Treakle (eds.), *Demanding Accountability*; Hicks et al., *Greening Aid?*.
[13] Gutner, *Banking on the Environment*.

2.2   *Regulation by governments: the* Common Approaches
for officially supported export credits

Similar to World Bank environmental policies, the environmental rules of export credit agencies are the result of public pressure exerted on governments. This activist campaign originated in the United States and then spread to other OECD states. Following a 1992 Congressional mandate, the United States Export–Import Bank established environmental standards in 1995 and thereby created a burden for US exporters seeking support from the Export–Import Bank that their competitors in other countries did not have to deal with. A combination of US diplomatic initiatives in the G7 and OECD and activist campaigns targeted at other OECD states led to the establishment of the *OECD Recommendation on Common Approaches on Environment and Officially Supported Export Credits*, which require members' ECAs to examine projects for their environmental impact prior to granting cover. The *Common Approaches* apply to transactions with repayment terms of more than two years. Its provisions stipulate environmental review of projects in which individual ECAs have a share of more than 10 million Special Drawing Rights (SDR) or which are located in sensitive areas. Although the *Common Approaches* do not contain quantitative or qualitative criteria for deciding whether environmental impacts can be considered acceptable or not, they reference a number of international standards, including World Bank environmental policies.

By making their support conditional on the fulfilment of environmental requirements, ECAs enlist domestic exporters' influence on project sponsors to bring projects into compliance with their environmental standards. This corresponds to what Gilboy calls 'compelled third-party participation':[14] exporters become liable for the environmental performance of the projects to which they supply goods and services if these are to be covered by ECAs. Using ECA cover as a lever, the government has thus delegated this regulatory task via its ECA to the exporter.

As the availability of ECA support can 'make or break' a deal by facilitating access to inexpensive financing, all major exporting nations have set up ECAs to assist their domestic supporters. Any tightening of ECA rules – environmental or otherwise – results in a disadvantage to domestic exporters vis-à-vis their international competitors. Not surprisingly, both OECD and non-OECD states have been reluctant to establish rules that could hurt

---

[14] Gilboy, 'Compelled Third-Party Participation', 135–55.

their economy. This reluctance is quite apparent when one compares the ECA policies of OECD states that are bound by the *Common Approaches* with the ECA policies of non-OECD states, which tend to have either weak environmental rules or none at all. In order to assess the potential maximum impact of the OECD rules, one needs to compare the share of ECA financing that comes from OECD and non-OECD states, respectively. As the overall share of non-OECD support rises, the likelihood of environmentally problematic projects receiving support increases. This means that the *Common Approaches* can only be expected to affect environmental project performance in areas where OECD ECAs dominate in export financing.

2.3   *Industry self-regulation: the* Equator Principles

Unlike the World Bank and ECA rules, the *Equator Principles* for private banks were created without outright government intervention, though the World Bank Group's International Finance Corporation (IFC) played an important role in facilitating the rule-making process. Responding to public pressure and criticism of banks' roles in financing environmentally destructive projects, Equator Principles financial institutions (EPFIs) established the *Principles* as industry self-regulation to govern their environmental due diligence in project finance and to manage reputational risks associated with environmentally problematic projects. In agreeing to the *Principles*, signatories formally adopt ten principles based on the World Bank Group's environmental policies. This agreement, however, does not include a commitment to any authority or contracting party and no provisions exist to ensure compliance. The implementation of the *Principles* is left almost entirely to the adopting financial institutions. The *Principles* prescribe no specific procedures and rules beyond requiring the classification of projects according to environmental impact and subsequent environmental management plans for certain categories of projects. In the *Principles'* first version, adopting banks would only face minimal costs from the formal adoption of the *Principles* regardless of whether or not they intended to implement them in their operations. Increased disclosure and transparency requirements in the 2006 version of the Equator *Principles* provide outside actors with some tools to enforce compliance through 'name-and-shame' tactics.

The *Equator Principles* are an example of private regulation of the private sector, although they utilise and advance policies established by public actors for similar purposes. The regulatory task of bringing projects into compliance with the *Principles* is delegated to the project developer under close supervision by the lead arranger. This means that the *Equator Principles'* coverage is limited to those projects in which an EPFI serves as the lead arranger. Project finance deals that do not include Equator banks are unlikely to be subject to similarly strong environmental requirements, if any at all. Private banks that have not subscribed to the *Principles* do not have much incentive to consider the environmental impacts of supported projects beyond their own prudent risk management. In fact, the ability to finance projects with minimal environmental scrutiny may serve as a comparative advantage to non-Equator banks in markets that value low cost over high environmental performance. Therefore, an assessment of the *Principles'* effects on project finance should start with an analysis of EPFIs' market share. As their market share in a given region increases, the *Principles'* impact should increase as non-green finance alternatives are crowded out. Conversely, in regions where EPFI's market share is smaller, environmental concerns are much less likely to be given serious consideration, as project developers can easily find alternative sources of financing.

3.   Impacts of standards vary by region

A crucial difference between product or process standards and environmental standards for access to finance is the amount of leverage the rule-setter has over the regulatory target. When states or firms set product or process standards, their market leverage directly affects producers' or suppliers' decisions on whether to conform with the standards: the larger the regulator's control over the market, the greater is his power over the regulatory targets. Environmental standards for access to finance, however, do not regulate access to a shielded market, but merely to support by a cartel of financial institutions.[15] As long as the cartel does not have complete control over the finance market, any number of financial institutions not bound by the rules of the cartel can render them ineffective by providing alternative financing. With respect to ECAs and private banks, the cartels are imperfect. Only OECD-member ECAs are bound by the *Common Approaches*, thus allowing non-OECD ECAs such as the Chinese and Indian Exim Banks to play an increasing role in many finance markets. The *Equator Principles*, too, have only limited membership, primarily representing North American and Western European financial institutions. Environmental standards can be expected to

---

[15] See also Evans, *International Regulation of Official Trade Finance.*

prove effective only in markets that are dominated by financial institutions bound by such standards.

A key difference between the effects of MDB policies and those of private banks and ECAs is that all multilateral financing is subject to some environmental rules. Even in regions dominated by MDBs with weak environmental policies, these policies establish a baseline for environmental performance. The *Common Approaches* and the *Equator Principles*, however, only apply to projects for which sponsors seek support from Equator banks or OECD ECAs. Non-OECD ECAs and private banks that have not adopted the *Equator Principles* may not place any environmental requirements on supported projects at all and thus eliminate an environmental performance floor altogether in areas where they are competing with EPFIs and OECD ECAs. Thus, these standards only travel as far as there is demand for financing from OECD ECAs and Equator banks. This demand can vary widely by region, making the ECAs and private banks the relevant area of study in this chapter.

Table 11.1 illustrates the low prevalence of long-term OECD export credits in Sub-Saharan Africa. Very few projects requiring environmental review under the *Common Approaches* are supported in Sub-Saharan Africa. Between 1998 and 2003 only six (out of twenty-seven) Sub-Saharan Least Developed Countries (LDCs) generated annual export credit business in excess of 10 million SDR for one or more years, the minimum criteria necessary to trigger the *Common Approaches'* environmental screening process by volume (projects in sensitive areas require review irrespective of volume). Five OLICs (Other Low Income Countries), four Lower Middle-Income Countries (LMICs), and three Upper Middle Income Countries (UMICs) generated annual portfolios above 10 million SDR, thereby possibly including projects subject to the *Common Approaches*. Owing to the nature of Export Credit Group (ECG) reporting, it is not possible to identify the number or share of projects in Sub-Saharan Africa that actually received environmental screening. The OECD reports on environmental reviews are not broken down by recipient country or region.

While OECD ECAs' engagement in Sub-Saharan Africa is limited, the China Exim Bank (the Export–Import Bank of China) – which is not party to the *Common Approaches* – is active in power generation, mining, and energy projects throughout Africa. The China Exim Bank approved loans with a global volume of $20 billion in 2005, a twenty-fold increase from 1995.[16] This ranks the Chinese ECA among its top three OECD

---

[16] Bosshard, 'Export Credit Agencies and Environmental Standards'.

Table 11.1 *Long-Term Export Credits by Country Category (over five years) – (million SDR)*

Income Group	1998	1999	2000	2001	2002	2003	2004
LDCs	59 (0.5%)	205 (1.3%)	169 (1.1%)	700 (5.1%)	156 (1.2%)	179 (1.2%)	48 (0.3%)
Sub-Saharan LDCs	29 (0.2%)	54 (0.3%)	146 (0.9%)	626 (4.5%)	128 (1.0%)	168 (1.1%)	4 (0.0%)
OLICs	1,854 (14.9%)	1,495 (9.6%)	526 (3.3%)	638 (4.6%)	992 (7.6%)	1,936 (13.0%)	1,392 (7.5%)
Sub-Saharan OLICs	134 (1.1%)	186 (1.2%)	87 (0.6%)	36 (0.3%)	338 (2.6%)	109 (0.7%)	138 (0.7%)
LMICs	5,585 (44.7%)	5,320 (34.1%)	6,471 (40.9%)	5,259 (38.1%)	4,767 (36.5%)	3,584 (24.0%)	6,790 (36.4%)
Sub-Saharan LMICs	25 (0.2%)	125 (0.8%)	2 (0.0%)	31 (0.2%)	7 (0.1%)	2 (0.0%)	26 (0.1%)
UMICs	2,542 (20.4%)	4,280 (27.5%)	4,485 (28.4%)	3,608 (26.2%)	3,644 (27.9%)	3,472 (23.3%)	2,244 (12.0%)
Sub-Saharan UMICs	39 (0.3%)	188 (1.2%)	47 (0.3%)	264 (2.0%)	27 (0.2%)	127 (0.9%)	339 (1.8%)
HICs	15 (0.1%)	177 (1.1%)	222 (1.4%)	–	2 (0.0%)	77 (0.5%)	*
All Developing	**10,054 (80.6%)**	**11,477 (73.6%)**	**11,872 (75.1%)**	**10,205 (74.0%)**	**9,561 (73.2%)**	**9,248 (62.0%)**	*
All Sub-Saharan	**227 (1.8%)**	**553 (3.5%)**	**282 (1.8%)**	**957 (7.0%)**	**500 (3.8%)**	**406 (2.7%)**	**507 (2.7%)**

Source: OECD (2004), '2003 Report on Export Credit Activities', TD/ECG(2004)16/FINAL, Paris: Organisation for Economic Cooperation and Development, OECD (2005), 'Statistics on Export Credit Activities (up to and Including the Year 2004)', Tables 1 to 12 from TD/ECG(2005)13/FINAL, Paris: OECD. Author's calculation of Sub-Saharan figures; classification of economies from the July 2006 World Bank List of Economies (http://siteresources.worldbank.org/DATASTATISTICS/Resources/CLASS.XLS; accessed 14 December 2006); LDC classification from the United Nations LDC list (www.un.org/special-rep/ohrlls/ldc/list.htm; accessed 14 December 2006).

Note: * = cannot be clearly identified due to changes in OECD reporting.

competitors Korea ($22 billion in 2005), Japan ($20 billion in 2005), and Germany ($19.5 billion in 2005).[17]

NGOs criticise the China Exim Bank for its environmental record:

> The Exim Bank's portfolio includes projects such as the Merowe Dam in Sudan, the Imboulou Dam in Congo–Brazzaville, the Tekeze Dam in Ethiopia, the Lower Kafue Gorge Dam in Zambia, the Yeywa Dam in Burma, and the Nam Mang 3 Dam in Laos. China Exim has also signed deals for projects in other countries with human rights problems, including Nigeria (Papalanto and Omotosho power plants) and Zimbabwe (Zimbabwe Iron and Steel Company).
>
> … One case in point is Merowe Dam, Africa's largest new hydropower project, which is currently being financed by China Exim. Located in Sudan, the project will create a reservoir with a length of 174 kilometers, generate electricity with a capacity of 1,250 megawatts, and displace 50,000 people. In spite of the project's large dimensions and potential social and environmental impacts, no independent environmental impact assessment was ever carried out. One of the companies involved in the project prepared a brief environmental assessment report. In violation of Sudanese law, the technical arm of Sudan's Environment Ministry did not receive a copy of the assessment, and was not able to review and clear the project.[18]

Moss and Rose list a number of large pending projects that may involve support by the China Exim Bank:

- A possible $1.2 billion in new loans to Ghana, including $600 million for construction of the Bui dam;
- $2.3 billion in total financing for Mozambique for the Mepanda Nkua dam and hydroelectric plant, plus another possible $300 million for the Moamba-Major dam;
- A $1.6 billion loan for a Chinese oil project in Nigeria;
- $200 million in preferential buyers' credit for Nigeria's first communications satellite;
- A $2 billion line of credit to Angola, with the possibility of another $9–10 billion;
- Reports of loans and export credits for other projects in Congo-Brazzaville, Sudan and Zimbabwe.[19]

Clearly, the effectiveness of the *Common Approaches* in Sub-Saharan is limited by the existence of the China Exim Bank as an alternative

[17] OECD 2007, 'Statistics on Export Credit Activities (up to and Including the Year 2005)', OECD, Paris.

[18] Bosshard and Chan-Fishel, 'Western Banks Financing China's Export Import Bank'.

[19] Moss and Rose, *China Exim Bank and Africa*.

Table 11.2 *Top Ten Mandated Arrangers of African and Middle Eastern Project Finance Loans*

Position	Financial Institution	Loan Amount ($m)	Number of Deals	% Share
1	HSBC[1]	520.38	6	6.75
2	BNP Paribas	512.43	5	6.65
3	Calyon[1]	509.21	5	6.60
4	Société Generale	491.76	5	6.38
5	ANZ Investment Bank	449.95	4	5.84
6	Standard Bank	441.46	3	5.73
7	Abu Dhabi Islamic Bank	400.00	2	5.19
8	West LB[1]	364.61	4	4.73
9	Mitsubishi Tokyo Financial Group	320.22	4	4.15
10	Gulf International Bank	314.37	3	4.08

Source: *Ibid.*

Note:[1] Equator bank as of 30 June 2004.

throughout Africa. Sudan, for example, is receiving US$387 million in export credits from the China Exim Bank for the construction of the Merowe Dam – more than 11 times as much as all OECD export credits to Sudan between 1998 and 2005.[20]

Christopher Wright and Alexis Rwabizambuga have illustrated regional limitation of the *Equator Principles*. Almost all EPFIs are head-quartered in Europe and North America and their project finance business is also limited in scope. While a majority of Latin American project finance loans are arranged by EPFIs, Equator banks play a much smaller role in African and Middle East loans. None of the top ten arrangers of project finance in Asia has adopted the *Equator Principles*.[21] As Table 11.2 indicates, though three out of the top ten mandated arrangers of project finance in Africa and the Middle East are EPFIs, the remaining seven financial institutions are not subject to the *Principles'* environmental

---

[20] Leadership Office of the Hamadab Affected People, International Rivers Network, and The Corner House (2007), 'Memorandum on the Merowe Dam Project – Submitted to His Excellency Zhang Dong, Ambassador of the People's Republic of China to Sudan, at the Occasion of the Visit of President Hu Jintao to Sudan', International Rivers Network, Berkeley; OECD 'Statistics on Export Credit Activities (Up To and Including the Year 2005)'.

[21] Wright and Rwabizambuga, 'Institutional Pressures, Corporate Reputation'.

requirements. Project developers can choose which bank to approach for financing of environmentally problematic projects.

Limitations on the potential impact of environmental rules for project finance clearly exist as this case study of Africa has shown. Both the *Common Approaches* and the *Equator Principles* are hampered in their effectiveness by the dominance of competing financial institutions that are not subject to these policies. Only MDB policies establish a baseline for environmental performance of projects that are underwritten by regional and multilateral development banks.

4. Uneven allocation of costs and benefits

For many developing countries, environmental concerns are secondary to the establishment of infrastructure. While it is generally accepted that donors have some influence over what is acceptable or unacceptable in terms of social and environmental externalities of development projects financed with aid money, this is not the case for ECA-supported projects. By definition, ECAs provide loans and insurance at market or near-market conditions and supported projects are usually of a commercial nature or they are funded with little or no aid involved. As such, it is not surprising that project sponsors and recipient country governments are concerned about their loss in autonomy and control if the exporting countries' ECAs require environmental impact assessments and potentially costly modifications to the projects' design despite compatibility with the recipient country's regulations. After all, costs that result from the compilation of assessments or from modifications to the projects are borne by the project sponsor or the recipient country.

Similarly, project sponsors bear the costs of environmental assessments required by EPFIs and mitigation of environmental externalities in projects subject to the *Equator Principles*. The cost of improved risk management for the Equator banks is externalised to their clients.

All three sets of rules are dominated by the interests of the providers of finance and only consider the interests of receivers in terms of providing for a better environment as an unspecified common good. Material interests of the receivers (for example, costs associated with preparing environmental assessments or providing mitigation measures) are disregarded. In all three cases, establishment of the policies was possible because of diffused costs and concentrated benefits. The reputational benefits of having implemented environmental policies go exclusively to the providers of finance, whereas the costs generated by these policies are borne by the receivers. In the case of ECAs, this required the establishment of common environmental rules among ECAs because unilateral environmental measures would have upset the cost–benefit balance by creating domestic costs in the form of forgone export opportunities.

5.   Greening finance: barking up the wrong tree?

As we have seen in the preceding pages, the effectiveness of financial institutions' environmental rules for project performance depends on the availability of alternative means of financing. Especially in Africa, the impact of the *Equator Principles* and the OECD *Common Approaches* appears to be very limited. This raises the question of whether financial institutions are an appropriate vehicle for improving environmental performance of infrastructure development in the first place, or whether other actors (public or private) may be more successful in greening infrastructure development. This question will be addressed in two dimensions. One concerns the overall relevance of MDBs, ECAs, and private project finance for infrastructure, industry, and resource extraction project development. The availability of different sources of financing would render MDB environmental policies, the *Common Approaches*, and the *Equator Principles* ineffective even if they had global coverage among their respective financial institutions. The other dimension is the effectiveness of environmental rules imposed by an actor that enters as late in the project cycle as financial institutions do. Incorporating environmental requirements in earlier project development stages may be more effective.

With regard to the first concern, one needs to consider the overall relevance of these financial institutions. A study by the IMF notes:

> Financial flows facilitated by official export credit agencies are large in comparison with official development assistance and gross lending by international financial institutions to developing countries.[22]
>
> However, relative to total capital flows to developing countries or exports, export credits supported by ECAs in industrial countries have been on the decline. Preliminary estimates suggest that new commitments by official ECAs amounted to near 35 per cent of total official and private lending plus foreign direct investment to developing countries in the early 1990s; the ratio declined to about 20 per cent in 2000–02.[23]
>
> New export credit commitments to low-income countries have been declining since 1995, and this trend has not been affected by the world economic cycle. The share of new commitments to low-income countries

---

[22] Wang *et al.*, *Officially Supported Export Credits*, 2.   [23] *Ibid.*, 7.

(excluding India) declined from 15 per cent in 1995–96 to about 8 per cent in 2000–03 ... Indeed, a number of ECAs have remained off-cover in many low-income countries, even in HIPCs that have passed the completion point (thereby receiving irrevocable debt relief committed under the HIPC initiative).[24]

Figure 11.1 clearly illustrates how capital flows subject to environmental requirements (ODA, MDBs, ECAs) are dwarfed by private capital flows that are not subject to such conditions. While the proliferation of environmental rules among development agencies, ECAs, and private banks has been a laudable development, their effectiveness must likely remain limited unless they spread beyond project finance to other types bank business and financial instruments, such as bonds.

Having addressed the competition to green financial institutions, I will now consider the suitability of finance as the carrier of environmental standards for project development. It is generally argued that environmental concerns should be addressed as early as possible in any planning process. Since financing for projects is typically sought once most project development has already been concluded, other actors that may be involved in planning at earlier stages in the project cycle may also be better suited than financial institutions to introduce environmental concerns into project design. Project developers, construction companies, and consulting engineers are among those actors who can affect project design earlier than financial institutions. None of these actors, however, has a strong incentive to favour stricter environmental rules.

Representatives of German industry lobby groups have suggested that an international agreement on environmental performance certification for construction projects would be more desirable than environmental requirements imposed by financial institutions. Their reasoning was that such an agreement could create strong environmental rules while also preventing competition among construction companies (and their ECAs) over the environmental aspects of bids submitted in response to international tenders. Absent such common rules, project developers would have no incentive to consider environmental aspects in project design, and competing foreign companies not bound by strict ECA rules could submit bids without costly environmental modifications.[25]

An environmental performance certification for project development agreed upon by states or adopted by the respective industry itself would

---

[24] *Ibid.*, 8–9.   [25] Interview with two German lobbyists, 20 January 2004.

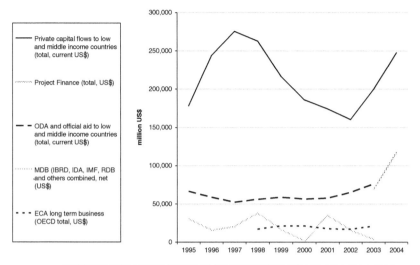

Business other than aircraft and defense (potentially subject to the *Common Approaches*)

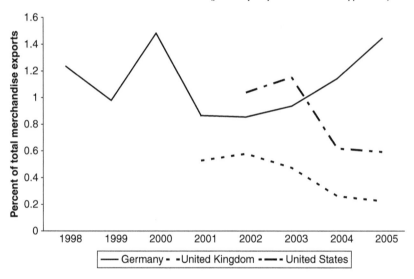

Figure 11.1 International Finance Volumes.

be a promising tool to green project development. Such rules would cover a broad range of projects regardless of their source of financing and geographic location. Lacking the creation of such an environmental performance regime through state intervention, however, project developers have

Source: OECD data, World Development Indicators, and Project Finance Yearbook.

little reason to consider environmental aspects beyond immediate risk management. Environmental impact assessments, stakeholder consultations, and environmental project modifications may all entail considerable costs that would cut into projects' profitability. Financial institutions were driven to adopting environmental rules by activist campaigns that could exert public pressure and exploit state leverage over the targets of their campaigns.[26] Project developers are largely immune to such pressures. Typically, they do not operate consumer businesses that would be prone to boycotts and they are not directly subject to Northern governments' political authority.

Consulting engineers and their international construction contracts could serve as a good vehicle for greening project development. Engineers are involved in project development from design to completion and adhere to internationally codified rules and procedures. Furthermore, increased project costs that may result from environmental requirements do not affect them. Perez also suggests that 'the international market for standard construction contracts is dominated by a small group of international organizations,'[27] lending itself to effective mobilisation. Incorporation of environmental rules into engineers' rules and procedures could result in as broad coverage as an agreement on project certification discussed above. While engineers and their professional organisations are not faced with as strong disincentives as project developers are in promoting environmental rules, they also do not have strong incentives to favour such rules. Similar to project development, their business is largely immune to consumer pressure and their professional organisations operate independent of state authority.

In this comparison, financial institutions fare poorly as carriers of environmental standards when compared to other actors. They can only affect projects late in the project cycle when most design decisions have already been made and their effectiveness is limited by the availability of other means of financing. Their status as environmental standard bearers is more the result of their vulnerability to public pressure than their suitability for such a role. Activists pressured financial institutions not because they were the perfect carrier of environmental rules, but because they were easy intermediate targets and promised considerable leverage over other, more remote actors.[28]

---

[26] Schaper, 'Leveraging Green Power'.
[27] Perez, 'Using Private–Public Linkages', 77–110.
[28] See also Schaper, 'Leveraging Green Power'.

6. Conclusion

Industry self-regulation and corporate social responsibility initiatives – the predominant forms of standards set by non-state actors – typically result from the regulatory shadow of the state, public pressure, or a combination of the two. Therefore, the bearers of non-state standards are not necessarily those that would be in the best position to address the underlying concern, but rather tend to be those private actors that are most vulnerable to public pressure or state authority.

Non-state standards can be expected to be most effective when their bearers can directly affect the source of the regulatory concern. That means that effective standard setting requires influential bearers that are vulnerable to public pressure or regulatory concerns that lie within the regulatory shadow of an interventionist state. Non-state standards may work well for consumer products and policy challenges in strong states, but less so for development projects in weak states.

In addition to our understanding of the limits of states' regulatory capacity, we need to develop an appreciation of the limitations of non-state actors' ability to achieve policy goals effectively. The argument presented here suggests that the proximity of an actor to a regulatory concern and its vulnerability to public pressure or state authority are important concerns in this regard.

References

Amalric, F. 2005, 'The Equator Principles: A Step Towards Sustainability', *Working Paper*, 01/05, January 2005, Center for Corporate Responsibility and Sustainability at the University of Zurich.

Bosshard, P. 2006, 'Export Credit Agencies and Environmental Standards: An Invitation to Join the Dialogue', *International Rivers Network*, available at www.irn.org/programs/finance/index.php? id=061220exim.html.

Bosshard, P. and Chan-Fishel, M. 2005, 'Western Banks Financing China's Export Import Bank: A Case of Environmental Money Laundering', *International Rivers Network*, Berkeley (CA).

Clark, D., Fox, J. and Treakle, K. (eds.) 2003, *Demanding Accountability: Civil Society Claims and the World Bank Inspection Panel*, Lanham, Rowman & Littlefield.

Evans, P. C. 2005, *International Regulation of Official Trade Finance: Competition and Collusion in Export Credits and Foreign Aid*, PhD Dissertation, Department of Political Science, Cambridge (MA), Massachusetts Institute of Technology.

Fox, J. A. and Brown, L. D. (eds.) 1998, *The Struggle for Accountability: The World Bank, NGOs, and Grassroots Movements*, Cambridge (MA), MIT Press.

Gilboy, J. A. 1998, 'Compelled Third-Party Participation in the Regulatory Process: Legal Duties, Culture, and Noncompliance', *Law & Policy*, vol. **20**, no. 2, 135–55.

Görlach, B., Knigge, M. and Schaper, M. 2007, 'Transparency, Information Disclosure and Participation in Export Credit Agencies' Cover Decisions' in S. Thoyer and B. Martimort-Asso (eds.), *Participation for Sustainability in Trade*, Aldershot, Ashgate, 241–58.

Gutner, T. L. 2002, *Banking on the Environment: Multilateral Development Banks and Their Environmental Performance in Central and Eastern Europe*, Cambridge (MA), MIT Press.

Gutner, T. 2005, 'Explaining the Gaps between Mandate and Performance: Agency Theory and World Bank Environmental Reform', *Global Environmental Politics*, vol. **5**, no. 2, 10–37.

Gutner, T. 2005, 'World Bank Environmental Reform: Revisiting Lessons from Agency Theory', *International Organization*, vol. **59**, no. 3, 773–83.

Hicks, R. L., Parks, B. C., Roberts, J. T. and Tierney, M. J. 2008, *Greening Aid? Understanding the Environmental Impact of Development Assistance*, Oxford University Press.

Moss, T. and Rose, S. 2006, *China Exim Bank and Africa: New Lending, New Challenges*, Washington DC, Center for Global Development.

Nielson, D. L. and Tierney, M. J. 2003, 'Delegation to International Organizations: Agency Theory and World Bank Environmental Reform', *International Organization*, vol. **57**, no. 2, 241–76.

Nielson, D. L. and Tierney, M. J. 2005, 'Theory, Data, and Hypothesis Testing: World Bank Environmental Reform Redux', *International Organization*, vol. **59**, no. 3, 785–800.

Perez, O. 2002, 'Using Private-Public Linkages to Regulate Environmental Conflicts: The Case of International Construction Contracts', *Journal of Law and Society*, vol. **29**, no. 1, 77–110.

Rich, B. 1994, *Mortgaging the Earth: The World Bank, Environmental Impoverishment, and the Crisis of Development*, Boston, Beacon Press.

Schaper, M. 2007, 'Leveraging Green Power: Environmental Rules for Project Finance', *Business and Politics*, vol. **9**, no. 3.

Schaper, M. 2009, 'Export Promotion, Trade, and the Environment: Negotiating Environmental Standards for Export Credit Agencies across the Atlantic' in M. A. Schreurs, S. D. Van Deveer and H. Selin (eds.), *Export Promotion, Trade, and the Environment: Negotiating Environmental Standards for Export Credit Agencies across the Atlantic*, Aldershot, Ashgate.

Schaper, M. (under review), *Delegated Delegation: Environmental Rules for Project Finance*.

Wade, R. 1997, 'Greening the Bank: The Struggle over the Environment, 1970–1995' in D. Kapur, J. P. Lewis and R. C. Webb (eds.), *The World*

Bank: Its First Half Century, Washington DC, Brookings Institution, 611–733.

Wang, J.-Y., Mansilla, M., Kikuchi, Y. and Choudhury, S. 2005, *Officially Supported Export Credits in a Changing World*, Washington DC, International Monetary Fund, 2.

Wright, C. and Rwabizambuga, A. 2006, 'Institutional Pressures, Corporate Reputation, and Voluntary Codes of Conduct: An Examination of the Equator Principles', *Business and Society Review*, vol. 111, no. 1, 89–117.

Limiting violence – culture and the constitution of public norms: with a case study from a stateless area

TILL FÖRSTER[*]

1. Introduction: statehood beyond the state?

From a Western perspective, the presence of the state as the dominant actor that sets or at least influences the setting of standards is often taken for granted – despite the recent shift to non-state actors in processes of standard setting addressed in this book. However, if one looks beyond the familiar realm of states that follow more or less the Westphalian model, it becomes apparent that in many regions, the state actually never had the authority that it seems to lose today in other parts of the world. In some cases, entire countries fall under this category. Somalia and a few other, mainly African countries are probably the best known examples. In other cases, it is a certain area within a country where the state has always been a somewhat ephemeral phenomenon. Such areas exist in many countries outside what is usually called the North. For instance, the outlying northern parts of the Sahelian countries have never been fully controlled by the colonial powers nor by the post-colonial state.[1] These areas, however, are not characterised by a power vacuum; on the contrary, the long struggles for domination have led to a particular situation that is often characterised as 'precarious statehood'[2] or as

---

[*] Prof. Dr phil. (Free University, Berlin), Institute of Social Anthropology, University of Basel; Basel Institute on Governance.

[1] Compare in general Trotha, 'Über den Erfolg und die Brüchigkeit der Utopie staatlicher Herrschaft', 223–51. On the history of the northern parts of the Sahelian countries, Klute, 'The Coming State', 49–72.

[2] There is no single definition of precarious statehood. For the purpose of this chapter, I understand it as the deficiency of the state's performance in crucial functional areas, i.e. security, political system/judiciary, administration and welfare. The state is only partially able to establish a legitimate monopoly of power and to protect its citizens. Compare in general Caplan, 'From Collapsing States to Neo-trusteeship', 231–44.

'para-statehood',[3] replacing the blunt and undifferentiated notion of the 'failed' or 'collapsed states'.[4] The latter states were understood as those that fail 'to provide security for the population, to guarantee rights at home or abroad, or to maintain functioning (not merely formal) democratic institutions'.[5] Of course, the reality is more complex, and what happens on the ground is often a question of degree and how to evaluate and describe the actual situation of the population.

Security issues illustrate the point fairly well. In many areas of precarious statehood, security is provided by competing actors and institutions, the state being just one among them. Police and other armed forces of the state are often not the dominant security providers, and sometimes, they are seen more as a threat than as a protection. In the majority of the cases that have been studied empirically, the market for security is not split up between large numbers of actors. Instead, the security market is usually dominated by a few competing actors; in other words, it is an oligopoly.[6] The situation in, say, an ordinary African city can vary considerably from one quarter to the other. Business districts are often protected by security firms and private policemen, while the public police is not very present there. According to the usual definition of public, that is, state authority, this could be interpreted as failure to maintain the monopoly of violence in particular urban spaces. On the other hand, government districts and the residential areas of high-ranking public servants are often very well protected by police and other armed bodies of the state, even in states that are rated as 'failed' according to usual western standards.[7] A striking example is Sudan, which was rated as 'the number one failed state' in 2007. The task of the police in these areas is precisely the same as that of private security agencies in other residential quarters – which is also why many citizens in such countries see the police as a free security service to state officials, while other, non-state servants have to pay for exactly the same service. In addition, there may be quarters that are dominated by a competition of an extremely wide

---

[3] Trotha, 'Die Zukunft liegt in Afrika', 253–79.

[4] The notion of the failed or collapsed state goes back to Zartman (ed.), *Collapsed States*.

[5] Chomsky, *Failed States*. Chomsky's book can be read as a radical critique of the USA as a 'failing state' according to the criteria mentioned above but also as a critique of the concept itself.

[6] See in a comparative perspective Mehler, 'Oligopolies of Violence', 539–48.

[7] Since 2005, Foreign Policy publishes yearly a Failed State Index according to twelve social, economic and political indicators: see www.foreignpolicy.com/story/cms.php?story_id=3865, 20 July 2008.

variety of other social actors that range from Muslim brotherhoods and Pentecostal churches to downright criminal youth gangs.

The lack of a monopoly of force and corresponding everyday violence can help us, in some regions and in certain times as extreme cases, to clarify the concept of standards in relation to general social norms. The spatial differentiation of an African city, to take the ordinary urban society again as an example, and also of the rural space surrounding it, is but one aspect of the complex reality that informs social life in areas of precarious statehood. Another is the difference of the norms and standards by which ordinary actors evaluate the social reality they have to cope with. It is obvious that violence has a different meaning for those who live in what would be called a shanty town in ordinary language and for those who live in a residential area of government civil servants. The level of everyday violence certainly differs from one quarter to the other, and so do the expectations of the people living there, and so do the normative assumptions on what is an acceptable level of violence and what is not. It is important at this point to distinguish clearly between four aspects: 1. The actual level of everyday violence and how it is evaluated and estimated by the actors; 2. How it is rated with regard to other areas where the level of violence may be higher or lower; 3. What level of violence is considered to be acceptable; and 4. What level is thought of as being desirable. Of course, all four aspects interact as they are all based on the experience of the actors and how the actors exchange their knowledge and ideas about violence and the state of the society.

The evaluation of violence is already linked to the level that the inhabitants of a certain city or a quarter therein have to cope with day after day. A hold-up that would disturb the daily life in a bourgeois setting may not receive much attention in, say, the area next to the harbour where such events occur on a daily basis. In other words, what is considered to be 'normal' does not attract particular attention, and awareness is focused on extraordinary events.[8] Of course, this does not mean that individuals do not suffer from such aggression and that they personally find it acceptable. What we are talking about is social awareness. In a social setting where hold-ups occur more or less regularly and

---

[8] In the phenomenological sociology of Alfred Schütz, such shifts in awareness and 'half awareness' are a central theme. In his analysis of intentional social action, awareness is only partially imposed by an event but also a choice of the actors based on their 'sedimented' experience and the taken-for-granted mindset in which potential courses of action are conceived. (Schütz and Luckmann, *Strukturen der Lebenswelt*. See in particular vol. 1, part III.B and vol. 2, part V.A.)

where the damage that is done does not exceed a certain level (to which I will come back in a moment), one more event of the kind seldom receives the same attention as, say, in one of the quiet gated communities in another quarter of the same city. The level of everyday violence has become 'normal' in certain settings, while it is considered to be 'abnormal' in others.

The argument also holds true for wider social contexts. Other examples come from regions where sedentary farmers and nomadic pastoralists live in a persisting tension. It is not exceptional that in such settings, violence becomes so ubiquitous that killing one's adversaries and getting killed by them is a possibility that permeates everyday life entirely. Of course, violence in such societies is almost always channelled towards outsiders, or to be more precise, to people that do not belong to one's own group.[9] It is a legitimate option to kill your enemy but not to harm your kin or any other member of the group. On the one hand, one has to get by with the fact that it may also be legitimate for others to kill you. Despite all existing restrictions, the 'normal' level of violence in such societal settings remains relatively high – and it often seems unbearable to Westerners.[10] Obviously, what is seen as 'a normal level' of violence depends to some degree on what everyday life looks like.

On the other hand, there seem to be absolute, anthropological limits to violence in society. Though already used to a relatively high level of everyday violence, the atrocities committed by various militias and their child soldiers during the civil wars in Liberia and Sierra Leone were, as far as we know, never accepted as 'something normal' by ordinary people.[11] It is, however, difficult to say when such limits are trespassed. Even when such anthropological limits exist – and I am convinced they do – the actual evaluation of everyday violence by the people depends on the historical situation that they have to cope with. Any answer to the

---

[9] The limits of the group within which solidarity and peaceful interactions are expected differ considerably. The classical description by Edward Evans Pritchard traces the changing limits of solidarity in the blood feuds among the Nuer of Sudan (Evans Pritchard, *The Nuer*). Another more recent example from West Africa is Sten Hagberg's study of such confrontations in Burkina Faso (Hagberg, 'Dealing with Dilemmas', 40–56). A partially comparative study from Europe is Boehm, *Blood Revenge*.

[10] Sometimes, international or Western-based NGOs try to suppress such violence because of their own normative assumptions of how ordinary social life should look like – and involuntarily often stimulate more violence because the actors cannot engage in the usual regulations. A striking example has recently been analysed in the Ethiopian Rift Valley (Mulugeta, *The Transformation of Conflicts*).

[11] See, for instance, Mats Utas for Liberia (Utas, *Sweet Battlefields*, 119–67).

anthropological question of what level of violence is and always will be unacceptable needs a comparative study of different cases in different societies. The empirical question that one has to address first is that of acceptable limits of violence in a particular society. In a social setting of lingering conflicts, as the pastoralist–farmer interactions mentioned above, the level of acceptable violence is often bifurcated: a violent social climate can dominate the interactions with outsiders while the interior of the groups may be comparatively peaceful. One could indeed argue that the peacefulness on the inner side is a complement to the brutality outside – and may make the latter tolerable. On the other hand, there are social settings that leave little space for such compensation. Civil war in cities may serve as an example.[12] There is no doubt that there are actual differences in the level of violence. There are more and less violent times and more and less violent places within a given society, and there are also differences from one society to the other.

I cannot answer the general, anthropological question where the bearable limits of violence are, but what one can assume is that there must be a kind of network of stable relationships that helps the individuals to survive as human beings and that counterbalances the violent, often unpredictable situations of social interaction elsewhere. The way these networks look is an issue that I will address more deeply later. Suffice to say now that the persistence of such social networks during warlike crises also points at how a society as a whole changes and survives in such situations.

More important for the purpose of this paper is that there are empirically observable 'standards of violence' in different societies, or more precisely standards of limited violence. The term has a disturbing undertone because one may think that it means to approve of violence, but that is not the case. What I mean by standards in this context is the level that seems to be acceptable to the majority at a certain moment in the history of their society, that is, when the actors do not (yet) see a necessity to react to what might be seen by others as an unacceptable spread of everyday violence. It is a level that they want to maintain at least. To understand the concept, it is necessary to distinguish clearly between the evaluation of the factual situation by the actors and their normative weighing of it.[13] Standard in this context refers to the former, that is,

---

[12] Such situations are difficult to study, but there are some good examples collected in Nordstrom *et al.* (eds.), *Fieldwork Under Fire*.

[13] Compare in general Popitz, *Soziale Normen*.

the evaluation of the actors. Besides how they as actors try to assess and rate the degree of violence, standard, as already mentioned, refers to what they feel is still acceptable or bearable – not what they wish to have. Standard in this understanding is a generalisation about what the actors expect from each other – not about what they think is a morally rightful practice. A standard informs social practice but it is not a normative statement on how the members of society want their social life to look. This is not to say that they see a certain degree of everyday violence as desirable – it simply means that the members of a society have learned how to cope with such violence and also with the violent actors which, for good or for evil, they have to live with. A standard is different from a normative assumption on social life. It is, however, influenced by normative views, persuasions and convictions.

From an anthropological point of view, this relationship between social standards and social norms is central to the understanding of how social practices unfold in a particular situation. It is not a plain, easy relationship because there are almost always competing social norms within one society, as outlined in the sketch of the ordinary city above. At times, standards are shared but not the basic normative assumptions by which they are judged. The inhabitants of a better-off quarter and a shanty town may agree upon the dimension of violence in their city or on what are dangerous places in different parts of the city. But what the members of a bourgeois milieu see as a decay of society, may fall into the realm of a competitive social order for others or may simply be seen as 'usual' by still others. In other cases, basic social norms are shared, but the inhabitants disagree on the actual amount of violence, that is, the evaluation of the situation is different, and perhaps the standards of what is taken as an acceptable level of violence, too.

It is obvious that there must be discussions, confrontations and negotiations on how to cope with violence in a complex and often confusing societal situation. There are political and social arenas, threads of talk and rumour, all kinds of media and countless other stages where such issues might surface. There are endless spheres of exchange and communication. But of course, not all spheres have the same societal significance. And this is precisely where the state comes back in. The state as an institution is, since the colonial conquest of the world at the end of the nineteenth century, the most important political institution that shapes and informs societal processes of negotiation in all parts of the earth. The state is, however, more than an institution to exert domination. It introduces and fosters practices of exchange and negotiation. In the ideal Western democracy, the state's parliament is the privileged arena for such exchanges, by election a representative mirror of the entire society and thus legitimated to decide on behalf of it. However, any classical analysis of political systems immediately shows that such an institutional framework is not universal, and certainly not the rule outside the West.[14] The political legitimacy of many post-colonial states in Africa was rarely based on elections but much more often on social legitimacy, that means on the co-optation of influential social actors within a patrimonial setting. 'Political bosses', writes Patrick Chabal, 'were "legitimate" because they could provide for their clients access to state resources'.[15]

It is clear that social legitimacy of such a kind does not match normative, Western models of the state. But more important is that the procedures and many institutions of the state, mainly inherited from the colonial powers and then largely sustained by the international political system,[16] did not cease to exist with the ascent of autocratic leaders or with the weakness of the post-colonial state and its failure to exert a monopoly of force over the whole of their territory. The modern institutionalisation of the state was and still is necessary for several reasons. One was certainly that a modern image had to be retained, both because of the international partners and the domestic population. It was impossible to maintain the position of a sovereign state in the international system without the usual modern institutions and the administrative procedures related to them. The other, domestic side was that, with the 'totally reordered political space'[17] through colonial domination, the local population expected political participation within the framework of a modern state, too. Both sides had to be satisfied.

[14] See with regard to Africa the still-impressive classical political analysis by Patrick Chabal (Chabal, *Power in Africa*, in particular 136–49). Chabal identifies five political crises in Africa, of which the crisis of legitimacy and representation is one.

[15] Chabal, *Power in Africa*, 141. Chabal does not say much about elections in post-colonial African states but writes that 'elections rarely provide sufficient depth of representation, other avenues have to be found' (*Ibid.*, 142).

[16] The survival of African states through international support in analysed thoroughly by Christoph Clapham (Clapham, *Africa and the International System*).

[17] Young, *The African Colonial State*, 9. There is a debate in African history and political science about rupture and continuity through colonial domination. Where Young sees rupture, scholars such as Jean-François Bayart and Patrick Chabal emphasise continuity from the pre-colonial era through colonial domination to post-colonial modes of domination in Africa.

It was a major advantage in the power game to be able to switch between two modes of 'legitimate' domination – one that officially followed the modern model and another, patrimonial model that co-existed with the former. The latter was based on a completely different type of legitimacy, that of reciprocal exchange of goods and services between patrons and clients. It had its own language, its own forms of dealing with power and protection, and its own advantages in terms of economic, social and cultural capital. However, many administrative procedures closely associated with the modern institutionalisation of the state persisted, too. They endowed certain social practices with predictability and stabilised the social order where pure patrimonialism, that is, responsibility only to the ruler, would have failed.

Practices that implicitly or explicitly refer to the state as an institution can be analysed as the peculiar form of statehood that the institution of the state adopts in society.[18] Such practices may still be useful when the state has faded away, as in many regions of Africa. They would still facilitate certain interactions in the public sphere, and they would continue to endow meaning to social practices that were once linked to the state. It is not inappropriate to say that statehood continues to exist when the state as an institution is no longer existent.[19] But more often than not, statehood is then practised by non-state actors. What this means for the constitution of norms and standards is the subject of the case study that follows.

2. Actors

Northern Côte d'Ivoire belongs to the regions where the state as an institution is no longer present. Officially – and that means from the Southerners' point of view – the main bodies of the post-colonial *République de Côte d'Ivoire* are still there, that means in all parts of the territory of the post-colonial state, including the rebellious Northern half. But reality is different and depends largely on time and place. When the country split into two halves in the late rainy season of 2002, most civil servants that were not born in the North left for the Southern parts still under the domination of the so-called legitimate government. In particular the armed bodies of the former post-colonial state disintegrated more or

---

[18] I adapt this conceptualisation from Joel Migdal (Migdal, *State in Society*).
[19] I analyse such practices more deeply in a forthcoming publication ('Statehood in a Stateless Society' in Bauer and Dobler (eds.) forthcoming, *Trust in States*).

less immediately after 19 September, the day the insurgency started. The
remaining factions of the police and the gendarmerie were soon dissolved
because of suspicions that they still supported the Southern, the so called
legitimate government. Some former members of the police and the
gendarmerie joined the troops of the rebel forces while others tried to
make a living from various other sources.[20] The security situation changed
over the months and years since September 2002, but in one regard, it did
not differ much from the situation before: apparently, there was one
dominant actor – first the state and then the rebellion – but *de facto*
neither actor could claim a monopoly in the legitimate use of force.
Their legitimacy as well as their capability to exert this force was questioned by other corporate actors and often by the majority of the population, too.

Before and after 2002, 'the state' and 'the rebellion' as main actors had
to compete with other providers of security, which I will describe in a
moment. Despite the complexity of the situation and many people's
uncertainty of how to assess it, there were widely accepted standards of
security that emerged from the interplay of these various actors. And by
the end of 2006, after more than four years of insurgency, a different kind
of social and political order has emerged in the northern part of the
country.[21] The standards were partially based on the normative basic
cultural assumptions of the people, but they also adapted to the rapidly,
later slowly changing situation on the ground. It is this societal setting
that makes the northern parts of Côte d'Ivoire, like other regions of
precarious statehood, so fascinating for an analysis of the processes of
standard setting. There are few, at times no, dominant actors that may
exert a decisive influence on such processes, and in addition, they often
cannot enforce adherence to such standards. Both are clearly the outcome of social processes and checks and balances.

Before analysing the constitutions of such norms and standards in
northern Côte d'Ivoire, a word must be said about the conceptualisation
of processes of standard setting. It seems to be obvious that the provision

---

[20] I cannot go into the strategies of survival of this particular group, suffice to say that these
strategies covered many activities, from the *import direct* of commodities from Togo and
Guinea (i.e. without paying customs) to 'security services' that would have been labelled
as criminal acts under normal circumstances.

[21] I started to do fieldwork in the northern parts of Côte d'Ivoire in January 2007 and came
back in January and February 2008. My description of the new social order thus refers to
the years 2007 and 2008. Fieldwork was funded by the Swiss National Fund and carried
out together with Kerstin Bauer.

of security is almost always a business. Security providers are not always paid in cash, but they have other advantages such as, say, vehicles and food. Among the rebels, they got a combination of all three, depending on their rank and position within the novel political and military order. The requisition of cars by young rebels over the first months after September 2002 was an issue of daily conversations. But they were not the only ones who profited from the insecurity. 'Private' security services were again present soon after the signing of the ceasefire on 17 October 2002 and in particular after the 'declaration of the end of the war' by both parties on 4 July 2003.[22] A few Lebanese never left their stores and always had their watchmen, but more security firms rushed in when some bigger companies re-established branches and agencies in the north. However, not all security providers were established as companies in the narrow sense of the word. There were gangs that threatened shop owners in some quarters of the cities and in particular in the peri-urban space where the rebels were less visible. Their activities came closer to intimidation and blackmail to extort money for the 'protection' they offered. Such markets, Georg Elwert argues, emerge when the state is not able to limit the use of violence in a social or physical space. The demanded commodity is, however, security, not violence.[23]

All these actors generate an income from such services, and it is certainly appropriate to analyse the provision of security in economic terms, that is, as a market. The practices of the actors are defined by the logic of material profits, and obviously, security markets as in northern Côte d'Ivoire are highly profitable. However, there are some actors that do not fit into this scheme. Two examples can be cited: one is the so-called *groupes d'autodéfense*, the 'self-defence groups' that are familiar to most ordinary people in northern Côte d'Ivoire but which do not exist everywhere, and the other is the hunters' associations, the famous *dozo* or *tozobele*.

The first example shows that such groups may be based on mutual solidarity, in this case on what their members learned during the common rites of passage. The term *groupes d'autodéfense*, however, neither

---

[22] A chronology of the Ivoirian crisis between September 2002 and the peace treaty of Ouagadougou in March 2007 was published by the French journal *Nouvel Observateur* at http://tempsreel.nouvelobs.com/actualites/international/afrique/20070327.OBS9176/chronologie_de_la_crise_ivoirienne.html (30 July 2008).

[23] See again Mehler, 'Oligopolies of Violence'. It would be a gross misunderstanding of the everyday to call this market a 'market of violence', as Georg Elwert has suggested (Elwert, 'Gewaltmärkte', 86–101).

refers to such rites nor has a direct equivalent in one of the local languages. It has become what I would call local French or, as some of my interlocutors said, a word of *franco-ivoirien*. What, then, is meant by *groupes d'autodéfense*? And how is it that the French word has become part of everyday language? To answer the first question, one needs to look at the village level where rites of passage are still practised, or at least known to everyone. The key institution here is the *poro*, a so-called secret society into which young men were initiated at about the age of 20 to 25. Membership, and thereby initiation, was more or less obligatory when a young man was coming of age. Since the Senufo, which account for more than three-quarters of the rural population in northern Côte d'Ivoire, were by and large an acephalous society, the *poro* was one of the very few institutions that cut across the boundaries of the lineages.[24] It linked the segments of society that were based on descent, and it fostered ties of solidarity between men of different ancestry.[25]

The young initiates of *poro* had to work in teams based on an ascription of the young men to an age set. The main metaphor for the activities of *poro* was 'work'. The men had to fulfil communal work such as the building of bridges and the clearance of roads and pathways that, in pre-colonial times, were the only links between their village and the wider world. Their main duty, however, was the defence of the village in case of war. They carried weapons and had to fight against the soldiers of Samori Touré, the last founder of a Manding empire, when he conquered their land shortly before the arrival of the French. There was neither pay nor any remuneration other than the recognition as adult and responsible men. It was a communal duty that received the highest regard by the old men and women of the village. The colonial power then banned all firearms, and the young men had to carry wooden mock rifles instead of the real ones when they were performing their duties. The *poro* persisted as a religious and ritual organisation, but it nonetheless fostered the mutual co-operation across lineage ties.

About a century later, in the early 1990s, young men in many villages started to gather in informal groups that protected their towns during the night when bandits and criminals were expected to attack the settlement.

---

[24] The other two institutions were the earth priests as representatives of the first settlers and the dense network of alliances created through marriage. A comprehensive description and analysis of the *poro* is provided in Förster, *Zerrisssene Entfaltung*.

[25] Descent was matrilineal until the early twentieth century but became patrilineal under the partial influences of Islam and Christianity. Today, most Senufo living in an urban setting have adopted patrilineal descent.

It was, so the ordinary people said, a time of incredible insecurity – a time much more dangerous than the decades before. The groups of young men that were now protecting their communities monitored every move in the village and at its fringes where the wilderness of the savannah came close to the last houses. They erected barriers at the roads entering the village, sometimes imposed curfews, and they again carried guns.[26] The weapons were first produced locally, but already in 1991, I was offered an Israeli Uzi submachine gun 'for self-protection at a reasonable price', as the trader told me. He proudly said that he bought it in Mali from some Tuareg coming from Libya.

There was no direct continuity between the age sets of the *poro* who had defended the Senufo villages a hundred years ago and the informal groupings of the 1990s. But the organisational model was very much the same. Most of the young men who became members of such self-defence groups were also members of *poro*, and though the two institutions were kept apart, they all shared a considerable experience in how to act together as a group under difficult conditions. Though there was no central command, they could convene their members within a few minutes – and they were good at organising discrete surveillance around the villages and could integrate into big units of more than a hundred men when necessary. They were strong enough to face criminal gangs trying to penetrate into the villages at night. Night watches were organised on a rotating basis: every man had to serve for two or three nights and was then replaced by another member of the group. Accountability was loosely structured: as a corporate body, the young men were not responsible to a particular person or institution. But they saw themselves as representatives of their communities, and if they captured a thief or another person that was suspect of evil intentions, they brought him or her to the old spokesman of the village[27] or the quarter. Such persons were then tried by a group of elders who represented the major lineages. As individuals, the men were embedded into the hierarchies of the

[26] Such barriers at village entries are shown in the documentary *Nafoun – oder es gibt kein Feuer* from 1992 (produced by Paul Schlecht), broadcast the same year by the former Südwestfunk Baden-Baden.

[27] Often but not necessarily this spokesman was the so-called *chef de village*, a hereditary position with little political influence. The office was often introduced by the colonial administration because it needed intermediaries between the *chefs de canton*, the lowest level of the administration, and the ordinary villagers. See for colonial Upper Volta, of which the southern parts belonged to Côte d'Ivoire until 1947, Spittler, *Verwaltung in einem afrikanischen Bauernstaat*, in particular 74–88.

respective *poro* societies where they had to follow the orders of the age set above them. The *poro* was also the place where they were held account-able if they violated the ethics of what the elders called 'an upright man'.

The name *groupes d'autodéfense* came from outside,[28] while many of the locals spoke of *ton*, a Manding word meaning 'voluntary association' in a very wide sense. It could cover anything from ephemeral groups that joined only once or twice for agricultural labour to well-established local political associations with written statutes. The French word was clearly more precise, and that is probably also why it entered into everyday discourse. In the bigger cities, such associations were comparatively rare. After 2002, they were absent in Ferkéssedougou, an important railway and road junction where all the traffic to Mali and Burkina Faso had to pass. In Korhogo, they existed for some time after the coup d'état of 1999 but later withdraw to the peri-urban space around the densely inhabited quarters of the city. To some degree, these settlements at the urban periphery possessed the closely knit solidarity networks of villages.[29]

But wherever such self-defence groups existed, they were organised as networks based on solidarity and reciprocity. They were all based on a segmentary mode of organisation and had no direct economic agenda.

Another example of non-profit security providers are the well-known hunters' associations in many West African countries. They were a major actor during the war in Sierra Leone and Liberia, and since the early 1990s they have also been present in Côte d'Ivoire, where they are known under the Manding word for hunter, *dozo*.[30] Furthermore, hunters' associations exist in every part of the Manding-speaking area, that is, in Guinea, Mali, and many parts of Guinea Bissau, Senegal and Burkina Faso. Their organisation may differ, but almost all of them claim an origin in pre-colonial times and many claim that they directly go back to the medieval empire of Mali and its legendary founder Soundiata Keita. When he won the battle of Kirina in 1235, there were of course no firearms, but the hunters always appropriated new technologies quickly.

---

[28] The word was better known in towns and the urban area of Korhogo, the major city in the north of the country. I cannot trace the origin, but the explanation of one of my interlocutors probably comes close to what happened: he said that the name came from the international NGOs that were operating in the country since the turn of the century.

[29] These areas are sometimes conceived as a series of 'rural communities' based on the same extended kin relations and reciprocity networks as remote villages. Compare for a similar conceptualisation Marris, *Family and Social Change*.

[30] See the special issue 'Mande Hunters, Civil Society and the State' of *Africa Today*, vol. 50, no. 4, 2004.

More than six centuries later, when French Captain Joseph Gallieni conquered the Western Sudan region between 1876 and 1882, most hunters already carried guns, and some had modern rifles that came from the British colonies at the Guinea coast.[31]

The hunters' associations in Côte d'Ivoire were not only present in the Manding-speaking areas in the north-west of the country, they had spread well into the neighbouring populations that were of a different origin and also spoke entirely different languages. While the *Malinké*, as they were called by the French colonial administration, had a political organisation based on small but centralised principalities and kingdoms with patrilineal succession, the neighbouring Senufo, also a colonial name, had an acephalous social organisation mainly based on matrilineal descent. Though both had to provide intermediary rulers to the colonial administration, the Senufo basically maintained their segmentary social organisation throughout the colonial period and also after independence. An exception was the city of Korhogo, the administrative post of the French and later by far the biggest city in the north of the country. Already the colonial administration had made the local village head man, Péléforo Gbon Coulibaly, a *chef de canton* and later *chef suprême Sénoufo*. The position gave him considerable influence in the colonial administration, and his successors soon held high positions in independent Côte d'Ivoire. The mayors of the city always came from the family, while other members were ministers and held other high offices. The family and its allies were still one of the major political actors when the Ivoirian crisis started in the 1990s.

However, it would be difficult to classify them as 'neo-traditional' actors.[32] Certainly, on the one hand, they always referred to their roots in the local society and still continue to do so. They participate in many rituals that would be labelled 'customary' from outside. For instance, they are often present when an elder dies in the city or in the not too far peri-urban area. And if a high-ranking member of the family is not available, they send at least a representative. They also made use of the widespread metaphors of kin solidarity to sustain the net of political ties to village elders. The mayor was often addressed as 'father of Korhogo' or even the Senufo, or he called himself the 'older brother' of the employees

---

[31] See the illustrations in Gallieni, *Voyage au Soudan Français*.
[32] The concept of neo-traditional ruler is more fully explained in Klute and Bellagamba (eds.), *Beside the State*. See also Dieter Neubert, chapter 2.

of the city council.[33] But when it came to modern discourses, he often adopted another language – one of outright intimidation that left little room for misunderstanding. Ordinary people saw this more or less as the expression of a hidden agenda – one that put his and his family's interests first.[34] Though he regularly distributed money to his clients during receptions at his residence or at official occasions, he was also said 'to eat alone'. This metaphor indicates that he did not follow the rules of redistribution that the general audience expected from a 'traditional' ruler.

The hunters' associations were not under the control of any of the post-colonial political actors. Not unlike the voluntary self-help associations, the hunters were organised along segmentary lines. They were more visible than the former because of the 'traditional' attire that they had to wear. But they also had discrete modes of communication, and in case of a conflict with the local administration, they could more or less immediately join forces and show up in units of several hundred people. The effectiveness of their segmentary organisation was stunning and a fact that many state actors until the end of the 1990s had difficulties to believe – until they suddenly had to face a crowd of hunters around their *sous-préfecture* or *préfecture*, demanding what they considered to be right.

Despite their claims to a century-long history, the Ivoirian hunters' associations of the 1990s and later seldom had a direct link to the past in the Senufo-dominated North. In many places – villages, towns and in particular cities – *dozoya* associations, literally 'what hunters do', were re-founded after a period of decline in the late 1980s and early 1990s. Already under the old regime of Houphouët-Boigny and his successor Henri Konan Bédié, they adopted many functions from the police and the gendarmerie. They erected road blocks to control illicit traffic, persecuted criminals across the countryside and patrolled in many a suburb

---

[33] The use of such metaphors is a parallel to the national level. The president, in particular the first president after independence, Félix Houphouët Boigny, was usually called *père de la nation*, or simply *le vieux*, a colloquial term for the oldest male of the family. Compare Schatzberg, *Political Legitimacy*, 8–35 and *passim*.

[34] An episode of this kind was the temporary suppression of the many informal 'fuel stations' (wooden racks with bottles filled with petrol) in and around Korhogo in the early 1990s in favour of small dispensing machines, officially because of safety reasons. Rumours went that the new machines were all owned by the mayor himself. This data is based on my fieldwork from 1990 to 1996.

to prevent evildoers to penetrate.[35] All these activities did not belong to the spectrum of the historical *dozoya*, though there always was a military component in it. The contemporary *dozo* are much more a hybrid type of actor that legitimises and immunises its activities by claims to an unquestionable historical legacy. What hunters do, however, is always addressing the here and now, that is, life under the conditions of precarious statehood.

What is more important is that the hunters, very much like the age sets of the *poro* and the self-help groups at village level, were known as men that had gone through meticulous initiation rituals and therefore had adopted an ethic of honesty, braveness and accountability. They would never, so almost everyone believed, do anything wrong or blackmail or harm an innocent person. There are endless stories about hunters performing the most extraordinary things to give justice to the underprivileged and poor people – becoming invisible to trace criminals was one of the easier things to do. Local politicians often co-opted the hunters' associations and tried to profit from the high reputation for their own business – something which was often criticised by ordinary people. What was of primary importance for most people was that the presence of hunters almost always limited violence in their sphere of action. When the 'dangerous times' in the 1990s showed their grim face of spreading everyday violence, a considerable number of villages as well as quarters in Korhogo explicitly invited hunters' associations from elsewhere to help them to establish a *dozoya* of their own. Around the turn of the century, when the political crisis reached its first peak, and more so after 2002, many people said that they were safe because they were in a quarter under the surveillance of the *dozo*. An informal standard was established and, certainly with exceptions, respected by most of the actors.[36] In 2007, a fairly stable civil order had emerged: the rebels and their soldiers were acting outside the city of Korhogo while the city was left to the *dozo* who

---

[35] See Hellweg, 'Encompassing the State', 3–28, and Hellweg, 'Manimory and the Aesthetics of Mimesis', 461–83. The data presented here, however, is from my own field research. See as an example for *dozo* policing the arrest of 23 bandits on 4 August 2008 (published by *Fraternité Matin*, http://news.abidjan.net/article/?n=299681, 13 August 2008).

[36] To some degree, the presence of the UNOCI and the *opération Licorne*, the peacekeeping forces of the United Nations and France, also had an impact. But these forces seldom intervened in the daily business of keeping ordinary violence at bay. Many of my interlocutors in 2007 complained that the UNOCI did not do anything at all – except for self-enrichment.

kept violence at a low level. Indeed, many people said that the city was safer than when the state was still a dominant actor.[37]

My first point is that these actors do not fit into the conceptualisation of security as a profitable market that then generates a certain standard of security as the outcome of strategic interactions between the most powerful actors. The findings also contradict the assumption that the disappearance of the state as an institution automatically leads to 'an open space for violence' that is then filled by actors with a predominantly economic agenda.[38] It is necessary to understand that, at least in this area of precarious statehood, neither the hunters nor the self-defence groups had ostensible economic agendas, and the logic of their practices is not one of profit-seeking and utilitarian rationality. But if standards did not emerge from the interplay of powerful security providers, where else did they come from?

At first glance, the answer seems to lie in the discourses that sustained the perception of security and insecurity. Being a reliable person, an honest man who would not betray the trust that the others pinned on him is a social expectation that can affect a whole societal setting. The more such expectations are communicated within a certain milieu, the more they will inform the practices of those to whom they are addressed. But that is a short-sighted argument since it does not take the impact of other practices into account. Discourses may have a decisive effect on social reality if the latter is understood as how the actors perceive the world and how they attribute meaning to it. In other words, discourses are often powerful agents that frame culture. However, cultural perspectives often have to face a reality that contradicts what we think about it and makes the actors' attitudes worthless.

3.   Trust and negotiation

The first few months after the rebellion in Côte d'Ivoire were a time of high insecurity – in the North as well as in the South. It was nearly impossible to travel across the country. Roadblocks were erected everywhere, and it was

---

[37] From my own experience, I would subscribe to such statements. In January 2007, I first hesitated to go out at night but soon learned that this was by no means as risky as I believed it to be.

[38] This is again the conceptualisation put forward by Elwert, 'Gewaltmärkte'. He also coined the term 'gewaltoffene Räume'. Needless to say that such conceptualisations can be read as statements about human nature. Elwert seems to fall back on Thomas Hobbes' assumption of a violent state of nature as 'war of all against all' that re-emerges once the state withdraws from a certain area.

nearly impossible to know how much time one needed to pass and what kind of difficulties the travellers would have to face. In the southern parts of the country, the *Jeunes Patriotes*, a national youth association that had close relationships to president Laurent Gbagbo and his party,[39] were famous for their armed hold-ups and also for the threatening of passengers at the illegal roadblocks that they were running along the major arteries linking the hinterland to the economic capital of Abidjan. The roadblocks were an important source of income for many young men. Checking cars, trucks, buses and passengers became a kind of profession. Many young men said in local French that they became *barragistes*, literally 'barriers'. Most people in northern Côte d'Ivoire attributed the atrocities that they had heard of or that they sometimes had witnessed themselves[40] either to them, the Young Patriots or to the loyal police and other auxiliary troops of the president. The situation in the North was not much better at the time. The rebels also erected roadblocks and suspected many buses and lorries of carrying hidden 'loyalists' back into the South where they would then take up their arms again to fight against the 'Northerners'. However, they did not act against people that were clearly from the northern parts – something they often tested by addressing them in one of the local languages.[41]

Traders were cut off from the harbour of Abidjan, and the trade with commodities from the South came to a halt. They all complained about the losses that they had to face. The transport of agricultural goods towards the South, in the first place cotton as the major cash crop of the region, also stopped. In particular female greengrocers, who mainly produced for the urban markets of Abidjan and a few other cities in the South, saw their salads and vegetables rotting on the ground.[42] They were

---

[39] On the role of youth associations in the crisis see Marshall-Fratani, 'Der Geist aus der Flasche', 27–31, and Konaté, 'Les enfants de la balle', 49–70.

[40] Eye-witness accounts of such events and atrocities and the traces they left in the collective memory will be the subject of a separate article.

[41] Still in January 2008, when I ran into a checkpoint of the rebels on my way to a town in the hinterland of Korhogo, the two young men at the roadblock immediately stopped to search the car when I addressed them in Senari, the language of the Senufo of the area. Language had become a 'reliable' marker of identity, and I was thus identified as 'a northerner'.

[42] The economic isolation of the rebel-held zone was also one of the reasons why many politicians of the South thought that the rebellion would simply collapse after a few days – a gross underestimation of the agency and flexibility of the traders. They soon found new alleys for their trade in Ghana, Togo and Guinea where they did not pay customs. In 2007–08, many commodities were considerably less expensive than in the South.

also the first to resume long-distance transport. The first trucks that left for Abidjan, the drivers remember, were full of market-women and their goods while no man yet dared to go. But that situation was no solution for the bigger traders: the unpredictability was unacceptable for any long-term engagement in business, many entrepreneurs complained.[43] In particular the fluctuation of 'fees' that had to be paid at checkpoints rendered any cost accounting hazardous. And while they had no impact on the situation in the South, the carriers in the North wanted at least the part under the control of the rebels to become a better place for doing business. Their spokesman was a rich and well-known businessman from Korhogo, Kassoum Coulibaly, who, among many other enterprises, also owned TCK, the biggest bus company in the North.[44] It was only a man of his standing, many smaller traders told me, who could negotiate better conditions with the rebel movement.

His counterpart on the side of the rebellion was Martin Kouakou Fofié, then the highest-ranking rebel commander in Korhogo, renowned for his ruthlessness and cruelty.[45] Fofié was and still seems to be a person of considerable influence in the whole North because of his unflinching loyalty to Guillaume Soro, secretary general and head of the political wing of the rebel movement and since April 2007 prime minister of the government of national unity. Collective remembrance about how the negotiations were carried out differs in several details, but it is consistent with regard to one: apparently, Kassoum Coulibaly – CK, as he is called by many – went to see Fofié in his notorious camp CTK, for *Compagnie Territoriale de Korhogo*. It is not clear how many representatives from both sides actually participated in the meeting, but according to popular under-standing, the others were but accessories and the real issue was that the two men had to confront each other in order to find a compromise that could serve as a basis for the future. As already mentioned, my aim is not so much the reconstruction of a real event but much more how the ordinary people imagine it. The popular imagery thus sees negotiation very much in

---

[43] The statement is based on the everyday remembrance of traders in Korhogo in 2007 and 2008.

[44] The company had adopted the acronym of TCK, i.e. 'Transport Coulibaly Kassoum'.

[45] Martin Kouakou Fofié is sought for war crimes and violations of human rights by paragraphs 9 and 11 of UN resolution 1572 (2004) and 1633 (2005): 'Forces under his command engaged in recruitment of child soldiers, abductions, imposition of forced labour, sexual abuse of women, arbitrary arrests and extra-judicial killings, contrary to human rights conventions and to international humanitarian law', www.un.org/News/Press/docs/2006/sc8631.doc.htm, 30 July 2008.

the lines of 'big man' against 'big man' (*grands types*), not so much as a process in which many stakeholders are involved. And if one side has a significant advantage of the outcome, it is more often than not attributed to the smartness of this one big man, not to the ability of many. He was one of those who could provide patrimonial protection, and the apparent success of his intervention on behalf of the other transporters contributed again to his social and political legitimacy to act as their representative.

More important for my topic is, however, the fact that these negotiations led to the establishment of reliable standards at most checkpoints in the North. In addition, their number was reduced to only a few along the routes leading into the southern parts of the country. Every bus and lorry driver then knew approximately how much he was expected to pay: 5,000 CFA at the entrance and again at the exit of the two big cities of Korhogo and Bouaké, 1,000 CFA for a private car, and 250 for a medium-sized motor cycle. At minor roads, the 'fees' were lower. It was also agreed that there should be no controls within the city. On the other hand, it would be inappropriate to speak in the aftermath of the 'implementation of an agreement'. It was much more a process by which the usual amount to pay became part of everyday knowledge. When actors were referring to this emerging standard, they did so with reference to everybody's obligations – either towards the rebellion or toward Kassoum as 'the father' of the transporters and the royal family in Korhogo.[46] By January 2007, it was a well-established practice. Bus drivers did not need to wait for long when they were entering Korhogo or another city in the central North if they paid the sum that was expected from them.[47] Of course, there was a range within which the amount fluctuated. It depended on how the drivers communicated with the rebels, if they had a 'brother' among them, but also on the mood of the young men at the checkpoint and their financial situation.[48] However, it was obvious that there were limits: drivers who were told to pay very high amounts could refuse and actually did so.[49] They would

---

[46] The short article written by Hamadou Ziao on the traditional chiefdom of Korhogo and the role of Kassoum Coulibaly is a striking example of that language (www.linter-ci.com/article.php3?id_article=5624, 29 July 2008).

[47] Unfortunately, I cannot tell from my own experience if the statement that this was valid 'everywhere in the North' came close to reality. I heard from some bus drivers that it was 'more difficult' in the region of Odienné, in the far North-West of Côte d'Ivoire.

[48] Most of the rebels are very young, often still teenagers or in their twenties.

[49] My information on such practices mainly comes from direct observation and what drivers in Korhogo told me about the change of transport conditions since 2002.

tell the man at the checkpoint that the request was unacceptable. They had a good chance of getting away without paying more than usual. By 2007, travelling in the North was easier than in the state-controlled South. There were fewer checkpoints than before the beginning of the crisis in 2002, and far less than in the government-controlled parts of the country.[50] Overland transport had become predictable again. Passengers, drivers and, last but not least, entrepreneurs trusted these standards. They calculated what they needed for a certain journey, thus building up new trading networks – not towards Abidjan but to destinations that they now approached because of the difficult transport conditions in the south of their own country. Traders bought Chinese motor cycles in Lomé and sold them very successfully in Korhogo and many other places. Market women started to sell yams to Burkina Faso and Mali where, they now proudly claim, the quality of yams improved and are now available at lower prices than ever before.

Still more interesting is another element: the standard 'fees' were called *les tarifs*, as if such tariffs were stipulated by some superior authority. In addition, many actors claimed that what had emerged as a standard until 2007 should serve as an example to a possible future administration. They vehemently stated that they did not want the police and the gendarmerie back because their controls were more arbitrary than what they had now. In other words, they held normative ideas on how a state and its administration should function, namely with regard to corruption. Though almost everyone said that it was 'impossible' to eradicate corruption completely, they maintained that ideally, a state should be free from it. All of my interlocutors were aware that such practices still existed in the North, but many of them also said that they were better off with the standard that they now had achieved. It was an acceptable level of corruption.[51]

4. Conclusion

Statehood as a particular type of governance is still present in the normative thinking of many actors in stateless northern Côte d'Ivoire.

---

[50] Travelling from Djebonoua, the frontier village between the two parts of the country, south to Abidjan meant going through some twenty checkpoints where, until recently, all passengers had to get out of their vehicles and were often harrassed by the *Jeunes Patriotes*, the police or whoever was running the post.

[51] For an excellent analysis of this phenomenon in Nigeria see Smith, *A Culture of Corruption*.

There are discourses about who should do what and how, and what should not be done. Though all actors are aware that reality does not meet the ideal they have in mind, they also claim that it is necessary to come closer to it than under the 'old regime' and the present government in the South. As social norms, such basic convictions of how social life should look need a complement in real life.

The new social order that has emerged since the country split into two halves in 2002 has led to fairly reliable standards. The most important is certainly the security issue. Security is not solely the outcome of the interplay of a limited number of actors in an unregulated market. It is partially based on a segmentary mode of organisation that informs the practices of at least two important actors. This segmentary organisation is embedded in the reproduction of culture. Cultural values such as honesty and braveness and social norms of solidarity are appropriated from older institutions and then cast into new and hybrid institutions as self-help groups and the hunters' associations regaining strength with the security services that they provide to the ordinary city population. In everyday discourses, the historical roots of the *dozo* legitimate them as 'traditional' and immunise them against the critique of other actors who have different agendas.

Free overland transport and the limitation of fees at roadblocks as public standards emerge from another kind of process. In this case, it is the interplay of social norms, the popular imagery of political negotiation and neo-patrimonial obligations that leads to the establishment of reliable standards. Though the main actors follow economic agendas, the process is again at the intersection of cultural and social reproduction. Unlike the first, it maintains, as a practice, a direct link to statehood. The standards refer to normative ideas about the political order, but in the end, they are reproduced through practice – and it is this practice that contributes to the maintenance of a normative image of the state.

According to our modern understanding, all groups and associations described and analysed in this contribution belong to the non-state side. Such a distinction does not make much sense if one narrows it down to the state as an institution. It is useful, though, if one looks at statehood as a practice that has a reference to an institution, informed by the norms underpinning that institution. As such, the distinction is action-oriented: statehood is then embedded in the practices of actors – regardless of their institutional affiliation. But when one looks at how this practice interacts with other norms and institutions, it is perhaps more appropriate to understand the state versus non-state distinction as a call for a radical alternative in social analysis.

References

Bauer, K. and Dobler, G. (eds.) forthcoming, *Trust in States, Trust without States: How the Privatization of Security Affects Social Trust.*

Boehm, Ch. 1984, *Blood Revenge: The Anthropology of Feuding in Montenegro and other Tribal Societies,* Lawrence, University of Kansas Press.

Caplan, R. 2007, 'From Collapsing States to Neo-Trusteeship: The Limits to Solving the Problem of "Precarious Statehood" in the 21st Century', *Third World Quarterly,* vol. **28**, no. 2, 231–44.

Chabal, P. 1994, *Power in Africa,* 2nd edn, New York, St. Martin's Press.

Chomsky, N. 2006, *Failed States: The Abuse of Power and the Assault on Democracy,* London, Hamish Hamilton.

Clapham, Ch. 1996, *Africa and the International System,* Cambridge University Press.

Elwert, G. 1997, 'Gewaltmärkte: Beobachtung zur Zweckrationalität der Gewalt', *Kölner Zeitschrift für Soziologie und Sozialpsychologie* (Sonderheft 37, T. v. Trotha (ed.), *Soziologie der Gewalt)* Köln, 86–101.

Evans Pritchard, E. 1940, *The Nuer,* Oxford, Clarendon Press.

Förster, T. 1997, *Zerrisssene Entfaltung: Alltag, Ritual und künstlerische Ausdrucksformen im Norden der Côte d'Ivoire,* Köln, Köppe.

Gallieni, J. S. 1885, *Voyage au Soudan Français (Haut-Niger et pays de Ségou) 1879–1881,* Paris, Hachette.

Hagberg, S. 2005, 'Dealing with Dilemmas: Violent Farmer-Pastoralist Conflicts in Burkina Faso' in P. Richards (ed.), *No Peace – No War,* Athens, Ohio University Press, 40–56.

Hellweg, J. 2004, 'Encompassing the State: Sacrifice and Security in the Hunters' Movement of Côte d'Ivoire', *Africa Today,* vol. **50**, no. 4, 3–28.

Hellweg, J. 2006, 'Manimory and the Aesthetics of Mimesis: Forest, Islam and State in Ivoirian Dozoya', *Africa Today,* vol. **76**, no. 4, 461–83.

Klute, G. 1996, 'The Coming State: Reactions of Nomadic Groups in the Western Sudan to the Expansion of the Colonial Powers' in G. Klute (ed.), *Nomads and the State, Nomadic Peoples,* vol. **38** (special issue), 49–72.

Klute, G. and Bellagamba, A. (eds.) 2008, *Beside the State: Emerging Forms of Power in Contemporary Africa,* Köln, Köppe.

Konaté, Y. 2003, 'Les enfants de la balle. De la FESCI aux mouvements des patriotes', *Politique Africaine,* vol. **89**, 49–70.

Marris, P. 1961, *Family and Social Change in an African City,* London, Routledge.

Marshall-Fratani, R. 2004, 'Der Geist aus der Flasche. Die Rolle der rebellierenden Jugend beim Konflikt in Côte d'Ivoire', *Der Überblick,* vol. **40**, no. 1, 27–31.

Mehler, A. 2004, 'Oligopolies of Violence in Africa South of the Sahara', *Nord-Süd-Aktuell,* vol. **18**, no. 3, 539–48.

Migdal, J. 2001, *State in Society: Studying how States and Societies Transform and Constitute one Another,* Cambridge University Press.

Mulugeta, A. 2008, *The Transformation of Conflicts among Ethiopian Pastoralists*, PhD thesis, University of Basel.

Nordstrom, C. *et al.* (eds.) 1995, *Fieldwork Under Fire: Contemporary Studies of Violence and Survival*, Berkeley, University of California Press.

Popitz, H. 2006, *Soziale Normen*, F. Pohlmann (ed.), Frankfurt am Main, Suhrkamp.

Schatzberg, M. C. 2001, *Political Legitimacy in Middle Africa*, Bloomington, Indiana University Press, 8–35.

Schütz, A. and Luckmann, T. 1979, 1984, *Strukturen der Lebenswelt*, 2 vols., Frankfurt am Main, Suhrkamp.

Smith, D. J. 2007, *A Culture of Corruption and Popular Discontent in Nigeria*, Princeton University Press.

Spittler, G. 1981, *Verwaltung in einem afrikanischen Bauernstaat*, Wiesbaden, Steiner.

Trotha, T. v. 1999, 'Über den Erfolg und die Brüchigkeit der Utopie staatlicher Herrschaft: Herrschaftssoziologische Beobachtungen über den kolonialen und nachkolonialen Staat in Westafrika' in W. Reinhard (ed.), *Verstaatlichung der Welt? Europäische Staatsmodelle und außereuropäische Machtprozesse*, München, Schriften des Historischen Kollegs, Kolloquien 47, 223–51.

Trotha, T. v. 2000, 'Die Zukunft liegt in Afrika: Vom Zerfall des Staates, von der konzentrischen Ordnung und vom Aufstieg der Parastaatlichkeit', *Leviathan, Zeitschrift für Sozialwissenschaften*, vol. **28**, no. 2, 253–79.

Utas, M. 2003, *Sweet Battlefields: Youth and the Liberian Civil War*, Uppsala, University Dissertations in Cultural Anthropology, 119–67.

Young, C. 1994, *The African Colonial State in Comparative Perspective*, New Haven, Yale University Press.

Zartman, W. (ed.) 1995, *Collapsed States: The Disintegration of Legitimate Authority*, Boulder, Lynne Rienner, Boulder.

PART III

The authority and effectiveness of actors and standards

13

Standard setting for capital movements: reasserting sovereignty over transnational actors?

PETER HÄGEL*

1. Introduction

Standard setting with regard to capital movements has never been a state monopoly, at least for countries that maintain relatively open economies. From the first stock exchanges to contemporary rating agencies and hedge funds, institutional and technological innovations that allow capital to be allocated have been driven mostly by the ingenuity of private actors. In a historical perspective, the relationship between private capital owners and rulers appears as an eternal cat-and-mouse game, with the former looking for the best investment opportunities and the latter trying to subjugate these to their own objectives, especially revenue and economic stability.[1]

The regulation of cross-border capital movements therefore constitutes a fascinating policy area for analysing the relationship between states and transnational actors. Capitalists rarely bother about borders if the grass is greener on the other side of the fence but their degree of autonomy depends on states' ambitions and capabilities to exercise authority and control over private capital movements. While transnational actors have become important subjects in the study of world politics, most research privileges them as autonomous. They are being examined in their efforts to create private rules or standards and to influence state actors in order to reach their material or normative goals. Consequently, models of the interactions between transnational and state actors rarely foresee the reverse: states

* Assistant Professor, Department of International and Comparative Politics, The American University of Paris, France. The author would like to thank Anne Peters and Richard Beardsworth for very helpful comments on earlier drafts of this chapter.
[1] See Ferguson, *The Cash Nexus*; Frieden, *Global Capitalism*.

influencing transnational actors to further their own interests. This relationship needs further investigation because states have been very active in reasserting their sovereignty vis-à-vis transnational actors.[2]

In the wake of several waves of financial sector liberalisation, early globalisation debates concentrated on the seemingly free movement of capital and how it reduced the authority and control of states. Since the 1990s, however, states started new initiatives to re-regulate capital flows. Comprehensive measures against money laundering, terrorist financing and corruption have created wide-ranging obligations for transnational actors, especially financial service providers, in how they do business. At the same time, such re-regulation often emerges in ways that defy traditional notions of sovereignty. International regimes are increasingly driven by the necessity, rather than the voluntary decision, to co-operate among states in order to achieve effective regulations. In Europe, states rely on supranational European Union (EU) legislation. The United States expands its national jurisdiction by claiming and enforcing its laws extraterritorially. Weaker states – often, but not only, in the Global South – are confronted with regulatory demands from the former actors. Therefore, sovereignty is changing from being a universal concept to one that needs to be differentiated and qualified, for example as interdependent, supranational, imperial or partial sovereignty.

2. Theoretical perspectives on sovereignty and transnational actors

Though sometimes seen as something absolute (either one has it or not), sovereignty is better understood as a benchmark – a norm constituting what, ideally, a modern state should claim and attain: final authority within its territory and non-intervention from abroad. The more states conform to this benchmark, the more sovereignty is the organising principle of world politics. Whereas the 'claiming' refers to the scope of state authority, the 'attaining' relates to the extent of state control in realising these claims. Understood in such a way, sovereignty is, and always has been, a question of degree that leaves room for historical and cross-national variation.[3] In this respect, it is crucial to conceptualise final authority as the meta-political authority to decide

---

[2] See Cohen, *Resilience of the State*.   [3] See Lake, 'The New Sovereignty'.

what falls into the political realm of the state and what is left to others.[4] Leaving or delegating the regulation of certain areas to private actors can thus be seen as a sovereign decision. During the times of the Westphalian Treaties (and still today), it concerned primarily the separation of religion and state; more recently it concentrates on delimitations between states and the private economy. From the perspective of sovereignty, standard setting by private actors is then a form of governance that takes place either because states choose to delegate it or because states fail to govern specific areas in which private actors demand co-ordination.[5]

For a long time, questions about variations of sovereignty were conspicuously absent from International Relations (IR) theory. With the onset of globalisation debates, however, research and publications problematising sovereignty flourished. After early Cassandras proclaimed the end of sovereignty, the established schools of IR – realism, liberalism and constructivism – developed their own, more nuanced versions of how sovereignty might be transformed, instead of simply persisting or disappearing.

Where classical realism (and even more so neo-realism) takes sovereignty more or less for granted, Stephen Krasner presents a conceptualisation that is strongly anchored in realist assumptions and at the same time expands the framework.[6] According to Krasner, sovereignty is 'organised hypocrisy' – an enduring yet weak norm that has to succumb and adapt to the interests of powerful states:

> For rulers making choices in an anarchic environment in which there are many demands, multiple norms, power asymmetries and no authoritative decision-making structures, adhering to Westphalian sovereignty might or might not maximise their utility.[7]

For him, the clearest examples of sovereignty violations are instances where powerful states intervene, coercing and imposing their preferences, in the domestic affairs of weaker states. Deviating from a strictly realist viewpoint, he also considers, to a lesser degree, states' voluntary limitations of their authority via invitations and contracts.

Such contracts are at the heart of the liberal model of sovereignty transformations. Emphasising the liberal concerns with international

---

[4] See Thomson, 'State Sovereignty'.
[5] See Mattli and Büthe, 'Setting International Standards'; Mattli and Büthe, 'Accountability in Accounting?'; Sinclair, *The New Masters of Capital*.
[6] See Lake, 'The New Sovereignty'. [7] See Krasner, *Sovereignty: Organized Hypocrisy*.

interdependence and co-operation, changes in the status of sovereignty are essentially seen as bargains:[8]

> Sovereignty no longer enables states to exert effective supremacy over what occurs within their territories: Decisions are made by firms on a global basis and other states' policies have major impacts within one's own boundaries ... What sovereignty does confer on states under conditions of complex interdependence is legal authority that can ... be bargained away in return for influence over others' policies and therefore greater gains from exchange.[9]

Thus, delegations of authority to inter- or supranational institutions take place according to states' cost–benefit analyses. Sovereignty is being pooled among member states in order to achieve collective benefits. But delegation can also imply deregulation and privatisation, if states limit their authority vis-à-vis private actors, because they expect benefits like economic growth in return.

Finally, constructivists examine how

> [s]tates' claims to sovereignty construct a social environment in which they can interact as an international society of states, while at the same time the mutual recognition of claims to sovereignty is an important element in the construction of states themselves.[10]

Depending on whether they concentrate on agents or structures, they highlight either how actors redefine the normative content of sovereignty, or how sovereignty as a basic norm shapes world politics.[11,12]

Emphasising different aspects of why and how state practices change particular aspects of sovereignty, realist, liberal and constructivist re-conceptualisations are helpful in moving beyond a static understanding of sovereignty. But each of them continues to exhibit a state-centric perspective and none of them provides a clear framework of how non-state actors might challenge state sovereignty.[13] Even the liberal approach – which, with its emphasis on state responses to interdependence, pays the most attention to private actors – forgets to address key questions: can the delegation of authority be reversed and when does declining control lead to a loss of authority?

---

[8] See Keohane, 'Hobbes's Dilemma'; Mattli, 'Sovereignty Bargains'.
[9] See Keohane, 'Hobbes's Dilemma', 176 et seq.
[10] Biersteker and Weber, 'Social Construction of State Sovereignty', 2.
[11] Biersteker and Weber, *Sovereignty as Social Construct*; Philpott, *Revolutions in Sovereignty*.
[12] Sørensen, 'Sovereignty: Change'; Werner and Wilde, 'The Endurance of Sovereignty'.
[13] Hägel, 'Regieren ohne Souveränität?'.

The state-centredness on the main IR theories stands in stark contrast to research globalisation that identifies private actors as the protagonists behind intensifying transnational flows that are said to undermine state control over domestic rules and thus diminish state authority.[14] In the analysis of transnational actors' roles in world politics, two perspectives dominate. A first perspective examines how transnational actors establish non-state governance, for example in the setting of private standards or the development of private contract law, circumventing the need for intergovernmental regimes, which could eventually substitute state authority.[15] Secondly, transnational actors' role in world politics is seen in attempts to shape international governance by influencing states' foreign policies and the international organisations set up by states.[16] What unites both perspectives is a dichotomy between transnational actors and states in which the relationship between them is unilateral. Transnational actors are treated as autonomous actors that stand apart from states, either trying to influence or to circumvent them. Just as mainstream IR theories have neglected to incorporate private actors into their frameworks, research on transnational actors usually does not foresee state actors influencing private actors.[17] But from the vantage point of sovereignty and its transformations, the conflicting authority and control claims between these two are crucial.

3.   Reasserting sovereignty?

The regulation of private capital movements represents a fascinating policy area to investigate mutual influences between states and transnational actors. Among the various spaces of transnational exchange that lie behind globalisation, the vast and complex networks of financial flows are among the most important. Against the background of wide-ranging liberalisation and exponential growth of international capital markets after 1970, early globalisation debates focused on capital mobility as a new structural feature of the world economy and how it reduced the authority and control of states.[18]

---

[14] Sassen, *Losing Control*; Strange, *The Retreat of the State*.
[15] Cutler, *Private Power*; Cutler *et al.* (eds.), *Private Authority*; Hall and Biersteker (eds.), *The Emergence of Private Authority*.
[16] Keck and Sikkink, *Activists beyond Borders*; Klotz, 'Transnational Activism'.
[17] Hägel and Peretz, 'States and Transnational Actors'.
[18] Andrews, 'Capital Mobility and State Autonomy'; O'Brien, *Global Financial Integration*; Strange, *Retreat of the State*.

The institutional and technological innovations that made the transnational expansion of financial markets possible resulted for the most part from private standard setting. At the consumer level, it was the growth of credit cards and their organisation within the two major interbank associations, Visa and MasterCard, that greatly facilitated crossborder transactions from the 1960s onward.[19] At the corporate level, the evolution of the Society for Worldwide Interbank Financial Telecommunication (SWIFT) came to provide the core infrastructure. Initiated in 1973 by 237 commercial banks in order to improve data exchanges between them, SWIFT has since then developed technology, software and standards that are at the centre of global finance.[20] Its SWIFTNet FIN is a financial messaging service that distributes international demands for payments, securities trading and other financial transactions among customers (mostly banks, brokers and investment managers). Whereas other inter- and intrabank financial messaging networks are used for domestic transactions, SWIFTNet FIN is the primary vehicle for cross-border operations. In 2008, SWIFT connected more than 8,830 financial institutions in 209 countries and territories, handling more than 3.8 billion messages.[21] Both SWIFT and the major credit card organisations have been highly successful in establishing private standards for the format, the content and the processing of financial transactions, which allow capital to circulate easily and safely across borders and between different private actors.

States participated in financial globalisation mostly via deregulating their financial sectors and abolishing of capital controls, which had become widespread after the Second World War.[22] To a large extent, this can be explained by the liberal perspective of sovereignty bargains: since states want international trade and investment for growth, their ability to distinguish between trade- and investment-related transactions and speculative flows weakens as the number of transactions increases, fundamentally undermining capital controls.[23] According to Goodman and Pauly, 'For governments, the utility of controls declined as their perceived costs thereby increased'.[24] In other words, while states

---

[19] Evans and Schmalensee, *Paying with Plastic*.
[20] For the evolution of SWIFT, see: www.swift.com/index.cfm?item_id=1243.
[21] SWIFT, *Annual Report 2008*.
[22] Helleiner, *Reemergence of Global Finance*; Schulze, *Political Economy of Capital Controls*.
[23] Accordingly, many countries with lower levels of international financial integration still maintain capital controls today.
[24] Goodman and Pauly, 'Obsolescence of Capital Controls?', 51.

withdrew their authority over transnational capital movements, private actors created new standards that promoted them and both did so in the expectation of profits and prosperity.

Yet soon it became clear that not only speculative transactions but also the proceeds from crime, bribes and terrorist financing became as free as the coveted trade and investment flows.[25] The voluntary retreat from capital controls thus produced serious repercussions in areas where states had not foreseen a 'sovereignty bargain'. As their abilities to control crime-related transactions within the wider sea of financial flows became very limited, states' authority in criminal matters suffered accordingly. If a state passed laws against money-laundering, bribery or terrorist financing domestically, their effectiveness was rendered nil once such transactions crossed borders into territories that did not criminalise these practices. On the one hand, this loss of control and authority had its very basis in the sovereign state system, since opportunities for evasion existed only because some states offered more lenient regulatory environments for private actors than others. On the other hand, the overall outcome of regulatory competition constituted an empowerment of private actors and their capital movements that was independent of individual states' behaviour.[26] Over the past two decades, however, states have engaged in comprehensive re-regulation. Various measures against money laundering, terrorist financing and corruption created new (inter-)governmental standards that transnational actors, especially financial service providers, need to comply with.[27]

3.1   Anti-corruption regulation

Initiatives against the corruption of foreign officials had already been launched in the late 1970s within the frameworks of the United Nations (UN) and the Organisation for Economic Co-operation and Development (OECD) – without attracting much support. In 1989, an ad-hoc OECD Working Group was asked to look into the problem and to evaluate the member states' laws. The outcome was an OECD 'Recommendation on Bribery in International Business Transactions'

---

[25] Altvater and Mahnkopf, *Globalisierung der Unsicherheit*; Naim, *Illicit*.

[26] The clearest manifestation of this is the so-called offshore world (Palan, *The Offshore World*).

[27] Hägel, *Geldwäschebekämpfung*; Hägel, 'L'incertaine mondialisation'; Helleiner, 'State Power'; Simmons, 'International Politics of Harmonization'.

from May 1994. It remained quite vague but it did set the agenda. Significant support for the issue came from the transnational non-governmental organisation (NGO) Transparency International, founded in 1993 with the mission to mobilise against corruption.[28] Further deliberations inside the Working Group focused on criminalising the corruption of foreign officials and abolishing the tax-deductibility of bribes paid abroad. A revised Recommendation in May 1997 incorporated these points and foresaw the monitoring of their implementation via self-evaluations and peer review. Directly afterwards, negotiations continued to turn the criminalisation of bribing foreign officials into hard law, resulting in the OECD Anti-Bribery Convention from December 1997.[29] In the EU, two Protocols amending the EU Convention on the protection of the European Communities' financial interests and an additional Convention on the fight against corruption were signed during the same year. More encompassing are the Council of Europe (CoE, 1999) and UN (2003) Conventions against corruption, which aim at expanding the criminalisation of this practice around the globe.[30]

3.2 Fighting money laundering

Proposals to deal with money laundering first appeared within the international fight against drugs: as CoE recommendations in 1980, within Interpol and as a statement by the Basel Committee on Banking Regulations and Supervisory Practices.[31] The 1988 UN Vienna Convention then criminalised the laundering of proceeds of drug-related crimes and called for confiscation provisions. Two years later, the CoE stretched the criminalisation to the laundering of proceeds from all crimes in its 1990 Strasbourg Convention. Simultaneously, a G7 initiative set up the Financial Action Task Force (FATF) in Paris, an informal expert forum that developed 40 recommendations (FATF-40) in 1990. These address regulatory controls for private financial institutions with

---

[28] Galtung, 'A Global Network'.   [29] Sacerdoti, 'Das OECD-Übereinkommen'.

[30] See: 17 December 1997 OECD Convention on Combating Bribery of Foreign Public Officials in International Business Transactions; 26 July 1995 Convention on the Protection of the European Community's (EC) Financial Interests; 26 May 1997 Convention on the Fight against Corruption involving Officials of the EC or Officials of the EU Member States; 27 January 1999 Council of Europe Criminal Law Convention on Corruption; 31 October 2003 UN Convention against Corruption.

[31] Gilmore, Dirty Money.

the aim to deter and detect the laundering of proceeds from drug-related crimes: obligations to identify customers, keep records and report unusual or suspicious transactions to Financial Intelligence Units (FIUs) that decide whether to send reports to law enforcement authorities. Regular self-assessments and mutual evaluations among the FATF members ensure peer pressure through a name and shame approach that is also extended to non-members, via a black-listing mechanism that identifies non-cooperative countries and territories (NCTTs). Reviews of the FATF-40 in 1996 and 2003 expanded their scope to the laundering of proceeds from many other crimes (including corruption) and to the control of non-financial institutions, for example traders in high-value goods and legal professions. Essentially soft law, the FATF recommendations have by now become a global standard that has been adopted almost all around the world.[32] In the EU, three money laundering directives turned large parts of the international provisions into European Community (EC) law in 1991, 2001 and 2005.[33] Globally, the 2000 UN Palermo Convention against transnational organised crime integrated similar regulations into binding international law.[34]

3.3   Combating terrorist financing

After the attacks on the United States on 11 September 2001 (9/11), the anti-money laundering strategy of going after the money was used to combat transnational terrorism.[35] There, however, the logic of anti-money laundering is reversed, as legal revenues can be used to finance terrorism. Nevertheless, since efforts against money laundering and terrorist financing both rely on filtering out illicit transactions, it seemed to make sense to expand the FATF-regime in such a way as to include

---

[32] Stessens, *Money Laundering.*   [33] Hägel, *Geldwäschebekämpfung.*

[34] See: 1988 UN 'Vienna' Convention against Illicit Traffic in Narcotic Drugs and Psychotropic Substances; 1990 CoE 'Strasbourg' Convention on Laundering, Search, Seizure and Confiscation of the Proceeds of Crime; 2000 UN 'Palermo' Convention against Transnational Organised Crime; 10 June 1991 EEC Directive on Prevention of the use of the Financial System for the Purpose of Money Laundering; 4 December 2001 EC Directive amending Council Directive 91/308/EEC on Prevention of the Use of the Financial System for the purpose of Money Laundering; 26 October 2005 EC Directive on the Prevention of the Use of the Financial System for the Purpose of Money Laundering and Terrorist Financing; www.fatf-gafi.org.

[35] In the context of previous efforts against terrorism, countries had already agreed to an UN Convention for the suppression of the financing of terrorism in 1999, which aimed at criminalising such practices internationally.

terrorist financing into the criminalisation, prevention and reporting requirements that had been established against money laundering.[36]
Within its nine special recommendations on terrorist-financing, the
FATF introduced a new focus on NGOs (recommendation VIII) according to which 'countries should ensure that they cannot be misused'
for financing terrorism.[37,38] In addition, the US executive order 13224
(23 September 2001, based on the International Emergency Economic
Powers Act) to freeze the assets of specially designated legal and
natural persons suspected of terrorist financing was elevated to
become a universal obligation via UN Security Council Resolution
1373 (28 September 2001).[39] In the EU, this resolution was transformed
into Council Regulation 881/2002 on 27 May 2002.

4. Sovereignty transformed

These developments can be interpreted as states reasserting sovereignty
over transnational private actors, as they establish new standards that
private actors need to integrate into their businesses. But such a perspective would fail to take into account how these re-regulations emerged in
ways that defy classical notions of sovereignty. Thus, the new international regimes are increasingly driven by the necessity, rather than
the voluntary decision, to co-operate among states in order to achieve
effective regulations. A key feature of money laundering, terrorist financing and corruption is that these practices take place at the intersection of
legal and illegal business and thus their regulation affects many other
commercial activities.[40] Therefore, under circumstances of economic
interdependence and international competition, unilateral measures
against business offences can have negative consequences for national
competitiveness and trade.

---

[36] Clunan, 'Fight Against Terrorist Financing'; Greenberg *et al.*, *Terrorist Financing*; Pieth,
'Criminalizing the Financing of Terrorism'.
[37] Available at www.fatf-gafi.org/document/7/0,2340,en_32250379_32236947_34267143_
1_1_1_1,00.html.
[38] McCulloch and Pickering, 'Suppressing the Financing of Terrorism'.
[39] Available at www.state.gov/s/ct/rls/fs/2002/16181.htm. The Council of Europe
Convention on Laundering, Search, Seizure and Confiscation of the Proceeds from
Crime and on the Financing of Terrorism (16 May 2005) – as previously in the case of
money laundering – adopted a similar approach.
[40] McCulloch and Pickering, 'Suppressing the Financing of Terrorism'; Ruggiero, *Crime
and Markets*.

4.1   Global co-operation and governance

Short of turning towards autarchy and risking substantial economic losses, states need multilateral approaches to guarantee a level playing field. The fact that all attempts to reassert state authority over private capital movements have taken place through the establishment of new international standards – via the UN, the OECD, the FATF as well as various regional organisations – proves the point. Liberal theories capture the co-operative aspect of these regimes with their concepts of sovereignty bargains and 'sovereignty as participation':

> This ... concept of sovereignty as participation means that disaggregated sovereignty would empower government institutions around the world to engage with each other in networks that would strengthen them and improve their ability to perform their designated government tasks individually and collectively.[41]

But it would be more precise to speak of interdependent sovereignty rather than sovereignty. In the context of deep levels of global financial integration, multilateral negotiations are not just an option – they are the only one.

4.2   The role and interests of the United States

Still, the roles of states within the establishment of international regimes differ – some are more interdependent than others and some have more capacities to be makers while others remain takers of international regulation. In the financial realm and its regulation, the United States stands out.[42] With regard to both the corruption of foreign officials and money laundering, the United States has been the first country to criminalise these practices. As moral vanguard and powerful defender of its interests, it then pushed for criminalisation abroad. In the wake of the Watergate and Lockheed scandals, the Foreign Corrupt Practices Act (FCPA) in 1977 made it a criminal offence for American businesses to bribe foreign officials.[43] While the Bank Secrecy Act of 1970 had already established basic accounting and reporting rules for financial institutions, a comprehensive strategy of *going after the money* was enacted in 1986 with the Money Laundering

---

[41] Slaughter, *A New World Order*, 34; see also Chayes and Chayes, *The New Sovereignty*.
[42] Simmons, 'Politics of Harmonization'.
[43] Greanias and Windsor, *The Foreign Corrupt Practices Act*.

Control Act as a central part of the *war on drugs*.[44] The FCPA put American companies at a disadvantage in international commerce vis-à-vis companies from all the other states that allowed bribery abroad. Similarly, the customer identification, record keeping and reporting requirements against money laundering inhibited multi-million dollar expense claims for the US financial services sector.[45,46] These drawbacks provided the rationale for America's efforts to spread its norms internationally so that other countries would join the costly fight against corruption and money laundering.[47] In the case of combating the financing of terrorism, American influence is equally present. But in the direct aftermath of the 9/11 attacks, international collaboration within the UN Security Council and the FATF was as much a question of pressure as one of solidarity, which explains the rapid adoption of the above-mentioned measures.[48]

US power in this respect is closely related to its willingness to employ its own laws extraterritorially, on the one hand, and the attractiveness of its economic and financial markets, on the other. The latter's importance and size make two *sticks* very effective in influencing other states. The first is the possibility to punish deviance in the American market. Since many foreign companies, especially banks, have subsidiaries in the United States, these can be asked to gather evidence from their parent company or other subsidiaries abroad for use in US investigations. With the issuing of subpoenas that imply significant fines for failing to comply with the provision of evidence, such demands become forceful instruments.[49] Even stronger is the threat to generally deny foreign companies access to the US market. The amendment of Senator John Kerry to the 1988 Anti-Drug Abuse Act introduced this option into American law (31 USC 5311). It allows the President to prohibit institutions from participating in the American financial system (which includes the important world-wide clearing and wire transfer systems CHIPS and Fedwire), if they originate from a country that is non-cooperative in the fight against drug-related money laundering. Though this option has never been used so far, Kerry writes proudly that,

---

[44] Frank, *Die Bekämpfung*.
[45] Reuter and Truman, *Chasing Dirty Money*, 93 et seq.
[46] Also, transnational money laundering, especially with regard to drug trafficking, threatened to make the American laws ineffective.
[47] Abbott and Snidal, 'Values and Interests'; Helleiner, *Global Financial Reregulation*.
[48] Greenberg *et al.*, *Terrorist Financing*.
[49] Nadelmann, *Cops Across Borders*, 335 et seq., 357 et seq.

[a]dministration officials tell me that the very hint of such an approach by the United States has already pushed several countries in the Caribbean and Western Europe to begin imposing real regulations to combat the launderers.[50]

In the case of corruption of foreign officials, a similar pressure was constructed with the threat to raise bribery as an international trade policy matter, which could potentially include trade sanctions.[51]

In addition, the United States is offering two *carrots* to co-operative allies. First, American 'cops across borders' offer manifold training and assistance services via foreign offices of US law enforcement agencies:

> In an effort to ensure global compliance with international standards, the United States helps build capacity, both bilaterally and through a number of different multilateral fora. On a bilateral basis, the United States regularly delivers anti-money laundering and counterterrorist financing technical assistance, including legislative drafting, FIU development, judicial and prosecutorial training, financial supervision and financial crime investigatory training.[52]

Similar provisions exist to spread anti-corruption measures.[53] Second, material incentives for co-operation in investigating and confiscating criminal assets derive from the American offer to share the proceeds.

> From its inception in 1989 through March 2002, the international asset-sharing programme administered by the Department of Justice has resulted in the forfeiture by the United States of $389,229,323.00, of which $171,467,512.00 has been shared with 26 foreign governments that cooperated and assisted in the investigations.[54,55]

---

[50] Kerry, *The New War*, 153. These measures have been reinforced with the post-9/11 Patriot Act (Greenberg *et al.*, *Terrorist Financing*, 12 et seq.)

[51] Tarullo, 'The Limits of Institutional Design', 677 et seq. Another leverage reinforced the United States' ambitions during the OECD negotiations: Transparency International supported the American government's cause, collaborated with several US multinational corporations and started to advocate strongly for the Convention. As such, it acted as moral entrepreneur, a role that has already been identified as important in previous international criminalisation campaigns. Moral pressure proved to be powerful, because it resonated among sensitive publics within Western European states, due to several national corruption scandals, e.g. in France and Germany (Glynn, Kobrin and Naim, 'The Globalization of Corruption', 22 et seq.).

[52] USDoT and USDoJ, *2003 National Money Laundering Strategy*, 11; see also Nadelmann, *Cops Across Borders*.

[53] United States Department of Commerce, *Addressing the Challenges of International Bribery*, 2 et seq.

[54] The Treasury administers another international asset-sharing programme that shared $30,562,451 with other countries from 1990 to 2002 (USDoT and USDoJ, *2003 National Money Laundering Strategy*, 84).

[55] USDoT and USDoJ, *2003 National Money Laundering Strategy*.

Though it is common to refer to American influence in the international initiatives against money laundering and corruption, this only becomes convincing when one looks at the actual threats and incentives that allowed the formation of *coalitions of the willing*. As it spreads its domestic rules abroad, American sovereignty takes on imperial dimensions.[56] This attribution has to be qualified because in the case of re-regulating capital flows, American efforts are primarily about ensuring its domestic authority rather than ruling other countries. The first comprehensive examination of how courts in the United States apply extra-territoriality shows that, in general, the central motivation seems to be the protection of the effectiveness of its domestic rules, so that a loss of control due to cross-border interactions does not lead to a loss of American authority.[57] Nevertheless, in expanding its national jurisdiction through the promotion and enforcement of its laws extraterritorially, the United States demonstrate a particular reaction to interdependence that is better understood as imperial sovereignty.

4.3   The European Union – supranational and self-centred

This becomes clearer in comparison to the EU's approach towards money laundering, terrorist financing and the corruption of foreign officials. Neither the directive on the free movement of capital (1988) nor the second banking directive (1989), which together deregulated financial services in the EU, mentioned any concerns about money laundering. Basically, the EU's first money laundering directive was a reaction to the international initiatives, in order to avoid that divergent national implementation would disrupt its internal market. Commenting on the proposal in 1990, Geoffrey Fitchew, then Director-General for Financial Institutions and Company Law within the European Commission, referred to the Kerry amendment and explained:

> The US authorities were pressing other states to comply with this legislation and introduce similar requirements themselves. European Community States did not accept that the United States were entitled to impose these requirements extraterritorially and regarded this kind of reporting requirements as costly and ineffective. In order to continue effective dialogue with the US authorities it was important for the Community to be seen having its own effective measures in place to combat money laundering.[58]

---

[56] Ferguson, *Colossus*.   [57] Putnam, *Courts Without Borders*.
[58] House of Lords, *Money Laundering*, 29.

With regard to corruption, the EU's focus was largely self-centred. Aware that significant parts of its budget were being lost to fraud, the *protection of the Communities' financial interests* became an important issue during the early 1990s.[59] The resulting conventions prohibit the corruption of foreign officials but are limited to officials of the EU and its member states. This perspective was carried into the OECD negotiations:

> The Europeans submitted a draft treaty text that … defined the core offense as corrupting a public official of another country but only if that country was also a party to the convention … This provision was borrowed from parallel negotiations toward an EU treaty that would prohibit bribery of officials of the EU and of other member states but not of any nonmember state.[60]

Likewise, EU action against the financing of terrorism focused mainly on transposing the UN and FATF rules into EU law so as to avoid harmful intra-EU heterogeneity.[61] At the same time, this happens within the EU in a context of integration, which has long since turned interdependence into a supranational political system.[62] The quasi-constitutional nature of the EU's founding treaties and the final authority of the European Court of Justice in interpreting these treaties go beyond a pooling of sovereignty. As such, sovereignty in the EU is best characterised as supranational – at least in those policy areas where binding decision making takes place at the EU level.[63] However, so far the EU's ambitions remain mostly regionally limited and EU measures to re-regulate private capital flows have mainly served to incorporate international provisions into binding EU law.

4.4 Weak states

Yet another perspective applies to weaker states – often but not only in the Global South – which are confronted with regulatory demands from those states that establish the international regimes. The *black-listing*

---

[59] White, *Protection of the Financial Interests.*
[60] Abbot and Snidal, 'Values and Interests', 167 et seq.
[61] Vlcek, 'Acts to Combat the Financing of Terrorism', 505.
[62] Weiler, 'The Community System'.
[63] While 'supranational' is a commonly highlighted feature of the EU, the use of the term sovereignty with regards to the EU might raise eyebrows. Of course, neither is the EU likely to turn into a federal state any time soon, nor have the member states lost their international standing as sovereign states. Nevertheless, the fact that EU law-making represents final authority that is territorially bounded seems to warrant the notion of sovereignty, even if it is limited to designated policy areas.

mechanism of the FATF, which identifies non-co-operative countries and territories in the fight against money laundering and – as a last resort – threatens to enact counter-measures, is the most obvious procedure. Since its inception in 2000, 23 countries have been named non-co-operative and countermeasures have been recommended against Nauru, Myanmar and – very briefly – Ukraine. In response to this pressure, all these NCCTs have changed their legislation to conform to the FATF demands, so that no country is currently identified as non-co-operative.[64] Moreover, anti-money laundering efforts have become part of both the World Bank's and the International Monetary Fund's (IMF) monitoring and technical assistance programmes.[65] The same holds true for anti-corruption efforts, which have been integrated into the conditions that the IMF and the World Bank attach to their development finance.[66] Accordingly, in the case of weak states that are forced to adopt international standards in whose construction they did not participate, sovereignty is best qualified as partial.

5.   What about control?

At the same time as sovereign authority is being reasserted – at least in an interdependent and/or imperial manner by those states constructing the intergovernmental regimes and standards that re-regulate capital flows – control remains dubious. This concerns broader questions on the enforcement and effectiveness of criminalisation in the context of economic regulation. If one looks at the results of legislation against transnational money laundering, terrorist financing and corruption, control appears meagre.[67] Of course, some significant successes are listed in the annual reports of every state's law enforcement agencies. But the comparative studies and evaluations for key countries show very limited overall enforcement.[68]

---

[64] Available at www.fatf-gafi.org/document/51/0,2340,en_32250379_32236992_33916403_1_1_1_1,00.html.

[65] Available at www1.worldbank.org/finance/html/amlcft/ and www.imf.org/external/np/exr/facts/aml.htm.

[66] Eurodad, *World Bank and IMF Conditionality*; Marquette, *Corruption, Development and Politics*.

[67] Cuéllar, 'The Mismatch'; Naylor, *Wages of Crime*.

[68] No comprehensive cross-country comparison of enforcement results against money laundering, terrorist financing and the bribing of foreign officials is available. Existing studies are limited to some advanced economies – which should nevertheless be a good

In most countries, very few of the private sector's suspicious activity reports (SARs) concerning money laundering and the financing of terrorism lead to successful investigations. Specialised money laundering professionals seem to be much less prevalent – or detected – than expected. Case analysis shows that, very often, the laundering of criminal income is done by the offenders themselves or by close relatives.[69] With regard to the bribing of foreign officials, there have been hardly any convictions for the new criminal offence among the signatories of the OECD member states, though in several cases (for example Siemens in Germany, fined around one billion Euro in 2008) heavy-weight investigations are under way.[70] Daniel Tarullo, former US Assistant Secretary of State for Economic and Business Affairs from 1993 to 1996 and as such one of the major officials to push for the OECD convention, tends towards the view that most countries only accepted the convention because of US pressure and without much will to effectively implement it.[71]

However, the track record of the United States is not too impressive, either. Between its entry into force in 1977 and 2002, there were only 28 criminal convictions under the FCPA by the Department of Justice and 13 actions by the Securities and Exchange Commission.[72] With regard to money laundering in the United States, draconian punishments and powerful incentives for law enforcement agencies – being allowed to keep large parts of forfeited assets for their own local budgets – have produced some results in the direction intended by the new laws.[73] But the number of SARs relating to the financing of terrorism remains low, similar to other countries. Up until mid-year 2006, depository institutions in the United States had filed only 2,735 SARs in which the suspected activity was said to be the financing of terrorism.[74] Almost all successful cases presented by the US authorities seem to derive from rather classical investigations and not from following the money trail

---

indicator since it is mostly these countries that were behind the establishment of the international regimes and that should have the most resources to put them into practice. Cuéllar, 'The Tenuous Relationship'; Hägel, 'L'incertaine mondialisation'; Kilchling (ed.), *Die Praxis der Gewinnabschöpfung*; Reuter and Truman, *Chasing Dirty Money*.

[69] Bundeskriminalamt, *Lagebild Organisierte*, 28–31; Cuéllar, 'Tenuous Relationship', 404 et seq.

[70] OECD, *Mid-Term Study*, 61.   [71] Tarullo, 'The Limits of Institutional Design'.

[72] OECD, *United States: Phase 2*, 42–53; Cragg and Woof, 'U.S. Foreign Corrupt Practices Act'.

[73] Frank, *Die Bekämpfung*; Naylor, *Wages of Crime*, 248 et seq.

[74] See FinCEN, *SAR Activity Review*.

of terrorism.[75] Finally, the value of all blocked assets relating to designated terrorists and terrorist organisations had summed up to only $13,793,102 as of 2005 – among which almost half belonged to Hamas.[76]

This does not mean that money laundering, terrorist financing and the bribing of foreign officials are negligible practices or that their criminalisation is useless. But it abates the assertion that the global regimes against them have had decisive impacts. Maybe more time is needed for law enforcement agencies to adapt to the new regulations. But where the corruption of foreign officials is concerned, general problems of extraterritorial law enforcement – why and how to investigate something that happens abroad – will remain difficult. With regard to money laundering and terrorist financing, new prevention and enforcement measures might always stay one step behind private actors' new concealment techniques. For both practices, the continuing diversification of business activities also creates new opportunities for blurring the distinction between legal and illegal commerce. Under conditions of intense globalisation, it seems as if reasserting sovereignty is more about authority claims than about regaining control over private actors' transnational capital flows. In view of this, ever-more sophisticated countermeasures are being proposed that would further deepen global regimes from the legislative (criminalisation) to the actual enforcement level.[77]

5.1   Taking direct control

Considering the past determination of the United States to combat illicit capital flows and the manifest difficulties in actually doing so, it is not surprising that the 9/11 terrorist attacks served as a starting point for a venture into a new enforcement dimension. In the direct aftermath of the attacks, the US government started an investigation into terrorist financing that went well beyond previous attempts at international harmonisation efforts and directly targeted one of the key private actors – SWIFT.

A co-operative limited-liability company under Belgian law, SWIFT appears to function only as something like a postal service between

---

[75] USDoT and USDoJ, *2003 National Money Laundering Strategy*, 34–36.
[76] OFAC and USDoT, *Terrorist Assets Report*, 8.
[77] Cuéllar, 'The Mismatch', 453 et seq.; Tarullo, 'The Limits of Institutional Design'.

financial institutions. For this reason, it had previously been exempt from any of the regulations that apply to 'real' financial institutions.[78] Susan Strange has seen global financial transaction networks like SWIFT as the new backbone of global capitalism, which indeed they are.[79] What she did not consider was the option that such centralised systems also potentially establish straightforward avenues for state control. Thus, studies about the feasibility of a Tobin-style tax on capital movements concluded that, technically, it would be feasible to administer such a tax if it were integrated into the information technology systems of international financial services messaging, clearing and/or payments systems.[80] While, so far, a Tobin tax has not been among US priorities, the possibility to investigate terrorist financing by looking directly into the files of SWIFT proved to be an opportunity not to be missed.

As the New York Times revealed in June 2006, a secret operation started some weeks after 9/11, ordering SWIFT by administrative subpoenas – 64 until summer 2006, based on the US International Emergency Economic Powers Act – to hand over parts of its traffic data to the United States' authorities.[81,82] The operation is executed by the Central Intelligence Agency (CIA) under the oversight of the United States Treasury Department, whose staff disseminate and analyse the SWIFT data, looking for transactions linked to the financing of terrorism:

> Starting with tips from intelligence reports about specific targets, agents search the database in what one official described as a '24/7' operation. Customers' names, bank account numbers and other identifying information can be retrieved, the officials said.[83]

As Stuart Levey, Under Secretary for Terrorism and Financial Intelligence in the United States Department of the Treasury, testified,

> the Terrorist Finance Tracking Programme exemplifies government at its best. ... In response to a subpoena, SWIFT makes available to us a subset

[78] Actual capital transfers are being executed via clearing and settlement systems like CHIPS (for $ transactions) or Clearstream (for securities). Since 2003, an oversight committee for SWIFT has been established by the central banks of the G10 countries, led by the central bank of Belgium, which is mostly concerned with monitoring the stability of the system.

[79] Strange, Mad Money, 24. [80] Spahn, Zur Durchführbarkeit.

[81] Lichtblau and Risen, 'Bank Data Is Sifted'.

[82] Commission de la Protection de la Vie Privée, Avis No 37/2006 du 27 septembre 2006.

[83] Lichtblau and Risen, 'Bank Data Is Sifted'.

of its records that it maintains in the United States in the normal course of its business (United States Treasury Department 2006: 3).[84]

The revelation of the programme's existence immediately provoked strong criticism, especially among the European Parliament and European data protection agencies.[85] On the one hand, the United States government maintains that its actions are fully legal, because the data it accessed was stored within US territory (though legal challenges by American citizens are still pending).[86] On the other hand, in November 2006, the EU's Article 29 Working Party – the advisory body on data protection and privacy – found that SWIFT had violated EU legislation on data protection[87] by exporting all its data, including purely intra-European messages, to the United States where it could be accessed by the Terrorist Finance Tracking Programme (TFTP).[88]

From 2002, increasing worries at SWIFT about the legality of the data transfers led to the installation of several mechanisms to protect SWIFT data. These included oversight by an independent auditor (Booz Allen Hamilton)[89] and the use of special software to restrict access to targeted investigations and prevent wholesale access to the SWIFT data.[90,91]

---

[84] The New York Times article hints at the possibility that in the beginning, directly after 9/11, SWIFT might have been a willing partner, citing one source as saying that 'the subpoenas were intended to give Swift some legal protection'. All official responses from SWIFT, however, emphasise that their compliance was enforced by the subpoenas (*Ibid.*; SWIFT, *Response to the Belgian Privacy Commission's Advisory Opinion.*)

[85] Commission de la Protection de la Vie Privée, *Avis No 37/2006 du 27 septembre 2006.*

[86] While SWIFT's headquarters are in a suburb of Brussels, its data processing – with all data stored for 124 days – is mirrored (inter alia as back-up files) in its second operation centre in the United States.

[87] Directive 95/46/EC of the European Parliament and of the Council of 24 October 1995 on the protection of individuals with regard to the processing of personal data and on the free movement of such data; OJ L 281, 23 November 1995.

[88] Council of the European Union, 'Processing and Protection of Personal Data', 3 et seq.

[89] The independence of Booz Allen Hamilton, whose business contracts and senior management exhibit strong ties to the United States intelligence agencies, has been questioned in a Memo by the American Civil Liberties Union and Privacy International for the Article 29 Working Party of the European Commission, see: www.privacyinternational.org/article.shtml?cmd[347]=x-347-543749.

[90] Immediately after the publication in the NYT, the Belgian Privacy Commission started an investigation in order to find out whether SWIFT had violated Belgian privacy laws (Commission de la Protection de la Vie Privée 2006). The main issue in question is whether SWIFT should be considered as a data controller with an impact on the content of the messages it transmits or simply as a data processor without any control over the messages sent through its network. While the Belgian Privacy Commission argued in favour of the former, SWIFT defended the latter viewpoint (SWIFT 2006).

[91] Commission de la Protection de la Vie Privée, *Avis No 37/2006 du 27 septembre 2006*, 5 et seq.

Following deliberations at the EU level and consultations with the United States, an agreement was reached in July 2007 to further guarantee compliance of SWIFT's data transfers with EU law. SWIFT has to inform its customers about potential breaches of privacy by the TFTP and it had to make sure that its data in the United States meets the requirements of the so-called Safe Harbour.[92] In addition, the United States Secretary for the Treasury has unilaterally described the procedures and protections with regards to the TFTP in so-called representations, which foresee the appointment of an eminent European who will monitor the use of SWIFT data by the TFTP.[93]

Despite these safeguards, the SWIFT affair demonstrates how a powerful state succeeds in reasserting its sovereignty over the private headquarters of transnational capital movements. Instead of relying upon private actors to report suspicious transactions or to use the threat of criminalisation, as in the case of previous measures against money laundering, corruption and terrorist financing, the United States use their authority to gain direct access to, and control over, the SWIFT data.

6. Conclusion

In the context of the de-monopolisation of governmental standard setting, the evolution of SWIFT can be seen as a major achievement by private actors to establish non-state standards for international financial transactions. Today, even governmental payments systems like Fedwire for the US dollar and TARGET for the euro are using SWIFT's standards. Yet, as the recent United States intervention (see above) shows, such non-state governance never operates in a sovereignty-free space. This holds true for transnational capital movements more generally, which, after wide-ranging liberalisation and deregulation from the 1970s to 1990s, have now become subject to new intergovernmental standards against money laundering, corruption and terrorist financing.

However, the transnational nature of capital movements, especially when combined with the competitive pressures among states to attract

---

[92] The EU's Safe Harbour principles are signed by companies to ensure that personal data transferred to the United States are being handled in a way that is adequate to EU levels of data protection. See Shea 2008.

[93] In March 2008, Jean-Louis Bruguière, a French judge with long experience in counter-terrorism matters, was chosen for the task (Council of the European Union, 'Processing and Protection of Personal Data').

capital for economic growth, makes most states' claims to sovereignty precarious. If states want to reassert their sovereignty vis-à-vis transnational actors, then international co-operation is a must rather than an option. The new international regulations for capital movements should therefore be regarded as expressions of interdependent sovereignty. This notion extends the liberal concept of sovereignty bargains to emphasise the more compulsory, rather than purely voluntary, nature of regulatory co-operation. In the EU, this kind of co-operation has reached a level of authority that warrants categorising it as supranational sovereignty, though it is limited regionally and to specific policy areas. The United States, in contrast, relies more and more on extra-territorial extensions of its laws when it see its domestic authority threatened by transnational interdependence. Its efforts to spread its laws abroad and to turn them into international regulations exhibit an understanding of sovereignty that can be qualified as imperial. Weaker states that are pressured into adopting the new international standards, on the other hand, see their sovereignty partially reduced.

While accepting that state sovereignty is enduring precisely because it is malleable, so qualifying and differentiating sovereignty responds to calls to pay more attention to states' unequal status in world politics.[94,95] Just as the liberalisation of capital movements since the 1970s was strongly influenced by decisions taken in the United Kingdom and the United States, which hosted the most important financial markets, the United States as today's superpower also plays a key role in current efforts to re-regulate.[96] Their recent capture of SWIFT's global data is significant evidence that financial globalisation and digital transnational networks have not emancipated private actors from state sovereignty. It might be argued that much of the international re-regulation of capital movements seems to have been more about reasserting state authority than control, because the actual enforcement of the new laws has produced only limited success so far. But the SWIFT case makes it clear that, given the political will, powerful states are able to take control of non-state governance structures and use them to their own advantage.

[94] Werner and Wilde, 'The Endurance of Sovereignty'.
[95] Strange, *The Retreat of the State*; Lake, 'The New Sovereignty'; Lake, 'Escape from the State of Nature'.
[96] Helleiner, *Reemergence of Global Finance*; Simmons, 'Politics of Harmonization'.

References

Abbot, K. W. and Snidal, D. 2002, 'Values and Interests: International Legalization in the Fight Against Corruption', *Journal of Legal Studies*, vol. **31**, no. 2, 141–78.

Altvater, E. and Mahnkopf, B. 2002, *Globalisierung der Unsicherheit: Arbeit im Schatten, schmutziges Geld und informelle Politik*, Münster, Westfälisches Dampfboot.

Andrews, D. M. 1994, 'Capital Mobility and State Autonomy: Toward a Structural Theory of International Monetary Relations', *International Studies Quarterly*, vol. **38**, 193–218.

Biersteker, T. J. and Weber, C. (eds.) 1996, *State Sovereignty as Social Construct*, Cambridge University Press.

Biersteker, T. J. and Weber, C. 1996, 'The Social Construction of State Sovereignty' in T. J. Biersteker and C. Weber (eds.), *State Sovereignty as Social Construct*, Cambridge University Press, 1–21.

Bundeskriminalamt 2003, *Lagebild Organisierte Kriminalität 2002: Bundesrepublik Deutschland (Kurzfassung)*, Bundeskriminalamt, Wiesbaden.

Chayes, A. and Chayes, A. H. 1995, *The New Sovereignty: Compliance with International Regulatory Agreements*, Cambridge, Harvard University Press.

Clunan, A. L. 2006, 'The Fight Against Terrorist Financing', *Political Science Quarterly*, vol. **121**, no. 4, 569–96.

Cohen, S. 2006, *The Resilience of the State: Democracy and the Challenges of Globalization*, Boulder, Lynne Rienner.

Commission de la Protection de la Vie Privée 2006, *Avis No 37/2006 du 27 septembre 2006*, Commission de la Protection de la Vie Privée, Brussels. Available at: www.privacycommission.be/communiqu%E9s/AV37-2006.pdf.

Council of the European Union 2007, 'Processing and Protection of Personal Data Subpoenaed by the Treasury Department from the US Based Operation Centre of the Society for Worldwide Interbank Financial Telecommunication (SWIFT)', Press Release 11291/2/07 REV 2. Available at: www.consilium.europa.eu/ueDocs/cms_Data/docs/pressData/en/misc/95017.pdf.

Cragg, W. and Woof, W. 2002, 'The U.S. Foreign Corrupt Practices Act: A Study of Its Effectiveness', *Business and Society Review*, vol. **107**, no. 1, 98–144.

Cuéllar, M.-F. 2003, 'The Tenuous Relationship Between the Fight Against Money Laundering and the Disruption of Criminal Finance', *Journal of Criminal Law & Criminology*, vol. **93**, nos. 2–3, 311–465.

Cuellar, M.-F. 2003, 'The Mismatch Between State Power and State Capacity in Transnational Law Enforcement', *Stanford Law School Research Paper* No. **70** (November 2003), Stanford Law School.

Cutler, A. C. 2003, *Private Power and Global Authority: Transnational Merchant Law in the Global Political Economy*, Cambridge University Press.

Cutler, A. C., Haufler, V. and Porter, T. (eds.) 1999, *Private Authority and International Affairs*, New York, SUNY Press.

Eurodad 2006, *World Bank and IMF Conditionality: A Development Injustice*, Eurodad Report June 2006. Available at: www.eurodad.org/uploadstore/cms/docs/Microsoft_Word__Eurodad_World_Bank_and_IMF_Conditionality_Report_Final_Version.pdf.

Evans, D. S. and Schmalensee, R. 2005, *Paying with Plastic: The Digital Revolution in Buying and Borrowing*, Cambridge, MIT Press.

Ferguson, N. 2001, *The Cash Nexus: Money and Power in the Modern World, 1700–2000*, New York, Basic Books.

Ferguson, N. 2004, *Colossus: The Rise and Fall of the American Empire*, London, Penguin.

FinCEN 2006, *SAR Activity Review – By the Numbers 7* (November 2006). Available at: www.fincen.gov/sar_review_by_the_numbers_issue7.pdf.

Frank, R. 2002, *Die Bekämpfung der Geldwäsche in den USA: High-Tech-Gewinnaufspürung, drakonische Strafen und radikale Gewinneinziehung – Ist der Amerikanische Ansatz ein Vorbild für Deutschland?*, Frankfurt am Main, Peter Lang.

Frieden, J. A. 2006, *Global Capitalism: Its Fall and Rise in the Twentieth Century*, New York, W. W. Norton & Company.

Galtung, F. 2000, 'A Global Network to Curb Corruption: The Experience of Transparency International' in A. M. Florini (ed.), *The Third Force: The Rise of Transnational Civil Society*, Tokyo/Washington, D.C., Japan Center for International Exchange/Carnegie Endowment for International Peace, 17–48.

Gilmore, W. C. 1999, *Dirty Money: The Evolution of Money Laundering Countermeasures*, 2nd edn, Strasbourg, Council of Europe Publishing.

Glynn, P., Kobrin, S. J. and Naim, M. 1997, 'The Globalization of Corruption' in Elliot, K. A. (ed.), *Corruption and the Global Economy*, Washington, D.C., Institute for International Economics, 7–27.

Goodman, J. B. and Pauly, L. W. 1993, 'The Obsolescence of Capital Controls? Economic Management in an Age of Global Markets', *World Politics*, vol. **46**, no. 1, 50–82.

Greanias, G. C. and Windsor, D. 1982, *The Foreign Corrupt Practices Act: Anatomy of a Statute*, Lexington, Lexington Books.

Greenberg, M. R., Wechsler, W. F. and Wolosky, L. S. 2002, *Terrorist Financing: Report of an Independent Task Force Sponsored by the Council on Foreign Relations*, New York, Council on Foreign Relations.

Hägel, P. 2003, *Geldwäschebekämpfung durch die EU*, SWP-Studie S37, Berlin, Stiftung Wissenschaft und Politik.

Hägel, P. 2005, 'L'incertaine mondialisation du contrôle: La France et l'Allemagne dans la lutte contre la corruption et le blanchiment', *Déviance et Société*, vol. **29**, no. 3, 243–58.

Hägel, P. 2005, 'Regieren ohne Souveränität? Neue Perspektiven zum Wandel einer umstrittenen Institution', *Berliner Journal für Soziologie*, vol. **15**, no. 1, 121–30.

Hägel, P. and Peretz, P. 2005, 'States and Transnational Actors: Who's Influencing Whom?', *European Journal of International Relations*, vol. 11, no. 4, 467–93.

Hall, R. B. and Biersteker, T. J. (eds.) 2002, *The Emergence of Private Authority in Global Governance*, Cambridge University Press.

Hall, R. B. and Biersteker, T. J. 2002, 'The Emergence of Private Authority in the International System' in R. B. Hall and T. J. Biersteker (eds.), *The Emergence of Private Authority in Global Governance*, Cambridge University Press, 3–22.

Helleiner, E. 1994, *States and the Reemergence of Global Finance: From Bretton Woods to the 1990s*, Ithaca, Cornell University Press.

Helleiner, E. 1999, 'State Power and the Regulation of Illicit Activity in Global Finance' in H. R. Friman and P. Andreas (eds.), *The Illicit Global Economy and State Power*, Lanham, Rowman and Littlefield, 53–90.

Helleiner, E. 2000, *The Politics of Global Financial Reregulation: Lessons from the Fight against Money Laundering*, CEPA Working Paper No. 15 (April 2000), New York, Center for Economic Policy Analysis/New School for Social Research.

House of Lords 1990, *Money Laundering*, House of Lords Select Committee on the European Communities, Session 1990–01, 1st Report (HL Paper 6), London, The Stationery Office.

Keck, M. E. and Sikkink, K. 1998, *Activists beyond Borders: Advocacy Networks in International Politics*, Ithaca, Cornell University Press.

Keohane, R. O. 1995, 'Hobbes's Dilemma and Institutional Change in World Politics: Sovereignty in International Society' in H.-H. Holm and G. Sørensen (eds.), *Whose World Order? Uneven Globalization and the End of the Cold War*, Boulder, Westview, 165–86.

Kerry, J. 1997, *The New War: The Web of Crime that Threatens America's Security*, New York, Simon and Schuster.

Kilchling, M. (ed.) 2002, *Die Praxis der Gewinnabschöpfung in Europa: Eine vergleichende Evaluationsstudie zur Gewinnabschöpfung in Fällen von Geldwäsche und anderen Formen Organisierter Kriminalität*, Ed. iuscrim, Freiburg i. Br., Max-Planck-Institut für ausländisches und internationales Strafrecht.

Klotz, A. 2002, 'Transnational Activism and Global Transformations: The Anti-Apartheid and Abolitionist Experiences', *European Journal of International Relations*, vol. 8, no. 1, 49–76.

Krasner, S. D. 1999, *Sovereignty: Organized Hypocrisy*, Princeton University Press.

Lake, D. A. 2003, 'The New Sovereignty in International Relations', *International Studies Review*, vol. 5, no. 3, 303–23.

Lake, D. A. 2007, 'Escape from the State of Nature: Authority and Hierarchy in World Politics', *International Security*, vol. 32, no. 1, 47–79.

Lichtblau, E. and Risen, J. 2006, 'Bank Data Is Sifted by U.S. in Secret to Block Terror', *New York Times*, 23 Jun.

Marquette, H. 2003, *Corruption, Development and Politics: The Role of the World Bank*, Basingstoke, Palgrave.

Mattli, W. 2000, 'Sovereignty Bargains in Regional Integration', *International Studies Review*, vol. **2**, no. 2, 149–80.

Mattli, W. and Büthe, T. 2003, 'Setting International Standards: Technological Rationality or Primacy of Power?', *World Politics*, vol. **56**, no. 1, 1–42.

Mattli, W. and Büthe, T. 2005, 'Accountability in Accounting? The Politics of Private Rule-Making in the Public Interest', *Governance*, vol. **18**, no. 3, 399–429.

McCulloch, J. and Pickering, S. 2005, 'Suppressing the Financing of Terrorism: Proliferating State Crime, Eroding Censure and Extending Neo-colonialism', *The British Journal of Criminology*, vol. **45**, no. 4, 470–86.

Nadelmann, E. A. 1993, *Cops Across Borders: The Internationalization of U.S. Criminal Law Enforcement*, Pennsylvania State University Press.

Naim, M. 2005, *Illicit: How Smugglers, Traffickers and Copycats are Hijacking the Global Economy*, New York, Doubleday.

Naylor, R. T. 2002, *Wages of Crime: Black Markets, Illegal Finance, and the Underworld Economy*, Ithaca, Cornell University Press.

O'Brien, R. 1992, *Global Financial Integration: The End of Geography*, London, Pinter.

OECD 2002, *United States: Phase 2: Report on the Application of the Convention on Combating Bribery of Foreign Public Officials in International Business Transactions and the 1997 Recommendation on Combating Bribery in International Business Transactions*, OECD, Paris.

OECD 2006, *Mid-Term Study of Phase 2 Reports: Application of the Convention on Combating Bribery of Foreign Public Officials in International Business Transactions and the 1997 Recommendation on Combating Bribery in International Business Transactions*, OECD, Paris.

OFAC (Office of Foreign Assets Control) & United States Department of the Treasury 2006, *Terrorist Assets Report, Calendar Year 2005, Fourteenth Annual Report to Congress on Assets in the United States of Terrorist Countries and International Terrorism Program Designees*. Available at: www.ustreas.gov/offices/enforcement/ ofac/reports/tar2005.pdf.

Palan, R. 2003, *The Offshore World: Sovereign Markets, Virtual Places, and Nomad Millionaires*, Ithaca, Cornell University Press.

Philpott, D. 2001, *Revolutions in Sovereignty: How Ideas Shaped Modern International Relations*, Princeton University Press.

Pieth, M. 2006, 'Criminalizing the Financing of Terrorism', *Journal of International Criminal Justice*, vol. **4**, no. 5, 1074–86.

Pieth, M. and Eigen, P. (eds.) 1999, *Korruption im internationalen Geschäftsverkehr: Bestandsaufnahme, Bekämpfung, Prävention*, Neuwied/ Kriftel, Luchterhand.

Putnam, T. L. 2006, *Courts Without Borders: The Domestic Sources of U.S. Extraterritorial Regulation*, Columbia University, New York mimeo, Department of Political Science.

Reuter, P. and Truman, E. M. 2004, *Chasing Dirty Money: The Fight Against Money Laundering*, Washington D.C., Institute for International Economics.

Ruggiero, V. 2000, *Crime and Markets: Essays in Anti-Criminology*, Oxford University Press.

Sacerdoti, G. 1999, 'Das OECD-Übereinkommen 1997 über die Bekämpfung der Bestechung ausländischer Amtsträger im internationalen Geschäftsverkehr' in M. Pieth and P. Eigen (eds.), *Korruption im internationalen Geschäftsverkehr: Bestandsaufnahme, Bekämpfung, Prävention*, Neuwied/Kriftel, Luchterhand.

Sassen, S. 1996, *Losing Control? Sovereignty in an Age of Globalization*, New York, Columbia University Press.

Schulze, G. 2000, *The Political Economy of Capital Controls*, Cambridge University Press.

Shea, C. 2008, 'A Need for Swift Change: The Struggle between the European Union's Desire for Privacy in International Financial Transactions and the United States' Need for Security from Terrorists as Evidenced by the Swift Scandal', *Journal Of High Technology Law*, vol. **8**, 143–68.

Simmons, B. 2001, 'The International Politics of Harmonization: The Case of Capital Market Regulation', *International Organization*, vol. **55**, no. 3, 589–620.

Sinclair, T. J. 2005, *The New Masters of Capital: American Bond Rating Agencies and the Politics of Creditworthiness*, Ithaca, Cornell University Press.

Slaughter, A.-M. 2004, *A New World Order*, Princeton University Press.

Sørensen, G. 1999, 'Sovereignty: Change and Continuity in a Fundamental Institution', *Political Studies*, vol. **47**, no. 3, 590–604.

Spahn, P. B. 2002, *Zur Durchführbarkeit einer Devisentransaktionssteuer*, Bonn, Gutachten im Auftrag des Bundesministerium für Wirtschaftliche Zusammenarbeit und Entwicklung. Available at: www.wiwi.uni-frankfurt.de/professoren/spahn/tobintax/.

Stessens, G. 2000, *Money Laundering: A New International Law Enforcement Model*, Cambridge University Press.

Strange, S. 1996, *The Retreat of the State: The Diffusion of Power in the World Economy*, Cambridge University Press.

Strange, S. 1998, *Mad Money*, Manchester University Press.

SWIFT 2007, *SWIFT Annual Report 2006: Achieving More, Together*, available at: www.swift.com/index.cfm?item_id=61861.

SWIFT 2009, 2008 Annual Report: Sharing Strength, available at: www.swift.com/about_swift/publications/annual_reports/SWIFT_Annual_report_2008.pdf.

Tarullo, D. 2004, 'The Limits of Institutional Design: Implementing the OECD Anti-Bribery Convention', *Virginia Journal of International Law*, vol. **44**, 665–710.

Thomson, J. E. 1995, 'State Sovereignty in International Relations: Bridging the Gap between Theory and Empirical Research', *International Studies Quarterly*, vol. **39**, 213–33.

United States Department of Commerce 2004, *Addressing the Challenges of International Bribery and Fair Competition 2004*, The Sixth Annual Report Under Section 6 of the International Anti-Bribery and Fair Competition Act of 1998, United States Department of Commerce, International Trade Administration, Washington, D.C.

United States Department of the Treasury & United States Department of Justice 2002, *2002 National Money Laundering Strategy*, United States Department of the Treasury/United States Department of Justice, Washington, D.C.

United States Department of the Treasury & United States Department of Justice 2003, *2003 National Money Laundering Strategy*, United States Department of the Treasury/United States Department of Justice, Washington, D.C.

United States Treasury Department 2006, *Testimony of Stuart Levey, Under Secretary Terrorism and Financial Intelligence, U.S. Department of the Treasury before the House Financial Services Subcommittee on Oversight and Investigations, July 11, 2006*, available at: www.fas.org/irp/congress/2006_hr/071106levey.pdf.

Vlcek, W. 2006, 'Acts to Combat the Financing of Terrorism: Common Foreign and Security Policy at the European Court of Justice', *European Foreign Affairs Review*, vol. **11**, 491–507.

Walker, N. (ed.) 2003, *Sovereignty in Transition*, London, Hart.

Weiler, J. H. H. 1981, 'The Community System: The Dual Character of Supranationalism', *Yearbook of European Law*, vol. **1**, 257–306.

Werner, W. G. and Wilde, J. H. 2001, 'The Endurance of Sovereignty', *European Journal of International Relations*, vol. **7**, no. 3, 283–313.

White, S. 1998, *Protection of the Financial Interests of the European Communities: The Fight Against Fraud and Corruption*, The Hague, Kluwer Law International.

14

Certification as a new private global forest governance system: the regulatory potential of the Forest Stewardship Council

STÉPHANE GUÉNEAU[*]

1. The failure of intergovernmental negotiation processes on forests

As 'global public goods' that benefit numerous states and cannot be controlled by any one, forests present a particular challenge to national regulators. In response, governments began in the early 1980s to negotiate on forest regulation.[1] These intergovernmental coordination efforts aimed to create binding and hierarchical measures for implementing international policies at the national level[2] and produced forest management and protection standards.[3] They therefore resulted in the creation of a 'regime', that is, 'a set of principles, standards, rules and decision-making procedures, whether explicit or implicit, around which actors' expectations converge in a specific area of international relations'.[4] However, from the beginning, it was a regime weakened by fragmentation.

1.1 A fragmented international architecture

The architecture of international forest regulation is complex and segmented, due to the overlapping responsibilities for forest issues among

---

[*] Research Fellow, CIRAD (French Agricultural Research Centre for International Development), Montpellier; Visiting Professor, Sciences-Po, Institute for Sustainable Development and International Relations (IDDRI), Paris; MSc (Economics, University of Montpellier); Doctoral Candidate (Management and Administration in Environmental Sciences and Policies, Paris Institute of Technology for Life, Food and Environmental Sciences (AgroParisTech).
[1] See Kern, *Global Governance.*   [2] Young, *Global Governance: Drawing Insights.*
[3] Skala-Kuhmann, *Legal Instruments*; Chaytor, *Global Forest Policy*; Humphreys, 'The Evolving Forest Regime'; Tarasofsky, *Assessing the International Forest Regime*; Gulbrandsen, 'Overlapping Public and Private'.
[4] See Krasner, *International Regimes.*

different institutions and instruments. The forest negotiation process at the 1992 Rio Earth Summit resulted in non-binding texts, including the Forest Declaration and Chapter 11 of Agenda 21, and continues today under the auspices of the United Nations Forum on Forests (UNFF). Two other multilateral instruments are specifically devoted to forests: the International Tropical Timber Agreement (ITTA) and the FAO Committee on Forestry. Other non-specific international mechanisms incorporate provisions that are essential for forests. In particular, the Kyoto Protocol to the United Nations Framework Convention on Climate Change (UNFCCC) regards forests as carbon sinks and the prevention of deforestation as a means of combating carbon emissions. The Convention on Biological Diversity (CBD) developed a special work programme on forest biodiversity, the World Heritage Convention deals with the protection of the world's most remarkable forest ecosystems and the Convention on International Trade in Endangered Species (CITES) regulates trade in certain species of wood. Even the Convention to Combat Desertification contains provisions on the role played by forests in the preservation of arid and semi-arid ecosystems, whereas Convention 169 of the International Labour Organization (ILO) includes the rights of indigenous people, who are of great importance in tropical forested areas.

1.2   North–South differences and the crisis of multilateralism

Fragmentation led several governments and forest experts to recommend a binding multilateral agreement to centralise and co-ordinate international efforts on forest protection. However, their efforts were hampered by intense divisions in the negotiation between the global 'North' and 'South'. In short, developed 'Northern' countries considered forests to be part of a global heritage requiring international protection. They argued that the lack of global rules in relation to forest protection could lead to the rapid disappearance of richly biodiverse forest ecosystems. By contrast, developing countries in the 'South' argued that forests were natural resources over which they had sovereignty, and that their economic development depended partly on those resources. Consequently, at the 1992 Earth Summit in Rio, the international community was unable to reach a consensus on the substance of a global forest agreement. The vastly different goals of developed and developing countries prevented a positive outcome.

In recent years, other changes in the international system have inhibited forest protection initiatives. The crisis in multilateralism has had a profound impact. Unilateralism was evident in the United States' refusal to ratify major multilateral environmental agreements, especially the UNFCCC and in objections to the current order by developing countries. Brazil, for example, has remained steadfast in its refusal to accept any binding multilateral forest agreement that could constitute an obstacle to its agribusiness export-oriented development model.

It was therefore not surprising that, at the last session of the UNFF in 2006, governments agreed that propositions made by the international community would be voluntary and that discussions on a binding multi-lateral instrument would be postponed – until 2015. It was therefore not surprising that, at the last session of the UNFF, governments agreed that propositions made by the international community would be voluntary. The numerous attempts to conclude the negotiations by a binding agreement failed. In sum, though international negotiations on forests continue, it is clear that major stumbling blocks still exist.

1.3   The shortcomings of the international regime

Despite the lack of an international consensus on forest regulation, an international regime based on soft law has gradually developed around the elements described by Guldbrandsen.[5] Though an important achievement, this regime contains major weaknesses. First, governments failed to agree how they should implement substantial measures to protect forests and the interests of indigenous populations and local communities. Second, enforcement tools are weak: with reporting the main mechanism for monitoring the implementation of international proposals, there is insufficient pressure on governments to meet their current commitments or to make further undertakings with regard to forest conservation and management. Third, there are no consensual multilateral rules aimed specifically at the trade in forest products from well-managed forests.

Environmental NGOs have been extremely active in highlighting these weaknesses.[6] Their lobbying ensured forest matters were acknowledged

---

[5] According to Gulbrandsen, the regime includes: the ecosystem approach; the principle of protected areas; the recognition of local knowledge of forest resources and the need for equitable sharing of benefits arising from their use; the recognition of the role forests play in climate change; the consensus between states on a series of good forest management criteria and indicators resulting from nine different regional negotiation processes; the implementation of non-binding international principles through national forest programmes and a reporting system allowing states to demonstrate their commitment to and progress made in terms of forest policy. See Gulbrandsen, 'Overlapping Public and Private Governance'.

[6] Wilson and Guéneau, *Gouvernance mondiale des forêts*.

by the CBD and some NGOs successfully christened the sixth Conference of the Parties of the CBD, held in La Hague in 2002, the 'Ancient Forest Summit'. At the close of the negotiations, most NGOs condemned the non-binding nature of the CBD work programme and revised their hopes for the international forest negotiation process accordingly. Nonetheless, through their media campaigns, their partnerships with public authorities and their use of market instruments to improve regulation, the role of NGOs in global forest governance has continued to grow. In their changing role, NGOs are making vital contributions to the emergence of new global forest governance systems.

2.   New global governance systems

The concept of global governance was developed by James Rosenau as early as 1987 and has since inspired a great deal of research. Updating ideas in regimes theory about 'governance without government', Rosenau foresaw a means of regulating human activities that emerges despite a lack of international mechanisms administered by the official authorities.

Though it is well established and researched, the subject of 'global governance' remains highly controversial. Definitions of governance abound – Pattberg cites ten[7] – and are used in relation to many different forms of coordination between many different types of actors: NGO participation in international decision-making processes, international public–private partnerships, the growing role in world politics of trans-national companies, to name just a few. According to Pattberg, the concept of governance has in fact become something of a buzzword in international relations.[8]

These different forms of coordination called 'governance' have at least one thing in common, however: they underline several ways in which public action has changed.[9] First, the concept of governance implies a rejection of traditional political models, in which government authorities are solely responsible for managing public affairs. It thus differs from the classical notion of government, where government represents the insti-tution and governance the act of governing.[10] Second, the concept of governance permits, and even emphasises, the range and diversity of

[7] Pattberg, *Global Governance.*   [8] *Ibid.*
[9] Holec and Brunet-Jolivald, *Gouvernance: Note de Synthèse.*
[10] Rosenau and Czempiel, *Governance without Government.*

actors involved in managing public affairs. So, it is able to acknowledge that the boundaries between public and private are redefined with the transfer of responsibilities between the state, civil society and market forces. Finally, the concept of governance presupposes interaction and negotiation between diverse stakeholders, making it possible to look beyond conflicting interests and towards consensus.

2.1   Transnational advocacy networks

Building on Rosenau's work, several authors have concentrated on the privatisation of governance, that is, the growing role of private bodies in the regulation of transnational activities. One line of research has concentrated on transnational advocacy networks. Its aim is to analyse the way in which collections of private bodies could influence global policy, elevating issues as new priorities through militant action or lobbying at international negotiations.[11]

These networks are particularly active in the field of forestry with all major environmental NGOs counting forest programmes among their priorities for action. For example, forest protection campaigns were particularly strong in the run-up to the Rio Earth Summit in 2002, and can be credited with leading some OECD member countries to attempt bans on tropical timber imports. More recently, high rates of deforestation in the Brazilian Amazon prompted Greenpeace International to launch a campaign aimed directly at soy producers and the governor of the state of Mato Grosso. The recent report emphasises the responsibility of the agricultural commodity giants, ADM, Bunge and Cargill, which control 60 per cent of the soy production in Brazil and supply more than three quarters of all the soy used for animal food in European processing industries.[12] In an earlier 'crackdown' in May 2005, Greenpeace blocked the Cargill soy grain terminal for several hours in Santarém deep in the Amazon rainforest. A month earlier, in Europe Greenpeace activists occupied several McDonald's restaurants, accusing the multinational company of fuelling the destruction of the Amazon to grow soy to feed the chickens used in its products.

This campaign was given a great deal of media coverage and affected Brazil's soy industry, already in a state of crisis due to the government's

---

[11] Keck and Sikkink, *Activists Beyond Borders*; Arts, 'Political Influence'; O'Brien *et al.*, *Contesting Global Governance*.

[12] See Greenpeace, *Eating up the Amazon*.

monetary policy. McDonald's and other companies quickly demanded that Brazilian soy traders belonging to ABIOVE (Brazilian Association of Vegetable Oil Industries) cease trading products that contribute to Amazon deforestation. In a statement made on 24 July 2006, ABIOVE and ANEC (National Association of Grain Exporters) announced their commitment to stop trading products grown in areas within the Amazon biome that are deforested after the date of the announcement. During the two-year moratorium, both associations commit to work with the government and organisations representing producers and civil society. They will prepare an action plan including a mapping and monitoring system, develop strategies to encourage producers to comply with Brazilian law and work with stakeholders to develop new instruments for their operations in the Amazon biome.

2.2   Public–private partnerships

The role of non-state actors in global governance is also being considered from the perspective of their contribution to political processes with public authorities. Certain authors regard public–private partnerships and 'global public policy networks' as new forms of governance for global environmental issues.[13]

These new forms of governance also represent a significant element of the regulatory architecture relating to forests. Alliances between governments, NGOs and the private sector are developing on a geographic or sectoral basis and are winning considerable support from bilateral and multilateral donors. For example, in Africa, the Congo Basin Forest Partnership was launched during the World Summit on Sustainable Development in Johannesburg in 2002 by the United States' and South African governments. In all, twenty-nine partners are associated in this initiative, including other governments, international institutions, forest research institutes, NGOs and private sector representatives.

An example of a sectoral alliance is Forest Law Enforcement and Governance, a partnership established by the World Bank, thirteen governments, NGOs and private sector representatives to combat illegal logging. NGOs have made the fight against illegal production one of their main campaigns, highlighting the role of forest crime in deforestation, loss of tax revenue and increased poverty (for example, according to WWF, 50 per cent of Cameroon's logging operations are illegal and

---

[13] Reinicke and Deng, *Critical Choices*; Börzel and Risse, 'Public-Private Partnerships'.

80 per cent of Brazil's timber is produced illegally.[14] The FLEG aims to combat forest crime through voluntary partnership agreements that provide mechanisms for verifying the legality of timber and greater civil society involvement and incentives for loggers to implement laws.

Producers can also work towards legality by developing independent verification systems with NGOs. This is the case with the Congo Basin forest concession monitoring system (FORCOMS) developed by the Interafrican Forest Industries Association (IFIA) in collaboration with several NGOs. This system uses certification to identify companies that comply with the law. Companies participate voluntarily in complying with laws and commitments to sustainable forest development, set out by a multi-stakeholders steering committee. The World Resources Institute is responsible for auditing how these requirements are met and awarding certificates accordingly. Any breaches are reported to the media and if the company still fails to comply after one month, its certificate of legality can be withdrawn. The legality certificate is attached to the other documents required to export products.

2.3   Private governance systems

It is only very recently that scholars have turned their attention to regulation processes which are exclusively private, that is, generated through transnational dialogue between different kinds of non-state actors (for example NGOs and companies). These private configurations are new in so far as they do not seek to influence public policy via media campaigns or participation in public–private coalitions. They also differ from other forms of private governance, which are made possible by governments implicitly or explicitly delegating part of their decision-making powers (for example self-regulation processes that companies develop to improve their corporate social responsibility).[15] Instead, these processes result in global rules, outside any state framework.

For Cashore, states have no decision-making power faced with what he calls non-state market-driven governance systems.[16] In these systems, political decision-making processes are based on the manipulation of global markets by non-state bodies. Pattberg describes this new phenomenon as the institutionalisation of private governance: 'This

---

[14] Toyne *et al.*, *Timber Footprint.*   [15] Cutler *et al.*, *Private Authority.*
[16] Cashore, 'Privatization of Environmental Governance'.

institutionalisation of private governance is different from ad hoc partnership or strategic alliances because it involves the notion of shared norms and principles as well as the prescription of roles and responsibilities.'[17] So, in forestry, 'good management' standards are increasingly being defined by non-state actors, especially within multi-stakeholder consultation forums.

One such forum is the Forest Stewardship Council (FSC). Created as an independent non-profit organisation in 1993, the FSC is governed by a board of directors representing nationally diverse actors from different forestry backgrounds – environmentalists, forestry companies and indigenous peoples' organisations (notably states are not included). The FSC sets forest management standards through negotiations after comparing different points of view and though the standards are potentially applicable to a wide range of actors, participation in the scheme is voluntary. Certification is the FSC's primary means of ensuring its standards are implemented. FSC-International establishes principles and criteria of compliance and accredits independent third-party certification bodies through ASI (Accreditation Services International), an organization created by the FSC and the MSC (Marine Stewardship Council) to deliver accreditation and other relevant services to the FSC and other certification schemes worldwide. Accredited certifying bodies then check whether individual operators comply with the FSC forest management standards and, if so, issue a certificate guaranteeing compliance. Certification bodies can also certify operators against indicators drawn up by national FSC initiatives if such initiatives are in existence and have been recognised by FSC-International.

As an international multi-stakeholder forum, the FSC can be seen as contributing to efforts to build a global civil society. The FSC's internal governance rules aim to guarantee all participants identical participation conditions and to ensure transparent decision making. The members of FSC-International are divided into three chambers – economic, social and environmental. Their votes are weighted equally regardless of the number of participants in each chamber, ensuring parity of representation between Southern and Northern members in each chamber, whatever the number of voters from the North or the South. The forum for dialogue set up by the FSC is open to all – organisations and individuals – but the voting weight of individual members must not exceed 10 per cent. The various systems for mediating conflicting interests within FSC-International can therefore be

[17] Pattberg, *Institutionalisation of Private Governance.*

seen as an attempt to find a democratic solution to collective problems at the global level.

3.   Some limitations on the FSC's potential as a private global governance institution

3.1   Governing through the market?

Through his analysis of forest certification, Cashore made a significant contribution to conceptualising the new forms of private global governance, for which authority is diffuse and located in the marketplace.[18] According to this liberal view of the regulation of public affairs, it is consumers – through their willingness to pay more for certified products than for conventional products – who will encourage producers to improve their forest management practices. However, market research conducted to date indicates that consumers are seldom inclined to pay a premium for certified products, even though they are increasingly concerned about the destruction of tropical forests and now know more about certification systems.[19] Even in Europe, where environmental awareness is strongest, consumers demand very little in the way of certified forest products.[20]

To circumvent this problem, the NGOs behind the FSC have carried out active campaigns targeted at retailers and importers. By committing to buy only FSC-certified timber, major private companies have created demand. The social pressure generated by these campaigns has led stakeholders to accept an institutionalised compromise concerning the way in which certification is to regulate the forest sector.[21]

Nevertheless, the FSC certification market is efficient only in sectors where distributors are in a position of oligopoly. For example, in the civil construction sector, trade in timber and by-products is concentrated among certain specialised companies, which can demand that their suppliers obtain FSC certification. In some countries, sales are scattered among a large number of SMEs and so there is no bottleneck. Further, demand for certified products is highest in European markets and is growing in Canada and the United States. However, the major markets of Asia and Latin America are not yet receptive to certified forest

[18] Cashore, 'Privatization of Environmental Governance'.
[19] Ozanne and Vlosky, 'Willingness to Pay'; Ozanne and Vlosky, 'US Consumer Perspective'.
[20] FAO, *Forest Products Annual Market Review*.   [21] Lafrance, 'La certification'.

products.[22] The market for certified forest products is therefore growing in countries where environmental awareness is particularly high and in sectors where private multinational groups are particularly well established. This chiefly concerns the pulp and paper market, which is dominated by a small number of multinationals, certain markets for wood products sold retail by major 'do it yourself' chains (Home Depot, B&Q, etc.), and several large furniture distribution chains (Ikea, etc.). The restricted certification market still constitutes a serious limit to the FSC's scope as a forest governance system.

Another limitation exists at the supply level: since retailers do not assume the cost of certification by increasing the sale price for their products, this cost is passed on to producers. Why should these producers increase their production costs and reduce their profits by engaging in costly forest certification programmes? The reason for tropical producers to obtain certification is therefore essentially to maintain their access to American and Northern European markets. However, factors independent of certification, such as the price or the quality of forest products, still largely condition international trade in tropical timber. Timber retailers point out that it is very difficult to source FSC-certified timber, especially from tropical forests.[23] In some cases, companies were obliged to top up their timber deliveries sourced from certified forests with timber from non-certified forests in order to find the quantity and quality of tropical timber ordered.[24]

Finally, it is worth noting that a large part of world timber production is excluded from these certified forest product markets, since less than 10 per cent of timber is traded internationally.[25] Forest products are predominantly sold and used by domestic consumers, many of whom do not know, or do not care, about the conditions in which timber is produced. In developing countries consumption levels are still very high and markets for timber often informal if they exist at all. This intrinsic limitation of the FSC's scope as a private global governance system is discussed by Thornber and colleagues.[26] They conclude that the FSC is primarily relevant for producers operating in the business economy and has little effect on rural producers situated outside the market economy, despite the fact that these actors play a vital role in the dynamics of forest cover change, especially in tropical areas.

[22] FAO, *International Trade in Forest Products and Services*.
[23] LCB, *Position sur l'écocertification*.   [24] Counsell and Loraas, *Trading in Credibility*.
[25] FAO, *Situation des forêts du monde*.   [26] Thornber *et al.*, *L'accès difficile*.

In September 2006, the area of FSC-certified forest reached seventy-nine million hectares in 74 countries. The number of countries concerned is clearly representative of a success, as is the area of forests certified or managed against FSC standards. But in relation to the four billion hectares of forest around the world, the possibilities for forest governance provided by FSC must be kept in perspective.

3.2   Governing through standards? The discrepancy between international standards and the local context

The certification process contributes to forest law enforcement in countries where the forest management services are weak. A sanction system exists, whereby the certificate may be withdrawn at any time if the forest company no longer complies with FSC standards. Certification bodies can also be sanctioned through temporary or permanent withdrawal of their accreditation. For example, FSC accreditation was temporarily withdrawn from the Dutch certifier SKAL in 2001.[27]

However, the effectiveness of the system must not be judged solely on the basis of its strengths in enforcement, but also on its acceptability by a wide range of actors. In places where forest ownership is characterised by small, highly fragmented areas, forest producers are strongly opposed to the FSC certification system. Opposition to the FSC system is even stronger when forest management traditions are firmly rooted in history and owners manage their property generation upon generation, as is the case in France.

Certification costs also penalise small-scale operations.[28] These costs include the costs of preliminary assessments for certification, the costs of managing changes needed to obtain certification and the cost of the yearly audit. Some of these costs are fixed and therefore result in scale effects: the smaller the forest operation, the higher the proportion of these costs in the total price of the certified product and the greater the disadvantages of certification. Large operations find it easiest to bear these costs and remain competitive. Therefore, the discrepancy between international standards and local contexts limits the FSC's scope as a global governance institution.

This discrepancy is particularly noticeable in tropical countries. According to Atyi and Simula, some of the main obstacles to the

---

[27] Kern, *Global Governance*.   [28] Guéneau, 'La forêt tropicale'.

proliferation of certification in tropical countries is the lack of flexibility in certification standards, the disregard for the context in which natural resources are used and conflicts between national legislation and certification rules.[29] In fact, the FSC has developed far more quickly in boreal and temperate forest areas than in tropical areas. Where certification has been used in tropical areas, it has tended to be in industrial plantations; the FSC also had little impact on small-scale operations and community-managed forests. For example, between 2000 and 2005, the area of FSC-certified industrial plantations in Brazil represented around two thirds of all certified forest areas in Brazil.[30] These factors limit the FSC's ability to impose binding rules, including those in international agreements, as pointed out by researchers Kern and Pattberg.[31]

North–South divisions are also apparent in the FSC's decision-making and standard-setting bodies. The geographical distribution of FSC members changed very little between 1993, when the FSC was set up, and late 2005. Currently, North American and European representatives make up around 60 per cent of all FSC members; this was already the case in 1993. Moreover, certain large forested countries and regions are un- or under-represented, for example Russia, Finland and the Congo Basin.

The FSC has attempted to rectify this imbalance through weighted voting: Southern participants always control 50 per cent of all votes in each chamber, whatever their actual number of representatives. However, the balanced voting system is not itself sufficient to remedy imbalances in power and knowledge between Northern and Southern representatives. Southern actors are in the minority in debates and may be less able to identify and oppose decisions inimical to their interests due to their lack of access to technical resources. Low level of participation by representatives from tropical countries also limits their ability to contribute to agendas and standards in ways that closely reflect their concerns. Then the criterion chosen by the FSC to define the 'Northern' and 'Southern' categories (average per capita income) results in the inclusion of some transitional countries, such as Poland and Hungary, in the 'Southern' category. Thus half of all votes are given to less than 15 per cent of the world's population, the richest group, and voting blocs do not distinguish Northern forests (boreal and temperate) from tropical

---

[29] Atyi and Simula, 'Forest Certification'.
[30] Figures available on the FSC-Brazil website (www.fsc.org.br/).
[31] See Kern, *Global Governance*; Pattberg, *Global Governance*.

forests, where conservation challenges are far more pronounced.[32] It is also worth noting that Southern members are represented by a high proportion of individuals: in late 2005, the figures stood at 59 per cent, 53 per cent and 71 per cent respectively in the environmental, social and economic chambers. Democratic procedures often cited in support of the FSC may actually mask the under-representation in FSC decision-making bodies of socially organised groups and private sector represen-tatives from tropical countries.

These factors undoubtedly help to sustain the discrepancy between the FSC's international standards and the local context in which they are applied. The FSC has attempted to reduce this discrepancy by fostering the national initiatives in tropical countries, which could adapt the FSC's principles and criteria using good management standards suited to local contexts. To reduce *per capita* auditing and certification costs FSC-International has promoted 'group certification' through the intermedi-aries (for example forest co-operatives, companies or consultants) and, in 2004, approved new standards for small and low-intensity managed forests (SLIMFs). So, FSC rules and standards are now more flexible and better suited to the local contexts in tropical countries and FSC-accredited certifying bodies are also more present in tropical areas than in the past.

The adaptation of the FSC's rules has allowed certain groups of actors to obtain certification more easily. For example, 1.5 million hectares of indigenous lands in the Brazilian Amazon were certified according to FSC standards in late 2006. The most extensive tropical forest certifica-tion ever, it was obtained by Kayapo Indians, who principally farm Brazil nuts, on the basis of FSC standards for non-wood forest products. Nevertheless, some scholars argue that there are still problems with forest certification initiatives for community forest management. Garcia Drigo and colleagues show that the reasons motivating commu-nities to obtain FSC certification are short-term increases in income and the possibility of protecting their lands against new settlers.[33] But the new occupants within the communities often prefer to clear the land of trees in order to set up extensive cattle ranching operations, rather than to manage the forest according to FSC principles. Furthermore, certifica-tion projects for community forests are strongly dependent on financial and technical assistance from NGOs and donors. The communities may

[32] Dingwerth, 'Global Governance and the South'.
[33] Drigo *et al.*, 'Community-Based Forest Management'.

not be sufficiently aware of the financial risks associated with certification and so market low-quality products that find no buyers in the marketplace.[34]

3.3 Certification as a means of fighting illegal logging?

Over recent years, the area of forest under management in the tropics has grown considerably – at least on paper. According to ITTO, 96.3 million hectares (or 27 per cent) of permanent natural tropical forests used for production are currently covered by management plans. In reality, however, many plans are unimplemented and, despite the regulatory bans on development in several tropical countries, many forest producers log using illegal practices.[35] Enforcement of forestry laws is also weak due to insufficient personnel, the remoteness of resources and the confusion created by multiple laws, decentralisation and other political processes.[36]

Theoretically, certification could provide a means of countering this threat – after all, compliance with national laws is a condition for obtaining FSC certification. However, the wide gap between FSC standards and actual management practices in tropical forests means that there are few real incentives for foresters to work within legal frameworks to achieve certification. One Amazon forestry company speaks of operational costs being 30 per cent higher in certified forests than in conventionally logged forests and other forest operators that comply with laws contend that they are in fierce competition with those who continue to use illegal practices.[37] In the Brazilian Amazon, many timber-processing companies are obliged to purchase their own forest land simply so they can guarantee they are selling FSC-certified products.

3.4 The problem of land tenure insecurity

Another disincentive to certification in tropical forests is land tenure insecurity. Land disputes are still common in tropical forested countries. As a result, producers are often unwilling to implement costly management plans, even less to meet demanding certification standards that

---

[34] *Ibid.* [35] ITTO, 'Status of Tropical Forest Management'.
[36] *Ibid.* [37] See Gullison, 'Forest Certification'; Espach, 'Does Private Regulation Work'.

they may not be able to comply with in the long term.[38] In Brazil, illegal occupation of private forest areas is common practice, as is the falsification of land titles. In June 2005, for example, some 2,000 people settled on Amazon property belonging to the Martins Group, whose forests are managed in line with FSC standards.[39] These new occupants cleared trees and jeopardised the company's wildlife re-introduction plans. There have been several other cases of land disputes between certified forestry companies and local commu-nities.[40] Brazilian authorities also regularly suspend logging permits in certified areas as they wait to clarify the land tenure situation. Faced with the complexity of this situation, some Brazilian companies are abandoning their forest activities in favour of lower-risk activities. These land tenure problems are also observed in the small number of FSC-certified community forests.

3.5   The problem of forest land conversion

Another factor limiting the FSC's scope as a private global governance system is the cost/benefit ratio for FSC-certified forest management methods. The economics behind this are simple: owing to high discount rates in developing countries, the timber harvested in the distant future should have only a low value that does not justify investment in the technical forest management model required for certification. This argu-ment, often used in Anglo-Saxon literature, is nevertheless challenged by several authors.[41] Karsenty and Nasi believe that if we take account of technological progress in industrial timber processing, the economic rent that is regularly recreated makes long-term investment in the manage-ment of natural forests attractive.[42] The same authors add that forest management also has an impact on short-term economic results due to higher labour productivity and lower operating costs. Several compara-tive studies between reduced impact logging and conventional logging seem to support the arguments of Karsenty and Nasi. According to Barreto, Holmes and their colleagues, the productivity gains and waste

---

[38] Becker, *Barriers to Forest Certification.*   [39] Pinto, 'Sem-toras ameaçam'.
[40] Lachefski and Freris, 'Precious Woods'; Carneiro, *O Dinheiro é Verde?*; Fanzeres and Murrieta, *Stakeholders' Viewpoints.*
[41] Niesten and Rice, 'Gestion durable des forêts'.
[42] Karsenty and Nasi, 'Les "concessions de conservation"'.

reduction resulting from well-managed operations gives them economic advantages over conventional operations.[43]

Nonetheless, sustainable management for timber production is less profitable for the different stakeholders (governments, dealers and local communities) than other forms of land use (ITTO, 2006). Owing to high discount rates and land tenure and political insecurity representative of tropical countries, the opportunity costs of long-term forest management are very high in relation to the conversion of forestland to farming uses.[44] In fact, certification gives the FSC very little control over the conversion of forests into pastureland and farmland, which is actually the main cause of deforestation in numerous tropical countries.

4. The FSC's regulatory effects

4.1 Behavioural effects

The FSC's growing impact on global forest management is often demonstrated using indicators such as the area of forest certified, the number of certificates issued and their respective progress. For example, by late 2006, almost 900 FSC forest management certificates had been issued by FSC-accredited monitoring bodies. These figures are often presented as evidence of the FSC's success, even though they do not 'prove' that certification influenced certificate-holders to improve their forest management practices.

Whether or not certification allows companies to develop green marketing strategies without actually making any substantial changes in their practices remains a highly controversial question. Several researchers have attempted to provide answers using specific indicators, such as the corrective action recommended by certification bodies during the initial audit process.[45] This research shows certification bodies that have asked companies engaged in a certification process to implement corrective actions in several environmental and social fields.

In Brazil, the assessment report drawn up by the Scientific Certification Systems (SCS), a monitoring body on forest management

---

[43] Barreto *et al.*, 'Costs and Benefits of Forest Management'; Holmes, *Custos e Benefícios Financeiros*.

[44] Gullison, 'Forest Certification'.

[45] Thornber, 'Global Trends in FSC Certificates'; Gullison, 'Forest Certification'; Newsom *et al.*, 'Does Forest Certification Matter?'.

certification for the Cikel company, showed that considerable behavioural changes in the company's practices were required.[46] SCS asked the company, inter alia, to define areas used by traditional Quilombo communities for their subsistence hunting and gathering activities. This demarcation then required formal acceptance by the communities. Other initiatives have focused on social measures (improving workers' rights, compulsory local recruitment, etc.) or environmental measures (developing a wildlife characterisation map, defining monitoring indicators for rare and endangered wildlife, etc.).

Nevertheless, significant differences exist between tropical regions. In the Brazilian Amazon, monitoring procedures are more attuned to environmental and social issues than in Africa.[47] For example, special attention is dedicated to the reduction of accidents among workers. On the other hand, the technical prescriptions required to elaborate the forest management plans – for example maps – are more detailed in Africa.

Furthermore, as certain authors point out, many companies already demonstrated 'better than average' forest management practices before being certified.[48] This is particularly true for certified public forests, when forest authorities are powerful enough to apply management standards and to monitor their effectiveness. However, it is also the case for certain private tropical forests, when NGOs, financial backers and research institutes provide technical assistance and funding to improve forest management. According to Pattberg, almost a third of operators engaged in a forest management certification process in Germany already complied with FSC standards before the certification process began.[49] A survey conducted in Brazil and Argentina by Espach reports that FSC certification results in relatively few changes in practices.[50] As Richards points out, the broader the gap between a company's forestry practices and the practices needed to obtain FSC certification, the lower the incentives to become certified.[51] In other words, companies with the poorest forest management practices are least inclined to improve through certification.

[46] Bauch et al., Avaliação de Certificação.
[47] Cassagne, L'Aménagement des Concessions.   [48] Atyi and Simula, 'Forest Certification'.
[49] Pattberg, 'Transnational Organization(s) as Governance'.
[50] Espach, 'Does Private Regulation Work'.
[51] Richards, Complex Socio-Political Settings.

4.2   Side effects

Certification may also have side effects, that is, unwanted consequences that can be directly linked to the emergence of the FSC and whose effects on global governance were unanticipated and do not correspond to the goals initially announced by the FSC.

The FSC's first 'side effect' concerns the structural problems of international inequality. FSC certification has had far more success in Northern countries than in tropical (Southern) countries where, paradoxically, biodiversity is richest and the forests most endangered. According to FSC-International, over 82 per cent of FSC certified forest areas are in Europe and North America. Only 3 per cent of these areas are in Africa (2.5 million hectares, of which 1.7 million alone are in South Africa) and 4 per cent in the Asia-Pacific region. These North–South disparities are partly explained by cost differentials between developed countries and developing countries. According to Gullison, certification costs for large forestry companies in the United States or Poland stand at $0.02 to 0.03 per cubic metre, compared to $0.26 to 1.10 in tropical countries and over $4.00 for small-scale producers in Latin America.[52]

These differences become material when tropical forest products compete on the same markets with temperate and boreal timber and other materials such as PVC and aluminium (for example for joinery). The requirements of certain actors on the major European Union markets, who force suppliers to systematically engage in certification, can act as prohibitive measures for tropical timber. Hence, we cannot completely exclude the possibility that certification is used for strategic purposes by some actors to push out or exclude competitors from markets. This assumption must, however, be supported by further economic analysis.

The exclusion of uncertified tropical timber from European markets could have a further side effect: increased exportation to markets that do not value good forest management practices. So, should it become the norm for the main markets, especially in Europe, to demand certified products, tropical suppliers and producers could be forced to turn their export flows towards buoyant markets that are less sensitive to environmental considerations (a prime example being China). Economic agents in tropical countries could also be tempted to sell their companies to foreign investors, who are not inclined to improve their environmental practices in light of their preferential access to markets with little concern

---

[52] See Gullison, 'Forest Certification'.

for environmental issues. Worse still, if the barriers to European markets are too high, tropical forest owners could be tempted to convert forests to different, more profitable uses, such as farming or livestock ranching, that would result in the removal of forests completely.

In the pulp and paper industry there is also an uneven geographic distribution of FSC timber. So, certain paper pulp production units, whose customers have opted for FSC certification, encounter difficulties sourcing timber from forests managed according to FSC standards. In France, for example, relatively few forests are certified by the FSC since many forest owners and the State Forestry Office (ONF) have opted for a competing certification system. This means that many French pulp and paper factories are obliged to source timber from abroad to meet orders from European paper manufacturers demanding the FSC label. Paradoxically, this situation could lead to serious environmental impacts linked to the transportation of timber.

And so a further side effect of the private global forest governance system is the emergence of voluntary certification systems that compete with the FSC. During the 1990s, several private initiatives were founded in North America (SFI or Sustainable Forestry Initiative in the United States and CSA, Canada Standard Association) and in Europe (PEFC or Pan-European Forest Certification Scheme). Other voluntary certification programmes were launched by governments, especially in developing countries. These initiatives were all established in direct response to the possibility that economic actors or states could lose control over forest governance due to the creation of the FSC.

Most of the certification systems competing with FSC have been grouped within the PEFC (the Programme for the Endorsement of Forest Certification Schemes). This programme has become an international mechanism for the mutual recognition of voluntary national certification initiatives. In the PEFC the standards that serve as a reference for certification are the forest management criteria and indicators resulting from a dozen regional intergovernmental negotiation processes. These include the Helsinki process set up in 1993 for Europe, the Montreal process set up the in same year for North America, the Tarapoto process set up in 1995 for the Amazon and the African Timber Organization's criteria and indicators defined in 1996.

PEFC standards contain mandatory procedures for improving practices. They are not as stringent as FSC standards, which set performance levels that apply to all forest operators. The area of forest managed according to PEFC standards is growing rapidly. PEFC now covers over two thirds of the total area of certified forest in the world, with FSC counting for 28 per cent.

Several private and public forest owners and managers who support the PEFC system believe it to be more legitimate than FSC as a global governance institution, since it is based on official negotiations between states, rather than discussion forums; in their opinion, FSC is manipulated by NGOs that act as pressure groups. Further, accreditation of monitoring bodies that issue the PEFC certificate is carried out by national accreditation associations belonging to the International Accreditation Forum (IAF), which guarantees that these bodies are competent, impartial and obtain recognition of their competence at the international level. This is not the case for the FSC, which is itself responsible for accrediting independent certification bodies. Finally, the PEFC is open to diverse stakeholders even though it was created by private forest owners and operators. In France, for example, the leading environmental NGO, France Nature Environnement, is a member of PEFC-France. The fact that NGOs belong to PEFC undeniably strengthens its legitimacy but the FSC supporters still argue that the PEFC remains a certification programme designed by and for private sector representatives.

Analysing the development of the FSC and the PEFC in parallel, it appears that there has been a certain convergence between the two systems. The PEFC has evolved towards internationalisation and greater openness to members of civil society. The FSC, on the other hand, has set up more flexible procedures allowing for better linkage between its global principles and criteria and the specific local contexts. Nonetheless, there remains a vast gulf between the two systems that is likely to prevent formal mutual recognition. First, strong tensions between the two systems in the past have scarred the relationship in ways that are yet to heal. Second, profound differences still exist between the two systems, with the FSC's certification system based on performance indicators and the PEFC's system based on compliance with procedures. Consequently, FSC certification requires all certificate holders to comply with one set of national standards, whereas PEFC certification allows for significant local differences within forest management units. Third, the FSC uses systematic on-site inspection to monitor compliance with standards, a much stricter procedure than the PEFC's examination of documents, particularly management plans. Having regard to these differences, it is unlikely that the two certification systems will converge in the foreseeable future.

What conclusions can we draw from the impact of the development of the FSC's rival certification systems on its influence as a global governance institution? In a sense, the creation of the PEFC can be explained as an attempt to compensate for some of the FSC's weaknesses as a global governance institution. PEFC standards were quickly accepted by a significant number of operators who felt the FSC was insufficiently attentive to their specific situations. We could thus conclude that the FSC consolidated global forest governance by triggering the emergence of other competing certification schemes. The FSC's rival certification programmes allow for forest sector regulation by codifying forest managers' practices and consolidating their implementation by means of independent monitoring mechanisms. In response, it could be argued that PEFC standards do not demand that certified forest managers reach a given performance level. But this does not alter the fact that they should require an improvement in practices, which is far better than no improvement at all.

Then again, the competitive struggle between the two systems may limit the FSC's possibilities for regulating the actors who choose PEFC certification and, for the reasons mentioned above, PEFC certification seems to generate fewer improvements in forest management methods than FSC certification though comparative research is still lacking.[53] Moreover, the proliferation of certification programmes, and therefore of logos, could confuse consumers and weaken the credibility of all efforts to encourage responsible consumption. Producers who want or need both certificates encounter higher transaction costs, as they are required to pay both certification fees even if the certifying body could issue both certificates in a single audit. Finally, governments may promote private voluntary schemes to support national timber industries and, within those industries, organised industrial lobbies may use certification to gain a competitive advantage or restrict market access for foreign companies. For example, the French government has traditionally favoured PEFC, partly by backing the certification of public forest management through PEFC standards, and partly by providing financial support to this private voluntary initiative.

4.3   Political effects

The FSC's political effects can be understood by considering its cognitive and discursive functions. By creating forums for multi-stakeholder

---

[53] Ozinga and Krul, *Footprints in the Forest.*

dialogue, the FSC acts as an institution for 'cognitive and discursive governance':[54] NGOs improve their knowledge of the problems affecting companies they previously labelled as unscrupulous, and companies learn to better understand the position of NGOs they previously considered radical. These forums for dialogue provide a means of settling disputes that were hitherto based largely on ignorance and misinformation.

The FSC is also an example of what Callon and colleagues called the 'new arenas of technical democracy' since it requires actors to engage in learning, information-sharing and lay expertise processes.[55] This dimension is particularly important in the forest sector, where decision-making processes take place in a context of scientific uncertainty. The sustainable management of forests is a complex issue, which varies in space and time and suffers from serious disagreements even within the international scientific community. For example, in tropical areas, the uncertainty characterising long-term forest dynamics makes it difficult to assess the impact operations will have on the state of the forest after two rotation cycles.[56] The development of forest management standards must also take into account diverse expertise on issues that are still subject to considerable scientific controversy, such as measuring biodiversity value. In this uncertain world, building forums for dialogue is a way of revealing social demands and collective preferences, and consequently fostering the emergence of new discursive regimes that permeate political processes.

The FSC has thus helped to influence international forest debates and policy, with certification even becoming one of the main subjects of international forest negotiations.[57] At the national level, the creation of FSC national initiatives and multi-stakeholder working groups – which may include governments – can have a significant political impact. In some countries, these are often the only forums for discussion and consultation that exist on forest issues. Within these forums, debates go far beyond the problem of forest certification.[58] When there are no national initiatives making it possible to organise debates and foster the emergence of social demands, the individual certification procedures developed by the FSC include the compulsory consultation of local actors and complaints

---

[54] Pattberg, 'Transnational Organization(s) as Governance'.
[55] Callon, *Agir dans un Monde Incertain*.
[56] Karsenty, *Les instruments économiques*.
[57] See Bass, 'Certification as a Manifestation'; Bass, 'Global Forest Governance'.
[58] Guéneau and Bass, 'Global Forest Governance'.

procedures for local NGOs. This means that in many countries, the rights granted to local NGOs through the FSC process are greater than those they are given under national legislation.[59] FSC thus plays a role in supporting the emergence and consolidation of civil society in some countries.

The FSC also has a political impact through the dissemination of an institutional model to an ever-wider range of sectors. Numerous initiatives have copied the FSC's structure and operational style, in the fisheries sector (MSC, Marine Stewardship Council), in marine aquarium organisations (MAC, Marine Aquarium Council), in tourism (STSC, Sustainable Tourism Stewardship Council), and in several agricultural sectors (RSPO, Roundtable on Sustainable Palm Oil; RTRS, Roundtable on Responsible Soy).

Another of the FSC's political effects can be appreciated through its integrative functions. This 'governance through integration' concerns the way in which private voluntary regulation schemes fit into public policy measures and, vice versa, how public policies can find scope for implementation via FSC.[60] These integrative functions are not specific to the FSC, since in many other sectors public action is largely supported by private regulation initiatives, either for improving the effectiveness of public policy instruments, or for public policy making. This is the case, for example, in organic farming, which was originally a private voluntary initiative and is now largely regulated by law.

In the forest sector, private certification initiatives have begun to influence public action through the greening policies recently launched for public markets. Several European governments committed to only using timber of verifiable origin from well-managed, certified forests. Some countries, such as Denmark, have embraced the FSC system. On the other hand, in France, government regulations adopted in April 2005 states that, by 2010, all public procurement of tropical timber will come from forests managed sustainably. The French approach does not therefore promote one certification programme over another. Both the French approach and others could produce indirect effects by favouring local certified timber, which is in abundant supply, over tropical certified timber.

This risk of protectionism implied in certification has been discussed on several occasions in international negotiations. The growing integration of environmental concerns in public procurement has, for many years, been

---

[59] Kern, *Global Governance*.
[60] See Pattberg, 'Transnational Organization(s) as Governance'.

the subject of a debate on WTO compatibility. According to the WTO's international trade rules, an importing country cannot ban imports of a product under the pretext that the production processes and methods (PPMs) used for this product have an environmental impact in the exporting country. Each country holds the sovereign right to draw up its own environmental policy, whether their trade partners like it or not. However, public procurement is a special case, in that several – but not all – WTO member countries have signed a multilateral agreement on public procurement. The provisions of this agreement hold that PPMs may be part of the technical specifications for public procurement contracts provided they create no unnecessary barriers to trade. The question of what may be considered as unnecessary remains open, of course, meaning that in the absence of case law, it is difficult to know how the WTO Dispute Settlement Body would judge a complaint for discriminatory practices.

Furthermore, these public procurement policies are not limited to states, as a growing number of local authorities in Europe have announced their intention to purchase only timber sourced from forests managed according to FSC standards. In France, the Nord-Pas-de-Calais Regional Council and several city councils have also taken such steps. By promoting voluntary certification at different levels of forest governance, the FSC has thus provided a lever for local actors in timber-consuming countries who feel excluded from international forest regulation processes.

The FSC can directly impact forest legislation, especially in countries where the dismantling of state services no longer allows them to provide some traditional functions. For example, South African forest monitoring operations have been entrusted to the FSC and in Mexico a forest law has been inspired by FSC standards.[61] Finally, through the agreement reached between WWF and the World Bank in 1998, the FSC has a direct influence on political processes at the international level. One of the objectives of the agreement between the World Bank and WWF was to reach 200 million hectares of certified forests by 2005. This target has been reached, since in July 2005, the area of certified forests for all programmes stood at 244 million hectares.

5. Conclusions

The FSC can fill many gaps left by the failure of multilateral inter-governmental forest negotiations. Its demanding standards are binding,

---

[61] See Pattberg, *Global Governance*.

monitored and accompanied by sanctions (certificate withdrawal) in case of non-compliance. So, the FSC improves the behaviour of actors engaged in forest management. The system also brings the interests of certain stakeholders closer together by institutionalising compromises between environmentalists and the private sector in order to achieve a certain 'social peace'. The open, transparent, participatory and balanced FSC bodies offer an attractive democratic alternative in the absence of international binding mechanism. Further, the FSC significantly influences political processes at the local, national and supranational level. It is a missing link between trade and environment as it allows consumers of forest products to favour well-managed forests over those resulting from production processes that harm the environment.

That said, the FSC has not remedied the regime's weaknesses entirely and has generated some of its own side effects. Private governance systems that are based on standards and market forces are intrinsically limited. As we have seen, the FSC is only partially capable of resolving all the tension between actors concerned by forest issues. FSC certification is predominantly relevant to the largest companies that are firmly established in global markets and are in the best position to improve their behaviour. Several actors that did not take part in standard-setting processes feel excluded from the system, or have purposefully differentiated themselves in order to recreate a parallel global governance system with other sources of legitimacy. Despite the precautions taken by the FSC to ensure transparency and equity and to balance the participation of actors in decision-making and standard-setting bodies, a broad gap remains between the FSC's international standards and the local context in which they are applied. Furthermore, trade in certified forest products reveals discriminatory practices, especially when they are backed by states, for example through subsidies or public procurement.

Viewed globally, the behavioural improvements noted are in fact fairly close to situations observed before the application of FSC standards. The more environmental and social damage caused by practices, the further they are from reaching FSC standards, and the less likely economic agents are to be motivated to improve them through the FSC's governance system. In reality, the FSC is an instrument that falls within the framework of corporate social responsibility: it highlights the good practices of actors whose previous behaviour, while not necessarily 'politically acceptable', was not the most threatening to forests.

The FSC has an indisputable influence over political processes, in terms of leading the public debate, learning processes and the profession-alisation of actors. It is a market instrument and a political tool for states which, in a context where the 'deliberative imperative' is the norm, redeploy their action around these new forms of private governance.[62] Enthusiasm for these new forms of action, with their liberal undertones, nevertheless carries certain risks. It focuses civil society on economic actors and distracts them from national authorities and international negotiations. The lack of pressure from civil society diminishes attempts at international coordination, despite the urgent need for collective action to solve problems of common interest. It focusses civil society on coordination issues and distracts them from strategic action to reduce the tropical deforestation. A specific research on efficiency issues within the FSC negotiation process could help the FSC to reach this main objective. Nevertheless, public policies also seem vital for the improve-ment of forest management practices, particularly through land tenure clarification and the implementation and monitoring of forest manage-ment plans. Through action such as land tenure clarification or the implementation and monitoring of forest development plans, public policies nevertheless seem vital for the improvement of forest manage-ment practices. But do they receive enough support?

References

Arts, B. 1998, 'The Political Influence of Global NGOs', *Case Studies on the Climate Change and Biodiversity Convention*, Utrecht, International Books.

Atyi, R. and Simula, M. 2002, 'Forest Certification: Pending Challenges for Tropical Timber', *ITTO Technical Series*, no. 19, Yokohama.

Barreto, P. *et al.* 1998, 'Costs and Benefits of Forest Management for Timber Production in Eastern Amazonia', *Forest Ecology and Management*, no. 108, 9–26.

Bass, S. 1996, 'Certification as a Manifestation of Changing Roles in Forestry', *Making Forest Policy Work*, Oxford Forestry Institute.

Bass, S. 2002, '*Global Forest Governance: Emerging Impacts of the Forest Stewardship Council*', Berlin, SUSTRA Workshop on Architecture of the Global System of Governance of Trade and Sustainable Development.

Bauch R. E. *et al.* 2004, *Avaliação de Certificação do Manejo Florestal das Florestas Naturais da Cikel Brasil Verde S.A.*, Brasilia, SCS.

---

[62] Blondiaux and Sintomer, 'L'Impératif Délibératif'.

Becker, M. 2004, *Barriers to Forest Certification in Developing Tropical Countries*, University of Toronto, Faculty of Forestry.

Blondiaux L. and Sintomer, Y. 2002, 'L'Impératif Délibératif', *Politix*, no. 57.

Börzel, T. A. and Risse, T. 2005, 'Public–Private Partnerships: Effective and Legitimate Tools of International Governance?' in E. Grande and L. W. Pauly (eds.), *Complex Sovereignty: Reconstituting Political Authority in the 21st Century*, University of Toronto Press, 195–216.

Callon, M. *et al.* 2001, *Agir dans un Monde Incertain: Essai sur la Démocratie Technique*, Paris, Le Seuil.

Carneiro, M. D. S. 2004, *O Dinheiro é Verde? A Construção Social do Mercado de Madeiras Certificadas na Amazônia Brasileira*, Universidade Federal de Rio de Janeiro, Instituto de Filosofia e Estudos Sociais.

Cashore, B. and Bernstein, S. 2005, 'Non-State Global Governance: Is Forest Certification a Legitimate Alternative to a Global Forest Convention?' in J. Kirton and M. Trebilcock (eds.), *Hard Choices, Soft Law: Combining Trade, Environment and Social Cohesion in Global Governance*, Aldershot, Ashgate.

Cashore, B. 2002, 'Legitimacy and the Privatization of Environmental Governance: How Non-State Market-Driven (NSMD) Governance Systems Gain Rule-Making Authority', *Governance: An International Journal of Policy, Administration and Institutions*, vol. 15, no. 4, 503–29.

Cassagne, B. 2006, *L'Aménagement des Concessions Forestières en Amazonie Brésilienne et dans le Bassin du Congo: Un Echange d'Expérience*, La lettre de l'ATIBT, no. 24.

Chaytor, B. 2001, *The Development of Global Forest Policy: Overview of Legal and Institutional Frameworks*, Genève, IISD – WBCSD.

Counsell, S. and Loraas, K. 2002, *Trading in Credibility: The Myth and Reality of the Forest Stewardship Council*, London, The Rainforest Foundation.

Cutler, C. *et al.* 1999, *Private Authority and International Affairs*, State University of New York Press.

Dingwerth, K. forthcoming, 'Global Governance and the South: The Affirmative Procedures of the Forest Stewardship Council', *Global Governance*, vol. 14.

Espach, R. 2005, 'Does Private Regulation Work in Developing Countries? Private Environmental Regulatory Programs in the Argentine and Brazilian Chemical and Forestry Industries', *Tuck School of Business at Dartmouth College Conference on Institutional Mechanisms for Self-Regulation*, Berkeley, University of California.

Fanzeres, A. and Murrieta, R. S. 2000, *Stakeholders' Viewpoints of Forest Certification Processes in Brazilian Amazon: An Opportunity of Reflection for FSC's Secretariat*, Belem, Board, Members and Supporters, Belem.

FAO 2005, *Global Forest Resources Assessment*, FAO, Rome.

FAO 2006a, *Forest Products Annual Market Review 2005–2006*, FAO, Rome.

FAO 2006b, *International Trade in Forest Products and Services*, FAO, Rome.

FAO 2007, *Situation des forêts du monde*, FAO, Rome.

Gale, F. 2006, 'Regulating the Market in an Era of Globalisation: Global Governance via the Forest Stewardship Council', Newcastle, *Australasian Political Studies Association (APSA) Conference*.

Garcia Drigo, I. *et al.*, 2006, 'Community-Based Forest Management Certification in Brazil: A Sustainable Initiative?', Saint Quentin en Yvelines, Colloque Gestion concertée des ressources naturelles et de l'environnement.

Gendron, C. *et al.* 2002, 'L'action des nouveaux mouvements sociaux économiques et le potentiel régulatoire de la certification dans le domaine forestier', *Les cahiers de la Chaire collection recherche*, no. 08, UQAM, Montréal.

Gendron, C. and Turcotte, M.-F. 2005, 'Configuration des nouveaux mouvements sociaux économiques: Résultats préliminaires', *Les Cahiers de Chaire collection recherche*, no. 07, UQAM, Montréal.

Greenpeace 2006, *Eating up the Amazon*, Greenpeace, Amsterdam.

Guéneau, S. 2006, *Livre blanc sur les forêts tropicales humides*, Paris, La documentation française.

Guéneau, S. 2002, 'La forêt tropicale: entre fourniture de bien public global et régulation privée, quelle place pour l'instrument certification?' in S. Maljean-Dubois (ed.), *L'outil économique en droit international et européen de l'environnement*, Paris, La documentation française.

Guéneau, S. and Bass, S. 2007, 'Global Forest Governance: Effectiveness, Fairness and Legitimacy of Market-Driven Approaches' in S. Thoyer and B. Martimort-Asso (eds.), *Participation for Sustainability in Trade*, Aldershot, Ashgate.

Gulbrandsen, L. H. 2004, 'Overlapping Public and Private Governance: Can Forest Certification Fill the Gaps in the Global Forest Regime?', *Global Environmental Politics*, vol. **4**, no. 2, 75–99.

Gulbrandsen, L. H. 2005, 'The Effectiveness of Non-State Governance Schemes: A Comparative Study of Forest Certification in Norway and Sweden', *International Environmental Agreements: Politics, Law and Economics*, vol. **5**, no. 2.

Gullison, R. E. 2003, 'Does Forest Certification Conserve Biodiversity?', *Oryx*, vol. **37**, no. 2.

Haufler, V. 2003, 'New Forms of Governance: Certification Regimes as Social Regulations of the Global Market' in E. Meidinger *et al.* (eds.), *Social and Political Dimensions of Forest Certification*, www.forsbuch.de, Remagen-Oberwinter.

Holec N. and Brunet-Jolivald, G. 1999, *Gouvernance: Note de Synthèse*. Available at: www.urbanisme.equipement.gouv.fr/cdu/accueil/bibliographies/gouvernance/note.htm.

Holmes, T. P. *et al.* 2002, 2nd edn, *Custos e Benefícios Financeiros da Exploração Florestal de Impacto Reduzido em Comparaçãoà Exploração Florestal Convencional na Amazônia Oriental*, Belém, Fundação Floresta Tropical.

Humpheys, D. 1999, 'The Evolving Forest Regime', *Global Environmental Change*, vol. 3, no. 9, 251–4.

ITTO 2006, 'Status of Tropical Forest Management', *ITTO Technical Series*, no. 24, Yokahoma.

Karsenty, A. and Nasi, R. 2004, 'Les "concessions de conservation" sonnent-elles le glas de l'aménagement forestier durable?', *Revue Tiers Monde*, no. 177.

Karsenty, A. 1999, *Les instruments économiques de la forêt tropicale: le cas de l'Afrique centrale*, Paris, Maisonneuve et Larose.

Keck, M. E. and Sikkink, K. 1998, *Activists Beyond Borders: Advocacy Networks in International Politics*, Ithaca, Cornell University Press.

Kern, K. 2004, *Global Governance Through Transnational Network Organizations. The Scope and Limitations of Civil Society Self-Organization*, Berlin, WZB Discussion paper.

Krasner, S. 1983, *International Regimes*, Ithaca, Cornell University Press.

Lachefski and Freris 2002, 'Precious Woods Amazon (PWA) and Gethal; Certification of Industrial Forestry in the Native Amazon Rainforest' in S. Counsell and K. Loraas (eds.), *Trading in Credibility: The Myth and Reality of the Forest Stewardship Council*, London, The Rainforest Foundation, London.

Lafrance, M.-A. 2005, 'La certification dans le secteur forestier: qui en profite réellement?' in *Configuration des nouveaux mouvements sociaux économiques: Résultats préliminaires*, Montréal, Les Cahiers de Chaire collection recherché, no. 07, UQAM.

LCB 2005, *Position sur l'écocertification*, Paris, French Working Group on Tropical Rainforests.

Meidinger, E. 2003, 'Forest Certification as a Global Civil Society Regulatory Institution' in E. Meidinger *et al.* (eds.), *Social and Political Dimensions of Forest Certification*, www.forsbuch.de, Remagen-Oberwinter.

Newsom, D. *et al.* 2005, 'Does Forest Certification Matter? An Analysis of Operation-Level Changes Required During the SmartWood Certification Process in the United States', *Journal of Forest Policy and Economics*, no. 9.

Niesten, E. and Rice, R. 2004, 'Gestion durable des forêts et incitations directes à la conservation de la diversité', *Revue Tiers Monde*, no. 177.

O'Brien, R. *et al.* 2000, *Contesting Global Governance: Multilateral Economic Institutions and Global Social Movements*, Cambridge University Press.

Ozanne, L. K. and Vlosky, R. P. 1997, 'Willingness to Pay for Environmentally Certified Wood Products: A Consumer Perspective', *Forest Products Journal*, vol. 47, no. 6, 39–48.

Ozanne, L. K. and Vlosky, R. P. 2003, 'Certification from the US Consumer Perspective: A Comparison from 1995 and 2000', *Forest Products Journal*, vol. 53, no. 3, 13–21.

Ozinga, S. and Krul, L. 2004, *Footprints in the Forest: Current Practice and Future Challenges in Forest Certification*, Bruxelles, FERN.

Pattberg, P. 2005, 'Transnational Organization(s) as Governance: A Comparative Analysis of Private Rules beyond the State', *International Organizations and Global Environmental Governance Conference*, Berlin, The Global Governance Project.

Pattberg, P. 2004, *The Institutionalisation of Private Governance: Conceptualising an Emerging Trend in Global Environmental Politics*, Global Governance Working Paper No. 9, Berlin, The Global Governance Project.

Pattberg, P. 2006, *Global Governance: Reconstructing a Contested Social Science Concept*, GARNET Working Paper No. 04, University of Warwick.

Pinto, R. J. 2005, 'Sem-toras ameaçam as florestas certificadas', *O Diario do Para*, 1 July.

Reinicke, W. and Deng, F. 2000, *Critical Choices: The United Nations, Networks and the Future of Global Governance*, Ottawa, International Development Research Centre.

Richards, M. 2004, *Certification in Complex Socio-Political Settings*, Washington DC, Forest Trends.

Rosenau, J. N. 1987, *Governance without Government: Systems of Rule in World Politics*, Los Angeles, Institute for Transnational Studies, University of South California.

Rosenau, J. N. and Czempiel, E.-O. 1992, *Governance without Government: Order and Change in World Politics*, Cambridge University Press.

Skala-Kuhmann, A. 1996, *Legal Instruments to Enhance the Conservation and Sustainable Management of Forest Resources at the International Level*, Bonn, BMZ – GTZ.

Tarasofsky, R. 1999, *Assessing the International Forest Regime*, Gland, IUCN Environmental Policy and Law Paper, no. 37.

Thornber, K. 1999, 'Overview of Global Trends in FSC Certificates', *Instruments for Sustainable Private Sector Forestry*, London, IIED.

Thornber, K. *et al.* 2000, *L'accès difficile aux avantages de la certification. Discussion des incidences sur l'équité*, Joensuu, European Forest Institute, Document de discussion no. 8.

Toyne, P. *et al.* 2002, *The Timber Footprint of the G8 and China. Making the Case for Green Procurement by Government*, Gland, WWF.

UNEP 2001, *Global Biodiversity Outlook*, Montreal.

Wilson, A.-M. and Guéneau, S. 2003, *Gouvernance mondiale des forêts: Une évaluation à partir de l'analyse de la position des organisations non gouvernementales*, Paris, Iddri.

Young, O. R. 1997, *Global Governance: Drawing Insights from the Environmental Experience*, Cambridge, MIT Press.

15

Private standards in the North – effective norms for the South?

EVA KOCHER[*]

1. Introduction

1.1 Social standards and CSR policies

The globalised world offers companies opportunities to capitalise on global labour markets: production can be organised globally in proprietary businesses or by means of an elaborate supply chain. However, the transnational organisation of business activities can also entail substantial risks. Both the press and the public have increasingly taken an interest in events that occur in far-off parts of the world and these incidents can turn into risks in consumer markets in industrialised nations. Just imagine the following scenario: the Clean Clothes Campaign claims that, according to accounts by female workers, a Central American textile producer was locking pregnant women in the cafeteria as punishment for failing to reach their production targets. The factory was closed in 2005 after being unionised. Whilst these allegations are being heard in the courts of the Central American country in which they occurred (in cases brought by, among others, the local trade union), they have simultaneously reached the attention of the German public, because the textile producer in question supplies a sportswear company based in Germany. Human rights groups such as the Clean Clothes Campaign (but also the local union and a local women's association) have invoked, among other things, the German sportswear company's code of conduct, which guarantees compliance with national laws, protection against discrimination and freedom of association. Their recourse to the code is grounded in the requirement of the German company that their business partners and suppliers also sign the code

[*] Professor, Faculty of Law, European University, Frankfurt (Oder), Germany; Dr. iur. (University of Hamburg).

as part of their contractual relations. The German company had also joined the Fair Labour Association (FLA), having certified its code and conducted (announced) the requisite work inspections; the FLA was also criticised for its role in the rights violations. The German company subsequently lobbied the Central American government to pay outstanding wages and compensation, though it also stated that it does not wish to assume any financial responsibility itself.[1]

This case exemplifies the issues concerning the global debate on the imposition of social standards by transnational companies and demonstrates the central role played by private standards and corporate codes of conduct. It is a typical example of the de-monopolisation of standard setting in the field of labour relations.

The case described is only one example of transnational social standards set by private actors. The transnational privatisation of standard setting is generated by the absence of effective and transparent systems of national and international law. International law, after all, only binds states; the relevant national law of the country of production, however, governs transnational production by private companies. It is often the case that European companies (as well as European consumers) are uncertain as to the subject and content of the applicable rules.[2]

However, the interest in legal certainty would not of itself lead private actors to set social standards. The decisive factor is pressure from external actors such as human rights groups. The 'Clean Clothes' case is a good example of how transnational companies selling branded goods may be exposed to external pressure in their consumer markets. In these instances, companies work with, and consider the interests of, civil-society and professional actors, quite early in the process of setting standards and their expectations play an indirect role in this process at the very least. Though it is questionable whether we can speak of standard setting by networks,[3] it is clear that transnational advocacy networks[4] comprising human rights groups, Northern and Southern trade unions, consumer organisations, actors in development policy and investment and rating agencies are instrumental in standards development.[5]

---

[1] Modelled on the 'Hermosa Case' from El Salvador in the dispute with adidas (Zimmer 2006).
[2] de Schutter 2004: 3.   [3] For more on the concept of networks see Börzel 1998.
[4] Keck and Sikkink 1998.   [5] Rodríguez-Garavito 2005.

At least since 2000 such corporate policies have been considered under the label of CSR (corporate social responsibility). Originally identified as having a focus on sustainability and the environment, it is becoming increasingly common for CSR strategies to include social standards.[6] The adoption of CSR policies has also become a matter of course for companies seeing themselves as global players.

Actors in financial markets have particularly contributed to a bandwagon effect. In the interviews we conducted as part of the ESTER project,[7] company representatives repeatedly mentioned a 'herd principle': '[CSR] policy is something you simply have to have nowadays.'[8] In the words of another company representative:

> Since I've been on board, since 2000, that is, [CSR] has played an increasing role, one I see in ... my own work ..., CSR, in my subjective view, is booming. ... So, there are a lot of requirements from outside the company, from the professional raters and rankers, and I'm inundated with questions ... You might almost say one a week at the moment. We [the Sustainability Department] are also responsible for responding to rankings involving sustainability aspects, and we're inundated with 25 rankings a year ... that are important to the financial market analysts or ... investment. Even though this is not yet a major segment of the market, you can still put a figure on it. It's growing.

With the integration of transnational social standards into CSR policies, a number of additional assumptions have entered into standard setting. The most common definition of CSR is contained in the European Commission's Green Paper of 2001: 'Corporate social responsibility is essentially a concept whereby companies decide voluntarily to contribute to a better society and a cleaner environment.' The Commission's support for voluntarism presumes that 'being socially responsible means not only fulfilling legal expectations, but also going beyond

---

[6] For the concept see Bassen, Jastram and Meyer 2005.

[7] The European research project 'ESTER' is an empirical study undertaken to determine whether the concepts included in CSR will serve to strengthen and export the 'European social model' or instead threaten it (for the European social model: Blanke and Hoffmann 2006). In the summer of 2005, research teams in seven European countries each conducted about 40 interviews with representatives from different corporations, trade unions, employee representatives on the shop floor level, advocatory NGOs, consumer organisations, business associations, etc. The study by no means intends to be representative, but rather hopes to glean deeper insights into the possible motives and approaches taken by different actors from these anonymous interviews.

[8] All quotes translated from the original German interviews.

compliance [...].'[9] The notions of *voluntarism* and *compliance beyond legal expectations* are supposed to clarify, in particular, the relationship between voluntary corporate standard setting and statutory regulation – a difficult relationship considering that corporate self-regulation represents potential competition to the state's previous monopoly in the area of social standard setting.

But to what extent does this competition actually exist? What is the impact of de-monopolisation on the authority and effectiveness of standards? In the case of transnational social standards these questions also assume significance in relation to development policy: does private standard setting by companies (in co-operation with other actors) from the North enter into competition with standard setting by states in the South; or, does private standard setting in the North strengthen the regulatory capacity of state norms established in the South?

1.2 Paralegal[10] CSR instruments

The instruments of standard setting in the CSR context are of a legal, or at the very least, a paralegal nature. In these corporate undertakings, such as codes of conduct, transnational companies promise that certain minimum social standards on working conditions will be met in their transnational production operations, that is, in their overseas establishments and/or supply chain. Since CSR implies voluntariness, these unilateral voluntary commitments communicate self-empowerment as a standard setter.[11] In addition, corporations also include these same standards in their commercial contracts with their Southern suppliers and in their employment contracts with staff or contracts with executives.

Supporting and reinforcing the standard-setting process, certification agencies (for example, Social Accountability (SA) 8000, Fair Labor Association (FLA), Rugmark Label) award private labels.[12] An ISO

---

[9] COM 2001: 366; see also COM 2006: 136.
[10] The term 'paralegal' is used to indicate instruments that appear on the surface to be legal without yet having their legal character affirmed in technical terms.
[11] Herberg 2001.
[12] Scherrer, Greven and Frank 1998; Großmann, Busse, Fuchs and Koopmann 2002; Hepple 2005. Cp 'Social Accountability International', (www.sa8000.org/SA8000/SA8000.htm); cf. Fair Labor Association, 'Workplace Code of Conduct' (www.fairlabor.org/all/code/index.html).

standard on social responsibility (ISO 26000) is currently being developed and may be due to become available by 2010.[13]

Unilateral corporate codes of conduct have been joined in recent years by a new, negotiated instrument called international framework agreements (IFAs) concluded between transnational companies and global union federations. In many cases, the agreements are also signed by European works councils or (where they exist) by world works councils.[14] In this way, private standard setting assumes contractual form. This suggests that social standards contribute to the formation of transnational law, or are even part of the *lex mercatoria*.[15] But does this mean that *law* is actually emerging outside or beyond the nation state? Or is the legal form merely being mimicked? Is it only being toyed with?

2. Legal authority of corporate standards

The first question is whether private social standards fulfil the societal functions of *law*, or, more specifically, of legal *social standards*, that is, market-correcting juridification.[16] In contrast to the field of commercial contract law, in the case of social standards law performs the functions of behavioural control and corrective regulation of corporate conduct.[17] In these fields, legal authority is intimately linked to regulatory capacity. If we wish to know the extent to which the de-monopolisation of governmental standard setting leads to competition between private and public standards, we must first enquire into the regulatory capacity of these standards.

2.1 Characteristics of legal norm enforcement

Judging the degree of compliance with private social standards is not easy. It is not possible to rely on the authority of legitimate democratic legislation alone. The guarantee of social standards is not necessarily in the interest of those addressed by the norms (companies and employers) and influencing their conduct is not a simple task, alone for domestic legal systems. Keeping track of suppliers and supply chains can, even

---

[13] Hällström 2006.
[14] For their legal quality see e.g. Kocher 2006; Seifert 2006: 219; Sobczak 2004: 39.
[15] On this see Stein 1995; Cutler 2003; Callies 2004.
[16] Zangl and Zürn 2004: 248.   [17] Kocher 2007: 72–90.

with the best intentions, break down at many points.[18] In some cases, standards are systematically breached.[19] Consequently, it has not yet been demonstrated that self-regulated social standards have actually led to an improvement in working conditions.

However, monitoring *compliance* is not ultimately the best way to judge the effectiveness and authority of standards.[20] Breaches of the norm are part of the very concept of the *norm*, especially in the regulation of social standards. Legal authority is not synonymous with compliance at shop-floor level. Legal authority does not presuppose enforcement but legal enforceability; and this in turn implies enforceability by way of (para)legal proceedings.[21]

Legal enforceability means that the interpretation and application of the norm fall to third parties or institutions that are independent of those addressed by the norm and who set the norm.[22] While in areas such as commercial or international law, communicative equivalents and negotiation procedures may exist which are able to create the necessary legal authority, this is not true for regulatory standards. Legal enforceability in these areas depends on delegated procedures.[23] This means that implementation, monitoring and conflict-resolution mechanisms must be available in conflict situations in which rights are granted, that is, in which private interests can be mobilised to enforce the norms and where the parties protected by the norm are entitled to assert their interest in compliance.

Regulatory standards that lack such delegation mechanisms cannot be termed legal or paralegal, but are rather promotional, political, technical or even economic in character. Political, technical and/or economic enforcement mechanisms[24] compete with legal mechanisms of control and may be equally effective. However, they use another type of logic; they are each supported by different actors and sources of power. The application of political processes and negotiation tactics results in a dispute settlement process that is mainly oriented towards satisfying

---

[18] Fichter and Sydow 2002.   [19] E.g. Köhnen 2002.

[20] O'Rourke 2003: 1; see also Brown, Weiss and Jacobson 1998: 4 for the distinction between implementation, compliance und effectiveness.

[21] Kocher 2007: 113.

[22] Abbott, Keohane, Moravcsik, Slaughter and Snidal 2000: 408; Brütsch 2002: 170; Zangl and Zürn 2004: 21.

[23] At least in the absence of collective representation and collective bargaining (cf following section on IFAs).

[24] See Callies 2004: 160.

certain interests and building consensus. Legal instruments with delegated methods of application on the basis of rights, by contrast, result in the battle over different applications and interpretations of the rules, being characterised by legal arguments.[25] Juridification thus creates the specific legal connection between legitimacy in standard setting and authority in enforcement:[26] legal arguments explicitly refer back to standards which are regarded as legitimate and implicitly point to enforcement mechanisms.

2.2   Norm enforcement in the context of CSR: delegation?

The legal character of the transnational *lex mercatoria* is accordingly derived primarily from transnational arbitration.[27] Arbitration provides a parajudicial process characterised by the delegation of norm enforcement, rights protection, entitlement and legal argumentation to a private body. However, as of yet, none of the CSR standards incorporated into transnational business contracts have become the subject of arbitration; arbitration still deals exclusively with questions of transnational commercial contract law.[28] Transnational social and environmental standards, as basic human rights, would be important steps towards a constitutionalisation of the *lex mercatoria*. Constitutionalisation – the embedding of commercial regulation in guarantees of basic human rights as well as democratically legitimate institutional settings – has been deemed necessary for the further development of transnational law. Nevertheless, constitutionalisation has yet to advance beyond the development of abstract *ordre public* clauses.[29]

Implementation and monitoring of CSR standards function in different ways . A number of company-owned implementation and enforcement instruments, ranging from the training and instruction of suppliers to random checks or systematic and even external monitoring and auditing have been developed. Internal implementation mechanisms include, for example, the control of personnel policy in foreign branches and dependent companies, the use of quality and process management,

---

[25] Kocher 2007: 34–44; Zangl and Zürn 2004: 16.
[26] Zürn and Koenig-Archibugi 2006: 243. (In the end, the terms 'legitimacy' and 'authority' go back to Weber, Wirtschaft und Gesellschaft, Chapter III.).
[27] Stein 1995: 29, 70; Cutler 2003: 26.
[28] See Berger, Dubberstein, Lehmann and Petzold 2002.
[29] Zangl and Zürn 2004: 35; Calliess 2004: 175.

the introduction of specific management systems or building awareness amongst suppliers. Inspection methods that rely solely on internal monitoring and spot checks for quality control measures are still widespread. Some companies have started to offer local seminars and courses for suppliers and management teams at local sites as a first step towards external monitoring. Auditing also provides a more independent type of external mechanism involving outside actors. In some industries it is a requirement that both suppliers and transnational headquarters undergo an audit.[30]

Certification agencies that award social labels, such as the FLA, have also contributed to the standardisation of implementation and inspection/monitoring procedures in recent years. These agencies generally require a certain degree of external monitoring and the auditing of production units and suppliers on location. Sometimes NGOs act as auditors in these instances. Companies accredited with the FLA have to agree to annual internal and external monitoring involving some local NGOs.[31]

However, in practice, it is much less common for companies to involve external actors than some reports on best practice would suggest. In fact, mechanisms to enforce social standards are only employed where companies genuinely fear bad publicity associated with their supply chains; in such cases, external auditing is a matter of risk management.[32] For the majority of companies CSR policies are simply developed to satisfy the push from capital markets to jump on the CSR bandwagon; they rarely employ such additional enforcement or monitoring mechanisms.

However, actors in capital markets are also demanding more than mere event-driven, internal checks on compliance with corporate standards. Their questionnaires implicitly expect implementation to be both professionalised and formalised, that is, that the process of implementation and inspection is institutionalised. A striking feature in this regard is the increasing importance of management systems and mainstreaming mechanisms. Management systems have established themselves as the relevant technical standard for the integration of social responsibility into economic strategies. However, those parties who set the standards (companies) retain control of implementation and, thereby, the concretisation and interpretation of standards. Paralegal

---

[30] Köpke and Röhr 2003; Hepple 2005: 75.
[31] O'Rourke 2003: 1; Hepple 2005: 75.
[32] Colucci 2000: 277–89; van Liemt 2000: 185.

delegation of the application and enforcement of norms hardly ever takes place.

2.3   International framework agreements: trade union involvement

The second feature of paralegal norm enforcement is that an actor's behaviour is controlled by reference to rights, entitlements and private interests. It is also rarely encountered in practice. In the implementation of unilateral codes of conduct, workers or workers' representatives are seldom formally involved in implementation and monitoring procedures.[33] This is true independently of the condition if internal monitoring has been instituted or if more robust monitoring mechanisms are in place (such as random checks, external auditing, and other review procedures).[34]

Specific mechanisms have been developed in international framework agreements which involve trade unions in a more meaningful way. In more recent international framework agreements companies are increasingly setting the standards together with global union federations and Works Councils are jointly responsible for the standard and collaborating on enforcement. Joint responsibility generally starts by setting up joint working groups, arranging regular meetings, and agreeing upon complaint and reporting mechanisms.

However, the degree of formalisation and institutionalisation in these cases is significantly lower than in management systems. This may be related to the fact that international framework agreements are an expression of co-operative labour relations in which employment rights are monitored more informally. For example, a works employee representative explained in an interview that, above all, reliance was placed on 'our networks at union level' to obtain information about specific breaches. Since the global union federations have only limited monitoring resources,[35] these mechanisms assume that employees and local trade unions are effectively using the space created for organising locally.[36] In some cases, international framework agreements at the global level have resulted in the recognition of unions by local management, or the establishment of independent factory committees or works councils.[37] The actual opportunity offered by these international

[33] Dickerson 2001.   [34] Hepple 2005: 75.
[35] Müller, Platzer and Rüb 2006.   [36] Cf Weinz 2006.   [37] Baylos Grau 2006: 82.

framework agreements lies in the effective promotion of freedom of association and organisation of trade unions at a local level. By supporting the creation and activity of important local actors, the agreements create a reflexive mechanism that involves local actors in the implementation of norms and thus enhances the effectiveness of norm enforcement.[38]

One problematic aspect of this is that the vast majority (49 out of 55) companies with international framework agreements[39] are of European origin and are headquartered in a European country.[40] Close cooperation with trade unions on a global level seems to be a practice closely associated with the European social model.[41] Furthermore, although these framework agreements lead to employee involvement in enforcement, that is, involvement of those whose interests are protected by the standard, these instruments are not as a rule associated with a juridified delegation of enforcement. Collective representation partly steps in and may, in some cases, even be considered an adequate functional equivalent to third-party delegation.

Still, in summary, it may be said that mechanisms for the enforcement of transnational social standards remain mostly political in nature, lacking a paralegal character. Compliance pull is largely of a political nature.[42] Societal pressure continues to be one of the key reasons for rule observance.

3.   Private rules between international law and local domestic law

But juridification is not only characterised by regulatory functions. After all, law does not only perform the social functions of regulating and controlling behaviour. Legal systems realise individual and societal interests, and contribute to the construction of identities.[43] Legal forms are capable of creating their own dynamic in this respect: legal legitimacy alone can create, or at least support, authority and effectiveness.[44]

---

[38] For the concept of 'reflexive' law see Kocher 2007: 81–83.
[39] Recent data from December received from the French 'Observatoire sur la Responsabilité Sociale des Entreprises' in March 2007.
[40] Cf Greven 2006: 12.   [41] Blanke and Hoffmann 2006.
[42] Cutler is also sceptical 2003: 72.   [43] Heger, Boyle and Meyer 2005: 180.
[44] Zangl and Zürn 2004: 248; see also Kerwer 2006: 80; Zürn and Koenig-Archibugi 2006: 243.

3.1 International law as a regulatory model: a success story of international law?

Legal legitimacy and the legal communication code are characterised by a rationalised universalist code and other universalist notions.[45] Thus, the legal legitimacy of transnational social standards rests primarily on rules agreed upon elsewhere, especially in international law.

In the area of transnational social standards, actors have developed a common understanding of minimum transnational standards around the ILO core labour norms and regulations on industrial health and safety. According to the pertinent ILO declaration of 1998, 'ILO core labour norms' means the abolition of child and forced labour,[46] non-discrimination[47] and a guarantee of freedom of association and collective bargaining.[48] Minimum standards on working times, wages, health and safety and other working conditions are also often included. Framework agreements and some unilateral codes also mention standards on work-force qualifications. Overall, the ILO core labour standards seem to represent the lowest common denominator for German corporations when it comes to regulating social standards in private instruments.[49] The international framework agreements concluded by global union federations include, without exception, these core labour norms. As a rule, the IFAs explicitly name the relevant ILO conventions; in contrast to unilateral corporate codes of conduct, which often only make implicit reference to the international law of the ILO.[50] The OECD Guidelines for Multinational Enterprises, following a revision in 2000, incorporated the core labour norms as central social standards.[51] The UN Global Compact, which was initiated in 2000 and has since been quite a success with OECD transnational companies, also understands minimum standards to be the ILO core labour standards.

Targeting transnational companies as actors, the ILO set out to improve the dissemination and enforcement of the ILO conventions

---

[45] Heger, Boyle and Meyer 2005: 184, 188; Kocher 2007: 102–20.

[46] V. ILO Conventions No. 29 (on forced labour, 1930), No. 105 (on the abolition of forced labour, 1957), No. 138 (on minimum age, 1973), and No. 182 (on the prohibition of the worst forms of child work, 1999).

[47] V. ILO Conventions No. 100 (on equal pay, 1951), and No. 111 (on non-discrimination at work, 1958).

[48] V. ILO Convention No. 87 (on freedom of association, 1948), No. 98 (on collective bargaining, 1949). More: Engels 2000.

[49] Kocher 2004: 27.

[50] Senghaas-Knobloch 2004; Hepple 2005: 73.   [51] Blanpain 2000.

when it identified its core labour norms.[52] To this extent, corporate standard setting can be viewed as a way to actually enforce international law. Some of our interviewees also pointed out that target setting does not add new substantive standards but merely ensures that standards that are already set are enforced. Thus, private standard setting does not perhaps even claim to establish its own transnational social standards, but furnishes existing standards with enforcement mechanisms.

This indirect effect of the ILO conventions is a success story for international law, albeit a relative success. Their inclusion in corporate codes of conduct and international framework agreements is some kind of privatisation: by translating standards from international law into private standards, companies have taken the application and enforcement of such norms into their own hands; thereby, companies also reserve the right to define and interpret the standards for themselves.

3.2   Translating public into private standards: the example of freedom of association

The difficulty in translating a standard under international law into a civil-law norm can be seen most clearly in the standard about freedom of association.[53]

This standard is central. For one thing, it represents the collective aspects of labour relations that lie at the heart of international labour law and the ILO conventions.[54] For another, the freedom of association has the quality of a procedural provision, entitling unions to represent the interests of individual employees. Since individual employees are not in a position to offer significant opposition to the economic power of their company employers, they can only dress the imbalance of bargaining power by acting collectively through the trade unions. Thus, it is the employee representatives who can contribute to the enforcement of standards in accordance with the logic of rights. The freedom of association and right to collective bargaining thus makes room for actors who are indispensable for procedural and reflexive enforcement.

---

[52] On the dispute about this strategy and its subjects, see Alston 2004 and Langille 2005.
[53] Hepple 1998/1999: 358; Justice 2000.
[54] For more on freedom of association, see Servais 2005: 117.

However, labour associations are, by definition, organisations that advocate for employee interests, when these conflict with the interests of corporate employers.[55] Hence, the employer cannot be relied upon to facilitate unionism. ILO Conventions 87 and 98 therefore create obligations on states with regard to the freedom of association and collective bargaining. It is the domestic legal system which must guarantee freedom of association and such a guarantee presupposes legal and institutional safeguards for union organisations, particularly in conflicts and disputes with employers and private companies.

When social rights are not upheld by the state, there are serious questions about how a private company can guarantee these same rights. Is it possible for a private company to actually promote or even guarantee the freedom of association of such organisations? It is unclear what it means when a corporate code of conduct gives an undertaking that '[t]he freedom of association and protection of the right to organise is also guaranteed in those countries in which freedom of association and the right to organise is not acknowledged as a right'.[56]

Our interviews provide some indication of how companies deal with this problem in interpreting the guarantee of freedom of association. For example, when asked about the implementation of the guarantee of freedom of association in China, one company representative stated:

> We say there needn't be a union at the location, and if having a union is prohibited by law, then our standard is not met. It becomes difficult the moment the employees approach us and say, 'We want a union'. Luckily, there isn't anything like that right now, thank goodness.

The same speaker also remarked:

> The important thing for us, and this is also what we demand as a standard, is that employees in one way or another get the opportunity to represent their interests vis-à-vis company management. And, in some respects, these can be very simple things; it can be the management of complaints. I have a box and I can stick a letter in it, or I'm the responsible person from among my ranks who can then, let's say, can appear before management.

Another company representative emphasised that it is not possible for a corporation to assume a mediating role on behalf of its union partner

---

[55] Servais 2005: 117.
[56] Quoted from Declaration on Social Rights and Industrial Relationships at LEONI para 1.2).

vis-à-vis its suppliers, it was the union's role to represent employee interests. From the company's perspective, where such disputes arise, an
attempt can be made to 'break down this very complex difficult question
to the company level'. 'An open communication process' that allows
grievances to be aired and within which complaints could be appropriately
dealt with was considered to be 'a very beneficial process'. Thus, internal,
company-operated complaints mechanisms were identified with the promotion of freedom of association.

There are other problematic aspects associated with the guarantee of
freedom of association by corporate entities. In response to these issues,
some companies have installed factory committees supposed to represent employees, or have demanded this of their suppliers. These mechanisms represent potential competition to union representation and have,
at times, been deliberately established by companies as competition to
trade unions.[57] Incidentally, ILO Convention No. 135 for the protection
of in-company union representatives, which aims to prevent such competition and guarantee the independence of in-company employee
representative bodies, is not, as a rule, part of corporate codes of conduct.

At any rate, it is becoming clear that the translation of international legal
standards into corporate standards requires detailed translation work in
each case. The text of transnational codes of conduct can therefore only
provide limited guidance when determining the specific meaning of
'freedom of association and collective bargaining' in the corporate context.

3.3   Reservations in favour of national law and application in practice

A further opening for the interpretive power to define and shape the
standard in implementation is the reservation in favour of national law. In
codes of conduct and international framework agreements, there is always
an assurance that national standards will be met.[58] Such provisions frequently include a reservation in respect of local/national law, 'national
regulation' or 'local practice'. In a typical formulation, 'The work hours
correspond at least to the respective national legal requirements or to the
minimum standards of the respective economic sectors.'[59]

---

[57] Jakobsen 2006.   [58] Herberg 2002: 45.
[59] Quoted from the Declaration on Social Rights and Industrial Relationships at
Volkswagen of 6 June 2002, § 1.6 (German version published in 'Arbeit und Recht'
2002, 343).

Only a handful of private standards contain favourability clauses.[60] One example of a genuine minimum standard with a favourability clause is that 'employees must not be required, except in extraordinary circumstances, to work more than 60 hours per week including overtime or the local legal requirement, whichever is less'.[61]

Often the wording of the corporate code does not provide a clear answer to the question of whether the corporate standard will take precedence over local law and local practice at the place of production, or if, instead national law will determine the interpretation of the standards. This question has important practical relevance as transnational corporate standards are sometimes (but by no means always) set higher than the labour laws of countries in the South.

The difficulty in reconciling potential contradictions between self-imposed obligations and national laws was mentioned in several of our interviews. The exchanges revealed that, in practice, there is a pragmatic interplay between the governing law at the production site and the standards set by transnational companies. For example, one corporate code of conduct appeared to lay down a maximum 48-hour working week, which could be extended to 60 hours provided overtime was paid. National labour law, however, permitted a 60-hour working week. A representative from the German company interpreted the code of conduct as calling for a gradual reduction of working hours to a 60-hour week. This kind of approach has frequently been legitimised on the basis that it demonstrates 'respect' for local customs, which could also be termed a 'cultural objection'. As stated by one corporate representative on the question of the transfer of social standards:

> [F]irst, what we don't want, and, what we can't do anyway: take abroad or export, just like that, certain cultural things that have developed naturally in Germany.

Another corporate representative, who also publicly declared adherence to universal ILO standards, including non-discrimination, stated:

> '[O]n culture – we always go at it with our German way of thinking. A Pakistani will either hire only men or only women. He'll never mix them because he's a Muslim. Like hell he will. So either he employs only men or he employs only women ... and then we have classic discrimination. How are we going to deal with this? If he employs men and women together, he has a much bigger problem.

---

[60] Hepple 2005: 73.
[61] Quoted from Standards of Engagement, adidas-Salomon, of January 2001.

The reverse occurs where transnational advocacy networks campaign against poor implementation of national law (as in the 'Clean Clothes' case discussed in the introduction). In these cases, networks set the agenda and transnational corporations allow themselves to be drawn into the agenda. As a result, companies champion compliance with national legislation on unfair dismissal or the guarantee of time off during menstruation.

In summary, the wording of codes of conduct and international framework agreements provides only an abstract hint on how they will be applied specifically. In the application of corporate standards, a more relative, less universal, approach emerges.

4.   Reflexive transnational law or window-dressing?

4.1   Reflexive transnational law?

A mark of legal provisions is their generality. They do not generally contain concrete technical specifications but general and specific rules. As a result, every regulatory system is made up of a cascade of legal principles, rules and directives. The way in which they relate to one another and to other more 'universal' principles of law constitutes a characteristic feature of the legal code.[62]

Vaguely worded corporate standards cannot be disqualified from the category of 'legal standards' simply because they are unclear.[63] This vagueness does mean, though, that knowledge of the applicable general principles still says little about their application in a specific conflict. To this extent, monitoring and implementation are crucial to the proper functioning of the normative system.[64] The way a rule is applied and enforced is vital when determining the quality of the normative system. Unilateral codes of conduct and international framework agreements draw their legitimacy from universal principles and national law and, with their implementation, this legitimacy is translated into authority.

As stated above, the predominant implementation and monitoring systems for private social standards are controlled by companies. It could, of course, be said that this is a reflexive mechanism which involves the addressee of the norm in norm implementation. Reflexive law displays many advantages over traditionally hierarchical forms

---

[62] Kocher 2007: 28–38; Simma and Zöckler 1996; Heger Boyle and Meyer 2005: 184.
[63] McCrudden 1999: 199; Winter 2005: 33.   [64] See Herberg 2005: 91.

of control.[65] However, in the case of transnational social standards, companies are not only the addressees of the norm, but also the norm setters. Such a reflexive mechanism that only involves the parties setting and addressed by the norm and not those parties protected by the standard (employees and their representatives), lacks legitimacy and cannot guarantee legal authority. Legitimacy drawn from international and national law is not complemented by application and enforcement processes that help to translate legitimacy into authority. The enforcing and legitimising elements of law are in disequilibrium.[66]

4.2 Playing with the legal form?

If we embrace the general idea that paralegal structures could emerge even without state and judicial recognition, it is possible to recognise that a process of juridification is taking place here.[67] Corporations can actively contribute to the emergence of transnational social standards by *playing* at the role of legal actors.[68]

The ritualised staging of law and legal systems in private standard setting[69] is a dangerous game. It may help establish a paralegal system but pretending to the existence of law exploits the communicative and legitimising functions of law in a dangerous way.[70] This pretence of law is not generally translated into authority, which gives rise to new regulatory problems and challenges such as transparency in consumer markets as problems of fair competition arise where the promises the legal form entails cannot ultimately be kept.

On the other hand, private standard setting concerns the regulatory capability and authority of legal actors in the countries of the South. With the de-monopolisation and privatisation of the legal form, a dual reference emerges for national actors in the South. With the development of transnational standards, corporations become actors in the field of development policy. By invoking the legitimacy of international and local national law, corporate standards compete with national legal

---

[65] Kocher 2007: 81–83.
[66] Within the meaning of Zangl and Zürn 2004: 260.
[67] Unlike McCrudden 1999: 199. For the recognition as 'soft law' in accordance with the letter of the law see e.g. Kocher 2002; Kocher 2005.
[68] Cochoy 2007.   [69] Heger, Boyle and Meyer 2005: 198.   [70] Cutler 2003: 102.

systems without guaranteeing the appropriate authority. This produces a risk of erosion. Accordingly, Hepple in no way expects a 'race to the top', but, fears instead 'rather a different kind of "race to the bottom"'.[71] Independent monitoring and effective national and international complaint mechanisms are necessary measures in the prevention of such a race.[72] Local actors, especially employees and their representatives must be empowered to act in this area.[73] A participatory approach to implementation and monitoring, and the involvement of legitimate actors must be fostered. This realisation draws attention back to international framework agreements and the standard of freedom of association, constituting the most important procedural element in a more effective strategy. It can serve as a vehicle for the provision of greater procedural justice, legitimacy – and authority.

References

Abbott, K. W., R. O. Keohane, A. Moravcsik, A.-M. Slaughter and D. Snidal 2000, 'The Concept of Legalization', *International Organization*, vol. **54**, no. 3, 401–19.

Alston, P. 2004, 'Core Labour Standards and the Transformation of the International Labour Rights Regime', *European Journal of International Law*, vol. **15**.

Bassen, A., S. Jastram and K. Meyer 2005, 'Corporate Social Responsibility. Eine Begriffserläuterung', *Zeitschrift für Wirtschafts- und Unternehmensethik*, vol. **6**, 231–36.

Baylos Grau, A. 2004, 'Los acuerdos marco de empresas globales: una nueva manifestación de la dimensión transnacional de la autonomía colectiva', *Revista de Derecho Social*, no. **28**.

Baylos Grau, A. 2006, 'La responsabilidad legal de las empresas transnacionales', *RDS-L (Revista de Derecho Social – Latinoamérica)*, 69–99.

Berger, K. P., H. Dubberstein, S. Lehmann and V. Petzold 2002, 'Anwendung Transnationalen Rechts in der internationalen Vertrags- und Schiedspraxis', *Zeitschrift für Vergleichende Rechtswissenschaft*, vol. **101**, 12–37.

Blanke, T. and J. Hoffmann 2006, 'Gibt es ein Europäisches Sozialmodell? Voraussetzungen, Schwierigkeiten und Perspektiven einer europäischen Sozialpolitik', *Kritische Justiz*, 134–50.

Blanpain, R. 2000, 'Review of the OECD-Guidelines for Multinational Enterprises', *Bulletin of Comparative Labour Relations*, vol. **37**, 29–66.

Börzel, T. A. 1998, 'Organizing Babylon – on the Different Conceptions of Policy Networks', *Public Administration*, vol. **76**, 253–73.

---

[71] Hepple, 1998/99: 360.   [72] Hepple 2005: 272–73.   [73] Goolsby 2001.

Brandl, S. and B. Stelzl 2005, 'Internationale Arbeitsbeziehungen – Globalisierung als Chance für die deutschen Gewerkschaften?', *WSI-Mitteilungen*, 82–89.

Brütsch, C. 2002, 'Verrechtlichung der Weltpolitik oder Politisierung des Rechts?', *Zeitschrift für Rechtssoziologie*, vol. **23**, 165–83.

Buckel, S. 2003, 'Empire oder Rechtspluralismus? Recht im Globalisierungsdiskurs', *Kritische Justiz*, 177–91.

Callies, G.-P. 2004, 'Transnationales Handelsvertragsrecht: Private Ordnung und staatlicher Rahmen', in B. Zangl and M. Zürn (eds), *Verrechtlichung – Baustein für Global Governance?*, Dietz-Verlag, Bonn, 160.

Cochoy, F. 2007, 'La responsabilité sociale de l'entreprise comme "représentation" de l'économie et du droit', *Droit et Société*, vol. **65**, 91–101.

Colucci, M. 2000, 'Implementation and Monitoring of Codes of Conduct. How to Make Codes of Conduct Effective?', *Bulletin of Comparative Labour Relations*, vol. **37**, 277–89.

Commission of the European Communities 2001, *Green Paper – Promoting a European Framework for Corporate Social Responsibility*, COM(2001) 366 final.

Commission of the European Communities 2006, *Communication Implementing the Partnership for Growth and Jobs: Making Europe a Pole of Excellence on Corporate Social Responsibility (European Alliance)*, COM(2006) 136 final.

Compa, L. and T. Hinchliffe-Darricarrère 1995, 'Enforcing International Labor Rights through Corporate Codes of Conduct', *Columbia Journal of Transnational Law*, vol. **33**, 663–89.

Cutler, C. A. 2003, *Private Power and Global Authority: Transnational Merchant Law and the Global Political Economy*, Cambridge University Press.

Dickerson, C. M. 2001, 'Transnational Codes of Conduct Through Dialogue: Leveling the Playing Field for Developing-Country Workers', *Florida Law Review*, vol. **53**, 611.

Engels, C. 2000, 'Codes of Conduct. Freedom of Association and the Right to Bargain Collectively', *Bulletin of Comparative Labour Relations*, vol. **37**, 219.

Fichter, M. and J. Sydow 2002, 'Using Networks Towards Global Labor Standards? Organizing Social Responsibility in Global Production Chains', *Industrielle Beziehungen*, vol. **9**, 357–80.

Goolsby, J. H. 2001, 'Is the Garment Industry Trying to Pull the Wool Over Your Eyes? The Need for Open Communication to Promote Labor Rights in China', *Law & Inequality: Journal of Theory and Practice*, vol. **19**, 193–227.

Greven, T. 2006, 'Auf dem Prüfstand: Gewerkschaftsstrategien zur Regulierung globaler Konkurrenz', *WSI-Mitteilungen*, 10–15.

Großmann, H., M. Busse, D. Fuchs and G. Koopmann 2002, *Sozialstandards in der Welthandelsordnung*, Nomos, Baden-Baden.

Hallström, K. T. 2006, 'ISO Enters the Field of Social Responsibility (SR)', in G. F. Schuppert (ed.), *Global Governance and the Role of Non-State Actors*, Nomos, Baden-Baden, 117–56.

Heger, Boyle, E. J. W. and Meyer 2005, 'Das moderne Recht als säkularisiertes globales Modell: Konsequenzen für die Rechtssoziologie' in J. W. Meyer (ed.), *Weltkultur. Wie die westlichen Prinzipien die Welt durchdringen*, Suhrkamp, Frankfurt am Main, 179–211.

Hepple, B. 1998/1999, 'A Race to the Top? International Investment Guidelines and Corporate Codes of Conduct', *Comparative Labor Law & Policy Journal*, vol. **20**, 347–63.

Hepple, B. 2005, *Labour Laws and Global Trade*, Oxford and Portland, OR, Hart.

Herberg, M. 2001, 'Codes of Conduct und kommunikative Vernunft. Rechtssoziologische Überlegungen zu den umweltbezogenen Selbstverpflichtungen transnationaler Chemiekonzerne', *Zeitschrift für Rechtssoziologie*, vol. **22**, 25–52.

Herberg, M. 2005, 'Re-Embedding the Disembedded. Die Umweltstandards multinationaler Konzerne in der globalen Steuerungsarchitektur', *Soziale Welt*, vol. **56**, 399–416.

Jakobsen, K. 2006, 'Netzwerke und multinationale Konzerne in Brasilien', WSI-Mitteilungen, 52–55. Streitigkeiten über Fabrikkomitees?

Justice, D. W. 2000, *The New Codes of Conduct and the Social Partners*, International Confederation of Free Trade Unions, available at www.cleanclothes.org/codes/00–01-justice.htm.

Keck, M. and K. Sikkink 1998, *Activists Beyond Borders: Advocacy Networks in International Politics*, Cornell University Press, Ithaca, NY.

Kerwer, D. 2006, 'Governing Financial Markets by International Standards' in M. Koenig-Archibugi & M. Zürn (eds), *New Modes of Governance in the Global System. Exploring Publicness, Delegation and Inclusiveness*, Palgrave Macmillan, New York, 77–100.

Kocher, E. 2002, 'Private Standards between Soft Law and Hard Law – The German Case', *The International Journal of Comparative Labour Law and Industrial Relations*, vol. **18**, no. 3, 265–80.

Kocher, E. 2004, 'Selbstverpflichtungen von Unternehmen zur sozialen Verantwortung. Erfahrungen mit sozialen Verhaltenskodizes in der transnationalen Produktion', *Recht der Arbeit*, 27–31.

Kocher, E. 2005, 'Unternehmerische Selbstverpflichtungen im Wettbewerb', *Gewerblicher Rechtsschutz und Urheberrecht*, 647–52.

Kocher, E. 2006, § 4, Rn 97 in O. E. Kempen and U. Zachert (eds), *Tarifvertragsgesetz. Kommentar für die Praxis*, 4th edn., Bund-Verlag, Köln.

Kocher, E. 2007, *Funktionen der Rechtsprechung*, Mohr, Tübingen.

Köhnen, H. 2002, *Haben Menschenrechtsverletzungen ein System? Wal-Mart's Verhaltenskodex und die Realität bei Zulieferern in ausgewählten Ländern*, Hans-Böckler-Stiftung, Düsseldorf.

Köpke, R. and W. Röhr 2003, *Codes of Conduct. Verhaltensnormen für Unternehmen und ihre Überwachung*, PapyRossa, Hamburg.

Körner-Dammann, M. 1991, *Bedeutung und faktische Wirkung von ILO-Standards – dargestellt am Beispiel Südafrika*, Nomos, Baden-Baden.

Langille, B. A. 2005, 'Core Labour Rights – The True Story', *European Journal of International Law*, vol. **16**, 409–37.

Liemt, G. v. 2000, 'Codes of Conduct and International Subcontracting: A "Private" Road Towards Ensuring Minimum Labour Standards in Export Industries', *Bulletin of Comparative Labour Relations*, vol. **37**, 177.

McCrudden, C. 1999, 'Human Rights Codes for Transnational Corporations: What Can the Sullivan and MacBride Principles Tell Us?', *Oxford Journal of Legal Studies*, vol. **19**, 167–201.

Müller, T., H.-W. Platzer and S. Rüb 2006, 'Weltbetriebsräte und globale Netzwerke – Instrumente internationaler Solidarität?', *WSI-Mitteilungen*, 5–9.

O'Rourke, D. 2003, 'Outsourcing Regulation: Analysing Nongovernmental Systems of Labor Standards and Monitoring', *The Policy Studies Journal*, vol. **31**, 1.

Rodríguez-Garavito, C. A. 2005, 'Nike's Law: The Anti-sweatshop Movement, Transnational Corporations, and the Struggle over International Labor Rights in the Americas', in B. de Sousa Santos and C. A. Rodríguez-Garavito (eds), *Law and Globalization from below. Towards a Cosmopolitan Legality*, Cambridge University Press, 64.

Scherrer, C., T. Greven and V. Frank 1998, *Sozialklauseln. Arbeiterrechte im Welthandel*, Münster.

Schutter, O. de 2004, 'The Accountability of Multinationals for Human Rights Violations in European Law', *Center for Human Rights and Global Justice Working* Paper, no. 01/04, New York University, New York.

Seifert, A. 2006, 'Die Schaffung transnationaler Arbeitnehmervertretungen in weltweit tätigen Unternehmen', *Zeitschrift für ausländisches und internationales Arbeits- und Sozialrecht*, 205–24.

Senghaas-Knobloch, E. 2004, 'Zwischen Überzeugen und Erzwingen – Nachhaltiger Druck für Geltung und Wirksamkeit internationaler Arbeits- und Sozialstandards', in B. Zangl and M. Zürn (eds), *Verrechtlichung – Baustein für Global Governance?*, Dietz-Verlag, Bonn, 140.

Servais, J.-M. 2005, *International Labour Law*, Kluwer Law International, Den Haag.

Simma, B. and M. Zöckler 1996, 'Law-Making by Universal Organizations' in B. Baron von Maydell and A. Nußberger (eds), *Social Protection by Way of International Law. Appraisal, Deficits and Further Development*, Duncker and Humblot, Berlin, 69–86.

Sobczak, A. 2004, 'La responsabilité sociale de l'entreprise, menace ou opportunité pour le droit du travail?', *Relations Industrielles – Industrial Relations*, vol. **59**, 26–51.

Stein, U. 1995, *Lex mercatoria, Realität und Theorie*, Vittorio Klostermann, Frankfurt am Main.

Tapiola, K. 2000, 'The ILO Declaration on Fundamental Principles and Rights at Work and its Follow-up', *Bulletin of Comparative Labour Relations*, vol. 37, 9–16.

Weinz, W. 2006, '*Globale Rahmenvereinbarungen zwischen Gewerkschaften und Konzernen*', in J. Martens (ed.), Corporate Accountability – Zwischenbilanz und Zukunftsperspektiven.

Winter, G. 2005, 'Die Umweltverantwortung multinationaler Unternehmen' in G. Winter (ed.), *Die Umweltverantwortung multinationaler Unternehmen*, Nomos, Baden-Baden.

Zangl, B. and M. Zürn 2004, 'Make Law, Not War: Internationale und transnationale Verrechtlichung als Baustein für Global Governance', in B. Zangl and M. Zürn (eds), *Verrechtlichung – Baustein für Global Governance?*, Dietz-Verlag, Bonn, 12–45.

Zangl, B. and M. Zürn 2004, 'Verrechtlichung jenseits des Staates – Zwischen Hegemonie und Globalisierung', in B. Zangl and M. Zürn (eds), *Verrechtlichung – Baustein für Global Governance?*, Dietz-Verlag, Bonn, 239.

Zimmer, R. 2006, 'Eine offene Rechnung', *Mitbestimmung*, 30–33.

Zürn, M. and M. Koenig-Archibugi 2006, 'Conclusion II: Modes and Dynamics of Global Governance', in M. Koenig-Archibugi and M. Zürn (eds), *New Modes of Governance in the Global System. Exploring Publicness, Delegation and Inclusiveness*, Palgrave Macmillan, New York, 236–54.

16

International corporate social responsibility standards: imposing or imitating business responsibility in Lithuania?

EGLE SVILPAITE*

1. Introduction

Corporate social responsibility (CSR) has become a mantra for countless businesses, societies and national governments. As states and international organisations have begun to perceive their limits and their relative lack of power in dealing with globalising businesses, cultures and societies, so they have heralded voluntary self-regulation as a means of bringing more flexibility and competency into global governance. Moreover, as CSR practices are increasingly standardised at the international and national levels, regulation may also be transformed, with voluntary standards embodying a model of shared global governance.

For people in developing countries and countries in transition, the growth of international CSR standards could have particular advantages. It has often been argued that voluntary business and CSR standards could produce a functioning measure when governments fail. So, in places like Africa or Eastern Europe, international business may be more likely to produce advanced corporate cultures and respect for human rights than weak administrations. Further, for countries undergoing complex political, economic and social changes, the notion of CSR is a challenge to traditional ways of regulation.

Its popularity and potential notwithstanding, there are considerable challenges in using CSR as a governance tool. Where CSR is proposed as a means of improving governance, there is a threshold question of what function CSR will serve in existing relations between business, state and society. Can states with weak administrative capacities effectively use

* Dr. iur. (Mykolas Romeris University, Lithuania); LLM (European Law, University of Lund, Sweden); Dipl. iur. (Vilnius University).

CSR to advance respect for human rights and the rule of law? Can CSR standards that have been made by and for multinational corporations really substitute or complement state regulation within national borders or internationally? If not, is CSR just a *placebo*?

This chapter considers these issues in the context of Lithuania's post-Cold War transformation. Lithuania began its political, economic and social transformation almost two decades ago with the proclamation of independence from the Soviet Union and, though it became a growing European market, its interest in Western-style CSR policies is quite new. After briefly discussing the development and the general features of CSR in section 2, we will consider the emergence of CSR policy and practices in Lithuania in section 3, particularly the reasons for the relatively late arrival and low profile of CSR standards in Lithuania. Finally, in section 4 we examine the reliability of CSR policies, drawing on the Lithuanian examples, before drawing conclusions in section 5.

2. The origins of CSR and its elasticity as a concept

The development of the concept of 'responsible business' is often associated with the need to restrain the growing powers of business and owes much of its history to the development of business culture in the United States.[1] Corporate scandals involving corruption, sweatshops and gross social and environmental negligence triggered civil society movements that pushed corporations to adopt ethical business practices.[2] These movements were fundamentally interested in turning the attention of (big) business to its social and environmental impacts, as well as with increasing the voluntary contribution of business to social welfare beyond maximisation of the profits and the requirements of national laws.[3]

At the same time, the idea of CSR duly served deliberations over the reform of costly, inefficient and rigid regulatory strategies of the states, unable to promptly and expertly follow the speedy development of business practices in the context of globalisation.[4] This problem was particularly pertinent in European social welfare states where many

---

[1] Matten and Moon, 'Pan-European Approach', 336–38; McInerney, 'Regulation Before Responsibility', 176–77; Vogel, *The Market for Virtue;* Zerk, *Multinationals*, 15, 244–45.
[2] Corporate Watch Report, *What's Wrong*, 6–8; Haufler, *A Public Role*, 9; Zerk, *Multinationals*, 23.
[3] Bantekas, 'Responsibility in International Law', 311; Yakovleva, *Responsibility in the Mining Industries*, 9.
[4] McInerney, 'Regulation Before Responsibility', 178–79, 182–83.

social and environmental issues, which were matters for self-regulation in the USA, constituted an integral part of state legal regulatory regimes.[5] CSR gave new impetus in the search for more flexible and less burdensome regulation and business expertise and so was often invoked as a justification for voluntary self-regulation.[6]

The growth in popularity of self-imposed corporate obligations coincided with globalisation and the resultant growth in strength of multinational corporations. The cross-border activities of multinationals and their increasing power presented a challenge to states' capacities to control business activities and to enforce international human rights obligations.[7] Concerns with businesses transcending national borders were taken up by international and regional organisations, such as the United Nations,[8] ILO,[9] OECD[10] and EU,[11] and reflected in nongovernmental initiatives, such as the Global Reporting Initiative, the AccountAbility standards or the forthcoming ISO 26000 standard, which will provide 'guidelines for social responsibility' within the ISO framework.[12] Despite these efforts, an effective, comprehensive regulatory regime for transnational corporate responsibility never came into being. After years of discussion, the 'overall agenda for CSR' had become extremely complex and more 'confused and fragmented'.[13]

---

[5] Matten and Moon, 'Pan-European Approach', 338–40.

[6] McInerney, 'Regulation Before Responsibility', 177–80.

[7] Jenkins, 'Corporate Codes of Conduct', 1–6; McInerney, 'Regulation Before Responsibility', 176–82; Vogel, *The Market for Virtue*, 8–10; Zerk, *Multinationals*, 37.

[8] The failure of the process for drafting a comprehensive Code of Conduct on Transnational Corporations was followed by the general dismissal of an ambitious set of norms on the responsibilities of transnational corporations and other business enterprises with regard to human rights adopted by Sub-Commission on the Promotion and Protection of Human Rights in 2003 (see more extensively e.g. Utting 'Rethinking Business Regulation', 16). The UN Secretary General successfully proposed ten liberal but ambitious principles for the corporate agenda as part of the Global Compact Initiative.

[9] For instance, the 1998 ILO Declaration on Fundamental Principles and Rights at Work and 1977 Tripartite Declaration of Principles Concerning Multinational Enterprises and Social Policy.

[10] Arguably the OECD's most influential instrument is the Guidelines for Multinational Enterprises.

[11] Commission Green Paper 2001; Communication from the Commission 2002; Communication from the Commission 2006. See also European Parliament resolution of 13 March 2007.

[12] See the ISO's preparatory work on its social responsibility standard, available at http://isotc.iso.org/livelink/livelink/fetch/2000/2122/830949/3934883/3935096/home.html?nodeid=4451259&vernum=0 (consulted 27 September 2007). See Bantekas, 'Responsibility in International Law', 317–23.

[13] Roome, 'Pan-European Approach', 320.

The stakeholders and interests included in corporate responsibility were broadening beyond the social issues with every new wave of concerns: from working conditions, fighting corruption and environmental impact to lifelong learning and universal human rights.[14] As a result, there is still no generally accepted definition, the phrase meaning 'different things to different people'.[15]

International efforts at standardisation have also created differences in understanding about the scope and substance of CSR.[16] For example, the European Union has limited CSR to the integration of social and environmental concerns into business operations, whereas the Global Compact broadens the scope of responsible business activities to human rights.[17] The ISO proposes an even more complex structure in its draft ISO 26000 standard, at the core of which is ethical behaviour and compliance with international and national laws.[18] CSR policies are also developing along cultural, social and economic lines, so much so that it may now be necessary to speak about country-specific CSR policies and practices.[19]

---

[14] Bantekas, 'Responsibility in International Law', 327–37; Roome, 'Pan-European Approach', 320–22; Vogel, *The Market for Virtue*; Utting, 'Rethinking Business Regulation', 2–4.

[15] Crowther and Rayman-Bacchus, 'Introduction', 2; Zerk, *Multinationals*, 30–31; Crane and Matten, 'Corporate Social Responsibility', xix–xxi.

[16] For a comparative study, see MacLeod, 'Reconciling Regulatory Approaches'. A number of institutions aiming to develop comprehensive CSR regimes are beginning to co-operate. For example, the ISO and the Global Compact Office have agreed to collaborate extensively on the development, promotion and support of the new ISO International Standard on Social Responsibility. The new standard will be consistent with the Global Compact's ten principles, among other instruments, www.iso.org/iso/en/commcentre/ pressreleases/2006/Ref1010.html (consulted 22 November 2006). The UN Global Compact Office and the OECD Secretariat have also prepared a document entitled the 'UN Global Compact and the OECD Guidelines for Multinational Enterprises: Complementarities and Distinctive Contributions', which reveals the synergies between the OECD's Guidelines and Global Compact, available at www.oecd.org/dataoecd/23/2/ 34873731.pdf (consulted 22 November 2006). See also Zerk, *Multinationals*, 29–31.

[17] www.globalcompact.com/AboutTheGC/TheTenPrinciples/index.html (consulted 27 September 2007). Commission Green Paper, 'Promoting a European Framework'; Commission Communication, 'Implementing the Partnership for Growth'.

[18] See TG 4 – Draft Text on SR Definition, ISO/TMB/WG SR TG4 N0054, 16 February 2007, available at http://isotc.iso.org/livelink/livelink?func=ll&objId=4590941&objAction= browse&sort=name (consulted 27 September 2007). See also the press release, available at www.iso.org/iso/en/commcentre/pressreleases/2006/Ref1010.html (consulted 22 November 2006), 7.

[19] Roome, 'Pan-European Approach', 322–30.

Unifying these divergent interpretations of CSR is the expectation that a company or business organisation should voluntarily go *beyond* what is required by law and make extra efforts and contributions towards the welfare of a particular society and environmental sustainability.

That said, there is still considerable uncertainty over the content of the term 'CSR': What do we mean exactly when we talk about 'socially responsible organisations'? How much and what should a company undertake before it can claim the 'socially responsible' label? And can society entrust corporations to protect human rights when CSR means so many different things and is fundamentally voluntary, based as it is on business goodwill? As emerges in the following discussion of the Lithuanian experience, social responsibility amongst business can only develop into mechanisms having a real effect on business responsibility when state and society are capable of holding business responsible for their public promises within the ambiguous CSR framework.

3.   The origins of CSR standards and business culture in Lithuania

3.1   Building the state, economy and society: explaining the late arrival of CSR standards in Lithuania

The attention paid to corporate social responsibility in Lithuania is a fairly recent phenomenon. For a variety of economic, political and social reasons, the instruments and policies of western CSR emerged at a later stage in the country's development and thus played a minor role in the government's initial efforts to build a state which efficiently enforces human rights and allows for a functioning rule of law.

3.1.1   State building

The restoration of independence at the beginning of the 1990s transformed Lithuania's political, economic and social systems. Socialist conceptions were replaced by free market ideologies, which aimed to minimise the state's role in regulating social affairs. The ideological transformation had numerous practical effects. Economically liberal governments reintroduced private ownership and began dismantling the complex social security system, in which the state or its wholly owned companies were supposed to provide public infrastructure, goods and services, from lifetime employment and pensions, to free medical services, free education and recreational facilities.

The transition to the market economy was rapid and rocky. As changes took place quickly, many Lithuanians did not have time to adjust to the new conditions, nor could government or society develop effective supplementary governance structures. Privatisations were effected by inexperienced and sometimes ignorant public officials in situations of poor transparency, lack of competency and information. Abuses of power were frequent. Desperate for foreign investment, the state was generous with foreign companies, asking little in exchange for important concessions, such as exclusive rights, tax exemptions and the conferral of special legal status, which sometimes approach the level of constitutional norms.[20]

Moreover, few early Lithuanian governments were equipped to run a country in a free market economy and thus were ill-prepared to (re)build the Lithuanian state. The government opted for meticulous regulation of many aspects of commercial life, including production and labour standards. This quickly produced a web of confusing, often contradictory and out-of-date regulations. Weaknesses in judicial and administrative organs and rapidly changing regulations meant that the rule of law was also slow to develop. State officials were rarely held to account for poorly considered and badly implemented laws, abuses of power, corruption or incompetence. Transparency, co-operation with business, public consultation over draft laws and regulations were not priorities for lawmakers. This simply fed widespread distrust and antagonism towards regulatory authorities from ordinary Lithuanians and the business community.

3.1.2   Developing a business culture

Lithuanians also faced the challenge of rebuilding their business culture using only their achievements and (more frequently) mistakes as a guide. Increasing interest in CSR in Western Europe at the time of independence had no parallel in Lithuania. To the contrary, Lithuanian business

---

[20] Perhaps the most striking example is the 1999 FDI agreement in favour of Williams International regarding the privatisation of the AB Mažeikių nafta oil refinery. The government not only granted different priority rights and guarantees, fixed the transportation tariffs, but also changed national laws and assumed numerous and disproportionate obligations, including an obligation not to make decisions that might aggravate the business environment for the next ten years. See 'Mažeikių nafta spaudžia Vyriausybę', Verslo žinios 2001, no. 217, 3 December, 6; 'Pritarta išvadoms dėl Mažeikių naftos', 16 June 2004, Verslo žinios, no. 116, 5.

people and their foreign consultants expounded a particularly strict version of neo-liberal economics, in which total deregulation was promoted as the best method for achieving social goods. Many self-made business people abandoned socially oriented policies and acquired government assets for personal use or resale. The predominant and almost exclusive concern with fast profits left no room for concerns about society and environment. Business ethics, transparency, even law-abiding behaviour, did not figure.[21]

During this time, Lithuania also experienced an increase in abusive or exploitative employment practices. Employees in the new economy lacked the information or experience necessary to defend their rights and, for historical reasons, did not trust trade unions to represent them.[22] Even now, 17 years after independence, unions have not become popular enough to be entrusted with the building of the social partnership between employers and employees.[23] This extreme distrust is even more severe in relation to the government and legal system as demonstrated by the 2007 spring Eurobarometer survey, which found that Lithuanians distrust all public institutions, where 79 per cent distrust the Parliament and 67 per cent the Government.[24]

Foreign investors did not rush to fill the governance gaps. Though often portrayed as bringing higher corporate standards to former Soviet countries with weak administrative capacities, in Lithuania they seemed equally disinterested in pursuing voluntary social and environmental practices or taking significant steps to promote the ideas of corporate social responsibility espoused by their parent companies in other parts of Europe and the United States.[25,26] In fact, many foreign companies came to Lithuania to benefit from cheap but skilful labour and to participate in a new market with less demanding social, ethical and environmental standards.[27] Foreign companies considered the creation

---

[21] Vasiljevas and Pučėtaitė, 'Foreign Corporation and Privatization', 198–99.

[22] Vasiljeviene and Vasiljevas, 'Lithuania – The Roadmap', 187; Pušinaitė et al., 'Darbo vietos etika', 180–81.

[23] According to different surveys, only between 10 and 15 per cent of employees belong to trade unions.

[24] Standard Eurobarometer 67, Lithuania, Spring 2007 (in Lithuanian). Available at: http://ec.europa.eu/public_opinion/archives/eb/eb67/eb67_lt_nat.pdf (consulted 30 September 2007).

[25] This tendency has been also observed in other former socialist bloc countries such as Hungary; see Fekete, 'Hungary', 145.

[26] UNDP, *Corporate Social Responsibility in Lithuania*, 39.

[27] Pučėtaitė and Vasiljevas, 'Foreign Corporation and Privatization', 337.

of new jobs and transferral of Western business know-how and technologies as their best possible contribution to Lithuania's welfare.

On the other hand, Lithuania to a certain extent represented a relatively 'neutral' country for the western culture of CSR practices. There were no severe, systematic violations of fundamental human rights in business practices in Lithuania (involving child labour or killings). Therefore, it did not attract considerable attention from global ethical consumer movements or governments in the Western countries where the production of our factories was sold.

3.1.3   On the way towards civil society

However, the greatest barrier to CSR in Lithuania, as in many other former Soviet bloc countries, was the absence of so-called 'social capital' and an active civil society.[28]

At the time of greatest change, Lithuanians were struggling to assimilate political and economic developments. Meanwhile, there was no tradition of societal critical thinking and organised pressure on the government and business to keep decision makers in check. People were brainwashed by free market prophets that profit is the only aim of the business in a free market economy as there cannot be such a thing as 'business with a human face'. Companies profited, using a cheap labour force, widespread 'matter-of-course' violations of employees' rights (such as illegal employment practices, unpaid overtime, forced unpaid vacations, humiliation, widespread illegal payments of undeclared salaries, etc.), or engaging in unfair commercial practices. The notion of socially responsible business was not known to the overall majority of Lithuanians.[29] The market economy started to function in Lithuania plainly at the cost of 'social responsibility'.

Many of the above-stated factors impeding the development of the CSR could have been improved had there been sufficient knowledge about the CSR and especially its positive practices. Lack of information and inadequate emphasis on changing business patterns in the West were also very important indicators for missing CSR discourse in Lithuania.[30] Apathetic and ignorant media contributed to such an informational vacuum.

---

[28] UNDP et al., *CSR Practices in the New EU Member States*, 21.

[29] Vasiljeviene and Vasiljev, 'Lithuania – The Roadmap', 186–87; Pušinaitė et al., 'Darbo vietos etika', 180–81.

[30] Ekonominės konsultacijos ir tyrimai, *Socialinės atsakomybės tendencijos*; Davulis, 'CSR Practices'.

3.2   The development of responsible business: what drove CSR in Lithuania

3.2.1   Legal and political environment

After the period of failures and recession, economic development in Lithuania gained speed. In recent years Lithuania has established itself among the world leaders in GDP growth and enjoys relatively high global ratings in economic freedom, global competitiveness and other indices, though economic growth also increased energy consumption and pollution.[31] Unfortunately, with the recent financial crisis, Lithuania does not enjoy many of the achievements, while business practices that tended to embody the ideas of CSR before 2008 change.

Unlike some Western European governments, none of the Lithuanian governments seriously considered deregulation and corporate self-regulation.[32,33] The state imposed on companies mandatory legal requirements in many fields, often leaving no or very limited discretion to contractual partners to choose different rules of behaviour (for example thorough regulation of employment relations, social allowances and compulsory social insurance, state pensions, hygiene and safety standards, minimum salary, main principles of corporate governance, etc.).

The CSR ideas were finally brought into the Lithuanian governance vocabulary with the transplantation of foreign standards that were either developed or fostered by international organisations, particularly the EU, OECD, ILO and UN.[34]

Among the government's first efforts at social dialogue and social partnership with business and the community was the creation of the Tripartite Council in 1995, stemming from our participation in the ILO treaties.[35] It comprises representatives of the Government, representatives of employers and trade unions. The Tripartite Council became one of the major public–private forums for debating employment and economic matters such as the monthly minimum wage, conditions of employment and requirements for social security payments. Then, in

---

[31] UNDP, *Corporate Social Responsibility Practices in Lithuania*, 16.

[32] At the end of 2006 and inspired by the EU's better regulation agenda, the Government of Lithuania finally adopted strategic directions to reduce state regulation.

[33] UNDP et al., *CSR Practices in the New EU Member State*, 9; Vasiljeviene and Vasiljevas, 'Management Models', 35.

[34] *Ibid.*

[35] In 1995, the first agreement on the establishment of the Tripartite Council was signed between the government, trade unions and employers' organisations and in 2005 it was replaced by a new agreement.

2000, the Lithuanian government established the National Commission on Sustainable Development to introduce principles of sustainable development into state governance. In 2003, the government adopted the National Strategy on Sustainable Development and since 2004 the indicators on sustainability have been monitored and published by the Department of Statistics. Nonetheless, until recently, no comprehensive actions were undertaken to introduce and promote CSR in Lithuania, as evidenced by the fact that none of these early efforts were discussed in the language of CSR.

In 2003, the National Contact Point under the OECD framework was established to promote and monitor the implementation of the Guidelines on Multinational Corporations in Lithuania. The Ministry of the Economy was placed in charge of the Guidelines, though the OECD initiative did not make CSR more prominent in public discourse.

Lithuania's accession to the European Union in 2004 necessitated the harmonisation of the national legal framework with the EU *acquis*. Lithuania greatly improved its environmental standards as a result of accession.[36] However, despite gentle promotion by the EU, Lithuania was less keen to develop 'soft governance' tools for improving business responsibility. The objectives of promoting and fostering CSR were finally included in the 2004–2008 and 2006–2008 Government Programmes, though no clear commitments were made.

With the assistance of the UNDP Lithuanian Office, the Ministry of Social Security and Labour finally adopted a policy paper on CSR in December 2005. The paper set forth concrete measures for encouraging the development of the CSR in Lithuania during the period 2006–2008. The document, which is based on the Global Compact initiative and the EU recommendations, identifies three priorities for the state in the field of CSR. They are:

1. raising awareness and improving knowledge about CSR
2. improving CSR implementation capacity
3. increasing transparency, reliability and effectiveness of CSR practices, methods and means, as well as improving the legal framework for CSR.

Following the release of the policy paper, the Ministry established a special commission for co-ordinating the development of CSR in Lithuania and launched a webpage for raising awareness about CSR on the website of the Ministry of Social Security and Labour.

---

[36] UNDP, *Corporate Social Responsibility Practices in Lithuania*, 36.

However, in the absence of a comprehensive governmental policy on the role of CSR, even this endeavour was a limited success. The government still had not defined the role of CSR as a policy tool in the (de) regulation of the Lithuanian economy and had not developed a comprehensive plan with key persons responsible for co-ordination of such policy measures.[37] So, while the Ministry of Social Security and Labour was launching its policy paper, other key Ministries, such as the Ministry of Economy and the Ministry of Environment,[38] remained rather passive, their actions and policies related to CSR were unco-ordinated and developed on an ad hoc basis. There is no correlation between different documents adopted by different institutions within the CSR promotion framework. Moreover, the special CSR co-ordination commission acts on a voluntary basis and has no effective instruments to interfere in the affairs of other state institutions in order to co-ordinate CSR policies and means. There are no guidelines how this commission and the National Commission on Sustainable Development are to co-ordinate their activities. It was not possible for business to find comprehensive information about the CSR and state incentives in the field through one information channel. Thus it can be concluded that continuous political support for the comprehensive formulation and systematic implementation of the CSR policy is missing.

3.2.2   Civil society

Lithuania's civil society movement is yet to develop into a major source of pressure for greater CSR and this is an important reason for the lack of interest in CSR practices in Lithuania now.[39] The main problem, as Štreimikienė and Vasiljevienė pertinently identified in their research, is that 'to many Lithuanians, the emphasis on humanistic ethical dimensions of the economy by scientists or researchers sounds socially romantic or utopian'.[40] What is more, Lithuanian consumers lack the knowledge, experience and even the willingness to push for greater CSR, as their counterparts have done in Western countries.[41] In Lithuania,

---

[37] UNDP et al., CSR Practices in the New EU Member States, 23–24.

[38] The Ministry of Environment is responsible for the Strategy on Sustainable Development and Green Procurement. On 8 August 2007, the government adopted a National Programme on the Implementation of Green Procurement. It stipulates gradual increases in the proportion of government procurements subject to environmental protection criterion between 2008 and 2011.

[39] UNDP, Corporate Social Responsibility Practices in Lithuania, 9.

[40] Štreimikienė and Vasiljevienė, 'Etiniai darnaus vystymosi aspektai', 190.

[41] Gruževskis et al., Įmonių socialinės atsakomybės vadovas, 5.

calls for public protest and product boycotts gain the support of few hundred people at most.[42]

Further, existing civil society organisations are limited in their ability to put pressure on government or business, as their operations are often fragmented and they are commonly dependent on corporate donations.[43] Indeed, a number of NGOs were established directly by business[44] and themselves operate with little transparency.[45] In the absence of a strong social pressure for CSR, the influence of civil society on business is low. In 2007, only 14 per cent of the small and medium enterprises surveyed conceded that NGOs had any influence on their decision making, whereas 60 per cent said NGOs had no influence.[46] However, NGOs, their activities and campaigns are slowly gaining traction; a recent study showing that the number of NGOs is growing, even if the number of people participating in the NGOs' activities remains low.[47]

Even so, there are signs that the concept of CSR has begun to take root in Lithuanian society. One of the critical factors behind the 'CSR

---

[42] That said, in 2007 the Ministry of Environment refused to issue permits to multinational companies to grow genetically modified plants in Lithuania in response to protests against genetically modified organisms; see also UNDP, *Corporate Social Responsibility Practices in Lithuania*, 21–22.

[43] UNDP et al., *CSR Practices in the New EU Member States*, 9.

[44] For instance, Investors' Forum was an initiator of the National Global Compact Network and is a key promoter of CSR in Lithuania. It unites more than thirty of the largest and most active investors in Lithuania and defends their interest by seeking to improve business conditions in Lithuania. Another organisation and member of Global Compact is Iniciatyvos fondas (the Initiative Fund) that was established in 2007 by Invalda, which is said to be one of the largest investment companies in Lithuania. The aim of the fund is 'to develop various programs for different social groups and to encourage social responsibility and initiative'. See further www.iniciatyvosfondas.lt/main.php?lan=EN&id=9 (consulted 23 September 2007).

[45] UNDP, *Corporate Social Responsibility Practices in Lithuania*, 22–23, 36–37.

[46] Ekonominės konsultacijos ir tyrimai, *Socialinės atsakomybės tendencijos*; UNDP, *Corporate Social Responsibility Practices in Lithuania*, 37.

[47] Lietuvos piliečiai jaučiasi bėjėgiai – teigia ekspertinis tyrimas 2006, 12 December, available at www.bernardinai.lt/index.php?url=articles/56321 (consulted 19 September 2007). Among the most active movements are Piliečių Santalka (Citizens' Front, www.santalka.lt), which aims to provide civic supervision of state authorities, to actively comment on draft laws and promote societal critical thinking. The Civil Society Institute also analyses public policy (www.civitas.lt) and the Human Rights Monitoring Institute promotes 'the development of an open democratic society based on human rights principle' (www.hrmi.lt). The Lithuanian Green Movement (www.zalieji.lt/english/about) and the Tatulos programme promote ecologic agriculture and consuming (www.organic.lt/lt/).

awakening' is the alarming rate of migration from Lithuania. EU membership resulted almost immediately in a labour shortage in Lithuania and it is estimated that since 1990, more than 400,000 Lithuanians, or 10 per cent of the total population, have left the country.[48] The major reason for emigration is the possibility of obtaining higher wages; however, it is likely that exploitative employment practices and the poor treatment of employees by Lithuanian employers are also reasons for the emigration. Many economic emigrants boast of 'being treated as human beings' in their new workplaces and destination countries. This quickly changed an attitude among Lithuanian employers: in just the first year after EU membership, employers began 'recalling' their legal, social and other responsibilities to their employees, that is, increasing the salaries or proposing more attractive working conditions.[49]

Another important incident in the development of CSR awareness and rhetoric took place in 2006 and challenged the widespread and longstanding practice of making illegal salary payments in 'little envelopes'.[50] In March 2006, Dalia Budrevičienė, an employee of meat company *AB Krekenavos agrofirma*, publicly confronted Viktor Uspaskich, a shareholder and controversial politician, to ask when the company would stop paying its employees part of their salary illegally in 'little envelopes'. Ms Budrevičienė was immediately dismissed from the factory and charged with slander of the company's director; she and her family reported that they did not feel safe.

Within days, this confrontation had evolved into a broad and heated public debate involving a diverse range of corporate stakeholders. Many company employees denounced Dalia Budrevičienė for exposing the illegal payments and effectively denying them the extra money they received in the little envelopes. State authorities responded to Ms Budrevičienė's complaint by initiating an investigation and inspecting the company's affairs. Lithuania's nascent civil society organisations responded quickly too. Some NGOs offered Ms Budrevičienė financial support and Kęstutis Čilinskas, the President of the Human Rights Monitoring Institute, offered his services as legal advisor and

---

[48] Department of Statistics to the Government of the Republic of Lithuania, www.stat.gov.lt/lt/news/view/?id=1767 (consulted 28 September 2007).

[49] UNDP, *Corporate Social Responsibility Practices in Lithuania*, 21.

[50] Different surveys estimate that from 13 to 40 per cent of Lithuanian employees receive part of their salaries undeclared, in little envelopes; see information available at www.info.lt/index.php?page=naujienos&view=naujiena_arch&id=69269 and www.balsas.lt/naujienos/verslas/straipsnis12339 (consulted 28 September 2007).

representative before the courts. Ms Budrevičienė was able to successfully challenge the company's decision to terminate her employment
contract and the charges of slander. In December 2006, Human
Rights Monitoring Institute awarded Ms Budrevičienė the title of
Human Rights Champion 2006 for high moral standards and public
spirit.

The rising emigration and 'little envelopes' scandal brought about
two important changes in Lithuanian employment practices. First,
immediately after the Budrevičienė scandal broke in June 2006, the
State Tax Inspectorate under the Ministry of Finance established a
confidential hotline and began encouraging Lithuanians to report payments in 'little envelopes' and other breaches of the tax laws. In just a
few months, the Inspectorate recorded its most successful year of
fighting illegal salary payments and other breaches of tax laws.[51]
Second, by the end of 2006, the Department of Statistics identified a
significant increase in the average salary in Lithuania, especially in
industries and sectors in which employees commonly receive only the
statutory minimum wage.

However, two years after the 'little envelopes' scandal, there has been
little change in attitudes which are crucial to the emergence and efficient
functioning of CSR: a sense of individual responsibility and responsible
consumerism. In general, price remains the main consideration for
Lithuanian consumers, as was apparent in the recent rejection of
'fair trade' products by supermarket chains and consumers.[52] Many
people support illegal salary payments as they are reluctant to pay a
large part of their salary to a government they do not trust. Indifference
to such breaches is greatest outside the cities in poorer regional areas.[53]
With great competition for employment, people often lack the confidence to complain even if they perceive a breach of their rights. The
Human Rights Monitoring Institute found in its 2006 survey that
58 per cent of respondents still did not know where to apply if their
rights have been breached, 78 per cent of respondents who suffered
human rights violations did not believe anyone could help them and
more than 30 per cent of respondents thought that the courts and
police were the institutions that violate human rights most.[54] Against

---

[51] Skėrytė, 'Vokelių dalytojam'.   [52] Važgauskaitė, Sąžinės ir piniginės.
[53] Davulis, 'CSR Practices'; Pušinaitė et al., 'Darbo vietos etika', 182.
[54] The survey is available at www.hrmi.lt/admin/Editor/assets/ZT_menuo_2006_Vilmorus_
pristatymas.pdf (consulted 28 September 2007).

this background, it is not surprising that after more than two years, Ms Budrevičienė remains unemployed.[55]

3.2.3   Business initiatives and attitudes

Foreign actors, such as investors, foreign contractors and international organisations, played an important role in the promotion of 'explicit' CSR discourses and practices among Lithuanian businesses, even if this has occurred later in the country's development and their CSR practices differed.[56] As the UNDP Baseline Study confirmed, foreign partners stood behind many CRS-type actions of Lithuanian companies as they had been introduced by foreign (multinational) companies to their Lithuanian subsidiaries or subcontractors.[57] For example, *Philip Morris* acquired a tobacco factory in Lithuania and has been considered as a model for corporate social awareness in Lithuania.[58] After reorganising the factory's operations, the company paid significant additional severance payments to redundant employees and has since become known for its fair wages, professional training, voluntary private pension schemes and other benefits.[59] The company also actively takes part in various cultural, social and philanthropic activities.

However, many other investors expressed their social awareness mainly through philanthropy, employee re-qualification or training activities, and their CSR practices were fragmented.

Some foreign companies ignored their global philosophy of corporate responsibility in their Lithuanian activities. For example, *Danisco Sugar* secured its investments in the Lithuanian sugar industry through a questionable privatisation process and then took controversial decisions about factory closures with minimal transparency, pressuring the government to monopolise the market.[60] As Davulis observes, the closure of the factories would have been a social disaster amongst company employees and suppliers of sugar beet in the poor local region.[61] Trade

---

[55] As she told one interviewer, the companies withdraw their job offers as soon as she introduces herself, see www.info.lt/index.php?page=naujienos&view=naujiena&id=92529 (consulted 28 September 2007).

[56] Vasiljeviene and Vasiljevas, 'Management Models' 34–35; Matten and Moon, 'Pan-European Approach', 341–45.

[57] UNDP, *Corporate Social Responsibility Practices in Lithuania*, 17, 33.

[58] Davulis, 'CSR Practices'.   [59] *Ibid*.

[60] Binkauskas, 'Investuotojai ir šantažuotojai'; Bagdanavičiūtė, 'Sutartis ėmė apkarsti', 5; Bagdanavičiūtė, 'Simboliniai 2.500 USD', 3; Bagdanavičiūtė, 'Danisco Sugar', 4.

[61] Davulis, 'CSR Practices'.

unions, mass media and the local community protested, the government intervened and ultimately *Danisco* kept the factories open. However, the protests cost the trade union activist and president his job and soured the relationship between *Danisco* and the government. The company was threatening to reconsider its investment promises for many years.[62]

The privatisation and reorganisation of the telecommunication monopolist *AB Lietuvos Telekomas* in 1998 was also a notable example of non-transparent privatisation and management decisions bypassing society.[63,64] Later the company started to support a variety of social initiatives.[65]

The explicit engagement of business in 'CSR' has become more prominent and less fragmented due to the work of the Lithuanian office of the United Nations Development Programme (UNDP).[66] In April 2005, UNDP partnered with the *Investors' Forum* to establish a *National Network on Socially Responsible Business* with eleven leading companies. Then, in June 2005, UNDP facilitated the official launch of the Global Compact in Lithuania, involving around forty companies and organisations.

Business attitudes towards CSR in Lithuania have been assessed by several surveys in 2005 and 2007. The 2007 UNDP baseline study revealed high levels of awareness about CSR among larger companies and considerable fear among small and medium-sized enterprises about the costs of CSR and reluctance to engage in CSR dialogue.[67] According to the 2007 survey on the CSR attitudes of small and medium enterprises (SMEs), 47 per cent of SMEs are not familiar with the term 'corporate social responsibility'.[68]

Further, respondents who knew about CSR tended to adopt narrow or self-serving definitions that add little to legal requirements.[69] Finally, companies often misperceive their one-way discussions with stakeholders

---

[62] *Ibid.*; Piketas prie Danijos ambasados, Verslo žinios.

[63] Arguably, the recent decision to change the company's name was influenced by negative publicity, which was itself attributable to the company's failure, over many years, to communicate with the public. However, in 2006 after the change in strategy, former Lietuvos Telekomas, now AB 'TEO', received the major award at the Baltic Market Awards organised by the OMX's exchanges in Vilnius, Tallinn and Riga. The company was recognised with the award for Best Investor Relations in the Baltic Countries.

[64] Pučėtaitė and Vasiljevas, 'Privatization in Lithuania', 325–26.   [65] *Ibid.*, 30.

[66] UNDP, *Corporate Social Responsibility Practices in Lithuania*, 8, 19.   [67] *Ibid.*, 33.

[68] Ekonominės konsultacijos ir tyrimai, *Tendencies of Social Responsibility*.

[69] UNDP, *Corporate Social Responsibility Practices in Lithuania*, 33–35; Vasiljeviene and Vasiljevas, 'Management Models', 35.

during conferences and PR campaigns as stakeholders' dialogue and mistake sporadic philanthropic activity and establishment of 'daughter' NGOs as real CSR.[70] The Lithuanian business culture (for example non-transparent business practices) is also a very important obstacle for the penetration of CSR.

According to the 2005 survey on attitudes to CSR in Lithuania, most companies linked socially responsible conduct to ethical practices and transparency in operations, whereas complying with the laws and caring for employees', shareholders' and clients' interests were considered as other most important tasks of the employers.[71] Environmental protection was named by only one third of respondents as a social responsibility[72] and only 41 per cent of Lithuanian companies that responded to the survey had implemented the ILO's *Core Labour Standards*.[73] According to the 2007 survey of SMEs, performed by organisation Ekonominės konsultacijos ir tyrimai, in rating the importance of certain activities, SMEs considered the health and safety of workers and the improvement of working conditions (including training, social security guarantees) to be very important (54 and 43 per cent respectively). By contrast, only 27 and 21 per cent attached the same level of importance to waste reduction and cleaner environment.[74] Those familiar with CSR generally considered it too costly and alien to the practices of SMEs.[75] In fact, many small and medium companies regularly claimed that they are only being able to stay in business because they pay minimum salaries (often with illegal extra bonuses in 'little envelopes') and do not comply with social security, tax, labour or other laws, which allegedly kill entrepreneurship.[76]

That said, there are signs that more local companies are beginning to integrate socially responsible practices into their business activities.[77]

---

[70] UNDP, *Corporate Social Responsibility Practices in Lithuania*, 22–23.

[71] 'What Does Business Think about Corporate Social Responsibility?', 61–62.

[72] Notably, small companies do not associate protection of the environment with socially responsible behaviour.

[73] 'What Does Business Think about Corporate Social Responsibility?', 70.

[74] Ekonominės konsultacijos ir tyrimai, *Tendencies of Social Responsibility*.

[75] 'What Does Business Think about Corporate Social Responsibility?', 81; Ekonominės konsultacijos ir tyrimai, *Tendencies of Social Responsibility*.

[76] Navickaitė, 'Atlyginimai vokeliuose'.

[77] The examples in the text below are based on the information included in UNDP Baseline Study (UNDP, *Corporate Social Responsibility Practices in Lithuania*, 45–50; the publication Kas kuria Lietuvos ateitį? Įmonių socialinė atsakomybė 2007, and information available on companies' domains.)

Already in 2005, the majority of the Lithuanian companies surveyed regarding their attitudes to CSR claimed to be engaged in employee training (99 per cent), social projects (55 per cent) and environmental projects (68 per cent).[78,79] This was reflected in the wide range of activities companies were engaged in:

- *AB SEB (Vilniaus bankas), AB Šiaulių bankas, AB TEO, UAB Lietuva Statoil* were educating various stakeholders outside the traditional target group (that is, their employees).
- Food processing companies *UAB Rūta* and *AB Danisco Sugar*, construction company *UAB Constructus* and furniture manufacturing company *UAB Narbutas & Ko* were imposing and assessing compliance with social, environmental, ethical or other quality standards in their supply-chains.
- *UAB Lietuva Statoil* and *UAB Commercial Union Lietuva Gyvybės Draudimas* were choosing their suppliers in part on the basis of their policies on the environment and social responsibility and their other social activities.
- Brewery *AB Švyturys-Utenos alus* had introduced a deposit system of the glass containers before the government could guarantee its effective functioning in accordance with the adopted laws.
- *MG Baltic* corporate group together with stakeholders had established a café, *Mano Guru*, for employing and training young people who successfully finished a drug rehabilitation programme.
- *AB TEO* had established three prizes for National Advancement in Partnership, Science and Culture.
- *UAB Constructus* was not using certain construction materials, which were legal but whose environmental impact had not been established.
- Textiles and clothing company *AB Utenos trikotažas* was gradually modernising its manufacturing process and thereby decreasing the environmental impact of its activities, while chemical manufacturer *AB Achema* had installed zero-waste technology.
- Smaller companies were adopting socially responsibility practices too. For example, UAB Mėta produces certified ecological herbal products.

---

[78] However, in a 2007 investigation of SMEs, 63 per cent of companies reported that they do not implement any social responsibility programmes (Ekonominės konsultacijos ir tyrimai, *Tendencies of Social Responsibility*.)

[79] 'What Does Business Think about Corporate Social Responsibility', 71–78.

Though not yet the norm in Lithuania, many foreign and national companies and their associations have adopted codes of conduct or ethics.[80] Already in 2005, 78 per cent of respondents claimed to have a code of conduct, albeit a verbal code in 40 per cent of cases. Approximately one quarter (23 per cent) of respondents could not say whether they had a code of conduct at all.[81]

A number of national companies were also quick to adopt ISO 9001 or 14001 standards (and, to a much lesser extent, other standards), having discovered positive implications for their relationships with Western trading partners.[82] However, the adoption of these standards was often viewed as a mere formality and was not treated as a potential basis for a new corporate culture.[83] Thus, it is no surprise that only in 2006 *AB Utenos trikotažas* was the first to acquire SA 8000 standard on social accountability in Lithuania, which is directed at the enforcement of international agreements in the fields of human rights and labour regulation. Remarkably, the company sought certification at the request of their Swiss trading partner, *Remei*.[84] A SA 8000 certificate has also lately been issued to a TNT company operating in Lithuania, this pursuant to TNT's global corporate strategy.[85]

The idea of ethical investment is only emerging. The Corporate Governance Code adopted by Vilnius Stock Exchange in 2006 and applicable to listed companies does not extend its reporting beyond the protection of shareholders' interests, efficient and transparent management and disclosure of corporate information.[86] Eco-labels are also becoming ever more popular among food producers, with a company *Ekoagros* performing independent certifications of food products.

---

[80] For instance, an investment company, AB Invalda, adopted both a code on social responsibility and a code of ethics. The relevant codes have also been adopted by many business associations, such as Lithuanian credit unions, brewers, insurance brokers, construction companies, etc. 'What Does Business Think about Corporate Social Responsibility?', 64.

[81] *Ibid.*, 64.

[82] For the numbers, see UNDP, *Corporate Social Responsibility Practices in Lithuania*, 30–32.

[83] UNDP *et al.*, *CSR Practices in the New EU Member States*, 44.

[84] From presentation 'Utenos trikotažas' at the Annual Global Compact Conference *Driving Forces for CSR.*

[85] See further www.tnt.com/country/lt_lt/about/tnt_naujienos/latest/Socialines_atsakomybes_sertifikatas.html (consulted 22 September 2007).

[86] Although banks are generally rather inactive in this area, some, such as AB SEB (former Vilniaus bankas), AB Šiaulių bankas and Nordea, evaluate environmental risks from the project finance perspective.

Nonetheless, such products face difficulties finding their place on shelves in big retail shops where the labels 'eco', 'bio', 'organic' are used without restriction and often without justification or certification by independent experts.[87]

For the time being, few companies in Lithuania could claim to have a plan for the strategic systematic incorporation of CSR policies into their activities; most tend to engage in CSR-like activities on a case-by-case basis, using the CSR discourse to supplement their marketing, public relations, environmental or personnel management strategies and campaigns.[88] Most businesses operating in Lithuania are concerned with the internal aspects of CSR-like activities, such as motivation of their employees or occasional philanthropic activities, such as the promotion of cultural and sport events.[89,90] No CSR report has been produced so far.[91] The Communication on Progress reports submitted as part of the Global Compact initiative tend to be formal confirmations that lack detailed evidence of how companies are abstaining from activities that conflict with the ten principles.[92]

Underlying these conflicting trends is the paradoxical attitude of business in Lithuania towards government regulation and social responsibility. On the one hand, business expects government to encourage CSR with 'regulatory initiatives, tax breaks and financial injections'. On the other, they strongly distrust the government and criticise its capacity to effectively regulate their activities.[93] As UNDP Baseline Study revealed, 'most business associations tend to view CSR as a zero-sum game where the companies are to be compensated for engaging in the socially-responsible behaviour'.[94] It is therefore not surprising that, in the opinion of business representatives, it is the government's responsibility to encourage proliferation of CSR practices and the main obstacle to CSR in Lithuania is the lack of appropriate regulation.[95]

---

[87] UNDP, *Corporate Social Responsibility Practices in Lithuania*, 32–33.
[88] *Ibid.*, 33–34, 37.
[89] Remarkably, the UNDP Baseline study found that some companies do not regard these activities as 'CSR', which they believe to be environmental impact management, see UNDP, Corporate Social Responsibility Practices in Lithuania, 33.
[90] Gruževskis *et al.*, *Įmonių socialinės*.
[91] UNDP, *Corporate Social Responsibility Practices in Lithuania*, 9.
[92] An exception are reports by UAB 'Statoil Lietuva', AB 'TEO', AB 'SEB Vilniaus bankas'.
[93] UNDP *et al.*, *CSR Practices in the New EU Member States*, 24.
[94] UNDP, *Corporate Social Responsibility Practices in Lithuania*, 9.
[95] 'What Does Business Think about Corporate Social Responsibility?', 81, 83.

3.2.4   Education, media and public resources

In recent years, a discourse around CSR has gradually emerged in Lithuanian academic and business circles and publications, intensifying during 2004 and 2005.[96] Different courses on business ethics and CSR have been introduced in a number of educational institutions, publications, surveys and studies.[97] Moreover, there are growing numbers of workshops and conferences[98] on social responsibility,[99] as well as blogs and websites for promoting CSR and debating issues relating to the environment, cultural heritage and human rights.[100]

Whilst noteworthy, these initiatives are of a limited impact on business practices due to the lack of close co-operation and synergy between the academic community and business. Other weaknesses identified in the UNDP Baseline Study include the limited scope of promotional activities, which are organised on a very general level, frequently by and for big companies at the exclusion of other corporate stakeholders and members of society. Information dissemination is also said to be very general.[101] Further, Lithuanian media and academics remain more

---

[96] Vasiljeviene and Vasiljevas, 'Management Models', 34.

[97] E.g.'What Does Business Think about Corporate Social Responsibility?'; Gruževskis et al., *Įmonių socialinės atsakomybės vadovas*; UNDP, *Corporate Social Responsibility Practices in Lithuania*.

[98] For instance, UNDP Lithuanian Office has been organising annual CSR conferences for a number of consecutive years already. They are often assisted by the Investors' Forum, which has also organised its own events. AIESEC organised three conferences on responsible business for students; the Lithuanian Confederation of Industrialists organised eleven Ethics Forums.

[99] It is worth noting that most publications are devoted to business ethics, rather than CSR. The Centre of Business Ethics at Vilnius University is extremely active in the field of business ethics education and research, including CSR. Its researchers N. Vasiljevienė and A. Vasiljevas are among the most productive in this field. Another specialised institution is the Institute of Environmental Engineering at the Kaunas University of Technology, which offers programmes on sustainable development and training on the environmental management. See further UNDP, *Corporate Social Responsibility Practices in Lithuania*, 26–27, 55–56.

[100] Among the first sites to promote CSR were those of the Ministry of Social Security and Labour (www.socmin.lt) and the Global Compact initiatives for a Lithuanian audience (www.globalcompact.lt). However, they do not publish comprehensive and systematic information on CSR. Interesting examples of private websites include http://ekoblogas. wordpress.com, which discusses positive solutions to ecological problems and promotes ecological awareness. At the beginning of 2007, a website www.atsakingasverslas.lt ('responsible business') was launched by a company Ekonominės konsultacijos ir tyrimai with the financial assistance of the EU as part of a project to develop a catalogue of the best practices on business social responsibility and promote CSR among SMEs in Lithuania.

[101] UNDP, *Corporate Social Responsibility Practices in Lithuania*, 19–20.

interested in reporting breaches of national laws by the companies than critically assessing voluntary corporate undertakings, promises and practices on social responsibility; even though they are increasingly interested in business ethics and critical publications on unfair corporate practices, corruption, illegal salary payments, malpractices and the like are quite common.[102] So, companies claiming to be socially responsible have in practice little or no external criticism to discredit their slogans or force them to improve their performance.

4.   In search of the CSR future perspectives in Lithuania

At this stage of Lithuania's development, when the language of CSR is finally emerging, the government faces an important decision: should it trust business to regulate itself, agreeing effectively to share the responsibility for monitoring and enforcing compliance with human rights, labour and environmental standards? As will emerge, there are a number of reasons for thinking it unlikely that business self-made CSR standards could serve as enforceable instruments for the contribution to sustainable development, social and environmental concerns in Lithuania, at least without agreement on the quality of the content of standards and the mechanisms for their implementation, accountability and enforcement.[103]

4.1   Unclear content of the CSR standards

The major problem with the CSR is a lack of clarity about the content of the CSR standards. To begin with, it is often difficult to establish which standards apply to a given company or business activity: is it the standards recognised by and within the frameworks of international organisations such as the OECD, EU, or UN, the standards drafted by the company itself in a code of conduct or the standards prepared by other private actors for other initiatives, such as the Global Reporting Initiative? Even when it is clear which standard applies, stakeholders may face considerable difficulties in determining the subject matter of the specific obligations and their scope.[104]

---

[102] The UNDP Baseline Study identified the business dailies, Verslo Žinios and Lietuvos Rytas and the biggest Internet news portal www.delfi.lt as including the largest number of articles, see UNDP and Public Policy and Management Institute 2007, 27.

[103] McInerney, 'Regulation Before Responsibility', 190–91.

[104] Davidsson, 'Legal Enforcement', 542–43. The European Parliament noted that the variety of CSR initiatives might serve as a 'disincentive for companies to pursue more credible CSR

For that reason, the CSR label is often misused. For example, every company claims to be socially responsible if it: a) adheres to ISO 14001; or b) joins Global Compact where a company can essentially undertake no steps of improving its activities for two consecutive years until it might be delisted as inactive (for example minority of the Lithuanian Global Compact participants submitted a report on their perform-ance);[105] or c) simply states on its website without making it more explicit that it is socially responsible (for example Swedbank (Hansabankas) in Lithuania before joining Global Compact), or d) a supplier of electricity that under the CSR policy cover urges its consu-mers to pay the debts for the electricity consumption (AB 'Rytų skirst-omieji tinklai') or publishes a manual on ecologic agriculture (Danisco Sugar). Many of these claims have little if anything in common with socially responsible behaviour. Very few if any of the companies opera-ting in Lithuania and claiming to be socially responsible can demonstrate today that they have a CSR strategy, stakeholders' engagement practices, CSR-related performance management, qualitative public disclosure and independent CSR assurance.[106] Most of the market participants just borrow the concept and use it to describe their ad hoc social initiatives.

The wide and flexible definition of CSR leads to another problem: the lack of comprehensive coverage.[107] The voluntary nature of a standard implies that companies are free to choose whether, where, when, and to what degree they are socially responsible. All matters are at the discretion of business, from the field of application, stakeholders, language of the commitment, time of engagement to termination of the engagement. In affording companies this discretion, governments give up their power to impose and enforce minimum standards with regard to important rights in whole sectors of the economy.[108] For example, in such a system, a

actions or more ambitious CSR policies': see European Parliament resolution of 13 March 2007, para 5.

[105] The Global Compact claims to be 'the world's largest voluntary corporate citizenship initiative' with over 4,000 companies and organisations participating. However, the Global Compact Office has already listed 779 participants as inactive (www.unglobal-compact.org/COP/inactives.html) and 445 participants as non-communicating participants, indicating that they have failed to submit a Communication on Progress or engage in dialogue on integrity measures; see www.globalcompact.com/CommunicatingProgress/non_communicating.html (consulted September, 2007).

[106] UNDP, *Corporate Social Responsibility Practices in Lithuania*, 41–42.

[107] Davidsson, 'Legal Enforcement', 537; Jenkins, 'Corporate Codes of Conduct', 26–27; McInerney, 'Regulation Before Responsibility', 190.

[108] McInerney, 194.

company committed to improving its employment practices would choose to do so through often very selective employee education and of training employees, subsidised lunches and ad hoc philanthropic initiatives rather than through comprehensive external assessments or restructuring of the business to guarantee core ILO labour standards. Already some companies tend to treat their CSR obligations as satisfied with 'saving paper and electricity campaigns'[109] or simply provision to the employees of suitable work clothes.[110]

As was aptly summarised by the Corporate Watch in their 2006 report, 'CSR has created a language shift, a re-brand and a new caring image, but no substance'.[111] Thus, unfortunately, in many cases talk of CSR is empty rhetoric. In Lithuania, companies that now increasingly speak in favour of social responsibility themselves engage mainly in traditional forms of philanthropy. Moreover, CSR commitments in Lithuania often amount to simple declarations that a company complies with the laws and is not engaged in unfair commercial practices.

4.2   Divergent CSR practices and commitments

A further problem is that companies often treat CSR standards as relevant only to one part of their activities and so engage in practices that contradict their stated commitments to CSR.[112] In Lithuania, companies employ contradictory initiatives, supporting free market advocates and failing to publicly disclose or promote CSR policies, practices or cultures.

4.2.1   Engaging in contradictory initiatives

In relation to the CSR activities in Lithuania, the examples of contradictory initiatives include:

- Efforts by foreign and national investors under the auspices of the association *Investors' Forum* to secure amendments to immigration laws that would enable migration of cheaper and less demanding labour

---

[109] Interview with the owner Dobilas Kežys of a company Pas Dobilą, a member of the Global Compact, available at www.bernardinai.lt/index.php?url=articles/55364.

[110] Vaitiekūnienė, 'Socialinę atsakomybę atranda smulkieji', 16.

[111] Corporate Watch Report, *What's Wrong With Corporate Social Responsibility?*, 12.

[112] As the European Parliament noted, 'the concept of "beyond compliance" may enable some companies to claim social responsibility while at the same time not respecting local or international laws', see European Parliament resolution of 13 March 2007, para 3.

forces into Lithuania from the third countries. The *Investors' Forum* formally promotes responsible corporate practices in Lithuania.

• Lithuanian retail chains, construction, sewing and other companies providing support to the community through ecological initiatives, charity concerts for children, or local hospitals, whilst often requiring employees to work unpaid overtime or for the minimum wage, paying undeclared salaries, etc.

4.2.2   Supporting free market advocates

The second distortion of CSR in Lithuania is the support by business of free market advocates as seen particularly in the relationship between supposedly responsible businesses and the Lithuanian Free Market Institute (LFMI).[113] One of the most well-established and active NGOs in the country, the LFMI is a private institute, which promotes the idea of a deregulated market and small government, often at the expense of the social welfare agenda. The LFMI has publicly questioned and criticised the role of CSR in the development of the Lithuanian economy. In August 2006, the President of the Institute R. Šimašius published an article entitled 'Irresponsible Social Responsibility' in which he fiercely rejected the idea of CSR. He declared that '(b)usiness' social responsibility is an invention, which consumes but not creates welfare, which erodes but not strengthens society itself'.[114] Experts at the Institute have criticised the government's goal of promoting CSR.[115] And yet, the largest proportion of the Institute's income comes from companies that promote CSR and/or are members of the Global Compact initiative. In fact, representatives of 'socially responsible' companies (for example AB Swedbank (Hansabankas), AB SEB (Vilniaus bankas), ERGO insurance company) have delegated representatives to participate on the Board of the Institute, which is said to consist of 'persons who uphold the Institute's mission and provide an active contribution with their ideas to the mission's accomplishment'.[116]

---

[113] Utting, 'Rethinking Business Regulation', 19.

[114] Šimašius, 'Irresponsible Social Responsibility'.

[115] See the position of the Lithuanian Free Market Institute 'Dėl Vyriausybės programos "Santarvės ir gerovės vardan"', available at www.lrinka.lt/index.php/meniu/leidinys_laisvoji_rinka/leidinys_laisvoji_3841rinka/straipsniai/naujienos_2006_liepa__rugsejis/ (consulted 30 September 2007).

[116] www.lrinka.lt/index.php/menu/about_lfmi/board/643 (consulted 26 September 2007).

4.2.3   Failure to disclose or promote CSR policies or practices

The third distortion of CSR is the failure to disclose or promote CSR policies or practices. This is especially evident in efforts by multinational holding companies to publicly introduce CSR vocabulary or corporate governance policies to their Lithuanian business partners or subsidiaries. Even now, a number of multinational companies have not translated their websites into Lithuanian and, even if they have done so, Lithuanian information portals often omit information on corporate governance and social responsibility.[117] Many companies and organisations seem to treat their membership of the Global Compact as a formality, failing to produce reports or, if subsidiaries of transnational corporations, publishing only the report of the parent company. In this case, the corporation's global reports are not adapted to reflect the progress of locally operating subsidiaries.[118]

In addition, before UNDP began promoting the Global Compact in Lithuania, only one company had joined the initiative.[119] Few member companies have inserted the ten 'Universal Principles' in their mission statements and over half of the companies and institutions that joined the Compact in 2005 failed to submit a Communication on Progress Report, including the initiators of the *National Global Compact Lithuanian Network – Investors' Forum*. Just over half of the participating companies consider the Compact and new CSR commitments important enough to inform about them on their websites and when they do, information on the Global Compact commonly figures in the 'old news' sections.[120]

---

[117] See, for example, the websites of Berlin-Chemie, Danisco Sugar, Ericsson, Ernst & Young, ERGO, Nestle and Philip Morris (consulted before September 2007).

[118] For instance, 2006 and 2005 Sustainability reports posted on the Global Compact site on behalf of Danisco Sugar companies operating in Lithuania are simply the same global sustainability reports of the entire Danisco group (which is posted on behalf of every participant of GC) and there is not a single mention of the local subsidiaries or their activities in Lithuania, while the notable exception is UAB 'Lietuva Statoil', which submitted an exclusively local report). UNDP Baseline study also confirmed this tendency for the whole region; see UNDP et al., *CSR Practices in the New EU Member States*, 48.

[119] This and the following numbers are based on the data available at globalcompact.com as of 23 September 2007. There is a discrepancy between information on the membership of Global Compact in different resources: according to data available on the UNDP Lithuania website 45 companies and organisations joined GC, globalcompact.com reports only 43; however, it should also be noted that different companies are included in globalcompact.com and UNDP Lithuania lists.

[120] Similar practices were observed by UNDP concerning subscription to codes of conducts drafted by the Lithuanian business associations. See UNDP, *Corporate Social Responsibility Practices in Lithuania*, 32.

Following global trends, poor communication about CSR in Lithuania also includes non-transparent decision making and misleading labelling. Often consumers, employees and shareholders cannot verify whether the company is truly observing its stated principles of social responsibility, the 'social', 'organic' or 'ecological' quality of the products or their origin, because they do not have access to information about the company's policies or procedures.[121] Although the Internet has made it more difficult for companies to conceal information available elsewhere, this publicly available information is more commonly relevant to Western European markets and not to the Lithuanian brands.

4.2.4   The nature of CSR commitments

Even if companies were consistent in their stance towards CSR, there is another reason for questioning CSR's utility as a governance tool: the nature of the commitment. As they are voluntary, the codes of conduct, guidelines, ethical standards and other CSR instruments belong to the category of soft law, meaning that their obligations are non-binding. The words companies use to describe how they are socially, environmentally or for human rights *responsible*, often have little to do with *responsibility* in the sense of obligation or commitment but are more expressions of concern and awareness.[122]

Naturally, there are standard arguments for the non-binding nature of CSR standards.[123] However, these are at odds with the very aim of CSR to be a means of ensuring human rights and the dignity of the individual, respect for the environment and conditions at work. The greatest paradox is that we speak about *responsibilities* that do not imply an obligation, an undertaking, or a right to a beneficiary, as the content of such social or ecological 'undertaking' is elastic. As Haufler observed, 'the problem that governments and publics have with these voluntary

---

[121] Corporate Watch Report, *What's Wrong With Corporate Social Responsibility?*, 16.

[122] Corporate Watch Report, *What's Wrong With Corporate Social Responsibility?*, 9. For instance, the MG Baltic corporate group simply states that it applies the highest requirements to its activity concerning the impact of its operations on nature, society, its security and public spirit (www.mgbaltic.lt/lt.php/visuomene_ir_mes/26, consulted 16 November 2006). A company supplying electricity, AB Rytų skirstomieji tinklai, claims that it 'seeks to contribute to the welfare of the society and creation of a nice environment, providing people with the possibility to enjoy the benefit of electricity, the light and beauty it sheds' (www.rst.lt/lt/?itemId=1005068, consulted 18 January 2007, translation by the author).

[123] Utting, 'Rethinking Business Regulation', 15; McInerney, 'Regulation Before Responsibility', 184–85.

initiatives is precisely that they are voluntary, with often weak enforcement mechanisms'.[124]

That companies are not eager to treat their public CSR commitments
seriously is evident from many cases. Many of them are very active in
lobbying against the introduction of national and international rules
which would regulate their voluntary undertakings and provide for
monitoring.[125] The oft-cited 2002 US Supreme Court case of *Nike* v.
Kasky and especially briefings from corporations revealed that corporations did not treat their public communication seriously and did not
consider themselves bound by their public statements on human rights,
environment or social issues even if very clear and specific statements
were made.[126]

Moreover, in the absence of an agreed standard definition, each and
every corporate stakeholder will introduce an individual *notion* of CSR,
with different *content* and differently drawn *boundaries* for CSR.
Companies can be (and are) very selective not only in the scope, but
also about the degree of their engagement and international institutions
encourage this practice by fiercely rejecting steps to regulate and monitor
the implementation of CSR.[127] Consequently, the idea of social responsibility tends to drift into the sphere of 'marketing strategy' and reduce
the idea of responsibility to an almost mythical ideal. However, it is
difficult to find logical explanations for downplay of ambitious and
very concrete CSR statements on the excuse of 'non-legal' and 'voluntary'
arguments.[128]

Likewise in Lithuania, CSR was introduced and promoted as implying
purely voluntary initiatives, quite distinct from law and mandatory
legal norms. Initial discussions of CSR made no reference to developments concerning mandatory regulations or the enforcement of CSR
policies from other national jurisdictions and at the international
level.[129]

---

[124] Haufler, *Public Role for the Private Sector*, 2; Slack, 'Putting Teeth'.
[125] For instance, business actors were largely responsible for the failure of the UN Norms on
the Responsibility of the Transnational Corporations. They considered the norms unnecessary and unacceptable. See further, e.g., Utting, 'Rethinking Business Regulation',
16; Corporate Watch Report, *What's Wrong with Corporate Social Responsibility*, 13.
[126] Collingsworth, 'Corporate Social Responsibility', 669–82. See (Appellate Brief) Brief
of Exxonmobil, Microsoft, Morgan Stanley, and Glaxosmithkline as Amici Curiae in
Support of Petitioners (28 February 2003), available at Westlaw or at www.reclaim
democracy.org/nike.
[127] McInerney, 'Regulation Before Responsibility', 190.
[128] See Zerk, *Multinationals*, 58–59.   [129] *Ibid.*, 32–36.

4.3   Enforcement

Finally, the problem of voluntarism leads to a question of accountability and enforcement. In the absence of instruments to make organisations accountable and to enforce commitments, they are able to choose whether they take action to implement or enforce their promises or policies or ignore them.[130] The defence of voluntary nature of the CSR standards allow the companies to be quite relaxed about the consequences for the non-observance of their 'responsibility' declarations.[131]

Moreover, according to McInerney '[t]urning over power to control (that is, regulate) socially harmful practices to the private sector through CSR initiatives effectively undermines the development of state capacity not only to regulate but also to expand the domestic economy and mitigate social harms'.[132] Thus, in Lithuania, where business now seized a leading role for the promotion of CSR and the government is rather passive, a concept might be abused.[133] The reality of this danger is demonstrated by the newest proposal by the Lithuanian Confederation of Industrialists to introduce a law allowing companies to claim tax incentives for any action defined as a social initiative (for example the company's investment in work tools and infrastructure, as already required by law, or merely preparing a code of ethics). Under the proposal, companies would not be required to demonstrate a strategy or systematic implementation of social responsibilities before they would become entitled to the financial benefits.[134]

Therefore, when the civil society organisations are weak, the state must strengthen its regulatory capacity and develop institutions able to fight against harmful and speculative corporate policies.[135] The state should demand a systematic approach from companies before they could use the CSR label and, with the assistance of the legislation and courts, make business responsible for their public promises.[136]

---

[130] Jenkins, 'Corporate Codes of Conduct', 25.

[131] This issue was among the biggest concerns in the Report of the Special Representative of the Secretary-General 2007.

[132] See McInerney, 'Regulation Before Responsibility', 193.

[133] UNDP, *Corporate Social Responsibility Practices in Lithuania*, 9–10.

[134] The draft law on the encouragement of social initiatives within the framework of CSR is under preparation and is not officially registered with the Parliament yet. The draft text in Lithuanian can be found at www.lps.lt/index.php?c=20070917164300 (consulted 27 September 2007).

[135] See McInerney, 'Regulation Before Responsibility', 193–94.

[136] Corporate Watch Report, *What's Wrong With Corporate Social Responsibility?*, 25.

5. Conclusion

Over the years, CSR has grown into a very complex phenomenon, with many multiple dimensions and manifestations.[137] The multiplication of CSR standards, the wide, vague and changing concept of CSR as well as the abuse of its voluntary nature, have devalued the notion to the point that it is not necessarily possible to regard the proprietor of a standard as a more responsible corporate citizen. The notion of CSR has become synonymous with the elastic conscience of business. The danger of treating CSR as *a regulatory instrument* complementing legal regulation is that it replaces state instruments into very vague statements without clear accountability and means of redress against it.[138] For that reason, the CSR concept should not sell the idea of responsibility in principle, but rather be replaced by a concept of responsibility for *something* particular (that is, employment conditions, reduced level of pollution, etc.). Otherwise, in the words of the Corporate Watch Report, CSR will become a 'mechanism in the weakening of government' as it 'sidelines democratic decision making [... and ...] replaces the (dis)enfranchised citizen with the "stakeholder"'.[139]

As this general overview of the Lithuanian experience has shown, the mere existence of an international standard 'on the books' does not guarantee its application and effectiveness in the local environment, even if the same corporation invokes and promotes the standard elsewhere in the world. Voluntary business engagement in CSR practices depends very much on the peculiarities of the legal and political system as well as the society's ability to demand socially responsible behaviour. Currently in Lithuania the idea of CSR is poorly perceived by state officials, business and society and even more poorly observed by business. At present, the path to CSR often implies mere law-abiding behaviour, and the development of CSR therefore remains at the point of promotion and awareness raising rather than implementation.

Beyond this, a state with weak administrative capacity and a dormant civil society is less likely to harbour a business culture which is comprehensively and efficiently dedicated to the implementation of CSR. At present, business is attempting to take over the leading role in the CSR promotion and self-regulation of their CSR policies; however, this

---

[137] See Roome, 'Pan-European Approach', 317.
[138] Corporate Watch Report, *What's Wrong with Corporate Social Responsibility?*, 17.
[139] *Ibid.*

may lead to self-interested examples of CSR and discrediting of CSR as a policy tool. Thus, in the case of a rather passive society with a weak NGO sector, a crucial task for the state is the development of legislation and institutions able to take action against abusive and speculative CSR policies, at least by way of exposing fraudulent CSR declarations and providing society with a means of redress against misuse of corporate power. This is one of the most important tasks along with the promotion of CSR and the encouragement of responsible behaviour. In the long term, the state should establish a set of criteria that could demonstrate systematic integration and real performance against CSR policies and thereby validate the eligibility to the CSR label.

Finally, unless international voluntary standards become part of the culture in a particular society, CSR standards that are largely copied or 'borrowed' will not have a major impact and will more often lead to artificial responsibility. As R. Sims rightly observed, '[t]he issue is not having the standards, however. It is living by them on a daily basis.'[140]

References

Bagdanavičiūtė, V. 1999, 'Sutartis ėmė apkarsti', *Verslo žinios*, 17 March, no. **51**, 5.

Bagdanavičiūtė, V. 1999, 'Simboliniai 2.500 USD', *Verslo žinios*, 25 March, no. **57**, 3.

Bagdanavičiūtė, V. 2000, '"Danisco Sugar" nori vienatvės', *Verslo žinios*, 28 February, no. **40**, 4.

Bantekas, I. 2004, 'Corporate Social Responsibility in International Law', *Boston University International Law Journal*, vol. **22**, 309–47.

Binkauskas, G. 1999, 'Investuotojai ir šantažuotojai', *Verslo žinios*, 13 September, no. **162**, 4.

Collingsworth, T. 2004, 'Corporate Social Responsibility. Unmasked', *St. Thomas Law Review*, vol. **16**, 669–86.

Commission Green Paper 2001, 'Promoting a European Framework for Corporate Social Responsibility', COM(2001) 366 final.

Communication from the Commission 2002, 'Corporate Social Responsibility. A Business Contribution to Sustainable Development', COM(2002) 347 final.

Communication from the Commission 2006, 'Implementing the Partnership for Growth and Jobs: Making Europe a Pole of Excellence on Corporate Social Responsibility', (COM(2006) 136 final.

Corporate Watch Report 2006, *What's Wrong With Corporate Social Responsibility?*, available at www.corporatewatch.org.uk/?lid=2670 (consulted 29 September 2007).

---

[140] See Sims, *Ethics and Corporate Social Responsibility*, 40.

Crane, A. and Matten, D. 2007, 'Corporate Social Responsibility as a Field of Scholarship' in A. Crane and D. Matten (eds.), *Corporate Social Responsibility. Vol I. Theories and Concepts of Corporate Social Responsibility*, Sage Publications.

Crowther, D. and Rayman-Bacchus, L. 2004, 'Introduction: Perspectives on Corporate Social Responsibility' in D. Crowther and L. Rayman-Bacchus (eds.), *Perspectives on Corporate Social Responsibility*, Aldershot, Ashgate.

Davidsson, P. A. 2002, 'Legal Enforcement of Corporate Social Responsibility within the EU', *Columbia Journal of European Law*, vol. **8**, 529–56.

Davulis, T. 2003, 'CSR Practices throughout the Region. Comparing and Contrasting Areas that Have Been Differently Affected by the Economic Reforms and Changing Environment', Presentation in the EC and ILO Athens Conference on Socially Responsible Enterprise Restructuring. Exchanging Experiences and Good Practices, 3 and 4 April 2003, available at www.itcilo.it/srer/athens/presentations/12DAVULIS.doc (consulted 25 September 2007).

Ekonominės konsultacijos ir tyrimai 2007, *Socialinės atsakomybės tendencijos tarp smulkių ir vidutinių įmonių, Tyrimo ataskaita* (Tendencies of Social Responsibility between Small and Medium Enterprises, Report on Survey), available at http://www.atsakingasverslas.lt/docs/CSR_ataskaita_galutine.pdf (consulted 22 September 2007).

European Parliament resolution of 13 March 2007 on Corporate Social Responsibility: A New Partnership, P6_TA(2007)0062.

Fekete, L. 2005, 'Hungary: Social Welfare Lagging Behind Economic Growth' in A. Habisch et al. (eds.), *Corporate Social Responsibility Across Europe*, New York, Springer.

Gruževskis, B., Vasiljevienė, N., Moskvina, J. and Kleinaitė, I. 2006, *Įmonių socialinės atsakomybės vadovas*, available at www.socmin.lt/index.php?1344093231 (consulted 28 September 2007).

Haufler, V. 2001, *A Public Role for the Private Sector: Industry Self-regulation in a Global Economy*, Washington, Carnegie, Endowment for International Peace.

Jenkins, R. 2001, 'Corporate Codes of Conduct. Self-Regulation in a Global Economy', Technology, Business and Society Programme, Paper no. 2, United Nations Research Institute for Social Development.

Kas kuria Lietuvos ateitį? Įmonių socialinė atsakomybė 2007, supported by the UNDP.

MacLeod, S. 2007, 'Reconciling Regulatory Approaches to Corporate Social Responsibility: The European Union, OECD and United Nations Compared', *European Public Law*, vol. **13**, 671.

Matten, D. and Moon, J. 2005, 'Pan-European Approach – A Conceptual Framework for Understanding CSR' in A. Habisch *et al.* (eds.), *Corporate Social Responsibility Across Europe*, Berlin, Springer.

McInerney, T. 2007, 'Putting Regulation Before Responsibility: Towards Binding Norms of Corporate Social Responsibility', *Cornell International Law Journal*, vol. **40**, 171–200.

Navickaitė, L. 2006, 'Atlyginimai vokeliuose: akivaizdu, bet neįrodoma', *Kauno diena*, 30 March, available at www.info.lt/index.php?page=naujienos& view=naujiena_arch&id=69269 (consulted 28 September 2007).

Piketas prie Danijos ambasados 1999, *Verslo žinios*, 5 Oct., no. **178**, 4.

Pučėtaitė, R. and Vasiljevas, A. 2002, 'Foreign Corporation and Privatization in Lithuania. "Lietuvos telekomas" Case' in N. Vasiljevienė and R. Jeurissen (eds.), *Business Ethics: From Theory to Practice*, Vilnius, UAB 'Ciklonas'.

Pušinaitė, R., Gurkšnienė, R. and Liakas, A. 2004, 'Darbo vietos etika kaip įmonių veiklos tobulinimo sąlyga ir socialinės atsakomybės diegimo būtinybė' in A. Bučinskas *et al.* (eds.), *Transformacijos Rytų ir Centrinėje Europoje*, Klaipėda, Klaipėdos universiteto leidykla.

Roome, N. 2005, 'Pan-European Approach: Some Implications of National Agendas for CSR' in A. Habisch *et al.* (eds.), *Corporate Social Responsibility Across Europe*, Berlin, Springer.

Šimašius, R. 2006, 'Irresponsible Social Responsibility', *Veidas*, 3 August, available at www.lrinka.lt/index.php/menu/newsletter_the_free_market/ newsletter_the_free_market/articles/irresponsible_social_responsibility/ 3846 (consulted 2007).

Sims, R. 2003, *Ethics and Corporate Social Responsibility: Why Giants Fall*, Westport, Praeger.

Skėrytė, J. 2006, 'Vokelių dalytojams – neramios dienos', *Lietuvos žinios*, 13 June, available at www.ivaizdis.lt/res_zinpr_det.php?id=3759 (consulted 28 September 2007).

Slack, K. 2006, 'Putting Teeth in Corporate Social Responsibility', *Policy Innovations*, 21 November, available at www.policyinnovations.org/ideas/ innovations/data/CSR (consulted 12 January 2007).

Special Representative of the Secretary-General 2007, *Report on the issue of human rights and transnational corporations and other business enterprises 'Business and Human Rights: Mapping International Standards of Responsibility and Accountability for Corporate Acts'*, A/HRC/4/035, 9 February.

Štreimikienė, D. and Vasiljevienė, N. 2004, 'Etiniai darnaus vystymosi aspektai ir jų ryšys su socialinėmis ir aplinkosauginėmis darnaus vystymosi dimensijomis', *Organizacijų vadyba: Sisteminiai tyrimai*, vol. **32**, 189–206.

UNDP, Line, M. and Braun, R. 2007, *Baseline Study on CSR Practices in the New EU Member States and Candidate Countries*.

UNDP, Public Policy and Management Institute 2007, *Baseline Study on Corporate Social Responsibility Practices in Lithuania*.

AB 'Utenos trikotažas' presentation at the Annual Global Compact Conference 'Driving Forces for CSR: How to Sustain and Find New Opportunities', 30 November 2006, available at www.investorsforum.lt/uploads/new/SA% 208000Utenos%20trikotazas%203.ppt#18.

Utting, P. 2005, 'Rethinking Business Regulation. From Self-Regulation to Social Control', *Technology, Business and Society Programme Paper* No. 15, United Nations Research Institute for Social Development, available at www. unrisd.org/unrisd/website/document.nsf/ab82a6805797760f80256b4f005-da1ab/f02ac3db0ed406e0c12570a10029bec8/$FILE/utting.pdf).

Vaitiekūnienė, J. 2007, 'Socialinę atsakomybę atranda smulkieji ir vidutiniokai', *Verslo žinios*, 5 May, no. **83**, 16.

Vasiljevas, A. and Pučėtaitė, R. 2005, 'Socialinės įmonių atsakomybės ir efektyvaus žmogiškųjų išteklių valdymo įgyvendinimas dalykinės etikos priemonėmis' in *Organizacijų vadyba: Sisteminiai tyrimai*, vol **36**, 193–211.

Vasiljevienė, N. 2004, 'Organizacijų etika kaip vadybos optimizavimo įrankis', *Ekonomika*, vol. **67**, no. 2, 1–14.

Vasiljeviene, N. and Vasiljev, A. 2005, 'Lithuania – The Roadmap: From Confrontation to Consensus' in A. Habisch *et al.* (eds.), *Corporate Social Responsibility Across Europe*, Berlin, Springer.

Vasiljeviene, N. and Vasiljevas, A. 2006, 'Management Models in Organizations and Problems of CSR Promotion: Lithuanian Case', *Electronic Journal of Business Ethics and Organization Studies*, vol. **11**, no. 2, 34–41.

Važgauskaitė, J. 2006, Sąžinės ir piniginės dvikova, *Panorama*, 7 October, available at www.delfi.lt/archive/article.php?id=10889345 (consulted 25 September 2007).

Vogel, D. 2005, *The Market for Virtue. The Potential and Limits of Corporate Social Responsibility*, Washington, Brooking Institution Press.

'What Do Business Think about Corporate Social Responsibility? Part I: Attitudes and Practices in Estonia, Latvia and Lithuania', 2005, The Report prepared by a team led by Piotr Mazurkiewicz on the basis of survey by the World Bank and supported by the European Commission.

Yakovleva, N. 2005, *Corporate Social Responsibility in the Mining Industries*, Aldershot, Ashgate.

Zerk, J. A. 2006, *Multinationals and Corporate Social Responsibility*, Cambridge University Press.

17

Legal pluralism under the influence of globalisation: a case study of child adoption in Tanzania

ULRIKE WANITZEK[*]

1. Introduction

Family law in Tanzania, like in many other African countries, is strongly characterised by legal pluralism.[1] State law, customary laws and religious laws exist side by side. Under the influence of globalisation, particularly the increasing international mobility of people,[2] processes of further legal pluralisation can be observed.[3] This chapter analyses such pluralisation processes in cases of child adoption in Tanzania.

Under African customary laws, the role of parent is not only to be played by the child's parents but also by other relatives, such as aunts, uncles, elder siblings, or grandparents. Until recently, formal child adoption under state law was quite uncommon among Tanzanians because they did not seem to see a need for it. However, the increase in international migration and the requirements of foreign immigration laws are effecting a change. Under many immigration laws, adults are only allowed to immigrate with children who are their own, in the sense of

[*] Professor of Law, Institute of African Studies, Faculty of Law and Economics, University of Bayreuth, Germany. I am grateful to Prof Bart Rwezaura and Prof Gordon R. Woodman for the discussions we had on a number of specific points of this contribution. The cases discussed below under section 5, as well as further cases were collected in Tanzania in the summer of 2006 together with Prof Bart Rwezaura whose consent to use some of them in this separate chapter is appreciated. A full analysis of the cases is currently being worked out (Rwezaura/ Wanitzek, 'The Law and Practice Relating to Child Adoption in Tanzania: 1986–2006', work in progress). Heartfelt thanks to Ms Eliamani Mbise, then Registrar of the Commercial Court, presently Registrar of the High Court of Tanzania, for her logistical support during the research, Ms Naelijwa Mrutu and Dr Kennedy Gastorn for their help in preparing and organising the research, and Ms Tulinave Willilo, Ms Neema Mugassa and Mr Steven Biko for their research assistance.
[1] See, for instance Himonga 2008; Woodman 1996; Rwezaura *et al.* 1995; Sow Sidibé 1991.
[2] See Wanitzek/Woodman 2004, 2–3; Giddens 1990, 64.
[3] Von Benda-Beckmann/von Benda-Beckmann 2006, 11, 31.

being part of the adults' nuclear family. This would normally include children who have been formally adopted, but it would exclude children who are looked after by a relative under customary law. If such relatives wish to live and work in a foreign country, they often will only obtain the necessary visa and residence permit for the child under their care if they formalise the customary care and adopt the child under state law.

The number of child adoptions by Tanzanians has thus risen with the increasing international mobility of Tanzanians, with the consequence that public norms of child adoption have attained a significance which they did not have before and which they do not have in other contexts. At the same time, customary law continues to govern relationships within the family even after a child has been adopted under state law.[4] As a result, both state law and customary law co-govern the family relationships even though state and customary laws are based on different kinship concepts: state law mainly focuses on the nuclear family, while customary law focuses on the lineage.

This has contradictory effects.[5] When a relative has adopted a child under state law, state and customary laws provide very different answers as to who is the child's legal parent. This adds a new globalised dimension to the existing pluralistic legal field.[6] It is even more difficult than in domestic conflicts of laws to draw a clear line between the applicability of customary and state laws. Rather, when each legal system is under the influence of, and in interaction with, the other, new legal patterns emerge.[7]

2.   Care for children within the lineage

Under African customary laws, including those of Tanzania, child care is considered a collective responsibility of the lineage.[8] This means that

---

[4] See also Foblets 2005, 310.

[5] For another example of an 'accumulation of contradictory legal standards' in a setting of legal pluralisation under the influence of globalisation, see Turner 2006, 101 et seq.

[6] Cf. von Benda-Beckmann/von Benda-Beckmann/Griffiths 2005, 18.

[7] See Himonga 1995, chapter 9; von Benda-Beckmann/von Benda-Beckmann 2006, 8. These new patterns may be seen as a result of legal 'syncretisation' or as a 'hybrid law', see Wanitzek/Woodman 2004, 46 et seq., 54 et seq.; on the concept of 'hybridity' see Weißköppel 2005.

[8] Kreager 1980, 7 et seq.; Wanitzek 1986, 122 et seq.; Rwezaura/Wanitzek 1988, 159; Armstrong 1995, 333 et seq.; Nhlopo 1993, 36 et seq.; see also Rigby 1969, 247 et seq. on the relevance of kinship among the Gogo, and Abrahams 1981, 111 et seq. among the Nyamwezi in Tanzania.

relatives apart from the parents such as grandparents,[9] aunts, uncles, brothers and sisters, are held, and feel, responsible for children belonging to the lineage.[10] It is therefore quite common in the various Tanzanian communities for children to grow up with, and be looked after by, relatives other than their parents.[11] This is often the case even where the parents themselves are available to care for the child.[12] For instance, elderly grandparents may ask for a grandchild to assist them in their household chores or work on the farm, or an aunt may need a niece to help her look after her young children. The parents' poverty may cause them to give a child to a relative who can provide better educational opportunities.

In situations in which parents are not available to care for their children, as in the case of the death of one or both parents, it is common that responsibility for the child is taken over by a relative. Care by relatives is also the default consideration in cases of the parents' separation, divorce, and remarriage, births out of wedlock and to teenage mothers, abandonment, serious illness of one or both parents and other kinds of 'family crisis'.[13]

However, two qualifications must be made in presenting this system of the lineage's responsibility for children under African customary laws in Tanzania. First, such practices of care provided by relatives should not be idealised. In some cases, relatives either may be unwilling to fulfil their customary obligation towards the children in the lineage[14] or they may not fulfil this obligation properly. Further, empirical studies on the situation of children living with relatives in Tanzania have shown

---

[9] See, e.g., Raum 1940 (repr. 1996), 156 et seq. on the Chaga; an example from East Cameroon is given by Notermans 2004.

[10] See, e.g., Cory/Hartnoll 1945 (repr. 1971), 30, on the Haya, and Cory 1953 (repr. 1970), 102 et seq. on the Sukuma in Tanzania.

[11] Rwezaura/Wanitzek 1988, 155 et seq.

[12] Rwezaura/Wanitzek 1988, 156. In a study conducted in a West African community (i.e. the Baatombu of Northern Benin), Alber found that, according to the general views held within that community, relatives are even in a better position than parents to educate a child properly and to apply the adequate measures of discipline, Alber 2003, 487 et seq. On the change of this perception and practice among the Fée (Mokolleé) in Northern Benin see Martin 2007. Goody 1982, 8 et seq., distinguishes between five 'parent roles' which may be performed by different persons and therefore not necessarily all of them by the parents themselves: (1) bearing and begetting, (2) status entitlements, (3) rearing and nurturance, (4) training, and (5) sponsorship.

[13] Rwezaura 2000, 326, 330.   [14] Wanitzek 1986, 211 et seq.

numerous instances and forms of abuse of, and discrimination against, such children.[15] For instance, children have been exploited by relatives as housemaids at the expense of their education or with inadequate food and health care, even while the relatives' own children are well provided for.[16] The 'risks of child fosterage'[17] thus include the possibility of marginalisation of, and discrimination against, these children as compared to the relatives' 'own' children.

Second, contemporary conditions of life may mean that relatives are not able to take responsibility for the children of the lineage. Relatives may be too poor or there may be no adult relatives alive or those who are left may be too ill to care for the children. In some families all, or nearly all, of the members of the parents' generation are dead, or are seriously ill, due to HIV/ AIDS.[18] In such cases, grandparents may look after the children but may be handicapped by their old age,[19] or elder siblings may look after their younger siblings in so-called 'children-headed households'.

Those remaining children for whom nobody cares, who have no person to stay with, or who are neglected or badly treated by relatives may end up living and working in the street.[20]

Nonetheless, the customary obligation to care for children of the lineage if necessary is still widely accepted among the population. Studies conducted in Tanzania have shown that '[i]n recent years the HIV/AIDS pandemic and the rising rate of divorce and marital separations account for large numbers of children being brought up by persons other than their two parents'.[21]

Care for children by relatives is usually achieved by an informal arrangement agreed upon by members of the lineage. The involvement of state authorities, such as the social welfare office or the courts, is the exception rather than the rule. The numbers of cases of formal foster care under the supervision of the social welfare office, and of adoption orders by the High Court, are extremely low. Hence informal care by relatives is the most common arrangement for the care of a child by someone other than his or her parents. Formal child fosterage or child adoption under state law is the exception rather than the rule.

---

[15] Rwezaura 2000, 326 et seq. with further references; for an example from Uganda see Ssemmanda 2007, 71 et seq.

[16] *Ibid.*, 332.   [17] *Ibid.*, 330.

[18] Kaijage 1997, 331 et seq.; UNAIDS 2008; LHRC 2009, 106 et seq., 112.

[19] Le Vine/Le Vine 1981, 40.

[20] Rwezaura 2000, 332; LHRC 2009, 90.   [21] Rwezaura 2000, 326, 331.

3. The need for adoption in cases of international migration

It is a different situation, however, when a relative looking after a child of the lineage immigrates into a foreign country.[22] In such cases, they will often encounter problems obtaining the necessary visa and residence permit for the child because they are not the child's legal parent or guardian. For instance, where leave to enter the United Kingdom is sought for a child, authorities will first require entry clearance from the relevant British autority in the applicant's home country.[23] To qualify for clearance, the child must be under the age of 18 and must not lead an independent life; he or she should not be married and should not have established an independent family unit; and he or she should be able to be maintained without recourse to public funds in suitable accommodation.[24]

If *indefinite* leave is sought, the child should be seeking to enter in order to accompany or join either a *parent*, or *relative*, who is settled, or who is intending to settle. 'Parent' is defined to include (1) a step-parent in cases in which the birth parent is dead; (2) an adoptive parent if the adoption order is recognised in the UK;[25] and (3) an unmarried father whose paternity has been proved. If the child seeks to enter in order to accompany or join a *relative*, there should be a serious and compelling family or other consideration making the

---

[22] On the unclarity of the term 'immigrant', see Bledsoe 2004, 90–91.

[23] Lowe/Douglas 2007, 336, with some distinction as between indefinite and limited leave, see below. On British immigration law, see also Rosenblatt/Lewis 1997; Bank/Grote 2001; Rawlings 2004. Immigration control falls under the responsibility of the Secretary of State for the Home Department, usually acting through delegated officers, Rosenblatt/Lewis 1997, 1; see Bank/Grote 2001, 330 and Tietje 2004, 30–31 on the significance of this system. The principal piece of primary legislation is the Immigration Act 1971 as amended, printed in Rosenblatt/Lewis 1997, Appendix I, 47 et seq. It is complemented by the Statement of Changes in Immigration Rules (HC 395), as amended, pursuant to section 3(2) Immigration Act 1971, printed in Rosenblatt/Lewis 1997, Appendix II, 233 et seq. These important rules contain all the requirements which applicants must satisfy to obtain entry into the United Kingdom, Rosenblatt/Lewis 1997, 1. On the relevance of European directives and regulations pursuant to the Treaty of Rome of 1959, and of the Treaty itself, in the United Kingdom see Rosenblatt/Lewis 1997, 2.

[24] For children of persons with limited leave to enter or remain under paras 128–93 of the Statement of Changes in Immigration Rules (HC 395), see paras 197–99 of HC 395 (Rosenblatt/Lewis 1997, 283 et seq.); for indefinite leave see paras 297–300 of HC 395 (Rosenblatt/Lewis 1997, 312–14).

[25] Certain immigration rules govern applications for leave to enter or remain as an adopted child, see paras 310–16 of HC 395; Rosenblatt/Lewis 1997, 21 et seq.

exclusion of the child undesirable, and suitable arrangements should have been made for the child's care.[26]

For children seeking *limited* leave to enter or remain as dependants, there is no possibility of joining *relatives* who are not parents.[27] But if *parents* are seeking leave to enter or remain, then, as a general rule, any child will be permitted to enter or remain with the parents.[28]

Similar provisions exist in other countries. For instance in Germany, children including adopted children may join their parents.[29] But children such as nieces and nephews, sisters and brothers, or foster children are only permitted to join their relatives or foster parents resident in Germany in cases of exceptional hardship.[30]

These examples show that under immigration laws, such as those in Britain and Germany,[31] it is more difficult for a person to immigrate with a child from his or her lineage than with a child from the nuclear family. Although a child may join a relative other than a parent under certain conditions, the requirements are more demanding.

It would be no solution for the immigrating relatives to leave the child behind in the home country. Social security benefits in the foreign

---

[26] Para 297 of HC 395 (Rosenblatt/Lewis 1997, 312); see also Lowe/Douglas 2007, 336 et seq. There is no guidance in the immigration rules as to the approach to such considerations, and accordingly applications are dealt with on a case-by-case basis, Rosenblatt/ Lewis 1997, 8.

[27] See, e.g., paras 197–99 of HC 395, which are applicable for employees and only mention parents as the persons to be joined by the child, not relatives.

[28] Rosenblatt/Lewis 1997, 13.

[29] § 32 Aufenthaltsgesetz of 25.2.2008, BGBl. I 162.

[30] 'Außergewöhnliche Härte.' According to § 27 Aufenthaltsgesetz, family members are permitted to join the family under the protection of Art. 6(1) Grundgesetz (GG, i.e. the German Basic Law). 'Family' in the sense of Art. 6(1) GG includes foster parents and children, Jarass/Pieroth 2009, Art. 6 GG Rn. 6; Sachs/Schmitt-Kammler 2009, Art. 6 GG Rn. 16. § 32 Aufenthaltsgesetz deals with own children (including adoptive children) while § 36 Aufenthaltsgesetz, which grants entry only in cases of exceptional hardship, concerns other family members (i.e. other than spouses and own children). According to Renner 2005, § 36 Aufenthaltsgesetz Rn. 5, 'family' is to be understood here in the sense of the extended family and therefore includes, among others, nieces and nephews, sisters and brothers-in-law (not mentioned by Renner are sisters and brothers but it is assumed that they would also fall into the category of family members if sisters and brothers-in-law do so), and foster children.

[31] On the immigration laws of a number of other states, see Giegerich/Wolfrum 2001; on Dutch immigration law, see also Koens 1996; for the USA, see also Kischel 2004, 96, 119; for a general overview of the immigration laws of various European countries, see Tietje 2004, 29–37; on the relevance of European community law, see Raible 2001; on visas and European community law, see Guild 2001, 274 et seq.; on the relevance of the European Convention on Human Rights, see Giegerich/Wolfrum 2001, 24 et seq.

country are often granted only to those family members who stay within the territory of that state.[32] Therefore, a child who stays in the home country would not benefit. The relatives may not be able to afford sufficient regular remittances, even if they have found somebody to assume the everyday care for the child in the home country.

A number of Tanzanians looking after relatives' children seem to have actually encountered such difficulties or have otherwise been advised that they need to become legal parents of the child in order to be granted leave for the child to enter the country of destination. The only legal tool available to formalise the relationship and to produce a legal parent–child relationship between the relative and the child is the adoption of the child by the relative under state law. State law is therefore of central importance in the specific case of a relative looking after a child of the lineage who immigrates together with the child into a foreign country.

Under these circumstances, it is necessary to examine the concept of adoption under state law in comparison with the concept of adoption under customary law.

4.   The concept of adoption

Adoption usually means 'the creation of partial or full kinship relations by agreement and law instead of blood'. This includes 'the voluntary assumption of parental obligations by an individual who is not the biological parent of the person adopted'.[33]

4.1   Roman law

Numerous contemporary European laws relating to adoption have been developed on the basis of Roman adoption law. Adoption under Roman law was primarily intended to provide a family with an heir and thus secure the survival of the family (ancestor worship was also to be conducted by the heir). This function explains why, under Roman law, the adopted son obtained the full position of a legitimate son of the family in the case of *arrogatio* (meaning the adoption of a person who was not under parental authority) and *adoptio plena* (meaning the full transfer of

---

[32] With varying interpretation and implementation in the member states of the European Community, Apap 2002, 94.

[33] Krause 1976, 5, 12. For the adoption of an 'illegitimate' child by his or her natural parent, see *ibid.*

parental authority from the holder to another person). Under Roman emperor Justinian, another variation was developed, that is, *adoptio minus plena* (which meant partial transfer of rights and duties resulting from a parent–child relationship).[34] When adopted, the adoptee assumed the family name of the adopter, acquiring inheritance rights from the adopter and retaining inheritance rights in the birth family.[35]

4.2   European state laws

The Roman law models of *adoptio plena* and *adoptio minus plena* served in various countries as the basis of contemporary adoption laws. Until today, adoption exists, as far as its legal effect is concerned, mainly in these two variations: 'strong' or 'full' adoption (comparable to *adoptio plena*) creates new, full kinship relationships and completely severs the existing kinship relationships; 'weak' or 'partial' adoption (comparable to *adoptio minus plena*) maintains elements of the existing relationships to some extent.[36] As for child adoption, some legal systems have chosen either one of these two forms; others provide for them both.[37]

Until the First World War, adoption was of limited practical relevance in Europe. In fact, in numerous countries, including England, adoption was not legally recognised at all. English common law held parental rights and duties to be inalienable.[38] In other countries, such as Germany or France, adoption was provided for legally but was only rarely practised.[39] This changed with the First World War, which created a large number of orphans. Because of the growing need to formalise the considerable numbers of *de facto* adoptions taking place in such cases,[40]

---

[34] Dölle 1965, 563 et seq.

[35] Krause 1976, 12. See Neukirchen 2005 for further details.

[36] This may concern the relationship with relatives other than the parents and rights evolving out of the kinship relationships, such as inheritance rights.

[37] A list of countries is provided in www.bundeszentralregister.de/bzaa/adop_pdf/ adoptionsform-.pdf. See also Frank 1978 and the country reports in Bergmann/Ferid/ Henrich. England and Germany, for instance, provide for the 'strong' adoption of children while France provides for two types of adoption, i.e. 'full adoption', which involves the transfer of parentage, and 'simple adoption', which does not break all links with the birth family, see Ferid 1987, 407 et seq.; Hauser/Huet-Weiller 1993, 660 et seq.; Sonnenberger/Autexier 2000, 166 et seq.; Chaussade-Klein/Henrich 2005, 50.

[38] Lowe/Douglas 2007, 817.

[39] The numbers reported, for instance, for France before 1900 were less than 50 adoptions per year, and not many more were reported for Germany, Dölle 1965, 564.

[40] Lowe/Douglas 2007, 818.

states which had no law for child adoption, such as England, introduced these laws.[41] The numbers of adoptions in European countries increased tremendously in the following period. Subsequently, many more countries enacted adoption legislation.[42]

From the First World War onwards, the function of adoption changed in European society. While adoption was formerly seen mainly as a patriarchal instrument to secure male heirs to whom property, family names or titles could be transmitted, it later came to be viewed as a device to provide parents for orphaned children, and at the same time to give children to childless couples.[43]

At the time when this function characterised numerous European adoption laws, these laws were exported by the European colonial powers to their African territories within the process of 'reception' or 'diffusion' of European laws during the colonial period.[44]

4.3 African state laws: the Tanzanian example

Both Tanzania (Mainland) and Tanzania Zanzibar, the two partners of the United Republic of Tanzania, inherited their statutory adoption laws from England. After a short period of German colonial power ('German East Africa' during 1891 to 1918),[45] Tanzania (Mainland) (then known as Tanganyika Territory) was under British rule from 1920 to 1961,[46] when Tanganyika attained independence. Exactly one year later Tanganyika became a Republic. Zanzibar, which had been a Sultanate of Oman since the seventeenth century, was a British Protectorate from 1890 until independence in December 1963. Approximately one month later, in January 1964, a revolution by the Afro-Shirazi party led to the

---

[41] England: Adoption of Children Act, 1926. By comparison, in the United States the first state adoption statute came into force as early as in 1851, Krause 1976, 12.

[42] Such that it can now be said that '[t]oday, adoption is recognised all but universally', Krause 1976, 12.

[43] Krause 1976, 12. Adoption also came to be viewed, and used, as a device to take over illegitimate children of unmarried mothers who were stigmatised by the fact of birth out of wedlock, Dölle 1965, 564.

[44] On the 'reception' or 'diffusion' of law see Twining 2004 with further references.

[45] Consisting of the areas of what is now Rwanda, Burundi and mainland Tanzania.

[46] First as a British Mandated Territory under the League of Nations (Article 22 Covenant of the League of Nations) and later as a British Trust Territory under the United Nations (Article 77 UN Charter).

creation of the People's Republic of Zanzibar. In April, 1964 Tanganyika and Zanzibar united and established the United Republic of Tanzania.[47]

The British, as colonial rulers, first introduced legislation on child adoption in Tanganyika in 1942[48] and in Zanzibar in 1951,[49] modelled on English adoption law.[50] In 1953, the Tanganyika adoption law was amended, and the result, the Adoption Ordinance of 1953,[51] has remained in force in Tanzania (Mainland) until now. There have only been minor amendments,[52] though it was recently renamed as the Adoption of Children Act under the Revised Laws of 2002.[53]

To understand the operation and practical relevance of these adoption statutes, it is necessary to be aware of the dimension of legal pluralism which has become a major characteristic of family law in the United Republic of Tanzania.

The first level to be affected by legal pluralism is the Union. Child adoption is not listed as a 'Union matter' in the Constitution,[54] hence there are still separate adoption statutes for Tanzania (Mainland) and for Tanzania Zanzibar.

The second level of legal pluralism refers to the laws within each partner of the Union. In both Tanzania (Mainland) and Tanzania Zanzibar the system of family law is pluralistic, comprised of English-based statutory law *cum* common law, African customary laws and religious laws, especially Islamic law.

The constellation of laws is different in the two partners in the Union due to different religious majorities. In Zanzibar, the vast majority of the population is Muslim and so Islamic law tends to govern their family relationships. In other cases, statutory law and common law are applicable, depending on individual cases and circumstances. Because of the

---

[47] On the legal relationship between the two partners of the Union, see Mvungi 2003.

[48] Adoption of Infants Ordinance 1942, No. 5 of 1942, Cap. 14, Laws of Tanganyika, in force since 8.5.1942; and Adoption of Infants Rules, GN 321 of 1942.

[49] Adoption of Children Decree, Cap. 55, Laws of Zanzibar; and Adoption of Children Rules, GN 28 of 1956.

[50] Adoption of Children Act, 1926, see above.

[51] No. 42 of 1953, Cap. 335, in force since 1.1.1955. The Adoption of Infants Rules, GN 321 of 1942, remained in force according to sec. 5 of the Second Schedule to the Adoption Ordinance of 1953.

[52] GN 478 of 1962 and Act No. 4 of 1968.

[53] Laws of Tanzania. The Revised Edition of 2002 (R.E. 2002).

[54] See Article 4(3) and First Schedule to the Constitution of the United Republic of Tanzania of 1977 as amended. In addition to the Union Constitution, there is, for Zanzibar, its own Constitution (1984).

predominance of Islamic law in Zanzibar, child adoption under statutory law is not common. Islamic law does not recognise legal adoption,[55] although it has developed various substitute forms.[56] In Tanzania (Mainland), where the majority of the population are not Muslims, the various African customary laws govern the family relationships of the majority of people. For the third of the population who are Muslim, Islamic law applies in combination with customary laws.[57]

Both Tanganyika and Zanzibar, like many other African countries that had been under British colonial government, took over the English concept of strong adoption.[58] The legal effect of a Tanzanian adoption order is to sever completely the existing legal relationship between the child and his or her birth parents, and to create a new legal relationship between child and adoptive parents with all ensuing rights and duties.[59]

This form of adoption under statutory law, as inherited from the former colonial power and maintained in the statute book until today, has remained alien to the majority of Tanzanians. They preferred, and continue to prefer, other arrangements to provide alternative care for children without parents and to provide children for childless couples.

4.4 African customary laws

As far as the 'childlessness' of a particular couple or spouse is concerned, African customary laws contain various solutions. Polygyny is the basis for some of them. A husband may marry another wife if the first wife does not bear a child.[60] Another means of providing a childless woman

---

[55] Nasir 2002, 153 et seq.; Pearl 1979, 82.

[56] On the practice of *kafalah* in Morocco, for instance, see Bargach 2002.

[57] See Juma 2004, 184.

[58] As did also, for instance, Ghana (sec. 75 Children's Act 1998, Act 560), Kenya (sec. 171 Children Act 2001, No. 8 of 2001), South Africa (sec. 242 Children's Act 2005, No. 38 of 2005) and Uganda (sec. 51 Children Statute 1996, No. 6 of 1996). In addition, several African countries which were not under British colonial government also introduced strong adoption, such as Togo (Articles 208 et seq. Code des personnes et de la famille 1980). Both strong and weak adoption is possible e.g. in Benin (Articles 336, 337 et seq., 366 et seq. Code des personnes et de la famille 2002). For further countries, see the list of countries provided in www.bundeszentralregister.de/bzaa/adop_pdf/adoptionsform.pdf and the country reports in Bergmann/Ferid/Henrich.

[59] Sec. 12 (1) Adoption of Children Act (Tanzania Mainland); Sec. 13 (1) Adoption of Children Decree (Tanzania Zanzibar). Rwezaura/Wanitzek 1988, 133.

[60] See also an example from Swaziland provided by Kuper 1950 (repr. 1975), 89: Swazi customary law provided, under certain circumstances, for the transfer of a junior wife's son to a sonless senior wife.

with a child is the legal institution of 'woman-to-woman marriage' known in various African societies.[61]

As for the provision of a substitute family for a child in need, such children are generally cared for by members of their lineages.[62] This form of child 'adoption' under the customary laws of African communities[63] follows a different logic to European concepts. The common practice is for relatives to take over the parents' role so that children grow up with relatives instead of their parents. This may fall partly within the broad European understanding of the concept of adoption formulated by Krause: 'the voluntary assumption of parental obligations by an individual who is usually not the biological parent of the person adopted.'[64]

But if 'European' adoption also requires 'the creation of partial or full kinship relations by agreement and law instead of blood',[65] African understandings do not fit. Where relatives other than parents care for children of the lineage, the existing kinship relationship is not removed nor is it replaced by any other kinship relationship. On the contrary, the existing relationship provides the basis for the relatives' care of the child.

On the other hand, African communities have undergone a degree of change as far as their family structures and practices are concerned.[66] The nuclear family has gradually gained weight, particularly among the more educated population. So not only the specific status of kinship and belonging to a lineage matters but also, in some cases, the notion of belonging to the nuclear family.

The relationship between these two concepts of family and adoption in the contemporary practice of child adoption in Tanzania will be discussed in the next section.

---

[61] Rwezaura/Wanitzek 1988, 154: 'This arrangement [of the Kuria people of Tanzania] ... may be described as a relationship between a sonless house represented by an elderly married woman or widow, commonly referred to as a mother-in-law, and a young woman who stands as a daughter-in-law to the elderly woman. The main object of this relationship is for the young woman to provide a son to the house of the older woman. Traditionally, a co-wife's son or an agnatic male relative of the elder woman's husband was selected to cohabit with the young woman and assist her to bear children but he was not legally recognised to be the father of those children.' See also Rwezaura 1985, 160 et seq.; Akpamgbo 1977, 87; Krige 1974, 14; Tietmeyer 1985.

[62] See above section 2 and notes 8 et seq.

[63] See Bledsoe 2004, 102–03 on the subtle problems of terminology of 'adoption', 'foster care' etc. See also Kreager 1980.

[64] Krause 1976, 5, 12.   [65] Krause 1976, 5.

[66] Rwezaura et al. 1995; Chirwa 2002, 157, 167 et seq.

5.   Adoption practice in Tanzania (Mainland)

The growing international mobility of the Tanzanian population has led to an increase of the numbers of child adoptions by Tanzanians. A large number of Tanzanians who applied for adoption were working or studying, and living abroad. Some selected examples of applications for child adoption involving international migration will be discussed below.[67]

5.1   Care for children whose parents have died

In the first group of cases, the death of the children's birth parents presented the cause for action. In the first case an aunt, Victoria (51), adopted three children: two nieces, Anna (17) and Maria (13), and a nephew, Peter (16).[68] Anna was Victoria's sister's child while Peter and Maria were her brother's children to different mothers. Peter's mother had died soon after Peter was born in 1990 and Maria's mother had died in 1996 when Maria was three. Victoria's brother, the children's father, died in 2001 when Peter was eleven and Maria eight. Anna's father had died in 1994 and her mother also subsequently became very ill. For this reason, Victoria 'adopted the three infants in August 2002 with the mutual agreement among the family members'.[69] Since then all the three children were under her care. In January 2006, Anna's mother died. The only surviving members of the children's parents' generation were Victoria and another sister. Victoria was a senior officer at one of the Ministries in Dar es Salaam and was currently pursuing her PhD programme abroad. She was divorced from her husband, who had died in the meantime, and had one adult son (26) who also lived and studied in the same foreign country.

In 2006, Victoria applied before the High Court in Dar es Salaam for the formal adoption of the three children. The children's grandmother

---

[67] In all cases presented below the names have been changed and no indications have been made as to the ethnic group, foreign nationality etc. of the persons involved in order to protect their anonymity and make sure that confidentiality is fully secured. All cases are from Tanzania (Mainland).

[68] Dar es Salaam High Court, Misc. Civil Cause No. 62 of 2006.

[69] According to the guardian ad litem's report. The court shall appoint a guardian ad litem in order to safeguard the child's interests. He or she has to investigate, and report to the court on, the circumstances of the child and the petitioner and other matters relevant for an assessment whether the adoption order will serve the child's best interest, sec. 11 (2) Adoption of Children Act; rule 13 Adoption of Infants Rules; see Rwezaura/Wanitzek 1988, 131–32.

and their other surviving maternal aunt consented to the adoption. Equally, Victoria's son stated that he 'has no objection for his mother to adopt the infants as he knows that she is the only caregiver of the infants'.[70] The adoption order was granted by the High Court in Dar es Salaam in June 2006.

In the second case, two paternal uncles applied for the adoption of six orphaned siblings.[71] The children's father had died in 1996, and the mother in 1997, when the children were between three and thirteen years old. In a meeting of the children's paternal family in June 1997, immediately after the mother's death, it was agreed that the elder brother of the children's father, Lawrence (54), should take over the care for the four elder children while the two younger children should be cared for by their younger paternal uncle, Stephen (43).

By the end of November 2000, Stephen and his wife Magdalena (36) applied for the adoption of the two younger children, Joyce (9) and Willis (7), before the High Court in Arusha. Stephen was an engineer and Magdalena a medical assistant. They had married in 1992 and had three of their own children who were still attending primary school and nursery school. In a 'Certificate of Urgency' it was stated by the applicants' advocate that 'the applicants are to leave the country for [a foreign country] on 20th December 2000 for a long period; [and that] the applicants cannot get travel documents for the infant children in the absence of a court decision on the pending application.'

Soon thereafter, in early December 2000, Lawrence and his wife Desdemona (50) also applied for the adoption of the four elder children, Laetitia (17), Fortunata (16), Devota (15) and Happiness (12). Lawrence held a PhD in management, and Desdemona, a citizen of another African country, a degree in education. Both were self-employed and were living in Desdemona's home country. They had married in 1974 and had three of their own adult children, two of them still pursuing their university education. In words reminiscent of the case mentioned above, their Certificate of Urgency stated that the petitioners 'are to leave the country for [another African country] on 29th December 2000 for a long period; [that] the infants are scheduled to start schooling in [that country] in early January 2001; [and that] the petitioners cannot get valid travel documents for the infants in the absence of the Honourable Court's decision on this pending miscellaneous civil cause.'

---

[70] According to the guardian ad litem's report.
[71] Arusha High Court, Misc. Civil Causes Nos. 8 and 9 of 2000.

The children's paternal grandfather consented to the adoption of all six children. However, the court records did not contain any adoption orders.

Orphaning of young children is a common event in contemporary Tanzania,[72] primarily due to HIV/AIDS, though other causes of death are cited in some cases.[73] In both cases discussed above, the customary obligation of the surviving members of the parents' generation to care for the orphaned children was put forward by other remaining members of the lineage ('mutual agreement among family members'; decision within a 'clan meeting').[74]

The HIV/AIDS pandemic has actually increased the number of cases in which children need to be looked after by relatives other than their parents for the most serious reason.[75] Therefore, there is an increasing demand for aunts and uncles to perform the roles of 'mother' and 'father' in the way of fully and permanently replacing the orphans' late parents. This is a responsibility quite different from that of a relative who performs a parent's role while one or both of the child's parents are still alive and may be approached, if the need arises, at any time for any reason. Furthermore, in many cases not only are both parents unavailable, but the whole generation of the parents, and thus of potential alternative caregivers, is reduced in numbers by the pandemic, often to the extent of being nearly or fully extinguished. This has had a considerable impact on the situation of the remaining relative (as Victoria's son put it, 'the only caregiver of the infants'), who cannot resort to other members of the lineage for their assistance. On the contrary, they may even have to look after additional sets of orphaned children of the lineage.

In the above cases, the persons appointed by the members of the lineage to look after the orphans showed their acceptance of the obligation through their behaviour. Since they were all living abroad, they had to take the children along in order to fulfil their customary law obligation to care for the children. For immigration purposes under the foreign laws

---

[72] See, e.g., Rwezaura 2000, 348; LHRC 2009, 112.

[73] E.g. in the first case, Dar es Salaam High Court, Misc. Civil Cause No. 62 of 2006, three death certificates indicate other causes of death, while only the fourth death certificate refers to HIV/AIDS. It is however not possible to rely on the indications of causes of death in the certificates because for various reasons they do not always reflect the actual causes.

[74] Cf. Fleischer 2007 on the role of the extended family in decision-making in cases of migrants from Cameroon in Germany.

[75] See above, section 2.

concerned, they had to adopt the children to have them assigned as their own children so that they could be taken along. This could only be achieved under the state law relating to child adoption. State law was thus used as an instrument to fulfil the customary law obligation under the specific circumstances of international migration.

It is very rare for Tanzanians to adopt a child under state law if there is no immediate need for a formal adoption, such as the immigration requirements of a foreign country. Such need arises, however, in the situation of international migration. The *de facto* care by members of the lineage for their relatives' children, in fulfilment of their customary law obligation to take over the parental role for these children, does not count legally as a parent–child relationship in the eyes of foreign immigration laws. Numerous immigration laws distinguish between a person's own children and his or her relatives' children. It is not that they ignore the lineage but they distinguish between the nuclear family and the lineage, and privilege members of the former over the latter.

This creates a difficult situation for international migrants looking after relatives' children. If they want to continue caring for these children, they are forced to use a legal institution – that of child adoption under state law – only for the purpose of satisfying the demands of the foreign immigration laws. In the eyes of the foreign immigration law, this may even be a misuse of the law.[76] They are thus caught in a trap between family and kinship concepts embedded in the two legal systems, that is, the customary law concept, which requires inclusion of relatives' children, and the foreign state law concept, which provides for their exclusion. The Tanzanian state law relating to child adoption has to face the challenge of mediating between these two concepts.[77]

The potential connecting point between the two concepts is the principle of the best interest of the child. Under the Tanzanian Adoption of Children Act, the court must examine whether the adoption order would be in the best interest of the child.[78] Depending on the individual case and circumstances, it is, on the one hand, quite probably in the best interest of orphans to be cared for by close relatives whom they know

---

[76] See also Wray 2006.

[77] For recent innovative solutions to this problem in national children's acts see, e.g., the Ghana Children's Act 1998 (Act 560), which defines 'parents' as the natural parents and persons who act like parents vis-à-vis the child (sec. 124 Ghana Children's Act), see Daniels 2008, chapter 5 et seq.; and the Uganda Children Statute, 1996 (No. 6 of 1996), see Okumu-Wengi 1998, Ssemmanda 2007 and Hellum/Stewart/Ali/Tsanga 2007, xxxi.

[78] Sec. 7(1)(b) Adoption of Children Act. See also Rwezaura/Wanitzek 1988, 130–32.

well, who are able and willing to care for them, and who do care for them with the lineage's consent. The answer to the question whether this appears in a different light in cases in which these relatives go abroad depends again on the individual case and the individual circumstances.

On the other hand, one has to distinguish between the customary care for such children and adoption as understood by Tanzanian state law. Even where it is in the children's best interest to be cared for by their relatives under such circumstances, the question is still whether it is also in their best interest to be adopted by them. As shown above, Tanzanian adoption law follows the concept of strong adoption, which means a change of legal status of the child, that is, the existing parent–child relationship is replaced by a new parent–child relationship between the child and the relative who has adopted him or her. Similarly, all other existing family relationships based on the previous parent–child relationship are changed according to the new parent–child relationship. After having been adopted, these children are no longer their parents' children but the children of the adopting aunts and uncles. Siblings who have been adopted by different relatives are not siblings any more. This is not the idea of the customary law concept of care for children by members of the lineage. As a consequence, and contradictorily, in cases of international migration, the customary care for relatives' children can only be secured by using a legal instrument (adoption under state law) which denies the legal relevance of the very same customary care.

This contradiction between the motivation for child adoption in actual practice (that is, to enable the applicants to provide customary care for relatives' children) and the effect of the adoption itself (turning relatives' children into their own children) is even more relevant and disturbing in cases in which an adopted child's parents are still alive, a constellation to which we now turn.

5.2 Care for children whose parents are still alive

The first case in this group of cases concerned the adoption by a paternal aunt, Nadou (45), of her nephew, Nathan (3).[79] Nadou was the elder sister of the boy's father, who was 32. She held a university degree in education and worked as a high-ranking officer of an international organisation in another African country, after having worked with the same organisation in various other African countries. Nadou was married but separated from her

---

[79] Arusha High Court, Misc. Civil Cause No. 97 of 1998.

husband and had a daughter of 22 years. During one of her earlier stays abroad, Nathan's father, then 17 years old, had lived with Nadou for some time and had been under her guardianship.

In July 1998, Nadou applied for Nathan's adoption before the High Court in Arusha. Nathan's parents were both alive and married to each other. Both of them were 'unemployed'. In the Certificate of Urgency submitted to the court Nadou stated that 'I ... must shortly travel with [Nathan] to [another African country] where I work and currently reside, and his legal adoption would facilitate travel and other opportunities.' Nathan's parents consented to the adoption. The adoption order was granted in September 1998.

In the second case of this group of cases, a father, Daudi (37), applied for adoption of his daughter Prisca (7) before the High Court in Arusha.[80] Prisca had been born before her parents married and Daudi was not recorded on the birth certificate as father. When he was about to go abroad to train for a job, he decided to take Prisca along so that she could attend school in the foreign country. According to the Certificate of Urgency, 'this cause is of utmost urgency for the following reasons: 1. that I have already secured a school for the child in [the foreign country]; 2. that I'll be leaving very soon to [go to that foreign country] where I am also studying and I want to leave with the child.' His wife, Prisca's mother, consented to the adoption because, as she indicated, she was too poor to take care of the child herself. About a year later, in July 2005, the petition was withdrawn by Daudi's advocate because 'it seems the petitioner is not interested in pursuing this application as he has never contacted me since the filing of this petition'.

In both cases, the children's birth parents were alive, healthy, and available but they seem to have assumed that better education could be provided for the children abroad than in Tanzania. In Nathan's case, the court records do not contain any explicit statement by the parties about the motives for adoption. However, Nadou seems to have been economically much better off than Nathan's parents, and so better economic prospects may have been a motive for the adoption. Nadou also had a special relationship with Nathan's father, because she had looked after him during his adolescence. Moreover, since she had a daughter but no son, it is also possible that she had an interest in raising Nathan in order to have a 'son' as well.

---

[80] Arusha High Court, Misc. Civil Cause No. 5 of 2004.

The decision that Nathan should be cared for by his aunt instead of his parents may therefore have been based on a bundle of several motives, including to further the child's best interest. The family members seem to have assumed that it served the best interest of the child, especially in terms of better education and a safe economic situation, if the child was cared for by a relative. Under customary law this care did not affect the existing legal parent–child relationship. Under state law, by contrast, this relationship was extinguished by the adoption order. Here the 'price' for the care by a well-to-do aunt living abroad consisted of the loss of the legal relationship between the child and his parents. This casts the question of the child's best interest in a different light.

In Prisca's case, the father's attempt to adopt his daughter may have been due to the fear, or the information received, that the foreign immigration law would not allow him to take along his 'illegitimate' child. He could have 'legitimated' his daughter under customary law[81] but this would not have been documented by a state authority. And, since Tanzania state law does not provide for the legitimisation of children born out of wedlock, even not by the subsequent marriage of their parents, nor for the separate establishment of paternity,[82] adoption may have seemed to be the only solution.[83] Under the Adoption of Children Act, a parent may adopt his or her own child.[84] In the case of a child born out of wedlock, this creates a legal bond between father and child which does otherwise not exist between them according to the old English common law still applicable in Tanzania on this point.[85] The current legal position of children born out of wedlock is not in line with the UN Convention on the Rights of the Child of 1989 and the African Charter on the Rights and Welfare of the Child of 1990 which the United Republic of Tanzania has ratified. As such, Tanzania is under an obligation to respect and ensure the rights set forth in the Convention on the Rights of the Child and in the African Charter on the Rights and Welfare of the Child to each child within its jurisdiction without discrimination of any kind, irrespective of, among others, the child's

---

[81] See Sheria Zinazohusu Hali ya Watu [Law of Persons], 1st Schedule, Local Customary Law (Declaration) Order, 1963, GN 279 of 1963.

[82] Wanitzek 1986, 394 et seq.

[83] Which was chosen also in previous cases, e.g. in Dar es Salaam High Court, Misc. Civil Cause No. 22 of 1979.

[84] Sec. 3(3) Adoption of Children Act; see Rwezaura/Wanitzek 1988, 127, text at n. 12.

[85] Rwezaura/Wanitzek 1988, 140 et seq.

birth or other status.[86] The current state of the law is not in line with this requirement.

5.3   Care for children in an intercultural family context

While the applicants discussed so far were all Africans, we now turn to a group of cases in which one spouse applying for adoption was an African and the other a European or North American.

The first case concerns the adoption of Lulu, a 13-year-old girl, by her maternal aunt Rehema (35), who was the younger sister of Lulu's mother, and Rehema's husband Paul (57), a foreign citizen.[87] Lulu was born out of wedlock. Her father was known to her maternal family only by his first name and his whereabouts were said to be unknown. The birth certificate indicated her maternal grandfather's name as that of her father. Her mother died in 1991 when Lulu was still under one year old. Her mother's younger brother took over her custody. Lulu completed her primary school education in 2003.

In December 2003, Rehema and Paul applied for her adoption. They wanted to take Lulu along to the country in which Paul was working and the family was living, although they also had a house in Tanzania. Rehema had trained as a tailor and Paul was a technician, being employed by an international organisation for which he had been working in various countries including Tanzania. Rehema and Paul had married each other in 1989 and had one common son aged 14 years, while Paul had two further children aged 17 and 20 who were living in the same country in which their father was currently working. In the Certificate of Urgency Rehema and Paul stated that they were about to leave Tanzania early in 2004 to return to the country where they were actually living and that Lulu was required to start secondary school there in January 2004. The adoption order was granted in January 2004.

The second case is that of Marceli, a 13-year-old boy, who was adopted by his half-sister Neema (27) and her husband David (59), a foreign citizen.[88] Marceli and Neema had the same mother, but different fathers. Marceli was born out of wedlock. On the birth certificate his (and Neema's) maternal grandfather was indicated as the boy's father. His

---

[86]   See Article 2(1) UN Convention on the Rights of the Child and Article 3 African Charter on the Rights and Welfare of the Child; Makaramba 1998; Mashamba 2008.

[87]   Arusha High Court, Misc. Civil Cause No. 5 of 2003.

[88]   Arusha High Court, Misc. Civil Cause No. 5 of 2005.

actual father was married to another woman with three children but had separated from his wife and lived alone. He had no relationship any more with Marceli's mother. The boy had been in his mother's custody since his birth. Since 1999, Neema and David had supported Marceli by paying his school fees so as to enable him to attend a school outside Tanzania in a neighbouring African country. During school holidays he used to stay with his mother who was living in Neema's and David's house in Tanzania.

David held a PhD in engineering, and Neema had trained as a secretary. They had married each other in 2000 and had a six-year-old son and a two-year-old daughter. They owned a house and several plots of land in Tanzania and ran a tourism business between Tanzania and the husband's home country where they lived and wanted Marceli to live with them and attend school.

The application for Marceli's adoption was filed in the High Court in Arusha in June 2005 because Neema and David wanted Marceli to start school in David's home country in July of the same year. As stated in the Certificate of Urgency, 'the infant cannot travel in the absence of the honourable court's decision on this pending application'. The adoption order was granted in July 2005.

These are cases of children born out of wedlock whose fathers were not involved with their upbringing or not available to care for them. The maternal grandfather took over the father's role which was reflected on the birth certificates indicating the maternal grandfather as father. Under this system, which exists in many customary laws, the maternal family had to provide both 'mother' and 'father' for the children.

In the cases reviewed, this may have made it more difficult to maintain the children because a second potential source of support, that of the father's lineage, was also missing. Fortunately for them, the mothers' lineages in both cases presented above acquired some additional potential to fulfil their responsibility towards the family members. In both cases one of the young women married a foreigner who was not only well off financially but also ready to contribute to his in-laws' fulfilment of their customary obligations towards the children of the lineage. By not only marrying a daughter but also looking after a child of her lineage, these husbands expressed their acceptance of the responsibilities under customary laws of a member of their wives' lineages. So Lulu was moved from her maternal uncle's care to that of her maternal aunt and her foreign husband, and Marceli from his mother's care to that of his elder sister and her foreign husband. The timing of the adoption was school-determined in both cases: after completion of primary school, the children were to start their secondary school education in the foreign country.

The contradiction for African adoptive parents between customary care and adoption under state law did not exist for the foreign adoptive fathers in these cases as their cultural backgrounds were characterised by the same family concept as the state adoption law, that is, that of the nuclear family. As for the African family members involved, in Lulu's case there was no parent alive to be affected, although there were other relatives. In Marceli's case his mother lost her legal parent–child relationship with Marceli. Instead, the adoption order turned her into her son's legal grandmother, while his sister, 14 years older than he, became his legal mother. The 'value' of the new legal father for the child depended, both in Lulu's and Marceli's cases, on the stability and quality of the marriage between him and the child's aunt or sister, respectively, who was the connecting link between adoptive father and child.

However, the question is whether such legal changes to relationships within the family actually play a role within the families and communities concerned. Some Tanzanian observers of these and similar cases had the impression that the family relations within the lineage rather continued as they were before, without any visible change due to the adoption order granted under state law. If this was the case, it would put another question mark behind the current legal position: a solution to the problem of taking the children along to a foreign country can be obtained only at the price of new legal family relationships which may not be in line with the relationships actually lived among, and valued by, those family members.

6. Conclusion

The cases analysed in this chapter reflect an increasing use of state law for the purpose of adopting a child where there is international migration. State law appears as the means of fulfilling customary law obligations of relatives to care for children in the lineage: adoption was expected to facilitate the immigration of a child to a foreign country where the relative looking after the child was living. Adoption under state law served an urgent purpose, although it did not really fit the relationship between the adoptive parent and child. State adoption law was used where and when it was considered necessary to fulfil the customary obligation to take care of a relative's child, while the primary effects of adoption under state law, that is, extinguishing the existing, and creating a new, legal parent–child relationship, were not necessarily wanted. The results are family relationships which are neither those of customary law nor of state law, but represent a further and new variant. The Tanzanian situation of legal pluralism thus undergoes further pluralisation under the influence of globalisation through international migration.

References

Abrahams, R. G. 1981, *The Nyamwezi Today. A Tanzanian People in the 1970s*, Cambridge University Press, Cambridge.

Akpamgbo, C. O. 1977, 'A "Woman to Woman" Marriage and the Repugnancy Clause: A Case of Putting New Wine into Old Bottles', *African Law Studies*, vol. **14**, 87–95.

Alber, E. 2003, 'Denying Biological Parenthood: Fosterage in Northern Benin', *Ethnos*, vol. **68**, 487–506.

Apap, J. 2002, *The Rights of Immigrant Workers in the European Union. An Evaluation of the EU Public Policy Process and the Legal Status of Labour Immigrants from the Maghreb Countries in the New Receiving States*, Kluwer, The Hague.

Armstrong, A. 1995, 'A Child Belongs to Everyone: Law, Family and the Construction of the "Best Interests of the Child" in Zimbabwe', Innocenti Occasional Papers Child Rights Series, 11, available at www.unicef-irc.org/publications/pdf/crs11.pdf.

Bank, R. and R. Grote 2001, 'Vereinigtes Königreich von Großbritannien und Nordirland' in T. Giegerich and R. Wolfrum (eds.), *Einwanderungsrecht – National und International. Staatliches Recht, Europa- und Völkerrecht*, Leske + Budrich, Opladen, 305–31.

Bargach, J. 2002, *Orphans of Islam. Family, Abandonment, and Secret Adoption in Morocco*, Rowman and Littlefield Publishers, Lanham etc.

Benda-Beckmann, F. v. K. v. Benda-Beckmann and A. Griffiths 2005, 'An Introduction' in F. v. Benda-Beckmann, K. v. Benda-Beckmann and A. Griffiths (eds.), *Mobile People, Mobile Law. Expanding Legal Relations in a Contracting World*, Ashgate, Aldershot, 1–25.

Benda-Beckmann, F. v. and K. v. Benda-Beckmann 2006, 'The Dynamics of Change and Continuity in Plural Legal Orders', *Journal of Legal Pluralism and Unofficial Law*, no. **53**/54, 1–44.

Bergmann, A., M. Ferid and D. Henrich (eds.), Looseleaf collection, *Internationales Ehe- und Kindschaftsrecht*, Verlag für Standesamtswesen, Frankfurt/Main.

Bledsoe, C. 2004, 'Reproduction at the Margins: Migration and Legitimacy in the New Europe', *Demographic Research*, Special Collection 3, Article 4, 86–116, available at www.demographic-research.org.

Chaussade-Klein, B. and D. Henrich 2005, 'Frankreich' in Bergmann, A., M. Ferid and D. Henrich (eds.), *Internationales Ehe- und Kindschaftsrecht*, Verlag für Standesamtswesen, Frankfurt/Main.

Chirwa, D. M. 2002, 'The Merits and Demerits of the African Charter on the Rights and Welfare of the Child', *International Journal of Children's Rights*, vol. **10**, 157–77.

Cory, H. and M. M. Hartnoll 1945 (repr. 1971), *Customary Law of the Haya Tribe, Tanganyika Territory*, Frank Cass, London.

Cory, H. 1953 (repr. 1970), *Sukuma Law and Custom*, Negro Universities Press, Westport Conn.

Daniels, W. C. E. 2008, 'Ghana.' *International Encyclopedia of Laws. Family and Succession Laws*, Kluwer, Alphen aan den Rijn.

Dölle, H. 1965, *Familienrecht. Darstellung des deutschen Familienrechts mit rechtsvergleichenden Hinweisen*, Band II, Verlag C. F. Müller, Karlsruhe.

Ferid, M. 1987, *Das französische Zivilrecht. Familienrecht, Erbrecht*, Verlag Recht und Wirtschaft, Heidelberg.

Fleischer, A. 2007, 'Family, Obligations, and Migration. The Role of Kinship in Cameroon', *Demographic Research*, vol. **16**, 413–40, available at www.demographic-research.org.

Foblets, M.-C. 2005, 'Mobility versus Law, Mobility in the Law? Judges in Europe Are Confronted with the Thorny Question "Which Law Applies to Litigants of Migrant Origin?"' in F. v. Benda-Beckmann, K. v. Benda-Beckmann and A. Griffiths (eds.), *Mobile People, Mobile Law. Expanding Legal Relations in a Contracting World*, Ashgate, Aldershot, 297–315.

Frank, R. 1978, *Grenzen der Adoption. Eine rechtsvergleichende Untersuchung zur Schutzbedürftigkeit faktischer Eltern-Kind-Verhältnisse*, Metzner, Frankfurt.

Giddens, A. 1990, *The Consequences of Modernity*, Stanford University Press, Stanford.

Giegerich, T. and R. Wolfrum (eds.) 2001, *Einwanderungsrecht – national und inter-national. Staatliches Recht, Europa- und Völkerrecht*, Leske + Budrich, Opladen.

Goody, E. 1982, *Parenthood and Social Reproduction: Fostering and Occupational Roles in West Africa*, Cambridge University Press, Cambridge.

Guild, E. 2001, *Immigration Law in the European Community*, Kluwer Law International, The Hague.

Hauser, J. and D. Huet-Weiller 1993, *Traité de droit civil. La famille. Fondation et vie da la famille*, Librairie générale de droit et de jurisprudence, Paris.

Hellum, A., J. Stewart, Sh. S. Ali and A. Tsanga 2007, 'Preface: Paths Are Made by Walking: Introductory Thoughts' in A. Hellum, J. Stewart, Sh. S. Ali and A. Tsanga (eds.), *Human Rights, Plural Legalities and Gendered Realities. Paths Are Made by Walking*, Southern and Eastern African Regional Centre for Women's Law (SEARCWL), Weaver Press, Harare, xii–xliv.

Himonga, Ch. 1995, *Family and Succession Laws in Zambia. Developments since Independence*, LIT, Münster.

Himonga, Ch. 2008, 'Normative Systems and Individual Choice in Plural African Legal Contexts', paper presented at the International Workshop on Legal Pluralism, Cape Town, 7–9 September 2008, pp. 9.

Jarass, H. D. and B. Pieroth 2009, *Grundgesetz für die Bundesrepublik Deutschland. Kommentar*, Beck, München, 10th edn.

Juma, I. 2004, 'Unsystematic Growth of Islamic Jurisprudence in Tanzania – An Overview', *Recht in Afrika/Law in Africa/Droit en Afrique*, vol. 7, 177–94.

Kaijage, F. 1997, 'Social Exclusion and the Social History of Disease: The Impact of HIV/AIDS and the Changing Concept of the Family in North-Western Tanzania' in McGrath, S., Ch. Jedrej, K. King and J. Thompson (eds.), *Rethinking African History*, University of Edinburgh, Centre of African Studies, Edinburgh, 331–56.

Kischel, U. 2004, 'Länderbericht USA. Neue Entwicklungen im Einwanderungs- und Asylrecht' in E. Riedel (ed.), *Neuere Entwicklungen im Einwanderungs- und Asylrecht. Verfassungs-, Völker- und Europarechtliche Aspekte*, Nomos, Baden-Baden.

Koens, M. J. C. 1996, 'Family Migration in the Netherlands' in Lowe, N. and G. Douglas (eds.), *Families across Frontiers*, Martinus Nijhoff Publishers, The Hague etc.

Krause, H. D. 1976, 'Creation of Relationships of Kinship', in *International Encyclopaedia of Comparative Law*, Volume IV: Persons and Family, Mouton, The Hague, 3–101.

Kreager, P. 1980, *Traditional Adoption Practices in Africa, Asia, Europe and Latin America*, International Planned Parenthood Federation, London.

Krige, E. J. 1974, 'Woman Marriage with Special Reference to the Lovedu – Its Significance for the Definition of Marriage', *Africa*, no. **44**, 11–37.

Kuper, H. 1950 (repr. 1975), 'Kinship among the Swazi' in A. R. Radcliffe-Brown and D. Forde (eds.), *African Systems of Kinship and Marriage*, Oxford University Press, London etc., 86–110.

Le Vine, S. and R. Le Vine 1981, 'Child Neglect in Sub-Saharan Africa' in J. E. Corbin (ed.), *Child Abuse and Neglect: Cross-Cultural Perspectives*, University of California Press, Berkeley, 35–55.

Legal and Human Rights Centre (LHRC) 2009, *Tanzania Human Rights Report 2008. Progress through Human Rights*, Legal and Human Rights Centre, Dar es Salaam.

Lowe, N. and G. Douglas 2007, *Bromley's Family Law*, Oxford University Press, Oxford, 10th edn.

Makaramba, R. V. 1998, *Children Rights in Tanzania*, Friedrich Ebert Stifung, Dar es Salaam

Martin, J. 2007, 'Yakubas neues Leben – Zum Wandel der Kindspflegschaftspraxis bei den ländlichen Fée (Mokollé) in Nordbenin', *Afrika Spectrum*, vol. **42**, 219–49.

Mashamba, J. C. 2008, 'Realising Children's Rights in the Context of the UDHR in Tanzania', *The Justice Review*, vol. 7, 101–19.

Mvungi, S. E. A. 2003, 'The Legal Problems of the Union between Tanganyika and Zanzibar', *Eastern Africa Law Review*, vol. 28–30, 31–50.

Nasir, J. J. 2002, *The Islamic Law of Personal Status*, Kluwer International, New York, 3rd edn.

Neukirchen, Ch. 2005. *Die rechtshistorische Entwicklung der Adoption*, Lang, Frankfurt/Main.

Nhlapo, R.T. 1993, 'Biological and Social Parenthood in African Perspective: the Movement of Children in Swazi Family Law' in J. Eekelaar and P. Šarčević (eds.), *Parenthood in Modern Society*, Nijhoff, Dordrecht etc., 35–50.

Notermans, C. 2004, 'Sharing Home, Food, and Bed: Paths of Grandmotherhood in East Cameroon', *Africa*, vol. 74, 6–27.

Okumu-Wengi, J. 1998, 'Searching for a Child-centred Adoption Process. The Law and Practice in Uganda' in W. Ncube (ed.), *Law, Culture, Tradition and Children's Rights in Eastern and Southern Africa*, Ashgate, Aldershot, UK, 225–48.

Pearl, D. 1979, *A Textbook on Muslim Law*, Croom Helm, London.

Raible, K. 2001, 'Vorgaben und unmittelbar anwendbare Normen des supranationalen Rechts der Europäischen Gemeinschaft' in T. Giegerich and R. Wolfrum (eds.), *Einwanderungsrecht – national und international. Staatliches Recht, Europa- und Völkerrecht*, Leske + Budrich, Opladen, 37–72.

Raum, O. F. 1940 (repr. 1996), *Chaga Childhood A Description of Indigenous Education in an East African Tribe*. New Introduction by Sally Falk Moore, LIT, Münster.

Rawlings, R. 2004, 'Länderbericht Großbritannien. The Three "F's" – and Beyond' in E. Riedel (ed.), *Neuere Entwicklungen im Einwanderungs- und Asylrecht. Verfassungs-, Völker- und Europarechtliche Aspekte*, Nomos, Baden-Baden, 149–85.

Renner, G. 2005, *Ausländerrecht Kommentar*, Beck, München, 8th edn.

Rigby, P. 1969, *Cattle and Kinship among the Gogo. A Semi-Pastoral Society of Central Tanzania*, Cornell University Press, Ithaca, London.

Rosenblatt, J. and I. Lewis 1997, *Children and Immigration*, Cavendish Publishing Limited, London.

Rwezaura, B. A. 1985, *Traditional Family Law and Change in Tanzania. A Study of the Kuria Social System*, Nomos, Baden-Baden.

Rwezaura, B. A. and U. Wanitzek 1988, 'The Law and Practice relating to the Adoption of Children in Tanzania', *Journal of African Law*, vol. **32**, 124–63.

Rwezaura, B., A. Armstrong, W. Ncube, J. Stewart, P. Letuka, P. Musanya, I. Casimiro and M. Mamashela 1995, 'Parting the Long Grass: Revealing and Reconceptualising the African Family', *Journal of Legal Pluralism and Unofficial Law*, no. **35**, 25–73.

Rwezaura, B. 2000, 'The Value of a Child: Marginal Children and the Law in Contemporary Tanzania', *International Journal of Law, Policy and the Family*, vol. **14**, 326–64.

Sachs, M. and A. Schmitt-Kammler 2009, *GG Kommentar*, Beck, München, 5th edn.

Sonnenberger, H. J. and Ch. Autexier 2000, *Einführung in das französische Recht*, Verlag Recht und Wirtschaft, Heidelberg, 3rd edn.

Sow Sidibé A., 1991, *Le pluralisme juridique en Afrique: L'exemple du droit successoral sénégalais*, Librairie générale de droit et de jurisprudence, Paris.

Ssemmanda, H. W. 2007, 'Working with Custom. Promoting Children's Rights to Livelihood by Making de facto Guardians Responsible', in A. Hellum, J. Stewart, Sh. S. Ali and A. Tsanga (eds.), *Human Rights, Plural Legalities and Gendered Realities. Paths Are Made by Walking*, Southern and Eastern African Regional Centre for Women's Law (SEARCWL), Weaver Press, Harare, 59–77.

Tietje, Ch. 2004, Neue Entwicklungen im Einwanderungs- und Asylrecht. Völker-, europa-, verfassungs- und verwaltungsrechtliche Aspekte. Generalbericht, in E. Riedel (ed.), *Neuere Entwicklungen im Einwanderungs- und Asylrecht. Verfassungs-, Völker- und Europarechtliche Aspekte*, Nomos, Baden-Baden, 9–58.

Tietmeyer, E. 1985, *Frauen heiraten Frauen. Studien zur Gynaegamie in Afrika*, Renner, Hohenschäftlarn.

Turner, B. 2006, 'Competing Global Players in Rural Morocco: Upgrading Legal Arenas', *Journal of Legal Pluralism and Unofficial Law*, no. **53**/54, 101–39.

Twining, W. 2004, 'Diffusion of Law: A Global Perspective', *Journal of Legal Pluralism and Unofficial Law*, no. **49**, 1–45.

UNAIDS 2008, 'Regional and Country Profiles: Tanzania', www.unaidsrstesa.org.

Wanitzek, U. 1986, *Kindschaftsrecht in Tansania, unter besonderer Berücksichtigung des Rechts der Sukuma*, Renner, Hohenschäftlarn.

Wanitzek, U. and G. R. Woodman 2004, 'Relating Local Legal Activity to Global Influences: A Theoretical Survey' in G. R. Woodman, U. Wanitzek and H. Sippel (eds.), *Local Land Law and Globalization. A Comparative Study of Peri-Urban Areas in Benin, Ghana and Tanzania*, LIT Verlag, Münster, 1–79.

Weißköppel, C. 2005, '"Hybridität" – die ethnografische Annäherung an ein theoretisches Konzept' in R. Loimeier, D. Neubert and C. Weißköppel (eds.), *Globalisierung im lokalen Kontext. Perspektiven und Konzepte von Handeln in Afrika*, LIT Verlag, Münster, 311–47.

Woodman, G.R. 1996, 'Legal Pluralism and the Search for Justice', *Journal of African Law* vol 40, 152–67.

Wray, H. 2006, 'Hidden Purpose: UK Ethnic Minority International Marriages and the Immigration Rules' in Shah, P. (ed.), *Migration, Diasporas and Legal Systems in Europe*, Routledge-Cavendish, Abingdon etc., 163–84.

18

Towards non-state actors as effective, legitimate, and accountable standard setters

ANNE PETERS*, TILL FÖRSTER**,
AND LUCY KOECHLIN***

The three parts of this book have dealt with our lead questions on non-state standard setting: How can the relevant actors and processes be described and mapped? By what authority do they set standards? And are the processes and their outcome, the standards, effective and legitimate?

The chapters comprised in this volume explore different facets of standard setting, some looking at these questions from a more theoretical perspective, some discussing concrete case studies in various fields. Given the diversity of actors and the diversity of standard-setting processes, no single set of necessary and sufficient conditions for guaranteeing the legitimacy, accountability, and effectiveness of non-state standard setting could be identified. However, the importance of inclusiveness, transparency, and procedural safeguards has emerged as a common theme. Moreover, all chapters taken together have made it abundantly clear that the phenomenon of non-state standard setting forces us to question four boundaries which are used in legal, sociological, and political analysis: the boundaries between law and non-law, between the public sphere and the private sphere, between public law and private law, and between international, national, and local law.

* Prof Dr. iur., LLM (Harvard), University of Basel; Basel Institute on Governance.
** Prof Dr. phil., Institute of Social Anthropology, University of Basel; Basel Institute on Governance.
*** Lic. phil., MSc (LSE), Basel Institute on Governance and Institute of Sociology, University of Basel.

1. Actors and processes

1.1 The role of NGOs in standard setting

The case studies in this book have illustrated how NGOs participate in global standard setting. In a legal perspective, we can distinguish various types of standards and corresponding different types of NGO involvement. First, NGOs are engaged in the elaboration of ordinary inter-state international conventions (see the examples given in the introduction[1] and by Lindsey Cameron (Chapter 5), on the role of the ICRC). Here NGO involvement is largely informal. NGO forums are held in parallel to and separate from the intergovernmental standard-setting conferences, such as the Rio conference of 1992. So NGOs do not have any negotiating role whatsoever here. However, their direct lobbying at those conferences can be crucial.

The second type of standard setting occurs within international organisations or quasi-organisations, in particular in the framework of the highly institutionalised multilateral environmental agreements. Here, the governmental bodies or conferences of the parties create secondary law for the implementation of the respective regimes. To most of these bodies, NGOs are accredited in formal procedures and thus enjoy an observer (or in the Council of Europe: 'participatory') status.[2] This legal status is an intermediate one between exclusion and full participation as co-law makers. It entails various rights to be invited and to sit in meetings, to obtain information (agendas, drafts), speaking time, the allowance to distribute documents and the like.

---

[1] See Peters, Koechlin, Fenner and Zinkernagel, Chapter 1, section 2.1.

[2] See, e.g., Art. 12 c) OECD Convention (1960); Art. 13(2) Convention Establishing the WIPO (1967); Art. XI(7) CITES Treaty (1973); Art. 6(5) Vienna Convention on the Protection of the Ozone Layer (1985); Art. 11(5) of the Montreal Protocol on Ozone Depletion (1987); Art. 15(6) Basel Convention on the Transboundary Movement of Hazardous Waste (1989); Art. V.2. WTO Agreement (1994); Art. 10(5) Aarhus Convention (1998); Art. 22(7) UN Convention to Combat Desertifiation (UNCCD, 1994); Art. 23(5) Biodiversity Convention (1992); Art. 29(8) Cartagena Protocol on Biosafety (2000); Art. 7(6) UNFCCC (Framework Convention on Climate Change (1992); Art. 13(8) Kyoto Protocol (1997), and the secondary law, rules of procedures and guidelines concretising the respective treaty provisions. See for the Organization of American States (OAS): Permament Council of the OAS, Review of the Rules of Procedure for Civil Society Participation with the OAS, 31 March 2004, CP/CISC-106/04: The OAS and its different organs and sub-organisations establish general or special 'co-operative relations' or 'official working relations' with civil society organisations. See for the Council of Europe below note 71.

The crucial legal feature of NGO involvement in this type of standard setting is that NGOs are, in all bodies, denied voting rights. They only have a voice. Among international lawyers, it is controversial whether NGOs have, as a matter of customary law, a general entitlement to participate as observers (and thus to be heard) within the law-generating international institutions.[3] Such an NGO right to be heard would come to bear in institutions which have no or only deficient special rules of procedure. We submit that a customary right of NGOs to participate in the international legal discourse does not yet exist, because practice and *opinio iuris* have not sufficiently matured. But NGOs already enjoy a legitimate expectation that – once an institution has admitted them – the participatory conditions will entail two core components: oral interventions and written submissions.[4] Refusal of these rights must be specifically and concretely justified. In the current international legal system, the NGOs' voice is thus the functional equivalent to the formal law-making power which other actors (the international legal subjects) possess. Because of this legal function of NGOs' voice, there is a need to legally structure NGO participation.

Finally, NGOs sometimes draft private texts or propose norms (often in conjunction with academics), such as codes of conduct and guidelines, interpretative treaty commentaries, or principles, in the hope that they will be adopted by other international actors, cited, and accepted as contributing to the corpus of international law.[5] Examples are the numerous Rules of the International Law Association, the Helsinki Rules on the Use of Waters of International Rivers of 1966, the Limburg Principles on the Implementation of the International Covenant on Economic, Social and Cultural Rights of 1997, the Montreal Principles on Women's Economic, Social and Cultural Rights of 2000, or the Princeton Principles on Universal Jurisdiction of 2001.

Overall, despite the multiple NGO activities and their often forceful presence, 'states retain a tight grip on the formal law-making processes'.[6] Even in those areas where NGOs have had greatest impact, states control the agenda and the access to the law-making arenas, in particular through the accreditation procedures.

---

[3] See in the affirmative Charnovitz, 'Nongovernmental Organizations', 370; negatively Nguyen Quoc, Daillier and Pellet, *Droit international public*, 653.

[4] Tully, *Corporations and International Law-Making*, 207, 233; also Lindblom, *Non-Governmental Organisations*, 526.

[5] Boyle and Chinkin, *The Making of International Law*, 88–89, also for the examples.

[6] *Ibid.*, 95.

1.2   The role of business in standard setting

TNCs increasingly act as 'regulatory entrepreneurs' in various ways. In the elaboration of international conventions, business as business has no formalised role. It can only obtain an official observer or participatory status in international organisations or negotiating forums through the guise of NGOs, for example via the International Chamber of Commerce. Primarily, TNCs' role in inter-state law making is limited to lobbying. This mainly happens on the national level, where TNCs influence the prior negotiating position of home states, and also subsequent implementation.[7] The pressure of business interests is nowadays probably an indispensible motor of regulation.[8]

There are various further types of genuine business standard setting: first, economic private actors are participating in the elaboration of the so-called 'new *lex mercatoria*'.[9] This body of law (or soft law) is being developed mainly by commercial arbitral tribunals which are installed by the economic actors themselves. The relevant standards build on economic usage and on model contracts and standard terms provided by private merchant associations, by the International Chamber of Commerce (ICC), the Hague Conference on Private International Law, UNIDROIT and various other UN agencies, such as IMO and UNCITRAL. The new law merchant thus develops in the interstices between intergovernmental organisations or agencies and private bodies, and oscillates between private and public, and between hard and soft law.

Second, firms elaborate technical, product, and professional standards. Third, they adopt company or multi-stakeholder codes of conduct, notably in the field of labour, environment, and human rights (see Eva Kocher (Chapter 15) and Egle Svilpaite (Chapter 16)). A fourth type is 'civil regulation'[10] by TNCs and NGOs in 'private–private partnerships', or within 'trilateral' public–private partnerships, composed of governmental actors, civil society organisations, and the business sector. We will for the moment retain the established terminology of 'public–private', although

---

[7] See on the participation of TNCs only with the acquiescence, support or permission of governments Tully, *Corporations and International Law-Making*, 304–05, 321, 233.

[8] Nowrot, *Normative Ordnungsstruktur*, 235 and 237.

[9] See from the abundant scholarship on the lex mercatoria, e.g., Berman and Kaufman, 'The Law of International Commercial Transactions', 221 et seq.; Weise, *Lex mercatoria*; de Ly, *International Business Law*; Osman, *Les principes généraux*; Stein, *Lex mercatoria*; Galgano, *Lex Mercatoria*; Cutler, *Private Power*.

[10] Muchlinski, *Multinational Enterprises*, 550, with examples in the field of environmental protection at 549–56.

one of the principal conclusions we draw is precisely that non-state actor involvement in standard setting demonstrates the *problématique* of the underlying categories.[11] The classical example of trilateral standard setting is the creation of labour standards within the International Labour Organisation. In the law-making body of this organization, the international labour conference, not only government delegates (two for each member state), but also employer delegates and worker delegates (one for each member state respectively) are present, with the member states nominating the non-government delegates. The ILO has been fairly successful in adopting global labour standards. However, these have to be formally ratified by governments as multilateral conventions. So the governments retain control of various steps of the process. Modern examples for 'private–private' standard setting are the Forest Stewardship Council (FSC) standards (Stéphane Guéneau (Chapter 14)). Also, the Ethical Trading Initiative's (ETI) 'ETI Base Code of Workplace Standards'[12] has been elaborated by business in co-operation with various NGOs, such as Oxfam and Christian Aid. Finally, Rio Tinto's and Shell's human rights, social, and environmental standards with regard to business activity *inter alia* in Indonesia, Mongolia, and Nigeria were implicitly endorsed by Amnesty International. These and other forms of private–private and private–public standard setting are achieved by regulatory framing and close supervision of transnational private standardisers by public authority, or through collaborative 'standards ventures' between private and public actors.[13]

In a formal legal perspective, neither type of business self- and co-regulation produces ordinary hard law.[14] However, corporate codes, technical standards, and various shades of hybrid regulation are arguably in some respects functionally equivalent to state or inter-state hard law. This will be briefly discussed below in 2.2.

1.3   The remaining role of states in standard setting

Although globalisation has marginalised formal law as a steering mode, states and state-made law have displayed staying-power in global

---

[11] See below section 6.   [12] www.ethicaltrade.org.

[13] See, e.g., for (technical) standardisation in the EU and EFTA: 'General Guidelines for the Cooperation between CEN, CENELEC and ETSI and the European Commission and the European Free Trade Association' of 28 March 2003, OJ EC 2003/C 91/04, 7–11. In scholarship Mattli, 'Public and Private Governance', at 225.

[14] See for the legal significance of corporate codes of conduct Lundblad, 'Some Legal Dimensions'.

governance. This diagnosis must be nuanced by the observation that 'the' states do not form a homogenous group with identical attitudes vis-à-vis non-state standard setting. Typically, developing states are more sceptical of global non-state standards, because of their real or suspected northern bias. Leaving aside this nuance, four points can be made.

First, only states (governments, acting directly or via international governmental organisations, see Steven Wheatley (Chapter 8)) 'make' formal international (treaty) law, while non-state actors participate in international formal legal processes in a manner qualitatively and quantitatively different from governments. However, focusing the analysis on the exclusion of non-state actors from formal international law making arguably 'misses the political and social reality of their increased participation' and the impact of that participation on subsequent state behaviour. 'It would be myopic to insist on the classical view of states as the sole makers of international law; rather we must recognise the multi-layered, multipartite nature of the international law-making enterprise.'[15]

Second, the states often perform a 'formalising' role. State institutions progressively integrate informal, non-state-made standards into the legal system. Such a formalisation of non-state standards occurs, for example, through references in judicial decisions or in codes.[16]

Third, states increasingly assume a mediator role in standard setting. Where two groups of global players, namely TNCs and NGOs, typically have conflicting objectives, the state becomes less of an initiator or law maker and more of a mediator between competing forces.[17] Standard setting within PPPs (among governments, business and civil society organisations) may be apt to neutralise or at least mitigate the danger of one-sided standards. PPP standard setting thus increases process and output legitimacy.

To conclude, despite the weakness of many states and the 'failure' of some,[18] states still remain the dominant political institutions worldwide. At the international level, they are recognised as the legitimate actors representing the population in their territories. At the domestic level, the state is the major frame within which processes of political and societal change take place. Finally, if states retain the monopoly on the legitimate

---

[15] Boyle and Chinkin, *The Making of International Law*, 97.

[16] See for examples below section 2.2.

[17] Boyle and Chinkin, *The Making of International Law*, 61.

[18] The notion of the 'failed state' has been coined by Robert I. Rotberg and assumes that a state ceases to exist when it is no longer able to sustain the monopoly on the legitimate use of force within its borders. See Rotberg (ed.), *When States Fail*.

use of force, they are the only actors to enforce law by coercive means. While non-state actors have become rule makers, these rules are then 'flanked' by governmental law enforcement.

2. The effectiveness of non-state standard setting

One of our leading questions is whether non-state actors' standards are effective. Here we must distinguish two levels: the process of standard setting itself, and later compliance with the standards made by or in co-operation with non-state actors. The focus of this book is the first level, whereas compliance and enforcement issues are not our main theme. So the question is under what conditions and to what extent the involvement of non-state actors contributes to the making of global standards, and under what conditions it inversely protracts, delays, distorts or even prevents their coming into being.

2.1   Causality, legitimacy, and the shadow of hierarchy

The effects of non-state-actor input into formal law making are difficult to determine, because the main channels of non-state actors' influence are informal. It can hardly be measured to what extent NGO and TNC lobbying in formal international law-making processes influenced governmental attitudes and voting and thus ultimately shaped the outcome. Notably NGOs have probably been more successful in agenda setting than in actually impacting on the concrete results, that is, the definite language and content of concrete standards. So they probably play their most important role during the first stage of standard setting.

Overall, the impact of non-state actors on intergovernmental standard-setting processes, and also their capability to produce autonomous standards and to engage in co-regulation with governments, seems to depend on factors such as reputation, flexibility, receptivity to alternative perspectives, representativity, and reliability – in short, on factors which simultaneously contribute to their legitimacy. So effective standard setting is in this regard conditioned on legitimacy (see on legitimacy below, section 4).[19]

---

[19] The effectiveness of the standards once adopted seems to be a quite different matter. Non-state-made standards are not legally enforceable, except when they have been endorsed by states, or have been otherwise incorporated into the fabric of state-made law. However, on this level legitimacy plays as well: in the absence of legal enforcement measures, the crucial factor of effective standards application is legitimacy.

A well-known hypothesis is that effective standard setting by non-state actors requires the 'shadow of hierarchy'.[20] Only if a credible threat of governmental, 'hierarchical' law making exists, the non-state participants, who are situated in a non-hierarchical, 'horizontal' relationship, will agree on a standard.[21] Otherwise, so the hypothesis, endless bargaining and no or merely suboptimal outcomes will result. The only way out would be to introduce majority voting in standard setting. But this is, in most if not all forums, unacceptable to the participants.

This hypothesis should probably be nuanced. First, insights gained through New Institutional Economics demonstrate that not merely hierarchy and organisation, but property rights and transaction costs in specific social contexts structure the pattern and success of formal and informal institutions.[22] Second, under the conditions of a privatised and often criminalised state, the presence of a hierarchical order may lead right into the dissolution of existing and effective standards, as the case of Zimbabwe shows.

In some settings, for example with regard to industrial self-regulation in various sectors, case studies have confirmed the 'shadow' hypothesis. Industry self-regulation works best within political systems that encourage it, and works poorly when the political system works against it. Virginia Haufler has concluded that much of the responsibility rests with government: 'International industry self-regulation has the potential to encourage significant improvements but only in concert with traditional political processes.'[23] This finding has important consequences for standard setting and implementation in weak or repressive states. While a legitimate state renders standards more effective by incorporating them into its accepted social order, standards in areas of precarious statehood must draw effectiveness from other sources, for instance, from a normative social order based on religion. Generally speaking, non-state actor standard setting becomes more effective when it refers to a legitimate social and political order. If this legitimate social order is statehood, standard setting seems to be most effective when it is embedded in state governance.

There is one functional equivalent to hierarchy: exclusivity, coupled with secrecy.[24] In the absence of hierarchy, standard setting flourishes in

---

[20] Scharpf, *Games Real Actors Play*, 204–05.

[21] See also above section 1.3 on the role of the state in global standard setting.

[22] For seminal literature see North, *Institutions*; Ostrom, *Governing the Commons*.

[23] Haufler, *A Public Role*, 121–22.

[24] Although secrecy and exclusion may serve as a functional equivalent to hierarchy, it is also a feature common to hierarchy itself. As Max Weber classically outlined, secrecy is one of the prime characteristics of bureaucratic hierarchies, serving to entrench the

small exclusive clubs of participants who do not have important conflicts of interest. Closeness and homogeneity facilitate norm creation.[25] So in this regard, effectiveness and legitimacy (which calls for inclusiveness and transparency) are in tension, and trade-offs are inevitable.

2.2   The legal effects of non-state standards in relation to 'hard' (inter-)state law

As already pointed out, most non-state standards are, in a legal perspective, not in themselves legally binding, although they may be binding in a societal perspective. They are not enforceable by ordinary legal mechanisms, notably by courts. In the binary conception which clearly distinguishes law from non-law, the non-state standards (except the interstate treaties and conventions) must be counted as non-law. In the continuum view, which accepts that there may be a grey zone between law and non-law, the non-state standards mostly lie on the 'soft' or less law-like end of the scale.

Nevertheless, non-state standards fulfil important normative functions, which can be mapped according to their relation to hard law. First, non-state standards fulfil a pre-law function. They are often adopted with a view to the elaboration and preparation of future international law. Standards provide normative guidance, build mutual confidence, and concert societal and political attitudes. Both within nation states, and especially on the international scene, private sector experimentation in developing and implementing standards can create the basis for a (transnational) social consensus, which is the foundation upon which more appropriate regulation can be built.[26] Non-state standards are thereby pacemakers for subsequent hard law. The setting of non-state standards might thus be characterised as 'bottom-up' norm formation, as opposed to 'top-down' legislation.[27] The fact that the non-state actors are not linked to nation states, but transcend boundaries, and

autonomy and power of the bureaucratic apparatus against other social and economic forces. See Weber, *Economy and Society*, vol. 3, chap. XI on bureaucracy.

[25] Closeness and homogeneity also foster compliance (which is not our issue), because a crucial motive of complying with formally non-binding rules is concern for reputation, which in turn is greatest in smaller, homogenous groups ('clubs').

[26] See for industrial standards Haufler, *A Public Role*, 121.

[27] See Levit, 'A Bottom-Up Approach', 129 on the creation of standards in the finance sector: 'The process starts with a relatively small, homogenous lawmaking group, reminiscent of a private club … that creates substantive rules, which are essentially organic norms emanating from the practices of the respective practitioners … The lawmaking group also establishes procedural and remedial rules … The informal, practice-based rules ultimately embed themselves in a more formal legal system and become law.'

potentially act globally, makes non-state standard setting a natural tool for legal harmonisation. Non-state-driven harmonisation corresponds to the idea of subsidiarity. Arguably, it is more effective (and more legitimate – see on legitimacy below, section 4) than top-down harmonisation (via formal inter-state covenants). Its effectiveness is due to the fact that non-state standards contribute to a competition between different national and international regulatory models. This competition fuels innovation and increases the probability for finding better normative arrangements.[28]

Second, in situations where binding rules are unavailable or for other reasons inopportune, non-state standards can substitute legislation and thereby fulfil a para-law function. An example are the 'para-legal' labour standards analysed by Eva Kocher in Chapter 15. The notion 'para-law' can be read as a parallel to the concept of para-statehood.[29] The latter stands for a type of domination where non-state actors – as individuals or as corporate groups – have acquired, often by illicit means, certain rights and duties from the core of the state's administration (see Michael Miklaucic (Chapter 7)).

Third, non-state-made standards effectively complement hard law, by making it more concrete or by guiding its interpretation. Especially the operationability of inter-state treaties with their often broad and vague language may benefit from such concretisation. For instance, the Law of the Sea Convention of 1982 establishes the right of innocent passage (Art. 17), but does not say how wide or deep the navigable channel must be. The International Navigation Association (PIANC), which represents port, navigation, and shipping interests, sets the relevant standards for the shipping channels.[30] Further, 'diagonal' agreements between governments and firms (for example investment agreements) frequently refer to standards for products or for behaviour (for example in accounting or evaluation practices), to 'best industry practice' or to 'prevailing commercial usage', and thus incorporate these private standards. For instance, the International Financial Reporting Standards (IFRS), adopted by the International Accounting Standards Board (IASB),[31]

---

[28] See for the area of international financial regulation Grote and Marauhn (eds.), *The Regulation of International Financial Markets*, 317–18.

[29] Para-statehood (*Parastaatlichkeit*) as a concept has been developed by Trutz von Trotha, e.g. Trotha, 'Die Zukunft liegt in Afrika'.

[30] Example from Lowe, 'Corporations', at 25.

[31] The IASB is an independent, privately funded accounting standard setter based in London, UK. The Board members are private persons selected on account of their

have been incorporated into an EU-Commission Regulation of 2003 whose annexes, which contain the standards, are being continuously amended.[32] The typical legal consequence of these referrals and incorporations is that observance of the 'private' standards will give rise to a presumption of lawfulness. For instance, within the European Union, conformity with the technical standards elaborated under the so-called 'new approach' to technical standard setting triggers the presumption that the product is in conformity with the relevant European Directives and therefore allowed to circulate freely in the Common Market.[33] The same technique is used in national law. For example, the accounting standards of the DRSC (*Deutsche Rechnungslegungs Standards Committee*), a professional association, are referred to in § 342 cl. 2 of the German commercial code (*Handelsgesetzbuch*). Under this provision, the use of these standards for accounting establishes the legal presumption that the legally required accounting and book-keeping standards have been observed.[34] The result of all these examples are 'mixed' regimes, in which non-state standards fulfil a 'law-plus' function.

3. The authority of non-state standard setters

With regard to new standards set by (or with substantial involvement of) non-state actors the question arises who has the authority to set standards. Given our premise that the power and thus also the authority of the state – the traditional prime locus of political authority – is waning under the pressures of globalisation, the issue is how standard-setting authority is generated and enforced within the increasing complexity of policy arenas. As pointed out in the introduction, the term 'authority' is ambivalent.[35] Authority can denote, *inter alia*, both the power and the right to rule.[36] In the following, we will not mean by 'authority' the mere

professional competence and practical experience. The IASB is committed to developing, in the public interest, a single set of high quality, understandable and enforceable global accounting standards that require transparent and comparable information in general purpose financial statements.

[32] Commission Regulation (EC) No 1725/2003 of 29 September 2003 adopting certain international accounting standards in accordance with Regulation (EC) No 1606/2002 of the European Parliament and of the Council, OJ EC L 261 of 13 October 2003/1.

[33] Röthel, 'Lex mercatoria', 759.

[34] German *Handelsgesetzbuch*, provision as amended and in force since 1 May 1998 (BGBl. 1998 I, 784).

[35] Peters, Koechlin, Fenner and Zinkernagel, Chapter 1, section 3.6.

[36] *The Oxford English Dictionary*, 798.

capacity to enforce obedience (that is, naked power), but the right (or title) to legitimately influence action, opinion, or belief. Even the latter type of authority has different facets: we can distinguish formal authority, that is, the authority of actors who are endowed with authority by right, from *de facto* authority, that is, actors who merely claim to be endowed with authority, who endow themselves with a mantle of legitimacy to justify their actions.[37] So authority – as we understand it – always encompasses at least a claim to legitimacy. But authority, thus associated with (real or usurped) legitimacy, needs more than legitimacy: '[O]nly those who have real power can, in normal circumstances, have legitimate political authority.'[38]

The plethora of new coalitions and policy networks constitute new loci of authority in that sense, which are at least in part private.[39] Hall and Biersteker have described the emergence of private authority within a threefold typology: market, moral, and illicit authority.[40] This typology allows a nuanced understanding of the transformative forces behind the shifting relationship between public and private authority, with market authority capturing the effects of globalisation, and moral authority[41] encapsulating epistemic and normative shifts. Both market and moral authority have to some extent translated into regulatory authority, which is now shared with the state.[42] The third, probably most original of these types is 'illicit' authority, denoting what other authors have termed the criminalisation or the privatisation of the state.[43]

---

[37] Cf. Raz, 'Introduction', 3. Raz uses the terms 'legitimate' and '*de facto* authority'. This conceptualisation differs from Wheatley's distinction between epistemic authority and practical authority (see Wheatley (Chapter 8)). In Raz's terms, 'practical authority' would encompass both legitimate authority as well as *de facto* authority, which merely claims a right to legitimacy (on this point see also Barker, *Legitimating Identities*, in particular Chapter 5 on rebels and vigilantes).

[38] Raz, 'Introduction', 3.

[39] Cf. Cutler, *Private Power and Global Authority*, 2: The 'new transnational legal order' and 'privatized lawmaking' is 'transforming relations of power and authority in the global political economy'.

[40] Hall and Biersteker (eds.), *The Emergence of Private Authority*, 9.

[41] Different subtypes of private moral authority can be identified: expertise, neutrality, or normative superiority. Moral authority has accrued notably to NGOs in all three subtypes: on account of their expertise, their neutrality, and their laudable objectives.

[42] Hall and Biersteker (eds.), *The Emergence of Private Authority*, 209–10.

[43] See Bayart, Ellis and Hibou, *The Criminalization*; Mbembe, *On Private Indirect Government*. See from a more policy-oriented perspective the work by the World Bank Institute on state capture, seminally laid out in Hellman, Jones and Kaufmann, *Seize the State*.

The new loci of authority seem to respond directly to problems raised by inadequate standard-setting capacity and resources of the actors (and authorities) involved. Whatever shapes and forms such processes take, the contextuality of the right to rule (by setting standards) as well as the capability to rule matters. Private actors are increasingly involved in norm-setting activities in formerly public domains (see for instance in this volume Dan Assaf (Chapter 3), Egle Svilpaite (Chapter 16) or Marcus Schaper (Chapter 11)), whereas the state assumes greater involvement in formerly private spheres (for instance Stéphane Guéneau (Chapter 14), Ulrike Wanitzek (Chapter 17) or Peter Hägel (Chapter 13)). Maybe more pertinently, the acquisition of authority by both state and non-state actors are not autonomous processes. They feed off and respond to each other and thus mutually inform and implicitly or explicitly link up 'public' and the 'private' standards in many different ways. This phenomenon has always been observable,[44] but is especially visible in new areas of regulation (for case studies see Lucy Koechlin and Richard Calland, Chapter 4, and Lindsey Cameron, Chapter 5). However, it can be tentatively asserted that neither the source nor the scope of the authority of the actors involved allows any generic predictions on the effectiveness of the norms generated. In the following sections, some relevant insights drawn from the contributions in this volume on factors defining the authority and effectiveness of new standards will be discussed.

First, although all the contemporary patterns of rule making discussed here are highly uneven in terms of the 'hardness' (that is, their degree of formalisation and of enforceability), one common denominator can be identified: their logics are co-operative rather than adversarial. More precisely, there is a decline in hierarchical relations and a shift towards more synergetic relationships between public and private actors.[45] However, this holds true only for many governance and rule-making processes in advanced democracies, and with regard to rules and standards on issues which are of interest to the North (such as for instance environmental or social regulation). The co-operative mode of governance does not necessarily prevail in many countries of the South. On the

---

[44] For the development of the modern state shaped by the interaction and friction between public and private (economic) interests see the classic study by Schumpeter, *History of Economic Analysis*.

[45] For further elaboration see Knill and Lehmkuhl, 'Private Actors and the State'; BG Peters, 'Governance'.

contrary, one characteristic of so-called weak states is precisely that conflicts over the legitimacy and effectiveness of authorities are frequently addressed through adversarial and downright violent means. In other words, although partnership, dialogue and multi-stakeholder engagement may be key features of new standard-setting authority, they are by no means the only defining feature or process. More scholarly analysis is needed on other, seemingly illicit forms of standard setting, capturing the authority of actors hidden in a sphere that Michael Miklaucic (Chapter 7) pointedly termed the 'dark matter', or what Till Förster (Chapter 12) calls 'statehood beyond the state'.

Second, with regard to the problem of authority, the contributions in this volume demonstrate two things: no standard-setting actors were discerned whose actions and representations can be termed wholly illegitimate, that is, who operate solely through naked coercion. Although brute force and violence may well be one method of securing compliance and realising certain (mostly economic) objectives, even the illicit actors examined clothe themselves in a mantle of legitimacy ('*de facto* authority', as defined above), by providing either ideological alternatives and/or concrete output to the population. This mantle is not merely symbolic. Even in situations of violent conflicts, the claims to legitimacy are instrumental to the compliance that such actors attain (and vice versa), for the simple reason that all forms of power (even subjugation, the most naked form of exercising power) are at least facilitated by a minimal level of acceptance. This holds true for such diverse actors as rebels, who usually apply a mixture of ideological as well as coercive methods to secure compliance[46] (see the case study of the CPN(M) in Michael Miklaucic, Chapter 7); as well as for perfectly legal actors such as international organisations or NGOs, whose right and ability to make authoritative decisions are derived from international

---

[46] On this point Barker, *Legitimating Identities*, 89 is particularly clear by elaborating that 'rebels legitimate themselves as vigorously as do rulers … Nor is such legitimation restricted to those rebels who challenge existing government in its entirety by aiming for control of the state. Those vigilantes who seek by coercive direct action against other subjects or citizens to appropriate some of the functions of government by compelling others to act in accordance with their own political, religious, cultural or moral beliefs, will engage in a corresponding legitimation of themselves as the proper exercisers, in a bespoke manner, of governmental power.' See also Hall and Biersteker (eds.), *The Emergence of Private Authority*, 16 on the social legitimation of illicit authority (i.e. violative of domestic or international legal norms).

institutional settings and processes and from the immediate necessity of providing order and basic services (see for instance Dieter Neubert (Chapter 2)).[47]

The preceding – by no means ground-breaking – point, that the exercise of power is usually bolstered by claims to legitimacy (and thus constitutes authority) needs to be modified by a further observation. In most of the processes examined in this book, the authority of the actors is contingent not only on (existing or emerging) rules and processes, or even on their immediate problem-solving or coercive capacity, but also on structures that are beyond the immediate influence of these actors. In other words, the nature of their authority is informed by the patterns of globalisation as well as localisation. In many cases, the power of actors to set and enforce standards is decisively shaped by their relative ability to exert influence over patterns of global economic and political distribution. Susan Strange has developed the concept of 'structural power' to analyse this phenomenon. Structural power is the power to influence the patterns of the global political economy and, mediated through this global influence, also the structures within which national polities and people have to operate.[48] Structural power is not a monolithic force, nor is it masterminded by a single, unified group of actors. Rather, it consists of key spheres that fundamentally transcend and transform the private-public divide. According to Susan Strange, these are the ability to influence the provision of security, goods and services, finance and credit, and finally knowledge. Although the concept of structural power was developed to explain relative power shifts between nations, it also offers very useful insights into the dynamics of the authority between state and non-state actors. As, for instance, Marcus Schaper's contribution (Chapter 11) shows, the *de facto* authority of private and public trans-domestic regulation depends less on the formal legitimacy of the actors (although that is also a factor) but far more on their market authority. In this case, interestingly, the structural power (that is, their dominance in

---

[47] The different facets of the nature of authority become clear in Steven Lukes' definition of authority as a 'distinctive mode of securing compliance which combines in a peculiar way power over others and the exercise of reason' (Lukes, 'Perspectives on Authority', 205). Although authority plainly involves a network of control mechanisms, such as (the threat of) coercion, force, manipulation etc., 'reason is plainly involved: authority offers a reason and operates through reasoning' (*ibid.* 205). This would correspond to Hall and Biersteker's understanding of moral authority.

[48] A first outline of the concept of structural power can be found in Strange, 'The Persistent Myth', 121 et seq.

the financial market of the recipient countries) exerted by financial enterprises from non-OECD countries subverts the authority that new 'Northern' norms in environmental regulation can unfold in Southern countries. Conversely, the *de facto* authority of certain international actors may emanate directly from their key position in providing finance, credit, aid as well as knowledge (not least in terms of post-conflict paradigms) to recipient countries. Both examples highlight that the arenas of shaping authority have indeed undergone massive changes. The same could be demonstrated with regard to illicit actors, for example warlords who derive their *de facto* authority from their proximity to international markets (both legal and illegal) which provide the resources to finance their activities.

What needs further exploration, then, is the legalisation of illicit actors in official positions. A pertinent example is provided by the phenomenon of warlords, who, judged by local standards, may or may not enjoy social acceptance and recognition, but certainly violate international human rights standards by exercising armed control over territories. They conduct extensive (and mostly illegal) economic activities within these territories. Although they are clearly illicit actors who act in opposition or in parallel to the state, they are frequently co-opted into formal public functions. Owing to their *de facto* authority within the national territory of the state, warlords are included in formal political institutions, for instance through their appointment as ministers. The underlying rationale of such inclusion is, first, to extend the state's control over its own territory via the warlords, and, secondly, to tame their illicit power. This happens in many post-conflict countries, the most well-documented case being Afghanistan, whose cabinet has included known warlords. Such practices are at least tacitly condoned by the international community. They are distinct from the criminalisation of the state or state capture, which denote informal processes of the appropriation of the state and the state's resources by private illicit actors. Rather, they constitute the reverse side: private illicit actors are co-opted by the state, thus avoiding an armed confrontation with and legal sanctioning of the warlords.

Although the national and international political reasoning behind these processes is well understood, the effects of such formally legitimised boundary crossing between legal and illegal are seriously under-problematised. Potentially, repercussions on the legitimacy of the state are to be expected. Popular perceptions might be that the public interest is betrayed by caving in to powerful individuals, providing them with a formal mantle of legitimacy and, moreover, endowing them with formal authority and access to state resources on top of their *de facto* authority. This hypothesis also invites further empirical research on factors shaping the social recognition of actors and standards. At this point it is important to observe that not only is the distinction between public and private at best blurred and *in extremis* redundant,[49] but conventional distinctions need to be reconceptualised – for instance global and local factors, or structural and cultural factors, as Till Förster demonstrates in Chapter 12. It will require deeper and probably more innovative analysis to capture the economic and political structures constraining and enabling specific forms of authority.

Third, several chapters turn to an increasingly pertinent question, namely the formalisation of *de facto* authority exercised by non-state actors, in particular through the introduction and implementation of accountability and transparency principles that allow some degree of democratic control. For instance, Monica Blagescu and Robert Lloyd (Chapter 10) argue persuasively for the introduction of not only cross-sectoral, but also measurable accountability standards for the very reason that international actors – independent of the sector of origin – exercise *de facto* and *de iure* authority. From a different theoretical perspective, Steven Wheatley (Chapter 8) and Marcus Schaper (Chapter 11) come to the same conclusion, namely that the *de facto* authority of certain standard setters (and the standards themselves) needs to be legitimised and rendered accountable through transparent decision making or their deliberation in acclaimed international bodies.

What is striking, fourth, is the degree to which the relationship between authority, legitimacy and effectiveness has loosened. The key conclusions of the chapters in this volume show at least indicatively that the legitimacy and authority of the actors themselves is at best a necessary, but by no means a sufficient condition of effective norms. Although most chapters touch upon this problem, the actual effect of the new norms and standards is extremely uneven. Two different phenomena need to be distinguished: the first is the situation where the actors may be endowed with formal authority but not with sufficient real power. Most pertinently, this is the case with many public institutions which lack capacity, expertise or resources to both develop and implement adequate norms (for instance strained or dismantled public institutions, see Marcus Schaper (Chapter 11) or in areas of great technological

---

[49] The example of warlords provides another neat illustration of the tangled relationship between public and private.

complexity, such as critical security infrastructure (see Dan Assaf (Chapter 3)). Without necessarily claiming that the authority of the state as such is in decline, we cannot ignore that public institutions are faced with massive governance challenges. The resolution of complex problems requires the kind of new approaches and resources witnessed in initiatives such as EITI (see Lucy Koechlin and Richard Calland (Chapter 4)). We shall turn further down to the impact of such processes on the authority of the standard-setting actors involved. Just highlighting one aspect, the impact of such processes on the effectiveness of public institutions is *a priori* open: it may bolster their credibility, expertise as well as endowments through the structured and formalised exchange processes (see for instance Eva Kocher (Chapter 15) or Lucy Koechlin and Richard Calland (Chapter 4); or it may weaken them further by diverging authority to other, non-state or international actors (see again Marcus Schaper (Chapter 11)).

Fifth, a lateral theme of many of the chapters is the issue of control and accountability of standard-setting actors – not just the 'how', but also the 'who'. The time-honoured question of political science, namely *'cuis custodiet ipsos custodes?'*, has lost some of its salience, for the custodians have become hidden or invisible: they have disappeared behind abstract and convoluted configurations of contractual and factual power-sharing arrangements, as Dan Assaf shows in an exemplary and highly pertinent area (Chapter 3). The question has mutated to who is exercising author-ity, and whether there is one denotable authority that can be identified and which is both able to enforce compliance as well as render account. Given the tangled interdependencies of the public and private actors in key policy-making arenas, no straightforward answers can be supp-lied here. More empirical enquiries are needed to unravel these interrelationships.

Sixth, it can be argued that many standard-setting processes in hitherto unregulated areas have been initiated without any real intention of having any effect, but purely for the sake of window dressing. This is observable in all types of self-regulatory as well as in multi-stakeholder initiatives (even in governmental regulatory activities, but this is not our prime concern). The reason is that actors need to be seen 'to do' some-thing when faced with public pressures and demands by their stake-holders. Julia Black's analysis (Chapter 9) of the trilemmas that regulatory regimes face when confronted with conflictual accountability demands is insightful and innovative in its endeavour to penetrate the underlying rationales of standard-setting authorities. More obviously, such dilemmas exist in the private sector, where enterprises have undergone a steep learning curve in dealing with and responding to accountability and transparency demands by the public or by certain constituencies, especially with regard to the impact of their activities in environmental or social terms. In this case, actors both from the public and private sphere seek to re-assert their authority (or more precisely: assert their authority in new arenas) by demonstrating their capacity to respond adequately to these concerns, as the discourse on Corporate Social Responsibility or standards of corporate governance reveals succinctly. The debates within this discourse on the 'real', underlying intentions indicate that the global public has become very suspicious about claims that such actors make: they may have the authority to introduce, for instance, disclosure systems, but do they actually have the will or incentive to enforce these standards? A prime example is provided by public and private accountability standards, such as the ones the Global Accountability Project evaluates and compares (see Monica Blagescu and Robert Lloyd, Chapter 10): most actors fall short of the standards they implicitly or explicitly claim to defend. This shows the need for understanding more clearly the underlying dynamics driving these processes.

One example that may support the case for a more thorough analysis of the actors, the sectors they are embedded in, and their underlying motives is provided by the Extractive Industry Transparency Initiative. As Lucy Koechlin and Richard Calland (Chapter 4) observe, the standard-setting process of EITI is unique and remarkable for tackling a sensitive and complex topic, and for involving actors from all sectors and across the globe. Indeed, this is arguably an exemplary case of a new type of co-operative, cross-sectoral, inclusive standard setting. The achievement of consensus building among very diverse actors over issues on which there are bitter debate and deeply adversarial positions has been notable. However, even the initial impetus (and the resources at the disposal) of the initiative may not be sufficient to sustain its credibility, especially around the three central issues: the effective implementation by the governments, the validation by the corporations, and the control by civil society. Here we neatly fall back into classic divisions between the sectors, that is, between the spheres of (legitimate) authority as well as the *de facto* power of the respective actors. In spite of the commitment to a common process and objectives, the involved actors are defined by their own, sector-specific rationales. In other words, although the multi-stakeholder initiative manages to mediate deep-seated divisions between actors, the logics informing the actions of the participating actors (that is, with regard to the actual implementation of and compliance with the principles) may ultimately be stronger than the common objective. Hence, gathering all the relevant, legitimate and effective authorities around a table may not be sufficient to actually generate effective, 'authoritative' norms. These processes, however, are yet so fresh and underresearched that it is too early to conclusively discern decisive factors shaping the authority of norms generated in this way, beyond the tentative conclusions offered in this volume.

4.   The legitimacy of non-state standard setting

Legitimacy is essential for non-state-made standards, because the less enforceable rules or standards are, the more they depend on legitimacy for being voluntarily complied with.

4.1   Social and normative legitimacy

As pointed out in the introduction to this book,[50] 'legitimacy' is on the one hand a social concept (to be legitimate here means to be in fact accepted or recognised), and on the other hand a normative concept (to be legitimate here means to be worthy of being recognised). Legitimacy as a social concept can be measured empirically, whereas legitimacy as a normative concept is assessed on the basis of a value judgment. Both concepts are analytically independent from each other. For instance, if a (hypothetical) TNCs' code of conduct for a production site in India recommends the use of child labour, this is in social terms legitimate, when all the employees (or other relevant communities) support it. The recommendation of child labour is, however, normatively illegitimate when measured against the International Convention on the Rights of the Child.

The normative legitimacy of non-state actors and the standards they make depends on the metric or yardstick that is applied. There are basically three types of yardstick: moral, legal, and even factual ones. Depending on the yardstick, a non-state standard is normatively legitimate if it satisfies our moral judgment, conforms to positive law, or finally when it is socially accepted[51] and/or brings about

---

[50] See Peters, Koechlin, Fenner and Zinkernagel, Chapter 1, section 3.4.

[51] The fact of social acceptance does not only constitute legitimacy in the sociological sense, but may also be an indicator of normative legitimacy under the premise that popular attitudes must be taken seriously.

beneficial effects in reality ('output legitimacy').[52] These metrics are not entirely independent, but feed off each other, can compensate each other, or conflict with one another. Therefore common-sense judgments on normative legitimacy often combine them. For instance, a standard that has been adopted in 'fair' procedures, including participation and publicity, gains both legal and moral legitimacy from this. Or, to give another example, one requirement for NGO accreditation with ECOSOC is that it is of 'recognized standing within the particular field of its competence'.[53] So here factual acceptance is a criterion for formal accreditation, which in turn conveys legal legitimacy to an NGO. 'Overall' normative legitimacy is a matter of degree. A standard is not only legitimate or illegitimate, but it may be more or less legitimate (morally, legalistically, or factually, or all taken together).

Legitimacy (both normative and social) is first and foremost a relational category. The general anthropological basis is the flexibility of man and his many possibilities to socialise, and in extension to constitute communities and societies. He needs a social order that provides orientation and reliability in everyday interactions. Social regulation and obligations, however, have to be reasonable because there are always possible alternatives to an existing social order. One such reason can be the basic assumptions of a coherent worldview as it is embedded in religious belief. A social order based on such unquestionable convictions is convincing and, at times, even compelling. It appears as a legitimate social order to those who share the assumptions that underpin it. A social order is not (socially) legitimate because it provides orientation or because it reduces uncertainty in everyday life – that could be done by any regulation. It is legitimate because it meets the life-worldly understanding of those who follow that order. There are many possible legitimate social orders with a normativity of their own. If, for instance, actors believe in the basic principle of representation, they would only take democratic orders as legitimate. But if they see principles of reciprocity and segmentary organisation as the fundamental basis of society, legitimacy would be judged on the balance of goods and services rendered to each actor (see Till Förster (Chapter 12)). Law which is based on the

---

[52] So effectiveness is not always in tension with legitimacy, but in turn contributes to output-legitimacy.

[53] UN ECOSOC, *Consultative Relationship between the United Nations and Non-Governmental Organizations* (UN Doc A/RES/1996/31) (resolution passed at the 49th plenary meeting of 25 July 1996), para. 9.

legitimate order of a democratic state is, in an anthropological perspective, only one possibility among many. Normative orders can also super-impose each other, as was almost always the case under colonial domination.[54] What we are facing today in processes of globalisation is to some extent similar: one understanding of legitimacy, the modern concept of democratic legitimacy, seems to dominate all others. This will be discussed in the next section.

4.2   Democracy, transparency, and inclusiveness

Today, it is generally assumed – and at least verbally supported even by totalitarian governments – that democratic procedures, coupled with safeguards for the protection of basic human rights, are the best guarantee to secure the overall legitimacy of standards which guide and structure peoples' lives and thus affect their needs, interests, and rights. Both state and non-state standard setting should therefore be – if possible – democratic. But democratic legitimacy (which is frequently criticised as an empty signifier) is neither a necessary nor a sufficient condition of legitimacy. Diverging notions of legitimacy may be more relevant for non-state actors that are often embedded in local societal contexts and cultures (see Ulrike Wanitzek (Chapter 17)). The presence of different types of legitimacy in a particular context of contact then refers to the interaction of different societies in processes of globalisation.

Another example of only thinly democratic legitimacy is the traditional mode of inter-state law making, as it evolved in an era of monarchies. The basic legitimatory norm of traditional international law (notably international treaties and customary international law) has not been democracy, but state sovereignty. States, the law makers, were considered as legitimate per se, and therefore the states' consent, expressed by their government, was deemed a sufficient basis of legitimacy for international law. In the modern 'democratic' reading of that mechanism, states are considered to represent their citizens. In that view, state sovereignty means also popular sovereignty. However, this equation does not reflect global reality, where undemocratic states participate in international law making, and where some states have so little bargaining power that their consent is not free and informed. In reality, then, international law making does not very well correspond to the democratic ideal.

---

[54] For a contemporary case study see in this volume Wanitzek, Chapter 17.

Against this background, the objection that non-state standard setting is undemocratic and thus per se unjustified is unpersuasive on three grounds. First, as just pointed out, it disregards the fact that many states are undemocratic as well, but are still allowed to participate in international standard setting on an equal footing with democratic states. Second, as long as standards are only 'soft law' and not enforceable, their impact is less serious, and therefore they need less democratic credentials. Third, as long as non-state actors only have voice in standard setting, but not a vote, their contribution is less decisive, and therefore their own legitimation need not satisfy the strictest standards. So the lack of formal democratic credentials of NGOs, technical experts, professional associations, TNCs, and various public–private or private–private partnerships does not constitute an absolute factor of illegitimacy of their standard-setting activity. It might be compensated by other forms of accountability (absent democratic elections). The accountability problems of non-state actor standard setting will be discussed below (section 5).

Besides (and as a part of) the democratic deficit of non-state law making, its exclusivity and intransparency deserve special consideration. A broad participation of potentially affected groups increases the likelihood that the resulting norms will ultimately safeguard or enable the egalitarian enjoyment of needs, interests and rights. Inclusive processes thereby contribute to the legitimacy of the resulting rules. The involvement of civil society organisations in standard setting is therefore a prime means to make those standards more legitimate.

The partial secrecy of non-state standard setting creates a legitimacy problem, because without information, potentially affected persons cannot hold the standard setters accountable. Accountability is an element of legitimacy, because it forces standard setters to respond to the needs and interests of individuals (see on accountability below section 5). So transparent standard setting is apt to contribute to the legitimacy of standards. This means that agendas, proposals, votes in committees, minutes of sessions, and drafts for standards should be generally publicised. Refusals to publish or to grant open access should be based on concrete grounds of privacy, third-party interests, or overriding public interests (such as security). The onus must be on the refusing body. However, opening up of the standard-setting fora will make standard setting more difficult, because the striking of certain compromises and package deals are more difficult in public. So, as already pointed out, some legitimacy gains will have to be traded off against the efficiency of standard making.

The creation of technical standards (for products, services, banking, accounting etc.) by professionals and experts, eventually in collaboration with selected government representatives, seems at first sight particularly undemocratic: this is not democracy, but technocracy. The standard-setting bodies have a very limited membership. Smaller firms have little influence, and consumers are almost completely excluded. Larger firms use the standards as a means to 'endorse' the composition and formats of their own products. Finally, technical standard setting depends on private sector funding. This creates a conflict of interest which also taints the legitimacy of the standards. Therefore, attempts to improve the legitimacy of technical standard setting aim precisely at inclusiveness and more transparency.[55] The trend is to combine the input of a smaller group of experts with broad consultation processes. In fact, most current technical standard setting comprises detailed procedural safeguards, which have been partly influenced by legal instruments, partly by the ethics of the engineering and other professions, and which have emerged through a global process of normative borrowing between the public and private spheres at various levels. According to Harm Schepel,[56] these procedures provide at a minimum for the elaboration of draft standards in technical committees with a balance of represented interests (manufacturers, consumers, social partners, public authorities), a requirement of consensus on the committee before the draft goes to a round of public notice and comment or consultation,[57] with the obligation on the committee to take received comments into account, and a ratification vote, again with the requirement of consensus rather than mere majority, among the constituency of the standards body, and the obligation to review standards periodically.

---

[55] See for the EU and EFTA the 'General Guidelines for the Cooperation between CEN, CENELEC and ETSI and the European Commission and the European Free Trade Association' of March 2003 (above note 13).

[56] Schepel, *The Constitution of Private Governance*, 6.

[57] Two examples: the International Organization of Securities Commissions (IOSCO), a forum for co-ordinating approaches to securities regulation, has introduced the 'IOSCO Consultation Policy and Procedure', published by the IOSCO Executive Committee in April 2005, accessible via www.iosco.org. Art. 5.10 of the Charter of the EU's CESR (Committee of European Securities Regulators) states: 'The Committee will use the appropriate processes to consult (both *ex ante* and *ex post*) market participants, consumers, and end users which may include, inter alia: concept releases, consultative papers, public hearings and roundtables, written and Internet consultations, public discourse and summary of comments, national and/or European focused consultations. The Committee will make a public statement of its consultation practices.'

To sum up: the general legitimacy issue of non-state standard setting is that its legitimacy flows neither from state sovereignty (as manifested in state consent) nor from popular sovereignty or democracy. But this problem can be mitigated to some extent, if not remedied, by procedural integrity, transparency, inclusive deliberations, a good knowledge base, and ethos. We will now turn to two types of non-state actors specifically.

4.3   The legitimacy of NGO standard setting

As political actors, NGOs enjoy normative legitimacy under the three yardsticks mentioned above. They possess legalist legitimacy when their actions refer to international law, or by accreditation. They enjoy moral legitimacy due to their aims, mission and values, and due to the credibility of their laudable aspirations. Their legitimacy derived from acceptance is visible in a large membership and broad donorship. These factors vary with the type of NGO. For activist or service NGOs performing disaster relief, or direct environmental action, effective performance of their tasks is an important source of legitimacy. Advocacy NGOs can in theory also enjoy output legitimacy with the caveat that here drawing causality and attributing tangible success is very difficult. The probably more important legitimacy factor of advocacy NGOs is therefore credibility.

How does NGO participation in standard setting contribute to the legitimacy of the processes and their outcome? NGOs furnish information, offer expertise, vocalise interests, and often act as opposition (we will come back to this below). All this improves the quality of debates and of texts. These functions can be fulfilled by NGOs because and as long as they are independent.[58] Thus, the involvement of independent NGOs in standard setting is apt to increase the legitimacy of standard-setting procedures, and the standards themselves.

However, the input of NGOs in global standard setting might also be illegitimate on several accounts. The most popular criticism is that NGOs do not enjoy any democratic mandate by (global) citizens, but are self-appointed. However, the democratic function of NGOs is not to be representatives in a parliamentary sense. In contrast, NGOs pursue single issues or special interests. They speak (or claim to speak) for

---

[58] Cf. CoE, *Fundamental Principles on the Status of Non-governmental Organisations in Europe and Explanatory Memorandum* (November 2002) para. 10: NGO must be free to take positions contrary to stated government policies.

minorities, for vulnerable groups, or for otherwise voiceless entities, such as nature. In most cases, NGOs have been founded precisely in order to counter the will of the majority, and to act as opposition. A democratic mandate by a global citizenry would not serve, but actually run counter to this function.

This functionality requires to give NGOs a voice, but not necessarily a vote in the standard-setting processes. Voice is the modus of deliberation. Voice is legitimate, because its impact on the outcome of the standard-setting process is informal and less weighty. It correspondingly needs less formal legitimacy, but is sufficiently justified by the reputational and moral legitimacy. Unsurprisingly, it is precisely a feature of pluralist law-making processes on the national or supranational level to offer interest groups the opportunity to participate and give input into the process without requiring any democratic mandate.[59] An NGO vote, in contrast, would not be legitimate, first, because of the NGOs' lacking democratic mandate. Second, NGOs' typical selectivity of interests and one-issue character makes them, unlike governments, which pursue and balance a host of competing interests, unfit for package deals or compromises in standard setting. Put differently, NGOs are structurally ill-suited to participate in the governance modus of bargaining. Granting them a vote would therefore hamper the process and thus decrease its functional legitimacy.

The legitimacy of NGO voice does not require representativity in terms of a democratic mandate conferred by a (more or less virtual) global society.[60] The NGO voices will complement and contradict each other, and will thus contribute to pluralist global deliberations, not to a parliamentary democracy. However, these deliberations are not self-evidently fully legitimate. Who is authorised to define the interests and weigh them, if this does not happen in a formal democratic process? Moreover, besides the usual prevalence of better-organised and more powerful interest groups, the geographical imbalance (dominance of 'northern' NGOs) decreases the legitimacy of the global deliberative process. All things considered, it can still be said that as long as NGO participation in global standard setting is limited to voice and does not

---

[59] See for law making in the EU: 'Towards a reinforced culture of consultation and dialogue – General principles and minimum standards for consultation of interested parties by the Commission', COM (2002), 704 final, Communication from the Commisison of 11 December 2002.

[60] Oberthür, *Participation of Non-Governmental Organisations*, 219; Rebasti, 'Beyond Consultative Status', 43.

include a vote, the legitimacy gains of NGO involvement clearly outweigh the legitimacy problems.

A related democratic legitimacy problem is that many NGOs lack an internal democratic structure. The ECOSOC guidelines, which have in practice been the most influential model for participatory schemes with other UN bodies and for organisations outside the UN, postulate that consultative relations can only be established with NGOs having 'a democratically adopted constitution'.[61] However, this requirement is not enforced by ECOSOC's accreditation committee. In reality, only a handful of more than 2,700 NGOs currently accredited with ECOSOC can be said to be democratic.[62] The newer Council of Europe 'Principles on the Status of NGOs in Europe' state that while the management of an NGO must be in accordance with its statutes and the law, 'NGOs are otherwise sovereign in determining the arrangements for pursuing their objectives'.[63] According to the Explanatory Memorandum to these Principles, the internal structure is 'entirely a matter for the NGO itself'.[64] The Principles thus do not require NGOs' internal democracy for participation in the Council of Europe.

The leniency with regard to the internal structure of NGOs, and the rejection of any internal democracy requirement, can be defended with two arguments. First, there are viable substitutes for internal democratic control. Donors 'vote' with their cheque-book, and members can – unlike the citizens of a state – easily realise their exit option and thereby bring their opinions on the NGO policies to bear. Second, numerous non-democratic states also have the right to vote on international standards. Why should requirements for NGOs be stricter? The formalist answer is that states are the direct addressees of international law, and are obliged to implement and enforce it. Therefore, so the argument goes, they have a legitimate interest in influencing those standards, and should be entitled to co-determine them, independently of their internal government structure. In contrast, NGOs are not international legal persons, therefore no legal duties arise for them from international law, and therefore NGOs do not have an intrinsic legitimate interest in shaping the standards that will bind others, not them. However, this 'state privilege' in standard setting is premised on the idea that the state is analogous to a natural person, and

[61] UN ECOSOC 1996, *Consultative Relationship* (above note 53), para. 10.
[62] Kamminga, 'What Makes an NGO "Legitimate"', 186.
[63] CoE 2002, *Fundamental Principles* (above note 58), para. 45.
[64] CoE 2002, *Fundamental Principles, Explanatory Memorandum* (above note 58), para. 33.

as such entitled to self-determination which translates into participation in rule making. This analogical premise is problematic, because states are not unitary actors, and do not enjoy rights for their own sake, which would be morally comparable to natural persons' fundamental rights to political participation. Therefore, the formalist answer given above is unsatisfactory. It follows that NGOs should not be treated stricter than states. Their participation in standard setting is (more or less) legitimate, largely independent of their internal structure.

A different legitimacy problem is the blurring of the societal and market sphere through a commercialisation of NGOs. NGOs may *de facto* become professional service agencies.[65] More importantly, broad accreditation rules of international organisations potentially allow TNCs to masquerade as NGOs and thus participate in standard setting. For instance, the ICC (International Chamber of Commerce) can have itself represented by firms, which resulted in waste traders participating as ICC members in negotiations on the Basel Convention on the Transboundary Movements of Hazardous Waste, and producers of ozone-depleting substances representing the ICC in issues relating to the Montreal Protocol. Also, TNCs have been involved in *Codex alimentarius* standard setting where they seek to use the Codex to legitimise standards, definitions, and the composition of their own products.[66] Another line is blurring: 'quangos' (quasi non-governmental organisations) are emerging, and ECOSOC increasingly accredits NGOs which are sponsored and controlled by government and that are thus not independent.[67] This governmentalisation is most relevant for service organisations.[68] For instance, a considerable amount of governmental development aid is delivered via NGOs. It is not entirely clear that this policy leads to efficiency gains. In some cases, reliance by governments on NGOs may here mask the inactivity of governments, and actually weaken output legitimacy, especially when NGOs *de facto* become part of national bureaucracies. More important is the abuse of the NGO garb by governments, especially in the human rights field. Numerous NGOs, for

---

[65] For instance, AI has been criticised for a 'trade with human rights violations', because the Danish section of AI sells to investors information on the human rights situation in potential host countries.

[66] All three examples from Krut, *Globalization and Civil Society*, 24.

[67] United Nations 2004, *We the Peoples: Civil Society, the United Nations and Global Governance, Report of the Panel of Eminent Persons on United Nations–Civil Society Relations* ('Cardoso Report'), A/58/817 (11 June 2004), para. 127.

[68] See for the complementary process of the privatisation of the state below, section 6.

example Chinese para-state mass organisations in the Commission on Human Rights, only serve their state of origin or registration by constantly praising and imitating it in general or country-specific debates. They thus form a 'servile society at the UN'.[69]

Probably the most serious legitimacy problem of NGOs as a group is the dominance of the North in all international organisations where NGOs are involved in standard setting and implementation. NGOs originating from or based in the rich industrial countries have a far from disproportional impact in global standard setting. And universal NGOs, such as Amnesty International, mostly do not have governance mechanisms to ensure that the make-up of the executive is geographically representative of the organisation as a whole.

In order to improve the legitimacy factors of inclusiveness and broad participation, measures to counteract the skewed impact of NGOs from the North are needed. Additional financial and technical support must be given to southern NGOs. In contrast to such targeted capacity building, quota systems seem problematic, because they tend to hinder the bottom-up emergence of NGOs for new items and thereby run counter to the NGO involvement's early warning and oppositional function.

Intensified monitoring, evaluations, streamlining, and the formalisation of the existing accreditation procedures by governments risk endangering the NGOs' independence, which is their primary element of legitimacy. It is therefore even argued that accreditation (that is, the conferral of an 'observer' or 'participatory' status within international organisations) is an outdated paradigm which should altogether be given up.[70] However, if only for practical reasons, there must be some channelling of NGO involvement in global standard setting, otherwise the system would collapse. It is therefore necessary to maintain accreditation in principle. In order to cut back abuses and illegitimate political considerations, the task should be removed further from the governments (of which bodies such as the ECOSOC committee on NGOs are composed), and instead entrusted to the secretariats of international organisations which are more distanced from governments.[71] This 'depoliticisation' of the accreditation procedure

---

[69] De Frouville, 'Domesticating Civil Society', 73.

[70] Noortmann, 'Who Really Needs Art. 71?', 118.

[71] See CoE, *Participatory Status for International Non-governmental Organisations with the Council of Europe* (Res(2003)8 of 19 November 2003) (adopted by the Committee of Ministers at the 861st meeting of the Ministers' Deputies), paras. 12–14: the decision to grant participatory status is taken by the Secretary General with a no-objection procedure by governments.

was one of the main proposals of the Cardoso Report on UN–civil society relations,[72] but did not meet approval in the General Assembly.[73]

Next, more emphasis should be laid on self-policing, which would not only improve the legitimacy, but also the accountability of NGOs.[74] Accreditation and self-regulation need not be mutually exclusive, but could be combined in varying degrees.[75] Sectoral NGO codes of conduct can be devised for different areas. An example is the Code of Good Practice for relief and development agencies.[76]

Finally, coalition building is a means to strengthen the legitimacy of NGO input in standard setting, because this increases the diversity, the social acceptance, and the effectiveness of NGOs. An example is the 'Coalition for an International Criminal Court', which had a great impact on the elaboration and adoption of the Rome Statute of the International Criminal Court.

4.4   The legitimacy of business involvement in standard setting

We have seen that business participates in global standard setting through companies, branch associations, or through professionals and experts. The basis of legitimacy of this standard-setting activity is not, as usually for private actors, their private autonomy and consent. Standards have a general scope. They address and bind not only the norm-creators themselves (like a contract), but third parties, which are not the authors of these norms. The actors do not only regulate themselves (their own future action), but intend to regulate other (mainly business) actors, who have not participated in the standard setting themselves. Therefore consent alone cannot form the legitimacy basis for the standards.

An additional basis of legitimacy could be delegation by governments. If the states had permissibly delegated the standard-setting authority to private actors, these standards would presumably be legitimate, because of the overall legitimacy and authority of states to produce norms. However, is the extensive and highly dynamic and private standard

---

[72] Cardoso Report (above note 67), paras. 120–28 and proposal 19.
[73] General Assembly Plenary Debates of 4 and 5 October 2004, UN Doc GA/10268 and GA/10270.
[74] See on accountability problems of NGOs below, section 5.6.
[75] Rebasti, 'Beyond Consultative Status', 47.
[76] 'People in Aid: Code of Good Practice in the Management and Support of Aid Personnel' (2003), elaborated by relief and development NGOs. See on the self-policing of humanitarian NGOs also below, section 5.6.

setting we witness really merely a delegated exercise? The delegation perspective is just the beginning, not the end of the question for the basis of legitimacy of non-state, especially genuinely private, standard setting.

In a more practical perspective, it can be said that the involvement of business in standard setting is apt to increase the effectiveness of the processes, and thus their output legitimacy. Especially in the highly complex context of global economy, national governments lack the information and the capacity to regulate issues which transcend the nation state. The involvement of global business actors might compensate for this loss of regulatory capacity. Business actors bring in their expertise and their skills to design economically viable solutions. In fact, governmental standard setting has arguably become dependent upon the economic data and technical solutions offered by firms. Further, the involvement of TNCs in the setting of standards creates a sense of ownership and therefore facilitates their later implementation. Finally, their more formalised inclusion could eliminate the informal attempts to influence global standard-setting and governance processes, such as the tobacco industry's campaign against the UN and WHO.[77]

On the other hand, business's involvement can also make standard setting less effective, because it protracts, delays or distorts standards, or may offset initiatives by others. But the most obvious danger of the participation of TNCs in standard setting is that this amounts to making the fox guard the henhouse. TNCs are primarily profit-driven, and their novel role as 'corporate citizens' is at best a secondary one. Firms do not per se pursue any – however defined – (global) public interest, but first of all seek to make money. As UNICEF Executive Director Carol Bellamy pointed out in response to the then UN Secretary General Kofi Annan's far-reaching proposals to engage the United Nations more with business: '[I]t is dangerous to assume that the goals of the private sector are somehow synonymous with those of the United Nations, because they most emphatically are not.'[78] TNCs are interested in co-operating with international institutions in standard setting not for the common good, but because global standards will minimise trade barriers resulting from national regulation, because they hope to influence global standards in their favour, gain prestige ('bluewash'), and finally because they can use the standard-setting forums to

---

[77] See WHO, Tobacco Company Strategies to Undermine Tobacco Control Activities at the World Health Organisation: Report of the Committee of Experts on Tobacco Industry Documents, Geneva, July 2000.

[78] Carol Bellamy, 'Public, Private, and Civil Society', Speech of 16 April 1999.

directly sponsor their own products. TNCs also seek to embed 'best practices' to squeeze out competitors, which blurs the line between agreements on standards among firms and unfair anti-competitive understandings.

Nevertheless, even corporate profit-driven activity may have beneficial spill-over effects for the public: it satisfies consumer needs, gives employment, and increases wealth. It is therefore also in the public interest not to subject business to standards that kill off their incentive to make profit. Also, the dangers of TNCs' involvement in standard setting, notably the danger of capture by profit interests, is to some extent mitigated by the fact that global business is by no means a monolithical bloc with uniform objectives. For instance, during the negotiations of the Kyoto Protocol, which was quite intensely lobbied by business, the energy sector and the insurance sector had opposing interests,[79] which meant that their antagonist inputs contributed to a more balanced solution.

All considered, there still is the real danger that international standard setting is unduly commercialised through business involvement. A remedy might be public–private–private standard setting, in which NGO involvement might compensate for legitimacy deficits engendered by marketisation, to which we turn now.

4.5   The legitimacy of trilateral standard setting in PPPs

One way to enhance the legitimacy of standard setting is to make sure that the process of developing and implementing standards is a shared endeavour among (inter-)governmental institutions, businesses, and NGOs.[80] Hence trilateral PPPs might constitute standard-setting forums in which governmental, NGO, and business contributions could outweigh each other's deficiencies. Notably international organisations and NGOs can mutually derive legitimacy from each other. The NGO allegiance gives an aura of independence and credibility while the affiliation to an international organisation gives its reports weight and authority. However, a number of cases where companies or even governments 'borrowed creditability' from NGOs has led to criticism. Legitimacy is gained through joint standard setting only when the parties remain independent from one another and sufficiently distant.[81]

---

[79] Nowrot, *Normative Ordnungsstruktur*, 235 with further references.
[80] Haufler, *A Public Role*, 119; Muchlinski, *Multinational Enterprises*, 550; Boyle and Chinkin, *The Making of International Law*, 92.
[81] Crane and Matten, *Business Ethics*, 374.

Finally, even if PPP rule making may be more inclusive than purely (inter-)governmental standard setting, it still suffers from the lack of formal accountability.[82] Generally, PPPs tend to be rather intransparent and selective. One of the major legitimacy problems of PPP activity is probably the choice of relevant stakeholders, and the weighting of the stakeholders who should be involved in standard setting and implementation. And as far as the effectiveness or output legitimacy of the PPP standard setting is concerned, PPPs' standard setting can result in mere problem shifting. Also, it may lead to a lowest common denominator, and it may exclude other stakeholders.[83]

All things considered, and given the fact that states are as yet the only formal representatives of citizens, are still – as a group – the most powerful global actors, and are (in most areas of the world) important repositories of political, social, and cultural identity, global standard setting must remain, in order to maintain a sufficient level of legitimacy, linked to states. The ultimate standard-setting responsibility should not be transferred to non-state actors. However, the involvement of non-state actors is an important additional source of legitimacy. It should consequently be broadened, structured, and to some extent formalised.

5.   The accountability of non-state standard setters

Accountability[84] is – as legitimacy – a relational concept which is socially and discursively constituted. As Julia Black (Chapter 9) demonstrates, regulatory regimes are not passive recipients but active participants in the accountability discourses.

5.1   Functional accountability

Accountability serves three interrelated functions: to safeguard interests, to prevent the concentration of power, and to enhance learning and effectiveness.[85] Notably Monica Blagescu and Robert Lloyd (Chapter 10) emphasise the third function and insist on accountability as a transformative process which is beneficial to the actors themselves. Accountability mechanisms are therefore functional when they provide sufficient

---

[82] Dingwerth, 'The Democratic Legitimacy', 78.

[83] Börzel and Risse, 'Public–Private Partnerships', 210–11.

[84] See for the notion of accountability Peters, Koechlin, Fenner, and Zinkernagel, Chapter 1, section 3.5.

[85] Cf. Bovens, 'Analysing and Assessing Accountability', 462.

information for the forum about the behaviour of an accountable actor, when they offer enough incentives for an actor to commit itself, to refrain from abuse and to be responsive, and when they allow for enough feedback, responsiveness, and learning. By fulfilling these three functions, accountability schemes enhance legitimacy (see above, section 4).

The 'One World Trust' Report of 2003[86] identified eight 'core dimensions' of accountability: member control, procedures for appointment of senior staff, compliance mechanisms, evaluation processes, external stakeholder consultation, complaint mechanisms, corporate social responsibility, and access to information. Building on this report and on the Global Accountability Index, Monica Blagescu and Robert Lloyd (Chapter 10) boil those dimensions down to four necessary components of a functioning accountability scheme: transparency, participation, evaluation, and complaint and response. Each component is itself strengthened through its interaction with its others, and meaningful accountability only results when all are effective. According to the survey of One World Trust and according to Monica Blagescu and Robert Lloyd (Chapter 10), all three types of global non-state actors, international organisations, TNCs, and NGOs do not score significantly differently on those accountability parameters. Other chapters as well have revealed serious accountability gaps in non-state standard setting (see notably Steven Wheatley (Chapter 8) and Dan Assaf (Chapter 3)). They also demonstrate that there is no one-fits-all accountability mechanism for the various kinds of global non-state actors. However, parallel problems can be identified, and maybe common principles and designs could be envisaged as a response.

5.2   Accountability for what?

The first element of accountability is the (meta-)standard to which an accountable standard-setting actor must conform ('Accountability for what?', in the words of Dan Assaf (Chapter 3)). Potential relevant standards for global non-state actors are public international law (notably human rights treaties), soft law, or finally domestic law.

With regard to international organisations, a major accountability gap lies in the fact that the organisations are not a party to international human rights covenants, and therefore not subject to the respective contractual compliance and enforcement mechanisms. Intensified international organisations' standards and enforcement measures, especially

---

[86] Kovach, Nelligan, and Burall, *Power Without Accountability?* (see table at 3).

UN sanctions, have in the recent years endangered human rights, especially social rights to food or access to medicine, or procedural rights to a fair trial. But the UN Security Council, the World Bank, the WTO, or NATO cannot be held accountable via the ordinary human rights complaint procedures for violations of such rights. This has created an accountability problem which is only recently being tackled. As far as TNCs and NGOs are concerned, public international law does not apply to them, because these actors are not formally recognised as international legal persons. Hence, international human rights covenants do not directly and in themselves constitute a standard of accountability for these actors. So here we have a similar accountability gap as in international organisations.

Of course, TNCs and NGOs are 'chartered' under the law of a specific state, and are therefore accountable under the standards of the relevant domestic law. However, especially TNCs may evade regulation. Also, the national standards are diverse, do not necessarily live up to the international standards, and therefore do not constitute a consistent and even accountability regime. Against the background of numerous reproaches of human rights violations by TNCs, especially in developing states (for example the use of forced labour in Myanmar, or the support of the Apartheid regime in former South Africa), 'soft' international human rights standards applicable to TNCs have been adopted by the OECD[87] and the UN.[88] Finally, firms have committed themselves to codes of conduct in the fields of environment, human rights, and labour (see notably Eva Kocher (Chapter 15) and Egle Svilpaite (Chapter 16)). For NGOs, self-regulation is only slowly emerging as an element of accountability (see Lindsey Cameron (Chapter 5) and below[89]). Overall, it seems as if certain, cross-cutting standards of accountability have already been articulated in transnational civil society, even where there is no applicable international law.[90]

5.3   Accountability to whom?

The most important accountability controversies relate to the accountability forum, that is, to the question: Who is entitled to hold

---

[87] OECD Guidelines for Multinational Enterprises (DAFFE/IME/WPG (2000) 15/FINAL).

[88] UN ECOSOC Sub-Commission on the Promotion and Protection of Human Rights, *Norms of the Responsibilities of Transnational Corporations and Other Business Enterprises* of 13 August 2003 (UN Doc E/CN.4/Sub.2/2003//12/Rev. 2).

[89] Section 5.5.   [90] Grant and Keohane, 'Accountability and Abuses', 35.

power-wielders accountable? Here the reproach of an 'accountability mismatch' is salient.[91] It is claimed by many that while non-state actors are not unaccountable, the problem is that their accountability exists vis-à-vis the wrong constituencies, and/or that it is skewed towards the most powerful stakeholders. This disagreement about the proper accountability forum is at least in part rooted in diverging paradigms of accountability. Two principal models have been identified:[92] 'delegated accountability' to the 'shareholders' (that is, to the source of power or the delegating body) as opposed to 'participatory accountability' to 'stakeholders' (a term to which we will revert in a minute). These two models of accountability require responsiveness to different groups ('constituencies'). Arguably, an effective accountability system should combine elements from both: delegated and participatory accountability.[93]

According to Steven Wheatley (Chapter 8), the concept of accountability has expanded in recent years to include *inter alia* the idea that governments should pursue the wishes or needs of their citizens – accountability as 'responsiveness'. Increasingly, accountability is seen as a 'dialogical activity', requiring officials to 'answer, explain and justify, while those holding them to account engage in questioning, assessing and criticising'. The hypothetical communicative community of an international governance regime – 'those affected' – have the right to participate in decision-making processes, directly or through representatives. Engagement with international civil society actors, 'we the people's representatives', is understood to provide some form of legitimacy for the exercise of political authority, linking political institutions with the wider public in the process of collective will-formation to ensure that relevant interests and perspectives are included in decision-making processes, in particular those of hitherto marginalised or excluded groups.

Other chapters in this book which touch accountability have likewise abandoned the traditional narrow idea of accountability which exists only vis-à-vis the source of power or 'shareholder'. All – if only implicitly – assume that the global standard-setting actors are accountable to a broader set of both internal and external stakeholders. 'Stakeholders' are all those who are or might be affected by the standards

---

[91] Levit, 'A Bottom-Up Approach', 200 for the sector of financial standard setting.
[92] Grant and Keohane, 'Accountability and Abuses', esp. 31.   [93] *Ibid.*, 42.

set by the actor, be it an international organisation, a TNC or an NGO.[94] Individuals or groups are affected when they are benefitted or harmed by the standards, in particular when their rights are violated. As already mentioned, Steven Wheatley submits that international organisations must not only be accountable to their member states' governments, but also to global civil society (see on international organisations' stakeholders also below, section 5.5). TNCs are not only accountable to their shareholders, but also to employees, customers, business partners, and societies in which the companies operate. Finally, NGOs are accountable not only to their funders and states of incorporation, but also to their beneficiaries.

However, all actors must perform a stakeholder analysis: Who are the relevant stakeholders? And what weight should their concerns be accorded? For normative and practical reasons, it is necessary to assess and to prioritise the stakeholders and their inevitably competing demands. First, because of the different types and degrees of affectedness, stakeholders literally have very different 'stakes', and it does not seem fair to grant each of them an identical say. Second, the circle of stakeholders is potentially infinite, when 'affectedness' is not limited by certain requirements of intensity or directness. If all stakeholders are taken into account, standard setting would be killed by an accountability paralysis. So here a reasonable balance between the need for adequate input and the need for swift decision making must be struck. An example are the EU principles on consultation in the European law-making process: here the EU Commission, in determining the relevant parties for consultation, is bound to ensure 'adequate coverage' of 'those affected by a policy, those who will be involved in the implementation of the policy, or bodies that have stated objectives giving them an interest in the policy'. The Commission should also take into account factors such as the need for specific experience, expertise, or technical knowledge, a proper balance of social and economic bodies, and specific target groups, such as ethnic minorities.[95]

---

[94] Seminal for the 'stakeholder theory' of the firm: Freeman, *Strategic Management*, 46. See for a definition of TNCs' stakeholders para. 22 of the ECOSOC Sub-Commission norms on human rights responbilities of TNCs (above note 88).

[95] 'Towards a reinforced culture of consultation and dialogue – General principles and minimum standards for consultation of interested parties by the Commission', COM (2002), 704 final, Communication from the Commission of 11 December 2002, 11–12, and 19 on the definition of the target group(s) in a consultation process.

To sum up, there are real tensions not only among different claims communities (as Julia Black (Chapter 9) elaborates), but also among the different models of accountability. The 'pluralist' solution to the accountability problem of competing accountability forums is to allow each constituency to challenge decisions, also in standard-setting procedures, but not to formally veto them.[96] This proposal fits well to the conferral of voice, but not of vote, to non-state actors, as we suggested in the discussion on their legitimacy.

5.4   The sanctions

The third element of accountability is the sanctions or disempowerment mechanisms. These may be legal, political, financial, or reputational. They may be formalised (fines, disciplinary measures, civil remedies, penal sanctions), or merely informal, such as pressuring to resign.

The most common and most effective political sanction, namely democratic elections, are lacking on the global plane, and global elections by a global citizenry are unfeasible. This is a central accountability (and thus legitimacy) problem of non-state global standard setting, and of global governance generally. But could the lack of the political sanction of global elections be compensated for by legal (more precisely: judicial) sanctions in the form of complaint mechanisms against standards? Would the accountability of non-state standard setters be increased by creating enforceable rights for individuals and firms against those standards? We doubt that, because both types of sanctions differ in important respects. Accountability through complaints functions – as opposed to accountability through elections – only *ex post*, not *ex ante*, is necessarily rights-based and cannot take into account other interests without a legal basis, and concerns individual cases, not general policies. Complaints are therefore hardly a functional equivalent to democratic elections or referendums, and cannot substitute those participatory devices.

5.5   Specific accountability problems of international organisations

International organisations are, in the traditional, state-centred view, accountable to their member states (as their 'shareholders') only. One problem in this context is that some organisations do not grant equal

---

[96] Krisch, 'The Pluralism of Global Administrative Law', 249.

rights to member states (the most conspicuous example being the veto-power of the five permanent security council members and the ponderation of votes in the Bretton Woods Institutions). A related problem is that even organisations whose members have formally equal voting rights practise informal decision making (for example in the notorious WTO 'green rooms') which effectively marginalises or completely excludes less powerful states. In this traditional perspective, the third accountability problem of international organisations is the 'runaway' or '*Zauberlehrling*' phenomenon, that is, the danger that an organisation escapes control by the member states and acquires too much institutional and bureaucratic autonomy. This can happen on account of 'mission creep' (dynamic expansion of competencies) and/or excessively long chains of responsibility. A slightly different problem is that of capture (for example the World Bank by the 'global capital'), which also distances the organisation from its rightful 'shareholders'.

A deeper problem exists, at least in the eyes of cosmopolitan critics. These critics emphasise that the ultimate accountability forum for international organisations should be the (global) citizens, not states. The traditional argument that citizens are represented by their nation states, and should therefore be entirely 'mediated' by their states in the international arena, is – in the eyes of cosmopolists – flawed on two grounds. First, the lines of accountability to the citizens are too long and indirect to allow for effective accountability. Second, many member states of international organisations are not democratic, and can therefore not rightfully claim to act for their citizens. In Chapter 8, Steven Wheatley points out that in fact most international organisations have introduced informal mechanisms to engage (to some extent) with external actors, including international civil society organisations and those potentially affected by their policy decisions. Accessible websites are the clearest manifestation of this.

Besides the problem of the proper accountability forum for international organisations, other accountability aspects deserve examination. An academic report of the International Law Association (ILA) recommended the following rules and practices to secure what it called the 'first level' of accountability of international organisations: transparency, a participatory decision-making process, access to information, a well-functioning international civil service, sound financial management, reporting and evaluation. These principles are at the same time principles of good governance. Additionally, the ILA report highlighted the principle of good faith, constitutionality and institutional balance, supervision and control, the principle of stating the reason for a particular course of action, procedural regularity, objectivity and impartiality, and due diligence.[97] It is noteworthy that these recommendations correspond to the more general requirements of accountability applicable to all actors, as identified above (section 5.1). As already mentioned, some empirical research has investigated to what extent selected international organisations fulfil these requirements. Contrary to popular opinion, international organisations are relatively transparent, in particular when compared to TNCs and NGOs.[98] Good information disclosure policies appear to be related to the amount of external pressure that has been applied to an organisation. The World Bank and WTO, for example, have been targeted by protesters and have consequently produced useful information disclosure statements.

This finding is a good reason for demanding further formalisation of NGO participation, and for the integration of national parliaments into the standard-setting activities of international organisations as a means for strengthening their accountability.[99] However, increasing NGO participation in international institutions also causes opportunity costs. Unless the value of outreach, inclusiveness, and participation exceeds these costs, global governance would be weakened, not strengthened.[100] It is therefore indispensable that the participation modes become more focused, streamlined, and eventually selective.

5.6   Specific accountability problems of NGOs

NGOs are legally accountable to their 'chartering' governments, and also reputational and financial accountability for NGOs exists. As they operate in a market for donors and depend on private funders, they could not exist without social acceptance, anyway. However, especially financial accountability as a source of legitimacy is ambiguous. It plays for NGOs which advocate 'sexy' issues, or those which attract potent, notably industrial donors, and these are not necessarily the most urgent ones.

Only to a limited extent, NGOs satisfy the cross-cutting principles of transparency, participation, evaluation, and complaint and response.

---

[97] ILA 2004, *Accountability of International Organisations*, Final Report, Part One, Berlin.
[98] Kovach, Nelligan, and Burall, *Power Without Accountability*, at 31–32 on the basis of a case study of selected international organisations.
[99] Rebasti, 'Beyond Consultative Status', 69–70.
[100] Cf. Cardoso Report (above note 67), para. 25.

They are thus only weakly accountable along those lines. Especially NGO transparency is often restricted in important areas. As a group, they provide less information about their activities than international organisations and TNCs.[101] Notably the beneficiaries are rarely informed about how the money is spent.

As far as the accountability forum is concerned, many NGOs have an excessively broad and undefined constituency, which precludes accountability vis-à-vis that constituency. For instance, many NGOs make broad claims to speak on behalf of 'the oppressed', 'the excluded', or 'youth and nature'. These NGOs cannot refer back to their 'constituency' for guidance. The beneficiaries cannot agree or disagree with certain actions or language on behalf of them. Even more importantly, there is no clear way to resolve differences in views between two NGOs that each claim to 'represent' an equally broad constituency.[102]

Self-policing is not well developed with NGOs. It seems most advanced for humanitarian NGOs, which had to face criticism of their response to the Rwandan genocide. They developed several mechanisms of accountability: a code of conduct, a humanitarian charter, a set of technical standards, and a 'quasi-ombudsman' called the Humanitarian Accountability Project (HAP), a learning network for sharing the lessons learnt from humanitarian operations, and other mechanisms.[103]

Specific guidance for NGO-accountability can be gathered from the influential ECOSOC resolution of 1996,[104] and from the more recent principles and rules of the Council of Europe.[105] The ECOSOC states as one principle to be applied in the establishment of consultative relations that the accredited NGOs shall have 'a representative structure and possess appropriate mechanisms of accountability to its members, who shall exercise effective control over its policies and actions through the exercise of voting rights or other appropriate democratic and transparent decision-making processes'.[106] In reality, however, many NGOs are accredited which do not conform to this principle.

The Council of Europe's principles state that NGOs' 'structures for management and decision-making should be sensitive to the different

---

[101] Kovach, Nelligan and Burall, *Power Without Accountability?*, 33.
[102] Krut, *Globalization and Civil Society*, 25.
[103] Further references in Slim, 'By what Authority?'.
[104] UN ECOSOC 1996, *Consultative Relationship* (above note 53).
[105] CoE, *Fundamental Principles on the Status of Non-governmental Organisations in Europe and Explanatory Memorandum* (November 2002).
[106] UN ECOSOC 1996, *Consultative Relationship* (above note 53), para. 12.

interests of members, users, beneficiaries, boards, supervisory authorities, staff and founders'.[107] The principles also contain provisions on
'transparency and accountability', which hold that NGOs should generally have their accounts audited by an institution or person independent
of their management.[108] According to the explanatory report to those
fundamental principles, it is 'good practice' to submit an annual report
on accounts and activities.[109]

However, many formal accountability requirements create additional
costs for NGOs, which disproportionately burden NGOs from the Global
South. This fact is all the more important as the underrepresentation of
the southern NGOs is currently one of the main legitimacy problems of
NGO involvement in global governance. So here the different factors
of legitimacy must be balanced.

5.7 Specific accountability problems of TNCs

As already mentioned, firms now generally assume a (limited) accountability vis-à-vis external stakeholders. This extension of the accountability forum is justified, because firms have become political actors. In times
of liberalisation and privatisation, they often perform functions which
have previously been considered as 'public'. Their business activity
touches upon the interests and rights not only of employees, but also of
consumers, taxpayers, contractors, and of other groups affected by business operations. However, the extension so far remains an abstract
matter of principle. The precise degree and form of accountability
vis-à-vis those broader groups of stakeholders depends entirely on the
national laws and practices, and varies from company to company.
Global accountability standards in this regard are only in *statu nascendi*.
Thus, the OECD Principles of Corporate Governance of 2004 ask for
'disclosure and transparency'.[110] They also mention stakeholders (without defining them), and notably employee participation, but refer back to
the 'laws and practices of corporate governance systems'.[111]

---

[107] CoE 2002, *Fundamental Principles* (above note 58), para. 46.
[108] *Ibid.*, paras. 60–65.
[109] CoE 2002, *Fundamental Principles, Explanatory Memorandum* (above note 58), paras.
66–68.
[110] OECD 2004, OECD Principles of Corporate Governance, Principle V. See in scholarship
on transparency and disclosure as a crucial strategy to enhance TNC accountability
Backer, 'From Moral Obligation to International Law'.
[111] OECD Principles (above note 110), Principle IV with annotation at 47.

So the main accountability mechanism for industry comes down to the threat of governmental regulation. Problems therefore rather result from a lack of governmental regulation than from the irresponsibility of TNCs.[112] This is serious with regard to those global TNCs operating in weak or failing states. It also creates an accountability deficit for those companies which operate transnationally and which can therefore relatively easily escape national regulation.

Owing to the weaker legal accountability of firms acting on the global level, market and reputational accountability becomes all the more important. But reputational accountability seems to hold well mainly for firms which depend on brand name products. It is doubtful whether consumption choices really function as 'purchase votes' and as effective sanction. A limiting factor is that the people who are most directly negatively affected by the activities of a TNC are often not the same people who are able to exert their consumer power. Moreover, boycotts require considerable consumer awareness and presuppose a real choice of products.[113]

Business has, in collaboration with international organisations and NGOs, made important progress towards accountability through self-policing. For instance, the Global Reporting Initiative (GRI), founded in 1997, is a multistakeholder initiative which seeks to provide a framework, that is, the 'Sustainability Reporting Guidelines' for sustainability reporting, which can be used by businesses of any size, sector, or location.[114] At the World Economic Forum of 2003, representatives of the most important global TNCs adopted a Framework for Action in which they called on business leaders to 'develop a graduated program for external reporting'.[115]

Also, the Global Compact,[116] initially conceived by the UN Secretary General as a learning platform for global business, has matured into a rudimentary accountability regime for TNCs.[117] Since 2003, firms participating in the Global Compact are expected to demonstrate their commitment to the Global Compact by 'Communications on Progress' in which the outcomes are measured using as much as possible indicators

[112] Haufler, *A Public Role*, 119.
[113] Kovach, Nelligan and Burall, *Power Without Accountability?*, 15–16.
[114] www.globalreporting.org. See also the ICC's 'Business Charter for Sustainable Development'.
[115] World Economic Forum, Global Corporate Citizenship: The Leadership Challenge for CDEOs and Boards (2003), Part II: A Framework for Action, Principle 4 (Transparency).
[116] www.globalcompact.org.   [117] Nowrot, 'The New Governance Structure'.

such as the GRI guidelines.[118] A more formalised complaint procedure for handling complaints on 'systematic or egregious abuse of the Global Compact's overall aims and principles' was introduced in 2005.[119] Another example are the 'Equator Principles', a financial industry benchmark for determining, assessing and managing social and environmental risk in project financing, adopted by financial institutions in 2006. One of the principles concerns consultation and dialogue. The banks that have committed themselves to the Equator Principles pledge not to provide loans to projects where the borrower, the respective government, has not 'consulted with affected communities in a structured and culturally appropriate way'.[120]

Specific accountability issues may arise for public–private partnerships. Dan Assaf (Chapter 3) argues that public–private partnerships in the protection of critical information infrastructure (CII) seriously lack accountability. Accountability is, according to Assaf, directly related to the degree of similarity of objectives and goals among the partners in a PPP. However, in the CII sector, the objectives typically diverge because of certain underlying characteristics of that sector. Because most of the CII is entirely owned by the private sector (telecommunication, cyber-technology, etc.), the principal objective for the public sector to enter into a PPP with the private sector is to obtain and share information with the owners of the CII, information which it could otherwise not lay its hands on. However, sharing information with the public sector and, especially, with other private partners in the PPP may often involve revealing critical trade secrets and other privileged company information.

---

[118] UN GC, *Policy for 'Communications on Progress'*, as of 13 March 2008.

[119] See the 'Note on Integrity Measures' of 29 June 2005. Despite apparent quasi-judicial features of the complaint mechanism (e.g. the complaint will be forwarded to the participating company concerned, requesting written comments), the Global Compact Office stresses that it 'will not involve itself in any way in claims of a legal nature'. The office may, in its sole discretion, offer good offices, ask the regional office to assist with the resolution of the complaint, refer the complaint to one of the UN entities guarding the Global Compact principles, and reserves the right to remove the incriminated company from the list of participants in the Global Compact (Attachment 1 to the report by the Global Compact Office 'The Global Compact's Next Phase' of 6 September 2005, part 4).

[120] *Equator Principles*, Principle 5: 'Consultation and Disclosure'. The principle also states that for projects with significant adverse impact on affected communities, that consultation must 'ensure their free, prior and informed consultation and facilitate their informed participation, as a means to establish, to the satisfaction of the [borrowing financial institution], whether a project has been adequately incorporated affected communities' concerns.' www.equator-principles.com.

Consequently, the private sector shies away from this particular objective of the PPP arrangement and its interests are thus directly opposite to those of the public sector in this particular PPP. Even legal measures to encourage the private sector to share more information (by excluding information shared in the CII PPPs from the Freedom of Information Act in the US) did not resolve this problem.

To conclude this section, the accountability of non-state actors in standard setting is problematic not only on a technical level, but raises deep questions of the proper structure of global governance.

6.   The public and the private

The distinction of public and private and the way this dichotomy is linked to the state has informed Western political practice since antiquity. It has also been a key issue for the academic analysis of society, politics and law. But what the contributions to this book show is that it is increasingly difficult to assign actors to either side – except when one reduces their respective positions exclusively to their official institutional affiliations. In ongoing practices of standard setting, though, one may easily rely on false assumptions if one looks exclusively at institutional affinities. The findings thus question the grand dichotomies that stand behind the state versus non-state distinction, in particular the public–private divide. What we witness is that there are more and more actors whose agendas are neither determined by public nor by private ties and obligations; they follow mixed agendas. This is sometimes and very broadly attributed to the growing interconnectedness of actors in a globalising world where processes of standard setting are no longer dominated by states and their agencies.[121]

6.1   Is public versus private an appropriate descriptive category?

Most of the case studies in this book have confirmed the hypothesis that fundamental transformations in global governance have enhanced the significance of the private sphere in the creation and enforcement of standards which regulate behaviour in more than one state.[122] They also make clear that standard setting is no longer organised along the lines of

---

[121]   A theorist who argues that processes of globalisation will inevitably lead to such a new political order is Martin Albrow (Albrow, *The Global Age*, in particular Chapter 8).

[122]   See Cutler, *Private Power and Global Authority*, 1, for commercial law.

state versus non-state actors. The formation of standards and norms takes place in spheres where the state and its institutions and representatives are dominant, but there are more and more spheres where other actors dominate. This is obvious when one looks at countries and regions outside the Western world, as the examples from Africa in this book show. Dieter Neubert (Chapter 2) describes how new social actors emerged in the colonial and post-colonial history of the continent, and he analyses their growing significance in the negotiation of standards. In particular the many international, national and local NGOs have an influence on such processes that can hardly be overestimated. This shift in processes of standard setting is a general tendency that might be less obvious in highly developed Western democracies but nonetheless points at a worldwide change in how societies maintain a social and normative order and how they relate to other societies and to international institutions such as the UN and its bodies.

From a general conceptual point of view, this book's chapters all point at a similar set of questions: what is the future of standard setting, if public institutions and in particular the state will no longer be the dominant actors in the making of standards? And, from a more theoretical point of view: is the usual distinction between public and private still useful as an analytic category when the actors participating in processes of standard setting do not maintain that distinction? The dichotomy might well be misleading if one looks, for instance, at how Eva Kocher (Chapter 15) and Egle Svilpaite (Chapter 16) describe and analyse the relation of private business to the public sector as highly ambivalent, expecting regulation from the state and simultaneously distrusting it because of its apparent difficulties to cope with local practices. In addition, many 'private' actors such as the already-mentioned NGOs and at times even companies claim that they act more in the 'public' interest than the state. The state, however, is sometimes seized by private stakeholders and represents their particular interests.[123] Many African countries could serve as an illustration of such a privatisation of the state, and Myanmar, where the state has become the booty of the military, would also be a case in point.

---

[123] A well known metaphor for the privatisation of the state is 'the politics of the belly', coined by Jean-François Bayart is his landmark publication 'The State in Africa' (Bayart, *The State in Africa*). Another metaphor is the 'criminalization of the state' as analysed by Bayart and others (Bayart, Ellis and Hibou, *The Criminalization*).

This debate is informed by inherent, but often hidden understandings of public and private as a basic dichotomy in Western thought. For the purpose of our inquiries, we will reduce the many existing and often competing notions of the 'public' and the 'private' to only two models. Model I is based on the assumption that the state as a centralised, unified and potent institution represents the public interest and thus is the only sphere that can legitimately claim to be a public actor. This model in the end goes back to the early modern notion of sovereignty, where the 'public' power of a (more or less) legitimate institution rules over 'private' individuals and associations. This understanding of public and private is also at the root of the modern notion of the state as already implicitly conceived in the Peace Treaties of Westphalia from 1648. Private actors are thus all actors – be they corporate or individual – that do not engage in such processes of standard setting on behalf of the state as the only possible public institution. All other institutions, for instance NGOs, by definition remain private institutions that cannot and do not pursue public interests. This understanding also informs our modern conception of state administration as public and the market economy as private.

Model II, the other model, is based on the accessibility to ongoing processes of societal self-determination and thereby to processes of standard setting. This model assumes that it is the right of all competent members of society to participate as citizens in such processes. Societal (including legal) norms and standards are thus the outcome of participatory engagement that is both independent of the state and of the private as opposed to the state. The public realm in this sense is embedded in another sphere – the public sphere where the state is an actor among others that then would belong to civil society. The public sphere is thus distinct from the state, and precisely because of its independence it guarantees the accessibility to processes of standard setting. It is only with such an understanding of the public that some actors, as for instance international human rights NGOs, can claim to act on behalf of the public interest.

Both models embrace different notions of the political community. While in model I, the state is the dominant if not the only political community, model II takes it that a political community grows out of a participatory process and has no clear-cut boundaries. While in the first model, standards are mainly set by legitimate representatives within the realm of the state, the second adopts another much more fluent view. Social norms and standards are negotiated and at times sanctioned in the public sphere. There is another difference between the two models. The first, sovereignty-focused model distinguishes unambiguously between the rulers and the ruled, while the second model sees processes of societal self-determination, including political decision making and the setting of social norms and standards, much more as open to anyone who wants to engage in what can be called political action. There is no clear-cut distinction between those who rule and those who are ruled, as both can and sometimes have to adopt varying positions in such processes. However, the chances of participatory engagement are almost always unevenly distributed among the possible actors – which does not necessarily mean that the state again comes in as the dominant actor. It depends on the situation that frames the actions and may lead to novel practices of negotiating norms and standards, as the contribution of Michael Miklaucic (Chapter 7) shows. There are situations where the state re-emerges as the dominant actor in processes of standard setting, while it may remain marginal in other situations – in particular when other, non-state actors have proved to be more efficient. Steven Wheatley (Chapter 8) illustrates this in his analysis of examples from history and today's globalising world.

The question that arises from this discussion is: have the situations in which norms and standards are usually debated and generated changed? And how and to what degree has this affected the chances of state and non-state actors to engage in such processes? To answer these questions, one needs to look closer at where the actors have their social background and from where they claim their legitimacy. In Chapter 17, Ulrike Wanitzek analyses how local, national and international standards of child fosterage interact. What is striking in this context is that local norms of kinship relations directly relate to practices that are, on the one hand, subject to regulations by the national laws of Tanzania and, on the other hand, by that of other nations. The link is often the migration of kin to distant, mostly European countries. What has changed is the degree of interrelatedness or, as theorists of globalisation tend to put it, the 'flows' that link actors with different normative backgrounds. It raises the awareness for the specificities of one's own society and thus leads into a highly ambivalent situation: the more the actors know about others' standards, the more they become aware of their own – and, in situations of questioned identity, stick to them. This interplay of local, regional, and global levels has been termed as 'glocalisation' by Roland Robertson and later by many other theorists of globalisation.[124] The growing interrelatedness of actors at local, regional and global levels is, however, not a new

---

[124] Robertson, *Globalization*, 173 et seq.

phenomenon, and its conceptualisation as 'glocalisation' can hardly claim to be highly original. But it is useful since most of us still think in terms of different spatial levels of societal integration.

Ulrike Wanitzek's example has immediate relevance for individual actors. But as a conceptual pattern that leads empirical enquiries, the opposition of local versus global is as slippery as public versus private. The question where to situate an actor, that is, more on the global or more on the local side, will always remain a question of how to weigh background, means and ends. Is it safe to say that an NGO is local because it only operates in a particular city in a particular country when it refers to international standards of human rights or when its funds come from elsewhere? Again, the distinction of local versus global is based on a preconception of how actors relate to a specific background, to each other, and how this affects the processes of negotiation of social norms and standards.

If one takes a spatial differentiation of social and cultural affiliation as an appropriate conceptualisation of today's world, it would be a truism to claim that situations in which norms and standards are produced and shaped have changed – since there simply is more need for regulation. But the growing significance of non-state actors in such processes is only indirectly linked to processes of globalisation. It is more linked to the fact that the growing interconnectedness brings more actors together that have a different understanding of public and private. The different understandings of public and private become more apparent in processes of globalisation, but they are not caused by it. This takes us back to the former argument. The blurring of the public and the private, as it is often called, is a challenge to our theoretical conceptualisation of processes of standard setting and how we translate it into empirical enquiry.

6.2   Why do we continue to use the distinction of public versus private?

If the distinction of public and private is already conceptually blurred, the more it is when it comes to analysis of real situations on the ground. Let us look at one such situation. Many NGOs arguing for 'universal human rights' standards aim at the implementation and respect of these human rights in a particular place belonging to a particular country, say in some outlying province in a state that is hardly capable of controlling this place and that enjoys only limited legitimacy among its own population out there. First, violations of human rights may be committed by the state and its administration, even if the state's administration is disintegrating rapidly. But frequently, they are also committed by private actors, although these are not formally bound by human rights conventions which directly bind only the contracting states. In addition, TNCs based outside this particular country may also play an important part since they are likely to replace the state's fading monopoly of violence by private military companies that they again may hire locally or somewhere else (Lindsey Cameron (Chapter 5)). The situation is becoming increasingly complex with the number of actors present in the place.

At first sight and according to model I, the international NGOs would be private actors because they are clearly and overtly acting against the state to which the province belongs if they monitor violations that are committed by the local administration. The administration would then be the public arena where such violations should be persecuted – even if the judiciary system is not working properly. Of course, the NGOs will then argue that the state in this country does not represent the public interest at all because it has been appropriated by a small and privileged group of people who privatised the state and who have no legitimacy to talk for the population. They would thus base their argument on the second model of the public sphere. The understanding of who is a private and a public actor differs enormously.

However, one might argue that at least the understanding of who is a state and who is a non-state actor will be coherent and easy to cope with. But again, the situation may soon look much more complicated than at first sight. The state in whose province the violations take place may see the activities of the NGOs as an outsider's intervention and may redefine the NGOs' presence in terms of foreign domination – one that is in the end guided by the interest of another state, the US for instance. Let us then assume that TNCs (which are 'private' actors in model I) have agreed on human rights standards under the umbrella of binding international legal norms and let us assume, too, that these companies actually try to respect such standards. They would thus implement public standards – though as private actors. If then the local administration is still seen as the extension of a privatised state – one that is mainly based on neo-patrimonial reciprocal obligations between individuals within formally public institutions, it leads to a complete blurring of what is private and public and who is a state and a non-state actor. Simultaneously, one could claim that many of these non-state actors are also indebted to the public sphere, that is, to the discussions and debates that shape the understanding of how a society should cope with its own future. In the end, because of the state as one of the primary spheres of political practice, the NGOs are also related to the state – or more precisely to several states. The interaction between TNCs and NGOs could also serve as an example: the NGOs may be based in a certain country but oblige the company to subscribe to the human rights standards that these particular NGOs try to implement worldwide. Even if, say, the NGOs are not present in the country where the company operates, it would thus have an impact as a public actor – through a private company.

One may argue that this blurring is more a conceptual than a practical problem, but what is more important is that the distinction shifts as the actors apply it to a specific situation. In the end, it could be argued that all actors in such a field are more or less 'private' and thus non-state actors since it is virtually impossible to draw a clear line between the state and the private interests that its representatives may pursue. Again, the best-known examples come from Africa, where the state was sometimes privatised by politicians as a source of private rents: 'Public' officials were acting on private agendas, thus turning the state into a shadow of other interests.[125] In cases such as Mobutu's Zaire, the state and its institutions became a means for private economic and often illicit enterprises.[126] As a system, the shadow state was often imposed by politicians together with other non-state actors. Shadow states often maintain an official system of governance, law and 'public' institutions as a façade hiding the other, private agenda of those who are in power. Though states such as the former Zaire and Sierra Leone seem to be extreme cases, the tendencies are more widespread than Western scholars usually assume.

But the challenge lies elsewhere, because the controversy leads into multifaceted arguments about how to analyse and judge the complex settings of state and statehood that led to the formulation of the concept. First, one needs to keep in mind that not all external actors labelled as 'private' according to model I are necessarily companies that have a

---

[125] The concept of the shadow state was first introduced by William Reno in his seminal work on 'Corruption and State Politics in Sierra Leone' (Reno, *Corruption and State Politics*). Though developed with regard to West Africa, the concept also applies to many other regions, for instance to many successor states of the former Soviet Union in Central Asia and even to some southern parts of Italy. See, among others, Wolch, *The Shadow State*; Beissinger and Young (eds.), *Beyond State Crisis?*.

[126] See the more general introduction of Jean-François Bayart, Stephen Ellis and Béatrice Hibou to *The Criminalization of the State in Africa* (Bayart, Ellis and Hibou, *The Criminalization*, in particular 18–31). On Mobutu's Zaire, see Leslie, *Zaire*.

straightforward profit-making agenda. Many of them could be NGOs and international networks that seek to introduce and maintain certain standards of, say, education and public health.[127] They are 'public' actors according to model II and often follow agendas that they have discussed at the international level with other NGOs and with other states, and it is not rare that they co-ordinate their actions in a given country. Such networks actually may modify the ways a shadow state provides access to its territory and how it governs its resources, for instance by environmental standards demanded by the North. Simultaneously, the very same networks may undermine the ability of such states to enforce their own policies, be they hidden private agendas or not.

The point is that the same mode of interaction between the state and non-state actors can be conceptualised and evaluated according to different, opposing moral norms. If the influence comes from NGOs and other actors that follow international standards and agreements, we tend to see their influence as benevolent, coming from what we would then call 'global civil society'[128] – otherwise, we would perhaps talk of an erosion of statehood and finally conclude that the process has led to the formation of a shadow state. In other words: the evaluation is normative. It is again a judgment according to our Western understanding of state and statehood, describing other states as deficient if they are not adopting the same institutions, procedures, goals and moral norms as ours.

This apparent contradiction is informed by the two models outlined above and by the identification of the state with the public. Obviously, this dichotomy leads us into conceptual difficulties. So why, then, do we still think in terms of public versus private and state versus non-state? We believe the answer lies first in the moral normativity of what we have so far called the public sphere and in the undifferentiated character of the dichotomy itself.

The short answer to the first point is what anthropologists call 'culture'. We are living a culture of legitimate domination, that is, we assume that a particular understanding of legitimate domination is valid for us and other actors and we expect such attitudes from our co-citizens and, more

---

[127] In Africa, education and public health are often the two sectors that need public standards more than any other sector of governance. Compare Sutton and Arnove (eds.), *Civil Society or Shadow State?*, l.

[128] We are aware that the concept of civil society does not fit all countries and states because it implies a shared understanding of the public sphere among all participating actors, which cannot be taken for granted. See with regard to Africa Comaroff and Comaroff, *Civil Society and the Political Imagination*. We will come back to this in a moment.

generally, from all contemporaries. And by doing so, many anthropologists would add, we are taking for granted what actually is a precarious achievement. We who are used to the idea that the state is or at least should be the privileged sphere where we, as citizens, make decisions that are meant to apply equally to everyone in the society will maintain a normative understanding of the state as long as it can claim legitimacy through, among other things, the representation of the will of the majority. If one looks at society per se, it does not matter much if the theory of the state is based on the notion of contract or on the supremacy of the state as an institution as long as it can successfully claim legitimacy. We extend our understanding to other states unless we have convincing evidence that these other states do not fulfil our own criteria of legitimacy and participation. All those are convictions that are deeply rooted in our culture.

But what does it mean then 'to live a culture'? Is our understanding of state and non-state, of private and public, simply rooted in culture? To some extent, we learn this understanding and the moral norms on which it is based when we are brought up. But that argument does not suffice to explain the continuity of such basic cultural convictions. We could acquire other convictions, which is precisely what many human rights organisations hope for when they engage in a country. The other argument is that, once a social order is established, it has a value of its own because it provides predictability in situations of uncertainty. But again, we would argue that this is not enough to explain the persistence of basic cultural convictions as the equation of state and public. There are other social and political orders that would also provide predictability – and the neo-patrimonial order of the shadow state in Africa does so, too. There is a need for another explanation – one that shows why it is useful for us to maintain the distinction of state versus non-state.

6.3   Is it useful to maintain the distinction of state versus non-state actors?

There are certainly situations where the distinction between state and non-state actors, regardless of which model informs the distinction, is not of great help to understand how actors relate their practices to each other. In particular when the agendas aim, on all sides, at the same and at times hidden interests and goals, it does not matter much if a particular actor belongs to the state as an institution or if he is, in western normative terms, a non-state, private actor. If, say, the actors all seek a dominant position in a security market – which is not unusual under conditions of precarious statehood – their practices and interactions are often not significantly affected by their institutional backgrounds.[129] In such cases, it can be more useful to analyse the implicit understanding of the respective motives and intentions of the actors from a purely emic perspective, that is, from their local point of view. This makes sense because social reality is made up of actors' points of view, that is, how they conceptualise and think about the situation that they have to cope with. The security standards that such actors may agree on often only cover a limited space, and they also may not last very long. In addition, they may remain questionable in the eyes of international actors who may also be present in the area and who follow their own, internationally recognised standards. But more often than not, such local security standards are the only reliable basis for further conflict transformation (see Till Förster (Chapter 12)).

Analysing such processes of standard setting mainly or even exclusively from the (local) actors' points of view is a classical anthropological approach. As all anthropological approaches, it tries to avoid any normative understanding of what happens on the ground – which means that the analysis does not introduce a state versus non-state dichotomy if the actors do not think in such terms. Though such an approach is certainly appropriate for basic research, and we would insist that it is actually needed for such a purpose, it also has its limits.

First, there is the methodological question to what degree a non-local scholar – and in particular a scholar who, as almost all scholars, has gone through a Western type of education – will be able to transcend his own conceptualisations of state versus non-state, of public versus private and other, related dichotomies. The answer that anthropology has for this question is clear and brief: no. Any scholarly analysis has to take the understanding of the scholar and also that of the audience that they address into account.[130] The latter are, so to speak, the concepts into which the analysis has to translate the local understandings of such processes of standard setting. In other words, it would not help very much to know about local concepts as long as we cannot relate them to our own understandings of such phenomena.

---

[129] William Reno has provided more than one account of such situations in his book on 'Warlord Politics and African States' (Reno, *Warlord Politics*). On the concept of security markets and its economic significance see Mehler, 'Oligopolies of Violence'.

[130] This was the major topic of the so-called 'Writing Culture Debate' in the 1980s. See Clifford and Marcus (eds.), *Writing Culture*.

Besides this epistemological argument, there is another argument that is perhaps more important in the context of this book: it is about the presence of statehood in areas and social spaces where the state, as an institution, is more or less absent. To understand this apparently paradoxical situation, we have to delve into the theory of state and statehood. Since Thomas Hobbes published his *Leviathan* in 1651, it is often claimed that a monopoly of force is a necessity for any social order because of the violent nature of man. But more so since Max Weber held his influential lecture at Munich University in the winter of 1918/19, immediately after the end of the First World War, the modern definition of the state as 'a human community that (successfully) claims the monopoly of the legitimate use of physical force within a given territory'[131] has become the standard understanding of the state in the social sciences.

If an institution that claims to be a state does not fulfil this one condition, we assume that it has ceased to be a state. Or we would rate states as states along this line, that is, how successfully they claim a monopoly of force within their territories.[132] Though it has incorporated other factors, too, the debate on weak and failed states still privileges this aspect. Because of the lack of a monopoly of force, it is argued, a failed state is no longer able to perform basic functions such as education, security, public health, or governance.[133] Hence, such states are seen as deficient with regard to the modern state as we know and experience it from day to day.

---

[131] 'Staat ist diejenige menschliche Gemeinschaft, welche innerhalb eines bestimmten Gebietes ... das *Monopol legitimer physischer Gewaltsamkeit* für sich (mit Erfolg) beansprucht.' Weber, 'Politik als Beruf', 506 (English transl. Gerth and Wright Mills, *From Max Weber*, 78). See for the concept of state in international law the Montevideo Convention on the Rights and Duties of States of 26 December 1933, 165 LNTS 25, Art. 1: 'The state as a person of international law should possess the following qualifications: a) a permanent population; b) a defined territory; c) government; and d) capacity to enter into relations with the other states.' In scholarship Crawford, *The Creation of States* (statehood requiring a defined territory, permanent population, and effective government).

[132] A well-known example is the Failed States Index, first published by Foreign Policy in 2005. See also the critique by Peter Riedlberger, 'Gescheiterte Staaten oder gescheiterte Statistik?' Accessible online via www.heise.de/.

[133] The critique of the failed state concept is nearly as old as the concept itself. See for the original concept Rotberg (ed.), *When States Fail*, and for a recent discussion Chomsky, *Failed States*. The critique comes from several sides, see, among others, Bøås and Jennings, '"Failed States" and "State Failure"'. They argue that the label of 'failed state' is mainly applied to states that seem to be a threat to Western interests while other states that show a similar weakness in the execution of the monopoly of violence and a similar prevalence of informal, neo-patrimonial structures are still not classified as 'failed'. For a similar assessment from another perspective see Hill 'Beyond the Other?'.

However, if we focus more on the process of the formation of the state and on its flipside, the disintegration of the state, than on the conclusive outcome, we would have to look more deeply into how people interact to shape that entity of the state as an institution of society. This perspective introduces another understanding of state and statehood, one that differentiates, as Joel Migdal has written, between '(1) the image of a coherent, controlling organization in a territory ... and (2) the actual practices of its multiple parts'.[134] Migdal explicitly speaks of an 'image' of the state as central organisation. He does so because an image provides an integrated character to what it depicts – or more precisely, to what it pretends to depict. In this case, Migdal writes, building on Edward Shils, it is persuasive because it invites the actors to see the state not as an amalgam of numerous institutions and practices but as an integrated, powerful and, perhaps more important than anything else, as an autonomous entity.[135] It means that actors may still have this image in mind when they act in precarious situations and even if they act in ways that contradict this image, as we will show later. Images are simultaneously figures of thought and representation. In addition, images may serve as residues of habitual memories because they maintain a certain constellation that helps the actors to reconstruct former experiences.[136] In other words: even if the state as an institution is no longer what we, in our normative understanding, expect it to be, statehood may still exist. It is bound to practices that the actors often still engage in, though there is no institution that would force them to do so.

If we adopt this differentiation between the state as an imagined institution and statehood as the reinforcing and sometimes also contradictory practices that shape this institution, we still maintain the factual normativity of the state but also acknowledge the agency of non-state actors. It is this interaction that we need to address more deeply.

6.4 Is there a conceptual alternative?

Many social scientists see the current debate on state and non-state actors as standard setters as a conceptual challenge. Statehood may exist where the state is no longer present, and state actors may follow

---

[134] Migdal, *State in Society*, 16.   [135] Shils, *Center and Periphery.*
[136] The debate on images and memory is complex and multi-faceted. Of particular help with regard to the imagination of the state as a societal institution is Paul Connerton (Connerton, *How Societies Remember*).

private agendas. But does this lead to another, novel formation of actors that does no longer follow the lines of state versus non-state?

Of course, one may refrain from any conceptualisation and adopt a less theorised attitude by claiming that a thorough description of the actors and their respective agendas would do, too. Such a descriptive approach is certainly needed as a reliable basis for any further research, but it still calls for an appropriate theory – at least in the sense of a reflective stance on our own, scholarly enquiry. In fact, there are several theoretical attempts to cope with the complexity of the present blurring of the state–non-state divide. Probably one of the best known is Hannah Arendt's distinction of the public, the private, and the social.[137] She argued that, while societies in the past could afford to rely on a binary distinction of public and private, today's societies have to acknowledge the rise of a third sphere, that of the social. This third sphere, she argues, is composed of autonomous public spheres or domains (in the plural), where actors may best express their political ideas and aims. One may link the post-modern rise of the term 'civil society' to what Hannah Arendt already analysed decades earlier. The more recent differentiation between an all-embracing 'public sphere' and distinct 'publics' can also help to clarify this spectrum of interrelated actors.[138] In this model, the public sphere is still the overarching realm where all members of society are invited to have their say on issues that will apply to everyone in society. Ideally, this public sphere incorporates the state which will then cast the outcome of the debates on norms and standards into an appropriate legislation. Publics (in the plural), on the other hand, also crystallise around shared interests and norms, but unlike the former, they do not or cannot claim authority for the entire society.[139] Their basis is collective – that is also why they are not fully private – but they address questions of limited relevance to the entire society. However, in the process of standard setting, their answers to these questions may later become valid for all members of society, but then, they would need to pass through the public sphere.

We believe that such a tripartite conceptualisation may serve as an appropriate conceptual tool for further investigations into the processes

---

[137] Arendt, *The Human Condition*; in particular part III 'Action', and part IV 'The Vita Activa and the Modern Age'.

[138] See mainly Wolfe, 'Public and Private in Theory and Practice'.

[139] All kinds of voluntary associations such as self-help groups, social movements, unions, parties, religious communities, but also ethnic, linguistic and other groups who base their identities on cultural difference may constitute such publics.

of standard setting. It has the advantage of being overt to empirical questions as, for instance: To what degree are such publics open to new members? How do they negotiate the norms that they share? How do they introduce their norms into the public sphere? On the other hand, it still acknowledges the normative ideas that, in Western history, are associated with the state.

One remark, however, has to address the relationship of such publics to the state. It is clear that our shared understanding of how a state should be part of 'the public' is affected by 'the publics' and how they engage in the processes of standard setting. But that also holds true the other way round: the engagement of non-state actors in processes of standard setting transforms them, too. The more they relate to such processes, they more they will be subject to them. It is not only the state that is transforming itself through such processes, the other, non-state actors also do so and will increasingly act like state actors.

6.5   Transnational law and global legal pluralism

In a legal perspective, the diagnosis that non-state standard setting erodes the public–private split does not only relate to the two distinct branches of law, namely public and private law, which are both state-made law to a large extent. It also, and more importantly, points to the fact that private entities no longer only make contracts which bind the (private) parties, but enact (or participate in the making of) general rules which potentially bind third actors.

Especially technical standards, including the financial standards as treated in this book by Peter Hägel (Chapter 13), are almost never either wholly public or wholly private.[140] The relevant standardisation bodies are sometimes public agencies, some are private trade associations, and most are something in between, locked together, and locked into the public sphere, by co-operation agreements, contract, membership of umbrella organisations, accreditation arrangements, and memoranda of understanding. Even where public authorities set product standards themselves, they have to rely on 'private' expertise. Conversely, even where standards are made by private bodies, they protect health and safety or other 'public' values.[141] Finally, these 'private' standards deploy

---

[140]   See on financial standards Augsberg, *Rechtssetzung zwischen Staat und Gesellschaft.*
[141]   Schepel, *The Constitution of Private Governance,* 4.

an extremely strong compliance pull, which resembles 'public' authority and enforceability.[142]

The result of this intermingling is what we might call 'transnational law'. This term was coined in the 1950s by Philip Jessup 'to include all law which regulates actions or events that transcend national frontiers. Both public and private international law are included, as are other rules which do not wholly fit into such standard categories.'[143] Transnational law, as we understand it in Jessup's tradition, is not necessarily an 'autonomous' third legal order 'beyond' domestic and public international law, but is a mixture of private and public, of national and international, of hard and soft law, whose hybridity, complexity, and irregularity seem to be the adequate response to the regulatory demands of our time. A theoretical framework to situate and explain the possibility of transnational law, and of 'interlegality', as Boaventura de Sousa Santos calls it,[144] is global legal pluralism. Legal pluralism has been defined as 'a situation in which two or more legal systems coexist in the same social field'.[145] This concept implies that law does not consist solely in the coercive commands of a sovereign power, but is constructed constantly through the contest among various communities. Pluralism thus accepts the existence of law without hierarchy, and presupposes legal relationships in which competing normative claims or interpretations are not 'killed off'.[146] Applied to the global sphere, legal pluralism assumes that the norms articulated by international, transnational, and epistemic communities are likewise 'law', because they influence both policy decisions and categories of thought over time.[147] In this perspective, non-state actors form such 'law-generating communities'. Gunther Teubner has explained this phenomenon as a result of globalisation in the language of systems theory as

---

[142] See Röthel, 'Lex mercatoria', 759, on technical standards within the EU.

[143] Jessup, *Transnational Law*, 2. See in recent scholarship Tietje and Nowrot, 'Laying Conceptual Ghosts of the Past to Rest'. The authors highlight four structural features of transnational (economic) law: deterritorialisation of regulation, vanishing distinction between legally binding 'hard' norms and rules that are in the strict sense non-legally binding, expansion of actors, and bottom-up norm formation.

[144] De Sousa Santos defines 'interlegality' as 'the intersection of different legal orders'. 'Interlegality is the phenomenological counterpart of legal pluralism, and a key concept in a postmodern conception of law.' De Sousa Santos, *Toward a New Common Sense*, 473.

[145] Merry, 'Legal Pluralism', 870. See also Griffiths, 'What is Legal Pluralism', 2, defining legal pluralism as 'that state of affairs, for any social field, in which behaviour pursuant to more than one legal order occurs'.

[146] Berman, 'A Pluralist Approach', 304.   [147] *Ibid.*, 327.

follows: the globalisation of law has created 'a multitude of decentred law-making processes in various sectors of civil society, independently of nation-states'. The new norms 'claim worldwide validity independently of the law of the nation-states and in relative distance of the rules of international public law. They have come into existence not by formal acts of nation-states but by strange paradoxical acts of self-validation.'[148] Crucially, globalisation has broken the 'hierarchical frame of the national constitution which represents the historical unity of law and state'. The difference between a highly globalised economy and weakly globalised politics has pressed for 'the emergence of a global law that has no legislation, no political constitution and no politically ordered hierarchy of norms which could keep the paradox of self-validation latent. This makes it necessary to rethink the traditional doctrine of sources of law. When the frame of rule hierarchy, with constitutionally legitimated political legislation at its top, breaks under the pressures of globalization, then the new frame which replaces it can only be heterarchical. It decentres political law-making, moves it away from its privileged place at the top of the norm-hierarchy and puts it on an equal footing with other types of social law-making.'[149]

Global legal pluralism implies that a single public world order is not only not feasible, but not even desirable. The problem is of course that such a pluralism, and the broad concept of 'law' going with it, does not provide a yardstick for determining which norm should prevail in the event of conflicts. And it does not answer the question who should decide these conflicts.

7.   Agenda for future research

Our research on non-state standard setting has raised a host of follow-up questions of legal doctrine and policy. For instance: do or should non-state standard setters enjoy international legal personality? Is their emerging right to participation in law formation a functional equivalent to legal personality? What are the precise legal implications of the non-state actors' legitimate expectation to have a 'voice' in the standard-setting processes? Is there a good-faith obligation for governments to duly take into account the input of NGOs? Are NGOs entitled to an answer? And what consequences can we draw for the structuring of the consultation process in standard setting? Which institutions should channel notably

---

[148] Teubner (ed.), *Global Law without a State*, xiii.   [149] *Ibid.*, xiii–xiv.

NGO involvement in global standard setting, and what should be the role of the United Nations or other international organisations in that regard? How can the accreditation procedures be depoliticised?

Another set of legal questions relates to delegation. Is the delegation of standard-setting authority to non-state actors permissible? How tight would governmental control have to be in order to speak meaningfully of delegated, as opposed to autonomous, standard setting? How far may such delegation go? Maybe only implementing or co-ordinating regulation, but not fully novel rule making can be delegated. Ultimately, non-state standard setting raises the theoretical question of the nature and the functions of law in a differentiated and novel societal context.[150]

On the empirical research agenda, equally interesting questions have emerged. On the one hand, it could be investigated under which conditions non-state standards are really pacemakers for subsequent 'hard' law. On the other hand, if the normative commitments of communities matter more than the formal status of these commitments, then empirical study is needed as to whether these statements are treated as binding in actual practice and by whom.[151] As Till Förster's contribution (Chapter 12) shows maybe most poignantly, the deeper understanding of how the social recognition of standards is generated goes far beyond a neat typology of sources of authority. Especially in societies of precarious or contested statehood – arguably large parts of the international community – the authority of private as well as public standards is informed by a web of culture and trust. Here, it is not merely the social desirability of regulation that influences the recognition and acceptance of such standards. Equally pertinently, social practices are shaped by the factual environment (levels of poverty, insecurity, vulnerability, violence, etc.) and hence the practical relevance of standards. However, these processes are more often than not highly contextualised micro-processes; far richer empirical studies are needed to draw generalisable conclusions on the conditions that shape the normative commitment of communities. This is a question of high empirical validity, in that factors informing such recognition need to be pinpointed on all levels: the conditions informing the recognition of standards on an international level right down to the local level, as well as the conditions which allow relevant local standards to percolate up to the national level.

---

[150] See for an excellent doctrinal analysis in the context of German law Bachmann, *Grundlagen ziviler Regelsetzung*.

[151] See in this sense also Berman, 'A Pluralist Approach', 323.

A further empirical question is whether the pluralisation of standard-setting actors and processes is continuing, or whether it has most recently started to revert, as Peter Hägel's Chapter 13 suggests. Indeed, the question of reversibility has been addressed at an early stage in the literature on private standard setting, discussing the conditions under which the reversibility of specific types of private authority is likely.[152] Given that the pluralisation of actors as well as standards is shaped by globalisation processes and hence mirrors all its complexities, disjunctures and contradictions, the question of reversibility still provides a rich agenda for future research. Saliently, it is context-specific whether this reversibility fosters or threatens social order and democratic accountability.

Another question arising from the contributions to this book is to what degree the internationalisation of processes of standard setting and the standards that they generate contributes to the emergence of a novel societal sphere that cross-cuts existing societies. Social scientists over the past two decades have sought to understand how individuals link to each other across national borders. Another question that arose from such studies is how individual actors relate to groups that cut across frontiers, both geographical and social. Participation in such groups means at least partially to subscribe to their social norms and standards – regardless of whether they are constituted by the ongoing interaction of the actors or if they already existed and are then adopted by one side or the other.

If one looks at the processes of standard setting, two empirical questions arise. One focuses on the fact that the interaction as such brings actors from different geographical and social origins together and obliges them to respect the other's viewpoint, thus fostering the emergence of shared norms and standards. This process is often addressed in studies of globalisation. In a somewhat affirmative attitude, it is often stated that such processes are characterised by the absence of a centre – actors from everywhere in the world can participate in such processes. At first sight, the observable facts seem to confirm the assumption that they all have equal opportunities to participate and to articulate their own ideas. No one who participates in such processes would then be able to dominate the others to an extent that would allow him to impose his own standards on the others. On the other hand, it is also obvious that such a conceptualisation of the flows of ideas and the debates on their significance for the constitution of norms and standards ignores more or less the fact that there is often an uneven balance

---

[152] For a systematic discussion see Hall and Biersteker (eds.), *The Emergence of Private Authority*, 213–17, in particular Table 7 at 218.

of power in global interactions, too. The empirical question thus can be stated very clearly: under the conditions of a globalising world, to what degree is the constitution of norms and standards subject to differences of power of the stakeholders? In other words: to what extent can one side or the other actually impose his own normative ideas on others and then declare that they are generally valid? This is a question that suggests a deeper analysis of the political economy of processes of standard setting.

The second question focuses more on the social side of processes of standard setting. In social theory, it is assumed that a certain repertoire of basic assumptions, convictions and social norms is necessary to integrate individuals and groups into a society. If this is true – and there are good reasons for such an assumption – it is possible to argue that the mere existence of processes of standard setting that cross-cut local, national and international boundaries is in itself a major cause for the emergence of what is often called a transnational social space. In this perspective, agency is no longer on the actors' side. They are much more subject to the processes that are governed by structural forces. The latter may remain invisible to the actors, but that does not mean that they do not exist. In the end, this second strand of inquiry would address the question if, again under the conditions of a globalising world, such processes of standard setting are informed by social agency at all or if they follow a systemic logic of economic forces.

A further pertinent empirical question is one addressed from different standpoints by Monica Blagescu and Robert Lloyd (Chapter 10) on the one hand, and Julia Black (Chapter 9) on the other, namely the question of how far accountability principles can be generalised across sectors and actors. Whereas the former authors postulate the desirability and indeed the democratic necessity of generalised standards, the latter points to the contradictory demands and constituencies that actors (in this case: regulatory bodies) can be faced with. In other words, a problem which is both undertheorised as well as empirically open is whether formalised and operationalised accountability mechanisms do indeed lead to increased transparency and public inclusion, or whether inversely the diverse constraints under which such actors operate make the effectiveness of organisational responses far more intractable and contingent. This is a tentative hypothesis which the conclusions of Lucy Koechlin and Richard Calland (Chapter 4) with regard to the EITI process support, but which would deserve further scrutiny.

The blurring of licit and illicit standards and actors has been well documented in our contributions. However, most of the examples and case studies focus on either clearly legal activities (such as environmental regulation) or clearly illegal activities (such as conducted by rebels and insurgents). In this context, an under-researched area is the phenomenon of illicit actors which are formally legitimised through their recognition by relevant state bodies. Michael Miklaucic (Chapter 7) attempts a typology of factors informing illicit actors, with the explicit objective of a more nuanced understanding of how to solicit their transformation from illicit actors to licit actors.

Other issues that need further exploration are the conditions under which sources of legitimacy can be shifted from the private to the public sphere and anchored in a democratic and accountable space. This research agenda extends from private international standards to standard setting by illicit actors.

On a theoretical level, such processes raise questions with regard to state building and state formation. Can the legitimacy of illicit actors be transformed by 'whitewashing' them through political acceptance and institutional inclusion? And what effect does this have on the credibility and legitimacy of the state? And lastly, and for our purposes perhaps most pertinently, which standards are bolstered by this phenomenon – does it truly neutralise the illicit power of these private actors and strengthen the territorial control of the state; or is not the reverse more likely, namely the official anchoring of private illicit interests within the realm of the public sphere, which is hence subverted both in terms of public authority as well as legitimacy? We believe that only a thorough rethinking of social and political analysis can answer this question.

The processes of standard setting examined in this book point at a well-known but nonetheless lingering problem of social analysis, the interaction of micro- and macro-perspectives. Some of the actors are, as the findings clearly demonstrate, acting at a very local level. Sometimes it is an ethnic group that does not count for more than a few per cent of a country's population, sometimes a quarter of a city where local standards and social norms are sustained by a limited number of actors. On the other hand, there are states as the most important actors at the international level, and even truly global actors such as the WTO. Many of these actors are linked through standard-setting processes, and it is obvious that they may operate simultaneously at more than one level. An NGO trying to implement apparently universal standards of, say, accountability in a certain state or region nonetheless has to face the diverging local social norms on the ground. It then may adopt a language, often a local language – understood in a very wide sense of the term – which the other actors in the place will understand. But adopting another language may mean adopting their ideas too, implicitly tolerating other standards. It appears to be a mere problem of political communication that has to be solved as the case arises. Even if only perceived as an ordinary problem of political communication, in the end it points at a structural predicament that arises in many processes of standard setting of our time, the micro–macro dilemma.

Many of the actors thus have to cope with a problem which is also familiar to social scientists: the interaction of the micro and macro level is pointing at an emergent social context created through the already-mentioned processes of globalisation. In other words: the whole of the ongoing interactions between the levels is more than the sum of individual encounters of actors. Every actor, regardless of state or non-state actor, needs to be understood in the context of the networks and obligations in which he is embedded, but this is not enough to address the novel social context that links the micro to the macro level through the agency of the actors.

From our perspective, the methodological challenge can be cast in two main questions: can micro-level analysis contribute to the understanding of macro processes of standard setting and vice versa? And what does this mean from a disciplinary perspective? The disciplines present in this book all have their methodological focuses which allow them to look more closely at one or the other level. They also focus more on the types of actors which may be more relevant to the level they are analysing. These perspectives generate different methodological approaches and make use of different methods. Suffice it to compare Dieter Neubert's (Chapter 2) and Egle Svilpaite's (Chapter 16) contributions to realise how different the methodologies can be. But in the end, we, as scholars, will be obliged to bring these approaches together – or to develop a range of linked and integrated methodological approaches that will allow us to move our understanding of standard setting beyond the established dualism of macro versus micro. Of course, there are attempts from the various disciplines[153] but there is not enough interdisciplinary discussion on how to integrate them to cope with the complexity of processes of standard

---

[153] In sociology, the work of Anthony Giddens and in particular his theory of structuration is probably the best known attempt to overcome the usual micro-macro bifurcation (Giddens, *The Constitution of Society*). In political science, Heinz Eulau has argued for an intensive study of what he calls micro-macro dilemmas (Eulau, *Micro-Macro Dilemmas*).

setting in the twenty-first century. So if there is one thing this study demonstrates, it is the need for continuing interdisciplinary dialogue and for new forms of interdisciplinary research on standard setting.

References

Albrow, M. 1997, *The Global Age: State and Society beyond Modernity*, Stanford University Press.

Arendt, H. 1958, *The Human Condition*, University of Chicago Press.

Augsberg, S. 2003, *Rechtssetzung zwischen Staat und Gesellschaft – Möglichkeiten differenzierter Steuerung des Kapitalmarkts*, Berlin, Duncker & Humblot.

Bachmann, G. 2006, *Grundlagen ziviler Regelsetzung*, Tübingen, Mohr Siebeck.

Backer, L. 2008, 'From Moral Obligation to International Law: Disclosure Systems, Markets and the Regulation of Multinational Corporations', *Georgetown Journal of International Law*, vol. **39**, 101–42.

Barker, R. 2001, *Legitimating Identities – The Self-Presentation of Rulers and Subjects*, Cambridge University Press.

Bayart, J. F., Ellis, St. and Hibou, B. (eds.) 1999, *The Criminalization of the State in Africa*, Oxford, James Currey.

Bayart, J.-F. 1993, *The State in Africa*, London, Longman.

Beissinger, M. R. and Young, C. (eds.) 2002, *Beyond State Crisis? Post-Colonial Africa and Post-Soviet Eurasia in Comparative Perspective*, Washington DC, Woodrow Wilson Center Press.

Berman, H. and Kaufman, C. 1978, 'The Law of International Comercial Transactions (Lex mercatoria)', *Harvard International Law Journal*, vol. **19**, 221–78.

Berman, P. 2007, 'A Pluralist Approach to International Law', *Yale Journal of International Law*, vol. **32**, 301–29.

Bøås, M. and Jennings, K. 2007, '"Failed States" and "State Failure": Threats or Opportunities?', *Globalizations*, vol. **4**, no. 4, 475–85.

Börzel, T. A. and Risse, T. 2005, 'Public–Private Partnerships: Effective and Legitimate Tools of International Governance?' in E. Grande and L. W. Pauly (eds.), *Complex Sovereignty: Reconstituting Political Authority in the 21st Century*, University of Toronto Press, 195–216.

Bovens, M. 2007, 'Analysing and Assessing Accountability: A Conceptual Framework', *European Law Journal*, vol. **13**, no. 4, 447–68.

Boyle, A. and Chinkin, Ch. 2007, *The Making of International Law*, Oxford University Press.

Charnovitz, S. 2006, 'Nongovernmental Organizations and International Law', *American Journal of International Law*, vol. **100**, no. 2, 348–72.

Chomsky, N. 2006, *Failed States: The Abuse of Power and the Assault on Democracy*, New York, Metropolitan Books.

Clifford, J. and Marcus, G. (eds.) 1986, *Writing Culture: The Poetics and Politics of Ethnography*, Berkeley, University of California Press.

Comaroff, J. and Comaroff, J. (eds.) 1999, *Civil Society and the Political Imagination in Africa*, Chicago University Press.

Connerton, P. 1989, *How Societies Remember*, Cambridge University Press.

Crane, A. and Matten, D. 2004, *Business Ethics – A European Perspective: Managing Corporate Citizenship and Sustainability in the Age of Globalization*, Oxford University Press.

Crawford, J. 2006, *The Creation of States*, 2nd edn, Cambridge University Press.

Cutler, C. A. 2003, *Private Power and Global Authority: Transnational Merchant Law in the Global Political Economy*, Cambridge University Press.

De Frouville, O. 2008, 'Domesticating Civil Society at the UN' in P-M. Dupuy and L. Vierucci (eds.), *NGOs in International Law: Efficiency and Flexibility*, Northampton, Edward Elgar Publishing, 71–115.

De Ly, F. 1992, *International Business Law and Lex Mercatoria*, Amsterdam, North Holland.

De Sousa Santos, B. 1995, *Toward a New Common Sense: Law, Science and Politics in the Paradigmatic Transition*, London, Routledge.

Dingwerth, K. 2005, 'The Democratic Legitimacy of Public-Private Rule Making: What Can We Learn from the World Commission on Dams', *Global Governance*, vol. **11**, 65–83.

Eulau, H. 1996, *Micro-Macro Dilemmas in Political Science*, Normann, University of Oklahoma Press.

Freeman, E. 1984, *Strategic Management: A Stakeholder Approach*, Boston, Pitman.

Galgano, F. 2001, *Lex Mercatoria*, Bologna, Società editrice Il Mulino.

Giddens, A. 1986, *The Constitution of Society: Outline of the Theory of Structuration*, Berkeley, University of California Press.

Grant, R. and Keohane, R. 2005, 'Accountability and Abuses of Power in World Politics', *American Political Science Review*, vol. **99**, 29–44.

Griffiths, J. 1986, 'What is Legal Pluralism', *Journal of Legal Pluralism and Inofficial Law*, vol. **24**, 1–50.

Grote, R. and Marauhn, T. (eds.) 2006, *The Regulation of International Financial Markets: Perspectives for Reform*, Cambridge University Press.

Hall, R. B. and Biersteker, T. J. (eds.) 2002, *The Emergence of Private Authority in Global Governance*, Cambridge University Press.

Haufler, V. 2001, *A Public Role for the Private Sector: Industry Self-regulation in a Global Economy*, Washington DC, Carnegie Endowment for International Peace.

Hellman, J., Jones, G. and Kaufmann, D. 2000, 'Seize the State, Seize the Day: State Capture, Corruption, and Influence in Transition Economies', *World Bank Policy Research Working Paper* **2444**, September 2000.

Hill, J. 2005, 'Beyond the Other? A Post-Colonial Critique of the Failed State Thesis', *African Identities*, vol. **3**, no. 2, 139–54.

Jessup, Ph. C. 1956, *Transnational Law*, New Haven, Yale University Press.

Kamminga, M. T. 2007, '*What Makes an NGO "Legitimate" in the Eyes of States?*' in Vedder (ed.), 175–95.

Knill, Ch. and Lehmkuhl, D. 2002, 'Private Actors and the State: Internationalization and Changing Patterns of Governance', *Governance*, vol. **15**, 41–63.

Kovach, H., Nelligan, C. and Burall, S. 2003, *Power Without Accountability?*, London, One World Trust.

Krisch, N. 2006, 'The Pluralism of Global Administrative Law', *European Journal of International Law*, vol. **17**, 247–78.

Krut, R. 1997, *Globalization and Civil Society: NGO Influence in International Decision-Making*, Geneva, United Nations Research Institute for Social Development.

Leslie, W. J. 1993, *Zaire: Continuity and Political Change in an Oppressive State*, Boulder, Westview Press.

Levit, J. 2005, 'A Bottom-Up Approach to International Law-Making: The Tale of Three Trade Finance Instruments', *Yale Journal of International Law*, vol. **30**, 125–209.

Lindblom, A.-K. 2005, *Non-Governmental Organisations in International Law*, Cambridge University Press.

Lowe, V. 2004, 'Corporations as International Actors and International Lawmakers', *Italian Yearbook of International Law*, vol. **14**, 23–38.

Lukes, S. 1990, 'Perspectives on Authority' in J. Raz (ed.), *Authority*, Oxford, Basil Blackwell, 203–17.

Lundblad, C. 2005, 'Some Legal Dimensions of Corporate Codes of Conduct' in R. Mullerat (ed.), *Corporate Social Responsibility: The Corporate Governance of the 21st Century*, The Hague, Kluwer Law International.

Mattli, W. 2003, 'Public and Private Governance in Setting International Standards' in M. Kahler and D. A. Lake (eds.), *Governance in a Global Economy*, Princeton University Press.

Mbembe, A. 2002, *On Private Indirect Government*, Dakar, CODESRIA.

Mehler, A. 2004, 'Oligopolies of Violence in Africa South of the Sahara', *Nord-Süd Aktuell*, vol. **18**, no. 3, 539–48.

Merry, S. E. 1988, 'Legal Pluralism', *Law and Society Review*, vol. **22**, 869–96.

Migdal, J. S. 2001, *State in Society: Studying how States and Societies Transform and Constitute one Another*, Cambridge University Press.

Muchlinski, P. 2007, *Multinational Enterprises and the Law*, 2nd edn, Oxford University Press.

Nguyen Quoc, D., Daillier P. and Pellet, A. 2002, *Droit international public*, Paris, L.G.D.J.

Noortmann, M. 2004, 'Who Really Needs Art. 71?' in W. P. Heere (ed.), *From Government to Governance: The Growing Impact of Non-state Actors on the International and European Legal System, Proceedings of the Sixth Hague Joint Conference held in The Hague, the Netherlands, 3–5 July 2003*, The Hague, T.M.C. Asser Press, 113–20.

North, D. J. 1990, *Institutions, Institutional Change and Economic Performance*, New York, Cambridge University Press.

Nowrot, K. 2005, 'The New Governance Structure of the Global Compact: Transforming a "Learning Network" into a Federalized and Parliamentarized Transnational Regulatory Regime', *Beiträge zum Transnationalen Wirtschaftsrecht*, vol. **47**, 5–50.

Nowrot, K. 2006, *Normative Ordnungsstruktur und private Wirkungsmacht: Konsequenzen der Beteiligung transnationaler Unternehmen an den Rechtssetzungsprozessen im internationalen Wirtschaftssystem*, Berlin, Berliner Wissenschaftsverlag.

Oberthür, S. *et al.* 2002, *Participation of Non-Governmental Organisations in International Environmental Co-operation: Legal Basis and Practical Experience*, Berlin, Schmidt.

Osman, F. 1992, *Les principes généraux de la lex mercatoria*, Paris, L.G.D.J.

Ostrom, E. 1990, *Governing the Commons*, Cambridge University Press.

The Oxford English Dictionary 1989, prepared by Simpson and Weiner, 2nd edn, Oxford, Clarendon Press.

Peters, B. G. 2005, 'Governance: A Garbage Can Perspective' in E. Grande and L. Pauly (eds.), *Complex Sovereignty: Reconstituting Political Authority in the Twenty-First Century*, University of Toronto Press, 68–92.

Raz, J. 1990, 'Introduction' in J. Raz (ed.), *Authority*, Oxford, Basil Blackwell, 1–19.

Rebasti, E. 2008, 'Beyond Consultative Status: Which Legal Framework for an Enhanced Interaction between NGOs and Intergovernmental Organizations?' in P.-M. Dupuy and L. Vierucci (eds.), *NGOs in International Law: Efficiency and Flexibility*, Northampton, Edward Elgar Publishing, 21–70.

Reno, W. 1995, *Corruption and State Politics in Sierra Leone*, Cambridge University Press.

Reno, W. 1998, *Warlord Politics and African States*, Boulder, Lynne Rienner.

Robertson, R. 1992, *Globalization: Social Theory and Global Culture*, London, Sage.

Röthel, A. 2007, 'Lex mercatoria, lex sportiva, lex technica', *Juristen-Zeitung*, vol. **62**, 755–63.

Rotberg, R. I. (ed.) 2004, *When States Fail: Causes and Consequences*, Princeton University Press.

Scharpf, F. 1997, *Games Real Actors Play: Actor-Centered Institutionalism in Policy Research*, Boulder, Westview Press.

Schepel, H. 2005, *The Constitution of Private Governance: Product Standards in the Regulation of Integrating Markets*, Oxford, Hart Publishing.

Schumpeter, J. 1975 [1942], History of Economic Analysis. *Capitalism, Socialism and Democracy*, New York, Harper.

Shils, E. 1975, *Center and Periphery: Essays in Macrosociology*, University of Chicago Press.

Slim, H. 2002, 'By What Authority? The Legitimacy and Accountability of Non-Governmental Organisations', *The International Council on Human Rights Policy International Meeting on Global Trends and Human Rights – Before and After 11 September*, Geneva, January 2002 (available at www.jha.ac/ articles/a082.htm).

Stein, U. 1995, *Lex mercatoria – Realität und Theorie*, Frankfurt am Main, Vittorio Klostermann.

Strange, S. 1987, 'The Persistent Myth of the Lost Hegenomy' in R. Tooze and Ch. May (eds.) 2002, *Authority and Markets – Susan Strange's Writings on International Political Economy*, Basingstoke, Palgrave Macmillan, 121–40.

Sutton, M. and Arnove, R. F. (eds.) 2004, *Civil Society or Shadow State? State/NGO Relations in Education*, Greenwich, Information Age Publishing.

Teubner, G. (ed.) 1997, *Global Law without a State*, Aldershot etc., Dartmouth.

Tietje, Ch. and Nowrot, K. 2006, 'Laying Conceptual Ghosts of the Past to Rest: The Rise of Philipp Jessup's "Transnational Law" in the Regulatory Governance of the International Economic System' in Ch. Tietje, G. Kraft and R. Sethe (eds.), *Beiträge zum Transnationalen Wirtschaftsrecht*, vol. **50**, 17–43.

Tietje, Ch., Brouder, A. and Nowrot, K. (eds.) 2006, *Philip Jessup's Transnational Law Revisited – on the Occasion of the 50th Anniversary of its Publication*, Halle/Saale, Universität Wittenberg, 17–43.

Trotha, T. v. 2000, 'Die Zukunft liegt in Afrika. Vom Zerfall des Staates, von der Vorherrschaft der konzentrischen Ordnung und vom Aufstieg der Parastaatlichkeit', *Leviathan*, vol. **28**, 253–79.

Tully, S. 2007, *Corporations and International Law-Making*, Boston and Leiden, Martinus Nijhoff.

Weber, M. 1985 [1922], *Wirtschaft und Gesellschaft*, Tübingen, Mohr (engl. transl. Weber, M. 1976, *Economy and Society* (ed. by G. Roth and C. Wittich), New York, Bedminster Press 1968).

Weber, M. 1988, 'Politik als Beruf' in J. Winckelmann (ed.), *Gesammelte Politische Schriften*, 5th edn, Tübingen, Mohr, 505–61 (English transl. 'Politics as a Vocation' in H. H. Gerth and C. Wright Mills (transl. and ed. 1946), *From Max Weber: Essays in Sociology*, New York, Oxford University Press, 77–128).

Weise, P.-F. 1990, Lex mercatoria, *Materielles Recht vor der internationalen Handelsschiedsgerichtsbarkeit*, Frankfurt am Main, Lang.

Wolch, J. 1990, *The Shadow State: Government and Voluntary Sector in Transition*, New York, The Foundation Center.

Wolfe, A. 1997, 'Public and Private in Theory and Practice: Some Implications on an Uncertain Boundary' in J. Weintraub and K. Kumar (eds.), *Public and Private in Thought and Practice*, University of Chicago Press, 182–203.

INDEX

For EU product safety concerns, contact us at Calle de José Abascal, 56–1°,
28003 Madrid, Spain or eugpsr@cambridge.org.

www.ingramcontent.com/pod-product-compliance
Ingram Content Group UK Ltd.
Pitfield, Milton Keynes, MK11 3LW, UK
UKHW042316180425
457623UK00005B/12